Writing Effectively

Writing
Effectively

SECOND EDITION

Beth S. Neman
WILMINGTON COLLEGE OF OHIO

1817

HARPER & ROW, PUBLISHERS, New York
Cambridge, Philadelphia, San Francisco, London,
Mexico City, São Paulo, Singapore, Sydney

Sponsoring Editor: Lucy Rosendahl
Project Editor: Eric Newman
Text Design: Rita Naughton
Cover Design: 20/20 Services Inc.
Cover Illustration: Vincent van Gogh, 1853–1890. *Iris*. Oil on paper, mounted on
  canvas. 62.2 × 48.3 cm. National Gallery of Canada, Ottawa.
Text Art: Don Martinetti and ComCom Division of Haddon Craftsmen, Inc.
Production Manager: Jeanie Berke
Production Assistant: Paula Roppolo
Compositor: ComCom Division of Haddon Craftsmen, Inc.
Printer and Binder: R. R. Donnelley & Sons Company
Cover Printer: Phoenix Color Corporation

Writing Effectively, Second Edition

Copyright © 1989 by Beth S. Neman, Inc.

Library of Congress Cataloging in Publication Data
  Neman, Beth.
    Writing effectively / Beth S. Neman. — 2nd ed.
      p.   cm.
    Includes index.
    ISBN 0-06-044807-5
    1. English language—Rhetoric.   2. Creative writing.   I. Title.
  PE1408.N418   1989
  808'.042—dc19   88–16464
                                                          CIP

88 89 90 91 9 8 7 6 5 4 3 2 1

To my students and
my family,
Albert, David, and Dan

Brief Table of Contents

Detailed Table of Contents

Convincing Your Readers Through Style

Guidelines and Checklists

Preface

Writing Effectively, Second Edition, is a student-centered, process-based, reader-focused text. It is structured so that students are led companionably step by step through the process of writing expository compositions, compositions that effectively engage their readers.

The text is student centered in that its every feature is designed to meet specific student needs. I address the student-readers directly; try to anticipate their questions, doubts, and problems; and encourage them to experiment in their writing. The abundance of exercises permits students to "Try Out" for themselves the principles the text endorses and to form their own judgments. More important, the exercises offer students plentiful opportunities to explore various strategies to fit their varying purposes and to find those strategies with which they are most comfortable personally. Students also especially value the comprehensive guidelines and checklists that conclude each section.

Writing Effectively is process based. Approaching writing as a process rather than a product, it offers practical guidance in mastering all the steps of prewriting, writing, and revising and provides recursive opportunities as well. In terms of contemporary composition theory, *Writing Effectively* adopts an eclectic process approach, including appropriate useful material from both the expressionist and the new rhetorical (i.e., structural) process approaches. Expressionist thought is influential, for example, in the important section on invention with its emphasis on free writing and also in the exercise-filled section on sharpening observation techniques to develop vivid and specific detail. On the other hand, because I believe that lack of focus and lack of adequate support are the most common and the most damaging problems inexperienced writers face, thesis, support, and other aspects of the structural perspective are central to this text.

Writing Effectively is reader focused, rhetorically oriented. Throughout, the text emphasizes writers' relationships with their readers. It conceives of the purpose of expository writing to be convincing readers that what the writer wants to say, the point he or she wants to make, is valid and worth their while. In the words of the text: "Convincing and satisfying your readers is the whole point of writing effectively."

NEW IN THE SECOND EDITION

The qualities that brought praise to the first edition have been retained in the second. The text's all-around teachability is intact, as is its research-based soundness. The companionable voice of its teacher-author remains, as does its ability to help students recognize, and thus avoid, the pitfalls that cause inexperienced writers to stumble. Remaining also are innovative features readers have found helpful, such as the "although" clause concept, exercises in sensual observation, the "George Washington"–inventory classroom exercise, a new approach to the precise use of imagery and other diction, an alphabetically accessible handbook, exemplification from essays available in the reader. And the volume is still comprehensive—including rhetoric, reader, and handbook, chapters on critical analyses and research papers, traditional and sentence-combining exercises.

The second edition should be even more teachable and more conducive to learning than the first because the text has been restructured and streamlined into a more pedagogically effective format. In addition, some changes have been made to build on the strengths of the original in response to suggestions of teachers and students. In the second edition, I make an even greater effort to accommodate individual styles of learning and teaching—in particular, to take into account both subjective and objective modes of thinking.

- The invention portion has been expanded in the second edition to serve the individual needs better both of those students who respond more readily to free writing and those who find inventorying and listing a greater spur to their creative thought.
- Furthermore, as early as Part One, the second edition offers students the option of outside sources by providing them information on how to use this material in their writing, thus freeing them from the limited confines of their own thoughts and experience.
- In order to accommodate a wide variety of learning interests, the research-paper chapter has been extensively revised toward an interdisciplinary focus. In the documentation portion, for instance,

the new MLA system is discussed in detail, and the systems of the American Psychological Association (APA) and the American Chemical Society (ACS) are also given significant mention.

· To vary the pace and add more pleasure to the learning experience, I have resequenced the contents of Part Two, interspersing sentence-combining chapters between the more overtly theoretical ones.

· Because many instructors like to teach from student samples and students often feel more comfortable with papers of those who are facing the same problems as they are themselves, I have expanded the student writing within the text and have added to the anthology of professional essays a selection of typical student papers, including a first-draft/revision sequence.

· A number of new exercises have been introduced, offering even more diversified opportunities for students to "try it out," to think through on their own what the text has to say. In addition, the assignments at the chapters' ends have been enriched by suggestions garnered from a survey of favorite assignments from faculty across the curriculum and across the nation.

CONTENTS

Part One: Writing the First Paper

Part One offers some exciting classroom experiences for those difficult first days. But the main purpose of this section is to help ease the first-paper paradox of students needing to be instantly familiar with the entire writing process. To give students the chance to build the confidence upon which their writing success depends, Part One provides, for the one or two weeks that precede the first assigned paper, the *essential* understandings for writing that paper—and indeed all others.

Part Two: Convincing Your Readers Through the Writing Process

Part Two sections that process into the three teachable—though admittedly somewhat artificial—writing stages of prewriting, writing, and revising so that instructor and students can approach specific writing problems analytically with appropriate exercises and activities. It then offers a final section, "Convincing Your Readers Through Style," which helps students learn to create their style through their conscious choice of syntax and diction.

In "The Prewriting Stage," Chapter 1 offers students a number of useful strategies to help them discover and organize their ideas. Chapter 2 breaks the pace and gives students what classroom experience indicates is a much-needed change in their intellectual activities with the introduction of sentence-combining exercises. In Chapter 3 I direct the students' thinking toward their readers and suggest tactics for incorporating their rhetorical purposes into their prewriting planning and into the paper itself.

In "The Writing Stage," Chapter 4 gives students practical advice and practice in the difficult tasks of starting up and concluding their essays. It also provides insight and guidance in structuring paragraphs or paragraph clusters so students may present their points most clearly. But the main emphasis in this chapter is on students' developing vivid and specific support for their points and a set of proven exercises in observation techniques to help them do so. In Chapter 5, students have the opportunity to further their understanding of point and support with a set of sentence-combining exercises specifically tailored for that purpose.

"The Rewriting Stage" has been divided into two chapters to reflect the significant distinction between holistic revision, Chapter 6, and editing, Chapter 7. *Writing Effectively* assumes that revising (in the first sense) is a natural culmination of the writing process. Thus, all the preceding text, in some way, leads to the sixth chapter. It is a particularly important one, for I believe that it is while rewriting—especially after teacher intervention—that students actually learn to write.

Discussion of mechanics and grammar has been reserved for Chapter 7. Research has shown that too-careful attention to mechanics while composing inhibits creativity (and can even lead to blocking) and that aiming at total correctness in the first draft is wasted effort. Confused syntax is often a mere reflection of confused thinking that disappears when the thoughts are untangled. But at the end of the process, knowledgeable editing and then proofreading are, of course, essential; and Chapter 7 provides a thorough review of syntax and a detailed treatment of the most salient mechanical problems.

The final section of Part Two, "Convincing Your Readers Through Style," helps students learn to improve their style by practicing a conscious choice of diction in Chapter 9 and of syntax in the sentence-combining exercises in Chapter 8.

A word should be said here about sentence-combining exercises, which, having survived even the adoration of faddists who proclaimed them a universal panacea, are now considered, simply, as among the most useful composition exercises available. Having been part of the carefully controlled sentence-combining research at Miami University,* I can add a personal endorsement. There is, I think, a good reason that these exercises, especially the contextual ones, tend to improve student writing. In isolating technique from content, they provide opportunities for making—and later for discussing—conscious stylistic and structural decisions without the

---

*See Morenberg, Daiker, and Kerek, "Sentence-Combining at the College Level: An Experimental Study," *Research in the Teaching of English*, 12 Oct. 1978, 245–50.

often-crippling impediment of personal ego-involvement. The exercises thus help develop sound authorial judgment. In the new *Writing Effectively*, where chapters containing sentence combining are interspersed, heightened student interest can be maintained, and the exercises can be used with maximum pedagogical efficacy.

Part Three: Writing Special Kinds of Expository Essays

Part Three helps students apply the knowledge they have gained about writing expository essays in general to the two such essays most frequently assigned in college classes, the research paper (Chapter 10) and the critical analysis (Chapter 11). Both chapters offer detailed, practical guidance, and both include some especially helpful features. Chapter 10, for instance, introduces note-taking and documentation procedures that all but eliminate inadvertent plagiarism. Chapter 11 includes a section on close reading that gives students a definite sense of what the analytical process is all about.

Part Four: A Sampler of Professional Essays and Student Papers

Part Five offers a selection of brief essays by professional writers, parts of which are quoted extensively as examples throughout the text. Including these essays makes it possible for readers to study examples in context and also to check the validity of any point the text makes about writing. Part Four also includes a small section of student papers, which supply the substance for a number of Try It Out exercises.

Part Five: Revision Guide

Part Five consists of alphabetically arranged, brief entries to answer any question a student is likely to raise about grammar, usage, capitalization, punctuation, or spelling. Because of the alphabetical arrangement, full exemplification, and extensive cross-referencing, the Guide is easily accessible.

Writing Effectively is based on what I have learned about the needs of beginning writing students from my own years of classroom experience and from my research into the experience of other teachers. I hope that you who study from it and you who teach it will gain both knowledge and pleasure from using this book.

ACKNOWLEDGMENTS

A second edition builds on a first edition, and I continue to be grateful to all those who contributed to and helped produce the first edition of *Writing*

Effectively. In particular, I again want to thank Nancy Bates, whose extensive knowledge enlightens and whose quick wit enlivens the Revision Guide; Daniel Neman, a student himself at the time, whose intelligent curiosity and humor are largely responsible for the quality of the exercises; and Beverly Kolz, the first edition's considerate, helpful, and able editor.

Writing Effectively, Second Edition, has benefited greatly from the wise advice and encouraging comments of scholars who kindly read the manuscript at its various stages. I am grateful to Mary Bly, University of California, Davis; William Dyer, Mankato State University; Sterling Eisiminger, Clemson University; William B. Guthrie, Wilmington College of Ohio; Patricia Licklider, John Jay College of Criminal Justice, City University of New York; Ron Nelson, Valencia Community College; and Karl Suess, Lincoln Land Community College.

I am especially appreciative of the considerate and wise counsel of my colleagues William Guthrie and James Cool and the students in their classes and mine at Wilmington College, who helped shape this text by thoughtful testing in the classroom. The guidance of English education students Anna Adams, Carol Arbogast, Shelley Beard, Lynn Lowell, Dan Pearce (who also worked on some exercises), and Suzanne Piezer was particularly helpful.

My gratitude also to Donna McClughen for her caring and efficient help in transcribing the work for revision and preparing the final manuscript.

And I would like to thank the skillful staff at Harper & Row who worked so effectively on this book, especially Allison Philips, editorial assistant; Eric Newman, project editor; Rita Naughton, designer; and Lauren Bahr, director of marketing. And finally I want to express my appreciation to my two editors: Phillip Leininger, whose professional expertise originated and guided this volume, and Lucy Rosendahl, whose intelligence, insight, and warm counsel helped to create this text.

Beth S. Neman

Before You Begin

Composition courses suffer from bad press; there is no question about it. Many students actually believe the bad notices and thus come into the course thinking of learning to write as either an impossibly difficult or a worthlessly easy task. Some of these students think it is impossible to learn to write because they see writing ability as a talent a person either has or has not, a gift with which only a few lucky geniuses have been blessed. Others think that learning to write is too mechanical a procedure to bother very much about. They believe that to write well a person need only follow an easily memorized formula that they are certain all composition teachers know but just fail to communicate. Though these views are widely held, they are both demonstrably false.

A well-written essay is derived neither from a mechanical formula nor from a stroke of genius. There is no magical way just to "fill in the blank" or "fulfill the specifications" and write anything but the dreariest of exercises. A glance at some of the articles in your favorite magazine (or at those in Part Four of this book) will convince you that no single formula or series of formulas could possibly account for the rich diversity of human thought they display. And although natural ability certainly helps a writer, the fact that a few people are particularly skilled does not suggest the futility of others' trying to learn to write well any more than the performance of a superb Olympic diver should restrain the rest of us from learning to swim.

The truth is that writing—like swimming or playing bridge or driving a car—is an activity that can be understood in terms of its overall purpose. Stripped of the mystique it has acquired, writing is simply the formulating of thought, the shaping of thought into sentences and arranging them on a page; its purpose—to convince readers that this thought is true or right or good.

Although writing is thus as learnable as any other skill, the process is rarely easy. For writing is inextricably bound up with thought, and thinking is just about the hardest thing we do. Nevertheless, I insist that learning to write, however strenuous the undertaking, will be worthwhile. First, if you learn to write effectively, you will be able to get your ideas across to others. Writing effectively will permit others not only to understand the essence of what you have to say, but also to appreciate its merits; and that means that never again should lack of writing skill prevent you from being credited for what you know or what you have accomplished. Second, you will increase your ability to think clearly and logically, for this kind of thinking necessarily precedes or coincides with the writing of effective, well-organized prose. And third, learning to write also offers a creative dividend: it puts you in touch with your own thought. For in exploring and ordering your thinking as you write, you will often discover exciting new ideas.

PART
ONE

Writing the First Paper

Writing is a single process. It can, nevertheless, be analyzed in three stages—prewriting, writing, and rewriting. Experienced writers tend to combine these stages as they compose, but almost everyone who writes well follows them. Thus to learn how to write effectively, you can look at the process as defined by these three stages and even break each stage into steps to consider one at a time.

There is a catch to this step-by-step approach, however. Although you can study the steps only one at a time, you will need to use them all for every composition you write—including the first.

This opening section should help you escape that catch. To prepare you for your first assignment, Part One introduces the most significant steps in the writing process. It especially emphasizes the essential early prewriting steps to get you off to a good start. In later chapters you will consider each step of the process more fully and carefully.

Let's begin.

Before You Write

YOUR PURPOSE AND YOUR READERS

What Do I Really Want to Say?

Starting to write is like setting out on a sea voyage. You experience a certain queasiness until you get your sea legs. To get your sea legs in writing, you need a firm grasp on what you hope to accomplish in the work you plan to write. In other words, you need to discover your purpose before you can begin to write effectively. As self-evident as finding your purpose would seem to be, it is easily overlooked. Although writing is a major part of my professional life, I find I often set out to write without thinking about my purpose at all. But then, when I become queasy, I say to myself (actually, right out loud, if no one is about), "Just what is it I really want to do here? What do I really want to say?" In answering these questions I usually manage to get the project launched; and so the technique of asking yourself such questions is one I heartily recommend to you.

CONVINCING YOUR READER

Answering "What do I really want to do?" requires deciding exactly what response you want your words and ideas to evoke in those who will read them. For instance, you might want a business letter to move your correspondent to offer a job interview, or an essay to dazzle your history professor into giving you an "A." More often your aim will be less personal: you want your reader to understand your subject and to find your approach to it acceptable.

In all your planning, writing, and revising, your first consideration should be how your words will affect your readers. To find out, put yourself in their place—be your own reader—and think how the words would affect you. Convincing and satisfying your readers is the whole point of writing effectively.

FINDING YOUR POINT

Answering the question "What do I really want to say?" pinpoints the matter you want your readers to understand, the idea you want to convince them is valid or worth their while. In expository writing, discovering what you want to say involves finding your thesis and the means to support it. The thesis is the heart of expository writing.

Expository Writing Defined. Although you may find the term "expository writing" unfamiliar, it describes the most familiar of all writing. It is the sort of writing found in textbooks and other works of nonfiction, in magazines, in many newspaper articles, the type of writing you are called upon to produce for college exams and business reports, the workaday, useful writing that makes the world's intellectual wheels go 'round. With expository writing you expound, explain, and set forth information and ideas. It is distinguished from narrative writing, the other major type of prose, by its organization. Narrative writing, which tells a story, is structured chronologically: "and then this happened, and then that happened." Expository writing, which makes a statement, is organized to state its point, its thesis, most effectively.

Thesis

The essence of what you mean to get across in a given work is called the thesis. It summarizes what your reader should come to believe. It is also, as I said, the organizational focus of expository writing. Conventionally, some statement of the thesis is placed toward the end of the introductory portion of a piece of expository prose and/or somewhere in the concluding segment. Sometimes the thesis is not stated in so many words, and occasionally it is only implied; but there can be no good expository writing without it. Without a thesis, expository writing is, literally, pointless.

These statements are strong—even though a careful thinker is reluctant to remark that anything *always* or *never* happens. Yet even a very careful thinker can confidently assert that good expository writing *always* has a thesis, either stated or implied.

EXAMPLES OF THESES

What does a thesis actually say? Let's look at a couple of theses and see. If you turn to page 411 and begin reading Shana Alexander's essay "Getting Old in Kids' Country," you will notice, in the conventional place at the end of what is clearly an introduction, a statement that seems to fulfill the thesis role:

Children today not only exist, they have taken over. (page 411, paragraph 2)[1]

Read on further and you will notice that all the material in the paragraphs following that statement tends to support it. Finish the article, and in its concluding portion you will find this more definitive statement of that point:

[1]Examples from essays reprinted in Part Four of this text are identified by page and paragraph number so that you can see how the example works within the essay as a whole.

> Today adults as a class have begun to disappear, condemning all of us to remain boys and girls forever. (page 414, paragraph 16)

Without question what we have isolated are two phrasings of Alexander's thesis.

Check the final lines of the introduction to Fred Golden's "Earth's Creeping Deserts" and you will find a similar purposeful statement:

> The creeping, seemingly relentless spread of the earth's deserts . . . [has become] a major environmental danger. (page 415, paragraph 1)

Notice that Golden also structures the paragraphs following his introduction to support his point. And see how Golden too uses the cumulative weight of this support to lead into a stronger rephrasing of his thesis in the essay's conclusion:

> To many countries, doing battle against the deserts is the only alternative to poverty, starvation and chaos. (page 417, paragraph 12)

ARGUMENTATIVE NATURE

Theses vary widely, ranging, as you can see, from declarations of whimsical fancy, like Alexander's, to assertions, like Golden's, of scientific ideas, factually phrased, experimentally verifiable. But the purpose behind every thesis, whatever its subject, is to persuade the reader of the truth of its ideas or, at least, that these ideas are worth considering. Thus all theses, without exception, are statements demanding development, explanation, demonstration.

This argumentative quality is fundamental to all theses. We can see it clearly in theses such as that of Walter Williams, who openly adopts an argumentative tone:

> The point of [these observations] *is* to question propositions concerning black socioeconomic progress which have now received axiomatic status. ("U.S. Blacks and a Free Market," page 441, paragraph 4)

Argument is clear, too, in the provocative accents of Meg Greenfield's thesis:

> [Our] response [to terrorism] is (by now) a ritualized series of diversions and evasions that subtly but quickly make us feel better while also making the hostages' situation worse. ("Accepting the Unacceptable," page 420, paragraph 1)

The Golden and Alexander theses may not seem to demand demonstration and development quite as aggressively as these last examples, but their readers will expect demonstration and development nevertheless. Every thesis requires explanation and support because, like the person from Missouri, every interested reader must be "shown." The whole of an effective composition confirms or furthers the point of its thesis.

TRY IT OUT

"Try It Out" exercises give you an opportunity to confirm for yourself what we are discussing. In some cases, as in question 1 below, you will be asked to refer to Part Four of this book, "A Selection of Essays." The essays in Part Four offer a sampling of good professional writing. Though chosen mainly for their interest, they can also serve as a proving ground for statements made in the text. For example, contrary to our text, some say that the thesis should be stated in the first sentence. You can settle this conflict (and others like it) by referring to Part Four and determining what the professionals do. "Try It Out" exercises encourage you to come to your own conclusions about good writing.

1. Like the Alexander and the Golden essays, the Williams and the Greenfield articles quoted in the section you have just read may be found in full in Part Four (see pages 441–443 and 420–422). Read both of them through and answer these questions about *each*:
   a. Do you agree that the quoted sentence (page 4) is indeed an introductory statement of the article's thesis? If not, which statement would you select? Or is there no introductory thesis statement?
   b. Where did you locate the thesis statement? Did you find it conventionally placed toward the end of the introduction?
   c. Did you find any other statement of the point the introductory thesis makes? If so, what is it? Where is the restatement of thesis placed?

2. When an essay has both a preliminary and a final statement of thesis, it is logical to assume that the final statement, the writer's last opportunity with the reader, would be a stronger, more complete statement of the thesis idea. Compare the two statements of thesis and comment upon the comparison in the Alexander and Golden as well as the Williams and Greenfield essays.

3. *An Extra Exercise for Skeptics.* Browse through the other essays in Part Four and see if you can find an essay that has no thesis. If you choose, go further afield and look in *Harper's* or *Esquire* or at articles of commentary in *Time, Newsweek,* or *Science* and continue your search. If you should find a thesis-less essay, bring it to class for discussion.

THESIS AND WORKING THESIS

As you have seen, the thesis of an essay, its point, can be phrased in a variety of ways. It can be stated explicitly or hinted at indirectly or even, rarely, only implied. But since the thesis is both the basis for a composition's persuasive strategy and the focus for its organization, you will find it helpful to phrase your thesis ideas as an arguable statement to serve as your "working thesis." Even if you do not use the exact wording of your arguable statement in your finished composition, you should find your "working thesis" a powerful planning tool.

How do you go about finding your thesis and constructing your working thesis? There are two basic ways. The subject you will be writing on will either spontaneously suggest a thesis idea, or it will not. If it should, then most of your prewriting time will be spent deductively, developing and sorting possible supporting ideas, the ideas that will help you make your point. As you work with these ideas, you will be refining and evaluating your thesis as well as building the structure of your paper. (For specifics on how to handle this process, see the four steps immediately following.) If no thesis occurs to you at once, then you will want to discover one inductively by making an inventory—a list—of your information or ideas on the subject, by analyzing the inventory into possible chains of supporting ideas, and then by deriving the thesis to which they lead. (This process is exemplified on pages 10–13.)

Finding Your Working Thesis Deductively

When you have a fairly clear notion of your writing topic, you can reason from that topic to your thesis. Although the quality of the thesis you develop will, of course, depend upon the quality of the ideas that form it, the following steps should help direct your thinking toward finding a workable thesis to express what you want to say.

STEP 1: NARROW YOUR TOPIC TO WORKABLE SIZE

Unless your paper is to be a very long one indeed, almost any suggested topic, from the proverbial "The Things I Did Last Summer" to a history assignment like "The Peloponnesian Wars," would be far too broad to be contained within it. More important, a paper written with no more focus than that of being "about" such a subject would be hopelessly diffuse. Furthermore, readers would not be able to find any purpose in such writing.

How do you go about narrowing your subject? By answering the question "What about it?" Ask yourself, "What about last summer?" ("Busy," "Lazy," "Satisfying.") What about the Peleponnesian Wars interests me most? What is most likely to interest others? ("Why the Athenians lost the Peloponnesian Wars.")

Now, why not experiment with this method yourself? On scratch paper, take any topic that comes to mind (page 9, no. 1, if you need ideas) and narrow it by asking the "What about it?" questions.

STEP 2: TURN THE NARROWED TOPIC INTO AN ARGUABLE STATEMENT

Sometimes changing a topic into an arguable statement is just a matter of wording. The phrase "The satisfactions of last summer" easily converts to the full sentence "Last summer was satisfying," an arguable proposition, though perhaps still broader than you might wish. To narrow it further, ask the "What about?" question again. "What about last summer was satisfying?" can produce "Last summer was especially satisfying to me because I discovered something important about myself." If the topic is phrased as a question or semi-question, the thesis lies in the answer to the question. "Why the Athenians lost the Peloponnesian Wars" can be answered by the arguable statement "The Athenians lost the Peloponnesian Wars because they had a foolish foreign policy."

Now try making the topic you narrowed in Step 1 into an arguable statement.

STEP 3: CLARIFY YOUR STATEMENT BY ADDING AN "ALTHOUGH" CLAUSE

Since theses by definition are "arguable propositions," each thesis carries the notion that something or someone opposes it, argues against it. When you think about it, it is this quality of opposing that gives the thesis its significance. You can define the point of disagreement and thus clarify your persuasive purpose by adding what I like to call an "although" clause. That is to say, you can phrase the opposing arguments as a subordinate clause[2] and attach it to the thesis statement to create a serviceable working thesis. Our sample theses (here underscored), together with their "although" clauses, might be worded:

- Although the Athenian civilization was undeniably superior to the Spartan, <u>the Athenians were foolhardy in their foreign policy and thus lost the Peloponnesian Wars.</u>

or
- Despite the undeniable superiority of the Athenian civilization, <u>the Athenians were foolhardy in their foreign policy and thus lost the Peloponnesian Wars.</u>

- For the other members of my family, nothing out of the ordinary happened last summer--it was a vacation much like all the others, but <u>to me it was a truly significant time. For the first time, I got a glimmering of real knowledge about myself and I began the slow process of growing up.</u>

In each of these examples, adding an "although" clause not only sharpens the point of contention but also clarifies the issues upon which the argument will depend. The Athenian loss of the Peloponnesian Wars becomes more meaningful when we realize how much more highly civilized and

---

[2]Such technical terms are explained in Part Five, the Revision Guide, where they are listed alphabetically.

Useful Facts About the "Although" Clause

- The clause need not begin with the word *although*. Note in the examples on page 7 that one clause begins with *despite*, and another uses *but* to oppose the thesis proper to the "although" material. You might also begin the subordinate clause with *though* or *even though*, or you could begin the thesis proper with *yet* or *still*, *nevertheless*, *however*, *on the other hand*, or any term that indicates the contrary.
- Ordinarily, there is no single correct "although" clause for a proposition. Usually you have a number of appropriate opposing perspectives from which to choose. For instance, the "although" clause in the third example on page 7 might as easily have been: "I didn't win any contests last summer or recover from a rare disease, but. . . ."
- Useful as the "although" clause part of the thesis is in constructing an essay, it need not appear in the finished composition. (In fact, though it is helpful to phrase your thesis exactly during the early stages of writing, you may decide that the thesis should not appear in the finished composition phrased in the original words of the working thesis.)

intelligent than their opponents the Athenians were considered to be. Even the wonders of a summer of self-knowledge and growth are put into sharper perspective when you consider that to the rest of the family last summer seemed much like any other.

Try adding an "although" clause to your experimental thesis.

STEP 4: EVALUATE YOUR THESIS

Once you have a thesis worded, you need to find out how useful it is likely to be. Try these tests:

- Is this proposition worth proving?
- Do I have (or can I get) enough evidence to develop it persuasively?

Formulating a potential "although" clause for a thesis you are considering can also be a useful way of evaluating whether the thesis proposition itself is worth writing about. Self-evident or clichéd theses do not make good compositions. Although a thesis certainly need not be blatantly controversial, a less-than-exciting composition will result from an attempt to argue that "Basketball players are tall" when no one has ever proposed otherwise. You could not truthfully claim about the height of the Boston Celtics that "Despite appearances to the contrary . . ." or that "Although authorities suggest differently . . ." or even that "We have substantial reason for believing otherwise, but. . . ." Thus, the value of "Basketball players are tall" as a thesis is, to say the least, questionable. Testing your thesis in this way can save you from spending time and energy working with an inherently uninteresting subject. On the other hand, exercise care not to discard a good thesis too quickly on these grounds. After all, the most exciting implicit opposition argument possible is "No one has ever pointed it out before, but. . . ."

You will also want to examine your potential thesis to see whether enough material is available to you to support it properly. Many well-worded theses would not make good compositions because they make an assertion about which little can be said. Some, such as "My roommate tosses our books on the floor" or "George Washington wore false teeth," are probably too specific to provide much more than a paragraph. Others, such as "The ptitze mold is a little-known organism," are self-limiting. Although such statements might serve well as introductory remarks or as ways of arousing interest, they cannot be illustrated and thus have little value as theses. Again, if you know nothing about ptitze mold and no information about it is accessible, the thesis "Ptitze mold is an interesting species" cannot yield an adequate composition. By the same token, a statement such as "Grass is not really green," though much more interesting than its opposite, must be discarded if, after investigation or serious thought, it turns out to be false.

A dividend comes with evaluating a thesis in this way. While you are thinking through possible evidence to see if you have enough material to make your thesis worth pursuing, you are also taking the preliminary steps toward the reasoning you will use to develop and support your thesis.

TRY IT OUT

1. In the preceding section of the text I suggest four steps to help you find your thesis and word it in a useful way. Write out the steps for the idea you experimented with on pages 6–8. Choose at least one of the following topics and take it through Steps 1, 2, and 3.

World Peace	Fraternities and Sororities
Mosquitos	The Soaps
The Women's Movement	Crime in the Streets
Nuclear Power Plants	Vegetarianism
Gadgets	China
College Athletics	Free Trade
Ghosts	Capital Punishment

2. Evaluate the theses you have created by applying both tests suggested in Step 4 (pages 8–9).

3. Evaluate the following for their usefulness as *working* theses, checking them against the evaluation tests on pages 8–9. Bear in mind that a good working thesis must be phrased as an arguable statement or proposition.
   a. My thesis is the effect of the Federal Reserve Bank on the stock market.
   b. Why John Donne wrote "A Hymn to God the Father."
   c. The sadness of life.

> **d.** Thomas Jefferson was the third president of the United States.
> **e.** The differences between the French and English political systems.
> **f.** Should inflation be defeated at the expense of full employment?
> **g.** Ernest Hemingway influenced Shakespeare.
>
> **4.** Choose from exercise 1 two items that you think have thesis potential. Then phrase them as good working theses.

Finding Your Working Thesis Inductively

The four steps suggested in the preceding section are helpful in formulating your thesis statement if you have a general idea about what your thesis is going to be or after you come to that idea. But often when you set out to write, you may have only the most superficial notion of what you want to say. And if you attempt to formulate your thesis at this stage in your thinking, you may well end up with the most superficial of essays. Under these conditions, in order to discover your thesis you will need to explore your topic inductively—that is, by assembling all the ideas you can on the subject and drawing your thesis from this list.

INVENTORY OF IDEAS

Specifically, you will want to gather information on the subject and make an inventory of your ideas. You can gather the information by doing research of all kinds—by observing the world about you, by talking to people, by experimenting, by reading, or by summoning the information from your own memory. When your subject takes you to outside resources, as it will in writing a research paper (see Chapter 10), then your inventory of ideas will be your note cards. When your ideas come mainly from your own thoughts, you can place them before yourself mentally or, better yet, jot them down. However you assemble the inventory, you will need to play with the ideas: divide, stack, and restack the cards; draw lines between the ideas on paper. Consider each notion or fact and relate it to the others. To do so, you will want to look for points of relationship. Which items are parallel or alike? Which items can be subordinated—that is, literally ordered or organized under others? You can form categories, eliminating some topics, adding others, until you begin to see a pattern (see the example on pages 11–12). Because structure and thesis are so closely related, the pattern will either suggest an organization out of which a thesis will be born or it will suggest a thesis from which you can derive an organization. Often as the pattern and the thesis begin to take shape, the dark will give way to dawn, and you will experience a sense that it is going to work out, that this particular combination will enable you to say something worth saying, something you would really like to say.

Let me show you how one freshman class as a group made an inventory of their ideas and how they developed their thesis from it. They decided to work on the topic "George Washington," which—though most did not consider it a particularly inspiring topic—did have the advantage of being one of the few subjects on which they shared common knowledge. In pooling this knowledge, they assembled the list of items shown in Figure I.1.

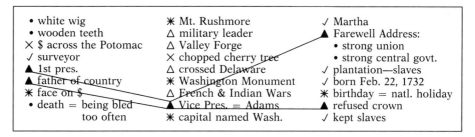

Figure I.1. Inventory of Ideas with Relationships Marked

This inventory of ideas is as miscellaneous a collection as you are likely to find; and yet, in its diversity, it is rather typical of the mixture of ideas in writers' minds as they start to compose. Can these varied facts be woven into a unified, logically structured paper? Well, yes, they can. First, however, the writer must discover the relationships among the diverse ideas. I'm not sure just what connections you would find among the George Washington ideas, but my freshman class, having first physically linked the items to one another by lines and symbols, came out with the clusters shown in Figure I.2.

| X cherry tree
X $ across Potomac | Δ military leader
Δ French & Indian Wars
Δ Valley Forge
Δ crossed Delaware | ✳ U.S. capital = Wash.
✳ Mt. Rushmore
✳ Wash. Monument
✳ face on $
✳ birthday = holiday |
| • wig
• teeth
• bled/death | ✓ surveyor
✓ Mt. Rushmore
✓ Martha
✓ plantation: slaves
✓ Feb. 22, 1732 | ▲ 1st pres.
▲ father of country
▲ farewell address
▲ Adams: Vice Pres.
▲ refused crown |

Figure I.2. Inventory Grouped by Clusters

As the class worked, discovering parallels and relating items to one another, they began to perceive their clusters as categories, categories that were, in turn, also related (see Figure I.3).

You may be wondering what these categories have to do with a thesis. The connection is, in fact, quite direct. An inventory of ideas contains what a writer knows or how the writer thinks about a subject. This list is then

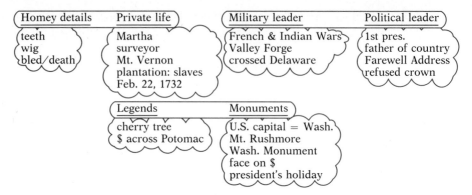

Figure I.3.   Inventory Items in Categories

both (1) the source that supplies the arguments that support the thesis and (2) the material from which the thesis is developed. Writers are not, of course, limited to their original inventory of ideas. They can, and often must, discard some original inventory items that are not directly relevant to their point as the thesis begins to make itself clear. Even so, this list is a writer's raw material. Thus, from the way you as the writer sort this material, from your way of seeing the relationships among ideas and facts in your inventory, should emerge what you really want to say about the subject—in short, your thesis.

As for the class that generated the sample inventory of ideas on George Washington, they worked their thesis out in a long and rather heated discussion that produced a whole sequence of suggested theses. Here are their working theses in the order they evolved:

- Washington was a great man.
- Washington was a hero in peace and a hero in war.
- Washington was a hero in the past and is a legend in the present.
- Washington was a hero in his day and is a legend in ours.
- Although Washington was a human being, even as we are, he was a genuine hero in his day and has become a legend in ours.
- Although Washington was not exempt from the flaws of humanity or the evil of his own culture, he became a genuine hero in his own day and is a legend in ours.

This method (sometimes called *brainstorming*) of taking inventory of one's ideas and then focusing in to discover relationships between the ideas takes much concentration and a certain agility of thought. But when you learn how to do it well, you can be assured that you will almost always produce a worthwhile thesis and a strong supporting structure.

TRY IT OUT

1. Study the following inventory of ideas, relate the items in it to one another, and place them in categories. Consider the categories and try to develop a thesis that could be supported by the facts and ideas listed in them.

   The Pilgrims[3]

Mayflower	went to Holland
1625	children losing heritage
Indian friends	sailed to America
corn	theocracy
religious freedom	cold winter
starvation	taking Indian land
illness	strict observance of Sabbath
Mayflower Compact	rough voyage
turkey	peace pipe
first Thanksgiving	no celebration of Christmas
plain dark clothes	enforced Puritanism on all
fled England	stocks
religious persecution	unbelievers banished

2. Brainstorm one of the following topics and gather your own inventory of ideas about it. Follow through to the thesis stage. Evaluate your thesis by the criteria suggested in Step 4 on pages 8–9.

Blind dates	South Africa
Plight of the farmer (auto worker, miner, etc.)	ESP (extra-sensory perception)
	Rock and roll
Terrorism	Yuppies
A pet	

ORGANIZING FROM YOUR WORKING THESIS

If you phrase your working thesis carefully, you can use it to organize your expository essay. Chapter 1 offers solid reasons why you will probably want to incorporate this organizing into some sort of written plan (or outline). But for now, while you are concentrating on your first essay, let me suggest only that a written plan, a shorthand way to designate organiza-

---

[3]This inventory of ideas, like that on George Washington, was suggested by the members of a composition class. After you have finished the exercise, if you would like to compare your thesis with those worked out by this class, see page 37.

tion, gives you a method of viewing the entire structure of the essay. It gives you a chance to think through your organization ahead of time, without taking away any of your freedom to make changes later in the writing process.

Making a Structural Plan (A Working Outline)

A plan of this sort can thus serve you as a powerful tool. How do you produce such a plan? The wording of your working thesis can provide the major clues. You see, since your thesis contains the essence of what you want to say, everything else in your paper must go to develop it or support it in some manner. Structurally speaking, your thesis is what all the parts of your composition depend upon and are subordinated to. We can even conceive of an expository composition as an equation where the various parts combine to yield the thesis:

$$\text{Part I} + \text{Part II} + \text{Part III} + \text{Part IV} \ldots = \text{THESIS}$$

If this reasoning is sound, then it should be possible literally to divide the thesis into its components and use the component ideas as your major topics. Briefly, you should:

1. Examine the language of your working thesis carefully and *analyze* its meaning.
2. Select the *key words and phrases* that point to the ideas in the thesis that will need support. Where the "although" clause is significant, find its key words, too.
3. Find that *support*—in your inventory of ideas or, if necessary, beyond.
4. *Subordinate* the support under the appropriate idea. (The art of organizing is the art of subordinating.)[4]

To see how this process would work in practice, let's try it out on the George Washington thesis that the class agreed upon:

· Although Washington was not exempt from the flaws of humanity or the evils of his own culture, he became a genuine hero in his own day and is a legend in ours.

1. Analysis: What exactly does this thesis commit its writer to prove?
   a. That Washington is justly considered a hero. (Subordinately: That Washington was also all too human.)
   b. To offer some explanation why.

---

[4]*Subordinate* derives its meaning from Latin roots meaning "to rank under or beneath."

2. Which key words and phrases will need support?
   a. In the thesis itself:
      That W. was a hero in his day
      That W. is a legend in ours
   b. In the "although" clause where significant (as it clearly is here):
      That W. had human flaws
      That W. reflected cultural evils
3. Is the evidence to support these ideas appropriately subordinated? (See the inventory of ideas categorized on page 12.)
   a. "[Although] Washington was not exempt from the flaws of humanity or the evils of his own culture"
      · He had human flaws
        - subject to vanity: powdered wig
        - subject to mortality: wooden false teeth, death by overbleeding
      · participated in cultural evils: kept slaves
   b. "[Still Washington] became a hero in his day"
      · A superb military leader
        - in the French & Indian Wars
        - at Valley Forge
        - at the Delaware
      · He was also an exceptional political leader
        - father of his country
        - first president
        - wise adviser in his Farewell Address
        - especially noble in refusing crown
   c. "[Furthermore, he has become] a legend in our [time]"
      · Glorified in cautionary tales
        - for his honesty: the cherry tree
        - for strength & skill: $ across Potomac
      · Memorialized in monuments
        - in the name of the U.S. capital
        - with a holiday birthday
        - on dollar bill
        - with Mt. Rushmore
        - with Washington Monument
   d. Why? Washington is truly heroic because of a special quality: [Figure out for concluding portion—something about turning down a crown?]

Some planning of this kind is essential. How extensive and how structured the planning needs to be depends upon you. Some people do best when they write it all out as fully as in our example. Others seem able to keep most of the plan in their heads, except when preparing a lengthy work. Experiment to find out how much written notation works best for you. As for me, if I were doing the Washington paper, I would prepare this brief plan to guide me:

Thesis: Although W. was not exempt from the flaws of humanity or the evils of his own culture, he became a genuine hero in his day and is a legend in ours.

I. Introduction
II. W. as fallible human being
   A. Flaws & mortality
   B. Evils of his culture
III. But W. now a legend
   A. Tales
   B. Monuments
IV. Deservedly so: W. genuinely heroic
   A. Militarily
   B. Politically
V. Conclusion: A special quality: Would not be king.

Did you notice that I reversed points III and IV? One of the greatest advantages in constructing a written plan is the flexibility it offers you. Like a blueprint, it gives you the opportunity to make your large structural mistakes in the plan, where they are easily corrected, rather than on the actual project, where change is achieved with much more difficulty.

Building your paper's structure from its thesis is a complex process. It may be helpful to study additional examples:

Thesis: For my family, last summer was nothing special, but to me it was the summer when I found out about myself and began to grow up.

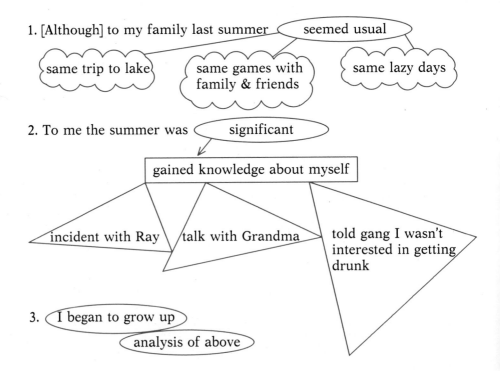

Thesis: Despite the undeniable superiority of the Athenian civilization to the Spartan, the Athenians were foolhardy in their foreign policy and thus lost the Peloponnesian Wars.

I. Introduction (poses the paradox)
II. Superiority of Athenian civilization
    A. Spartan culture
       1. Arts
       2. Philosophy
       3. Government   *or*
    B. Athenian culture
       1. Arts
       2. Philosophy
       3. Government

    A. Arts
       1. Sparta
       2. Athens
    B. Philosophy
       1. Sparta
       2. Athens
    C. Government
       1. Sparta
       2. Athens

III. Foolishness of Athenian foreign policy
    A. Example
    B. Example
    C. Example
    D. Example
IV. Loss of Peloponnesian Wars
    A. Chronological account
    B. Evaluation (emphasizing point in III as the cause)
V. Conclusion (generalization)

There are a number of additional techniques for handling the specifics of organizing, as you will learn in the next chapter, but for now the accompanying boxed section should be helpful.

Guidelines for Structure

1. *Make your plan brief so that your mind can comprehend it as a whole.* Since the human mind reaches its outer limits for easy comprehension and memory with five or six items, you may need to subordinate and coordinate ideas to keep within these limits.
   - Restrict yourself to four to seven major headings (including the introduction and the conclusion).
   - Restrict the subheadings as well. Resubdivide if a sequence becomes longer than five or six.
2. *Keep the plan (and thus the composition it will produce) unified and pointed toward its thesis.* Think of an organizational plan as a pie, for instance. The whole pie = the thesis. Divide it, and all pieces are still part of the whole pie. Just as a slice of apple pie can be nothing but apple, and a slice of cherry always remains cherry, so every

part of a composition (and of the plan that shows its organization) is committed to explaining or supporting its point, its thesis.

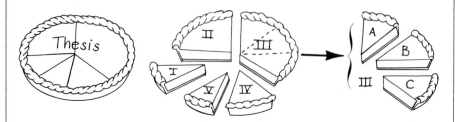

The analogy can also be carried from the whole pie to its slices. Divide one of the slices into smaller portions, and these small segments make up the larger piece just as the larger pieces make up the whole.

· Make sure, therefore, that all subpoints go to support or develop their points, and that all major points go to support and develop the thesis.

3. *Arrange your points (and subpoints) in the way that will most effectively support your thesis.*

· Deal with the "although" clause first—that is, clear the opposing arguments out of the way so that by the conclusion your point of view indisputably prevails.

· Arrange all items in a well-thought-out, logically defensible order.

4. *For a more tightly logical structure in the final composition, try wording your plan in phrases that are parallel in form.* For example, you might want to subdivide the point about Washington's being genuinely heroic:

Okay   Okay   BUT NOT
W. = Hero   W. = Hero   W. = Hero
   a. as a military leader   a. militarily   a. as a military leader
   b. as a political leader   b. politically   b. politically

Because of some oddity in the way our minds work, your finished composition will probably turn out to be less tightly constructed if you mix the terms in the plan.

TRY IT OUT

1. Carefully study the wording in the following working theses and derive organizational plans (outlines) from them:

   a. Although capital punishment has been proved to exert no deterrent effect upon crime, it should not be abolished because it serves some important economic and psychological needs of society.

   b. Despite the overwhelming popularity of capital punishment in a country ideally run by the wishes of the majority, the practice should nevertheless be abolished because it serves no useful purpose and is inherently uncivilized.

2. Write two theses based on the following topics, and derive organizational plans from them. Use the theses you created for the Try It Out exercises on pages 9 and 13 if you wish.

Pilgrims

The sixties

The soaps

A pet

The plight of the farmer (auto worker, miner, or others)

Little League athletics

Blind dates

ESP

Terrorism

Rock and roll

Yuppies

South Africa

ESTABLISHING A RELATIONSHIP WITH YOUR READERS

When you have discovered what you want to say and have found the material you will need to support or develop it, when you have formulated your thesis and have structured an effective organization around it, you will again want to consider your relationship with your readers.

A good way to think of writing is to picture a three-way relationship among writer, thesis, and reader, a relationship in which the *writer* tries to express ideas in such a way that *readers* are persuaded to accept the writer's view of the subject, the *thesis*. See Figure I.4.

Your readers, then, are the people you will need to convince. And it is to them, to actual human beings, that you will direct your words. Exactly who are these readers? Sometimes they are specific individuals. For example, if you have been asked to investigate a part of your company's operations and report back on your research, you will be writing for specific managers in your company. Since you may know these people personally, you will be able to direct your message to fit both their interests and what you suspect their reactions might be.

Sometimes your readers will be a group of people you do not know, but who share some important characteristics. At present, for example, I am writing to you and other college composition students. Though I may not know you personally, as I write I think about other students I know and thus try to speak to you (and them) in a natural way and address the ideas that you (and they) may be interested in learning about. Similarly, your

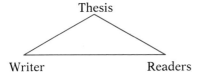

Figure I.4. Rhetorical Triangle

instructors may sometimes assign a paper to be addressed to a particular audience, and then you will have to assess the special needs or personality of this audience and try to aim your writing to fit them.

Far more frequently, however, you will be writing for a less specific group of readers. Like all the authors whose work appears in Part Four, you will be directing your writing toward a general audience of educated people, an audience like the readership of the newspapers and magazines for which most of our authors write, an audience, in short, of people much like yourself. Each of these readers has the same sort of thoughts and emotions, the same quirks and eccentricities, the same capacity to be pleased—and to be irritated—that we all possess. Thus, to know yourself and your colleagues is to know your readers. Chapters 1 through 9 specify techniques that authors have found helpful for reaching and convincing their readers, and Chapter 3 discusses this subject in detail.

Finding Your "Voice" as a Writer

We have not yet considered the third angle in the rhetorical triangle: you the writer—perhaps the most significant part of the communication cycle. Lou Kelly, writer and master teacher, exaggerates only a trifle when she contends: "The content of composition *is* the writer—as he reveals himself, thoughtfully and feelingly in his own language, with his own voice." No subject can speak for itself. All content—scientific, historical, intellectual, as well as personal—necessarily is conveyed to the reader in some sort of voice. That voice can be engaging or dull, or even the mechanical speech of a computer. Its tone can help readers along in interpreting or understanding the content, or it can get in the way of their comprehension. Although readers are not always consciously aware of the writer's voice, it is always there in one form or another, influencing their attitude in a significant way, either openly or subliminally.

USING THE APPROPRIATE VOICE

All writing is conveyed through a particular voice, and that voice influences the communication of the message it carries to the reader. How are you to make sure that the voice your writing projects carries the conviction you want it to have? The answer is twofold: (1) Make sure that your writing expresses your own voice, and (2) use that voice of your own which is most appropriate to your approach to your subject and to the occasion.

Your Own Voice.   Your writing should sound like you. It should not sound like an imitation of someone else because the tone will not ring true. Your ideas will also lose their credibility if you clothe them in artificial phraseology or express them in vocabulary inspired by Dr. Roget's thesaurus rather than your own experience. Nor should you attempt to so abstract yourself from your writing that all that remains is an impersonal, mechanical, often convoluted prose rarely seen anywhere but the classroom, the sort of writing that English professor Ken Macrorie, having read hundreds of student compositions, dubs "Engfish." Your writing voice should instead incorporate the qualities you most like about yourself. Writing is, after all, a conversation with a reader held under ideal conditions; for in writing you can always go back and clarify, go back and make amends, go back and insert that clever retort you never remember until the encounter is long over.

Your Appropriate Voice. Your writing should also reflect the voice of yours that is most appropriate to your subject and to your audience. You may not often think of yourself as having more than one voice, but a moment's reflection should convince you that you instinctively speak quite differently when you're out with your friends than you do when you are applying for a job.

Professional authors speak in various voices, too. George Will in "The Chicago Cubs, Overdue" speaks in a playful, semi-ironic tone and addresses the reader almost intimately:

> A reader demands to know how I contracted the infectious conservatism for which he plans to horsewhip me. So if you have tears, gentle reader, prepare to shed them now as I reveal how my gloomy temperament received its conservative warp from early and prolonged exposure to the Chicago Cubs. (page 438, paragraph 1)

The tone of this article is typical of Will, yet other tones are equally representative of his work. Notice the hard, almost angry realism in the voice that introduces another of his well-known essays, "Israel and Munich":

> Various Jewish religious observances commemorate calamities or narrow deliverance from calamities, and the short history of the Jewish state is replete with such experiences. Today, friction between Israel and the . . . administration is building up a dangerous charge of static electricity. No Israeli government casually risks the U.S. government's displeasure: diminished support for Israel could lead to a calamity from which there would be no deliverance. But the contagious crossness between Washington and Jerusalem that originated in Washington is a compound of Washington impatience and Israeli anxiety. The anxiety is more reasonable than the impatience.[5]

The essential difference between the voices talking to us from the two Will passages is "distance." In the first essay, Will seems very close to the reader. His tone is informal, and he uses the first person "I" and the second-person "you" in a familiar, conversational way. Distance between author and reader is far greater in the second essay. The I-you relationship is kept beneath the surface, providing a more objective tone. What Will writes is

[5]*Newsweek,* July 7, 1977. Printed by permission of Newsweek Inc.

presented not as a matter of personal idiosyncrasy, but rather as a matter of soon-to-be-demonstrated fact: "The anxiety is more reasonable than the impatience." And despite such typical examples of Will's pertinent and witty diction as "contagious crossness," the tone of his voice in the second instance is far more formal than in the first, as befits its more serious subject.

Like Will, you too can employ widely varying voices. But how will you know what voice to use and how to use it? Fortunately, you already know very well. Without even thinking about it, you naturally adopt the tone, vocabulary, and syntax appropriate to the occasion—whether it is an outing with Grandma or an evening of romance. And in personal writing, you probably have little difficulty finding the right voice in which to compose a letter to Grandma or to your new romance. If you can keep your intended readers in mind in much the same way when you write more formally, you should have little trouble with tone of voice here either.

MANAGING YOUR PRONOUNS

Though most of your ability to control your tone of voice is instinctive, you should also find some practical suggestions helpful. Chapter 9, pages 260–277, discusses how to choose the appropriate diction for specific readers and occasions. But probably the most important word choices you'll have to make concern which pronoun to use. Here you can be guided by the choices professional writers usually make. The following tips are derived from research in the work of many respected professional essayists:

Using "I."   If you have decided to write subjectively or informally or if the subject matter concerns your own life or opinions, feel free to speak in the first person. Much use of passive constructions and other sorts of unnecessarily complicated syntax result from writers' struggling to avoid the natural use of "I." You may have noticed that most of the writers of essays in this text use "I" and "we" comfortably.

Overusing "I."   On the other hand, some uses of the first person can lead to pitfalls of which you should be aware:

- Appearing self-centered. Just as in conversation, beginning each sentence with "I" or ending every phrase with "me" can imply an unattractive self-centeredness.
- Appearing indecisive and unsure. Adding an "I think" or an "I believe" to your statements does not really identify the statement as your opinion. The simple fact of your authorship does that. Frequent use of these phrases, rather, introduces a hesitancy or a tentativeness to your writing. If such hesitancy (or the becoming mod-

esty that this hesitancy sometimes implies) is your aim, well and good; but also realize that in creating such a tone, you lose a degree of persuasiveness from your statements.

Using "You." Reserve the pronoun "you" only for occasions when you want to address your readers directly. Using the "you" is appropriate in a "how-to" work (such as this book) or when you have chosen a distance very close to your reader or have adopted an unusually informal tone (as Will does so effectively in his Chicago Cubs essay). But for most expository writing, you are probably wise to avoid using the second-person pronoun. "You" meaning "one" or an indefinite subject, as in "Whenever you want to go out, it rains," is ordinarily incorrect in writing. Therefore—except in the most informal of essays—write "you" only when you truly mean "you, my reader."

TRY IT OUT

1. Look carefully at the opening paragraphs of Charles Stack's "If I'm So Smart, How Come I Flunk All the Time?" (page 425), Meg Greenfield's "Accepting the Unacceptable" (page 420), Ellen Goodman's "The Communication Gap" (page 418), and Lewis Thomas's "Late Night Thoughts" (page 428). All these essays are on scientific or sociohistorical matters, yet a distinctly personal voice speaks to its readers from each of them. As you read, consciously listen to the author's voice speaking to you through the written work.

   In a few well-chosen adjectives or brief descriptive phrases, try to characterize each of the authors' voices speaking through these samples and see if you can distinguish them from one another. Do you think, for instance, that a particular author reveals himself or herself to be compassionate? arrogant? intelligent? curious? knowledgeable? confused? authoritative? disagreeable? humble? angry? cynical? skeptical? foolish? well educated?

2. The essays in Part Four exemplify many uses of the personal pronoun. Study the following usages to determine (1) the effect of this use of the personal pronoun upon the tone of the sentence or paragraph in which it occurs, (2) its effect upon the author's voice in the article as a whole, and (3) the way that voice relates to the reader:

   "I" in (a) Will, page 438, and (b) Tucker, page 431.
   "We" in (c) Alexander, page 411, paragraphs 3 and 4.
   "Our" in (d) Tucker, page 431, paragraphs 4 and 5.
   "You" in (e) Turner, page 434.

3. Try varying your voice by writing two brief paragraphs on the same subject. In both paragraphs discuss either "Dormitory Life" or "The First Days of the Freshman Year." But write one for private distribution to next year's students and the other for inclusion in the *Official Freshman Handbook.*

When You Write

BEGINNING TO WRITE

How should you begin to write an essay? The answer is "very quickly"! And that answer is more than a joke. For if you are like most of us, once you have written something on the page, almost anything at all, the blank-page jitters begin to subside. Where should you start? Despite differences of opinion, the wisest judgment holds that, for most people, it is best to begin at the beginning—that is, with the introduction. Ignoring for the moment your freedom to change or delete anything you write, you should realize that with everything you say in your essay, you make a commitment to your reader—a commitment to follow up the statement, to explain, to support its premises. For this reason, it is usually wiser to write sequentially, to begin by writing your introduction.

Introducing

But what should an introduction contain? What is it supposed to do? To discover the answer, let's look at the introductions to essays written by professional authors. The following excerpts are introductions from some of the essays in Part Four.

> Remember high school English? Remember symbols? Remember the scarlet A? When you studied Hawthorne's *The Scarlet Letter,* you probably spent a lot of class time discussing Sin and Guilt. But it could be your English teacher missed the point. Jemshed Khan, an opthalmologist at the University of Missouri at Columbia, claims that too many of the book's readers are finding the same old profundities. What readers keep overlooking, maintains Khan, are all the signs of a great murder mystery. (Perry Turner, "What Killed Arthur Dimmesdale?" page 434)

> I went back to college this week or, to be more accurate, back to colleges. For five days I had an intensive course on the generation born circa 1960. I gathered enough material for a thesis on The Communication Gap Between

the Sexes, Phase II. On campuses covered with ivy and lined with palm trees, I met young women who've been encouraged to consider life plans that will include careers as well as families, aspiring as well as caretaking. I met young women who talk regularly with each other in and out of class about marriages of mutuality, about futures of equality.

But when I asked how often, how easily, these same women talked about their ideas and ideals with the men in their lives, I sensed an uneasy quiet.

Gradually, I realized that many of these students maintain a kind of conspiracy of silence with men. They secrete away some levels of feelings and hopes until it is "too late," until false expectations are already set. (Ellen Goodman, "The Communication Gap," page 418)

Outside the great conference hall in Nairobi, 16 fountains sent up sparkling plumes of water, and black Mercedes limousines glistened in the bright East African sun. Inside, some 1,500 delegates from 110 nations sat in air-conditioned comfort. The splendid setting of the meeting could hardly have clashed more jarringly with its purpose. At the U.N.'s invitation, the representatives had gathered in the Kenyan capital last week to discuss and devise ways of containing what an increasing number of experts regard as a major environmental danger: the creeping, seemingly relentless spread of the earth's deserts. (Fred Golden, "Earth's Creeping Deserts," page 415)

If we assume these examples to be fairly typical, what can we say about introductions? Even on the basis of this limited sample, we can at least rule out a couple of deep-rooted bits of folklore about introductions:

1. Clearly, an introduction is *not* always a single paragraph.
2. The thesis is *not* always (or even usually) the first sentence in a composition.

We might even hazard some generalizations:

3. Introductions usually contain a preliminary statement of thesis. In the examples:
   · What readers keep overlooking [in *The Scarlet Letter*], maintains Khan, are all the signs of a great murder mystery.
   · [Women students] secrete away some levels of feelings and hopes [from men] until it is "too late," until false expectations are already set.
   · The creeping, seemingly relentless spread of the earth's deserts . . . [is] a major environmental danger.
4. Statements of thesis usually come at or toward the end of an introduction (with any material following the thesis merely restating or amplifying it).
5. Introductions do *not* contain arguments or other kinds of support for the main point of the thesis.

From these introductions (and others you might want to take a look at), we can formulate some idea about the purpose of an introduction.

> **The purpose of the introduction to an expository work is to lead the readers to a statement of its thesis (or at least to approach its central idea), to provide them with enough background information for them to grasp it, and to do so in such a way that they will want to continue reading.**

How do writers manage to accomplish this purpose? Let me answer in terms of the three samples: Turner reminds readers of their own experience with the subject and then points out that the usual interpretation of it is the opposite of the thesis now being expounded by a noted scholar. Goodman approaches her thesis by describing the personal experience that led her to adopt it. And Golden attempts to arouse interest in his little-known problem by demonstrating its current importance through his description of an international meeting recently held on the subject.

Each of these authors seems to have considered what interested him or her about the subject or what about the subject seems to make it relevant right now. Each is careful to give readers the factual background necessary to understand the issue. But perhaps the most striking similarity in these three very different introductions is that at least two of them appear to be a development of the "although" clause of their theses.

The "although" clause to Turner's thesis is surely that

> [Although most] high-school English . . . classes discuss . . . Hawthorne's *Scarlet Letter* [in terms of] Sin and Guilt. . . .

This idea is amplified through the rest of the introductory paragraph up to the statement of the thesis. Similarly, Goodman's introduction is concerned with developing the "although" clause of her thesis:

> [Although] I met young women who talk regularly with each other in and out of class about marriages of mutuality, about futures of equality. . . .

Even Golden's introduction seems to have a hidden ironic "although" clause:

> [Although everything about the setting of the environmentalist meeting signified an extravagant waste of water. . . .]

Introductory use of "although" clauses is thus common in professional writing, as a glance at the introductions to the other essays in Part Four confirms. And this use should not surprise us too much. After all, the reason behind much expository writing is the desire to refute a contrary opinion. And there seems to be a natural tendency to want to begin an explanation where the writer's mind first takes hold.

How can you follow in the footsteps of such professional writers? You can begin by searching for the same sort of reasons for reader interest in your own thesis. Then, by composing your introduction to lead from these reasons to the statement of your thesis, you will draw your reader into the ideas of your essay. You might ask yourself such questions as these to get started:

1. What idea or event got me interested in this topic to begin with? Might it not also interest my readers?
2. What about my topic or my approach to my topic is relevant to readers at this time? Does my topic relate in some way to a subject of particular interest right now? (For example, to the women's movement? the election campaign? the coming of winter?)
3. What do I need to explain about my topic before my readers can understand my thesis?
4. Would expanding the "although" clause of my thesis make an interesting introduction?

Once you have decided upon the approach to your subject that might most intrigue your reader, compose your introduction so that it leads quickly from presentation of the ideas to statement of your thesis.

TRY IT OUT

1. Consider the introductions to three essays *other* than those by Turner, Goodman, and Golden sampled in the preceding section and answer these questions about them:
   a. Do any of your samples state the thesis in the opening sentence? If so, which?
   b. How many paragraphs long is each of your sample introductions?
   c. Does each of your samples have a statement of thesis? If not, which introduction omits it?
   d. Exactly where does each statement of thesis occur? What is the nature of any introduction material following it?
   e. Can any of your sample introductions be considered expansions of the "although" clauses of their theses? Which ones?

2. Work out a suitable introduction for a thesis developed from one of these following topics. You may use a thesis you wrote for an earlier Try It Out exercise if you wish.

The eighties	Terrorism	Yuppies
The soaps	Blind dates	Little League
ESP	Nuclear power	Women's role
Pilgrims	South Africa	Vegetarianism

WRITING THE BODY OF YOUR ESSAY

Your introduction will interest readers in your subject and pave their way to your thesis. In the body of your paper, your task will be to develop and support that thesis. If you have thoughtfully carried out the prewriting procedures, the actual writing of your paper should not be too troublesome. After all, you have already thought through the kinds of ideas you will use to support your thesis, and you will already have mapped out a logical way to organize that support. Your written plan or outline can be invaluable to you now. In fact, you could almost think about the actual writing of your paper as a fleshing out of your outline, giving substance and body to your plan.

But though your plan can be a most useful guide to rely upon, it is neither sacred nor unchangeable. Despite the good thinking that went into formulating it, you have not carved it in stone. An outline chiseled in granite would certainly be a millstone about your neck, holding you back from making needed changes. So, as you write and have the opportunity to explore your ideas more fully, keep your mind open to any other thoughts that may come, adjusting the plan to accommodate changes in your thinking. At the same time, remember that any new plan you come up with should be at least as logical and reasonable as the old.

Topic Sentences

Exactly how do you use your plan (or outline) to write the body of your essay? You take the thesis-supporting ideas, briefly noted as the points (and perhaps the subpoints) of your plan, and build them into the paragraphs or paragraph clusters that will make up the body of your paper. In fact, you will probably want to derive the topic sentences of these paragraphs from the ideas set forth in the points or subpoints of your plan.

The topic sentence of a paragraph, like the thesis of a composition, is that statement of the idea which all the rest of the sentences of that paragraph explain, support, or define.

Sometimes the topic idea is not completely spelled out in the topic sentence and sometimes it does not fill the entire sentence, but whether hinted at indirectly or stated in full, the topic idea awakens readers' expectations about what is to follow. Thus, if you are to guide your reader with understanding through the development of what you want to say, each of your paragraphs (or paragraph clusters) should have a topic sentence at or near its beginning, a topic sentence that should be followed by other sentences that either redefine or develop its point.

You may be surprised at my recommending topic sentences so unhesitatingly, for if you have ever come across the rule that "Every paragraph must be headed by a topic sentence," you may well have dismissed it as just another bit of folklore. But the truth is that, unlike other such dogmatic statements, this rule usually turns out to be valid. Research has demonstrated that professional authors control the direction of their writing by topic sentences at or near the start of most paragraphs or paragraph clusters.[6] Why not try a little research yourself? Check back over the last few paragraphs or forward over the next few, identify the topic sentences, and see how they focus their paragraphs.

The fact that professional writers regularly employ topic sentences should not surprise us because such sentences are remarkably useful to both writer and reader. We comprehend what we read mostly by processing a series of clues. Topic sentences provide perhaps the strongest of these clues, for they alert us to what will immediately follow. When we read a sentence, we subconsciously expect the next one to exemplify, explain, or illustrate it. When we read the beginning sentences of a paragraph, we look for their explanation and support in the rest.

Concrete Support

Support for topic sentences is also important. The persuasive power of an essay in large measure lies in the strength of its supporting material. Sometimes, however, beginning writers fail to appreciate this fact. Having made their point and rephrased it to their satisfaction, they often feel ready to get on to the next order of business without realizing that their readers may be left unconvinced and dissatisfied. But *all* good writing must "show" as well as "tell." A topic sentence such as "Capital punishment does not act as a deterrent" clearly needs to be documented with such evidence as statistical studies, quotations from court transcripts, or criminal case histories. But it is no less urgent to back up less argumentative topic or subtopic sentences such as "My brother keeps a messy room." Yes, Brother's room is messy, the reader might concede, but what is messy about it? In what specific way is it untidy? It is your job as writer to supply the answers—to explain and describe, to give examples and illustrations. You might support your statement with anecdotes or bits of conversation:

> · Ever since the day the frog jumped out at her, my mother avoids Brother's room altogether. She claims she is afraid to go in.

Or you might use specific sensory details:

[6]The exceptions are introductory or transitional paragraphs, which topic sentences rarely head, and the internal paragraphs of paragraph clusters, which are controlled by the topic sentence in the lead paragraph. Paragraph clusters include the smaller divisions into which long paragraphs are sometimes broken for visual reasons. For a fuller discussion, see Chapter 4, pages 113–114.

> · Tossed on top of the rumpled sheets and blankets on
> Brother's unmade bed and weighing down the limp heap of
> yesterday's soiled clothing were a spelling note-
> book, a Snoopy-bedecked lunch pail, two nearly shred-
> ded <u>Mad</u> magazines, and a gym shoe with a broken lace.

The more specific your examples, the more convincing your writing will be. Walter Williams in "Blacks and a Free Market" (page 442, paragraph 7), for instance, makes his strong argument about the excluding character of licensing even stronger when he provides his readers with the exact cost of a taxi license: $60,000. Fred Golden is not content to tell his readers that "Earth's Creeping Deserts" have covered great expanses of our planet and have affected the lives of many people; he tells us specifically how much and how many:

> More than a third of the earth's land mass is desert or desert-like, and one out of seven people—some 630 million—dwell in these parched regions. (page 415, paragraph 2)

And don't hesitate to cite specific names—even when they may be unknown to many of your readers. Particulars give a situation reality. We don't have to be familiar with Indian geography to respond to Golden's instancing of the Rajasthan region:

> In one part of India's Rajasthan region, often called the dustiest place in the world, sand cover has increased by about 8% in only 18 years. (page 415, paragraph 3)

And in the following example from a student theme, we don't have to know the writer's roommate to appreciate the specificity in the revised passage:

> · FIRST DRAFT: "Many of the students I have met at college
> are real characters."
> · REVISED: "My green-eyed, freckle-faced roommate,
> Robin, is a genuine eccentric."

Using Outside Sources as Support

Often when you support your point, you will need to use information not stored in your own head. You may find your information by interviewing, as Elizabeth Jane Stein did for her student paper (pages 458–461); or you may find it in books or other written sources. It is exceedingly important that you mention your source as you work with this material. If you are to use this information persuasively in your writing, then your readers must know and be able to evaluate its origin. And if you are to retain their trust, then they must be confirmed in their expectation that every idea and every phrase that you do not attribute to someone else is completely your own. Chapter 10 explains the most effective way of taking notes from outside material and details appropriate ways of using the material and of documenting it. You may well want to study that chapter before you do much work with outside sources. But for now let me outline what is essential for you to know in order to include reference material in your writing.

The first thing to keep in mind is that even when you are working with borrowed material, the essay you are writing is your own and the points you are making are your own; you are using the outside material, just as you often use your own thoughts, to substantiate and support your points. The only difference is that you must be careful to identify the source of your supporting material. Such identification is especially important to keep yourself free of any suspicion of the particularly nasty act of plagiarism. (See pages 303–304.)

Rules for Referring to Sources

1. Always *introduce* your subject in your own words.
2. Always *identify your source* as you present reference material, whether you are quoting it directly, stating it in your own words, or giving statistics.
3. If you are quoting directly—even so much as a phrase—always enclose the quoted material in *quotation marks* (or, if the quotation is of three lines or longer, indent it into a block).
4. When you write a formal paper, such as a college essay, *document your source* by including in parentheses the page number and the author's name (if not cited introductorily).

Note how the authors of the following examples quoted from the readings in Part Four invariably follow the first three rules. In citing the quotations for you, I follow the fourth documenting rule as well.

USING DIRECT QUOTATION

1. Introduce: Others were less convinced by Khan.
2. Name source: Eugene Arden, an English professor at the University of Michigan in Dearborn,
3. Use " marks: said that . . . Dimmesdale "was in fact becoming the most powerful and persuasive deliverer of sermons in New England—not a feat likely in a person dying of atropine poisoning."
4. Document: (Turner, page 435, paragraph 10)

USING PARAPHRASE (I.E., YOUR PHRASING OF YOUR SOURCE'S WORDS)

1. Introduce: It could be your English teacher missed the point.

2. Name source: Jemshed Khan, an ophthalmologist at the University of Missouri,

3. paraphrase; no " marks: claims that too many of the book's readers are finding the same old profundities. What readers are overlooking, maintains Khan, are all the signs of a great murder mystery.

4. Document: (Turner, page 434, paragraph 1)

USING STATISTICS

1. Introduce: I know that we have changed in tandem with the times.

2. Name source: When Helen and Alexander Astin did their study on incoming freshmen in 1971, 32 percent of the men and 31 percent of the women agreed that. . . .

3. Document: (Goodman, page 419, paragraph 11)

If you remember to stay in charge of your essay by always stating your topic and subtopic sentences in your own words, and if you always let your readers know when they are encountering someone else's words or ideas, then you will not go wrong in using outside support.

Your use of appropriate supporting detail is the key to success for your essay. Sources for backup of this kind that you may find most useful include:

- Facts
- Statistics
- Anecdotes
- Analogies and comparisons
- Well-reasoned arguments
- Evidence of the five senses
- Quotations

You will find a much fuller discussion of these ideas in "Supporting Your Point" in Chapter 4 (pages 116–124).

TRY IT OUT

1. Let's see how professional authors use topic sentences. Since introductory paragraphs are often structured in a different way, we will consider only internal paragraphs. What are the topic sentences of paragraphs 2 and 3 in E. B. White's "The Distant Music of the Hounds" (page 436)? What are the topic sentences of paragraphs 3 and 4 of Shana Alexander's "Getting Old in Kid's Country" (page 411)?

2. What concrete evidence do these authors provide to back up the ideas they express in their topic sentences? (You may find the terms listed on page 32 helpful here.)
   a. In White's paragraph 2? In paragraph 3?
   b. In Alexander's paragraph 3? In her paragraph 4?

3. Having seen how the professionals handle support, why not try it yourself? Write a paragraph supporting this topic sentence:

> A number of countries have developed ways to halt the onslaught of the desert.

Derive your support from Fred Golden's essay (pages 416–417, paragraphs 8–11). Make your points and support and document them appropriately, using the rules on page 31.

Hint: You might find it helpful to turn to Bret Gilbert's paper (pages 445–447) to see how a student uses another author's essay as source material to support his own quite different thesis.

CONCLUDING YOUR ESSAY

The conclusion of a composition has but one purpose: to bring the work to a satisfying end. The reader should be brought to experience a feeling of finality, an understanding of the author's point, and a positive—or at least open-minded—attitude toward that point. Sometimes this goal is accomplished within the body of the composition, especially in a very short essay; but more often an author feels the need to conclude more formally in a brief paragraph or two. Although from time to time you may come across compositions without formal conclusions, you will find that all the essays in Part Four do have them. The conclusion is located, after all, in the most influential position of a written work. It is the last thing the reader will read and will probably be the part most readily remembered. It thus should carry the essay's strongest, most persuasive phrasing of the writer's point of view.

How then should you approach the ending of your own paper? I would urge you to finish writing introduction and body—and then pause. Clear the cobwebs from your mind, then read back through the composition and get a real sense of what you have written. You have worked hard on the paper part by part, and you need an opportunity to get a feeling for the essay as a whole. Read it aloud if you can; savor its rhythms; make the revisions that seem indicated. After taking this pause, an appropriate way to end the work almost always suggests itself. With this approach, you can draw from the essay itself an understanding of what still needs to be said.

Some papers conclude by evaluating or interpreting the arguments or ideas they have presented; others offer the reader constructive suggestion for action or further thought. The most frequently included element in well-written conclusions is an eloquent statement (or restatement) of thesis. This statement can be even more effective if it echoes the ideas or phraseology of the points supporting the thesis argument throughout the paper. The material in the rest of the conclusion might also hold such echoes. Through restatement or echoing, the reader not only experiences a more satisfying sense of wholeness and unity but also receives a subtle reminder of the most persuasive points in the essay and all they had implied. (See also pages 124–132.)

TRY IT OUT

1. Read through E. B. White's "The Distant Music of the Hounds" (page 436). Which phrase or phrases in the conclusion are echoes of what has gone before? Which sentence rephrases White's thesis?

2. Does Walter Williams's conclusion to "U.S. Blacks and a Free Market" (page 443) tend most to evaluate, to interpret, or to restate the ideas of the essay? Or does it offer suggestions for further thought?

After You Write

RECONSIDERING

Most good writers replan and reconsider as they write, studies show; but a time comes when a writer reaches the end of a unit of work, completes a first draft. And then it is time to thoroughly reconsider. Let's assume that you have just completed that first draft. If writing were exactly like conversation, your act of communication would be over. Because you are writing, however, you have an added opportunity to make sure that you have said exactly what you want to say and, perhaps even more important, that your reader will understand what you have said exactly as you intended it.

If you can possibly arrange it, let some time elapse between your writing and your revising. The more time the better, because when you next look at your paper, you will be trying to see it not through the eyes of its anxious author but through those of an interested reader. So put it away for a couple of days. Or sleep on it. Or at least munch on a peanut-butter sandwich and think about something else. And then very, very carefully, read through your paper again. Chapter 7 offers a thorough discussion of the editing and proofreading skills you will want to develop as you become a more experienced writer. But for your early papers, let the accompanying checklist guide you in revising.

Checklist for Revision

Check for persuasiveness of thesis and structure

1. Does your overall organization permit your points and ideas to support your thesis? Could any parts be changed or adjusted to make your thesis more convincing or more appealing?
2. Is there a logical order behind the arrangement of your points?
3. Does every paragraph (cluster) have a topic sentence that helps develop your thesis?
4. Does every sentence help develop the topic sentence of its paragraph? Or would the ideas expressed in some sentences serve better to support the point of another paragraph? Are the sentences within each paragraph arranged in a logical order?
5. Is any material in the essay irrelevant to the support of your thesis? (Be merciless on this one.)

Check for effectiveness of voice and tone

1. Is the voice that speaks through the composition truly your own? Are the tone and distance of that voice appropriate to the subject? Are they appropriate to the relationship you want to achieve between yourself and your reader? Does this degree of distance remain consistent throughout the composition? Can any inconsistencies be eliminated?
2. Do you put your best foot forward in this composition? Do your most agreeable qualities show through? Do you let your genuine interest in, or enthusiasm for, the topic show?

Check for mechanics

1. Have you checked in the dictionary for the correct spelling of any word you're not sure about?
2. Have you checked in the Revision Guide (Part Five) any mark of punctuation or any point of grammar you are not certain about?

ASSIGNMENT

Using personal experience as the basis for generalization, write about one of the following suggestions (or another topic your instructor may provide). Check the list of steps following these suggestions for a useful approach to the assignment.

1. The transition between high school and college is often a crucial one—at least it certainly feels that way to most of us at the time. In a well-organized essay, try to define the freshman experience as you are encountering it.

   If you prefer, choose instead to focus on how it feels to be a member of your particular college or university community.

2. Think of an experience that changed your life or your thinking in some way: for example, a first encounter with racism, sexism, disabled people, serious illness, death, injustice, crime. Basing your work on this experience, write an essay that makes a statement about either your new approach to the problem you encountered or the change the experience wrought in you.[7]

3. Reread Lewis Thomas's "Late Night Thoughts on Listening to Mahler's Ninth Symphony." If you are a music buff, surely some musical composition moves you as Mahler's music moves Thomas. In a well-organized essay, describe this music, explain what it means to you as precisely as you can, and, like Thomas, draw some of its larger implications.

4. From your own experiences or those of people you know, write an essay explaining the reasons behind the current physical-fitness craze and showing why it will or will not last.[8]

5. Develop one of the theses you worked with earlier in this part into a full composition. Remember to draw on your own experience.

The steps suggested in this first part of *Writing Effectively* offer one good approach to writing a composition. Try writing your first paper by working consciously through the accompanying summary of these steps.

Steps in Writing a Composition

1. Analyze your purpose for writing, consider your probable reader(s), and select your subject accordingly. (See pages 2–3.)
2. Find the point you are interested in making about your subject by reasoning either from a general topic (pages 6–9) or from a group of particulars (pages 10–13). Phrase your point as an arguable statement. Include an "although" clause that acknowledges another approach to your thesis (pages 7–8).
3. Check your statement against the tests suggested on page 8, and if it still satisfies you, write it down as the working statement of your thesis. (Remember that your working thesis is an organizational tool that need not appear in those words in your paper.)

[7]Topic suggested by Professor Thomas Whissen of Wright State University.
[8]Suggested by Professor Jim Pictor of St. Francis College.

4. Analyze your thesis statement (as suggested on pages 14–16) to determine exactly what you will need to demonstrate. Select from your thesis the key words and phrases that will need to be supported, and compose an organizational plan based on these key ideas. Find that needed support (in your inventory of ideas or elsewhere), and in your written plan subordinate that support under the appropriate points (see pages 15–17).

5. Give further thought to the relationship you want to maintain with your reader in discussing this particular subject and to the voice most appropriate for this essay to project (see pages 19–23). Begin to write your essay.

6. Decide upon a meaningful and/or appealing way to introduce your subject (pages 24–26), and lead into a statement of your thesis toward the end of the introduction.

7. Support your thesis in the body of the paper by composing paragraphs from the ideas outlined in your organizational plan. Each supporting or amplifying point should be stated clearly in a topic sentence at or near the head of a paragraph (or paragraph cluster). Be sure to demonstrate and/or develop each of these points concretely and specifically (pages 29–32).

8. Read through what you have written. Reconsider and perhaps revise.

9. Draw your conclusion out from what you have already written (pages 33–34). Your ending should probably include restatement of your central point.

10. Edit your paper. Revise. Correct. Rewrite.

11. Proofread.

The theses the composition class created for the Pilgrim exercises on page 13 are:

· Although the Pilgrims encountered many hardships, they were able to overcome them because of their strength of character, a strength rooted in their deep religious faith.
· Although the Pilgrims believed in freedom, especially religious freedom, in America they set up a theocracy and restricted the religious freedom of others.

PART
TWO

Convincing Your Readers Through the Writing Process

In Part Two we will explore the writing process in detail. Here you will have the opportunity to find answers to the questions that our rapid survey in Part One may have raised in your mind. Here you should also discover practical strategies and techniques to help you write effectively. Part Two will help you make decisions about how to approach your topic and how to arrange your material, what to write and where to revise, and, above all, it should help you conceive of your purpose for writing in terms of the real human beings who will read what you have written.

Chapter
1

The Prewriting Stage

Inventing and Arranging Your Ideas

Good writing is produced when writers have something they truly want to express to their readers. Finding something significant to say, then, may well be the most important problem a writer faces. You may have seen the problem firsthand: A paper is assigned, and instantly all sparkle fades and student eyes go blank and worried. Perhaps you have experienced this blank feeling yourself. Except for those miraculous moments when inspiration—or something akin to it—seems to strike, all writers have to begin by giving some serious thought to what is called the "invention" of ideas.

DISCOVERING YOUR POINT AND THE IDEAS TO SUPPORT IT

Although *invention* is the term that has been used since the days of the ancient Greek philosopher Aristotle, it does not accurately describe the process of finding ideas. Nobody really *invents* ideas; people discover them. They bring ideas out of their subconscious into the light where their conscious minds can examine and work with them.

Brainstorming

Such a search can be made either freely or systematically. The free search of the mind has been called *brainstorming*. My research shows that writers brainstorm in two basic ways. One way is to take an inventory of all the ideas the brain might harbor on a subject and list them (just as we did when we explored our thoughts on George Washington in Part One). The other way is through the act of writing itself. For many, the very process of writing stimulates creativity. In finding words and in formulating sentences, writers discover ideas they didn't know they had. Subconscious ideas can be brought to the surface through the process called *free writing.* Individual writers tend to favor either inventorying or free writing for invention, but most employ both techniques to some extent. You will want to try out and practice both and then decide which is most useful to you.

FREE WRITING

Free writing is totally unrestricted, as its name implies. Only one thing is required of the free writer: to keep writing until a set time is up. When you are free writing, if you are going to get at the ideas in your subconscious, you must not stop to think, to rest your fingers, to relax your muscles; you must just keep writing. You should not look back at what you've written, should not make corrections. If you cannot think what to say, just repeat the last phrase over and over until a new idea comes.

To use free writing as an invention technique, concentrate on your topic or subject as you begin and write for a specified amount of time—say, ten or fifteen minutes as a start. Let the wording of the topic suggest ideas to you and follow those ideas wherever they lead you. Make no effort to correct your writing or to turn it into a regular composition. Instead, use it as a storage bank of ideas. When you have completed your free-writing period, underline or circle ideas that may be worth pursuing. Also be sure to look for and mark all graceful turns of phrase that you may want to incorporate when you actually write your essay.

Use your annotated free writing as you would use an inventory of ideas, and think it through. Does a principle begin to form that seems to incorporate most of the ideas or to which most of them can be subordinated? In short, does a thesis begin to take shape? Can you structure some of the other material around it?

Often it is helpful to try another free-writing session as a follow-up to the first.[1] This time you begin by writing down the idea (or ideas) that seem to stand out in your first free writing and then let your mind wander from there. The second attempt will probably turn out to be more structured than the first. From it you may be able to work out a plan that will lead directly to your first draft.

Free writing is not for everybody at all times. It is a good technique to try, however, if your mind feels especially blank or if you are confused about the subject you are to write on. And many people find it a helpful way

---

[1]Peter Elbow suggests this strategy in *Writing without Teachers* (New York: Oxford University Press, 1979), a book you might really enjoy if you are among that half of writers who find free writing a useful technique.

to begin on those days when even the thought of writing seems disagreeable.

Besides Brainstorming

You may want to look again at Part One to review the inventory-of-ideas strategy (pages 10–12). Both inventorying (or listing) and free writing encourage the free flow of thought. But at times you may want to explore your ideas in a more structured way. At such times it can be worthwhile to try some more formal schemes called "heuristics" (from the Greek word meaning "to find out"). Both kinds of brainstorming help put you in touch with your ideas; heuristics are techniques to help you clarify these ideas and get a firmer grasp on their content.

THE JOURNALIST'S FIVE *W*S

One of the most useful heuristics is derived from a memory device long used by journalists. Reporters learn from their cub days to consider the *W*s, the traditional journalistic questions: Who? What? Where? When? Why? and, if applicable, How? Every good news-story writer builds the "lead" around the answers to these questions. And the questions can be just as effectively asked by an expository writer during prewriting. Using the *W*s almost guarantees a fairly thorough survey of one's information. If the class working with "George Washington" had used the *W*s, their inventory of ideas might have been far more extensive. "Who?" for example, could have brought to mind not only "Martha" and "slaves" but probably also a number of other people important in Washington's life.

You can use the *W*s not only to expand your inventory of ideas, but also to narrow a topic and channel it in a specific direction. You can pose any one of the questions, answer it with whatever first comes to mind, and then ask the other questions in terms of that answer. Let's say that your topic is "First Love." You can start with the question "When?" and answer it "When I was twelve." Thinking now of that incident, you will answer the question "Where?" with "At summer camp." "Who?" will bring "Bill" or "Lisa," which should carry you on to the crucial exploration of "What?" and "Why?"

Some writers combine the questions for deeper probing. The "Why" combinations are especially penetrating. "Why this particular person?" for example. "Why at this particular place at that time in my life?" If this heuristic works for you, it should help you to narrow your subject to workable size, to review all aspects of it, and to delve deeply enough into it to discover its significance.

ARISTOTLE'S "TOPICS"

Almost twenty-four centuries ago, Aristotle worked out a strategy for discovering and developing relationships among ideas, a technique so useful that many writers find it hard to better even today. Aristotle suggested that support for any subject could be discovered by considering that subject in terms of modes of thought that he called "topics." The idea was for orators (or writers) to ask themselves questions about their subject that the "topics" suggested to them. Aristotle suggested five major topics that he further subdivided into seventeen subtopics. Those that are most useful to writers today include:

1. *Definition:* What kind of thing is my subject? To what grouping or category does it belong? How is it distinguished from other members of that group?
2. *Comparison:* How is this subject similar to others in its group? How does it differ from them?
3. *Causal relationships:* What does the subject cause or bring about? What are the effects, the consequences of this subject?
4. *Authority:* What do the experts have to say about my subject? How might you use these "topics" to invent theses and support?

Take, for example, the perennial subject of student essays, "My Vacation."

```
· Definition
  - Free time
  - Learning experience
· Comparison (with other kinds of free time, other
  learning experiences)
  - More time
  - More solitude
  - Different way of being with friends, family
  - Sun and sand and sea
· Effects
  - Vacation threw new light on my relationships with
    others
  - Gave me more time alone to think about them
  - The background of the great eternals lent every-
    thing new perspective
  - I learned some important things about myself
· Authority
      ?? Check Herman T. Epstein's brain-growth theory ??
```

Despite the triteness of the assignment, a thoughtful theme is in the making here once each idea is supported by specific details.

Effective as the "topics" are for generating and developing theses, they were designed originally for finding arguments to support controversial positions. Even now this application is where they can achieve their greatest effectiveness. Let us look, for example, at positions for and against legislation on equal rights for women and see how the "topics" might help a writer develop arguments. The question is: "Should equal rights for women be guaranteed by law?"

ARGUMENTS

Yes

From definition: Women, like men, are people and, therefore, should be regarded so in the eyes of the law.

From comparison (to the past):

1. Psychological difference: In the past women found their entire sense of identity and worth in the service they rendered to parents, husband, and children. Today women recognize that they need something from life in their own right. The law must, therefore, grant them personhood and equality so that they will have a fair chance to achieve their desires.

2. Economic difference: In the past, women had economic security. If they remained single, they continued as part of a larger family circle that would provide for them. If they married, their husbands took care of them financially. But now only the nuclear family remains, and it does not offer support to the unmarried relative. Married women now have to accept the possibility of divorce; and even if they remain married, the rise in the cost of living often requires two breadwinners. Women, therefore, now need to be economically effective just as men are.

From effect: If legislation is passed, justice will be served and the promises of "freedom and justice for all" will at last be fulfilled.

From authority:
The Declaration of Independence.
The Constitution (especially the 14th Amendment).
Betty Friedan, Gloria Steinem, Bella Abzug.

No

From definition: Men are men and women are women; and although neither should be favored, the difference should be legally recognized.

From comparison (to the past):

1. Psychological difference: In the past women found fulfillment in their traditional role. Now many women who choose to continue in that role are made to feel so degraded that they believe they must work outside the home, thus contributing to the downfall of the family and disintegration of the moral fabric of society itself.

2. Economic difference: In the past, when men were the major breadwinners and most women were content to be helpmates at home, massive unemployment existed only during infrequent economic depressions. But now many women have been persuaded to seek "personal fulfillment" in a job outside the home. In neglecting their own families, these women are also displacing other heads of families from their work, and our society suffers the ills of continuous unemployment. Legislation will further all these destructive trends.

From effect: If passed, all that is unnatural will triumph. Women will lose all their special privileges; they will be required to serve in combat, they will be forced to share lavatories with men, and they will lose all special financial protection in divorce and special physical protection in factories.

From authority:
The Bible.
Phyllis Schlafly, Marabel Morgan.

FREE WRITING PLUS

This heuristic combines the probing apparatus of some of the other strategies with free writing; it will be especially useful if you find free writing helpful. The idea is to choose a heuristic, and taking in turn each item—for example, the five *W* questions or each of Aristotle's "topics"—free write the ideas that come to you. For best results, spend no more than three to five minutes on any single perspective.[2]

RESEARCH

Sometimes the very best brainstorming does not work—cannot work—to bring up relevant ideas from your subconscious, simply because you don't have enough knowledge of the subject to have any relevant ideas in your subconscious. Similarly, there are times when all a heuristic can do is show you what sort of thing might support your point well—if only you knew something about it. At such times, you need to turn to research as a technique for invention.

How do you go about research? How can you find out what you want to know? First, formulate some questions. You cannot find answers until you ask effective questions. If you know too little about a subject to ask effective questions, then two courses are open to you. First, you can ask around. Bring up the topic in conversation. See if anyone in your acquaintance can give you a clue that might lead to a source of knowledge for you or that might point a way into the subject that you could pursue more systematically. Second, look up the topic in an encyclopedia or in a general reference work in the field. Although few encyclopedias have articles written in the depth needed for actually writing the paper, much invention-stirring material should turn up in such reference works.

Once you know something of what there is to know about your subject, you can formulate some questions and try to search out the answers to them. Where will you find the answers that will help you "invent" the paper? From people, books, or your own experimentation. The topic might suggest any or all of these resources. Your own questions will determine which.

If, for instance, you are working on a topic of political interest—say, whether military expenditures should be cut or increased—the precise questions you want answered will determine whether you should:

- Write your senators and representative to see where they stand; or
- Look in recent news magazines to learn what experts predict for this year's budget; or

---

[2]Elizabeth Cowan Neeld, in *Writing*, 2nd ed. (Glenview, Ill.: Scott, Foresman, 1986), develops a Free Writing Plus heuristic called Cubing, in which she suggests considering a topic as if it were a cube—that is to say, from each of its six "sides." Her six "sides" include: Describing it, Comparing it, Associating it (with other ideas), Analyzing it, Applying it, and Arguing for *and* against it.

- Find a book in the library's card catalog to get a historical perspective; or
- Survey your classmates (if your question is: What do students at my college think?).

Any of these research strategies will provide you with plenty of data for brainstorming up a thesis and also give it some solid support.

The suggestions in this chapter should keep you from the discouraging condition of not knowing what to say or how to go about supporting it. The following Try It Out section will give you a chance to experiment with these strategies for yourself.

TRY IT OUT

1. Choose one of the following topics and free write about it for twelve minutes.

Influence of rock stars	Scholarships for athletes
Rights of AIDS victims	The draft
UFOs	Sadism on TV
NASA and the United States space program	Subsidized day-care centers

Does a leading idea begin to present itself from your writing? If so, could this idea be developed to serve as a thesis?

2. Take one of these topics and ask yourself the five *W*s about it. Write down answers. Do the beginnings of an essay seem to emerge? What is its thesis?

3. Take one of the topics from number 1 (but *not* the one you used for number 2) and work it through Aristotle's "topics." Write a thesis from the results.

4. Which of the strategies we have discussed (including the inventory of ideas you learned about in Part One) seems most valuable in discovering a thesis and the main points you will use to support it? Why?

5. Write a paragraph supporting one of the points you have "invented" in these exercises. Discover the support you need for this paragraph by personal research. Try surveying the opinion of six to ten people—on your corridor, in the grocery, or elsewhere. But remember that this survey will give a very limited sample, valid only for those who live on your corridor or who were shopping that day. Be sure, then, to make only limited claims for this researched support in the paragraph you write.

ORGANIZING AND ARRANGING YOUR IDEAS

Another important part of planning is inventing an effective arrangement or organization for your ideas. It is true that you will continue to develop the essay's structure as you write, just as you continue to invent new ideas along the way. But the whole writing process becomes much easier for you (and the work itself much clearer to your reader) when you take a little time to put your ideas into some kind of rhetorical order before you begin to write.

Why Make a Scratch Outline?

It is even a good idea to scribble down your ordered ideas to guide you as you write. Perhaps you are skeptical. But if you will try a brief experiment, you can prove to yourself that some sort of written plan is close to essential for constructing anything but the very shortest work of writing. Albert Joseph uses the following experiment to convince the sophisticated—and highly skeptical—business people who enroll in his Industrial Writing Institute:

EXPERIMENT

Try the following problems, but *without using pencil and paper.* You can find the answers at the conclusion of this chapter.

1. Combine the letters A and B in as many ways as possible. (You discovered, I'm sure, the only two possible combinations.)

2. Combine the letters A, B, and C in all possible ways. (This would be much easier with a pencil. Were you able to find all six combinations?)

3. Now try all the combinations of the letters A, B, C, and D. (Congratulations if you were able to name the twenty-four combinations listed on page 65 without the help of pen or pencil. According to Joseph, only one out of one hundred adults is able to do so.)

The point of the experiment is that using memory alone to keep track of items of any complexity is extraordinarily difficult for most of us. And the moral is that if the composition you are going to write will have three or four ideas at least as complicated as A, B, C, D, you are well advised to order these ideas on paper before you start. In other words, you will do much better in organizing your writing if you rely upon a written plan, however sketchy.

MAKING YOUR SCRATCH OUTLINE

Making an outline need not be burdensome. If the word *outline* summons up a picture of a list of items numbered I to XXVI or of three painstakingly typed pages of topic sentences, we are not talking about the same thing at all. The kind of outline I have in mind is a brief written plan, meant for your eyes alone, in which you set down your ideas in a meaningful sequence to guide you in constructing your composition.

Choosing a Form.   Your outline should be a working tool tailored to your own needs. How you construct it is an individual matter. It can consist of anything from a brief list of numbered phrases to a set of attached balloons worthy of a Rube Goldberg cartoon (see samples on pages 16 and 52), as long as it spells structure to you.

Despite the personal nature of the outline form, I must offer a cautionary word. Even if you are usually most comfortable with complete sentences, you probably should be wary of sentence outlines (outlines composed of topic sentences). These plans take so much time to write that those who make them often develop such a vested interest in their phrasing that, in using the outlines, they compose their ideas to fit the words already established. A paper written from preconceived topic sentences tends to be not only inflexible in its thinking, but also stiff and awkward in its phrasing.

Beyond that advice, what system you use is immaterial. Bullets (•), dashes (--), asterisks (*), whatever, will do. Over the years, one system of outlining conventions has become fairly standard, and you might want to employ it. This system begins with roman numerals (I, II, III); indented under these are capital letters (A, B, C); and then arabic numerals (1, 2, 3); and then lowercase letters (a, b, c); and then, if needed, lowercase roman numerals (i, ii, iii). You will find examples of these conventions in this chapter (pages 51, 52, and 58) and throughout the book. I like it, despite the possibility of being charged with stuffiness, because it is a way of dividing my material that lets me see the divisions clearly and because it helps me discover patterns and parallels among my ideas.

What is most important to remember when making your outline—however you choose to designate the points—is that all of its points must go to develop the thesis. All the subpoints of a point must go to develop that point. And all the subsections of a subpoint must go to develop that subpoint.

Ordering Your Ideas

Besides showing the value of writing down your ideas to arrange them meaningfully, the experiment with the ABCD combinations on page 48 illustrates another significant point: the necessity for logical arrangement. People who were unable to figure out some logical sequence for combining the letters (such as ABC, ACB, BAC, BCA, and so on) probably didn't come close to getting all the combinations, while those who were able to find a pattern were well on their way to achievement. The experiment demonstrates, then, that in order for our minds to grasp the meaning of a series of ideas, we need to understand their relationship to each other.

The basis of any relationship between ideas is either coordination or subordination. That is, are the ideas equal or parallel? Or should one be subordinated to the other? An idea is subordinate to another if it supports, or can be categorized under, it. Organizing is almost impossible without subordination. It is the key to solving both major problems in constructing a piece of writing: the key to the problem of organizing both a large number of diverse items and a broad, undivided topic.

UNDERSTANDING SUBORDINATION

Although the principles of subordination seem to come naturally to some people, others find this subject—as central as it is—obscure and difficult to understand. One simple way to understand it is to compare it with the similar "common denominator" principle in fractions. If you want to add $\frac{1}{2}$, $\frac{1}{3}$, and $\frac{1}{6}$, you know that all three numbers have to be converted to a common denominator—that is, into sixths—in order to be combined. The same principle applies if you are trying to work with a number of diverse ideas. If you want to consider *mice* and *human beings* and *tigers,* for instance, you need to look for a common denominator for them, a category into which all will fit. You might decide to consider them all in the category *mammals.* In the language of organizing, you would, in both mathematical and zoological examples, *subordinate* the specific items under the general heading. Adding *canary* and *eagle* to your list would complicate the problem a little, since these animals are not mammals. But, just as you would broaden the common denominator to twelfths if $\frac{1}{4}$ were added to the list of $\frac{1}{2}$, $\frac{1}{3}$, and $\frac{1}{6}$, so too you would search for a broader category—*warm-blooded animals,* perhaps—to handle your additions.

In making these decisions, you are developing an organization. Subordinated in the conventions of the outline, these examples look like this:

```
I. Twelfths          I. Warm-blooded animals
   A. Halves             A. Mammals
   B. Thirds               1. Mice
   C. Fourths              2. Human beings
   D. Sixths               3. Tigers
      1. Halves         B. Birds
      2. Thirds            1. Canary
                           2. Eagle
```

Even though the ideas you will deal with in your writing are more complicated than simple fractions or kinds of animals, the principle remains the same. To treat diverse ideas in one paragraph, or even in one essay, you have to discover their common base and work with them by that standard. Think back on the procedure our example class used to bring order out of their jumble of facts about George Washington (pages 11–16). Despite the complexity of those items compared with fractions or categories of animals, the process the class went through was identical to the one just summarized.

ORGANIZING THE UNDIVIDED TOPIC

The analogy to working with fractions also holds true when you are faced with the opposite problem in organization: the large undivided topic, such as "Nuclear Disarmament" or "Freshman Year." Here you already have your common denominator, the topic itself. Your problem, just as in mathematics, is to find appropriate categories to divide it into. Just as in mathematics you would have to find the "factors that go in evenly," so too in organizing you have to discover divisions that encompass all the material.

How does this principle work in practice? Let's look at "Getting Old in Kid's Country" (page 411) to see how Shana Alexander handles the problem. Alexander's thesis is, "Kids have taken over [our society]." "How can I best approach this point?" Alexander must have asked herself: "How can I divide up my ideas?" She must have then answered: "Well, I can introduce it and interest folks in the subject; then I can support it; and then I can evaluate it." Once she had her topic structured in this general way, she must have done some thinking about subdividing further—especially the central portion in which she proves her thesis, for she takes up, individually, our admiration for kids' bodies, kids' food, kids' prizes, kids' heroes, kids' values. In short, Alexander probably worked from a structure much like this:

Thesis: Kids have taken over [our society].

    I. Introduction: Explanation
   II. Support & demonstration: We admire
       A. kids' bodies
       B. kids' food
       C. kids' prizes
       D. kids' heroes
       E. kids' values
  III. Evaluation
       A. Negative aspects
       B. Positive aspects
  IV. Conclusion

In supporting each of her subpoints, Alexander further subdivides her material. Examples subordinated to the idea of "Kids' food," for instance, she might have outlined as in Figure 1.1.

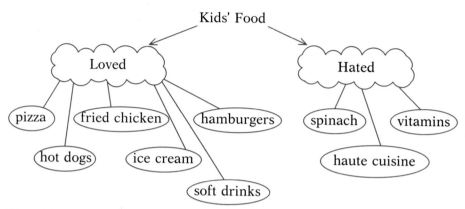

Figure 1.1   Subordination

KEEPING SEQUENCES SHORT

One other idea is worth remembering about organizing: Try not to include in any sequence more than five (or, at most, six) items before subordinating under subcategories. Any greater number of items in a sequence is hard to retain in the memory. Further, as your readers would find, when developed in paragraphs, more than five or six facts in a series become exceedingly tedious to read. But you will find as you write that very few lists of six or more points cannot be regrouped and considered under subheadings. American wars are much more effectively ordered in either of the following (or similar) ways than as a grouping of ten:

Use:

III. American wars
    A. 18th Century
        1. French-Indian War
        2. Revolutionary War
    B. 19th Century
        1. War of 1812
        2. Civil War
        3. Mexican War
        4. Spanish-American War
    C. 20th Century
        1. World War I
        2. World War II
        3. Korean War
        4. Vietnam War

Or:

III. American wars
    A. Major Conflicts
        1. Revolutionary War
        2. Civil War
        3. World War I
        4. World War II
    B. Minor Conflicts
        1. French-Indian War
        2. War of 1812
        3. Mexican War
        4. Spanish-American War
        5. Korean War
        6. Vietnam War

Not:

.

   III. American wars
      A. French-Indian War
      B. Revolutionary War
      C. War of 1812
      D. Civil War
      E. Mexican War
      F. Spanish-American War
      G. World War I
      H. World War II
      I. Korean War
      J. Vietnam War

TRY IT OUT

1. **Finding common denominators.** In what group do all the individuals in each of these sets belong?

    a. Dwight Gooden, Pete Rose, Joe DiMaggio, Babe Ruth
    b. Larry Bird, Kareem Abdul-Jabbar, Wilt Chamberlain, Oscar Robinson
    c. Chris Evert-Lloyd, Martina Navratilova, Boris Becker, John McEnroe
    d. O. J. Simpson, Walter Payton, Roger Staubach, Terry Bradshaw

Considering all the answers (a, b, c, and d) as a set, to what group do they all belong? Subordinate the items in number 1 appropriately and arrange them according to the conventional outline pattern.

2. Here is another list of specific items, but it also includes more general (or categorical) terms. Find the common denominators (use some of the included terms, if you wish) and construct a conventional outline by appropriate subordination.

    Dustin Hoffman, Lionel Richie, Singers, Meryl Streep, The Doors, Molly Ringwald, Bill Cosby, Actors, Bob Newhart, Rock groups, Robert Redford, Comedians, Phil Collins, Entertainers, The Beatles, The Rolling Stones, Bruce Springsteen, Richard Pryor, Goldie Hawn.

3. The next exercise is similar to one used by James M. McCrimmon at Florida State University. It gives you the opportunity to find an organization for material like that you may be working with in your courses. Suppose you are doing research on derivation of words. You have been told that among the most influential principles accounting for change in the meaning of words are: *generalization, specification, upgrading,* and *downgrading,* and you want to check it for yourself. So you have looked up the list of words in column A and discovered that each of them used to have the quite different meaning listed beside it in column B. It is up to you

to fill in column C with the principle that seems to account for the change in meaning:

A. Word	B. Original meaning	C. Principle of change
Chest	"coffin"	generalization
Constable	"stable caretaker"	upgrading
Girl	"young person of either sex"	specification
Immoral	"not customary"	downgrading
Meat	"food"	_____
Lewd	"ignorant"	_____
Starve	"die"	_____
Knight	"unsophisticated country dweller"	_____
Minister	"servant"	_____
Virtue	"manliness"	_____
Lust	"pleasure"	_____
Pretty	"sly, deceitful"	_____
Undertaker	"doer"	_____
Go	"walk"	_____

4. The material in Exercise 3 is a fair sampling of what you would find in wider research. You can thus consider it a fair inventory of ideas for an essay on the subject. Think of it in this way and (1) formulate a thesis from it, a thesis that could be supported by the evidence you discovered in working Exercise 3; (2) construct an outline to reflect the structure of a paper that you might write from that thesis.

SEQUENCING STRATEGIES

In working out a written plan for your composition, you may begin to wonder whether the order of points and subpoints actually matters much. The answer is that although the order of the subpoints is rarely crucial to the finished composition, the order of the main topics can often make a real difference. In any case, with or without a plan, you will necessarily select some items to be first and some to be last. And it is certainly better to make these decisions rationally and deliberately than to trust to chance.

The Rhetorical Principle

One test will always guide you rightly in arranging your ideas. Simply ask yourself: How do I organize this material to demonstrate or develop my thesis most effectively for my readers? In the paragraphs that follow, I describe some of the many strategies available to you. Each time you write, your choice should be the arrangement that will present your particular ideas most clearly and most appealingly.

SAVE THE BEST FOR LAST

According to findings in some psychological surveys, reader interest and reader memory are greatest for material at the end of a sample, next greatest for that at the beginning, and least for that in the middle. The most effective place to put your strongest point, then, is last—the last category you discuss, the last subpoint in a category. Thus, if you are writing with the intention of your reader continuing to the end and understanding the work as a whole, give your most telling idea that final emphasis, for it will be what your reader sees last and remembers best.[3]

"ALTHOUGH" CLAUSE

You will find the advice that you reserve last place for the most important idea especially useful when you are deciding where to put the "although" material. Since the "although" clause in the working thesis is subordinate to the thesis proper, the material supporting that clause should precede the thesis material in the finished work. Because the although material either states the opposition to your point of view or suggests an idea of far less importance to the paper, you certainly will not want to have this idea lingering in the reader's mind and clouding the effect of your main point when the reader reaches the end of the paper.

For a bad example, imagine that you are reading a well-argued paper against capital punishment, and just as you reach the final paragraphs and are beginning to be convinced, the essayist suddenly says: "On the other hand, proponents of capital punishment have some compelling ideas too, which I will briefly expound before concluding." Imagine your confusion with this turn in direction. Chances are, as you read the arguments on the other side, you will lose your sympathy for the writer's position irretrievably.

Surely then, it is wisest to get the "although" material out of the way as early as possible. Furthermore, as we have seen, such material frequently offers an effective opening for your composition (see pages 26–27).

But what do you do when the "although" material demands more than simple introductory treatment? When the subordinate clause of your thesis contains material that you will need to develop with some fulness in order

---

[3]Writers of business memos and reports, however, cannot reasonably expect their readers to comprehend the work as a whole. Under the press of time, busy executives customarily skim the beginnings and subheadings of most documents, limiting their complete reading to papers whose subjects coincide with their current needs. The rhetorical principle for business writing, therefore, dictates your placing the most important items first.

to strengthen and clarify the main point? Organizing then can be more complex; but whether you choose to stress the "although" material minimally or at some length, there are sound rhetorical reasons for saving the best—that is, the material that supports your thesis point—for last.

Debate Structure.   One good way to think of writing where the "although" material is emphasized is to consider a debate. The image of a debate simplifies your organizing problems because debates have a traditional structure. Variations in the following structure have been used by effective writers and orators since the days of the Roman orator Cicero. You may well find that it will work for you:

> · Suggest the opposition's ideas early in the paper.
> · *Then* argue your point of view.
> [· Perhaps present the opposition's objections and *then* refute them.]
> · Finish up with the undistracted reader committed to your point of view.

This ancient structural pattern serves Perry Turner's purposes in his "What Killed Arthur Dimmesdale?":

> Introduction
> > · Development of opposing idea: "Although" we used to think the *Scarlet Letter* was about Sin and Death. . . .
> > · Leading to thesis: Khan says it's really about murder.
> 1. Khan's arguments
> > · The arguments
> > · Scholarly support for Khan's arguments
> 2. Refuting opposing arguments
> > · First argument
> > > - Opposition
> > > - Khan
> > · Second argument
> > > - Opposition
> Conclusion:
> > - Khan and Hawthorne

Notice that the "although" side is always placed first (both in the Introduction and in Point 2) and that Khan's side, which Turner supports in this essay, always gets the final say.

Another way to think about organizing "although" material that demands emphasis is to treat it in terms of a comparison-or-contrast structural pattern. That is, you might consider structuring the "although" support material in contrast to material supporting the thesis proper. In the next section, comparison patterns will be discussed and exemplified in detail.

The Comparison Principle

A surprising number of theses lend themselves to arrangements that compare and contrast ideas. Besides using these structural patterns to explore the differences between the main part of a thesis statement and its "although" clause, you can use them to make an out-and-out comparison or to support one side of a controversial issue. You can apply them to the whole structure or to individual portions of it. Despite the enormous variety of possible subjects, there are only two basic comparative patterns: the alternating and the divided. You might organize a controversial issue in either of these patterns:

Divided pattern		Alternating pattern
I. Their side		I. Point 1
A. Point 1		A. Their side
B. Point 2		B. Our side
C. Point 3	or	II. Point 2
II. Our side		A. Their side
A. Point 1		B. Our side
B. Point 2		III. Point 3
C. Point 3		A. Their side
		B. Our side

You would face a similar choice if your paper involved looking at one subject in terms of another. If, for example, you were interested in developing the thesis "Although high school and college offer courses in the same subjects, the college courses are much more difficult," you would probably set up your structure in one of these ways:

Divided pattern		Alternating pattern
I. Introduction		I. Introduction
II. High school		II. Math
A. Math		A. High school
B. English		B. College
C. History	or	III. English
III. College		A. High school
A. Math		B. College
B. English		IV. History
C. History		A. High school
IV. Conclusion		B. College
		V. Conclusion

For an example of the comparative pattern serving to guide the development in one portion of a composition, recall the outline model about Athens and the Peloponnesian War on page 17. To show how remarkable it was that Athens lost those wars to a state like Sparta, the writer was obliged first to demonstrate Athens' superiority over Sparta:

```
I.
II. Superiority of the
    Athenian Civilization
    Divided pattern              Alternate pattern
    A. Sparta achieved much      A. The Arts
       1. Arts                      1. Sparta
       2. Philosophy                2. Athens
       3. Government        or   B. Philosophy
    B. But Athens achieved          1. Sparta
       much more                    2. Athens
       1. Arts                   C. Government
       2. Philosophy                1. Sparta
       3. Government                2. Athens
 III.
  IV.
   V.
```

Each of the two patterns has its advantages—and its drawbacks. If you want to make a number of points or if the points are not strongly distinguished from one another, the alternating arrangement can become repetitive, somewhat tedious, and sometimes even confusing. On the other hand, this arrangement allows you direct interplay between the two ideas that the divided way does not offer. A combination of the two is also possible. Perry Turner's "What Killed Arthur Dimmesdale?" offers examples of just such a combination. See the suggested outline on page 56, and notice how Turner makes use of divided comparison in the Introduction and the alternative pattern in Point 2. What pattern you choose should be determined by the nature of your material. You may want to think your subject through in both forms before deciding.

The Principle of Progression

Progression is another organizational scheme that writers often use. This approach includes a succession of items ordered according to a linear sequence: first to last, closest to furthest, best to worst, among others. You will find the principle of progression particularly valuable when you are trying to decide upon the arrangement of subpoints under a topic.

PROGRESSION BY THE PRINCIPLE OF IMPORTANCE

Perhaps the most useful form of progression follows our rule of saving the best for last. Here the sequence progresses from least important to most important. When no other arrangement suggests itself, you may well want to discuss your ideas by beginning with those least important to your argument and ending with those most crucial to it. This is the order Golden follows in "Earth's Creeping Deserts" as he adds facts, each more tragic than the last, to convince the reader of the magnitude of the Sahel calamity (page 415–416, paragraphs 5–6).

Inverted Pyramid.   For most expository writing, least-important-to-most is a strategy that will serve you well. But, as I mentioned earlier (footnote 3, page 55), in business writing where you cannot count on your reader taking the time to read your complete communication, the opposite progression, from most important to least, becomes your most reliable sequence. Whenever you need to write a business memo or report, I recommend considering first this strategy, called the inverted pyramid.

CHRONOLOGICAL PROGRESSION

Chronological arrangement, or ordering in a time sequence, is another highly useful progression. So much of our lives is related in some way to the passing of time that a writer quite naturally looks to a time order for arranging material that would otherwise seem unfocused. An anthropologist who wants to discuss ancient funerary practices might well arrange examples from the earliest date to the latest, beginning with those of Paleolithic peoples and continuing through time with those of the people of Ur, the Egyptians, the Etruscans, and finally the nobles of medieval Europe. When a psychologist needs an arrangement for discussing development of personality traits, a natural choice is the chronological sequence of newborn, infant, child, adolescent.[4]

Though you will also doubtless find many occasions to use a time progression, it does offer dangers you should be aware of. Just as thesis and argument is the basic structure in expository writing, chronological sequence is the basic structure in narrative writing or storytelling. Storytelling has primal appeal; it is the elemental composition, loved as much by primitive people and small children as it is by sophisticates. We all thus have a natural tendency to slip into storytelling when we write. This inclination makes it all too easy for us to rely heavily upon chronological organization, sometimes employing it when it is not appropriate. When writers give in to this narrative urge, they may find themselves developing every conceivable thesis in chronological order—even to the following ludicrous example:

> Thesis: Many children suffer traumatic effects when they learn that Santa Claus is an imaginary figure.
>
>   I. Introduction
> II. Santa's childhood
> III. Santa's youth

Faulty

[4]For the anthropological example, see J. H. Plumb's "De Mortuis," *Horizon* (Spring 1967); and for the psychological example, see Alan S. Katz, "Toward a Better Understanding of Passivity," *Boston University Journal* (Spring 1971).

```
 IV. Santa's adulthood
  V. Santa's old age
 VI. Conclusion
```

Yes, the chronological principle is as useful an organizing method as we have; nevertheless, be warned.

SPATIAL PROGRESSION

If the items you want to discuss are spatially related—the parts of a room, the places visited on a vacation, the states that may have offshore oil—you may find it useful to order them according to their closeness to, or direction from, one another. You might discuss them in the order that they occur going east (or north or south or west) from a point or going clockwise (or counter-clockwise). You might want to consider them according to their distance from a designated place, going from the farthest to the closest (or the other way around). Or you might think of them by their position up (or down) a mountain or along a river. Any progression of sequential sites will help your reader's mind through the organization of your ideas.

PROGRESSION FROM MOST TO LEAST (OR LEAST TO MOST)

Progressions of the type we have been examining are not confined to connections of time or space. We can apply a progression to any quantitative or qualitative relationship, any sort of least-to-most or best-to-worst. You might choose to organize your review of a museum collection by ranking the most garish to the most subdued paintings in the gallery; or you might want to make a zoological point by arranging your material in a sequence from the kind of caribou most likely to hibernate to the kind least likely to. Authors acquainting their readers with little-known facts often begin with the most obvious and proceed to the most unusual.

Other Useful Sequences

CAUSE AND EFFECT

Another arrangement that might further your purpose in a piece of writing is based on cause and effect. You might, for instance, start with an effect—such as World War I—and, one by one, trace the causes leading to it. Or you might start with a cause—such as World War I—and consider individually the effects it produced. You might even want to construct a chain of cause and effect: a cause leading to its effect, which in turn becomes a cause leading to other effects.

Ellen Goodman organizes "The Communication Gap" (page 418) with a variation on this cause-and-effect principle. On a recent trip to college campuses, Goodman discovered a lack of communication between women students and their closest male friends about issues that clearly were important to them. In examining her discovery, Goodman first considers the causes behind this curious silence and then sadly suggests some effects that it may well produce. The basic structure of her article thus involves:

· Introduction: The curious silence Goodman discovered
· Its causes
· Its potential effects

PROBLEM AND SOLUTION

The problem-solution structure is another useful organizational scheme. Using this method, you might set out a problem in the introduction, analyze it in the body of the paper, and offer a solution in the conclusion. Psychologist Charles Slack uses a variation of this pattern in "If I'm So Smart, How Come I Flunk All the Time?" Here he presents the problem of teacher bias in terms of students who have mastered a body of material and yet are receiving low grades. He describes the research he conducted to analyze the problem and reports on the solution the analysis suggested and on the research confirming that solution. His essay is organized in this way:

Problem—(Introduction)
   Indisputably knowledgeable though low-achieving students are victims of teacher bias
Analysis—of students' classroom behavior that elicited the teachers' positive & negative response
   1. Behavior of "Bright-Eyes"
   2. Behavior of "Scaredy Cats"
   3. Behavior of "Dummies"
Solution—Teach the "Dummies" the behavior of the "Bright-Eyes"
   1.
   2.
Evaluation—(Conclusion)

You may find the problem-solution structure not only a practical tool for essays in the social and physical sciences, but also a good way to organize a letter of complaint or suggestion. You might use it, for example, to persuade the people in charge to accept your solution to a problem you have discovered with some campus service or at one of the stores in your neighborhood shopping center.

CLASSIFICATION

Classification is a way of organizing material by assigning it to classes or categories of some kind. For our purposes, this method usually means breaking down a subject so that it can be analyzed in terms of its parts. You may find this approach particularly useful for organizing your subpoints. Slack, for instance (see the outline in the preceding section), uses this method twice in his essay: once to classify the types of students teachers respond to strongly and again to analyze the behavior associated with these types.

Classification can also provide a structure for an entire composition. Meg Greenfield uses it in "Accepting the Unacceptable" (pages 420–422) to analyze both portions of her double thesis. She structures her essay around her classification of the "permanent disadvantages" we face in responding to terrorism and of the "disadvantageous responses" we therefore tend to make:

> Introduction → leading to thesis: [We have] a permanent disadvantage in dealing with [terrorists] and . . . [a] penchant for deepening the disadvantage by the way in which we respond.
> Permanent disadvantages: 1.
>   2.
>   3.
> Disadvantageous responses: 1.
>   2.
> Results (Conclusion.)

The classification method works best when the categories chosen appear to grow naturally from the subject or the author's approach to it. Some subjects do seem to fall into categories as a matter of course, as, for example, executive, legislative, and judicial branches of government; animal, vegetable, and mineral; staff officers, line officers, and enlisted men and women; elementary school, high school, and college. More often, however, you, like the authors cited here, will have to impose classifications upon your material. For example: "We can identify four approaches to this argument," or "Those who knew this great woman remember her chiefly for one of these three qualities."

DIALECTICAL STRUCTURE

Dialectics is a word that once signified a broad range of methods for logical analysis. In our time, however, primarily because of work by Hegel and Marx, it has come to mean the sort of reasoning that involves combining or compromising two valid or accepted contrasting positions. In dialectics, the *thesis* states the first position (→), the *antithesis* the opposing position (←), and the *synthesis* the combined position (↔). Surprisingly enough, the thesis, antithesis, synthesis format of dialectical reasoning can be put to good use in organizing compositions. Consider, for example, the following plan:

> →   I. (Thesis: an accepted idea) To be educated, a student needs some acquaintance with "the best that has been thought and said in the world."
>   A. Proof
>   B. Proof
>   and so on

← II. (Antithesis: valid objection to I) But to be professionally qualified, a student must have a large quantity of specialized knowledge.
   A. Proof
   B. Proof
      and so on
↔ III. (Synthesis: a compromise) Therefore, many colleges insist on two years of undergraduate general studies in the liberal arts and two years of specialization in a major field.

The synthesis that concludes this plan might go on to become the thesis in yet another cycle of reasoning—perhaps a plan arguing for the additional years of specialization offered in a graduate course of study.

Final Thoughts on Arrangement

The list of ways to organize your compositions just detailed should be useful to you, but its usefulness should lie less in the knowledge it provides of the specific modes of ordering than in the glimpse it gives you of the richness and the variety of logical ways to organize. My aim is not for you to select any particular strategy or combination of strategies, but for you to choose some logically defensible order and to know why you choose it. The structure of your composition should seem organic, growing out of the material itself, not forced onto it. Your most important consideration remains presenting your thesis. In selecting your strategies, ask yourself at each stage, "Which ordering will present my material most naturally and with the greatest degree of logical consistency? What sort of organization will develop my point and my supporting ideas most convincingly?"

TRY IT OUT

1. Included as examples in this chapter are the bare bones of outlines for articles by Turner (page 56), Goodman (page 61), Slack (page 61), and Greenfield (page 62). Read two of these articles and flesh out the given outline by specifying the subtopics merely suggested there and by adding, where appropriate, examples for a further level of subordination.

2. Examine Alexander's article "Kids' Country" (page 411) and try to determine what principle(s) she uses in ordering her numerous examples. Would you have followed the same order she uses? If not, what principle would you have used?

3. Identify Elizabeth Jane's thesis in "The Blues Don't Knock . . ." (pages 458–461) and outline the structure she uses to develop it. Then try to identify a thesis and sketch in an outline in her preliminary draft (pages 462–468). What do you find?

4. Write a workable thesis about one of the following topics:

Seatbelt (motorcycle-helmet) laws	Scholarships for athletes
Subsidized day-care centers	"Buy American" campaigns
UFOs	Sadism on MTV
Influnce of rock stars	NASA and the United States space program

If you prefer, use the thesis that came out of your work with the topics in the exercises on page 47. Do, though, develop a working outline to structure support for this thesis. What strategy or combination of strategies did you use to order the points and subpoints of your outline? Why?

ASSIGNMENT

Paying particular attention to prewriting as outlined in "Writing the First Paper" and as discussed in this chapter, write a well-organized expository essay on the topic listed here that interests you most. Or, take a topic you have worked on as an exercise earlier in the chapter and develop it into a full essay.

1. Write an essay for or against the proposition: Life is harder for men. Working through Aristotle's topics (or another heuristic) devise the arguments you will need to support your thesis.

2. Select a problem on your campus: parking, registration procedures, the cafeteria, or the like. Join a group of your classmates and brainstorm the problem until you have collected an adequate Inventory of Ideas (alternatively, derive your Inventory of Ideas by free writing). Then, working independently, organize the ideas, find your thesis, and write a strong essay in which you analyze the problem and offer concrete suggestions for its solution.[5]

3. Compare your religious beliefs with those of a friend.

4. Do you agree with those who say that growing up is harder today than it was a generation ago? Write a well-organized essay defending your point of view.

5. Write a thoughtful essay with a clearly defined thesis comparing and/or contrasting one of the following pairs:
   a. Life in the 1960s and life in the 1980s.
   b. The best and the worst part-time jobs you have held.[6]
   c. Protestantism and Catholicism or Judaism and Christianity.

---

[5]Topic suggested by C. Russell of Rio Hondo College.
[6]Topic suggested by Fred H. Fischer of Imperial Valley College.

d. Weightlifting and isometrics for body building.
e. Greek and independent college life-styles.

Hint: If you choose one of the comparative topics (3, 4, or 5), remember that a good thesis cannot be developed from: "X and Y are different (or similar)." It should rather encompass your answer to the question "How" or "Why" or "In what ways" are X and Y different (or similar)?

Solutions to the Experiment (page 48)

1. AB, BA   = 2

2. ABC, ACB, BAC, BCA, CAB, CBA   = 6

3. ABCD, ABDC, ACBD, ACDB, ADBC, ADCB,
   BACD, BADC, BCDA, BCAD, BDAC, BDCA,   = 24
   CABD, CADB, CBAD, CBDA, CDAB, CDBA,
   DABC, DACB, DBAC, DBCA, DCAB, DCBA

Chapter 2

Thinking About Your Writing: A Sentence-Combining Interlude

Writing is funny. We don't feel about it as we do about the other things we do. If we work a math problem and discover we have made a mistake, few of us hesitate to rub out the mistake and continue on. But if we write a composition and find it needs extensive changing, most of us feel terrible. Asked to cut or prune our paper, we feel as if we're chopping off our fingers and toes. Our sense of self is that tied up with what we write.

This supersensitivity probably stems from the fact that thinking and writing are so closely related, and, naturally, we are all sensitive about our thoughts. Writing teachers have long speculated about how much easier learning to write would be if writing skills could be separated from a writer's thought. A few years ago one of them invented sentence-combining exercises, designed to do just that. By providing ready-made thought or content, these exercises give writers a pleasurable way to think about their writing. It gives them a chance to practice various wordings, phrasings, and even organization, and to find out—without anguish—just which choice is most effective, most persuasive.

In this chapter you will have the opportunity to do a little preliminary sentence combining so that you can see how the exercises work and how they can work for you.

HOW SENTENCE COMBINING WORKS

The meaning of language is contained in sentences. And since the purpose of sentence-combining exercises is to supply meaning, the exercises work through sentences. The sentence-combining approach assumes that all the sentences we speak or write are derived from the simple basic sentence: subject-verb-object. According to this theory, our minds combine these minimal sentences in complex ways to create an infinite number of possible sentences. In this view, the sentence "A troubled Hamlet gazed thoughtfully at the skull" is derived from the following three basic sentences (sometimes called "kernels"):

· Hamlet gazed at the skull.
· Hamlet is troubled.
· Hamlet's gaze is thoughtful.

These same kernels could also produce:

· `Hamlet, who was troubled, gazed at the skull thoughtfully.`
· `Thoughtfully, a troubled Hamlet gazed at the skull.`
· `The skull was gazed at thoughtfully by a troubled Hamlet.`
· `Hamlet, troubled, gazed thoughtfully at the skull.`

Sentence-combining exercises provide sets of such kernels and thus offer you a way to duplicate consciously the theoretical sentence-forming procedure.

You will not need special training to do sentence-combining exercises, for you are already something of an expert in the English language. You already have inside your brain the kind of rules that prevent you from ever creating such nonsentences as "Over game was the." Being a speaker of English, you have intuitive knowledge of the patterns of the English sentence and the ability to fit the thousands of words you know into these patterns. The aim of sentence-combining exercises is to strengthen your ability to do what you already do well by making you more aware of the process while you are doing it.

Abundance and Variety of Possible Combinations

In the sections that follow, you are asked to make effective sentences out of sets of simple kernels such as these:

· The game was over.
· The crowd was excited.
· The crowd left the stadium.
· The crowd filled the streets.
· The streets were narrow.

The most direct combination of these kernels gives you:

· `The game was over, and the excited crowd left the stadium and filled the narrow streets.`

But whether this is the most pleasing or most suitable sentence these kernels can yield, you can't know until you experiment with other options. These following possibilities come immediately to mind, but if you think about it, I'm sure you can find several more:

1. The game was over, and the excited crowd left the stadium and filled the narrow streets.
2. After the game was over, the crowd, which was excited, left the stadium and filled the narrow streets.
3. Leaving the stadium after the game was over, the crowd excitedly filled the narrow streets.
4. The narrow streets were filled by the excited crowd, who had left the stadium after the game.
5. Because the game was over, the excited crowd left the stadium and filled the narrow streets.
6. The game being over, the crowd left the stadium excitedly and filled the narrow streets.
7. As they left the stadium, the after-game crowds filled the narrow streets with excitement.
8. The game was over; the excited crowd left the stadium, filling the narrow streets.
9. The streets, which are exceedingly narrow by the stadium, are always filled with excited crowds when games are over.
10. The streets were filled with an excited crowd who had left the stadium. The game was over.

This set of sentence kernels about the stadium crowd—like every such set—offers the writer a remarkable number of options. To explore these options, feel free to experiment in the following ways: Here are some suggestions:

- Combine the kernels in any order that sounds good to you.
- Add appropriate function words (for instance, *after* as in examples 2, 4, and 7; *because* as in 5; *as* as in 7; *who* as in 4 and 10; *which* as in 9, and so on).
- Change the form of words (for instance, *excited* to *excitedly* in examples 3 and 6 and to *excitement* in 7; *filled* to *filling* in 8 and to *were filled* in 4 and 10).
- Add or delete a detail (for instance, the addition of *exceedingly narrow* and *always filled* in 9).
- Occasionally do not combine at all (let a kernel sentence stand as is, as in 10).

Don't hesitate to be creative. The more kinds of sentence structure you can learn to use comfortably, the richer your writing will become.

> **TRY IT OUT**
>
> **Combining Kernels.** In how many ways can you combine the following sentences without changing the content? Experiment with these kernels.
>
> **PARIS AT SUNDOWN**
>
> **1.** The sun sank down.
> **2.** It sank over the river Seine.
> **3.** A girl sat at a sidewalk café.
> **4.** The girl was American.
> **5.** The girl finished her coffee.
> **6.** She finished idly.
> **7.** The girl watched the passersby.
> **8.** She watched eagerly.
>
> Were you able to create at least eight combinations of these kernels? If so, you have done very well indeed. Even so, twice as many more combinations may be waiting to be discovered—the English language is that rich in possibilities.

EVALUATING COMBINATIONS

Having discovered the abundant combinations possible in even the simplest set of kernels, you may already understand that there can be no single "right" way to combine them and that there is *no* single "correct answer" to any sentence-combining puzzle. Still, you have probably also determined that some ways are better than others, and you may be wondering if some objective criteria can't be found to help you distinguish the best combinations. Clearly there are criteria, but they are rather subjective. And that is why comparing your work with others' and discussing the results is so important in sentence-combining practice. For through this sort of discussion, you will be able to develop a surer sense of what is effective with your readers and thus gain confidence in your own writing judgment.

To determine just how effective a particular combination is, you may safely rely on these three standards:

· Clarity and directness of meaning
· Rhythmic appeal
· Intended emphasis

CLARITY

The standard I judge most important is clarity, because clear communication is your first commitment to your reader. A sentence is good, therefore, when it clearly conveys its meaning and weak when it is ambiguous or difficult to understand. In applying this standard, ask first whether the sentence's subject, verb, and object are immediately perceivable. Sometimes too many, or oddly placed, words and phrases interrupting these three vital elements obscure the sentence's meaning. Sometimes added phrases or clauses, which would otherwise work to the sentence's advantage, cause problems by faulty punctuation. (Remember to surround such unessential interruptions with a pair of commas or dashes or parentheses—never use just one.)

Clarity also demands a certain logic of content. Of the American girl in the earlier exercise, you might say that she

> · . . . finished her coffee idly because she eagerly watched the passersby.

But it would be illogical to write the equally grammatical statement that she

> · . . . eagerly watched the passersby because she idly finished her coffee.

RHYTHMIC APPEAL

Rhythm is a good second criterion because of the subtle yet strong influence it can exert on readers. In evaluating, therefore, it is fair to judge a sentence as better when it is more rhythmically pleasing. A sentence loses its rhythmic appeal when its syntax is awkward or convoluted. Notice the awkwardness in this phrasing where the main clause is sandwiched between two adverbials:

Awkward
> · When the American girl idly finished her coffee,
> she sat at the sidewalk cafe
> while she eagerly watched the passersby.

A defect in parallelism is an even greater offense against harmony. Mark the miscellaneous mixture of grammatical elements in this example:

Faulty
> · The American girl sat idly at the cafe,
> was finishing her coffee, and
> she watched the passersby eagerly.

A harmonious sentence is pleasing, but a sentence that builds a compelling rhythm by repetition (rhythm *is* patterned repetition) can stir the emotions. The appeal seems to be universal, tied up with something that is deep and primitive in human nature. Judge sentences for their rhythmic qualities, then, especially at beginnings and endings and where a persuasive climax is called for. Emotion-producing rhythm can be achieved through syntactic parallels such as:

> · id ly finish ing her coffee
> · eager ly watch ing the passersby

To judge a passage for rhythm, read it aloud and listen for the accented beats in each sentence as you would for those in a piece of music. Notice contrasts in lengths of phrase—that of a long, rolling preliminary segment, for example, and its abrupt conclusion. High in rhythmic appeal is the following combination with its parallel -*ing* phrases and its long, dominant clause contrasting with the single-syllable beat of its relatively brief climactic finale. Notice also how repetition of the *s* sound contributes to the rhythm.

> · The American girl sat at the sidewalk cafe, idly fin-
>   ishing her coffee and eagerly watching the passers-
>   by, while the sun sank down over the river Seine.

INTENDED EMPHASIS

A third standard for judging the quality of a combination of kernels is whether it has appropriate emphasis. The emphasis that is appropriate depends on the exact meaning you intend. Such exactness of meaning must take precedence over all other considerations. For example, in most cases you would choose to call the subject of the sentence on the Paris café simply "an American girl." The construction is both direct and smooth and easily meets the other two standards. But if your purpose in the sentence were to emphasize the girl's nationality—to distinguish her from girls of other lands, for instance—then you would more appropriately write, "The girl, an American . . ." or "The girl, who was American. . . ."

To give you another example, suppose you were interested in directing your readers' attention to the relationship between girl and passersby—perhaps to develop her characterization or to foreshadow some later event. In such a case you would probably not use the parallel structure that rhythmic considerations might otherwise dictate (see page 70). Instead you might select a sentence with this emphasis:

> · While the sun sank quietly over the river Seine, an
>   American girl, who was idly finishing her coffee at a
>   sidewalk cafe, watched the passersby with great ea-
>   gerness.

Putting "watched the passersby" in the main clause, subordinating all the rest of the material to it, as well as giving it the emphatic final position, focuses the readers' interest squarely where you want it. Substituting the more forceful phrase *with great eagerness* for the word *eagerly* also helps achieve a greater consequence for the girl–passersby relationship.

At times you might even choose to write a sentence in the passive mood—to write, for instance, "The girl was lit by a glow from the setting sun," instead of the usually preferable active constructions of the preceding examples. Despite the excellence of advice to avoid the passive in order to achieve directness and clarity, the passive is a legitimate English construction. It is appropriately used when you want to emphasize the action that is being done to the object of the sentence: "The girl was illumin- ated. . . ."

Sentences written from the Paris-café kernels usually are focused on the girl, placing her as the subject. But you can choose other emphases. If your aim in the sentence is to give the reader a glimpse of one among several little Parisian scenes that will set the stage for later action, then you may choose to make the sun the subject and write a sentence like this:

- The sun, as it sank over the river Seine, also cast its
  glow upon an American girl who sat at a sidewalk cafe,
  idly finishing her coffee and eagerly watching the
  passersby.

Or if you wanted it to serve as one example in a paragraph developing a thesis about the universality of coffee not only as a beverage, but as a medium of social exchange, you might choose to write:

- Coffee is the beverage consumed by idle American girls
  eagerly watching passersby from sidewalk cafes as the
  sun sinks over the river Seine.

In summary, make your writing choices and evaluate your sentences and those of your classmates by how clearly and directly the wording conveys the intended meaning—including how precisely they reflect their intended emphasis—and by how smoothly and effectively the sentences sound their rhythms.

Evaluating Combinations in Context

Useful as these three criteria can be, they take on real meaning only in a specific writing situation. In fact, most evaluating questions can only be answered: It depends. Is a long sentence better or worse than a short sentence? It depends. Is it better to begin a sentence with a phrase or a clause? It depends. Is it better to put dependent clauses at the beginning or at the end of sentences? Again, it depends. What it depends upon is where the sentence fits into its paragraph, its purpose within the paragraph, and its relation to the other sentences in that paragraph. For instance, a compo- sition filled with brief sentences of the subject-verb-object variety would surely give the impression of immature writing, rather like that of a first reader:

- Here is a dog.
  His name is Spot.
  Run, Spot, run.

But such sentences can also provide an impressive note of contrast after a series of longer and more complicated sentences. With proper contrast, short sentences can also add a surprisingly dramatic touch:

> While the sun was setting in all its glory over the river Seine, an American girl sat in a sidewalk cafe watching the passersby with great eagerness. <u>The sun sank. The girl finished her coffee.</u>

Purpose, balance, and variety are the important considerations. For good sentences build upon one another. Their rhythms and their meanings flow from one to the other.

Furthermore, a phrasing that would make a good topic sentence for a paragraph might well be inappropriate for a supporting sentence. And certainly a sentence that is meant to serve as a transition should have a different phrasing from one that is intended to be climactic.

The answer to what makes a good sentence, then, is largely dependent upon the purpose of that sentence within the context of a whole composition. And for this reason, most of the sentence-combining exercises in this text give you the opportunity to choose your options within the context of paragraphs and short essays. Let's begin our sentence combining with a brief paragraph.

TRY IT OUT

Combining Kernels. Combine the following kernels into strong sentences making up an effective paragraph. The kernels are grouped to help you decide upon the size of individual sentences, but disregard these groupings if you wish.

THE PIZZA PARLOR

1. Sam is the pizza chef.
2. The pizza chef removes the pizza.
3. The pizza is hot.
4. The pizza is steamy.
5. He removes it from the oven.
6. The oven is oversized.
7. He removes it deftly.

8. The cheese is yellow.
9. The cheese bubbles.
10. It bubbles over the tomato sauce.
11. It bubbles over the pepperoni.
12. The pizza cools.

13. The waitress eyes the pizza.
14. She eyes it with hunger.
15. She eyes it with envy.
16. The waitress inhales the odors.
17. The odors are delicious.

18. The pizza is ready (finally).
19. The waitress delivers the pizza.
20. She delivers it with resignation.
21. She delivers it to the customers.
22. The customers are eager.
23. The customers are accepting.

ANALYZING YOUR WRITING

To work through the Pizza Parlor exercise, write down the various possibilities, read them aloud, and decide upon the particular options you feel will make the most effective paragraph. Then you will be ready to discuss your decisions and compare them with those others have made. Your instructor will probably ask three or four students to share their versions with you.

After you have had a chance to see your classmates' work and perhaps also to hear their paragraphs read aloud, the differences among them should become clear. To discover how these differences have been achieved—and how some might be avoided—ask yourself such questions as the following:

OVERALL IMPRESSION

1. Which version do you think is best? Why?
2. Which versions seem to handle the material most creatively? Have any of them changed or added to the original wording? If so, do the changes make an improvement? Why? Or why not?
3. Which versions have most variety in sentence structure? Which have tried the most unusual or interesting structures?
4. Which is the most rhythmically effective version? How is this effectiveness achieved?
5. Are any of the versions weak in coherence or in unity? How might these flaws be corrected?
6. In what major ways do the versions differ?

PURPOSE AND POINT

1. Do all the versions seem to have the same purpose? If no, how do they differ? If yes, what is that purpose?

2. Do the differences in style reflect a difference in purpose? Or simply different approaches to the same purpose?
3. How well do the various stylistic strategies serve their purpose? (If you think, for instance, that the aim in "Pizza Parlor" is to focus on the pizza and the reactions it evokes, which version best gives that emphasis?)
4. How might some versions be changed to communicate their points more effectively?

USING THE QUESTIONS

These sets of questions are to help you examine any of the paragraphs or essays you and your classmates will produce with sentence-combining exercises. The purpose of the following Part by Part set is to help you examine the work in close detail, to guide you in looking at it specifically part by part and even sentence by sentence. Because of the specificity of this type of study, general questions are less helpful. I have therefore included four paragraphs other students have written on "Pizza Parlor." The questions in Part by Part deal specifically with these sample paragraphs, but they are representative of the questions you might pose for any paragraph or essay.

SAMPLE STUDENT PARAGRAPHS

A. Sam, who is the pizza chef, removes the pizza deftly from the oversized oven. The pizza is hot and steamy. The cheese is yellow, and it bubbles over the tomato sauce and over the pepperoni. As the pizza cools, the waitress eyes it with hungry envy. She also inhales the delicious odors. When the pizza is finally ready, the waitress delivers it with resignation. The customers accept it with eagerness.

B. Sam, the pizza chef, deftly removed the hot, steamy pizza from the oversized oven. The yellow pizza cheese bubbled over the tomato sauce and the pepperoni. While the pizza cooled, the waitress, hungrily eyeing it with envy, inhaled the delicious odors; and when it was finally ready, she delivered it with resignation to the eager, accepting customers.

C. The hot, steaming pizza is deftly removed from the oversized oven by Sam, the pizza chef. The cheese bubbles over the tomato sauce and pepperoni. Hungrily, the waitress enviously eyes it, inhaling the delicious odors, while it cools. Finally it is ready, and she resignedly delivers it to the eagerly accepting customers.

D. Yellow cheese bubbles over tomato and pepperoni as Sam, the pizza chef, deftly removes the hot and steamy pizza from the oversized oven. Hungrily the waitress eyes the cooling pizza, and enviously she inhales the delicious odors. With resignation she delivers the pizza to the customers, who accept it eagerly.

PART BY PART

1. *Which begins best?* Do you prefer the Sam openings (A and B) or the pizza openings (C and D)? If you like the Sam openings, how do you feel about the "who" clause in version A? Does it add desirable emphasis? Or does it detract from a concise, direct approach? If you think the initial emphasis belongs on the pizza itself, do you like the passive method in C? Or do you prefer the way the D version focuses on the appetizing "bubbling yellow cheese" by subordinating Sam to a dependent clause placed later in the sentence?

2. *Which version has the most effective conclusion?* Do you like the conclusive ring of the brief final sentence in A? How do you feel about the directness in A's use of "accept" as an active verb and about the final parallelism A achieves with

   · . . . delivers it with resignation.
   · . . . accept it with eagerness

   Do you prefer that ending to B's ending where the waitress delivers the pizza

   · . . . with resignation to the eager, accepting customers

   or to C where she delivers it:

   · . . . resignedly to the eager, accepting customers?

   Do you find "resignedly" or "with resignation" more effective in this context? Or do you prefer D altogether, where the first phrase of the final sentence, "With resignation," parallels the "hungrily" and "enviously" beginnings of the preceding clauses? And how effective do you find D's concluding "who" clause?

   · With resignation she delivers the pizza to the customers, <u>who accept it eagerly</u>.

3. *What about the use of verbs?* Does turning the opening sentence passive in C help to advance the meaning? Or does it make the sentence vaguely indirect or awkward? Does changing the verb tense to the past (in B) seem to improve or detract from the rest?

4. *What about the length and complexity of the sentences?* Do you find the third sentence in B too long and complex? If so, where would you suggest breaking it up? How could it be better phrased? A has

a number of very brief sentences. Are they effectively employed? Would some be more productively combined? If so, which ones? And how? Or is there already sufficient variety in length and structure?

5. *How do the paragraphs stack up in a close analysis of stylistic features?* Let's compare the different handling of these two important kernels:

- `She eyes it with hunger.`
- `She eyes it with envy.`

A handles the situation in one striking phrase: "hungry envy." Do you find this phrase impressive? Why? How do you feel about C's surrounding the waitress with adverbs:

- <u>Hungrily</u> the waitress <u>enviously</u> eyes it.

Do you think this construction is excessive or awkward? If so, how would you suggest revising it? Do you prefer the alternative construction in B?

- `The waitress hungrily eyes it with envy.`

Do you find the parallelism of the treatment in D especially effective?

- `Hungrily, the waitress eyes the cooling pizza.`
- `Enviously, she inhales the delicious odors.`

Notice that D is a bit creative with the text. Do you feel that the changes and additions improve it?

More Practice

The next exercises offer more opportunity to explore the possibilities of sentence combining. They should help you become familiar with the thinking involved in building sentences and paragraphs and should also give you valuable experience in comparing the effectiveness of various constructions.

TRY IT OUT

Combining into Paragraphs. Combine the following sentence kernels into an effective paragraph. Experiment. The spaces between clusters of kernels are meant to help you to form your sentences, but feel free to disregard them.

BEATLEMANIA

1. The Beatles appeared in the 1960s.
2. Then the English-speaking world was seized by something.
3. This something was called "Beatlemania."
4. It was seized immediately.

5. Teen-aged girls heard a song.
6. They would swoon.
7. The song was by the Beatles.
8. The girls fell in love.
9. The love was mad.
10. They loved John.
11. They loved Paul.
12. They loved George.
13. Or they loved Ringo.

14. Teen-aged boys would not be outdone.
15. They copied the haircuts.
16. The haircuts belonged to the Beatles.
17. The haircuts were new.
18. They copied the clothing.
19. The clothing belonged to the Beatles.
20. The clothing was new.

21. The Beatles were on tour.
22. Then they would be met.
23. They would be met at the airport.
24. They would be met by a horde.
25. The horde was screaming.
26. The horde was of thousands.
27. The horde was fans.
28. The fans wanted a memento.
29. The memento was an autograph.
30. The memento was a lock of hair.
31. The memento was even a shred of clothing.

32. The Beatles managed somehow.
33. The Beatles managed this.
34. They survived these attacks.
35. They went on.
36. They enjoyed their fame.
37. They enjoyed their fortune.

TRY IT OUT

Combining into Essays. Compose effective brief essays by combining the following set of kernels. Don't hesitate to be creative.

ARSON

1. Arson is a crime.
2. The crime is one of the worst.

   3. The crime should be so considered.
   4. The crime arises.
   5. It arises solely from greed.
   6. The crime results.
   7. The only result is death.
   8. The only result is destruction.
   9. The destruction is of homes.
 10. The homes belong to people.
 11. The people are innocent.
 12. Arson is widespread.
 13. Here is an example.
 14. There were 114,000 fires.
 15. The fires were in 1979.
 16. The fires were in New York.
 17. Nearly 10,000 fires were set.
 18. The setting was intentional.
 19. Fifty people were killed.

 20. There were arson fires nationwide.
 21. The fires were in the same year.
 22. The fires killed 1,000.
 23. The fires caused damage.
 24. The damage was three billion dollars.

 25. Police believe this fact.
 26. Accidents cause some fires.
 27. Pyromaniacs set some fires.
 28. The profit motive causes most fires.
 29. Property owners order most fires.
 30. These property owners are heavily insured.

 31. One big-city landlord had an interest.
 32. The interest was in 250 buildings.
 33. The 250 buildings burned down.
 34. They burned over a five-year period.
 35. The landlord had associates.
 36. They collected more than five million dollars.
 37. The dollars were from fire-insurance claims.
 38. Arson fires are a crime.
 39. The crime is especially frustrating.
 40. The reason for this frustration is a fact.
 41. The fact is this.
 42. Prosecution is difficult.
 43. Only 5 percent result in conviction.
 44. The 5 percent conviction rate is from all arson investigations.

ASSIGNMENT

Write an essay on one of the following topics. Each of them gives you the opportunity to continue the thinking you put into the sentence-combining exercises in this chapter and to practice some of the techniques you developed in writing the exercises.[1]

1. Think of a place where you eat often—the dormitory, your home, or a favorite restaurant—and describe it in the same sensuously detailed way as you did the Pizza Parlor in the sentence-combining exercise on pages 73–74.

And/or

2. Write an essay comparing the Pizza Parlor in your sentence-combining paragraph with a place where you eat often (home, dormitory, or favorite restaurant). Include portions of your Pizza Parlor paragraph if you wish.

3. Think of your favorite musical group and, following the structure of the Beatlemania exercise, describe what you know about them—their backgrounds, their costumes, the reactions of their fans.

And/or

4. Write an essay comparing the Beatles, as described in your sentence-combining exercise, with your favorite musical group. Include portions of your exercise essay if you wish.

5. Study the way you used statistics to argue the point in your sentence-combining essay on arson. Then gather statistics on another subject that interests you, formulate a thesis, and write an essay in which you support that thesis with the statistics in a similar way. Remember to credit the source of your information (see pages 31–32 or 337–342).

---

[1]These topics were suggested by Professor William Guthrie of Wilmington College.

Chapter
3

Thinking About
Your Readers

Underlying all the strategies and techniques suggested in *Writing Effectively* is the notion that every piece of writing is a conversation with those who will read it. To make any of the strategies work for you, you as writer should always be conscious of your readers. You should hear your voice talking to them as you write and should constantly keep their needs in mind. You must be aware of your readers as people because writing well means communicating persuasively.

The concept of persuading readers is of the greatest importance to the writing process; rhetoric is defined, after all, as the art of persuasion. Yet students sometimes have difficulty accepting this notion and its implications about thesis. Here are some of the challenges students most often raise:

- Why is it so important for writers to think about their readers? Can't I just write?
- Must all expository writing really have a thesis? Why can't I just tell *about* my subject?
- Why do theses have to be argumentative?

Perhaps you have been asking some of these questions yourself. Let me suggest some answers.

THE POINT IN HAVING A POINT

Why Readers?

Maybe because English composition courses are skills courses and much of the writing in them is primarily for practice, students sometimes get so involved in trying to follow suggestions from text or teacher in just the right way that they lose track of the fact that they are writing to communicate with readers. But let me assure you, good writers do not write into a void. Every writing situation necessarily involves communicating with a reader.

If your purpose in writing is to secure a job interview, to get a refund for a faulty product, or to change your senator's vote, then you are probably in little danger of disregarding the correspondent you are trying to influence. Your audience may be much easier to overlook, however, when you are writing the papers likely to be assigned in college classes.

WHOM SHOULD COLLEGE PAPERS ADDRESS?

Most college instructors prefer that you think of their formal written assignments as scholarly papers written for the readers of a presumed journal in their discipline (at your own level of knowledge, of course). Although it is true that the chances of your history or literature paper's being published in a scholarly journal or read before a scholarly assembly are slight, publication of undergraduate papers is not unknown. In any case, scholarly thinking is a skill that takes practice to master, and most professors feel that scholarly writing is the best way to practice it. Whom should you write your college papers for, then? For your fellow scholars— who are, after all, your classmates, an audience whose reading needs you have only to look within yourself to understand.

Whether your readers are specifically known or the imagined audience of an imagined journal, the effectiveness of your writing depends upon how well you are able to anticipate and fulfill their reading needs.

Why a Thesis?

If you are now convinced that good writing presupposes readers, then it will be hard to deny the necessity of a thesis as the organizing principle in expository writing. For both components of thesis—focus and persuasiveness—take their force from the centrality of the writer–reader relationship.

FOCUS: WHY NOT JUST WRITE "ABOUT" THE SUBJECT?

Consideration for your readers demands that you focus your writing. Frankly, unfocused papers that just tell "about" something are confusing, often boring. Think of your own experience. Have you ever heard someone tell a story and just go on and on? He'll say, "And then . . . and then . . . and then . . . and then. . . ." And you will be thinking, "Come to the point, won't you—just come to the point," all the while wishing for some convenient opening to get away. Readers experience much the same frustration in trying to read an essay that just talks "about" a subject. Our minds cannot assimilate a quantity of unrelated ideas except with great difficulty, and then only by finding a focus that will relate the ideas to one another. As readers, we have a right to expect the writer to discover the focus for us. For this reason, good writers do not decide they would just like to talk about, say, aardvarks. Rather, they select in advance the particular point they want to make about aardvarks and then direct all their attention toward making that point. Imagine what Fred Golden's article (page 415), for example, would be like if he had decided just to write "about" deserts. He could have told all the interesting things he does tell about these parched regions, and yet if he had not focused our attention on his point about the "desert's cancerous growth," we would finish reading the essay and say, "It's nice to know all these facts about deserts, but *so what?*"

Because of the possibility of every reader's "So what?" all well-written expository works do indeed have theses. There truly is no reason for writing anything unless a point is to be made. And this necessity for a thesis is not a factor of length. Even works as long as the multivolume *Decline and Fall of the Roman Empire* are organized around a single thesis— though, of course, such works must have subtheses, too.

From time to time, you may come across an expository composition that seems to have no single sentence which states the thesis. Nevertheless, if it is a well-written piece, you will invariably find that there is one idea that underlies the whole, and around it the entire composition has been organized. In such works, the thoughtful reader has no difficulty identifying the author's point—the implied thesis—nor even in putting it into words.

PERSUASIVENESS: WHY NOT JUST "TELL" ABOUT THE SUBJECT?

Concern for readers is also the reason you should consider your writing purpose as persuasive. Even when you simply want to "tell" something, you still want to persuade your readers that what you are telling is worth their while. Considered broadly in this way, all good theses are argumentative. In fact, many of the most respected rhetoricians identify this persuasiveness as the essence of the thesis idea. Among them:

  · Sheridan Baker: "Put an argumentative edge on your subject—and you will have found your thesis."
  · David Skwire: "Your primary purpose is to persuade the reader that your thesis is a valid one."
  · Frederick Crews: "Your thesis doesn't have to be openly antagonistic,

but it should . . . defend one position against possible alternatives to it."[1]

Yet despite such expert confirmation, the challenge most often raised about the concept of thesis concerns its argumentative intent; and you, personally, may still find it difficult to believe that *all* expository papers must "contain," in Crews's words, "a thread of argument." You may feel that some assignments, such as "Defend or Oppose Capital Punishment" or "The Woman's Movement," can be viewed in this way but, candidly, may still not be convinced that Baker's "argumentative edge" must hold true for such noncontroversial topics as "Freshman Year at College" or "My Dog Spot." You may think that you are being advised to view all assignments as opposition papers, and you may find the notion preposterous.

In voicing this concern, you touch upon the crux of the whole thesis matter. Odd as it may seem, I really am suggesting that you regard all expository writing as if it were, in a manner of speaking, persuasive writing. I am saying that the downright persuasive paper is just a conspicuous example of what *all* good expository writing fundamentally is.

To demonstrate, let's take an example from a mode of writing removed as far as possible from the argumentative. Here are some undeniably lyric lines from a poem, the beginning of Wordsworth's sonnet "It Is a Beauteous Evening":

It is a beauteous evening, calm and free;
The holy time is quiet as a nun
Breathless with adoration; the broad sun
Is sinking down in its tranquility;
The gentleness of heaven broods o'er the sea;
Listen! the mighty Being is awake,
And doth with his eternal motion make
A sound like thunder—everlastingly.

Even a confirmed rhetorician would not claim that a lyric like this is obliged to have a thesis. And yet, if you look at the verse in these terms, you will notice that Wordsworth begins with something very like a thesis: "It is a beauteous evening . . . [and] holy," a contention that he argues most persuasively through the first eight lines. Wordsworth "argues" his "thesis" not only with factual statements, but also with all the devices of poetry at his command—with rhyme and meter, with simile:

The holy time is quiet as a nun
Breathless with adoration . . .

with alliteration and personification:

---

[1]Sheridan Baker, *The Practical Stylist* (New York: Harper & Row, 1986), p. 32; David Skwire, *Writing with a Thesis* (New York: Holt, Rinehart and Winston, 1985), p. 3; Frederick Crews, *The Random House Handbook* (New York: Random House, 1974), p. 23.

> . . . the broad sun
> Is sinking down in its tranquility;
> The gentleness of heaven broods o'er the sea

with onomatopoeia: "breathless," "a sound like thunder."

Through these devices, Wordsworth has not simply described an evening, but has offered powerful emotional arguments to prove its beauty and its holiness. There is, at least, something very like a thesis at work here, even in the least controversial of expository compositions. It is in this sense that all expository writing must be considered persuasive and all theses argumentative.

TRY IT OUT

1. Cheryl Jacobs's student paper (pages 448–450) is expressive in mood and personal in subject. Is it also an expository essay—that is, is it organized around a thesis? If so, what is her thesis?

2. List the major points she makes to support the thesis. What "evidence" does she cite to convince you of these points?

3. When Michael Reveal had gathered the information for his student paper (pages 454–457), he might have been tempted to just "write about" the Amish. Instead, he reviewed his material and, drawing a conclusion from it, found a point worth making about these people. What is this point? How does he support it?

Why Argumentative?

Your writing will benefit if you view it as persuasion in this way and approach your thesis as an argumentative statement. You see, your readers are likely to be a bit difficult to please or convince, skeptical, ornery (even as you and I). Therefore, if you—like Wordsworth—are writing about the beauteous holiness of an evening, you have the burden of somehow persuading your readers both of the evening's beauty and of its holiness. Besides being skeptical, these readers are likely also to be easily distracted or bored and thus may not continue reading if they suspect you are simply rehearsing the commonplace or the self-evident. They will, however, grow interested at the hint of controversy. Judge from your own experience. Don't you like to read about ideas that make waves and destroy the calm of the ideological ocean around you? Given the danger of boring readers, there is a tremendous advantage for writers who can acknowledge that even the least controversial theses are fundamentally argumentative. These writers build into their theses the tension between their main statement and their "although" clauses (whether implied or expressed) that will attract and maintain their readers' interest. And an interesting paper almost always results from resolving such tension.

CREATING TENSION WITH "ALTHOUGH" MATERIAL

How do you create such tension? You think of the point you want to make in terms of any contradictions that exist about it. To return to a familiar example, let's suppose you were assigned the paper on Washington discussed in Part One. You might very well survey the original inventory of ideas (page 12) and come to the thesis "George Washington was a great man." But since this statement is likely to turn out a paper every bit as exciting as that produced by the thesis "Grass is green," you would probably next want to consider working with its opposite: "Washington was not a great man." You would recognize quickly that this statement, although more interesting, is probably not supportable by the facts in the inventory of ideas. Being left with the "great man" thesis, then, you would search for any contrasting ideas within it that would make this conclusion worth the saying. Two such contrasts were suggested earlier in this book:

- `Great man, even though he was merely human like our-`
  `selves (problems with his teeth and his family)`
- `Great man, despite the recent antiheroic approach of`
  `revisionist historians`

Because the accepted idea often bores while the paradoxical notion almost invariably intrigues, you would probably choose one of these contradictions for your thesis or else find a similar contrast.

The tension between what we have been calling the "although" material and the main thrust of the thesis is present in every essay in our collection. It accounts to a large extent for the emotional power, for instance, of Lewis Thomas's "Late Night Thoughts":

- ALTHOUGH: [I used to take Mahler's Ninth] as a metaphor for reassurance, confirming my own strong hunch that the dying of every living creature, the most natural of all experiences, has to be a peaceful experience,
- YET: now . . . I cannot listen to the last movement . . . without the door-smashing intrusion of a huge new thought: death everywhere, the dying of everything, the end of humanity. (page 428)[2]

A similar tension enlivens Meg Greenfield's "Accepting the Unacceptable" and clarifies her point:

---

[2]This sentence, although conventionally placed and phrased, is only the apparent thesis of Thomas's essay. His actual thesis, unstated though strongly implied throughout, is: Nuclear weaponry is a mindless horror that drives the old to despair and the young, probably, to madness.

- ALTHOUGH (or perhaps because): [our] response to [terrorism] is a (by now) ritualized series of diversions and evasions that subtly but quickly make us feel better,
- YET: [this response] deepen[s] our disadvantage . . . while making the hostages' situation worse. (page 420)

If there is any single factor that all good expository essays have in common, it is probably this hint of argument that creates a tension, the resolution of which keeps the reader attentive to the end of the essay.

TRY IT OUT

1. Do you have any reservations about the validity of the following statements? If you do, briefly argue your point of view; if you agree with them, briefly tell why.
   a. It is hard to write well without keeping one's reader in mind.
   b. All expository writing should be organized around a thesis.
   c. A thesis must be, broadly speaking, argumentative.

2. Using the "although-yet" format exemplified earlier, define both the "although" material and the main thrust of the thesis in the following essays. (You may quote from the articles or use your own words as you choose.)
   - C. Tucker's "On Splitting" (page 431)
   - White's "The Distant Music of the Hounds" (page 436)

3. Think of some factual material you have learned about in one of your courses this term that might make an interesting brief essay. See if you can think of a way to create interest-arousing "argumentative" tension in your presentation of this material, and sketch out your idea in the "although-yet" format exemplified earlier.

"ALTHOUGH"-CLAUSE STRATEGIES FOR CONVINCING YOUR READERS

We have seen that, to some extent, the theses of all good expository writing are controversial. To determine just how controversial your thesis is, ask yourself how far your readers are likely to agree with it. You should be able to place it somewhere along the continuum in Figure 3.1.

The extent of agreement you expect from your readers should help you decide how much to emphasize the "although" material—the ideas of the opposing position as summarized in your "although" clause. The more controversial the thesis, the more care, and usually space, you will need to devote to the "although" clause.

Thus, in planning your paper, it is helpful to focus in on the "although" clause of your working thesis. Examine it to see how much con-

(u) Total agreement	(v) General agreement, but you offer something new	(w) Unknown material or complete neutrality	(x) Disagreement in part (the rest agreed or unknown)	(y) Disagreement without emotional involvement	(z) Hostile disagreement

Figure 3.1 The Controversy Continuum

troversiality it implies. For even though "although" clauses are contrary by definition, they can express or imply any position along the Controversy Continuum.

Many "although" clauses suggest that the thesis is not particularly controversial. Take, for example, the "although" portion of Charles Slack's thesis in "If I'm So Smart . . .":

> [Although] Homme (the researcher) was surprised to discover [the new scientific information]. . . . (page 425, paragraph 7)

This "although," like that of other reports of original research, merely implies that the thesis idea is newly discovered or probably little known to the reader. A similarly noncontroversial "although" clause might hint that "Although this material is well known, I have a new angle, approach, or interpretation to bring to it." Shana Alexander's development of her thesis that "Children today not only exist, they have taken over" (page 411) has this implication. An "although" clause might even suggest that "Although I am sure you will agree with me once I tell you or remind you of the conditions . . . ," as does Fred Golden's description of "Earth's Creeping Deserts" (page 415).

When you add "although" clauses of this sort to your theses, you are not making them controversial; you are not putting your readers in an adversary position. And, as you will see in the next section, you need not give particular emphasis in your essay to the ideas they contain. On the other hand, sometimes an "although" clause voices an opinion in total disagreement with its thesis. Recall, for instance, the "although" in Meg Greenfield's thesis (page 87) or those in the theses on capital punishment in the Try it Out on page 87. If you decide your "although" material makes the thesis controversial in this way, then you will want to think carefully about how you present these ideas. Here are some proven strategies that should help you.

Strategies for Handling Noncontroversial "Although" Material

When the "although clause" of your working thesis does not set up an adversary relationship with your readers, you are not obliged to include the "although" material in your finished composition. And many pieces of writing, especially very brief ones, do not. For example, in Barbara Sims's explication of "We Real Cool" (page 401) the underlying "although" clause suggests, as does that of many other critical analyses, that the author had not before found a completely satisfying interpretation of the poem; but though this idea is clearly implied, Sims never mentions it in the essay and instead goes directly into her own interpretation.

TO JUSTIFY PURPOSE

On the other hand, there are good reasons why you sometimes might want to use "although" material in your noncontroversial writing. Since it can justify your purpose in writing, you might want to use it in (or as) your introduction. Scholarly papers are often begun in this way because their usual purpose is to respond to earlier work. Frequently, they start by listing earlier accepted opinion or the results of earlier research on the topic. Perry Turner uses the material in this way to introduce his semischolarly essay "What Killed Arthur Dimmesdale?"

> When you studied Hawthorne's *The Scarlet Letter,* you probably spent a lot of class time discussing Sin and Guilt. But it could be your English teacher missed the point. Jemshed Khan . . . claims that too many of the book's readers are finding the same old profundities. (page 434)

And you too may find this conventional use of "although" material effective in writing papers for some of your college classes.

TO INTRODUCE

Other introductory uses for "although" material can furnish an interesting or offbeat approach to your thesis. If your thesis deals with a historical time or a faraway place, for instance, you might attract readers' interest by opening with "although" material relating it to the here and now. Or if your thesis is contemporary and present, you might take your "although" material from another time or place to emphasize your topic's modernity. Shana Alexander uses this strategy when she contrasts her modern thesis with a description from the past:

> Children are a relatively modern invention. Until a few hundred years ago, they did not exist. In Medieval and Renaissance painting, you see pint-size men and women wearing . . . grown-up expressions, performing grown-up tasks. (page 411)

All these strategies offer effective ways of using your "although" material to lead your readers into even noncontroversial compositions. But when your thesis is not particularly contentious, you will seldom want to continue the "although" matter beyond your introduction—except perhaps to give an echo of it just at the close (see "Frame or Circle Conclusions," page 131).

Strategies for Handling Controversial "Although" Material

The main problem with noncontroversial theses is that readers may wonder why you are taking the trouble to rehash known and accepted material. But when your thesis is openly controversial, you face the problem of winning over your readers from attitudes of disagreement ranging from indifference to hostility. The greater the disagreement, the greater the care you will need to take with the "although" material expressing that disagreement, and the more you will need to attend to the feelings and needs of your readers.

TWO APPROACHES: ARISTOTLE VS. ROGERS

Aristotle's advice that we must regard our readers as worthy opponents is often useful. And frequently as you determine your thesis and define its support, you will want to think of your readers as intelligent skeptics with a show-me attitude. But this approach may not always be the most effective one when you set out to convince readers of the value of what you have to say. Carl Rogers, a contemporary psychologist, adds modern psychological insights to Aristotle's ancient ones on writer–reader relationships. Rogers advises us to reach readers in areas where agreement might be worked out, to try for some commonality of ideas as a start. He writes:

> Mutual communication . . . leads to a situation in which I see how the problem appears to you, as well as to me, and you see how it appears to me as well as to you.[3]

In other words, Rogers recommends putting yourself in your readers' place. His advice is similar to the folk wisdom of native Americans that suggests "walking a mile in the other person's moccasins."

IN YOUR READERS' MOCCASINS

To put yourself in the place of readers who strongly disagree with your thesis, try to remember how you felt when you read or heard something that challenged your most deeply held opinions. If you can do so, you will recall that the feelings such challenges aroused were not comfortable. You will also remember how easily an opponent of some idea you valued could overstep the line and make you defensive—or angry.

It may be easier to put yourself in the place of your uncommitted readers. Try to remember the last time you were reading intensely controversial material that you had not yet made up your mind about. I'm sure you will recall wanting to weigh matters for yourself and not be unduly influenced by the writer. Perhaps you found yourself in sympathy with the

---

[3]Carl Rogers, "Communication: Its Blocking, Its Facilitation," in *On Becoming a Person* (Boston: Houghton Mifflin, 1961), p. 336.

side that seemed the underdog—that is, the side the writer opposed, the side that could not argue back. If these memories of yourself as a committed or uncommitted reader are at all vivid, they should lead you to two important conclusions about handling the "although" material. First, when you are urging a controversial thesis, you cannot afford to disregard or give only fleeting attention to the ideas of the opposition. And second, it is to your advantage to deal with their views fairly.

PRESENTING CONTROVERSIAL "ALTHOUGH" MATERIAL FAIRLY

You cannot expect to ignore the views opposed to your thesis and hope that your readers will be unaware of their existence. These views are bound to be passing through the minds of readers acquainted with the controversy. Further, you can be fairly certain that those who have not yet learned of it will be raising some of the opposition issues in their minds as you present your case. To make your views persuasive, then, you will probably have to expand your discussion of the opposition ideas beyond an introductory sentence or two. You would also be wise to accord these views some portion of respect. For however you may feel about the opposing point of view or about those who hold it, you will not be able to reach your readers—let alone convince them—except by scrupulous fairness. Because your readers expect you to give the other side a fair hearing, name-calling, sarcasm, snide remarks, or an abusive or superior tone in your discussion of that side will assuredly backfire.[4] No matter how justified writers feel such tactics may be, readers tend to react negatively to these attacks unless they already hold a deep conviction supporting the thesis. Recall your own reactions as a reader.

Fair, Not Neutral.   In speaking strongly for fairness, I do not mean that you need to give the illusion of neutrality. For one thing, if you manage to present all positions equally, you will leave your readers confused and dissatisfied. For another, fairness itself demands that your readers learn where you stand. Thus, the idea is to identify your position and present the other side's arguments in terms of your position without distorting the views of either side.

In "Late Night Thoughts," for example, Lewis Thomas states his negative position toward nuclear deterrence early and strongly so that, though he presents his "although" pronuclear-buildup material factually and fairly, his readers are nonetheless repelled by it.

> Now, with a pamphlet in front of me . . . published by the Congressional Office of Technology Assessment, entitled *MX Basing,* an analysis of all the alternative strategies for placement and protection of hundreds of these missiles,

---

[4]If you choose to write satire, as Art Buchwald and Russell Baker do, you need to be, if anything, even more controlled. For suggestions on handling irony, see page 98.

> each capable of creating artificial suns to vaporize a hundred Hiroshimas, collectively capable of destroying the life of any continent. . . . (page 429, paragraph 8)

He continues his discussion of the opposition material with an almost exaggerated matter-of-factness, having given his way of thinking enough emotional clout for that very matter-of-factness to begin to take on a sort of insanity:

> The man on television, Sunday midday, middle-aged and solid, nice-looking chap, all the facts at his fingertips, more dependable looking than most high-school principals, is talking about civilian defense, his responsibility in Washington. It can make an enormous difference, he is saying. Instead of the outright death of eighty million American citizens in twenty minutes, he says, we can, by careful planning and practice, get that number down to only forty million, maybe even twenty. . . . Of course, he adds, [the Russians] have the capacity to kill all two hundred and twenty million of us if they were to try real hard, and they know we can do the same to them. If the figure is only forty million this will deter them, not worth the trouble, not worth the risk. Eighty million would be another matter; we should guard ourselves against losing that many all at once, he says. (page 430, paragraph 10)

Thomas achieves his irony here not by misquoting his opposition, but rather by quoting repeatedly an idea that struck him, and he hopes will also strike his readers, as foolish. Only in the clause, "If they were to try real hard," do we briefly catch a glimpse of open hostility, and this is probably the weakest portion of the passage.

CONCEDING WHAT CAN BE CONCEDED

The heart of Carl Rogers's persuasive strategy (see page 90) is to root your points of controversy in the broadest base of agreement you can manage. Your readers are far more likely to give consideration to your differing viewpoint if you show your basic goodwill and your eagerness for theirs by conceding to their side whatever points you can honestly concede. Notice how skillfully William Raspberry employs this technique in beginning "Children of Two-Career Families":

> Maybe you have to be crazy to argue with two Harvard psychiatrists—particularly two such insightful psychiatrists as Barrie Greiff and Preston Hunter.

Working with Controversial Material

1. Be sure to give adequate coverage to the opposition's viewpoint.
2. You may, however, present their opinions from your own biased point of view.
3. It is, nevertheless, to your rhetorical advantage to present the opposition viewpoint fairly.

So before I register my small objection to their article in the May–June issue of *Harvard* magazine, let me say that nearly everything these two doctors have to say about the strains and stresses of dual-career families makes sense to me. (page 423, paragraphs 1–2)

Carll Tucker's "On Splitting" offers another example of how you might make readers more open to persuasion by gracefully conceding that the opposition has some right on its side, too. Tucker, who argues against divorce, begins by describing how angry he felt when two couples among his friends called to tell him they were getting divorced. He follows this description by conceding that divorce may not have been a bad idea in the case of his friends:

I did not feel anger at my friends personally: Given the era and their feelings, their decisions probably made sense. (page 431, paragraph 3)

Following this concession, he presents his "although" material in a fair—though, of course, not completely impartial—manner. Tucker is even willing to concede that, to a certain extent, his opposition is right:

In some respects, this freedom [to divorce without stigma] can be seen as social progress. Modern couples can flee the corrosive bitterness that made Strindberg's marriages nightmares. Dreiser's Clyde Griffiths might have abandoned his Roberta instead of drowning her. (page 432, paragraph 6)

Tucker's concessions take some of the sting out of his controversial position and thus help him argue his side more effectively. This strategy should be helpful to you as well.

ANTICIPATING AND ANSWERING POSSIBLE OBJECTIONS

When you are discussing an issue face-to-face, the other discussants have the opportunity to question your ideas or raise objections to your arguments. At the same time, you have the opportunity to answer each objection as they raise it and to put their minds at rest about any idea of yours that may distress them. Writing denies you this opportunity for immediate interchange. Putting yourself in your readers' place, however, can help you overcome this disadvantage. For, in trying to think as your readers might think, you should be able to anticipate their questions and supply answers, to foresee their objections and quiet them. Although covering possible reader objections is of major importance to argumentative theses, it can also be an effective technique when you do less controversial writing. For an example, glance again at the first section of this chapter (page 81). You will see that I have tried there to speak to the sort of objections to the thesis concept that you might be harboring.

Whenever you are writing, try to see your work through your readers' eyes and try to figure out the issues they may have difficulty understanding and the ideas they may have trouble accepting. Then raise these issues and ideas yourself and answer them in order to satisfy your readers' unspoken questions.

Strategies for Arguing Your Point Persuasively

1. Define the opposition material fairly.
2. Set forth your own position.
3. Concede what can be conceded.
4. Raise and answer possible objections—that is, argue what must be argued.
5. Present your own case.

Note: Points 1 and 2 and points 4 and 5 may be handled in reverse order, depending on circumstances.

TRY IT OUT

1. Put yourself in the position of the authors of the following essays in Part Four. Decide for each author just how controversial your thesis is likely to be. Then, weighing their degree of controversiality, place the theses appropriately on the controversy continuum on page 88.
   a. Greenfield, "Accepting the Unacceptable" (page 420)
   b. Raspberry, "Children of Two-Career Families" (page 423)
   c. Will, "The Chicago Cubs, Overdue" (page 438)
   d. Williams, "U.S. Blacks and a Free Market" (page 441)

2. How much attention do the authors of the four works cited in Exercise 1 pay to their "although" material? Be as specific as you can.

3. Explain Aristotle's and Rogers's approaches to their audience. Which seems most effective to you? (Does a person really catch more flies with honey than with vinegar?)

Extra credit. Which do you think works more effectively: Greenfield's Rogerian or Williams's Aristotelian approach (in the essays listed above)?

PRESENTING YOUR OWN CASE PERSUASIVELY

Your readers' concerns must be central in your handling of "although" clause material. They should also influence the way in which you support your own side of the thesis. In Chapter 4 we will talk about the kinds of support that should be most convincing. Here, the focus is on planning the strategies that will help you present your thesis persuasively. Probably the most useful way of thinking about these strategies is to return to the rhetorical triangle (see Figure 3.2) and think of the relationships between you, your thesis, and your readers in terms of your persuasive purpose.

In order to persuade as a *writer,* you will have to give your work

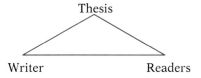

Figure 3.2. Rhetorical Triangle

enough personal authority to make it convincing. You will best be able to persuade your *readers* if you can get them to identify with you and your ideas. And to make your *thesis* itself persuasive, you need to give it the intellectual validity that will make it credible to your readers. Let's consider these three tasks individually in order to find strategies to help you accomplish them.

Giving Personal Authority to Your Writing

An effective way to make your point convincingly is to give it the weight of personal authority. How can you do that? You can start by letting your readers know your intellectual and moral qualifications for the job you have undertaken as their guide to the subject.

ESTABLISHING INTELLECTUAL AUTHORITY

If you have special expertise in your subject field, let your readers know. You need not fear to seem immodest. Readers of Ellen Goodman's "The Communication Gap" learn immediately that extensive person-to-person research backs up her conclusions:

> I went back to college this week, or, to be more accurate, back to colleges. For five days I had an intensive course on the generation born circa 1960. I gathered enough material for a thesis on The Communication Gap Between the Sexes, Phase II. . . . On campuses covered with ivy and lined with palm trees, I met young women. (page 418, paragraphs 1–2)

Goodman's reference to ivy and palm trees conveys the extent of her travels and hints to the reader that her visits to campuses may well have been occasioned by invitations to lecture, invitations that are reserved for an authority. She fits this information in modestly as a necessary part of her text rather than as an extra fact attached to it. And so we readers give Goodman the additional credit we tend to award when we can sense that the author is an expert.

Know Your Subject.   Even if you choose to be less personal or less specific, your readers will be able to discern the qualifications that give your work authority if you handle your material competently and knowledgeably. Charles Slack, for example, is a psychologist as well as a journalist, but although he gives no overt clues to his profession in "If I'm So Smart" (page 425), choosing to write the article in a popular rather than a scientific way, his competent handling of the material clearly demonstrates his full command of his subject.

When you have to write on a subject where you've had little previous understanding, it is hard to project such intellectual authority. Study is then your only course. For only when you master the subject well enough to be able to speak knowledgeably about it will you be able to write on it convincingly.

ESTABLISHING MORAL AUTHORITY

Another way to add to your personal authority as a writer is by projecting strength of character. To believe you, readers need to understand that you are the kind of person they can trust. You can win this trust in a number of ways.

Credit Your References.   An especially important way is to be absolutely precise in your use of reference material. If you quote as much as a brief phrase from another writer, designate it a quotation and credit its author. If you borrow an idea, never neglect to credit its source. (Chapter 10 will give you firm guidance in documentation.) Remember, unless you tell them otherwise, readers have the right to believe that every word you write and every idea you discuss are original with you. Should you give them reason to suspect differently, their faith in you and in your writing will be severely shaken.

Another means of giving moral authority to your work is to treat the opposition fairly, though in the still-partisan way discussed earlier. (See pages 91–92.)

Objective Observer or Impassioned Advocate.   Yet another way to establish your authority is to approach your subject in the stance of the Objective Observer or the Impassioned Advocate or both. The most effective writers have usually relied upon a combination of these roles. You may choose to approach your subject with the dry objectivity of Sergeant Friday in the 1950s television show "Dragnet"—"Just the facts, ma'am, just the facts." If you do, your readers will appreciate your insistence upon the unembellished facts and may be drawn to your interpretation of them. On the other hand, the righteous indignation of an Impassioned Advocate speaking out for justice carries a moral authority, too. If you can demonstrate with the objective facts that your indignation is indeed justified, you can wear your advocacy like a banner, and you just may be able to carry your readers with you. For a skillful example of such mingling, look at the paragraph by Thomas that I partially quoted earlier:

Combination of Objective Observer and Impassioned Advocate

Now, with a pamphlet in front of me on a corner of my desk, published by the Congressional Office of Technology Assessment, entitled *MX Basing,* an analysis of all the alternative strategies for placement and protection of hundreds of these missiles, each capable of creating artificial suns to vaporize a hundred Hiroshimas, collectively capable of destroying the life of any continent, I cannot hear the same Mahler. Now, those cellos sound in my mind like the opening of all the hatches and the instant before ignition. (page 429, paragraph 8)

Identifying Your Readers with Your Point

All people tend to respond more favorably to ideas they can identify with. You can use your knowledge of this human tendency to make your writing more persuasive. First, find some common ground with your readers and then present your thinking from that foundation. In "Accepting the Unacceptable," Meg Greenfield, for instance, uses the "we" form of address to identify with her readers as fellow Americans bewildered by the violence of terrorism. Her sharp criticism of the American response to terrorism is softened and made more acceptable by her talking about "our response" instead of an implied "your" response. She identifies too with the human need, her readers' need, not to be completely in the wrong. "The permanent disadvantage is not our fault" (page 420, paragraph 2), she writes as she goes on to explain and relieves her readers of all the guilt she can before honing in on the ills she would like to have "us" correct.

NEW JOURNALISM

Greenfield's technique is to identify with her readers; New Journalists pursue the opposite strategy, getting the reader to identify with them. They explain a circumstance or a thing vividly by describing both their own experiences with it and the impressions the experiences made upon them.

These authors hope that readers will share the experience described and then adopt the accompanying interpretation of it. Ellen Goodman, who often adapts this technique to her own style, uses a modified version in "Communication Gap" (page 418). If you should decide to work with this technique, however, be aware of one danger. Inexperienced writers must be careful not to use the method to excess and turn an essay about a topic into a story about themselves.

IRONY

Irony is such a difficult technique, so tricky to use, that you might want to wait until later in the term to try it. Nevertheless, it is surely an especially effective way of getting your readers to identify with you and your point of view. In writing ironically, you say or imply the opposite of what you believe to be true.[5] By requiring your readers to understand your actual intentions, you create a sly bond of conspiracy. It is as if you give a broad wink to your readers and flatter them by saying, "Those of you who are in the know will realize I am joking. I don't dare say how dreadful I think this matter is, but with *your* intelligence you will understand the strong criticism hidden in my words."

For example, when Walter Williams writes, "It is fairly certain that societal love cannot explain the assimilation of past disadvantaged groups" (page 442, paragraph 6), he expects his shrewd readers to understand that he is very far from being only *"fairly* certain," and that he doesn't believe in the reliability of "societal love." In fact, he really means, and expects his readers to know that he means, quite the contrary: that if disadvantaged groups had to wait for society to love them in order to prosper, they would never prosper at all. Similarly, E. B. White flatters his readers and brings them into alliance with him when he expects them to catch the implied criticism in his ironic phrase, "the silent-nighting of the loud speakers" (page 436, paragraph 1).

If you lay the groundwork carefully, you can also turn your opponents' own words against them, with a special ironic technique called *dramatic irony*. For instance, Lewis Thomas gives enough hints for his clever readers to understand that the "nice-looking chap . . . on television," whom Thomas paraphrases in the passage quoted below, is a dangerously foolish man:

> What about radioactive fallout? he is asked. Well, he says. Anyway, he says, if the Russians know they can only destroy forty million of us instead of eighty million, this will deter them. Of course, he adds, they have the capacity to kill all two hundred and twenty million of us if they were to try real hard, but they know we can do the same to them. If the figure is only forty million

---

[5]For a more technical explanation of *irony,* see the entry in Part Five, the Revision Guide.

> this will deter them, not worth the trouble, not worth the risk. Eighty million would be another matter. (page 430, paragraph 10)

In his repeated use of attribution tags—"Well, he says," "Anyway, he says," "Of course, he adds"—Thomas throws a broad wink to his readers that points up the inanity of the expression to which the tags are attached and thus casts doubt on the trustworthiness of the narrator. Similarly, Thomas's repeating the colloquial but nongrammatical phrases "not worth the trouble, not worth the risk" gets his readers to consider more closely the terrifying implications of "only forty million" deaths, which the phrases—and their speaker—try to minimize. Thus, Thomas uses dramatic irony[6] to emphasize what he considers the empty thinking of his adversaries and to win his readers to his point of view.

Though irony is not easy to handle, you may find it a useful tool. When you use it, however, be careful not to be either too broad or too subtle. If your irony is too broad and sarcastic ("The cafeteria food here is just grrreat!" for instance), you are in danger of having your readers accuse you of being unfair or simplistic. If, on the other hand, you are too subtle and do not give adequate clues to your real meaning, readers may very well take you seriously and think you mean just the opposite of what you intend.

APPEAL TO EMOTION

The way writers most frequently use to get their readers to identify with a point of view is an appeal to their common humanity. After all, only rarely will you have the chance to address a group of readers who are specifically defined. But whoever your readers may be, you can know for sure that they are human, and this knowledge can offer you insight into ways of persuading them.

You can, for instance, appeal to the feelings and sympathies that we all share. I am not, of course, suggesting that you add to those dismal appeals to greed, lust, and envy that are the shame of our television programming and much advertising. Rather, I advise that you reach your readers through your understanding of such universal human experiences as love; fear; sympathy with the young, the helpless, and the oppressed; and indignation against the violators of fairness and justice. William Raspberry, for example, assumes that readers of "Children of Two-Career Families" have had these human experiences and therefore share his humanistic values. His essay gains its strength from this assumption throughout, and in its conclusion he uses it to clinch his argument:

> The Harvard psychiatrists worry about cheating children out of their childhood. I worry about cheating them out of something more profoundly important: their self-respect as responsible, contributing human beings. (page 424, paragraph 16)

---

[6]Dramatic irony is discussed more fully on pages 394–395.

Thomas's "Late Night Thoughts" relies with terrifying effectiveness on our human fears: "the intrusion of a huge new thought: death everywhere, the dying of everything, the end of humanity" (page 428, paragraph 2).

Mystery, Humor.   Or depend on an entirely different sort of shared human values, the love of a good mystery. Turner relies upon this human characteristic to enliven literary criticism in "What Killed Arthur Dimmesdale?" and Slack uses it to build readers' interest in his report on social science research, "If I'm So Smart, How Come I Flunk All the Time?" He writes: "The only clue to the mystery was this common remark: 'The teachers . . . got it in for us'" (page 425, paragraph 4).

The love of laughter is another human emotion we share that writers find especially effective. We all like to laugh, and most of us admire the cleverness and wit that make George Will's Chicago Cubs essay both so delightful and so persuasive.

Case Studies.   You can win your readers by exemplifying your point in human terms. Impressive as statistics can be, they lack the human touch: 6.5 million, when it refers to human deaths in the Nazi camps, is a terrifying figure. But that number becomes far more meaningful when it is backed by a single case history, such as Anne Frank's diary, for Anne was a human being like us. In our essays, Slack (page 425) employs the case-study technique when he centers his research report on the story of an experimenter and his students, rather than on a scientific description of the experiment and its statistical results.

Sensuous Detail.   You can make this emotional identification more thorough by including the sort of vivid sensory detail that brings all your readers' senses into play. You might, for instance, follow the example Golden sets when he leads his readers into his rather technical "Earth's Creeping Deserts" with this sense-stimulating sentence:

> Outside the great conference hall in Nairobi, 16 fountains sent up sparkling plumes of water, and black Mercedes limousines glistened in the bright East African sun. (page 415, paragraph 1)

Imagery.   Some other good ways to secure your reader's emotional agreement are detailed in Chapter 9, which offers suggestions on how to use language and imagery persuasively. See especially pages 277–291.

Problems.   All these strategies for relating to your readers emotionally can be highly effective, but you can encounter serious problems in using them as well. The problems are those of excess. If you adopt an approach too greatly emphasizing feelings, your work may strike your readers as overly sentimental. If you are too powerful in your use of language and imagery, they may think of you as heavy-handed or insincere. The topic you are writing about should enter into your decision. The amount of emotional charge that might be completely appropriate for an essay on nuclear destruction could only be ludicrous applied to a composition on intramural soccer.

Giving Your Work Intellectual Validity

Yet a third set of strategies can help you persuade your reader. We have discussed the techniques associated with the author corner of the rhetorical triangle that help a writer establish moral and intellectual authority; and we've talked of the techniques from the reader corner that aid in getting readers to identify. Now let's turn to the techniques that should help provide intellectual validity for the work itself.

NO UNSUPPORTED STATEMENTS

Most important, you must be absolutely sure to give support for every point and every subpoint you make. You cannot expect your readers to believe your unconfirmed word. Every time you put forth a generalization, such as a conclusion about a broad class or category, you are making a silent promise to your readers that you will soon supply them with particulars that show the truth of what you have concluded. What are they to think when one unsupported generalization follows another with no particulars for either one? Nor can any amount of restatement satisfy readers' hunger for detail, for specific evidence. Your evidence may be as insubstantial as a personal anecdote: "All I remember about my wedding day in 1967 is that the Cubs dropped a doubleheader" (Will, supporting his loyalty to the Chicago Cubs: page 439, paragraph 9). Or it may be as indisputable as statistics or an authoritative quotation: "Washington's Worldwatch Institute estimates that the lives of perhaps 50 million people are jeopardized"; or "Warns U.N. Secretary General Kurt Waldheim: 'We risk destroying whole peoples in the afflicted area'" (Golden supporting the danger of desertification: page 415, paragraph 4). In any case, you will need to supply specific evidence of some kind, or you will assuredly lose both your readers' confidence and their interest. There is no way of getting around it: Supporting your every point is an inviolable rule of good writing.

SOURCES THAT ARE APPROPRIATE

To be persuasive, however, that support—of whatever variety—must be intellectually valid. If you choose to support your idea with a quotation, that quotation will have only the authority that the person you are quoting brings to it. In the example just presented, Golden's use of a secretary general of the United Nations to supply information about world drought supports his point effectively. Goodman gains similar authority for her views of the male–female relationship by citing the work of researchers Helen and Alexander Astin (page 419, paragraph 14).

Simply having a well-known name does not make a person an authoritative source outside of his or her own field, however. I might be willing to take the word of athletes, for instance, on the merits of athletic equipment or the fine points of a game, but their opinions on breakfast cereal or soap products or, for that matter, politics are of no more value than those of the rest of us. Nor will you find a self-serving quotation effective. Readers give little weight to a comment that clearly profits the person being quoted. They would discount, for example, views on deregulating oil prices expressed by the president of Exxon.

LOGICALLY VALID SUPPORT

In order to persuade your readers, the support you offer for your points must be logically valid. That is, a logical relationship should connect each of your points with the material you use to support them. Notice the clear-cut connection between the point (here italicized) and the support in this paragraph of Alexander's:

Point

Support

> *In Kids' Country, every day must be prize day.* Miss America, Miss Teen-Age America, Miss Junior Miss America, and probably Miss Little Miss America trample each other down star-spangled runways. Volume mail-order give-aways will shortly silt up our postal system entirely. All day long TV shows like *Concentration, Dating Game, Hollywood Squares,* and *Jackpot* hand out more toys: wristwatches, washing machines, trips to Hawaii. (page 412, paragraph 6).

Golden uses a more complex support:

Point

Example 1

Example 2

Results

Final Results

> Droughts and crop failures have always been a harsh fact of life in arid regions. *But the Sahel's calamity was worsened by distinctly modern factors.* Improvements in public health had vastly expanded population. New wells lulled the Africans into thinking they were no longer so completely dependent on the slim rainfall. They enlarged their herds and planted more cash crops like cotton and peanuts. For a while, the land withstood the strains. But when the rains ceased, the crops failed and the cattle stripped the fields of virtually every blade of grass around the overworked wells. Soon the thin layer of topsoil vanished, and there was nothing but rock, sand, and dust. The Sahara had won. (page 416, paragraph 6)

There is sound logic in the connections Golden draws as he relates his point about "modern factors," along with his two examples of these factors, to his conclusion about the eventual disaster resulting from these factors.

SOUND SUBSTANCE

It is good for you to develop writing strategies and techniques to help get your ideas across to your readers effectively so that they can appreciate the true merit in those ideas. But no quantity of technique can make ideas of little worth attractive or mask the writer's lack of knowledge or understanding. At base, the aspect of your essay that will contribute most to its effectiveness is sound substance: a worthwhile thesis backed by strong, solid support.

Chapter 1 should give you some ideas about how to explore your thoughts on a topic and how to organize them effectively. But before you write, make sure you know enough about your subject and have given it enough thought to speak knowledgeably and to make what you have to say about it worth the reading.

TRY IT OUT

1. Greenfield's "Accepting the Unacceptable," Williams's "U.S. Blacks and a Free Market," and Tucker's "On Splitting" have controversial theses. Choose one of these articles and list the persuasive strategies discussed in this chapter that the essayist employs.

2. How effectively does your author handle these strategies? How persuasive is the result?

3. Write a paragraph discussing the ethical issues involved in using rhetorical strategies to persuade your readers. Whether you believe this use is right or wrong, in supporting your point in *this* exercise, please use some of these strategies and label them in the margin.

ASSIGNMENT

Choose one of the following topics or another your instructor suggests and write an essay putting into practice some of the strategies of this chapter.

1. The feminist movement has tried to give women freedom of choice by emphasizing career and de-emphasizing family. Some critics (including Betty Friedan, a founding mother of the movement) feel that the de-emphasis of family has been too great and that now the choice of a completely family-centered life-style is being taken away from women. Write an essay explaining where you stand on the issue and why. This is a sensitive issue. Try using Rogers's principles of rhetoric to persuade your reader.

2. Another topic for which you will need the tact and sensitivity that Rogers suggests: Explain some significant characteristics, attitudes, and values

you share with your classmates and others that make you different from them. You will need a unifying thesis.[7]

3. When and to what extent is revenge justified? Write an essay in which you state and justify your position on the morality of revenge. Be concrete and specific in your support, and because this subject can arouse emotion, be especially wary in your handling of the "although" material.

4. This next assignment lets you explore the question of audience. Examine two or three issues of one of the following magazines: *Cosmopolitan, Commonweal, Nation, National Enquirer, The Village Voice, Ms., People, The New York Times Magazine,* or *The National Review.* By noting the ads, the content of the articles, the format, the style, and perhaps the ideological slant, decide exactly who the magazine's target audience is. Write an essay identifying the audience in terms of income, social class, age, sex, religion, interests, political and social values, recreational habits, anxieties, attitudes, and so on. Support your thesis with evidence derived from your observations.[8]

5. Respond to one of the essays in Part Four. Present the author's ideas fairly and agree or take issue with them. Support your views with specific and concrete details from your experience or your reading.

6. Develop into a finished essay any of the topics you began working with in a Try It Out earlier in the chapter.

---

[7]Topic suggested by Professor Michael Neuman of Capitol University.
[8]Suggested by Professor Ernest Fontana of Xavier University.

Chapter
4

The Writing Stage

Composing Your Essay

You have thought through the assignment and have made your decisions. You have, in short, completed the prewriting part of the writing process. And now you are supposed to be ready to write the essay itself. But that blank sheet of paper sits in front of you. I hope you are one of those who can plunge right into writing without too much anxiety. If you are not, understand that a large percentage of those who put pen to paper—including many professional writers—suffer similar tension. Donald Murray, a respected writer, admits that he "feels more terror facing the empty page" than he did in leaping from a plane when he was a paratrooper.

The feeling of being "pen-tied" is not new. Sir Philip Sidney, who lived in Shakespeare's day, described this peculiar agony perhaps more accurately than anyone when he wrote:

> Loving in truth, and fain in verse my love to show . . .
> I sought fit words . . . her wits to entertain,
> Oft turning others' leaves to see if thence would flow
> Some fresh and fruitful showers upon my sun-burned brain.
> But words came halting forth, wanting Invention's stay;
> Invention, Nature's child, fled step-dame Study's blows,
> And others' feet still seemed but strangers in my way.
> Thus, great with child to speak, and helpless in my throes,
> Biting my truant pen, beating myself for spite. . . .

Most of us (even those who make a special study of writing) know the feeling well. But the truth is that when you have finished your prewriting and have come at last to the moment of actually writing your paper, the hardest part of the task is already behind you. You have your thesis, you have your supporting ideas, you even have a good notion about how you are going to structure them. All you have to do now is find the words to express the ideas to your readers. All that remains is to introduce your point to them, develop it for them, and tie the essay together persuasively.

INTRODUCING YOUR POINT

It may help to approach the problem of introduction writing from the point of view of your readers. Before they begin reading your essay, they can have no idea of its subject. For all they know, it could be about anything at all. They will, therefore, not want to read too far without at least some rather strong hints as to the topic you are pursuing. Your first problem, then, is to find a quick way of excluding from their consideration all else in the world except that small part of it which you will discuss. Professional authors handle this problem in remarkably similar ways. A glance at the essays in Part Four will show that whatever the style and whatever the introductory ploy, all the authors follow the same procedure: (1) They manage to state the topic in so many words quite early; (2) they find a way to particularize or expand upon the simple topic; and (3) by the end of the introduction, they reveal the approach they are going to take to this topic—that is, most of them state their thesis. Here are a few examples:

Title	Topic	Abbreviated Thesis
"Distant Music" (page 436)	Perceiv[ing] Christmas through its wrapping	The miracle of Christmas is that . . . it [still] penetrates . . . the heart [despite everything].
"Kids' Country" (page 411)	Modern . . . children	Children today . . . have taken over.
"On Splitting" (page 431)	Marriages [that] hadn't made it.	What angered me was the loss of years and energy.

Setting up Your Thesis

From a practical standpoint, then, your problem is how you will suggest your topic and how you will get from topic to thesis. Sir Philip Sidney, whom we have heard on the agony of starting to write, concludes the passage on page 105 with advice that has never been matched:

"Fool," said my Muse to me, "Look in thy heart and write."

When it comes to writing introductions, *you* are your own richest resource. Think back and recall what first interested you in your subject. Was there a personal connection? Something that happened to you? A book you read? A movie or play that you saw? Does something in the topic connect to something currently in the news? Is there a subject much talked about just now that touches upon it? Is the topic an old one that you have just seen in a new light? Is it a tried and true topic that you now understand from a new angle? Is there something about the topic that cries for attention? Is there something about it that must be explained for your thesis to make sense? Do you disagree with the common view on the subject? Or with an important dissenting view? (These last questions, which lead into an "although" clause approach, can be particularly fruitful.)

Go over these questions or consider others like them that you invent for yourself. Follow up your thinking on the questions that appear most productive. Sharpen and develop this line of thought until it leads to a statement of your thesis. When you have put this reasoning on paper, you have written an introduction.

Using Introductory "Hooks"

By getting at the root of what interests you in your subject and conveying it clearly and in an appealing way to your readers, you will probably be able to interest them, too. This straightforward sort of introduction begins most professional essays. Sometimes, however, when the subject or the tone of their essays makes it appropriate, professional writers choose from a variety of strategies or devices to add interest to their introduction. Journalists call these strategies "hooks." Although you would be unwise to rely upon hooks too often or in an artificial way, they can add life and attractiveness to your approach to your thesis.

ANECDOTES

One of the most useful introductory strategies is the anecdote, the brief telling of an amusing or otherwise engaging incident. Most introductory anecdotes are the direct offspring of Sidney's "look-in-thy-heart" school of advice and are personal in character. They often relate the very event that brought the topic to the writer's attention. In using the anecdote, authors also take advantage of the universal appeal of stories and storytelling. Carll Tucker, for instance, begins his essay in this way:

One afternoon recently, two unrelated friends called to tell me that, well, their marriages hadn't made it. One was leaving his wife for another woman. The other was leaving her husband because "we thought it best." (page 431, paragraph 1)

INTRODUCTORY QUESTIONS

Another hook that authors use to attract their readers is the question. When you choose to begin with a question, you take advantage of two possibilities that are natural to this sort of sentence. First, since a question asks, it presupposes an answering, which gives you a quick route into the thesis (or into the "although" clause) by way of reply. Walter Williams sets up his "although" clause in this way:

Does black socioeconomic progress necessarily depend upon whether blacks are liked by whites? Does it depend on the continuance of massive federal expenditures? (page 441, paragraph 1)

Second, the question has an ability to involve your reader personally in whatever you have to say because, in itself, it reflects direct communication between author and reader. Slack, for example, intrigues his reader with this thought-provoking opening question:

Can twenty flunking students of varying intelligence raise their math and English a full year's level in only thirty working days? (page 425, paragraph 1)

POINTEDLY BRIEF STATEMENTS

Like an introductory question, a pointedly brief statement catches the eye and, with luck, the reader's interest, by its contrast to the other kinds of sentences around it. Because most mature writing is expressed in complex sentences made up of clauses and phrases of varying lengths, a blunt, affirmative statement containing only a few words can arrest the eye and startle the mind into attention. The simple phrasing of such brief statements gives them an almost proverb-like quality. The first words in Shana Alexander's essay are typical of this strategy:

Children are a relatively modern invention. (page 411, paragraph 1)

Some writers inject an informal, conversational quality into their brief opening remark. William Raspberry's "Two-Career Families," for example, begins:

Maybe you have to be crazy to argue with two Harvard psychiatrists. (page 423, paragraph 1)

INTRODUCTORY QUOTATIONS

You might choose to introduce your essay with a quotation. In "Two-Career Families," Raspberry takes issue with a theory discussed in a book he has recently read. He quotes the offending passage in his introduction:

> The only paragraph [from Barrie Greiff and Preston Hunter's article] that arched my eyebrows included this sentence: "Dual-career parents . . . shouldn't overburden their children with responsibility for themselves or their siblings, or for running the household; that only cheats them out of their childhood and confuses them about parental roles." (page 423, paragraph 3)

Although Raspberry slides into his quotation with preliminary remarks, such a preface is not always necessary. Many authors who use this hook begin their essays with the quotation itself and offer their explanations later on. A typical review from a popular magazine, for example, begins:

> "The schools are the golden avenue of opportunity for able youngsters, but by the same token they are the arena in which less able youngsters discover their limitations." John Gardner's book, *Excellence,* has to do with this plain fact. He wishes to make it plainer, to have the country face up to it, and to have educators deal with it wisely. (Harold Taylor, "Quality and Equality," *Saturday Review,* 44 [April 15, 1961], 72)

WIT AND HUMOR

Some of the most appealing introductions combine a clear setting out of the subject with an appropriately witty play on words. This quality of language, though highly effective, is difficult to pin down. George Will's opening sentence in "The Chicago Cubs, Overdue," with its sly metaphor on catching an illness, certainly has it:

> A reader demands to know how I contracted the infectious conservatism for which he plans to horsewhip me. (page 438, paragraph 1)

E. B. White's subtle handling of the pun in his opening sentence is also marked by wit:

> To perceive *Christmas* through its *wrapping* becomes more difficult with every year. (page 436, paragraph 1; emphasis mine)

Using (and Not Using) Hooks

Devices such as these do make an introduction more interest-provoking. But you must not feel that such pizzazz is necessary. If you should be inspired by an idea for such an opening that is both imaginative and appropriate to your subject, don't be afraid to experiment with it. But if such inspiration does not come, it is always a mistake to try to force it. For although you are right to admire a strikingly apt opening, you should not underestimate the value of a simple but solid lead into your thesis followed by a clear statement of the thesis itself.

Good introductions are as various as good essays. Still, the accompanying practical suggestions might help you in composing yours.

Guidelines for Your Introduction

1. Overall purpose: To present the thesis interestingly
   a. Specific purpose: To lead into the subject and generally into some statement of thesis
   b. Persuasive purpose: To interest the reader in the subject
2. Include:
   a. (always) A lead into the subject
   b. (almost always) A statement of (or some expression of) thesis
   c. (often) A statement of the "although" clause or an explication of the "although" material
   d. (sometimes) A clarification of approach or explication of structure
   e. (never) Arguments for the thesis
3. Arrangement:
   a. Thesis statement (or expression) last or nearly last
   b. If material follows the thesis, it should be limited to
      (1) Restatement or amplification of the thesis
      (2) A transitional sentence on structural matters

TRY IT OUT

1. Examine six introductions from essays in Part Four or from another sampling of magazine essays or another collection of articles. How many have:
   a. A straightforward lead into the thesis.
   b. An "although" clause type of opening, leading to a contradictory thesis.
   c. Some hook or special strategy to attract the reader. Describe the hooks that you have discovered. Do you find them effective?

2. Try constructing two effective one-paragraph introductions leading to two of the following theses. (Feel free to reword the thesis sentences to suit your own purpose.)
   a. Consuming sugar creates more health problems than is usually acknowledged.
   b. Despite the corruption of the boss-run City Hall, there are those who long for restoration of the old-fashioned patronage system, abuses and all.

c. Important though the computer is to our economy, it creates as many problems as it solves.

d. Men and women of differing religions are unwise to marry each other.

or

The problems of interreligious marriages are greatly exaggerated.

SUPPORTING YOUR POINT

Once you have completed the beginning of your paper, you have introduced and presented your point, your thesis. Now you have to support it. The ideas you have jotted down in your organizational plan, along with any thoughts they call to mind, should suggest the means of support and should help you structure that support. Your task at this stage is to explain, expand upon, and develop each of these ideas in order to present your thesis in the most convincing way.

In the next sections you will find suggestions of strategies and opportunities to practice techniques that should help you create effective support for each of your ideas. Nevertheless, when you begin to write, do not worry too much about keeping the precise particulars of this advice in mind. What you really want to do when you compose is to get your ideas flowing. Don't stop and consider every word, every sentence. Don't even be afraid occasionally to leave your plan behind and follow a thought wherever it seems to take you. Always realize that *you will have the opportunity to revise.* You can stop and make changes at the end of each natural division if you like—or whenever the flow of your ideas begins to dwindle. You should certainly plan to revise when you reach the end. Remember your rewriting can be as extensive as you choose.

Bearing in mind, then, that everything you write is subject to change, use your plan as a general guide, and write the body of your composition as freely as you can.

Paragraphs and Paragraph Clusters

When we speak of writing the body of a composition, we mean composing paragraphs. "Paragraph" is, of course, a term familiar to you:

A paragraph consists of material set off by spacing and indentation on a printed, typed, or manuscript page.

Although this definition is straightforward enough, the concept represented by the term "paragraph" is surprisingly problematic. The problem is that, in most respects, paragraphs are arbitrary divisions determined as much by the way a portion of written material looks on a page as by the meaning of the words in it.

Where a paragraph ends is based upon readability. Because the space following each paragraph offers a rest for the reader's eye and mind, how many words to include before that rest is needed depends on such mechanical conditions as the width of the column of type and the size of the lettering. For example, an able editor may decide to break up a passage of, say, 150 words about the popularity of soccer into three paragraphs if it is to be printed in a narrow newspaper column, or into two paragraphs for printing on the pages of a small book in a large typeface, but that same editor might leave it as a single paragraph if the material is to appear in a wide-column journal. Figure 4.1 shows how a passage from Alexander's "Kids' Country" might be variously paragraphed.

PARAGRAPH CLUSTERS DEFINED

Paragraphs are such inconsistent segments that you may well wonder how any consistent advice can be given about them. The truth is that if we insist upon talking about the literal paragraph as it is variously printed on a page, no advice can be valid because no unvarying description is possible.

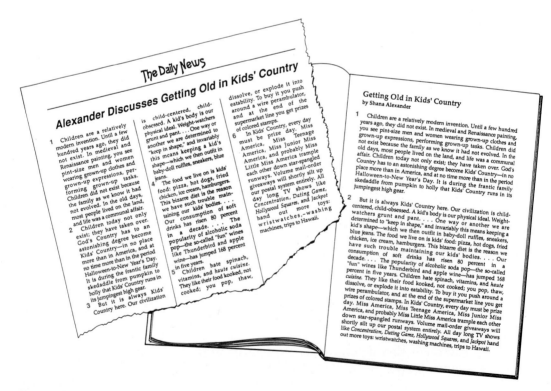

Figure 4.1   Type Format Affects Paragraphing

The form of short, semi-focused paragraph 5 in the newspaper version of Alexander's essay, for instance, has little in common with the form of the long, topic-sentenced paragraph 2, of which it is a part in the wide-columned version. On the other hand, if we can look beyond the arbitrary mechanics of typesetting and printing and concentrate on the passage as a whole—whether it appears on the page as one paragraph or as a string of paragraphs—we can recognize characteristic features.

The unit we are talking about here (and it is sometimes called "a paragraph" in rhetoric books) is a concept for which English has no universally recognized name. We might call this concept a "paragraph cluster."

A paragraph cluster is a unit of prose in which a limited topic is stated and developed.

Whether this unit is spaced on the page as one paragraph or a number of paragraphs, it is the major building block of expository compositions. And a very useful unit it is too. Scholarly research (which you can duplicate for yourself by studying the paragraphs in this book and elsewhere) shows that paragraph clusters in expository prose share the characteristics described in the accompanying box.

Well-written Expository Paragraphs (or Paragraph Clusters)

1. These units almost always have a topic sentence that presents the subject of the paragraph (or cluster).
2. The rest of the sentences of the paragraph (or cluster) relate to the topic sentence in one of the following ways:
   a. Lead into it
   b. Explain it, by expanding or restricting its meaning
   c. Support it
   d. Or support or explain a supporting sentence
3. The placement of the topic sentence can vary, but in paragraphs or clusters that are *not introductory,* the topic sentence ordinarily occurs at or near the beginning.
4. Introductory passages generally have these characteristics:
   a. The topic sentence ordinarily occurs at or near the conclusion of an introductory paragraph or cluster (see pages 24–26).
   b. In "although" clause introductory paragraphs (or clusters), the topic sentence frequently occurs somewhere near the center, following the "although" material. There it often has the effect of altering, even reversing, the meaning of the paragraph to that point.
   c. These introductory patterns sometimes occur within the body of an essay as well. In particular, they provide the pattern for some transitional paragraphs that introduce new sets of ideas.

Topic Sentences

What can you take from this knowledge of how good writers construct their paragraphs (or clusters) that will be useful in constructing your own? First, you can understand how important the topic sentence is for communicating your ideas to the reader. (See page 28 for a definition and discussion of the topic sentence.) You can also learn to help your reader by placing this extremely important sentence in the conventional position, where your reader expects to find it.[1] The other sentences in the paragraph unit can then perform their function of explaining or supporting your point. You will want to make sure that every sentence in the paragraph (or cluster) relates directly to your point and eliminate any that do not.

Most of your topic sentences should be effective statements of the points or subpoints in your organizational plan. As such, these sentences serve two functions:

· They set forth your point or subpoint clearly in a way that leads into or demands explanation or support.
· And they reflect, tie into, or support the thesis of your essay.

Consider a typical topic sentence in Alexander's essay, "Kids' Country":

The food we live on is kids' food. (page 411, paragraph 4)

Or see another example in Perry Turner's "Who Killed Arthur Dimmesdale?":

Other [scholars] were less convinced by Kahn's "possible truth." (page 435, paragraph 8)

These sentences, like all good topic sentences, "look before and after." The first example at the same time supports Alexander's thesis that America has become a "kids' country" and prompts the statistics on American eating habits that make up the rest of the paragraph. Similarly, the second sample both hearkens back (here in a negative way) to Turner's thesis and sets up the scholarly quotation that supports it as the topic sentence of this paragraph.

---

[1]After conducting extensive research on the subject, psychologist David Kieras concludes: "The topic sentence of a passage really should be first, because that is where a reader expects to find the important information." ("How Readers Abstract Main Ideas . . . ," a paper presented at the American Institute for Research, Washington, D.C., November 17, 1980. p. 7.)

Support and Your Reader

Topic sentences, no less than theses, make commitments to readers. When you write a topic sentence near the beginning of a paragraph, you indicate to your readers that you will satisfy any question that might come to their minds about what the statement means or why it is true. That is, you agree to explain the statement or its main ideas, to define them, to illustrate them until your readers find them clear. You also agree that you will provide enough supporting data, enough convincing examples, to make your readers follow your point and, if not agree to it, at least understand your reasons for thinking it is true.

You are probably wondering how you can keep this commitment. Here, I can offer some definite advice: First, let your mind play over your topic sentence. Perhaps add another sentence or two to clarify it—to make it more specific or to expand it. Do not, however, fall into the danger, so common to writers, of building a paragraph consisting of repeated restatements of or generalizations on your topic sentence.[2] When you are satisfied that you have made your point clearly, then see what supporting information comes to mind to illustrate it or to back it up. Perhaps you will think of a series of examples, such as Perry Turner used in a paragraph cluster in "What Killed Arthur Dimmesdale?"

> *It's also true that atropine produces symptoms much like those that start to plague Dimmesdale;*[3] flushing, for instance, and speech problems. At about the time Chillingworth set up shop as the town's physician, Dimmesdale's health began to deteriorate: "His form grew emaciated; his voice, though still rich and sweet, had a certain melancholy prophecy of decay in it; he was often observed . . . to put his hand over his heart, with first a flush and then a paleness."
>
> Atropine also makes the pupils dilate, and Hawthorne cagily observes that "whether it were his failing health, or whatever the cause might be, [Dimmesdale's] large dark eyes had a world of pain in their troubled and melancholy depth." And then there's the matter of Dimmesdale's deteriorating coordination, another symptom of incremental atropine poisoning. By the last scene, in fact, his walk resembles "the wavering effort of an infant." (page 434, paragraphs 5–6)

Or perhaps a single example that you could elaborate upon would back up your point more effectively. George Will uses this technique in his essay on the Chicago Cubs:

> Every litter must have its runt, but *my Cubs were almost all runts.* Topps baseball bubblegum cards always struggled to say something nice about each

---

[2]This problem is discussed in detail in Chapter 6, page 176.
[3]I italicize this topic sentence and those in the examples that follow.

player. All they could say about the Cubs' infielder Eddie Miksis was that in 1951 he was tenth in the league in stolen bases, with eleven. (page 439, paragraph 7)

On the other hand, you might find the best illustration for your point by narrating an anecdote, as E. B. White does in this paragraph from "The Distant Music of the Hounds":

> *The miracle of Christmas is that,* like the distant and very musical voice of the hound, *it penetrates finally and becomes heard in the heart*—over so many years, through so many cheap curtain-raisers. It is not destroyed even by all the arts and craftsness of the destroyers, having an essential simplicity that is everlasting and triumphant, at the end of confusion. We once were out at night with coon-hunters, and we were aware that it was not so much the promise of the kill that took the men away from their warm homes and sent them through the cold shadowy woods, it was something more human, more mystical—something even simpler. It was the night, and the excitement of the note of the hound, first heard, then not heard. It was the natural world seen at its best and most haunting, unlit except by stars, impenetrable except to the knowing and the sympathetic. (page 436, paragraph 2)

FINDING SUPPORT (OR BACK TO INVENTING AGAIN)

But what should you do when appropriate examples and illustrations do not come immediately to mind? You might turn again to one of the heuristics we discussed earlier (pages 41–47) and continue the inventing process. To activate what Agatha Christie's detective, Hercule Poirot, calls "the little grey cells," ask yourself the Aristotelian questions of definition, comparison, cause and effect, and authority, but apply them to the point of your topic or subtopic sentences.

Do not limit yourself to any one line of reasoning, however. Instead, let your mind range freely among all the questions. Perhaps the best approach is to try to decide just what expectations your topic sentence would arouse in your readers, what questions it would create in their minds. Then plan your support to answer all their unasked questions.

TRY IT OUT

1. The student papers by Michael Reveal (pages 454–457) and Sheila Kenney (pages 451–453) illustrate the major distinction in kinds of support, Mike backing his points with material from outside sources and Sheila using "evidence" from her own senses and experience. What is the topic sentence of Mike's paragraph 4? Cite the evidence he uses to support his point. Do you find it convincing? Why? What is the topic sentence of Sheila's first

paragraph? Cite her evidence. Do you find it convincing? Why? How does the appeal of this type of evidence differ from that of the support in paragraph 3?

2. Name two of the ways Cheryl Jacobs supports her points in her paper (page 448).

3. Think of yourself as a prospective reader of paragraphs headed by the following topic sentences. What questions would they raise in your mind? How would you suggest that a writer go about answering them in paragraph form?
   a. Mononucleosis, a disease affecting the liver and spleen, is an uncommonly disagreeable affliction that attacks many college students.
   b. Learning to write is not easy.
   c. Many educators have become disillusioned with what used to be called the "new math."
   d. Chicago is rightly known as the "windy city."

4. Write topic sentences for three of the following topics. Then, choose one sentence and develop a convincing paragraph from it, a paragraph that would interest a reader.

Sitcoms	Sickle-cell anemia
The draft	Adoption
Native American Culture	The Indianapolis 500
San Francisco (or city of your choice)	Euthanasia

   Use the guidelines on page 113 to help you with paragraph form. Develop your support material by working with at least two of the four sets of Aristotelian questions: definition (or classification), comparison (or analogy), cause and effect, or authority. (See Chapter 1, pages 43–45.)

MAKING YOUR SUPPORT SPECIFIC AND VIVID

You are probably now convinced that to write an effective essay you need to develop your thesis with paragraphs or paragraph clusters whose topic sentences support the thesis and are in turn each convincingly supported. But when you have reviewed some of your options for developing that support, you may still wonder about the content of the support. Initially, professional writing may seem to offer little help. If you examine the sample paragraphs cited in the last section, other paragraphs from the essays in Part Four, or other examples of professional writing, your overall impression must be one of overwhelming variety. You will find that supporting material comes from literature (classical, popular, and historical); from statistical data and recorded facts; from memories or everyday knowledge; from personal observation or fantasy; from interviews (see Elizabeth Jane Stein's student paper, pages 458–461), conversations, books, plays, television; from knowledge derived from the whole alphabet of scholarly disciplines from archaeology, botany, chemistry all the way to zoology. Nevertheless, amid all this diversity, supporting material in well-written paragraphs does seem to have two important characteristics in common: the illustrations, from whatever source, are always both specific and vivid. It may even seem as you examine writing samples that an abundance of vivid and specific detail is what makes expository writing effective.

Unrelieved generalization, in fact, may well be the chief hallmark of the inexperienced writer. For example, an inexperienced writer might approach George Will's notion of the influence an honored but ever-losing baseball team had on his life in this way:

> From early childhood, I was loyal to the local baseball team and their continuing misfortunes influenced my life in a negative way. Most little children would be moved by this discouraging experience, and I was no exception. During my youth all the teams but mine won championships. Nevertheless, I marked the occasions of my life by their misfortunes.

Although this is not a bad paragraph, it is far less effective than it could be. Instead of twice repeating the generalizations in the topic sentence, that sentence could be far better supported by adding details specific enough to explain it convincingly and vivid enough to involve its readers' imaginations. Here is the paragraph cluster as Will writes it:

> Like the boy who stood on the burning deck whence all but he had fled, I was loyal. And the downward trajectory of my life was set. An eight-year-old could not face these fires without being singed, unless he had the crust of an armadillo, and how many eight-year-olds do?
>
> Of the sixteen teams that existed in 1949, all have since won league championships—all but the Cubs. And which of the old National League teams was first to finish in tenth place behind even the expansion teams? Don't ask. Since 1948 the Cubs have played more than 6,000 hours of losing baseball. My cruel addiction continued. In 1964 I chose to do three years of graduate study at Princeton because Princeton is midway between Philadelphia and New York—two National League cities. All I remember about my wedding day in 1967 is that the Cubs dropped a doubleheader. ("The Chicago Cubs, Overdue," page 439, paragraphs 8–9)

Comparing the two paragraphs reveals the sources of the second's strength. Instead of the general term *early youth* in the first paragraph, Will speaks specifically of his "eight-year-old" self; instead of *local baseball team,* he specifies "the Chicago Cubs." Not content with simply stating that his life was *influenced negative*[ly] by his *discouraging experience,* Will turns to hyperbole and metaphor (that is, to exaggeration and comparison). He claims that his loyalty to the Cubs set his life on a "downward trajectory" by his eighth year. And, alluding to an old poem, he compares himself to "the boy who stood on the burning deck" and his loyalty to the losing ball team to the "fires" that would inevitably "singe" him—"unless," as he adds in another vivid image, the unlikely case that his eight-year-old self had "the crust of an armadillo." Will makes the abstract phrase *continuing misfortunes* more vivid by asking the rhetorical question: "And which of the old National League teams was first to finish in tenth place?" and then refusing to state the obvious; instead, he answers: "Don't ask." And he makes the phrase more specific by citing the "more than 6,000 hours of losing baseball" his team had "played . . . since 1948." For the generality of *marked the occasions* of my life, Will substitutes the particular: "In 1964 I chose to do three years of graduate study at Princeton." He is even more specific and vivid in his final example: "All I remember of my wedding day in 1967 is that the Cubs dropped a doubleheader." In short, Will has made his point convincing in this paragraph by supporting it with vivid, specific detail.

Developing Your Observing and Analyzing Skills

What works for professional writers should also work for you. How effective you are in creating expository paragraphs depends on how well you can think up vivid, specific detail and how appropriately you use it. Two skills are especially important in this effort:

- The ability to observe in the particular rather than just in the general
- The ability to find relationships, to uncover similarities within your diverse experiences and memories.

Both of these are skills that can be helped along by practice. The following sets of exercises are designed to provide you with such practice.

OBSERVING VISUALLY

Here are two ways that you can train yourself to be an intelligent observer: Observe the object, person, or scene (1) as a whole in relation to its surroundings, and (2) as the sum of its parts. In other words, think of yourself as first viewing it from afar and then examining it at close range. Try it out.

TRY IT OUT

1. Select an object to observe carefully. (A specific tree or a particular alarm clock, say.)
   a. Look at it from a distance.
      (1) See how it relates to the space and other objects around it, and record your observations. What can you say about its size? Its proportions? Its color? Its relative importance in its own context?
      (2) Does it remind you of anything from your own experience, from life, reading, movies, or television? Record also (however far-fetched they appear at first) the ideas the distant object calls to mind.
   b. Examine the object closer up.
      (1) Describe it carefully. List at least ten specific details about it. (Include details derived from senses other than the visual if you choose.)
      (2) Record also any comparisons that the close-up examination calls from your memory.

2. Choose a scene to observe carefully: a small segment of landscape or a room.
   a. Get some perspective on the scene.
      (1) Observe it from afar or think how it would look if you were seeing it from a distance. (You might imagine how you would view it through a telescope.) Describe it carefully in relation to its surroundings.
      (2) Record also any ideas that this scene might suggest to you.
   b. Place yourself within the scene.
      (1) Closely examine its various parts. You might even put some features of it under a mental microscope. List at least twelve specific details about it. (Record details derived from senses other than visual if you choose.)
      (2) Record also any comparisons that this close-up examination might call to mind.

OBSERVING BY HEARING AND SMELLING

Although without question for most of us the visual sense is the dominant observing power, good writers do not neglect any of their senses. Hearing and smell can be particularly useful. The following exercises will help you practice.

TRY IT OUT

1. Choose three locations. Include the scene you used earlier if you wish. In each one:
   a. Close your eyes and listen.
      (1) Write down every sound that you hear. (If you have trouble describing a sound, use a comparison or an analogy that will communicate what you have heard.)
      (2) What association(s) do the sounds call up in your mind?
   b. Breathe deeply or sniff about.
      (1) Identify the predominant odor(s) if you can. Describe it (them) specifically. If you cannot make the odor clear by descriptive words alone, use comparisons or analogies.
      (2) What association(s) do the odors bring to mind?

SELECTING INTELLIGENTLY

Not being able to "see the forest for the trees" is an old saying that sums up the problems inexperienced writers sometimes face when they have learned how to observe well enough to gather a great number of details but have not yet learned how to use those details discriminatingly. In using details, as in almost anything else, there can be too much of a good thing. You need to narrow down the dozens of sense impressions that are part of every situation to those few telling details that convey the sense of what you want to say. Specifically, in composing each of your paragraphs or paragraph clusters, focus on the meaning of your topic sentence and select only those details that support it.

TRY IT OUT

1. a. Return to the scene you used for observation in the visual exercise (and possibly also in the later exercises). What is the overall impression the place leaves in your mind? Perhaps it is a mood you sense there. Perhaps it is a thought that the place brings to mind.
   b. Compose a sentence in which you express this impression, this mood, or this thought.
   c. Examine your list of specific details describing the place, and check only those details that have to do with the ideas expressed in your sentence.
   d. Making this sentence your topic sentence, write a paragraph (or para-

graph cluster) in which you support your topic sentence with the details you have checked on your list.

The Bathers by Georges-Pierre Seurat (1859–1891). (*Source:* National Gallery Publications, The National Gallery, Trafalgar Square, London.)

2. **a.** Study the accompanying painting. What do you think the artist is trying to say in it? Phrase your answer as a sentence.
   b. Jot down all the details you can find in the picture that suggest that your interpretive sentence is correct. (If you find details that do not fit with your theory, be sure to revise the theory.)
   c. Write a paragraph interpreting the picture, using your revised interpretive sentence as its topic sentence and the details you have noticed as its support.

SEEING RELATIONSHIPS, DRAWING CONNECTIONS

Sometimes good writers do not draw the details with which they support their points directly from sense impressions or even from facts and figures. Sometimes they take them instead from memory. When George Will, for instance, needed support for his statement that the Chicago Cubs of his youth were a laughably inferior team, he remembered an old bubblegum baseball card that couldn't find anything to praise about one of the team members (page 439). When Walter Williams wanted to prove that it was much easier for a person to achieve economic security in the past than it is now, driving a taxi was the illustration that occurred to him. With this idea in mind, he researched the appropriate licensing facts and gave vivid and specific proof (page 442, paragraph 7).

Illustrations that illuminate the idea expressed in this way are rooted in the ability to see relationships, to make connections between what you want to say and the relevant portions of your experience or memories. Practice can help you develop your ability to use your imagination and memory in this way to convey your ideas to readers.

TRY IT OUT

1. a. Think of someone you know. What character in a book or in a movie or on television does he or she remind you of? In what *specific* ways are they alike? What are their points of difference?

  b. Write a paragraph describing your acquaintance (or friend or relative) in terms of the fictional (or historic) character so that a reader familiar with the character will be able to understand your friend or acquaintance as well.

A   B

A. *Madame Moitessier Seated* by Jean-Auguste-Dominique Ingres (1780–1867). (*Source:* National Gallery Publications, The National Gallery, Trafalgar Squate, London.)

B. *Portrait of Greta Moll* by Henri Matisse (1869–1954). (*Source:* National Gallery Publications, The National Gallery, Trafalgar Square, London.)

2. **a.** Carefully study pictures A and B on page 123. There may well be an underlying resemblance in the features of the women who sat as models for these two portraits. The works, however, were painted by artists widely separated in time and in artistic technique, who were influenced by widely differing ideas of fashion and beauty. Do you see the pictures as similar or as very different? Why do you think so?

  b. In deciding why you think as you do, you should discover a major point of comparison between the two pictures. What is it?

  c. Phrase your point of comparison as a topic sentence.

  d. Illustrate and demonstrate the truth of your topic sentence in a paragraph built on details in or suggested by the two pictures.

TYING IT ALL TOGETHER

The purpose of a conclusion is to conclude, to tie the whole experience of reading the essay together and to leave the reader with something to remember or ponder. The suggestions here should help you conclude your essay effectively.

Rereading Your Paper

Much has been said in this book about planning. Chapters 1 and 3, in fact, are completely devoted to the advance thinking that is the essence of the prewriting part of the writing process. Nevertheless, when it comes to writing the conclusion of your essay, I want to suggest that you do *not* plan it exactly beforehand. When you have finished writing the first draft of the introduction and body of the composition, take time out and read carefully through what you have written. Having reread and reconsidered, you can then let your ending flow out of what you have already said. For a number of reasons this procedure is a good one.

To begin with, it is possible that when you reread the composition, you may find that you have already said all you have to say—that anything else would be just filler. Especially in a very brief paper, a formal conclusion can be repetitive and unnecessary. It may be that instead of writing a concluding paragraph, all you will need to do is to be sure that the last paragraph in the body of your essay ends with a note of finality. (See, for example, Will's Cubs essay on page 438.)

Then, too, you cannot know before you have written the essay just what its conclusion should say. Writing itself is part of the invention process. Unless you follow your original outline in a robotlike way, the chances are that you will be reshaping some of your ideas while you are writing them. You'll want to leave yourself free to find the most effective way of concluding the composition you have actually written.

Most important, drawing your conclusion from your rereading of the rest provides your essay with a sense of wholeness. When you write the closing after rereading, you will not be tempted to add a pat ending. Instead, you will give your final reflections upon your thesis, your final coloring of the point you make in the paper and the ideas you have discussed in making it.

After rereading the essay, you may possibly discover that it already has a sense of completeness; if you do, you can, of course, simply stop. More often you will want to try for this sense of wholeness and completion by employing three basic concluding techniques: (1) You can restate your central point, your thesis, as shaped by the ideas through which you have developed it; (2) you can provide echoes of these ideas and even of the language in which you phrased them earlier; and (3) you can let your natural enthusiasm for your topic gather force as you reach the end so that it heightens the emotional intensity of your language. Let's look more closely at these techniques.

Final Statement of Thesis . . . and Beyond

The final presentation of your central point is probably the most important element of your conclusion. Your readers will expect that in closing you will give your thesis its clearest and most persuasive expression. When you reread the essay before writing your conclusion, you can phrase the thesis so that it will follow naturally from what you have written earlier. You can phrase it so that it summarizes, without repeating monotonously. The conclusion of Golden's essay is a good instance of thesis restatement:

> Some scientists feared that the document placed too much faith in technological—rather than "human"—solutions, but the plea nonetheless represents a milestone. For the first time, the international community is committing itself to the fight against the growth of deserts. While the document leaves action up to individual countries, the incentive to collaborate—perhaps even with old enemies—is great. *To many countries, doing battle against the deserts is the only alternative to poverty, starvation and chaos.* (page 417, paragraph 12; thesis in italics)

William Raspberry also closes with a simple but strongly worded reaffirmation of his thesis:

> The Harvard psychiatrists worry about cheating children out of their childhood. *I worry about cheating them out of something more profoundly important: their self-respect as responsible, contributing human beings.* (page 424, paragraph 16; thesis in italics)

ADDING A PRACTICAL APPLICATION

Although brief endings of this sort can be highly effective, in some of your writing you may wish to take your readers a step beyond your thesis.

You will then probably want to follow professional examples and continue on after restating the thesis to apply your point in some practical way. Walter Williams, for instance, who throughout his essay argues that the accepted view of black socioeconomic problems is destructive, concludes "U.S. Blacks and a Free Market" by briefly counterposing his own more constructive outlook. Let's look at his concluding paragraph cluster more closely:

> [First a transitional sentence concluding and summarizing his economic arguments:] Therefore, what has happened is that when blacks received the franchise, they found that many markets were closed and hence the traditional sources of upward mobility. [Then his restatement of thesis:] *For too many blacks dependency has been substituted for self-initiative for lack of a better insight into the problems that they face.* [And a final amplification of his thesis:] This misunderstanding has led their leadership to preside over the formulation of the first permanent welfare group in America's history. Ironically, this leadership, perhaps unwittingly, solidly supports labor laws that seriously handicap the most disadvantaged while it vociferously supports other laws which increase dependence. (page 442, paragraph 10)

Having stated his main point persuasively, Williams could easily have ended his essay here. Instead, because his thesis is limited to analyzing the problem, he chooses to go beyond his thesis and briefly outline his solution:

> What disadvantaged people need are freer markets and a return to the principles of the Bill of Rights—principles which the Supreme Court of the 1930s threw out when they gave the state and federal governments greater control over the individual's economic life. Black people need a fair chance to compete—nothing more and nothing less. (page 443, paragraph 11)

Offering a solution to the problem discussed, as Williams does, is only one of the ways you can carry your conclusion beyond restating the thesis. Another way is to suggest your own evaluation of the point you have made. For example, if you have written a critical analysis of a story and have explained what the author or scholar meant, you might well decide to follow up your summation with your own opinion of how well the author had achieved his or her end, or even your refutation of the ideas.

Similarly, you may want to suggest that your readers change their thinking or take action on your point. If you have argued that capital punishment is wrong, you may want to advise your convinced readers to write their state legislators. If you have explained the results of your science-course experiments, you may want to point out where future research still needs to be done. If you have shown that the campus cafeteria food is inedible, you might recommend petitioning the Dean of Students. Or if you have argued that you are well qualified for a job, you will probably want to conclude by asking for an interview.

Although endings that go beyond the present thesis to a future application or beyond a theoretical thesis to a practical application can be highly satisfying, you should *not* feel obliged to conclude in this way. Brief conclusions may be even more effective, especially for brief essays. Avoid filler. Avoid wordiness. Often when you have expounded your thesis clearly and persuasively, there is nothing more to say. At such times it is best simply to conclude.

Echoes

When you reread your paper just before writing its closing, its ideas and phrasing will be fresh in your mind. You are then in a position to echo these ideas and phrasing in your conclusion. Not only do such echoes give your readers a sense of unity that is both satisfying and persuasive, but they can also provide an under-the-surface summary of your most persuasive points. I do not, of course, recommend that you build your conclusion out of the last part of the old saw that says "Tell them what you're gonna say; say it; and then tell them you've said it." Closings such as "I have argued (1) . . ., (2) . . ., and (3) . . .; and therefore . . ." can be deadly, especially in a brief or nontechnical paper. It is quite a different matter, however, for these points to express themselves to the reader through connecting links with the rest of the paper.

What exactly are these links? Echoes are difficult to explain by means of brief quotation alone since by their very nature they reflect the whole. But let me suggest a way you can explore them for yourself. Examine the conclusion of one of the essays in Part Four. Select its key words and trace them or their counterparts throughout the whole work. If you focus on the closing paragraph of Thomas's "Late Night Thoughts on Listening to Mahler's Ninth Symphony" (page 430), for example, you may be struck by the familiarity of its first clause: *"If I were sixteen or seventeen years old."* If you then decide to trace it back, you will find the reason for the familiarity: this clause is a concluding echo of:

[paragraph 6:] *If I were* very young, *sixteen or seventeen years old,* I think I would begin, perhaps very slowly and imperceptibly, to go crazy.

[and of paragraph 9:] *If I were sixteen or seventeen years old,* I would not hear the cracking of my own brain, but I would know for sure that the whole world was coming unhinged.

Later in the Thomas conclusion you might notice the phrase *"things like that,"* which refers to the material in paragraph 10 about the "nice-looking chap['s]" unblinking calculation of "the outright death" of "only forty million . . . American citizens in twenty minutes." This phrase also echoes earlier references:

[In paragraph 4:] Not while *those things* are in place, aimed everywhere, ready for launching.

> [And in paragraph 5:] *This* [the deployment of nuclear weapons] *is a bad enough thing* for the people in my generation.

With this network of echoes, Thomas links for his readers' final consideration all he has said throughout the essay about the minds of youth and the madness of preparation for nuclear war.

Yet a third group of echoes in Thomas's conclusion, those referring to sound and music, work with those in the introductory portions of the essay to form a frame. The technique of the frame conclusion, often—as · here—associated with echo networks, is one of the more formal closing strategies discussed later in this section.

Heightened Language

Because all writing is essentially persuasive, a good conclusion not only leaves the reader with something to remember or ponder, but also with a sense of conviction. To gain this conviction, authors often close their essays with language that has more emotional intensity than they used earlier in the piece. They word their conclusions in a prose that is more rhythmic in phrasing and more metaphoric in content. Examples abound. There is scarcely an essay in Part Four in which the emotional impact of the writing does not intensify through the final sentences.

Sometimes the effect is achieved in the almost poetic rhythms created by parallel structure:

> It is there we perceive Christmas—and the sheep quiet, and the world waiting. (White, page 437, paragraph 4. Notice also White's effective repetition of "and.")

> The Harvard psychiatrists worry about cheating children out of their childhood. I worry about cheating them out of something more profoundly important: their self-respect as responsible, contributing human beings. (Raspberry, page 424, paragraph 16)

Sometimes the writer uses a rousing exhortation:

> Black people need a fair chance to compete—nothing more and nothing less. (Williams, page 443, paragraph 11)

Sometimes the emotional charge comes in a final, very brief sentence, which often contrasts with the lengthy ones preceding it:

> There is great joy in watching a tree grow. (Tucker, page 433, paragraph 10)

> Homme agrees: "In fact, results are guaranteed for life," he says. (Slack, page 427, paragraph 17)

Sometimes the impact can come from a rhetorical question:

> Is this pain and disillusionment being nurtured now in the soil of our silence? (Goodman, page 419, paragraph 19)

Sometimes the author uses metaphor:

> There is great joy in watching a tree grow. (Tucker, page 433, paragraph 10)

You may want to try to bring this sort of color to your endings. The chapters on style later in the book (see especially Chapters 8 and 9) give you some concrete ideas about intensifying language. And rereading your essay should also help. For rereading can rekindle your enthusiasm for your subject and thus prompt you to convey that excitement to your readers.

More Formal Concluding Strategies

In concluding some essays, though by no means all, authors may go beyond simply heightening language to employ more formal strategies. You should feel under no compulsion to try these techniques. Sometimes they can, in fact, lead to excess. Yet, when the devices are appropriate to the subject and tone of an essay and are not overdone, these strategies can be highly effective. Let us examine some that you might employ.

CONCLUDING QUOTATIONS

You might close your paper with a quotation. Sometimes you can find a quotation that adds the kind of ringing phrases to your conclusion that you feel shy about using yourself. Perry Turner, for example, in writing about *The Scarlet Letter,* quite naturally let a Hawthorne quotation sound his final words (page 435, paragraph 11). And Charles Slack ends his article, and supports his thesis, by quoting favorable evaluations of the experiment he describes (page 427, paragraphs 15–17).

You can also enhance a conclusion by quoting another author who states your point in a particularly telling way. If the author you quote is well known, you can enjoy the advantage of adding authoritative weight to your restatement of thesis. William Raspberry, for example, concludes an essay on equal opportunity by quoting from a recent book:

> Should blacks be given preferential treatment? Dorn finds the answer easy: "If equal opportunity is to produce racial equality, then it is clear that a period of compensatory inequality is required. . . . It simply makes no sense to pretend that 'equal' opportunity, as we now practice it, will lead us toward racial equality." (*Washington Post,* April 20, 1981)

Since one of your reasons for ending with a quotation would be to intensify the emotional quality of your concluding language, you might try ending with a line or two of poetry. The language of poetry is, almost by definition, emotionally charged. Quoting poetry is not an unusual way to close, although none of the essayists in Part Four adopts the technique. A *Time* article reviewing the effect of the 1960s counterculture offers a typical example. It concludes with the closing lines from W. B. Yeats's poem "The Second Coming":

> Ultimately, the great danger of the counter-culture is its self-proclaimed flight from reason, its exaltation of self over society, its Dionysian anarchism. . . . The Second Comings of history carry with them no guarantees of success, and a revolution based on unreason may just as easily bring a New Barbarism rather than the New Jerusalem. As Yeats so pointedly asked:
>
>> And what rough beast, its hour come round at last, /Slouches toward Bethlehem to be born? ("The Message of History's Biggest Happening," *Time*, 94 [August 29, 1969], 32–33.)

CONCLUDING ANECDOTES

Another effective way that writers sometimes end their work—and you might like to try it—is with an anecdote, a brief story. You may find in your reading a relevant anecdote that you could quote in closing your essay. Or you might very well relate an incident from your own experience that captures your point in narrative form. Wallace Stegner, for example, uses a telling anecdote to conclude an essay about the futility of overusing profanity:

> I remember my uncle, a farmer who had used four-letter words ten to the sentence ever since he learned to talk. One day he came too near the circular saw and cut half his fingers off. While we stared in horror, he stood watching the bright arterial blood pump from his ruined hand. Then he spoke, and he did not speak loud. "Aw, the dickens," he said.
>
> I think he understood, better than some sophomore girls and better than some novelists, the nature of emphasis. ("Good-bye to All That," *The Atlantic*, 215 [March 1965], 119.)

WITTY CONCLUSIONS

Authors often write witty conclusions because they know that readers are likely to be pleased, and perhaps persuaded, by works they can finish with a smile. It could be a smile of humor, stimulated by an anecdote like Stegner's. Or it could be a smile of appreciation, called forth by a display of wit. Perry Turner's conclusion to his "What Killed Arthur Dimmesdale?" brings out just such a smile. Having considered both sides of the case for Dr. Chillingsworth as the murderer, Turner concludes:

> So what *is* the truth here? It may be that the only indisputable truth in *The Scarlet Letter* will come from neither physicians nor professors of literature but from the author himself. "A man burdened with a secret," Hawthorne advises, "should especially avoid the intimacy of his physician." (page 435, paragraph 11)

The Paradox.   A special form of wit is the paradox (a true though seemingly contradictory statement). Readers often take delight in essays that end paradoxically. Often such endings twist an image presented earlier and thus can be thought of as "reverse-frame" conclusions. For example, Shana Alexander begins her essay with the notion that

> Children are a relatively modern invention. Until a few hundred years ago, they did not exist. (page 411)

By the time she reaches her closing, she has reversed her earlier assessment:

> If in the old days children did not exist, it seems equally true today that adults as a class have begun to disappear, condemning all of us to remain boys and girls forever, jogging and doing push-ups against all eternity. (page 414)

FRAME OR CIRCLE CONCLUSIONS

Some particularly satisfying conclusions complete a circle of thought begun in the early sentences of an essay. The essay is thus framed by a unifying introductory and concluding idea. Thomas, for instance, begins "Late Night Thoughts on Listening to Mahler's Ninth Symphony" with the title idea. He describes how Mahler's Ninth used to affect him when he was able to take somber comfort from its "open acknowledgment of death and dying." In the second paragraph he contrasts that feeling with the terror the music inspires now in the days of nuclear preparedness. That terror is, of course, the subject of the essay.

Having worked through his central ideas about that terror and the anguish it must work on the young, Thomas closes with a reminder of his beginning allusion. The echoes in his final sentence, where he speaks of "new kinds of *sounds*" that would be "different from any *music* heard before," carry readers back to his opening discussion of the Mahler symphony. Together they form a sort of musical frame surrounding the essay and act as a sounding board from which Thomas bounces his political ideas.

Although a frame construction does not necessarily require it, throughout the essay Thomas uses other references to music and especially to the Mahler to help develop his point. In paragraph 6, he writes:

> . . . the thought that keeps grinding its way into my mind, making the Mahler a hideous noise. . . .

Paragraph 7 is devoted entirely to close analysis of a portion of the symphony and serves as a transition to Thomas's discussion, beginning in paragraph 8, of the MX Basing pamphlet and the Civil Defense speech, the heart of his thesis support:

> There is a short passage near the very end of the Mahler in which the almost vanishing violins, all engaged in a sustained backward glance, are edged aside

for a few bars by the cellos. . . . I used to hear this as a wonderful few seconds of encouragement: we'll be back, we're still here, keep going, keep going.

Now, with a pamphlet in front of me . . . I cannot hear the same Mahler. Those cellos sound in my mind like the opening of all the hatches and the instant before ignition. (page 429, paragraphs 7–8)

All these internal echoes serve to strengthen the frame.

You will find similar framing images in a number of articles in this book, including the United Nations conference in Golden's "Earth's Creeping Deserts" and Harvard psychiatrists in Raspberry's "Children of Two-Career Families."

Conclusions: Final Advice

As exciting as such formal conclusions can be, most essays need no such flourishes. On the other hand, a great number, as we said, intensify meaning by heightening the language. What should *you* do? You should read your paper through and permit yourself to be—well, let's call it by its name—inspired in a quite natural way by what you have written in the introduction and the body. Then, if your rereading works as it can, you may find that without artificial striving you can achieve a genuinely effective conclusion. In any case, draw from your rereading a final statement of your thesis that has both solidity and clarity. That in itself is no small achievement.

The Title

When you have finished your essay, give it a title that suggests its content or, where appropriate, comments upon it in a clever way. Because a title may appear on a separate page, it should not be considered an integral part of the essay. Do not, therefore, depend upon the title to introduce the topic of your paper. A paper that begins, "This idea will lead to no good" arouses unnecessary curiosity while the reader fumbles for the title page to find out whether the writer is referring to capital punishment or kissing on the first date. Think of a title as a nice completing touch. Think of it as rather like the frosting on a cake: though it does not really affect the texture of the product, it gives gloss and finish.

TRY IT OUT

1. The word (and the idea) *silence* is repeated a number of times throughout Goodman's "The Communications Gap" (page 418) and is echoed in its conclusion. Trace and record the echo pattern.

2. Staple or tape paper over the conclusion of your last (or next) composition, and exchange it with that of a classmate whose conclusion is similarly covered. Read through your classmate's essay and write an appropriate ending for it. Compare the new closings with the original ones, examining features discussed in this section.

3. Suggest alternative titles for two of the essays in Part Four.

ASSIGNMENT

Following the suggestions set forth in Part One and the first four chapters, write an effective essay on one of these topics below or one suggested by your instructor.

1. Many students (and a good number of educators as well) object to education that consists primarily of students repeating back what an instructor has taught. If you are among these critics, write an essay justifying your objections from your own experience. Support your position with specific detail and sound argument. You may wish to conclude by suggesting an alternative educational style.

2. To what extent should friends be willing to change themselves to benefit their friendship? (Lovers to benefit their love relationship?) Write an essay embodying your answer to the question. Support your answer with specifics from literature—book or film—and/or from your observation of personal relationships.[4]

3. Choose a cartoon of some complexity from a magazine such as *The New Yorker* or from the editorial page of a newspaper. Identify the source and explain and interpret the cartoon. Support your interpretation by relating the specific details from which you derived your understanding of it.[5]

4. Defend or take issue with the following statement:
The English language, as it is used today, has an abundance of sexist overtones, but these do not reinforce discriminatory attitudes.
Whichever position you choose, illustrate the "although" clause and support your point with an abundance of specific examples.

5. Choose a quotation—perhaps a humorous one—that appeals to you in some way and use it to give focus to your essay.

[4]Topic suggested by Professor Michael Neuman of Capitol University.
[5]Suggested by Professor Charles D. Klingler of Manchester College.

   a. Write an introduction using the quotation you have chosen. The quotation should lead to your statement of thesis.
   b. Work two references to the quotation into the body of your essay.
   c. Use a further quotation from the same source to write your conclusion, creating a "frame" that ties your essay together.

6. Develop a topic you worked with in one of the Try It Outs into an effective essay.

Chapter
5

The Writing Stage

Practicing Composing Skills Through Sentence Combining

In this chapter you will have the opportunity to practice the skills we've been talking about, especially creating theses, developing support, and organizing your essays.

SENTENCE COMBINING TO HELP PROVE YOUR POINT

Writing effectively, as you know, means writing so as to convince your readers that what you have to say is worthwhile. To do so, you need to develop your thesis persuasively and support it convincingly. The sentence-combining exercises here are designed to give you practice in making rhetorical decisions of this sort. As you work these exercises, ask yourself: In this specific context, which of my choices will contribute most effectively to making my points, to supporting my thesis?

Using a Paragraph to Make Your Point

The following exercises ask you to construct an effective paragraph by creating a strong topic sentence from the given kernels and then, by composing supporting sentences, to develop the point of that topic sentence as effectively as you can.

TRY IT OUT

Combining an Effective Paragraph. In this first exercise, concentrate on phrasing the ideas expressed in the kernels so as to emphasize those which are most pertinent to the point of the paragraph and to create the tone most appropriate to the subject. No attempt has been made to scramble the ideas in this paragraph, but rearrange them if you choose.

THE DECLINE AND FALL OF THE TOMATO

A. 1. Today's tomato may be rosy.
 2. Today's tomato may be attractive.
 3. It is bland.
 4. It is dry.
 5. It tastes like cardboard.

B. 1. Mechanization, technology, and an expansion in the size of farms have combined.
 2. The mechanization is increased.
 3. The technology is dramatic.
 4. The expansion in farm size is impressive.
 5. The combining has been in recent years.
 6. The combining has contributed to cultivation.
 7. The cultivation is of a bland, processed-tasting tomato.

C. 1. Mechanization was introduced fifteen years ago into tomato cultivation.
 2. The coming of the mechanical harvester reduced the number of human harvesters.
 3. The number was reduced by 80 percent.
 4. The human touch lends a certain loving tenderness.
 5. That human touch is all but gone.

D. 1. The human touch was also part of the small tomato farm.
 2. The small tomato farm is a thing of the past.
 3. A sudden demand for tomatoes has forced American farmers.
 4. They must strive for quantity.
 5. They can no longer strive for quality.
 6. They must expand their farms.
 7. They must produce 50.5 pounds of tomatoes a year for every American.
 8. In 1920, they had to produce only 18 pounds of tomatoes for every American.

E. 1. The years have also brought spectacular breakthroughs in technology.
 2. These breakthroughs have allowed a certain way of breeding.

   3. Geneticists can now breed tomatoes for uniform ripeness.
   4. They can now breed tomatoes for high yield.
   5. They can now breed tomatoes for thick walls.
   6. They can be bred for low acidity.
   7. Chemists have also manufactured a substance.
   8. The substance ripens and reddens tomatoes.
   9. The ripening and reddening is faster than nature's.

F. 1. Now we eat tomatoes.
   2. These tomatoes have been mass-produced.
   3. These tomatoes have been artificially ripened.
   4. These tomatoes have been mechanically harvested.
   5. It is not a wonder.
   6. Such tomatoes no longer appeal.
   7. They do not appeal to our taste buds.

TRY IT OUT

Supporting the Topic Sentence. In this exercise, compose an effective paragraph by combining the kernels into sentences supporting a topic sentence. Because the supporting ideas have been scrambled to give you practice in ordering, you will probably want to rearrange them. That is, when you compose your own paragraph you will not necessarily want to place the contents of section B before that of C, nor that of C before D.

HAIR-TRIGGER TRICKERY

Topic sentence

A. 1. History has traditionally condemned Aaron Burr.
   2. He was the cold-blooded murderer in a duel.
   3. The duel was fatal.
   4. The duel was with Alexander Hamilton.
   5. New evidence suggests something.
   6. Hamilton, in fact, tried something in the duel.
   7. Hamilton rigged the duel.
   8. Hamilton died.
   9. His death was from his own scheming.

B. 1. Hamilton provided the pistols.
   2. The pistols were borrowed.
   3. They were borrowed from John B. Church.

    4. John B. Church was Hamilton's brother-in-law.
    5. But Hamilton owned a set of pistols himself.
    6. Hamilton's pistols were perfectly proper.
    7. They were dueling pistols.

C. **1.** Many historians now believe something.
    2. Hamilton deliberately set the hair trigger of his gun.
    3. Hamilton lowered his gun for a reason.
    4. He aimed his gun at Burr.
    5. Hamilton applied too much pressure.
    6. The pressure was on the sensitive trigger.
    7. The sensitive trigger caused a misfire.
    8. The gun fired several feet over Burr's head.
    9. Burr would not have known something.
  10. He would not have set his gun's hair trigger.
  11. Burr then had an opportunity.
  12. He could take proper aim.
  13. He could fire.

D. **1.** Hamilton and Burr concluded their feud.
    2. Their feud was long standing.
    3. The conclusion was a duel.
    4. The duel took place on July 11, 1804.
    5. The duel was in the morning.
    6. The duel was in Weehawken, New Jersey.
    7. Hamilton's shot struck a tree.
    8. The shot struck twelve feet above Burr's head.
    9. Burr's shot hit Hamilton in the liver.
  10. Burr's shot mortally wounded Hamilton.

E. **1.** Church's pistols have survived.
    2. A recent study of these pistols shows something.
    3. These pistols have a trick mechanism.
    4. The trick is a hair trigger.
    5. The mechanism can be set.
    6. The set mechanism makes something much easier.
    7. The gunsman can pull the trigger easier.
    8. The gunsman can thus fire the gun faster.

F. **1.** It happened in this way.
    2. Hamilton's trickery led to the result.
    3. Hamilton had a downfall.
    4. It was his own.

TRY IT OUT

Identifying the Topic Sentence. Before you can compose a paragraph from the next sets of sentence kernels, you will have to decide which set (or portion of a set) will make the most effective topic sentence and then arrange the others to support your choice.

SQUELCHING SNORES

A.
1. Robert Crossley has invented a cure.
2. The invention is recent.
3. The cure is more than 90 percent successful.
4. Its success is apparent.
5. The invention is a plastic collar.
6. The collar sends electrical impulses.
7. The impulses go into the sleeper's neck.
8. The impulses go off with each snore.
9. Crossley claims something.
10. The collar acts as a punishment.
11. The punishment is very mild.
12. The collar builds up a mental block.
13. The block is against snoring.

B.
1. More than 100 devices have been patented.
2. The devices differ.
3. The devices are designed for a purpose.
4. They should stop snoring.
5. Most of these devices do not work.
6. Some of these devices have straps or springs.
7. Some of these devices have flaps or prongs.
8. Some seem like punishment.
9. The punishment is cruel.
10. The punishment is unusual.
11. The offense is minor.
12. The offense is only snoring.

C.
1. Countless attempts have been made.
2. The attempts have been made throughout the years.
3. The attempts have been made for a purpose.
4. They would combat a problem.
5. The problem is snoring.
6. Snoring is an affliction.
7. The affliction is shared by one in every eight persons.
8. This number is estimated.

D. **1.** Many colonial soldiers were told something.
2. It was during the American Revolutionary War.
3. They should put musket balls in the backs of their night clothes.
4. There was a purpose.
5. The balls should discourage the soldiers.
6. Soldiers should not sleep on their backs.

E. **1.** Columnist Ann Landers gives advice today.
2. It is much the same advice.
3. Ann Landers substitutes table-tennis balls.
4. They substitute for the musket balls.

Making Your Point in Short Essays

The following exercises ask you to develop effective essays by combining kernels into sentences, appropriately constructed and organized. Always determine your thesis first, then structure your support in the way you decide is most persuasive.

TRY IT OUT

Paragraphing Your Essay. The kernels in the next exercise are grouped for placement in the introduction, the body, or the conclusion of an essay. It is up to you to order the ideas within these parts to make the most effective essay possible. What will be your thesis? You will probably want to decide right away so that you can point your introduction toward expressing the thesis idea and construct the topic sentences of your body paragraph(s) to support it. And you will want to compose your conclusion to give your point its most persuasive expression.

CINDERELLA BLUE JEANS

Introduction

A. **1.** The blue jean is a symbol.
2. The symbol is of American sturdiness.
3. The blue jean came from beginnings.
4. The beginnings were the humblest.
5. The blue jean is a piece of wearing apparel.
6. The apparel became desired.
7. It is the single most desired.
8. All the world did the desiring.

B. 1. A culture believes something.
2. "Mighty oaks from little acorns grow."
3. A culture favors the underdog.
4. The favor is perpetual.
5. In this culture a story should have appeal.
6. The story would be about the blue jean.
7. The blue jean is lowly.
8. The appeal is like that of a Cinderella.
9. This Cinderella is from true-life.

Body

V. 1. The business was modest enough.
2. This was at the start.
3. Then Strauss bought the rights.
4. The rights were for an idea.
5. Then Strauss patented the idea.
6. The idea was for a method of construction.
7. He put rivets on the pockets.
8. He put rivets at points of stress.
9. The rivets were of copper.
10. The rivets strengthened the pockets and the points of stress.
11. The jeans did not tear.
12. Then business picked up.
13. The increase was appreciable.
14. Levi Strauss and Company supplied the clothing.
15. The clothing was for most of the working West.
16. Some of the workers were lumberjacks.
17. Some of the workers were cowboys.

W. 1. Blue jeans began with a peddler.
2. The peddler was named Levi Strauss.
3. The peddler was impoverished.
4. The peddler was Jewish.
5. The peddler was an immigrant.
6. He decided on a move.
7. He would move West.
8. The move was in 1850.
9. The peddler took a quantity of material with him.
10. The material was canvas.
11. Strauss hoped to sell the canvas.
12. It would sell for tenting.

X. 1. Strauss soon found something.
2. The canvas was of the wrong kind.
3. The canvas was not for tents.
4. Strauss heard a miner complain.

    5. The miner could not find work pants.
    6. Work pants were not truly sturdy.
    7. Strauss measured the miner.
    8. The measuring cost six dollars in gold dust.
    9. Strauss fitted the miner.
   10. The fitting was with canvas trousers.
   11. The miner liked the trousers.
   12. The miner told all his friends.
   13. Strauss made pants for the friends.
   14. Strauss soon found himself in business.
   15. Strauss was in the pants business.

Y. **1.** In the 1960s there was a counterculture.
    2. This culture was international.
    3. This culture adopted blue jeans.
    4. This culture took the jeans as their own.
    5. Blue jeans became ubiquitous.

Z. **1.** Word spread.
    2. The word was about the pants.
    3. The pants had riveted pockets.
    4. The pants were immensely popular.
    5. The popularity spread to the East.
    6. Eastern city folk vacationed.
    7. They vacationed on western dude ranches.
    8. They took the news back home.
    9. The news was of the western Levis.
   10. Then easterners also started something.
   11. They wore blue jeans, too.

Conclusion

C. **1.** Blue jeans are pants.
    2. They are unpretentious.
    3. But they are sturdy.
    4. Jeans originated in leftover canvas.
    5. Jeans have become the uniform.
    6. The uniform is worldwide.
    7. The uniform is that of youth.

D. **1.** Today more than 83,000,000 Levis are sold.
    2. That number is sold each year.
    3. These Levis are genuine.
    4. Imitations are also sold.
    5. Probably twice that number are sold.
    6. That quantity is sold each year.

E. **1.** There are fashionable shops.
    2. The shops are in Paris.
    3. The shops are in London.
    4. The shops sport jeans.
    5. The jeans are prefaded.
    6. The fading is to just the right intensity of blue.
    7. The jeans are sold.
    8. The prices go over £50.

F. **1.** There is traffic.
    2. The traffic is in blue jeans.
    3. The traffic is lively.
    4. The traffic is on the black market.
    5. The black market is in Russia.
    6. The black market is in the Eastern European countries.
    7. Some blue jeans are authentically American.
    8. These jeans bring a great deal of money.
    9. Sometimes these jeans bring more than $200.

PERSUADING THROUGH SENTENCE COMBINING

The main problem in persuading others to adopt your point of view on an issue is that valid points can almost always be made on the other side. You can, of course, ignore the other side altogether, but you do so at your peril. For even if your audience has not heard of specific opposition arguments, they could hardly be fooled into thinking that the other side has no points to make at all. If you decide to include some of the opposition points, it is best to get them out of the way as soon as you can. First acknowledge gracefully what must be acknowledged, then refute soundly what can be refuted, and end with some rousing points of your own. During your discussion, you will want to phrase the opposition ideas with as little emphasis as possible and give the most persuasive phrasing to your own views. (See pages 90–94.)

TRY IT OUT

Gun Control. This exercise consists of two sets of sentence kernels arranged in columns representing alternative points of view. Combine the kernels into an effective essay arguing for *one* point of view. Although you are likely to use more material from one column than from the other, do not ignore the other column completely.

Pro–Gun Control Arguments	Anti-Gun Control Arguments
Introduction (Death Pre-Argument)	*Introduction* (Freedom Pre-Argument)

A.
1. Guns are instruments of death.
2. Guns have but one purpose.
3. Their sole purpose is this:
4. They kill living things.
5. Guns carry a threat.
6. The threat is inherent.
7. The threat is death.
8. Guns are thus used for a purpose.
9. They help commit crimes.
10. Their use for this purpose is easy.
11. Their use for this purpose is frequent.

B.
1. There is therefore a need.
2. The need is particularly urgent.
3. We must ban handguns.
4. At least we must register handguns.

Body (Crime Arguments: Anti-Handgun)

X.
1. Handguns are used to commit murder.
2. They are responsible for one murder in every two.
3. Approximately 72 percent of homicides are not premeditated.
4. These homicides are committed by citizens.
5. These citizens were previously law-abiding.
6. These citizens kill their lovers.
7. These citizens kill their friends.
8. These citizens kill their relatives.
9. The killings are done on the spur of the moment.
10. The killings are done during arguments.
11. The arguments are passionate.
12. These murders would not take place without a gun.
13. The gun is readily accessible.

A.
1. Every American has a right.
2. The right is constitutional.
3. The American can keep arms.
4. The American can bear arms.
5. America was made great.
6. America has this right.

B.
1. Americans conquered the wilderness.
2. Americans fought.
3. Americans kept America free.
4. Today a controversy rages over gun control.
5. This controversy is essentially a fight for something.
6. Americans should retain this freedom.
7. The freedom was hard-won.

Body (Crime Arguments: Pro-Handgun)

W.
1. Now there is a crime rate.
2. The crime rate is soaring.
3. Now guns are almost a necessity.

X.
1. Guns are needed for good reasons.
2. People must defend their lives.
3. People must defend their property.
4. People must protect themselves against crime.

(Anti–Handgun Control Arguments)

Y.
1. One handgun is used in committing a crime.
2. This handgun is used in one of 4,000 crimes.
3. The 4,000 are in the United States.
4. Criminals commit these crimes.
5. These criminals would have acted anyway.

Pro-Gun Control Arguments

Body (Crime Arguments: Anti-Handgun)

Y. 1. There are other forms of spur-of-the-moment violence.
   2. These forms are less final.
   3. Broken crockery can be swept up.
   4. Bruises can heal.
   5. Even stabbings are seldom fatal.
   6. There are odds on surviving a stabbing.
   7. These odds are five times greater.
   8. The comparison is with surviving a gunshot wound.

Z. 1. There would not be any guns.
   2. Then murders would be far fewer.
   3. Here is an example.
   4. Japan has a murder rate.
   5. That rate is 200 times lower than the U.S. rate.
   6. Japan prohibits handguns.

(Anti-Rifle Arguments)

L. 1. The problem is not posed by handguns alone.
   2. Rifles are a favorite weapon for massacre.
   3. The massacre is of animals.
   4. Many species are now extinct.
   5. These species were hunted.
   6. Several hundred more species are in danger of extinction.
   7. These species are also hunted.

Conclusion (Danger Arguments)

C. 1. Ownership of guns is increasing in the United States.
   2. The ownership is becoming more widespread.
   3. Little is done to check on the mental state of gun buyers.
   4. Little is done to check on the criminal record of gun buyers.

Anti-Gun Control Arguments

(Anti–Handgun Control Arguments)

   6. Even if guns had been outlawed.
   7. Even if there had been no handguns.

Z. 1. But this result is unlikely:
   2. Criminals would not go weaponless.
   3. Guns would be outlawed.
   4. Then only criminals would own guns.

(Rifle Argument)

L. 1. Rifles are a kind of gun.
   2. Rifles are needed to hunt animals.
   3. Hunting is a legitimate sport.
   4. Hunting is a means of obtaining food.

M. 1. Farmers use rifles.
   2. Farmers also use shotguns.
   3. They keep predators away from their crops.
   4. They keep predators away from their livestock.

N. 1. Many communities have a custom.
   2. They give a boy a gun.
   3. The gun is his first.
   4. The gun is a symbol.
   5. The symbol stands for the boy's initiation.
   6. The initiation takes him into manhood.

Conclusion (Freedom Argument)

C. 1. Some people wish to control guns.
   2. Some people wish to confiscate guns.
   3. These people have a desire.
   4. They may realize its meaning.
   5. They may not realize its meaning.

Pro-Gun Control Arguments

Conclusion (Danger Arguments)

D. 1. These guns serve no useful purpose.
2. Instead, they pose a danger.
3. They are a continuous threat.
4. They threaten nature.
5. They threaten society.
6. They threaten innocent life.

Anti-Gun Control Arguments

Conclusion (Freedom Arguments)

6. They want to impose regulations.
7. The regulations would be imposed on society.
8. This imposition is a type of thinking.
9. This thinking can lead to a police state.
10. There is a defense against a police state.
11. It is the best defense.
12. Individual citizens should have access to guns.

A Peacetime Draft. Arrange the sentences you compose from the next sets of kernels into an essay that will persuasively support one side of the issue of a peacetime draft. Feel free to omit any kernel that will not contribute to making your side convincing. You may also add details not given in the kernels where you feel they will help. Do not hesitate to rearrange the groups of kernels to your advantage. When in doubt, remember to put the "although" clause material first. Be creative and persuasive in your combining.

Pro-Peacetime Draft Arguments

Introduction

1. America needs a draft.
2. Here is the reason.
3. A threat might arise against the security of this country.
4. Then an army would be already formed.
5. That army would be already prepared.
6. Our country would be ready.

Body (Practical Drawbacks of a Volunteer Army)

1. A volunteer army is often less competent.
2. A volunteer army tends toward something:
3. It is filled with misfits.
4. It is sloppily trained.

Anti-Peacetime Draft Arguments

Introduction

1. A peacetime draft is not necessary.
2. A peacetime draft is not desirable.
3. A peacetime draft is not in keeping with a special spirit.
4. America was founded in this spirit.

Body (Practical Benefits of a Volunteer Army)

X. 1. A volunteer army would better serve our needs.
2. A volunteer army is made up of soldiers.
3. These soldiers want to be in the army.

Pro–Peacetime Draft Arguments

Body (Practical Drawbacks of a
Volunteer Army)

    5. It is therefore grossly
inefficient.
    6. It cannot be relied upon in an
emergency.
    7. A volunteer army is too small.
    8. A volunteer army is too weak.
    9. A volunteer army cannot keep
our nation safe.

(Practical Benefits of a Draft)

    1. Speed is needed in an
emergency.
    2. Efficiency is needed in an
emergency.
    3. A draft ensures speed and
efficiency.
    4. A draft makes soldiers available
for combat.
    5. The soldiers would be there in
large numbers.
    6. The soldiers would be qualified
for service.
    7. The soldiers would be well
trained.
    8. A draft can also prevent an
emergency.
    9. Enemy nations will know that
we are conducting a draft.
  10. Enemy nations will understand
something:
  11. Our draft provides us with a
formidable army.
  12. Enemy nations will respect our
strength.
  13. Enemy nations will therefore
hesitate to attack.

(Ideational Benefits of a Draft)

    1. The draft is also needed for
something else.
    2. It can contribute to the spirit of
the country.
    3. The spirit can become patriotic.
    4. Serving our country can
become an ideal again.

Anti–Peacetime Draft Arguments

Body (Practical Benefits of a
Volunteer Army)

    4. The volunteer army has an
overall willingness.
    5. The volunteer army has an
overall desire.
    6. The willingness and desire are
shared by three million
soldiers.
    7. This shared will provides
efficiency.
    8. This efficiency is greater than
that of a much larger army.
    9. The larger army would not
hold this attitude.

Y. 1. One fact is clear.
    2. Enormous masses of soldiers
are no longer needed.
    3. Masses do not fight a modern
war.
    4. What is needed instead?
    5. Relatively few people are
needed.
    6. These people must be
intelligent enough.
    7. These people must be well
enough trained.
    8. They must handle the
sophisticated equipment of
today's army.

Z. 1. One would not need to draft
everyone in sight.
    2. Money could be saved.
    3. This money could be spent for
something else.
    4. The money could be spent to
pay soldiers wages competitive
with those in the civilian
economy.
    5. The spending could thus entice
qualified and interested people
into joining the army.
    6. The spending could entice them
into making the army their
lifetime career.

Pro–Peacetime Draft Arguments

(Ideational Benefits of a
   Draft)

5. Self-discipline can become ideal again.
6. Draftees can learn democracy.
7. Draftees are from all levels of society.
8. In the army they work together.
9. They work as equals.
10. Draftees gain a sense of duty.
11. They devote a year or two of their lives.
12. They help their country.
13. They help themselves.

Anti–Peacetime Draft Arguments

Body (Practical Benefits of a
   Volunteer Army)

7. America could be well defended.
8. The defense would come at last.
9. The defense would be done by volunteer soldiers such as these.

(Practical Drawbacks of the Draft)

1. A draft is not desirable.
2. A draft will build a large military force.
3. This large force could tempt power-hungry generals.
4. These generals could flex the nation's military muscle.
5. The flexing might occur on any pretext.
6. The flexing might include invading another country.
7. The flexing might bring us into war.
8. The war would be caused by dangerous thinking.
9. The thinking would be that the draft makes us invincible.

(Ideational Drawbacks to a Draft)

1. A draft installs a system of servitude.
2. The servitude is involuntary.
3. Draftees are made to serve in the army.
4. Draftees may or may not want to serve.
5. Draftees can be forced to do things.
6. Draftees can be forced to go places.
7. Draftees can even be forced to kill other people.
8. The forcing is done against the draftees' will

Pro-Peacetime Draft Arguments

Conclusion

1. The draft makes something possible
2. America will be ready.
3. America can thwart aggression.
4. Aggression occurs.
5. America can defend itself.
6. America can defend its allies.
7. A draft will permit America to attain something.
8. A draft will permit the world to attain something.
9. That something is peace.
10. America and the world can remain at peace.

Anti-Peacetime Draft Arguments

Conclusion

1. Our country is founded on principle.
2. The principle is freedom.
3. We cannot protect freedom with a system of slavery.
4. A peacetime draft amounts to using slavery.
5. Slavery is supposed to guarantee freedom.

TRY IT OUT

Scholarly Persuasion. Although most of the compositions you are asked to write in college are not on topics as overtly controversial as those in the preceding exercise, you must remember that scholarly papers need to be persuasive, too. The final exercise in this chapter should help you make the kind of decisions necessary for writing effective scholarly papers. Combine the kernel sentences in the next exercise to construct an essay discussing the discovery of America. The kernels are arranged in three sets of arguments. Each of these arguments embodies a series of facts pointing to a specific conclusion about the discovery of the American continents. The following suggested procedure may help you construct your essay from the three arguments:

1. Read over the arguments and come to your own decision on their relative merit. (All are factual.)

2. Phrase your decision as a thesis. Be sure to include an "although" clause to subordinate the other arguments. Include your thesis in the introduction you construct from the kernels.

3. Organize the arguments to support your thesis in the best way, saving discussion of your argument for last.

4. Combine the kernels within each argument so as to make its point clearly, remembering to make your own argument most persuasive.

5. When your essay is complete, read it over carefully and write your own conclusion for it.

WHO DISCOVERED AMERICA?

Introduction

1. Tribes were already settled.
2. They settled throughout North and South America.
3. The tribes were "discovered."
4. There is a question of who "discovered" the tribes.
5. This question may seem a moot point.
6. It would seem so to the tribes.
7. The question fans a spark, however.
8. The spark is competition.
9. The competition is among people of non-American origin.
10. Who got there first?
11. Columbus is the best-known candidate for the prize.
12. But Columbus is not the only candidate.
13. Recent discoveries suggest . . .

Read through the material in the succeeding arguments, form your opinion, and *compose your own thesis.* Add your thesis to number 13 in the Introduction kernels or start a new sentence.

The Columbus Argument

1. It was two hours past midnight.
2. The night was dark.
3. It was night at sea.
4. Three ships had been sailing unknown seas.
5. The ships were small and wooden.
6. They had sailed for more than two months.
7. A shout came suddenly.
8. The shout came from the prow of the *Pinta.*
9. The shout proved something.
10. The earth was round.
11. The shout was "Land Ho!"
12. Christopher Columbus had discovered the New World.
13. The triumph came on October 12.
14. This triumph was the culmination.
15. The culmination was of a long personal struggle.
16. Columbus was Italian.
17. Columbus was fired by an unproven hypothesis.
18. Columbus was tempted by the tales of Marco Polo.
19. Columbus longed for something.
20. He would sail in search of India.
21. He had a quest for a patron.

22. The quest took eight years.
23. King Ferdinand and Queen Isabella of Spain agreed.
24. They agreed after long refusing.
25. They agreed in 1492.
26. They would sponsor his voyage.
27. The *Niña,* the *Pinta,* and the *Santa Maria* sailed.
28. They sailed out of Palos harbor, Spain.
29. They sailed on August 3.
30. The expense was justified.
31. The trust was justified.
32. The justification came two months and nine days later.
33. The Spanish sailors were unaware of something.
34. Their lack of awareness was ironic.
35. They trod a new soil.
36. This soil was completely unfamiliar to European civilization.
37. Columbus leaped ashore.
38. Columbus claimed the small Bahama island.
39. He claimed it in the name of Spain.
40. Then Columbus set off blithely.
41. He searched for Japan.
42. The treasures of the Orient were nowhere in sight.
43. Of course, this was true.
44. But a bounty lay at Europe's feet.
45. It was a far greater bounty.

The Chinese Argument

1. The sun sinks down beyond the ocean.
2. The sun is a red dragon.
3. A Buddhist monk turns his gaze.
4. His turning is resolute.
5. He is turning from the sun's flaming passage.
6. The passage is homeward to China.
7. The monk's ship sails east from China.
8. Morning comes.
9. The shores of a new land stretch before him.
10. They stretch in the haze.
11. The monk calls the new land "Fusang."
12. Today "Mexico" is the name of the new land.
13. Fang Zhongpu is a navigational historian.
14. Fang points out something.
15. Chinese merchants traveled.
16. They traveled beyond the Philippines.
17. They traveled as early as the eleventh century B.C.E.
18. The Chinese Kingdom of Wu had ships.
19. They had ships by the third century B.C.E.

20. These ships could carry 3,000 passengers.
21. The Chinese had ability.
22. Their ability is evident.
23. They could sail across the Pacific.
24. Their sailing ability is not the only supporting clue.
25. Two stone anchors have been found.
26. The anchors are of a distinctive type.
27. This type of anchor was carried on Chinese ships.
28. Ships with such anchors sailed in the fifth century.
29. The discovery was in American waters.
30. The discovery was recent.
31. The first anchor was found near the Palos Verdes peninsula.
32. The second anchor was found about 1,000 fathoms down off Point Mendocino.

The Viking Argument

1. The Viking long ship drifted.
2. The ship was slender.
3. The ship was wooden.
4. Its drifting was aimless.
5. Its drifting was through the churning mist.
6. Its drifting was among chunks of glacier.
7. The chunks were perilous.
8. The chunks filled the Northern Sea.
9. Ice and fog conspired.
10. They formed a soup.
11. The soup was thick.
12. The soup was frozen.
13. The soup was swallowed up by night.
14. The worried sailors could not glimpse their home.
15. Their home was a sea-road.
16. "Lucky Leif" Ericson beached his ship and his crew.
17. He beached them safely.
18. He beached them once again.
19. The sculpted sea monster bedded down.
20. The sculpting was on the prow.
21. The sea monster was savage.
22. The bedding down was tame.
23. The bedding down was beside the Labrador coast.
24. The Labrador coast was rocky.
25. Ericson had been bored by the prospect.
26. He was bored by another routine journey.
27. The journey would be from Iceland to Greenland.
28. Ericson had decided something.
29. He would try an unusual route.

30. The unusual route would be by way of the Hebrides.
31. The storms cleared from the unknown shore.
32. Ericson realized this:
33. He had lost his way.
34. He turned his ship.
35. He sailed toward his Nordic home.
36. Ericson arrived.
37. He announced his discovery.
38. The discovery was a new continent.
39. He called the new continent "Vinland."
40. Thorfinn Karlesefini was Ericson's countryman.
41. Karlesefini organized a colonizing expedition.
42. He organized it shortly after Ericson's return.
43. The expedition was complete.
44. It had three ships, 160 people, and some cattle.
45. The colonists stayed in their new home.
46. They stayed for three years.
47. They stayed until the natives drove them out.
48. They called the natives "Skraelings."
49. This tale is related in the *Saga of Eric the Red*.
50. The saga is famous.
51. The tale has long been intriguing.
52. The tale has long been unverified.
53. Helge Ingstad is an archaeologist.
54. Helge Ingstad excavated eight house sites.
55. The excavation was done in 1960.
56. The excavation was successful.
57. The sites are on the northern tip of Newfoundland.
58. Carbon dating proves something.
59. The ruins are Norse.
60. The ruins are remains of houses built around the year 1000 B.C.E.
61. The ancient saga has been confirmed.
62. The confirmation is at last.

ASSIGNMENT

Using all the persuasive strategies now at your disposal, convince an indifferent or neutral reader that your position on one of the following issues (or similarly controversial ones) is best.

    College athletic scholarships

    Test-tube babies

    Alimony

Patenting of scientifically created life forms
Nuclear power plants
Premarital chastity
Women clergy[1]
Life-support machines and/or euthanasia
A topic from today's newspaper headlines
A current campus controversy

[1]Suggested by Professor Jim Pictor of Saint Francis College.

Revising for Structure; Editing for Persuasion

After you finish writing your paper, you certainly have earned a hearty sigh of relief. Nevertheless, even after you have done a good job of composing the first draft, your work is not over. For if you have been able to let your ideas flow freely, if you have been able to push aside questions of mechanics and just let yourself write, then you will probably find a number of ways you can improve your initial effort. Although the revising stage of the writing process is, on the whole, not as difficult as either the prewriting or the writing stage, it is at least as important. Research into the composing process reveals that revision often involves just that: a re-vision, a reseeing, and thus a re-creating. During this final stage you create the essay your readers will actually see.

Probably the best way to go about revising is to work from large to small, from overall to parts, from structure to style. This ordering can save a good deal of effort, for in making major revisions you may very well eliminate material where smaller revisions would have been needed. Furthermore, research has shown that when a writer clarifies the thinking behind an awkwardly worded passage, more often than not the syntactical problems take care of themselves. Chapter 6 first helps you look at the possibilities for revising for structure, a process that sometimes involves considerable rewriting, re-creating. It then discusses ways you can edit your essay to strengthen its persuasiveness. Chapter 7 delves into some of the mechanics of style that will help you edit for correctness and then proofread your revised essay effectively.

Rewriting Effectively

Effective revisers understand a little magic: they know how to transform themselves from "the writer" to "the reader." Rewriting requires thinking about a draft with the cool and uninitiated mind of a reader, not the involved, knowing mind of the author. The better able you are to look at your work through a reader's eyes, the more effective will be your rewriting. Time helps in the transformation. Try, then, to put at least a night's sleep between finishing your first draft and revising it. If you cannot spare the time, at least remove your thoughts from the task. Talk to a friend about something else; do a bit of homework in a subject far removed; involve your imagination in an absorbing book or television show. Then, when the paper is less fresh in your mind and the precise details of its composition have faded from your memory, deliberately imagine yourself a detached reader and begin to revise.

REVISING FOR STRUCTURE

Traditionally, when writers have worked on revising the structure of their compositions, they have evaluated them for unity, coherence, and emphasis. These remain the most useful criteria. Here is how Donald Murray defines them:

> [Your essay] must have unity: it should all be about the same subject. It must have coherence: each point should lead to the next point. And it must have emphasis: the most important points should be in the most important places.[1]

The following sections offer suggestions on how you can review your first draft to make sure that it has the appropriate unity, coherence, and emphasis. They also advise you on ways you can revise your paper to correct any such deficiencies you might discover.

Revising for Unity

Your thesis is your best tool for achieving unity. If you have focused the entire paper upon demonstrating your thesis, the paper will automatically be unified. How can you tell? Why not read over all the topic sentences of your paragraphs to make sure that they somehow relate to "proving" your thesis? If they do, then your paper has an overall focus.

Nevertheless, your essay needs internal unity as well. To check for this unity, you will need to reread those topic sentences to be certain that each also sets up the subject of its particular paragraph. Then, within each paragraph unit, check to see if all the supporting material contributes to backing up the topic sentence.

---

[1] *A Writer Teaches Writing* (Boston: Houghton Mifflin, 1968), p. 11.

If you should find some paragraphs that do not directly support your thesis or some material in a paragraph that does not relate to the idea suggested in its topic sentence, I strongly urge you to eliminate it. No matter how interesting the extra material, if it distracts from the line of thinking you are pursuing, it can only do harm. If you cannot bear to give up a passage, you might try to find another point to which it relates more directly or to which it can be subordinated. But if it is truly unrelated to your present thesis, do not try to include it. Consider instead jotting the passage down in a notebook or journal so that you can put it to use in another paper some day.

If you sense a lack of focus in your essay but are having trouble locating the source of the problem, here is an almost mathematical way to look for the difficulty: Go back to your outline and revise it, if necessary, so that it corresponds exactly to the structure of your paper as you have written it. Then check the corrected outline for unity, using the modified versions of the following equations that are appropriate to your own situation:

- Do points I + II + III + IV $\cdots$ = your thesis?
- Do subpoints IIA + IIB + IIC $\cdots$ = Point II?
- Do sub-subpoints IIA1 + IIA2 + IIA3 = Subpoint IIA?
- And so on?

Where you find a discrepancy, rework your outline to correct it. Then revise your paper accordingly.

Professional writers have invented a handy technique for making major revisions of this sort that you may also find useful. It's called "cut-and-paste." What you do is cut out the portions of your first draft that seem to be out of order, and staple or tape them to scratch paper in the new positions before making the necessary internal revisions. If you are lucky enough to be revising on a word processor, you are electronically equipped to perform this operation easily.

TRY IT OUT

It is often easier to spot elements of disunity if they are not of your own making. The following exercises offer you practice in this sort of editing. The skill you gain can be transferred to your own work.

1. I have introduced a few distracting sentences into the following paragraph from Martin Luther King's famous "Letter from a Birmingham Jail."
   a. Identify the extraneous sentences and explain how they clutter the paragraph and interfere with its unity.
   b. Remove them and thus turn the paragraph back to the lean, strong prose King originally intended:

Faulty

Sometimes a law is just on its face and unjust in its application. Justice is the goal we all strive for. For instance, I have been arrested on a charge of parading without a permit. And arrest is a degrading and humiliating experience. Now there is nothing wrong in having an ordinance which requires a permit for a parade. Parades are enjoyed by children on the Fourth of July. They love to decorate their tricycles with red, white, and blue crepe paper. They love to wave their miniature flags and beat their miniature drums. When veterans parade on Memorial Day, they remind us of our great debt to those who sacrificed for our country. Of course, the police need to establish some order on parade days, so licensing ordinances need to be required. But such an ordinance becomes unjust when it is used to maintain segregation and to deny citizens the First Amendment privilege of peaceful assembly and protest.

2. Exchange your last essay (or your next one) with one of your classmates, and examine his or her paper for problems of unity or focus. Explain how these problems might be remedied.

Revising for Coherence

Problems with coherence stem almost entirely from a lack of that ability I mentioned at the beginning of the chapter—from the inability of some writers to put themselves in their reader's place and write their work from a reader's point of view. These problems come from writers' having what they want to say so clear in their own minds that they don't realize they have left out material needed to let readers make sense of their ideas. Such problems also come from writers' being so taken up with the order in which a set of ideas came to them that they do not realize these ideas would be clearer to their readers arranged in another sequence. To find and revise away problems of coherence, then, you need to act as a reader of your own writing. You need to ask yourself: Is this point really clear? Does it follow unmistakably from the preceding idea? Is something missing? If you are still not sure, have someone else read the draft and ask, "What do you understand this passage to mean?"

OVERALL COHERENCE

Begin your search for coherence by examining your overall structure to determine if all your points and subpoints are in the order that supports your thesis most reasonably. If you have any serious uncertainty here, ask others to look your paper over to see if they can easily follow your chain of thought. If you discover a problem, do not hesitate to cut and paste until the difficulty is eliminated.

COHERENCE IN PARAGRAPHS

Reasonable ordering of ideas is also important at the paragraph level. Scholars such as Francis Christensen and Alton Becker have conducted research to determine exactly what makes for coherent paragraphs. To further their research, each scholar has developed an analytical apparatus. As you revise, you may find their apparatus useful for diagnosing coherence problems that you sense within a paragraph but are unable to point to precisely.

TRI

Alton Becker's approach to the paragraph is relatively simple. He sees it in terms of the statement of a (T)opic, a (R)estriction on or a development of that topic, and an (I)llustration of the topic. More informally, his schema is known as TRI. He would analyze a typical paragraph, such as this one of Slack's in this way:

(T) "With few exceptions, our students acted like dummies," said Homme, "even though we knew they were ahead of the rest in knowledge.

(R) They were so used to playing the class idiot that they didn't know how to show what they knew.

(I) Their eyes wandered, they appeared absentminded or even belligerent. One or two read magazines hidden under their desks, thinking, most likely, that they already knew the classwork. They rarely volunteered and often had to have questions repeated because they weren't listening. . . ." (page 425, paragraph 8)

Although most good paragraphs fit the TRI structure, Becker's system also allows for an occasional TIRI, ITR, TRIT, or even IRT. Furthermore, Becker enhances the usability of his system by adding the symbols Q(uestion) and A(nswer) along with P(roblem) and S(olution). They work in this way:

(Q) Were the experiments a success?

(A)(T) The scientists said Yes but the students said No.

(I) When grades were measured using standardized tests under strict laboratory conditions, marks went up more than one year on the average. Meanwhile, back at the school, the students were still barely passing, at best.

(T) "The experiment was fine for the scientists. They proved their theory on paper and made a name for themselves, but most of us were still flunking in class," remarked one seventeen-year-old. (Slack, page 425, paragraph 3)

CHRISTENSEN'S METHOD

Although you may find the TRI method a useful tool for analyzing the structure of a paragraph that troubles you, you may feel that you need a more precise guide for recognizing the source of a particular problem in coherence. Francis Christensen's more complex method may serve you better here. Like Becker's, Christensen's research led him to focus on the topic sentence, which Christensen defines as "the sentence on which the others depend . . . the sentence whose assertion is supported or whose meaning is explicated or whose parts are detailed by the sentences added to it."[2] Except for paragraphs which begin with transitional material, Christensen found that paragraphs generally open with a topic sentence. This topic sentence is then developed in two possible ways: by sentences that are either coordinate with it or subordinate to it. "Coordinate" sentences, Christensen says, explain or restate the matter in the topic sentence. "Subordinate" sentences, he explains, exemplify, modify, or develop the topic material. He believes that each of the other sentences in a good paragraph is also developed in one of the two ways—in relation to either the sentence immediately before it or to the topic sentence.

Christensen suggests a paragraph analysis that permits you to understand this structure visually. In the following analyzed example from Turner, notice that coordinate sentences are assigned the same number. A subordinate sentence is given one number less than the sentence to which it is subordinate. The topic sentence is always numbered one. Notice also the parallel indentation.

> 1. Nobody likes to miss the point, and soon after Khan published his conclusions, scholars were hastening to concur.
>   2. Barbara Storms, for instance, a University of Chicago student of literature, rejoiced over Khan's reading:
>   3. "Gone is the heavy symbolic or allegorical structure put forward so often by literary scholars.
>   3. The reader is left with the kernel of a possible truth rather than the chaff of rhetoric that only leads to more questions."
>   2. Virginia McCormick, an English teacher at Allen High School in Allentown, Pennsylvania, took a less heady but no less approving tone:
>   3. "There is no reason," she declared, "that both theories—Dimmesdale's death as a result of a guilty conscience and his death as a result of herbal poisoning—cannot co-exist." (page 435, paragraph 7)

For a paragraph to be truly coherent, every statement must be either coordinate or subordinate with the statement preceding it or with the topic sentence. If a sentence does not fit in this way, it is clearly out of place—either in the sequence in which it occurs or in the paragraph (or cluster) as a whole. Christensen's system of analysis thus offers a practical method for discovering the exact source of coherence problems you may sense in your paragraphs.

---

[2]"Generative Rhetoric of the Paragraph," in *Notes Toward a New Rhetoric* (New York: Harper & Row, 1978), pp. 79–80.

LINKAGES AND TRANSITIONS

Structural coherence of the sort we have been discussing is basic to the coherence of your essay; but what if you have checked the paper thoroughly and, though you have found it structurally sound, it still does not read as smoothly and coherently as you would like? Your problem then might be a lack of appropriate linkage between your ideas.[3] Besides underlying coherence, you have to give your readers surface clues to help them connect your ideas together so that they can understand them. You can give these clues in two basic ways: repetition and transitional devices.

If you think about it, all sentences in the context of a paragraph or an essay should consist of old material and new material. The old material is necessary to provide continuity of thought and to prevent confusion. The new material is needed to develop ideas and to avoid monotony. Check, for example, the sentences in the commonplace paragraph preceding this one, the one headed *Linkages and Transitions* (or, for that matter, in almost any professionally written paragraph), and you will see that this principle holds true:

Old, Linking Material	New Ideas
1. Structural coherence of the sort we have been discussing is basic to the coherence of your essay;	but what if you have checked the paper thoroughly and, though you have found it structurally sound, it still does not read as smoothly and coherently as you would like?
2. Your problem then	might be a lack of appropriate linkage between your ideas.
3. Besides an underlying coherence,	you have to give your readers surface clues to help them connect your ideas together so that they can understand them.
4. You can give these clues	in two basic ways: repetition and transitional devices.

Clearly, grounding each sentence in matter that reinforces what the reader already knows makes for coherence.

Repetitional Links. Sometimes you can achieve this reinforcement by exactly repeating words or phrases (for example, the repetition of "coherence" and "coherently" in the sample paragraph). Sometimes you want to

---

[3]For a discussion of concluding "echoes" to link your conclusion with the ideas you have expressed throughout your essay, see pages 127–128.

repeat the idea but would rather change the wording to avoid monotony (as I did by interchanging "linkage" and "connect[ion]" in the example). Sometimes you want to substitute an appropriate pronoun in order to avoid endlessly repeating the same word (for instance, *it* for *paper* and *them* for *clues*). Whichever of the methods of repeating you use, you can think of the idea to be repeated as a colored thread that you weave through the tapestry of your essay, both to create the pattern for your ideas and to hold those ideas together. In checking over your paper for coherence, you need to make sure that these important threads are in place.

Transitional Devices.   The English language is rich not only in words and phrases that help writers tie ideas together, but also in those that point the reader to the particular relationships that hold among a writer's ideas. The brief paragraph on "Linkages and Transitions" just examined (though it certainly was *not* composed as an exemplary paragraph) offers a number of instances of these devices as well. "But" suggests a mild contradiction of the preceding idea. "What if" implies speculative possibility. "Though" suggests a concession to another point of view. "Still" implies that despite the obstacles raised, the concept expressed remains true.

Using devices such as these to help tie your work together will smooth out your transitions between sentences and between paragraphs and will make your essay read more fluently. The accompanying box of transitional words and phrases is a partial list of such devices and the general relationship to which each points.

The section on adverbials on pages 230–232 will give you the opportu-

---

Transitional Words and Phrases

Phrases of sequence: first, second, third . . .; first, then; after, afterward, since, before, when, whenever, until, as soon as, as long as, while, in [in 1923, in the summer, and so on], at [Christmastime, the end of a term, and so on], finally.

Phrases of affirmation: in fact, actually, indeed, certainly.

Phrases of negation: nevertheless, on the contrary, notwithstanding, on the other hand, despite, still, however, but, yet, conversely.

Phrases of concession: although, though, granted that, no doubt, to be sure, whereas, of course, doubtless, certainly.

Phrases of illustration: for example, for instance, to illustrate, in particular, specifically.

Phrases of addition: and, also, moreover, or (nor), furthermore, next, again, too, second (third, and so on), another, finally.

Phrases of qualification: frequently, often, usually, in general, occasionally, provided, in case, unless, when, since, because, for, if.

Phrases of summation: therefore, thus, in conclusion, to sum up, so, consequently, accordingly, all in all, in short, on the whole, in other words, then.

nity to make creative use of transitional devices such as these. But now, while you are thinking about revising for coherence, it is good to be aware of the improvement these phrases can make in an incoherent passage. Perhaps even more helpful is an understanding of the damage that faulty use of these transitional words and phrases can do to writing. Because these phrases point to very specific relationships, they cannot easily be interchanged. For instance, examine the following:

> · Jane held the smoking gun in her hand,

Faulty   · *Furthermore,* she was not the murderer.

Faulty   · *Consequently,* she was not the murderer.

"Nevertheless, she was not the murderer" would be a more reasonable choice of words. *Furthermore, consequently,* and *nevertheless* are all equally useful transitional words, and the sentence each is used in is syntactically correct. In relation to the first sentence, however, these two words make their sentences ridiculous. To save your work from equally disastrous results, be very sure that each of the transitional words you choose lends the sentence precisely the meaning you intend. If you have any question about what the transitional phrase implies, ask someone else to read through the passage.

TRY IT OUT

1. Analyze the following paragraph of Meg Greenfield's by the TRI method.

    (a) Finally, it is in the nature of this kind of terror that its victims—meaning all who don't practice, understand or condone it—will at once turn and run from its reality, insisting on seeing it as something different from what it is. (b) Terrorism attacks our compatriots on airplanes and that makes us sad or angry on their behalf. (c) But it also attacks our most fundamental, settled assumptions about how we can expect people to behave in relation to us, what we can count on them to feel and do—or not do. Those assumptions are central to our sense of personal security. (d) And so this kind of attack frightens and disorients us and we try very hard to describe or rename or wish it away. (e) We give terrorism a familiar face, an understandable motive, an explanation that makes it somehow less menacing. We try to doll it up to to look just like the family next door. (f) And meanwhile the terrorists continue to shoot the odd helpless passenger and pitch him out the airplane door. (page 420, paragraph 4)

2. Analyze the Greenfield paragraph according to Christensen's numbering and indenting method.

3. The following paragraph is also from the Greenfield article. Try analyzing it also according to the Christensen method.

It doesn't take long, you will observe, before we are all basing our conversation on unspoken premises that aren't much good from anyone's point of view— except that of the terrorists. In November of the first year of the Iranian hostage crisis you could hear people demanding that the captors entertain the prospect of delivering Christmas packages to their captured wards. Christmas arrangements! In November! What a way of saying that we were settling in for a nice long haul. Within a few hours of the TWA affair you could sense a crime like a net. The lunatic professoriat took to the air and expressed its usual hostage-crisis baloney; we commentators did much the same; the so-called experts on terrorism scratched their heads; we heard all about the legitimate grievances of the captors; we heard how the hostages were being treated well; we got used to the idea.

4. Trace the patterns of coherence in the first Greenfield paragraph (Exercise 1):
(a) List the transitional devices Greenfield employs, and explain their structural purpose.

Example: *Finally* signifies "last in a series."

(b) List repeated words, phrases, and ideas; list also pronouns that substitute for such words or phrases.

Revising for Emphasis

Because even the simplest composition contains a number of ideas competing for readers' attention, it is important to give the most significant of these ideas most emphasis. You have two main ways of achieving emphasis structurally: the proportion of work you devote to an idea and the position you place it in the essay.

EMPHASIS BY PROPORTION

To achieve quantitative emphasis, a good rule of thumb is to assign the space in the essay roughly in proportion to the importance of each idea to conveying your thesis to your reader.

The more important an idea is to your overall point, and to convincing your reader of that point, the more space you should devote to it.

This principle may seem obvious to you; but, unfortunately, it is one that inexperienced writers sometimes disregard.

The Writer's Fatigue Problem.   Too often, inexperienced writers begin their compositions with enthusiasm and cover the early points fully, only to find themselves running out of steam with scarcely the energy to summarize their final points briefly. Unfortunately, this mode of writing often creates papers that do not reflect their authors' intentions. If a writer organizes an essay's ideas in the usually effective order, from least to most important, the most important ideas, occurring later, will be the ones slighted should a decline in energy set in. The results are particularly disastrous when the problem occurs in an essay based upon the "although" clause structure, where the other side is explicated first, with the writer's point of view following and refuting it. Writer's fatigue serves here to emphasize the "although" side at the expense of the writer's own.

Three good strategies can help if you should discover the results of writer's fatigue in your essay:

1. When the early part of the first draft pleases you, leave it pretty much as written, and rewrite the final section(s) with the same care and spirit with which you began.
2. If the early part now seems wordy or overdone, you can cut it down and do less rewriting in the later parts. Be careful if you choose this alternative, though. Very often when the first portions are too profuse, the latter portions tend to be too scanty.
3. A third alternative is to shift your thesis itself to match the emphasis that your writing has taken. If the "although" position now seems more interesting than your thesis, you can change your stance. First write a new introduction and beginning section(s), and then rework what you had written earlier to serve as the main focus of the revised paper.

Because all these alternatives mean fairly extensive revision, it would probably be better to guard yourself against writer's fatigue in the first place. Thus, when you are writing a first draft and sense fatigue creeping over you, stop. Rest and refresh yourself before continuing.

EMPHASIS BY POSITION

Another way to emphasize an idea is to give it a prominent position in your paper. Beginnings and endings are the sections that readers are most impressed with and remember longest. They are the parts, therefore, that make the best showcase for your most important ideas. When you check over the paper, you will want to make sure that your thesis is either stated or prepared for early in your paper and that it is given a resounding declaration toward the end. You will also want to check your supporting paragraphs so that no idea of importance is permitted to get lost in mid-paragraph or midsentence. Be sure that all significant points have at least a sentence or two of their own and that you position them at the beginning or end of the paragraph.

Whether first or last position carries more importance depends a good deal on whether or not you expect your composition to be read in its entirety. Since few pieces of business writing get every reader's complete review, writing for business is a matter of saying the most important ideas at the very beginning—of the composition and of each paragraph. When you write for classes in college or for magazines or journals, on the other hand, you can expect the readers you win over in the beginning to stay with you to the end. For this audience, you can regard the essay as a unit and build toward a persuasive conclusion.

For our present purposes, then, the ending of your paper conveys greatest emphasis. You will want to give it an especially close look before making revisions. Guard particularly against shifting your emphasis at the close. Watch that you have not included any "by the way, I forgot to mention earlier . . ." sort of material in your conclusion. And be equally careful not to allow your "although" clause ideas to reenter at the end. Avoid:

Faulty
· In closing, therefore, it is clear that *my point* is true. On the other hand, much can to be said for *the alternative* point of view.

If you decide to continue on from your final statement of thesis, make sure that what you write follows naturally from and completes your main point in the reader's mind.

TRY IT OUT

1. On page 462 you will find the first draft of Elizabeth Jane Stein's student paper, "The Blues Don't Knock on Nobody's Door." Its problems are mainly structural. List the problems you find. How does Elizabeth Jane

correct them in the final draft? Do you think the changes make her paper more effective? Why?

2. Revise the following paragraph for structural problems. Use the overall essay thesis as a guide for composing your topic sentence and for editing the paragraph. (You may find it helpful to refer to the revision checklist as you work.)

Essay Thesis: *High unemployment can shred the social fabric.*

Faulty

All too often, a teenager will see keys in a car and decide to steal it. And he might break into a house and steal all of the valuables located there. Additionally, there is a high unemployment rate for teenagers which is turning them to a life of crime. Many crimes take place because they're committed by teenagers; nevertheless, they are restless from unemployment, and they lack the money they need for things like beer, junk food, video games, movies, their cars, records, sometimes college tuition, books, and drugs, which are furthermore against the law. However, frustration results, and he turns to specific acts of theft and violence.

Revising for Structure: A Summary Checklist

Key: Keep your thesis in mind.

TRY TO ACHIEVE:

Unity

1. Check to see that every paragraph, every sentence contributes to supporting the thesis.
2. Be sure that the sentences in each paragraph support the paragraph's topic sentence.

Coherence

1. Read your essay carefully to see if your ideas come across clearly and that they follow one another in a reasonable sequence. If you are not completely certain, ask someone else to examine the paper with these points in mind.
2. If in rereading you discover problems with coherence in the presentation of your major ideas, return to the outline and shift its points about until you discover a logical ordering. Then reorder the sections of your paper to fit it. Do not hesitate to cut and paste.
3. If your rereading discovers coherence problems within your paragraphs, reorganize the offending paragraphs. Discard any intruding material. If you have difficulty locating the specific problem, try the TRI or the Christensen method of analysis.

4. If your ideas are logically placed and yet the paragraphs still do not seem to hang together properly, examine your linkage systems.
   - Check to see if there is enough repetition to guide the reader through the pattern of your ideas.
   - Check to see that your transitional words and phrases relate your ideas to each other appropriately.

Emphasis

1. Make sure that the amount of space you have allotted to each idea coincides with its importance.
2. Be especially careful that your "although" material does not overpower your own point.
3. Make sure that you have placed your discussion of your major points at the end and/or the beginning of your essay and that you have not buried them in midparagraph or midsentence.

REVISING FOR PERSUASIVENESS

Many sections in this book focus on positive techniques for making your work persuasive. But here, when our concern is with revising, it is probably more helpful to ask the negative question: What might keep your writing from being as persuasive as it could be? From this point of view, as you go over the first draft, search for any elements of your paper that might interfere with readers' accepting what you have to say. To find these elements, you must make yourself acutely aware of your readers as people—as real human beings who can be both pleased and offended.

It is possible that you object to this approach. You may be thinking that if your facts are sound and well supported, nothing else should matter. And perhaps nothing else would matter if the essay were to be processed by a machine. But the truth is that your writing will be read by people whose judgments are humanly illogical enough to be influenced by their impression of you, the writer. Without even being aware of it, readers take in signals that help them make up their minds, signals quite apart from the merits of your arguments. They can be offended by the tone of an article, by its language, or by underlying attitudes they think it reveals. They can become bored by it or annoyed because they find it difficult to read or because it contains mechanical errors such as poor spelling or incorrect punctuation. Any or all of these conditions can distract your readers from what you are telling them. Let us look into these problems more specifically.

Offenses Against Taste

Taste is, as you know, an extremely slippery concept to grasp. The saying "One man's meat is another man's poison" is no less true because it is too often quoted. Your problem as a writer who must make choices based partly on your readers' taste is increased because often you do not know your prospective readers well enough to be sure of their taste. You certainly cannot know them precisely if you are writing for a journal or magazine (though reading a few issues can give you real insight into the values and ideas shared by the readership). And even if you write only for your instructor and your classmates, you can count on no clear uniformity of taste. You are better off, therefore, to avoid language that large numbers of your potential readers would find offensive.

RACIAL SLURS

Foremost among expressions that revision should rule out of your writing are slurs against racial, religious, or national groups or against any other group that has been subject to stereotyping. This is not to say that you cannot take issue with the opinions shared by a particular group. You can, for instance, express strong disapproval of terrorism without implying that all members of a particular ethnic group behave in an objectionable way. In fact, except for some stories with direct quotations, I can think of no occasion in which the use of an ugly slang term for a member of a racial, religious, or national group is appropriate. Nor are there many occasions when a legitimate rhetorical purpose is served by including stereotypical details about any group. No group has a monopoly on any characteristic, either good or bad, and it is not only false, but also boring to imply that it does.

SEXIST SLURS

Offensive as are the stereotypes claiming that all politicians take bribes and that all athletes are dumb, we need not take up each kind individually. But one sort of stereotypical thinking must be singled out for special mention because more than half the population is involved. I am referring, of course, to stereotypes about women. More and more we are coming to understand how tasteless sexist references can be. We need not dwell on the boorishness of such terms as *broad* or *chick* or on the contradictory notions that all women are weak and helpless and all women are domineering nags. Such lapses are easily rooted out. Unfortunately, some sexist thinking seems to be built into the language itself. And here you may offend quite unaware. The following hints can be helpful:

1. Use plurals wherever possible to avoid having to choose a sex-marked pronoun. For example, if you write "Students should complete *their* exams," you avoid the awkward "A student should complete *his or her* exam." (The rule that suggested turning all neutral pronouns masculine is now outdated, and the practice is offensive to many.)
2. Avoid expressions such as "lady lawyer." These carry the insulting

implication that the occupational term by itself refers exclusively to men. When you write, simply, "Susan is an engineer," there is no lack of clarity.

3. Choose the more general, rather than the masculine, term. For example, use *humankind* rather than *mankind* and *person* instead of *man.* Or select a genderless specific word, as in "a five-*member* team").

PROFANITY AND OBSCENITY

Think very carefully about your particular readers before you permit a word many people consider profane or obscene to reach the final draft of your paper. Those who are offended by this language make such a sizable group that unless you feel certain that you cannot achieve the desired effect without the expression, you will probably be wise to delete it.

Editing for Offensive Tone

Tone is the sound of the writer's voice talking to the reader. It is a particularly difficult element for writers to check for themselves. In fact, if you have a serious question about the tone of a paper, consider asking a friend to read it aloud to you. When you read it aloud to yourself, you may hear only the tone you meant rather than the one that the paper actually imparts.

Much that is offensive in writing tone is similar to the tones that most people find irritating in conversation. Conversations make us uncomfortable when they make us feel inadequate. In writing as in conversation, then, it is better to avoid an overbearing tone or a show-off manner. Conversation also becomes difficult when a speaker's bearing is unpleasant or when a sneering tone does not make us share in the disapproval expressed. It usually leads us to believe that the writer (or speaker) is mean-spirited, not to be trusted on this point, and probably not very sound in general. Similarly, a gushy tone does not convince us that the subject deserves such effusions, but rather that the writer (or speaker) is insincere and, again, not to be trusted. We shy away in the same way from an angry tone. David Worcester, an insightful critic, explains why tones that seem overly emotional tend to backfire:

> It is acute discomfort to be present where a man has fallen into a furious passion. If you are in such a situation, and the object of your acquaintance's rage has no connection with you, you will experience an instinctive craving to turn the painful situation into a ludicrous one. This is done by withdrawing all sympathy from the blusterer and by taking a more relativistic view of him as a lobster-faced baboon in a fit.[4]

[4]*The Art of Satire* (Cambridge: Harvard University Press, 1940), pp. 17–18.

To avoid consequences such as Worcester imagines, listen carefully for any trace of excessive emotion in your paper. If you should find any, more often than not you will be able to correct the flaw by omitting a word or two or by substituting a less inflammatory phrase. Should the problem go deeper and the questionable tone pervade your essay, you may want to reword the whole piece so that it reflects a more objective point of view. No matter how strongly you feel about a subject, if you can present the material objectively, you will be more convincing. There is much persuasive force in restraint.

Editing out Confusion

One of the easiest ways to earn your readers' ill will is to confuse them. Rewrite any passage that you have reason to think might not be clear. Do not hesitate to explain it thoroughly—even if you secretly think it will sound a bit as if you were explaining it for a six-year-old. Although you may understand your subject completely, chances are that it is unfamiliar to the reader.

VAGUE REFERENCE

From time to time we all fall into vagueness and unconsciously compose a passage without being fully clear on the matter ourselves. You can uncover such passages when rereading your essay by looking for the giveaway signal of "this," "that," "it," or "which" appearing with no definite word to refer back to (that is, with no antecedent). The following example is typical:

Faulty

· Jan had long wanted to spend a summer in Italy. <u>This</u> was on her mind all the time. <u>It</u> kept interfering with her studies. She finally made up her mind to take the trip, <u>which</u> surprised no one.

The underlined pronouns are used here—as similar ones are used in all such writing—to mean, vaguely, "all the stuff I just said." Readers find such indefinite reference exasperating because they sense that the writer is not completely sure about what is intended and is lazily relying upon the pronouns in order to escape having to be more specific.

To revise sentences such as these, you first have to give a name to the vague idea you are referring to. Ask yourself, What exactly do I mean by that pronoun? When you have decided, an easy solution is to use a demonstrative pronoun ("this," "that") as an adjective pointing to the name you have chosen:

· Jan had long wanted to spend a summer in Italy. <u>This</u> <u>desire</u>. . . .

An alternative is to substitute a specific idea for the indefinite pronoun. Let's continue with the example and revise "It kept interfering . . .":

> · Jan had long wanted to spend a summer in Italy. This desire was on her mind all the time. Dreams of Roman fountains and Venetian canals kept interfering with her studying.

Although using "which" in the vague way of the sample (*"which* surprised no one") is a more serious error than the others, you can correct it by similar means. You can name the idea it stands for:

> · She finally made up her mind to take the trip, a decision which surprised no one.

Or you can rephrase to edit out the "which" entirely:

> · That she finally made up her mind to take the trip surprised no one.
> · When she finally made up her mind to take the trip, no one was surprised.

Often when you search for a way to edit out instances of confusing reference, you come to firmer grips with what you want to say, and your work improves all around.

INCONSISTENCY

Be careful also to present your ideas consistently. In trying for objectivity, inexperienced writers sometimes confuse their readers about the point of the writing by seeming to advocate every idea they present. If you should uncover such a problem, revise so that your position is clear at the outset. Either explain that you will be presenting the best case for each alternative, or include in each presentation a clue to your own preference. Notice, for instance, how the word *well,* which Carll Tucker interjects into the following statement, leaves his readers with no doubt about where he stands on the event he narrates:

> One afternoon recently, two unrelated friends called to tell me that, *well,* their marriages hadn't made it. One was leaving his wife for another woman. The other was leaving her husband because "we thought it best." (page 431, paragraph 1; italics mine)

Inconsistency of voice is another way to confuse your readers, who are entitled to a sure sense of the voice that addresses them. For them to gain this sureness, you will need to provide a degree of unity of tone, time, and mode of address. If, for example, you begin your paper formally and then suddenly lapse into a style that is full of neighborhood dialect and slang, your readers will not know what to make of it. The jarring would almost be as if Thomas Jefferson had begun the Declaration of Independence in this way:

Faulty
> · When in the course of human events, a bunch of baddies start to throw their weight around with some of their relatives, it becomes necessary for those relatives to dissolve the political bands that have connected them.

Your readers will also be distracted by inappropriate shifts in tense. A dizziness is built into writing that hops about between the past and present. Examine, for instance, the following bad example:

Faulty
> · We <u>had begun</u> our trip when we <u>see</u> a tree. The tree <u>is growing</u> right in the middle of the road, which <u>was divided</u> at that spot and <u>heads</u> on the left for Burlington while it <u>wound</u> round to Clarksville on the right.

You can further confuse your readers by shifting back and forth in your point of view:

Faulty
> · <u>I</u> visited the mountains and <u>it</u> was much enjoyed. <u>You</u> get all choked up when <u>you</u> see so much beauty. <u>Mother and Uncle Joe</u> said <u>they</u> had never had so much fun. <u>There</u> is a plan to go back some day.

You need not strive for a total unity. (Chapters 8 and 9, in fact, point out effective ways to *vary* your tone.) But an overall consistency is necessary if you are to avoid confusing your reader. When you edit, therefore, keep a sharp eye out for inconsistencies like those in the preceding bad examples, and be ready to make whatever revisions are needed. The following exercise should give you some practice.

TRY IT OUT

Edit the following paragraph from a student essay. Watch especially for vague references and inconsistencies.

Steroids

Faulty
The use of steroids in athletics is a bad situation. Many of the world's best and most famous athletes are using them. Steroids is a drug that is illegal in the United States. Many athletes obtain it personally and used it while they are working out, which they think will benefit them and help them stay in good shape. But this will harm them later. Steroids can make you grow physically with steady use, but can also cause mutations and have side effects. Many offi-

```
cials are upset at their spreading use. They think testing
should be done in athletics. Howie Long, defensive end for
the L.A. Raiders, thinks steroid use by other athletes is
unfair. "They should play honest," he says.
```

Editing out Boredom

There is no doubt in my mind that writers lose more of their readers through boredom than through any other cause. For every reader who tosses an article aside in a huff because of foul language, there must be fifty whose minds simply drift away because of the dullness of the work. To revise your composition effectively, be on the lookout for a variety of possible sources of boredom.

BOREDOM FROM LONGWINDEDNESS

The most obvious cause of boredom is the presence of too much and too many: too much writing, too many unrelated ideas, too much repetition, too many words, too much overblown language. To prepare yourself to edit for succinctness, you might try a mental trick I have found helpful: pretend that the space available to you has been strictly rationed. To make the needed economies, eliminate any sentence that adds nothing new to your presentation; combine where there is overlap. Cross out any word that does not contribute to your meaning. Be especially wary of stock phrases with built-in redundancies—that is, phrases that say the same thing twice, such as *adequate enough, past experience, consensus of opinion, my own personal . . . , each individual person.* (For more examples, see "Redundancies" in the Revision Guide.) Change grammatical constructions so that the lengthier terms are eliminated. Use *-ing* nouns, for instance, instead of the longer and more syntactically complicated *-ation* nouns. Compare:

> · *Irrigating* the desert has made it bloom.
> · *The irrigation of* the desert has made it bloom.

Repetition.   One of the most boring aspects of longwindedness is repetition. Have you ever been in conversation with eagerly talkative people who say everything twice to make sure you hear it and once again because they begin to like the sound of it? If so, you can appreciate just how boring repetitive writing can be. And yet repetition can be one of the most powerful tools for producing coherence and emphasis in your writing (see pages 127 and 161). What then should you do when you are editing and discover a repeated idea, word, or phrasal pattern? You need to decide whether the repetition provides the emphasis or clarity you want or whether it merely clutters your work. Here's how:

Ask yourself frankly: In repeating this idea, am I helping my reader

"OH, HOW I HATE THE RE-WRITING!"

© 1985 by Sidney Harris

understand? Or do I really just hate to part with any of the phrasings I tried out when I was striving to explain the concept? If your answer is the latter, then grit your teeth and mercilessly eliminate the repetition.

Although the parallelism produced by repeating grammatical structures can be highly effective, as pages 247–255 demonstrate, uncontrolled repetition can drum monotonously. Read your paper aloud, and if you hear this monotony, you can be sure that you have fallen into a habit of using the same pattern over and over. Try reading this passage aloud, for example:

Faulty

· Rising quickly, Jan went outdoors. Seeing the sunshine, she smiled to herself. Stooping to pick some

```
flowers, she began to whistle. Whistling merrily, she
returned to the house.
```

Pages 215–245 show you ways you can keep your sentence structure from becoming monotonous in this way.

As for eliminating repeated words, a word of caution is in order before you run to your thesaurus or dictionary of synonyms. Do not use a word unless you're entirely sure of its meaning. Synonyms are never completely interchangeable. It is far better, for instance, to describe a pond as *shallow* three or four times than to try for variety by describing it as *insincere"* (see "Finding the Precise Word," page 260).

BOREDOM FROM LACK OF SPECIFIC DETAIL

Another sort of "too much" that results in reader boredom is too much generalization without enough specific support. When you edit your paper, make sure that you have not left one generalization unsupported. Watch, for example, for such sequences as the following from a student paper, where one generalization follows another without a hint of support:

Faulty

```
· Sports are enjoyable and exciting because of the phys-
  ical competition. Politics casts a shadow upon the
  real pleasure in sporting events.
```

Most of the time your readers will not object if you need to take an extra sentence or two to restate or clarify an especially difficult concept. But when you have amplified your point until it is crystal clear, you will still be obliged to offer some support for it. The first two sentences in the next paragraph from the same student paper leave the reader hungering for the detailed support that the rest of the paragraph never delivers:

Faulty

```
· Coaches should judge their players only on ability and
  not involve themselves in politics. Political con-
  siderations do not offer a fair base for judgment and
  can only hurt the players--and eventually the team.
  When politics interferes with sports, it has a way of
  destroying one's confidence and making an athlete
  feel useless. Politics may be the reason why some of
  the best players lose all interest in the game. Coaches
  should always pick players on the basis of their ath-
  letic ability rather than on politics.
```

If you should come across this sort of boring accumulation of generalities in your own work, supply concrete and detailed support (see pages 115–124) for the generalizations that add to the paragraph's point. Then eliminate the others or save them for another part of your essay.

TRY IT OUT

Rewrite the student's paragraph on politics in high-school athletics presented in the preceding section and, by specific examples and detail, provide it with the interest it now lacks. Eliminate anything that does not add to the overall effectiveness of the paragraph.

BOREDOM FROM OVERPERSONAL WRITING

Self-centered people are among the most boring of conversationalists. And they do little better as writers. On the other hand, the sound of a personal voice is one of the keys to effective writing. The distinction between a tone that has a strong sense of self and one that is self-absorbed is a difficult one to draw theoretically. Let me instead give you a specific example of an approach that I judged too personal.

A student came in for a conference about a paper he planned to write on the relationship between science and sexual behavior in the Laputa Voyage segment of Swift's *Gulliver's Travels* and in Huxley's *Brave New World.* He did not want to discuss the authors' intentions in setting up these relationships, but rather to give his opinion of such relationships and support it with details of how he came to have that opinion. I tried to persuade him to focus his paper more closely on the works. For there is no question in my mind but that a paper based on such premises would be boringly personal (quite aside from my wondering just what a recital of how he came to his opinion on sex and science would amount to). The paper, you see, would be about the student—and not really about Swift's Laputa and Huxley's brave new world at all.

As for a personal approach that might pass your editor's pencil, let me suggest my use of *I* in the anecdote just narrated. Although what is acceptable in tone is, as we have said, very much a matter of private taste, most readers would probably agree that the personal tone in the anecdote about the Swift-Huxley paper works out all right. They would judge that it contributes to rather than detracts from the point the example is intended to make. Whether or not you agree in this case, the criterion is a good test for overpersonal writing and should prove helpful in your editing.

BOREDOM FROM UNDERPERSONAL WRITING

No matter how dull overly personal writing can be, the writing with the most offensively boring tone is that which seems to have no personal author at all. Such writing speaks to its readers in the dehumanized drone of a machine, with no identifiable human author addressing the human reader. Nobody really does anything in such writing, or at least nobody seems willing to take responsibility for doing anything. Everything that happens seems compelled by some vague, nameless force:

Faulty   · It has been thought that . . .
Faulty   · It has been brought to mind . . .
Faulty   · There can be no doubt that . . .

Nobody ever complains:

Faulty   · Complaints have been made.

Nobody receives letters:

Faulty   · Letters are received.

Nobody conducts business:

Faulty   · Business is conducted.
Faulty   · Yours of the fifth inst. received and contents duly noted.

What is more, the vocabulary used in this mechanized writing is not the kind that conveys information from one human mind to another in a natural manner. It is composed instead of the stock phrases, words, and popular jargon you find programmed into computers (see cartoon).

Whatever could possess anyone to write such nonsense as "Yours of the fifth inst. received" or "A logistical interface of management referendums"? Inexperienced writers fall into machinelike writing such as this partly from a misinformed desire to avoid using "I" and partly in an equally misguided attempt to sound impressive. If you have any doubts at all that such attempts are misguided, let me reassure you. All effective communication of the world's business—whether in industry, in the classroom, or in

GOOSEMYER   by parker and wilder

GOOSEMYER by Brant Parker and Don Wilder. © 1980 Field Enterprises, Inc., by permission of North America Syndicate, Inc.

people's lives—is conducted by a thoroughly human "I" or "we" to an equally human "you," in language they all can understand and be affected by. The best way to avoid a machinelike tone is to watch for unnecessary passives and jargon, which are its major causes.

Editing out Unnecessary Passives. Much of the unappealing nonpersonal quality we have been discussing stems from structuring too many sentences in the passive voice. In English, the basic sentence has what is called an *active* structure; that is, it is composed of a subject doing something to an object:

· The boy *hit* the ball.

Most sentences can also be constructed in the *passive* form by switching object for subject and turning the verb passive (that is, by adding on a form of the verb "to be"):

· The ball *was hit* [by the boy].

But now the new subject remains passive, being acted upon; and the actor, relegated to a phrase at the end, no longer seems necessary. In fact, the actor is often dropped from the sentence altogether.

Of course, there are times when passive sentences—though on the whole less interesting—can convey your meaning more precisely. Sometimes, to continue the example, it is not the boy but the ball you want to concentrate upon:

· The *ball* was hit. It soared and soared.

Sometimes the active construction is simply inappropriate; only the passive can get across what you wish to say:

· The site of the accident was as devastated as a battlefield.
· The president was elected by a large plurality.

Nevertheless, if you use the passive habitually, your writing will probably become both dull and awkward. There are three reasons for this result.

1. The passive encourages that curious absence we discussed, of an agent or actor, of a human being in charge.
2. Because the passive is not the natural construction in English, it often leads to long and convoluted (twisted) sentence structures. Compare:

Passive	Active
A question is raised whether. . . .	I question whether. . . .
There exists the reason that. . . .	The reason is. . . .
It was the understanding of this committee that. . . .	The committee understood that. . . .

3. The kind of twisted prose that passive sentences set up often involves turning verbs into nouns that are elongated and sometimes pretentious, the words that give such writing its tone of pompous clutter. Compare:

Faulty

- *A reduction* in paperwork *would be brought* about by this plan. (long *passive* phrasing)
- This plan *would reduce* paperwork. (short, direct *active* phrasing)

Habitual users of the passive form pile up such constructions in awkward abundance. The four passive convolutions in the following example are typical:

Faulty

- *The suggestion is made* (1) *that the utilization of company money* (2) to pay for executive vacations in Hawaii *could appear suspicious to the Internal Revenue Service* (3) and make them think that *there may have been an improper disbursement of funds* (4).

To edit this sentence, first turn all the passive constructions into the active voice:

- *We suggest* (1) that if *the company uses its money* (2) to pay for executive vacations in Hawaii, *the IRS may suspect* (3) that the *company has disbursed its funds improperly* (4).

Next, in editing, compare your new sentence with the original one and decide whether it conveys the meaning you intended in a more direct way. In the case of the sample sentence, the revised version clears up the awkwardness, indirectness, and pretension of the original without changing its meaning.

Editing out Jargon and Gobbledygook.   Machinelike writing also stems from the overuse of jargon, the in-house terminology of a variety of disciplines. Even when wrenched from its technical context, jargon manages to maintain a pseudo-technical ring. Such terms, as *peer group, fixation, goal-directed,* and *function,* from psychology, or *feedback, input, breakthrough,* or *interface,* from computer science, are characteristic of jargon. When such terms are combined (often in twisted and unnecessarily complex syntax) with elongated words and forced diction, the product is a pompous nonsense humorously called "gobbledygook."

Some Typical Gobbledygook

prioritize	render operative
maximize	causative factors
facilitate	take cognizance of

utilize   energize
potentiate   synergize

Too often, inexperienced writers adopt gobbledygook to sound impressive or to enhance their image. But the truth is that far from making an impressive show, the user of such diction has become something of a figure of fun, fair game for the comedian's and the cartoonist's barbs. See the Goosemyer cartoon on page 178, for instance. Gobbledygook thus can mar your reader's perception of you and what you want to communicate. Therefore, except to express technical ideas within a specialized field, edit out the specialized term when a nontechnical word will convey all you mean to say. Very seldom, for instance, will *utilize* convey your meaning more precisely than *use,* or *transmit* be more meaningful than *send,* or *terminate* be preferable to *end.*

BOREDOM FROM OVERFAMILIARITY

All sorts of clichés annoy readers. They get bored when they feel that they can just about finish a writer's every phrase. If, as you edit, the words of a phrase seem to belong together, such as "torrential downpour" or "raining cats and dogs," make an attempt to keep your readers awake by substituting a word or phrase that accurately describes the situation but that they probably would not have thought of themselves. If you find stock phrases a persistent problem, see pages 295–297, where this subject is analyzed in more detail.

Overly Familiar Ideas. Unfortunately, ideas can be clichéd too. Readers become bored when they can accurately predict the content of the next several paragraphs just by reading a topic sentence. And though you should not automatically eliminate every idea anyone might consider commonplace, be aware, as you revise, that statements which simply express conventional wisdom or ideas that "everybody knows" to be true may be subject to criticism for lack of sincerity or lack of thought. You thus need to think through such ideas again.

First, examine yourself to be sure that you really mean the statement. Conventional wisdom is difficult to make interesting even when you sincerely believe it. If you disbelieve it or are indifferent to it, there certainly is no point in writing it. More likely, however, you do believe that the conventional statement you have written is true, at least to some extent. You may believe for instance, that "All babies are cute" or that "Playing football builds character" or that "Spring is a happy time." The problem here may well be overstatement. The solution is to qualify your remarks. There are very few statements to which "always" or "never" apply. *Most* babies are cute. Playing football *can* build character. Spring is *sometimes* the happiest season. And do not cheapen your genuine feelings by overstating them, as did the student who wrote: "I did not stop crying for a week after my gerbil died." Wherever you can, make your statement specific to the facts.

It is also a good idea to rethink your purpose in restating the well accepted idea. Since your readers probably have come across it before, be sure that you have something new to add that makes it worth their reading. Even if that something is only your assurance that the notion, common though it is, needs occasional reinforcing, go ahead with it. But if you really have no reason for expressing commonplace ideas, they are better edited out.

Revising for Persuasiveness: A Summary Checklist

Key: Keep your readers in mind
Try to avoid:

Offenses against taste

1. Edit out slurs against special groups (racial, religious, national, and so on).
2. Edit out sexist slurs. Avoid sexist use of pronouns and general terms that use "man" instead of "human" or "person."
3. Edit out profanity or obscenity unless you're sure of a receptive readership.

Offensive tone

1. Revise to avoid a tone that is overbearing or self-congratulatory.
2. Avoid an excessively emotional tone, whether it's angry and disapproving or gushy and overly effusive.

Confusion

1. Rewrite any passage that your reader may not find clear.
2. Make sure every pronoun points to *a particular word,* for which it is the substitute.
3. Be consistent in presenting of ideas, especially in conveying your point of view.
4. Be consistent in the voice with which you address readers.

Boredom

1. Revise to eliminate "too much and too many." Simpler is better.
2. Edit out unnecessary repetition of ideas, words, or phrasal structure.
3. Make sure every generalization is fully supported by specific detail.
4. Avoid overpersonal or underpersonal writing.
5. Edit out unnecessary passive constructions.
6. Edit out unnecessary jargon and all pseudo-jargon and gobbledygook.
7. Edit out clichés, evaluate platitudes.

TRY IT OUT

1. Edit the following sentence from the Goosemeyer cartoon on page 178. Eliminate the gobbledygook and rephrase in a clear, meaningful way:

   Mr. Farnestock, I believe at this point in time that a logistical interface of management referendums would be of significant manifestation.

2. Revise the following awkwardly written paragraph. How can you eliminate the awkwardness of the impersonal style? Ask yourself, Who is doing what? Try to get most of your sentences into an appropriate subject-verb-object relationship. Watch especially for inappropriate use of passive structure. (Don't forget also to prune any unnecessary words or awkward phrasing.)

Slugs

Faulty   Ugliness and nasty dispositions are characteristics of slugs. Prioritization of their day includes mucous trails, which they make, and slime fights that they engage in with other creatures. It is also common for them to have aggression within their own species. There are combats which occur deliberately and head to head frequently near shelter or on food. The head of the aggressor is lunged forward and its mouth is slashed downward and its jaw is guillotined downward and its victim is repeatedly struck until it is badly injured or viciously killed. Characterization of the mating of slugs also includes ritualistic aggression. All in all it is the main characteristic of slugs to be unpleasant. But the relationship of snails and slugs is close because slugs are snails without the decency of a shell. So what else would you expect?

3. The following student paragraph is marred by the wordiness, awkward syntax, and pompous diction of the impersonal style. Revise.

Faulty   One of the biggest problems today that modern students seem to have concerns a perceived inability on the part of these students to write papers and indeed lower subsections of papers--paragraphs and even sentences-- that are clearly intelligible by the reader. One of the biggest and chief problems that arises in these hard-to-read papers is that of verbosity, wherein the modern student will use many too many words in his paper to be easily

> understood, while actually the idea he is hoping and try-
> ing to express is, under close examination, shown to be
> in actuality quite simple.

4. Write a paragraph without using a single passive sentence.

ASSIGNMENT

Write a thoughtful essay on one of the following topics (or another that your instructor suggests). Before you write, give your ideas a chance to grow and mellow and then organize them carefully. While you write your essay, concentrate only on writing down your ideas. But when you have finished your first draft, revise it and edit it according to the suggestions given in this chapter.

1. Examine your values by writing about one of these topics:
   · Something genuinely important to you, though not necessarily to others.
   · Something of tremendous importance to others, but not to you.
   · Something that once seemed important to you, but does no longer.
   · Something you believe to be unfair.
   Although these topics are phrased in personal terms to help you begin your thinking and "invent" your support, you may want to take a less personal approach when you formulate your thesis. Watch for problems of overly personal and overly impersonal expression when you revise.

2. Read Slack's "If I'm So Smart . . ." (page 425). Summarize his points. Then, relating what he has to say to what you have observed in the classroom, develop your own thesis on the subject. Revise your essay according to the guidelines (page 182).

3. Imagine that another solar system has been discovered in a far corner of the Milky Way. In hopes of contacting other intelligent beings, NASA will be sending up a small probe, including a thirty-minute videotape explaining earth for them. You have been asked to submit a plan for that tape. Write a letter to the NASA officials explaining your plan and justifying it so that yours will be the plan accepted.[5]

4. Find out about something interesting that is going on in your community by interviewing someone involved, and write an essay making a point about it. In revising your first draft, be especially sure that your paper is tightly organized around your thesis. Interview-based papers sometimes have problems with focus because interviews can supply such a wide diver-

[5]From an idea of Professor Lauri Anderson of Suomi College.

sity of tantalizing information. You might find it helpful to read Elizabeth Jane Stein's student paper (pages 458–461), which is based upon just such an assignment.

5. Look through the titles of the Part Four essays. Choose one title to direct a free writing. Use that free writing to arrive at a thesis by one of the methods described in Chapter 1 or Part One. Write an essay on that topic. Set it aside for at least eight hours. Then revise thoroughly.

Chapter 7

Editing and Proofreading for Correctness

Since much of your editing job, as we have seen, is searching out and eliminating causes of reader annoyance, to edit effectively you will have to devote some thought to the less than exciting subject of mechanical error. Unfortunately, readers seem to be particularly annoyed by writing mechanics that do not conform to accepted standards for written English. It is true that errors in spelling, capitalization, punctuation, sentence structure, and grammatical usage are minor compared with the difficulties in structure and tone we have been discussing. And it is equally true that such errors (except for those in punctuation) rarely interfere with the actual communication of a writer's ideas. Nevertheless, for a large proportion of readers these errors present an almost impenetrable block between themselves and the writer's message. In fact, research demonstrates that some errors cause readers to form such negative judgments about the writer of a composition that they disregard the merits of the content. And English teachers are not the only readers who react in this way. Actually, as Professor Maxine Hairston discovered, many professionals such as engineers, judges, bankers, architects, lawyers, and corporation executives are even more distressed by errors in the mechanics of writing than are college instructors.[1] Without question, mechanical errors in a finished composition can severely damage its impact.

---

[1] *Successful Writing* (New York: W. W. Norton, 1981), pp. 244–246.

SAVE WORRY ABOUT MECHANICS FOR THE FINAL DRAFT

If errors in mechanics are relatively unimportant to your overall composition and yet if they are of tremendous consequence to a significant segment of your readers, what are you to do? Let me recommend that you go through the process of prewriting, writing, and rewriting your paper without giving the mechanics too much thought. Many of the errors in your original draft will vanish when you revise for structure and clarity, for these errors tend to creep in when you are still not completely sure of the ideas you want to express. But before you copy over the composition to present it to your readers in its final form, make as sure as you possibly can that it is free from errors and that it conforms to the standards of written English.

READER-DISTRESSING ERRORS

Readers do not find all errors equally disturbing. Professor Hairston's study confirmed earlier research that among the most distressing are errors of the sentence—especially run-on sentences and fragments and subject-verb disagreements. Other errors that seem almost as offensive are certain errors in comma usage and in capitalization. Spelling errors, when they are too abundant, and faulty parallelism also appear to be troublesome. Although errors can occur in many other areas, those just mentioned seem to be by far the most important to readers.[2]

Chapter 7 will therefore concentrate on those specific errors and areas. Here you will find enough linguistic background to help you make sense of the rules for "correct" and "incorrect." You can then more easily recognize mechanical errors and develop sound editing and proofreading strategies for their correction.

REALLY UNDERSTANDING THE ENGLISH SENTENCE

If you can understand, truly understand, the English sentence, you will not only find it much easier to edit for correctness, but, better yet, you will have a real advantage in developing your own effective writing style. (See Chapter 8.) During your schooling you have probably been exposed to a wide variety of the "shoulds" and "should nots" of English grammar. And you may well have found them overwhelmingly and confusingly diverse. I do not think you will feel this confusion if you understand English syntax as a logical unity. The following review, therefore, emphasizes the systematic structure of our language. Here, then, compacted into just a few pages, is "all you ever wanted to know" about English syntax.

---

[2]Professor Hairston's research also recognized the importance of errors due to nonstandard dialects and other errors of usage. Such errors are examined in the Revision Guide (Part Five).

The Essential Sentence: Subject-Verb-[Complement]

We will begin with the structure of the sentence because every unit in English syntax related to that structure and is, in fact, best defined by its function in it.

What exactly is a *sentence?* The essence of the sentence becomes clearest when we reduce it to its basics. Let's examine some examples of the shortest possible sentences:

· Birds fly.
· Babies coo.
· [You] Smile!
· Garbage smells.

These brief examples (the last included to avert any charges of sentimentality) contain everything a verbal structure needs to be a sentence. Each has a subject and a verb: *something doing or being.* The requirements for a sentence are met whether it is phrased as a statement:

· Birds will fly
  (subj.) (verb)

or as a question:

· Will birds fly?
  (subj.)
  (verb)

or even as a command where the subject, "you," is understood (not stated):

· [You] Jump!
  (subj.) (verb)

In essence, a sentence is an independently existing group of words arranged to express something doing or being.

Actually, as we know, very few sentences are as sparse as these. Most English sentences also include an object or quality needed to complete the verb (a complement) and thus express *something doing or being something.* Examples of this sort of sentence—again cut to the bare bones—include:

· Bats hit balls.
  (subj.) (verb) (obj.)

· The girl picked a daisy.
  (subj.) (verb) (obj.)

· The squirrel will climb the tree.
  (subj.) (verb) (obj.)

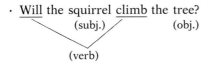

And that's really all there is to it. The configuration Subject-Verb-[Complement (Object)] is at the heart of the English syntactical system, and almost everything within that system can be explained in its terms.

CLAUSES AND PHRASES DEFINED

Clauses and phrases might both be defined as *meaningfully arranged groups of words* within a sentence. They are distinguished from each other by the presence or absence of subject and verb. Phrases do *not* have subjects and verbs:

- in the wind
- blowing in the wind
- blown in the wind
- to blow [in the wind]

But clauses, like sentences, must include both a subject and a verb.

An independent clause (also called *main clause*) is of itself a sentence, though it occurs within a larger structure. Given initial capital and end punctuation, it could stand alone as, for instance, in the sentence:

- The wind blows, and the waves pound.

Both "The wind blows" and "the waves pound" are independent clauses and can be transformed into true sentences by appropriate capitalization and punctuation.

- The wind blows.
  (subj.) (verb)

- The waves pound.
  (subj.) (verb)

A dependent clause (subordinate clause) must also have a subject and a verb. The subordinate clause cannot stand alone, however, because it is hindered by an extra word (a *subordinating conjunction*[3] or a *relative pronoun*) that attaches it to its main clause and signals its dependent relationship. For example, although "The wind blows" is a main clause, we can make a subordinate clause simply by adding a subordinating conjunction: *"That* the wind blows," *"When* the wind blows," and "[The wind] *which* blows" are all subordinate clauses. Incorporated with appropriate main clauses into sentences, they become:

---

[3]For more about subordinating conjunctions, see pages 219, 234, and 241.

- He   told me *that the wind blows.*
  (subj.) (verb)   (subj.) (verb)

- The waves pound *when the wind blows.*
   (subj.) (verb)   (subj.) (verb)

- The wind *which blows* makes the waves pound.
   (subj.) (subj.) (verb) (verb)

Parts of Speech

The Subject-Verb-[Complement (Object)] configuration explains the functions of the parts of speech—and the functions of the various kinds of phrases and clauses as well. **Nouns** are words that serve as the subjects or objects of sentences, clauses, or phrases. Observe, for instance, the functions served by the nouns in the following constructions:

- The *waves* pound the *shore.*
   (subj.)   (obj.)

- *Jack* told the   *boy*   the *tale.*
 (subj.)   (indirect obj.)   (obj.)

- in the *wind*
       (obj. of prepositional phrase)

- to sail the *ship*
        (obj. of infinitive phrase)

- Jack, a *man* after my own heart.
     (subj. of appositive phrase)

Pronouns serve the same functions when they substitute for nouns:

- *They* [the waves] pound the shore.
 (subj.)

- *Who* has seen the wind?
 (subj.)

- To *whom* do you wish to speak?
    (indirect obj.—or obj. of phrase)

Verbs are the words that express the doing or being of the subject. When we change their spelling or add an auxiliary, they also tell *when* the subject does or is:

- The wind *blows.* The waves *pounded* the shore. The beach *will be* sandy.

Adjectives describe or modify subjects or objects—that is to say, nouns:

- The *rough* waves pound the *sandy* shore.

Adverbs similarly describe or modify the verb:

· The waves *roughly* pound the shore.

Adverbs also mark the sentence for time, place, manner, or frequency by telling when or where or how often the subject acts or is:

· *Then* the waves pounded the shore *again* and *again.*

Nouns (and pronouns), verbs, adjectives, and adverbs carry the basic meaning. The remaining parts of speech (variously named depending upon the authority) are **function words** that serve primarily to shape sentences, clauses, and phrases and to hold them together. These function words include three kinds of conjunctions:

· Coordinating conjunctions (*and, but, or,* and so on) join groups of words together in more or less equal balance.
· Subordinating conjunctions (*after, because, when,* and so on) attach a dependent group of words (clause or phrase) to an independent one.
· Connectors (*therefore, however, nevertheless,* and so on) combine an adverbial with a conjunctive function.
· Prepositions (*under, over, in, out, to, from,* and so on) should also be considered function words. They link their object, a noun, and its modifiers to the rest of the clause or sentence.

Phrases

Prepositional phrases can serve as either adjectives or adverbs, depending on whether they describe a noun:

· The child *with the shovel* . . .
   (noun)   (adj. p.p.)

or a verb:

· . . . played *in the garden.*
   (verb)   (adv. p.p.)

Participial phrases—that is, phrases headed by the *-ing* or the *-ed* forms of the verb—act as adjectives because they describe nouns.

· The ship, *sailing swiftly, managed by its crew* . . .
   (noun)   (adj. phr.)   (adj. phr.)

Infinitive phrases, phrases headed usually by the *to* form of the verb, behave mainly as nouns—where they serve as subjects:

· *To err* is human.

or as complements:

· He learned *to swim.*

Gerund phrases, phrases headed by the *-ing* form of the verb, also serve as nouns. They act as subjects:

· *Playing chess* is lots of fun.

or as objects (here of a prepositional phrase):

· by *swimming competitively.* . . .

Appositive phrases, though they consist of a noun and its modifiers, actually have an adjectival function because they modify another noun and its modifiers:

· The haunted house, *a dilapidated Victorian monstrosity,* . . .
· Professor Offenbach, *my teacher,* . . .

And **adverbial phrases** serve, of course, as adverbs. Adverbial phrases are adverb clauses with their subject and verb removed. You might also think of them as participial phrases headed by an adverbial subordinating conjunction:

· *While sitting by the road* . . .
· *When drenched with rain* . . .

Subordinate Clauses

The three kinds of subordinate clause (adverb, adjective, and noun) are named for the part of speech they function as in a sentence.

Adverb clauses are headed by adverbial subordinating conjunctions (*when, while, since, because, if,* and so on). These clauses mark the sentence for time, place, manner, or frequency—and, in short, they behave like adverbs:

· *When the dance was over,* the band stopped playing.
· The band stopped playing *because the dance was over.*

Adjective clauses are the "who," "which," "that" clauses that describe nouns:

· Sally, *who was dressed in red,* answered the door.
· The clock *that was always late* chimed three times.

Adjective clauses are sometimes called *relative clauses* because the words that introduce them are *relative pronouns.* (These pronouns are *relative* because they relate or connect the clause to the rest of the sentence; they are *pronouns* because, by substituting for the modified noun, they usually serve as the subject of the clause.)

Noun clauses, which are introduced by words like *that, where,* and *what,* act as subjects or objects, the whole clause taking the place of a noun:

· She told me *that she was happy.* (as object of sentence)
· *That she was happy* was all too clear. (as subject of sentence)

· He was afraid of *what he could not understand.* (as object of preposition)
· *Where my love laughs* is *where I want to be.* (as subject and as object of sentence)

TRY IT OUT

The preceding summary gives you a systematic way of approaching syntax, but it is extremely concentrated and intense. Fortunately, there is an exercise for reviewing grammar that is helpful but not at all intense. Most students seem to have a good time working it.

Add-It-On Exercise. Though you can work this exercise alone as you might work a puzzle, most people find it more fun to try it in groups.

The serious purpose of the Add-It-On is to explore the possibilities of the simple sentence and to distinguish it from the compound, complex, and compound-complex varieties. We have already discovered the minimal boundaries of the simple sentence. This exercise will help you push the simple sentence to its maximal contours. In so doing, you will find just how much you can add to a simple sentence before it becomes complex or compound. For the most successful solution to this exercise, follow the directions with as much imagination as you can summon up. The sample solution shows you how one freshman class worked it out.

The Simple Sentence

1. Create a simple sentence in the unadorned subject-verb-subject pattern— the more absurd the subject matter, the better.
   Sample: Armadillos eat Fig Newtons.

2. Add adjective modifiers.
   a. Add at least one adjective.
   Sample: Clumsy armadillos eat *scorched* Fig Newtons.
   b. Add at least one adjectival prepositional phrase.
   Sample: Clumsy armadillos *with growling stomachs* eat scorched Fig Newtons.
   c. Add at least one participial phrase (either past *-ed* or present *-ing*).
   Sample: Clumsy armadillos with growling stomachs eat scorched Fig Newtons *dipped in paste-like catsup.*

3. Add adverbial modifiers.
   a. Add at least one adverb.
   Sample: Clumsy armadillos with growling stomachs *slowly* and *carefully* eat scorched Fig Newtons dipped in paste-like catsup.

b. Add at least one adverbial phrase or adverbial prepositional phrase.

Sample: Clumsy armadillos with growling stomachs slowly and carefully eat scorched Fig Newtons dipped in paste-like catsup *while falling off a cliff.*

(We are still dealing with nothing but a *simple sentence.*)

4. Compound the subject by adding at least one other subject.

Sample: Little lemmings and clumsy armadillos with growling stomachs slowly and carefully eat scorched Fig Newtons dipped in paste-like catsup while falling off a cliff.

5. Compound the object by adding at least one more complement to the verb.

Sample: Little lemmings and clumsy armadillos with growling stomachs slowly and carefully eat *popcorn and* scorched Fig Newtons dipped in paste-like catsup while falling off a cliff.

6. Compound the verb by adding at least one other main verb.

Sample: Little lemmings and clumsy armadillos with growling stomachs slowly and carefully eat popcorn and scorched Fig Newtons dipped in paste-like catsup *and play stud poker* while falling off a cliff.

All this and *the sentence is still a simple sentence!*

The Compound Sentence. How then can you make a compound sentence? Not by adding another subject or another verb, but by adding another *complete* sentence. The two main clauses can be joined by a coordinating conjunction, such as "and" or "but," or by a semicolon.

7. Make a compound sentence by adding another sentence to the first (and thus turning them both into the main clauses in a compound sentence).
    Sample: Little lemmings and clumsy armadillos with growling stomachs slowly and carefully eat popcorn and scorched Fig Newtons dipped in paste-like catsup and play stud poker while falling off a cliff, *but they are silly beasts.*
    (subj.)(verb)   (obj.)

The Complex Sentence. A complex sentence is a sentence that has a main clause and at least one subordinate clause. How do you turn your simple sentence into a complex one? One way is by changing your sentence into a subordinate clause by adding a subordinating conjunction. Amazing as it may seem, the entire concoction of lemmings and armadillos and catsup and poker and cliffs can be turned into a dependent clause—and thus no sentence at all—by adding as little as one word: "*When* little lemmings . . .," "*Until* little lemmings . . .," and so on.

8. *Complex Sentence with Dependent Adverb Clause.* Create a complex sentence by turning your original sentence into an adverb clause and attaching it to a suitable main clause, either before or after.
    Sample: Because little lemmings and clumsy armadillos with growling stomachs slowly and carefully eat popcorn and scorched Fig Newtons dipped in paste-like catsup and play stud poker while falling off a cliff, they are silly beasts.

9. *Complex Sentence with Dependent Noun Clause.* Create a complex sentence by adding a "that" (or similar term) to your original sentence and use it as a noun clause to serve as a verb's subject or object.
    Sample: That little lemmings and clumsy armadillos with growling stomachs slowly and carefully eat popcorn and scorched Fig Newtons dipped in paste-like catsup and play stud poker while falling off a cliff means they are silly beasts.

10. *Complex Sentence with Dependent Adjective Clause.* The whole sentence cannot be turned into an adjective clause, but the original sentence can become complex if we insert an adjective clause. Any adjective—word or phrase—is at base an adjective clause with the relative pronoun and verb

"to be" removed. Restore the pronoun and verb (*is, are, was, were,* or other forms of "to be") and the clause is created. The sentence then automatically becomes complex. Use this technique to turn your original sentence into a complex sentence with an adjective clause.

Sample: Little lemmings and armadillos, *which are clumsy and have growling stomachs,* slowly and carefully eat popcorn and scorched Fig Newtons dipped in paste-like catsup and play stud poker while falling off a cliff.

The Compound-Complex Sentence. The compound-complex sentence is a compound sentence with one or more subordinate clauses.

11. Create a compound-complex sentence, using the material from your original sentence.

Sample: Little lemmings and armadillos, which are clumsy and have growling stomachs, slowly and carefully eat popcorn and scorched Fig Newtons dipped in paste-like catsup and play stud poker while falling off a cliff; they are silly beasts.

For strategies and practice in using adjective, adverb, and noun constructions to vary and enliven your style, don't miss Chapter 8.

EDITING OUT ERRORS OF THE SENTENCE

Readers care about sentences. A capital letter is a signal to them that a sentence is beginning and triggers their expectations for all that conventionally goes on in the English sentence. A period (sometimes a question mark or exclamation point) lets them know that the sentence has come to an end. When their expectations for the sentence are not fulfilled in the usual way, readers often find themselves so puzzled that their minds wander from the writer's ideas and struggle instead with the form.

Now that you have an understanding of the structure of the sentence, you can recognize and edit out the kind of sentence fragments and run-on sentences that distract readers. These errors are ordinarily caused by a lack of knowledge about what actually constitutes a sentence. Often they come from relying on the old, nonfunctional definition that "a sentence is a complete thought," a definition that does not help much in deciding where to put the capital letter and the period. Run-ons occur when a writer mistakes two or more complete sentences for one "complete thought" and punctuates accordingly:

Run-on   · The day was bright the birds sang.

Run-on   · Joe crammed himself into the car, it was bursting already with passengers.

A fragment appears when a writer mistakes a nonsentence (usually a clause or a phrase) for a "complete thought" and punctuates it as a sentence.

Fragment	· Janet decided to accept the position. *Having given the matter serious consideration.*
Fragment	· *Although the fish were biting that day.* Henry gathered up his gear and trudged home. *Which he really had not wanted to do.*

Avoiding Run-on Sentences

Whenever you suspect you might have been treating more than one sentence as if they were only one, test each part by asking yourself: Does it have a subject? Does the subject control the verb? Is nothing added on to keep this subject-predicate combination from standing on its own? Each time you can answer yes to all three questions, you have a complete sentence. You cannot leave two or more of these sentences running together without punctuation, as in the bird example. Nor can you splice them together with commas as in the example about Joe and the car. Without changing any wording, however, you do have three editing options:

1. You can write the two as separate sentences:
   · The day was bright. The birds sang.
   · Joe crammed himself into the car. It was already bursting with passengers.
2. If you feel that the two ideas are so closely related that they should not be wish separated, you can keep them both in one sentence by placing a semicolon between them:
   · The day was bright; the birds sang.
   · Joe crammed himself into the car; it was already bursting with passengers.
3. Or if you would like to divide them only by a comma, you can do so if you add a coordinating conjunction *(and, but, so, for)* to the second sentence (clause):
   · The day was bright, *and* the birds sang.
   · Joe crammed himself into the car, *but* it was already bursting with passengers.

Please note that only coordinating conjunctions will work with a comma in this way. If you want to include a word like "however" or "nevertheless," you will have to select one of the alternative choices:

· The day was bright; *furthermore,* the birds sang.
· Joe crammed himself into the car. *However,* it was already bursting with passengers.

You might also consider a fourth option—subordinating one of the two sentences to the other by turning one into a dependent clause:

- *Because* the day was bright, the birds sang.
- Joe crammed himself into the car *that* was already bursting with passengers.
- Joe crammed himself into the car *although* it was already bursting with passengers.

Avoiding Sentence Fragments

When a group of words lacks a subject or its verb (or both), or when it has a word or two attached that prevents it from standing on its own (*that* birds fly, birds *that* fly, *although* birds fly, *when* birds fly, and so on), it is only a fragment of a sentence. Phrases and dependent clauses are always fragments. As a rule, such fragments should not be punctuated as sentences.

Once you have identified the fragments in your own work, you will usually have little trouble revising them. Ordinarily the fragment will attach quite naturally to the sentence that precedes it or that follows it. Let's look again at the examples beginning this section. The Janet example revises easily:

- Janet decided to accept the position, having given the matter serious consideration.

The first part of the Henry example is also easily edited:

- Although the fish were biting that day, Henry gathered up his gear and trudged home.

The second error in the Henry example, however, is typical of fragments that need rewording—here, changing into a sentence to stand on its own:

Faulty
- Henry gathered up his gear and trudged home. *Which he had not really wanted to do.*

Revised
- Henry gathered up his gear and trudged home. He had not really wanted to leave that early.

Unintentional fragments can mar your work. Nevertheless, you will find that fragments do sometimes have a place in serious writing. Occasionally, an experienced author will deliberately use one for emphasis, as Thomas does in the first example below, or to provide an informal tone, as Slack does in the second:

I cannot think that way anymore. *Not while those things are still in place.* (page 429, paragraph 4)

When grades still failed to rise, the scientists felt there might be some truth in what the young team members were saying. *Not that teachers were to blame, necessarily.* (page 425, paragraph 5)

Making Subjects and Verbs Agree

A third sentence error that jars many readers almost as much as fragments and run-ons occurs in the sentence or clause whose subject and verb do not agree in number. Singular subjects take singular verbs and plural subjects take plural verbs:

· When our cat is outside, the birds have to be careful.
  (singular)   (plural)

Notice the curious fact that although singular nouns have no -*s* endings, their appropriate present-tense verbs do; and while plural nouns end in -*s*, plural verbs in the present tense do not. Make sure that you have only one -*s* word to a pair and you can be confident that you're right.

Unless the dialect you speak is not the standard, you should have little trouble with subject–verb agreement in most sentences. However, when prepositional phrases complete the subject, as they often do, the nouns in those phrases may cause confusion. It helps to remember that the subject of a sentence cannot be in a prepositional phrase. When in doubt, mentally cross out all prepositional phrases and concentrate on the words that remain to find the subject that will give you the proper form for your verb:

· If the *house* in the woods *is* still standing,
       (singular)

· the *boys* from the scout troop *plan* to spend the night there.
      (plural)

Compound subjects, pronoun subjects, and single subjects that end in -*s* also can cause you problems when you must decide whether a verb should be singular or plural. For a list of rules governing these situations, check the Revision Guide entry "Agreement: Subject and Verb."

TRY IT OUT

Revise the following student paragraph. Eliminate sentence errors, but also edit out awkwardness stemming from some of the problems discussed in

Chapter 6: vague reference, overuse of the passive, and inconsistent verb tenses.

```
              The Legacy of Huey Long
The effect had by Huey Long on the state of Louisiana. It is
tremendous, his works can be seen even more fully now than
then. Hospitals, roadways, and social services for all is
Long's doing. Agriculture and Education also benefited.
Those people who don't know Long's name and haven't heard
of him before. They will probably wonder why the names of
the Long family so often graces buildings and bridges and
roads. Long channeled money from the biggest industries
in Louisiana back to the people it came from. He did this
through corporate taxes and high leasing rights. He
forced the building of roads, which he did by building
main roads with no access roads. Long was remembered as
the governor allowing free textbooks to school children,
he will never be forgotten by delta farmers. Because Long
revamped Louisiana's water control system. Long may have
been corrupt. But the good sides of his tenure as governor
is the many improvements he caused the making of in the
state.
```

Fixing Faulty Parallelism

Faulty parallelism is another error bothersome to readers. And when you edit it out of your work by making the discordant elements parallel, you gain a stylistic dividend. Successful parallelism adds sparkle to your style, as Chapter 8 explains.

The following are examples of the sort of mistakes in parallelism that can creep into a writer's work:

1. Among Peter's ambitions were a good job, to do well in college, and learning to fly a plane.
2. The tourists were unsure whether to unpack and settle in their hotel or if they should go out and see the sights of the town.
3. Brent's uneasiness was due to his being late and because he had forgotten the speaker's name.
4. Decide upon a goal that is reachable with a clear direction and purpose and which offers real satisfaction.
5. The politician's tour included munching on such ethnic delights as pizza and bagels and spanokepeta and some adorable Sicilian-American babies whom he kissed.

Fortunately, you can turn such faulty parallelisms into successful ones. Your key to this sort of editing is your understanding of the syntactic components of the sentence. All the items in a parallel series or balance must be syntactically equivalent; that is, adjective clauses must parallel other adjective clauses, prepositional phrases, other prepositional phrases, and so on. Let's look, for instance at sample 1 again. This nonparallel series contains a modified common noun ("a good job"), an infinitive phrase ("to do well in college") and an *-ing* participle phrase ("learning to fly a plane"). To correct this sentence, you need to make all parts of the series truly parallel by choosing one of the three syntactic forms and changing the other two to match. Try it yourself, then check your editing of this example and the others with the following suggested solutions.

1. Among Peter's ambitions were to get a good job, to do well in college, and to learn to fly a plane.
   or
   Among Peter's ambitions were getting a good job, doing well in college, and learning to fly a plane.
2. The tourists were unsure whether to unpack and settle in their hotel or to go out and see the sights of the town.
3. Brent's uneasiness was due to his being late and to his having forgotten the speaker's name.
4. Decide upon a goal that is reachable, that has a clear direction and purpose, and that offers real satisfaction.
5. The politician's tour included munching on such ethnic delights as pizza, bagels, and spanokepeta, and kissing some adorable Sicilian-American babies.

If you are interested in using parallelism to brighten your style, be sure to look at pages 247–257.

TRY IT OUT

Revising Parallelism. Correct the errors in the following sentences by turning faulty parallelism into the genuine article.

1. Having had a good night's sleep, our hotel manager was especially pleasant and the food was delicious.

2. Angela liked black-eyed Susans, ambling in the meadows, and to pick buttercups.

3. Simon P. Pettifog, a sleazy lawyer, was disbarred and charming.

4. I long to return to the cry of the loon, waking with the sun, and where the waves beat against the shore.

5. Vladimir Ilich Ulyanov had quietly practiced law in St. Petersburg, is an accomplished hunter, was reading revolutionary authors, and would become the man known as Nicolai Lenin.

6. The Village Inn Hotel was dingy, the rooms were dark and in disrepair, and they cheated on their bill.

7. In the morning she was happy, in the springtime, she was delighted, and she always enjoyed being in Poughkeepsie.

8. The fine restaurant served tournedos, escargots, and the waitress was nice.

EDITING FOR CORRECT CAPITALIZATION AND PUNCTUATION

Readers suffer from both too little and too much capitalization and punctuation. Their reading is, of course, disturbed when they don't find a capital letter or a punctuation mark where they expect to see one—say, no capital beginning a proper name or no comma after a *however* or a *nevertheless*. But their reading is even more severely disrupted when they find capitals, commas, and such where they should not be. When they discover such symbols randomly punctuating the text, they often cannot follow the flow of ideas. So the first rule of editing for capitals and marks of punctuation is:

When really in doubt, leave them out.

You will find more specific guidance in the following paragraphs.

Capital Letters

Always begin each sentence with a capital letter. Always capitalize "I" when you are referring to yourself. And always use a capital for the initial letter of a proper name. (If you have any doubt as to what is a proper name, look in the Revision Guide under "Capitalization.") You will rarely need to use capital letters outside of these occasions. Do not use them for emphasis. If you are among those writers who absent-mindedly begin many of their words with capital letters, take care to edit these random capitals out of your final drafts.

Commas

Some writers also scatter commas about. Readers find unnecessary commas especially intrusive, for a comma interrupts the flow of the text. A single purposeless comma placed between a subject and its verb or a verb and its object can make a sentence almost incomprehensible:

Faulty · She and her friends, knew that he would come.
Faulty · She and her friends knew, that he would come.

Edit out any commas that intrude in this way.

THE OVERALL, UMBRELLA, NEVER-FAIL COMMA RULE

On the other hand, a pair of commas ensures that interrupting material (parenthetical remarks, interjections, transitional words and phrases, appositives, nonessential relative clauses, participial and other explanatory phrases) are separated off. Commas keep such interruptions from interfering with the reader's understanding of the central subject-verb-object flow in the sentence. Thus, the overall rule to remember is:

Surround nonessential sentence interrupters with commas.

How can you recognize this material? If you can pick it up by its commas and remove it from the sentence, and the sentence continues to make good sense, you can be sure that you have a genuine interrupter.

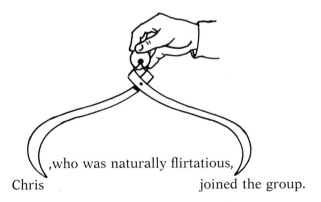

Chris ,who was naturally flirtatious, joined the group.

When you edit your work, make sure that all such material you use in midsentence is marked off *on both sides* by commas. When such material occurs at the beginning or the end of a sentence (or of an independent clause), you will, of course, need to use only one comma. The examples in the accompanying boxed section can serve as models.

Using Commas to Set Off Interrupting Material

- Even the civilization of Sumer, *the birthplace of written language,* declined and vanished.
- *Nevertheless,* artifacts of this civilization, having survived the centuries, can still be found in museums.
- The Oriental Museum at the University of Chicago, *for example,* has an impressive collection; *unfortunately,* it is little known.
- May the class take a field trip to Chicago, *Professor Marx?*
- Professor Marx, *who had long believed in the benefits of field trips,* booked reservations for his group on the first bus heading for Chicago.[4]

If you use adverbial clauses on phrases at the beginning of a sentence—rather than at the end, where their function of modifying the verb is regarded as "natural"—you can consider them also as interrupters and thus conclude them with a comma, as the accompanying boxed section explains and exemplifies.

Using Commas to Set Off Adverbial Introductory Material

- *When you begin a sentence with an adverb clause,* add a comma before you begin the main clause.
- You need not use a comma *when the adverb clause concludes your sentence.*
- *In the case of a number of prepositional phrases at the beginning of your sentence,* you have the option of clarifying with a comma.

OTHER COMMA USES

Commas are also used to mark the divisions in dates and addresses and to separate the words or phrases in a series. (The final comma before the "and" in a series is optional.) The models in the accompanying boxed section should be helpful as you edit.

---

[4]The interesting distinction between nonessential relative clauses, such as this one, which require commas because the enclosed material is semiparenthetical, and essential relative clauses, which do not, is discussed in detail on pages 218–219.

Using Commas in Series, Addresses, and Dates

- *On Sunday evening⊙April 10⊙1983⊙a soccer match was held on the beach at Santa Barbara, California.*
- *Joe⊙John⊙and Ellen all went to the match.*
- *Having sunned themselves on the beach⊙having splashed in the waves⊙having consumed an excellent supper⊙and even having watched a little of the match⊙they pedaled home.*

You will find more detailed discussion about using the comma in the Revision Guide under "Comma."

Semicolons

The semicolon, which consists of a period on top of a comma (;), is related to both marks. It signals a strong interruption—somewhat less strong than that of the period, but much more than that of the comma. Because its purpose is to interrupt the text so definitely, misplaced semicolons are particularly distracting to readers. The examples in the boxed section model their appropriate use.

Using Semicolons to Separate and to Tie Together

- The semicolon is like the period⊙its function is to separate independent clauses (sentences) from each other.
- But unlike the period, the semicolon also unites⊙it ties independent clauses together in a compound sentence without the need for conjunctions like *and* or *but.*
- The semicolon also acts as a stronger comma, dividing the sentence in a masterly way when commas are already present⊙and thus it is appropriate, if you have employed commas within the segments, to use semicolons to substitute both for the commas that divide items in a series and the commas that join with *and* or *but* to divide independent clauses in compound sentences.

Further Examples
- The moon rose⊙the stars came out; a coyote howled.
- The desert seemed empty⊙nevertheless, danger lurked everywhere.
- Some children enjoy cantaloupe, of course⊙but you can't really go wrong with ice cream for a kiddie party.

The purposes exemplified in these guidelines are the only ones for which the semicolon should be used. To keep from distracting your readers, make sure in editing that all the semicolons in your paper are used only in these ways.

Colons, Dashes, and Parentheses

This discussion of editing and punctuation we have emphasized eliminating excess. Some marks of punctuation, though useful in their way, seem to have a special tendency to be overused by inexperienced writers. The exclamation point (!), for instance, has little place in expository essays. Ellipses (. . .), too, while essential for indicating omissions in quoted material (see Chapter 10), have no other use in expository prose. You may find, however, that dashes, parentheses, and colons, though equally subject to overly enthusiastic use, can be helpful in your serious writing—providing you do not rely on them too heavily.

These three kinds of punctuation have some overlapping functions. Sometimes, then, you will have to choose among them. Here your sense of style must be your chief guide. To give you a sense of how professional authors make these decisions, all the examples in this section are from the professional work in Part Four.

Using Colons, Dashes, and Parentheses to Add or Explain

Colons signify "namely," "to wit," "that is," or "let me explain."
· The food we live on is kids' food: pizza, hot dogs, fried chicken, ice cream, hamburgers. (Alexander, page 411, paragraph 4)

Dashes (typed as two hyphens) can be used as an informal colon. They can also be used, like the comma, to include incidental information. Dashes enclose digressions:
· By September [the Cubs] had set a mark for ineptness at which others—but not next year's Cubs—would shoot in vain. (Will, page 439, paragraph 6)

And they add emphasis or change the direction of a sentence or both:
· This week many will be reminded that no explosion of atoms generates so hopeful a light as the reflection of a star, seen appreciatively in a pasture pond. It is there we perceive Christmas—and the sheep quiet, and the world waiting. (White, page 437, paragraph 4)

Parentheses, which are ordinarily more formal than dashes, are used to include scholarly apparatus or comment on a text.
· Smalley . . . who in his best year (1953) hit .249. (Will, page 439, paragraph 10)

But, like dashes and commas, they are also used to enclose incidental information and digressions.
· Conservatives (and Cub fans) know better. (Will, page 438, paragraph 2)

Effective though occasional use of this sort can be, relying too extensively on dashes and parentheses will give your paper an informality of tone that can border on the haphazard. Furthermore, too-frequent asides and digressions can seriously interfere with the flow of your ideas. Each time you come to one of these constructions as you edit your work, ask yourself: Would this information or digression be more effective if it were removed from the dashes or parentheses that enclose it and presented in a more straightforward way? If the answer is yes, make the appropriate changes.

TRY IT OUT

1. Edit the following student's paragraph, paying particular attention to your use of capital letters and commas.

College

Last fall, when I went to College I did not know, what to expect, from the New Life, I was entering in. Was it going to be all reading Books, studying French, and writing Papers, or was it going to be just one big Party, with Beer, raucous Dormitory Life, and friendly meetings, with Members of the Opposite Sex? As it turns out College Life has been, a combination of these. Sure I have to Study, a lot; especially my Capitalization and Punctuation but I have Time for fun too. Just last week, a Paper I had written on, Arthur Miller's <u>Death of A Salesman,</u> got ruined in a Water Fight. This proves I suppose, that one cannot mix, Business with Pleasure.

2. The student who wrote this next paragraph relied totally on the comma to punctuate his work. Some of the commas are appropriate, but others might better be exchanged for semicolons, colons, periods, dashes, or parentheses. Edit the paragraph, giving special emphasis to punctuation.

A "Mute, Inglorious Milton"

Many people think it's easy to write a novel, God knows I've tried to enough times, but it is, in fact, hard work, a rough estimate would be that only one-tenth of all people who start a novel finish it, and a smaller percentage yet, of which I am not unhappily a member, actually get published. Face it, most of us just aren't destined to be Great Authors, like Great Authors past, Fielding, Jane Austen, Hawthorne, Hemingway, but oh, what would I give,

```
and I would give a lot, I assure you, for just a little of
the fame, the glamour, the glitter, that attends even a
lesser author, a Horatio Alger, an Agatha Christie, a
Ford Madox Ford, but no, no, my pen is likely, fated, you
might say, to achieve no greatness other than winning at
tic-tac-toe.
```

Quotation Marks

Quotation marks also distress readers both in their absence and in their excess. Let's talk first about where readers expect to find them.

Primarily, readers expect quotation marks to designate quoted matter. Be certain, therefore, when you edit that every quotation of fewer than three lines—even it it is only a word or two—is surrounded by quotation marks. (For detailed advice on handling quoted material, see pages 332–333.) Quotation marks should also enclose titles of poems, songs, short stories, essays, and other writing not separately published, for example: Carll Tucker's essay, "On Splitting."

And because readers are almost equally distracted by extraneous quotation marks, make sure in your editing that you do *not* have them in the following situations:

1. No quotation marks around the title of your own essay unless the title you have chosen is itself a quotation.
2. No marks around quotations of three lines or longer that you have indented and quoted in block form. The indentation and the block form itself indicate quoted material.
3. Nor should you use quotation marks around the title of a book or other separately published work; underline these instead, as for instance: Treasure Island or Hamlet.
4. And it is not a good idea to surround with quotation marks words or phrases you are a little uncomfortable using, as for example, in the FAULTY: I think kittens are so "cute." Eliminate all such quotation marks as you edit. If you don't feel right about using the word or phrase without them, then you should probably choose another word or phrase.

TRY IT OUT

Edit the following paragraph, paying particular attention to the correct use of quotation marks.

Faulty

"My Favorite Poem"

I am not exactly proud of what I am going to "confide" to you. You see, my very favorite poem is certainly not "fashionable," and I am not even sure it is very "good." It is called <u>The Barefoot Boy</u>, and you can find it in an anthology, "The Poems of John Greenleaf Whittier." The reason I'm so fond of The Barefoot Boy is "sentimental." When I was a tiny tot, my father taught it to me and had me recite it at all family occasions. He would say, Come and recite your poem. And I would start at the beginning and just go on and on:

"Blessings on thee little man,
"Barefoot boy with cheek of tan;
"With your turned up pantaloons,
"And your merry whistle tunes,
"With your redlips redder still,
"Kissed by strawberries on the hill. . . ."

It may not be "especially good" poetry, but to this day, I still choke up when I hear: From my heart I give thee joy: / I was once a barefoot boy.

EDITING FOR CORRECT SPELLING

Misspellings, especially multiple misspellings, are also likely to distract your readers. Unfortunately, English is a notoriously difficult language to spell. "Sounding it out" does not always work with English because there are many discrepancies between sound and spelling. Most such problems stem from the tendency of English speakers over the centuries to simplify its sounds. For example, in the days when there really were knights in armor, "knight" was pronounced "ka-ni-ckt." Today, the spelling still reflects the medieval sound, even though the modern pronunciation no longer offers a key to it. Furthermore, as time has passed, all unstressed vowels in English words have tended to draw toward the single sound "uh." Though no doubt the following examples of unstressed vowels were once clearly distinguishable in speech, now they are all pronounced "uh":

· oct**a**gon fun**e**ral intell**i**gent oct**o**pus unpleas**a**nt plat**y**pus

These examples are typical. Thus, when you are faced with spelling the "uh" sound in a word that you do not have fixed in your visual memory, you have little ground upon which to base an intelligent guess.

English also owes much of its confusing spelling to the source of its amazing richness, the numerous words it has borrowed from foreign languages. A line from comedian Shelley Berman's skit "Franz Kafka on the

Telephone," demonstrates the confusion brought to English spelling by these foreign sound systems. In this line, Berman attempts to identify the letters that spell *pokerface:*

· POKERFACE. P as in *Psychosis.* O as in *Oedipus.* K as in *Knicknack.* E as in *Euphemism.* . . .

Despite the difficulties caused by an evolving language, correct spelling remains important to the success of your written work. To keep your writing free from spelling errors, it is best to be a reader with a natural eye and memory for the formation of words. Failing that, second best is to be conscious that you are not a naturally good speller and be willing to work on it. Some of my students have improved their spelling impressively through the following routine.

1. Learn the rules. Despite the irregularities of the English language, there are a number of spelling rules (listed under "Spelling" in the Revision Guide) that can help you eliminate unsureness on hundreds of English words.
2. Have a friend test you on the list of commonly misspelled words in the Revision Guide. Memorize the spelling of the ones you miss, for these are words that you use (and perhaps misspell) frequently.
3. As for the words you use infrequently, accept your lack of a speller's eye and check out every word you are not as sure of as you are, for instance, of C-A-T. When editing your final draft, circle all the words whose spelling you are not certain of, look them up, and correct where necessary.

Editing for Correctness

Only the errors that are most distracting to readers have been singled out for discussion in this chapter. They are, of course, only a fraction of potential errors. Because errors are so individual, the problems discussed here may not be yours. In editing for correctness, the most helpful thing you can do is to become aware of your *own* areas of weakness. Then you can train your editing eye to focus on those writing situations where you are likely to run into difficulty. If you find any points where you are uncertain, turn to the Revision Guide for clarification. The alphabetically arranged entries provide concise explanations and practical advice for successful editing.

PROOFREADING YOUR ESSAY

You have come to the final stage of the writing process. You have prewritten, written, and rewritten. You have revised your paper for structure, for persuasiveness, for correctness and style. You have given yourself time away from your paper, have read it again, and have, perhaps, revised yet again the draft that was to be final. You have typed your final copy (or, if

Revising for Correctness: A Summary Checklist

Key: Look up the correct form whenever you are unsure.

To Correct Errors of the Sentence

1. Edit run-on sentences.
2. Revise unnecessary or inappropriate sentence fragments.
3. Check for subject-verb agreement; be particularly careful of subjects that include prepositional phrases.
4. Make sure that all the elements in parallel series are the same syntactically.

To Correct Faulty Capitalization and Punctuation

1. Check for initial capitals and final periods.
2. Make sure every proper name is capitalized.
3. Edit out absent-minded capitals and those meant only for emphasis.
4. Edit out commas that interrupt the flow of the text.
5. Make sure interrupting material is set off by a *pair* of commas.
6. Add a comma after introductory subordinate clauses or other lengthy introductory material.
7. Check for needed commas in series, in addresses, and in dates.
8. Be sure to use a semicolon to separate the independent clauses in a compound sentence where there is no linking *and* or *but* or where either clause contains commas.
9. To keep the structure clear, use semicolons to divide a series where the components contain internal commas.
10. Use colons, parentheses, or dashes to make your meaning clear; but check to be sure you are not overusing them.
11. Make sure that every bit of quoted material is enclosed in quotation marks.
12. Edit out unnecessary quotation marks.

To Correct Spelling Errors

1. In this area of revision, it's best to know your weakness. When in doubt, look it up.
2. Learning spelling rules may help. Check under "Spelling" in the Revision Guide.

---

acceptable, hand copied it neatly and legibly). But you are *not yet* finished. You still need to proofread your manuscript.

Human beings make mistakes. And the chances that your paper contains no errors at all are almost nil—as careful as you have tried to be. The few minutes that you spend on proofreading may be the most valuable of the whole writing process. They may prove the difference between one evaluative grade and the grade above, between getting the job interview or not getting it, between getting the article published or not. The more time and effort you have already spent on your work, the less you can afford to neglect to proofread.

How to Proofread

Proofreading is slower and more concentrated than your usual reading. Do it aloud if you can. In any case, read your paper word by word. Concentrate on the text itself rather than the content. Keep your mind open for all errors, but watch especially for those in the following list, because they are the most common.

Proofread for:	Examples
1. added letters	intelligente
2. reversed letters or words	intelilgent The uproar has stopped not.
3. omitted letters or words	inteligent The uproar not stopped.
4. omitted or misplaced lines, passages, or paragraphs	
5. repeated letters or words	intellligent The uproar has has not stopped.
6. repeated lines, passages, or paragraphs	
7. the items on the Revising for Correctness Checklist (page 211). Be particularly watchful for errors in punctuation and spelling.	

Whenever you spot such an error, lightly pencil a dot in the nearest margin. Mark any questions you may still have about spelling or punctuation in the same way, and follow up with the Revision Guide or a dictionary.

How to Correct

If you are working with a word processor, your final corrections are easily made. Transfer the corrections from your hard copy to the machine and rerun whatever pages are necessary.

If your paper is typed or handwritten, you will probably not need to recopy. Unless you have discovered a large omission or misplacement, simply "white out" the error and correct. If such a procedure is not available to you, add careful hand corrections. The following copy-editing markings are standard and should be acceptable for small flaws:

- intelligente
- intellilgent
- inteligent
- intelligent
- The uproar has stopped not.
- The uproar not stopped.
- The uproar has has not stopped.

After you have made your corrections, proofread the corrected portions one more time, particularly if any pages needed recopying. And your paper is really finished!

TRY IT OUT

Carefully proofread the following paragraph. Then, working from a photocopy, correct it by hand, using the appropriate copy-editing markings. (If this were not an exercise, you would have to copy it over, of course.)

Snake charmers

indian snake charmers make thier living charming snakes out of their baskets and coins out the of pockets the of on-lookers. Charmers, who like to be called "snakers are trianed from childhood in the arts of snak catching Snake charming, and snake Showmrnship. They have passed down these art throughgh the snakker castes for thousands of yearss. egyptain pyramide texts pf about 2350 bce mentoin Serpent Charming? And buddhist writing pf about 2350 bce mentoin Serpent Charming? And buddhist writings indicate that charming was an establiched profesion by 300 B.C.E. Although a long time has passed; a long time has past, the technique has chagned ittle. The snkers play musci on they"re fluts and the rise up, swaying and bearing there fangs the tourists is impresed and pay well too see the show.

ASSIGNMENT

Choose one of the following and write an effective essay. When your paper has been written and revised, be sure to edit and proofread it carefully.

1. In a letter to the editor of your college newspaper, your city or home-town newspaper, or the editor of a national magazine or journal, comment on a recent item in that publication, or support or take issue with an opinion expressed there.[5]

2. The following pairs of contradictory words of wisdom show that even the wise can differ over values. Choose the pair that comments upon the values you wish to explore and write a well-organized, rhetorically effective expository essay supporting one of the suggested positions. Do not simply try to illustrate the proverb or quotation you select, but discuss the issue, analyze the values in question, and develop concrete evidence to support your position.
   a. Look before you leap.
      He who hesitates is lost.
   b. It matters "not that you won or lost, but how you played the game." (Grantland Rice)
      Winning isn't everything—it's the only thing. (Vince Lombardi)[6]
   c. War alone brings up to its highest tension all human energy and puts the stamp of nobility upon the peoples who have the courage to face it. (Benito Mussolini)
      War is hell. (William Tecumseh Sherman)
   d. Absence makes the heart grow fonder.
      Out of sight; out of mind.

3. This next topic also asks you to examines values, but in a more personal way: Write an essay in which you explore the extent to which you accept the religious, political, and/or moral views of your family, teachers, or preachers, and the extent you differ from them. Develop a well-defined, limited thesis and be very specific in supporting your position.[7]

4. Write an essay about the Great Depression of the 1930s based upon interviews with people who lived through that time. Organize your descriptions and impressions around a well-defined thesis.[8]

[5]I would be most interested in hearing about the letters that the newspapers and magazines accept for publication.

[6]You might also want to consider Leo Durocher's idea that "Nice guys finish last." (An addition by Michael Neuman of Capitol University.)

[7]Topic suggested by Professor D. W. Baker of Wabash College.

[8]Suggested by Professor Sheila Gullickson of Moorehead State University.

Chapter 8

Making Decisions About Sentences

Much of the persuasive power of writing comes from style. And although I would discourage your thinking much about style while writing your first draft, stylistic considerations should be an important part of your revising process.

Yet it is difficult to concentrate on style alone because it can never be totally distinguished from content, the expression from the expressed. But by looking closely at the *form* of the language used, we can nevertheless isolate style—at least in a particular passage—for separate consideration and study. If we can keep the content of two passages relatively constant, whatever differences we find must be attributable to style. Say, for example, you wanted to suggest that a girl you were writing about had negative feelings about leaving a place. Among many possible ways of expressing this thought you might choose to write either:

· The girl was reluctant to leave.

  or

· She just didn't want to go nohow.

The content of the statements—the girl and her feelings—remains the same in both sentences. But the styles of the two statements—the way the girl is observed and reported and, consequently, the way she will be perceived by the reader—are entirely different. The style of neither sentence accounts for the sentence's meaning, but the difference in the styles of the two sentences does account for the differences in meanings and the differing effects of the two sentences upon the reader.

Style and Sentence Combining. Viewed in this way, style can be considered a matter of the writer's choice—basically a choice of words (diction) and of sentence structure (syntax). Improving your writing style, then, becomes a matter of learning to make these choices wisely. The exercises in Chapter 9 will give you an opportunity to practice dictional choices. Sentence-combining exercises can serve as a laboratory for experiments in syntactical choice. As you have discovered, these exercises separate form from content. The exercises provide the content; your choices provide the style.

The review of grammar in Chapter 7 should have given you an overview of the breadth of your syntactical choices. Let's begin with the important adjectival options.

CHOOSING ADJECTIVE CLAUSES AND PHRASES

The adjectival function consists of modifying, describing, and developing the nouns that serve as the subjects and objects of sentences—and of clauses and phrases. The adjectival function is not only important but also allows varied approaches to expression—though this fact is not generally known to inexperienced writers. Such writers tend to restrict their adjectival modifiers to two positions, either using them as adjective complements:

- The baritone is *plump.*
- The baritone is *lusty.*

or sandwiching them between the article and its noun:

- The *plump* baritone
- The *lusty* baritone

Participial adj.   · The *singing* baritone
Participial adj.   · The *red-bearded* baritone

Both these uses can be effective, but the adjectival option is by no means limited to these two. Two other positions for adjective placement are equally appropriate though less frequently employed. These positions are directly before or directly following the noun and its article:

- *Plump and lusty,* the baritone . . .
- The baritone, *plump and lusty,* . . .

Yet another way of describing the baritone would be to do so through the use of an adjective clause:

- The baritone, *who is plump and red-bearded,* . . .
- The baritone, *who was singing happily,* . . .
- The baritone, *who was a lusty singer,* . . .

Or you might prefer to employ a prepositional phrase:

· The baritone, *in his red beard,* . . .
· *With his lusty singing voice,* the baritone . . .

Another alternative is to use an appositive, a descriptive phrase that stands as an equivalent to the noun described:

· The baritone, *a lusty singer,* . . .
· *A plump and red-bearded man,* the baritone . . .

The appositive is an interesting mix: it is nounlike in form and adjectival in function.

One of the most useful of all adjectival modifiers is the participial phrase, a phrase denoting the *-ing* or *-ed* form of a verb and used adjectivally immediately before or immediately after the word described:

· *Singing lustily,* the baritone . . .
· The baritone, *singing lustily,* . . .
· *Red-bearded and bronzed by the sun,* the baritone [sang lustily].
· [Yesterday we caught a glimpse of] the baritone, *red-bearded and bronzed by the sun.*

In the exercises later in the chapter, you will have the opportunity to experiment with all these options. And you can discover which constructions you feel are most appropriate to particular contexts. But first, let's examine these adjectival possibilities more closely.

Choosing Adjective Clauses

The purpose of the adjective clause is to add descriptive or explanatory information about a person, place, animal, or object in a way that subordinates this information to that in the rest of the sentence or clause. According to sentence-combining theory, such sentences are created from two kernel sentences about the same person, place, animal, or object by embedding the sentence to be subordinated in the other one and by linking them together with a relative pronoun (*who, which, that, whose,* or *whom*). Let's take, for example, these two sentences[1] about Theodore Roosevelt:

A. Theodore Roosevelt had been a colonel in the Puerto Rican campaign of the Spanish-American War.
B. Theodore Roosevelt became one of our most colorful presidents.

Depending on which aspect of Roosevelt's career you prefer for your focus, you could turn either sentence A or sentence B into a relative clause and

---

[1]To simplify matters, I will sometimes use extended kernels (as in A and B) for examples and exercises.

embed it in the other. If you wanted to emphasize Roosevelt the soldier, you would subordinate sentence B:

· Theodore Roosevelt, *who became one of our most colorful presidents,* had been a colonel in the Puerto Rican campaign of the Spanish-American War.

But if you wanted to focus on Roosevelt the president, you would subordinate sentence A:

· Theodore Roosevelt, *who had been a colonel in the Puerto Rican campaign of the Spanish-American War,* became one of our most colorful presidents.

You may be wondering what point there is in forming adjective clauses. After all, both sentences A and B are pretty good sentences on their own, and they seem to be typical of their kind. Actually, this construction offers a number of advantages:

1. It links related ideas more closely together and reveals that relationship.
2. It helps to structure the ideas in a paragraph by subordinating one to another.
3. It tightens the writing by combining two related sentences, and by eliminating duplication of the modified word or phrase, it helps to avoid nonpurposeful repetition.
4. It varies the sentence structure within a paragraph and enhances the rhythms of the paragraph. Often it provides a pause within the structure of the sentence and thus also offers variation in the rhythm of the sentence.

Although you would not wish to put an adjective clause in every sentence, it is a useful construction to have in your repertoire.

PUNCTUATING ADJECTIVE CLAUSES

Using adjective clauses involves judgment about appropriate punctuation. Sometimes they should be enclosed in commas and sometimes they should not be. Take, for example, this pair of sentences:

Faulty

A. Little boys who have bubble gum on their faces are in need of a bath.
B. Little boys, who have bubble gum on their faces, are in need of a bath.

Since pairs of commas indicate parenthetical or interrupting material not essential to the main meaning of the sentence, sentence B makes two unintended implications: (1) *all* little boys have bubble gum on their faces and (2) *all* little boys need a bath. Despite the possibility that these implications carry some degree of truth, they are clearly *not* what the author has in mind. The author obviously intends to limit those little boys in need of a bath to the ones who have bubble gum on their faces and thus should omit the commas.

To determine whether to use commas with an adjective clause, you need to decide whether the matter in the clause is necessary to the noun described or whether it is parenthetical or "extra." If it is "extra," then add the "extra" commas. A helpful hint: You always need commas when the clause describes a proper noun ("O'Hare Airport, which is the world's busiest"), and you never need them when you choose *that* for your relative pronoun.

SELECTING THE APPROPRIATE RELATIVE PRONOUN

Writers sometimes also find themselves confused about which pronoun they should use to introduce adjective clauses. There are a number of possibilities—*who, whom, whose, which,* and *that*—and they are similar to one another. But though the confusion is understandable, it need not be troublesome. Let us look, for example, at the following sentence, which contains several relative clauses:

> · On October 3, a hunter, *who had a habit of carelessly fingering the trigger of his gun,* just missed murdering one of Farmer MacGregor's cows *that happened to be ambling by,* almost demolished the patchwork quilt *which was hanging on Mrs. MacGregor's clothesline,* and actually hit two of the MacGregor piglets, *whose pathetic oinking could be heard for miles.*

Did you notice the particular pronoun that introduced each of the clauses?

> · "the hunter *who*" (*Who* refers to a person.)
> · "the cow *that*" (*That,* which can refer to either person or thing, is particularly appropriate here for an animal.)
> · "the patchwork quilt *which*" (*Which* always refers to an object.)
> · "piglets *whose* pathetic oinking" (*Whose* is the possessive pronoun. It stands in for nouns that take an apostrophe as "piglets" would here: "piglets' oinking," "the oinking of the piglets.")

The other relative pronoun, *whom,* the object form of *who,* is seldom used now. More and more it is being replaced by *that* in such constructions as "the partner *that* she chose" (instead of "the partner *whom* she chose"). Except for very formal usage, such prepositional constructions as "the person *to whom* he spoke" are being replaced by the now mostly acceptable "the person he spoke to."

One more point on this subject: *That* is usually preferred to *which* when the material introduced is not extra and doesn't require commas:

> · The home *that* I knew so well. . . .

is better than

> · The home *which* I knew so well. . . .

In fact, some good writers find *which* awkward and try to avoid using it too frequently.

TRY IT OUT

A. Combining Kernels. Combine each set of the following kernel sentences into a single sentence using at least one adjective clause.

Sample problem:
- The earthquake set the dishes rattling in the cupboard and the chandelier swinging from the ceiling.
- The earthquake registered 6 on the Richter scale.

Some sample solutions:
- The earthquake, *which registered 6 on the Richter scale,* set the dishes rattling in the cupboard and the chandelier swinging from the ceiling.
- The earthquake, *which set the dishes rattling in the cupboard and the chandelier swinging from the ceiling,* registered 6 on the Richter scale.

1. Babe Ruth hit sixty home runs in 1927.
   Babe Ruth started his baseball career as a pitcher.
2. I watched a man suspiciously all day.
   The man with beady eyes turned out to be the president of a major corporation.
3. Some aspirin is packaged under an advertised brand name.
   Some aspirin costs twice as much as other aspirin.
   Some aspirin is simply labeled "aspirin."
4. Some babies' limbs were deformed by thalidomide.
   Many of these babies have grown up to lead useful and productive lives.
5. Ludwig van Beethoven was completely deaf for a substantial part of his mature life.
   Ludwig van Beethoven wrote some of the most glorious music the world has ever known.

B. Compose Your Own. Compose your own sentences by adding at least one adjective clause to each of the following sentences. Be as creative and imaginative as you can.

Sample problem:
- The famous detective put down his pipe and concentrated on the evidence.

Some sample solutions:
- The famous detective, *whose exploits had been faithfully recorded by his friend, Dr. Watson,* put down his pipe and concentrated on the evidence.
- The famous detective put down his pipe and concentrated on the evidence *that was laid out upon the table before him.*

1. Tom never finds enough time to do his laundry.
2. The defendant pleaded not guilty to all the charges.
3. Carlos clutched his foot in pain.

4. Adam Smith can be considered the first capitalist.

5. As he was trained to do, the gorilla practiced daily on his symbol typewriter.

Reducing Adjective Clauses

Adjective clauses are, as we have seen, highly useful. On the other hand, at times they can be wordy and cumbersome, even awkward. To achieve economy of language, an appealing leanness in your prose, you may sometimes want to reduce an adjective clause to a briefer—and perhaps stronger—adjectival construction. Wherever the adjective clause uses the verb "to be" *(is, are, was, were),* you can reduce it to such a structure by eliminating the relative pronoun and the verb: For example,

- Sherlock Holmes put down his pipe, *which was* a blackened veteran of many investigations.

can become

- Sherlock Holmes put down his pipe, a blackened veteran of many investigations. (appositive phrase)

- Sherlock Holmes put down his pipe, *which was* blackened by much long and thoughtful use.

can become

- Sherlock Holmes put down his pipe, blackened by much long and thoughtful use. (participial phrase)

- Sherlock Holmes put down his pipe, *which was* black and sooty from many earlier investigations.

can become

- Sherlock Holmes put down his pipe, black and sooty from many earlier investigations. (adjective cluster, prep. phrase)

In every pair, both versions are good; both versions are correct. Many readers, however, would prefer the conciseness and directness of the second alternatives.

The following sets of exercises provide an opportunity for you to experiment with these adjectival alternatives. Before working each set, study the "Sample Options" well, then try practicing with some of the suggested patterns to get the flavor of the construction and to see just what they can do for your style.

CHOOSING ADJECTIVE CLUSTERS AND PHRASES

Adjective clusters and prepositional phrases offer some dramatic possibilities, especially when they are grouped at the beginning of a sentence or a paragraph.

SAMPLE OPTIONS

· *With sunshine in her eyes and moonlight in her smile,* Mary Ellen approached the gathering.
· *Solemn and stately,* the mansion had stood there on Yorkshire Moor for nearly three centuries.

On the other hand, you might prefer to use such phrases immediately following the term modified:

· Mary Ellen, *with sunshine in her eyes and moonlight in her smile,* approached the gathering.
· The mansion, *solemn and stately,* had stood there on Yorkshire Moor for nearly three centuries.

TRY IT OUT

A. Combining Kernels. Combine each set of the following kernel sentences into a single sentence using at least one adjective cluster or adjectival prepositional phrase.

Sample problem:
· The gnat was tiny.
· The gnat was elusive.
· The gnat had the power to sting.
· The gnat darted erratically.

Some sample solutions:
· Tiny and elusive, but with the power to sting, the gnat darted erratically.
· The gnat, tiny and elusive—but with the power to sting—darted erratically.

1. The dictator had a forcefulness of expression.
   The dictator had a power of persuasion.
   The dictator held his subjects' attention.
   The subjects' attention was unswerving.
2. James was lithe.
   James was sprightly.
   James was like a deer.
   James bounded through the meadow.
3. The tenement was old.
   The tenement was decrepit.
   The tenement collapsed unnoticed.
   The collapse left a pile of bricks and dust.

4. Gloria was like a statue.
Gloria stood in the sunlight.
The statue is graceful.
The statue is still.

5. The speaker was pompous.
The speaker was uninspired.
The speaker bored his audience with trivial details.

B. Compose Your Own. Compose your own sentences by adding at least one adjective cluster or adjectival prepositional phrase to each of the following sentences. See what effects you can achieve.

Sample problem:
· The ocean liner pulled away from the dock.

Some sample solutions:
· *With its flags waving, its whistle blowing, and its passengers cheering,* the ocean liner pulled away from the dock.
· The ocean liner *under cover of darkness* pulled away from the *dark and deserted* dock.

1. The hypocrite pretended to scorn what she really enjoyed.
2. Sir Gawain battled the Green Knight.
3. My sister is almost always a pest.
4. The preacher gave his sermon on sin.
5. The actor fumbled his way through *Hamlet.*

Choosing Appositive Phrases

Although appositives describe as adjectives do, they are really nouns equal to, and usually interchangeable with, the nouns they describe. For example, in "Abraham Lincoln, *a tall angular man,*" the appositive "a tall angular man" means the same as "Abraham Lincoln." Appositives can also be negative, as in "a nightingale, *not a lark.*" They can repeat the word described: "the sound, *the sound of a bell.*" And they can exemplify it when introduced by such expressions as *for instance, for example, particularly, especially, namely, including,* and *mainly.* In the samples that follow, notice the variety of your appositive and punctuation options.

SAMPLE OPTIONS

· *A tall, angular, awkwardly moving man,* Abraham Lincoln aroused mixed emotions among his constituents.
· Juliet tried to convince Romeo that he had heard a nightingale, *not a lark.*
· He went without eating. He fretted and fumed and worried for hours. Then *it* finally came: *a knock on the door.*
· Little Elmer waited all day for *the sound* that to him was as melodic as the playing of any symphony orchestra—*the sound of the ice-cream truck.*

- Although service songs, *such as "The Marines' Hymn," and "Anchor's Aweigh"* are memorized by every schoolchild in time of war, they are rarely heard in peacetime.
- College freshmen—*particularly those who are the only children in their families*—sometimes have difficulty in adjusting to the hubbub of dormitory life.
- Jo spent the summer reading horror stories, *few of which engaged either her intellect or her imagination.*

As the "Sample Options" show, you can use appositive phrases directly to add specific detail and suspensefully to create rhetorical climaxes at the ends of sentences. But you will probably find appositives most helpful of all in revising as a device for ridding your work of bothersome indefinite references, those annoying *this*'s without specific antecedents so common in academic writing. Take, for example, the following typical passage from a student paper:

Faulty
- The national emotional state evolved into the progressive movement in an attempt to harmonize the modern industrial age with traditional values. *This* is reflected in the thesis of Robert H. Wiebe's book, *The Search for Order, 1877–1920.*

Most of us know very well that *this* can't really refer to "all that," though we have trouble thinking of ways to avoid it. Using a "which" clause (". . . with traditional values, *which* is reflected in the thesis . . .") is even worse, for now it's the "which" that refers to "all that." An appositive construction, however, offers a graceful solution to the problem:

- The national emotional state evolved into the progressive movement in an attempt to harmonize the modern industrial age with traditional values—a fact that is reflected in the thesis of Robert H. Wiebe's book, *The Search for Order, 1877–1920.*

Appositive phrases are almost always enclosed by punctuation. But you will want to decide for each use whether the matter-of-fact comma, the more dramatic or more informal dash, or the very formal colon is the most appropriate punctuation to use.

TRY IT OUT

A. Combining Kernels. Combine each set of the following kernel sentences into a single sentence using at least one appositive phrase.
Sample problem:
- The Charge of the Light Brigade was a battle in the Crimean War.
- It was immortalized in a poem by Alfred, Lord Tennyson.
- It was a combination of unimaginable folly and heroism.
- It will stand forever as a symbol of the absurdity of war.

Some sample solutions:

· The Charge of the Light Brigade, *a battle in the Crimean War immortal-ized in a poem by Alfred, Lord Tennyson,* was a combination of unimaginable folly and heroism that will stand forever as a symbol of the absurdity of war.
· The Charge of the Light Brigade, *a combination of unimaginable folly and heroism,* having been immortalized in a poem by Alfred, Lord Tennyson, will stand forever as a symbol of the absurdity of war.

1. The pope is the spiritual leader of millions.
The pope issued an important papal decree.
2. My broken watch is a worthless piece of workmanship.
It always reads the same time.
The time is always 3:27.
3. Jack Ruby killed Lee Harvey Oswald.
Lee Harvey Oswald was the man who shot President Kennedy.
The killing was on national television.
4. The first rock-and-roll hit was *Rock around the Clock.*
Rock around the Clock was by Bill Haley and the Comets.
The first rock-and-roll hit is still the biggest-selling rock single ever.
5. *La Traviata* is an opera by Verdi.
Verdi's opera will be performed this year by many opera companies.
Examples of these companies are La Scala Milano and the Chicago Lyric opera.

B. Compose Your Own. Compose your own sentence by adding at least one appositive phrase to the following sentences. Experiment with creative ideas.
Sample problem:
· Last Wednesday the century-old tree in the center of the market square was destroyed by lightning.

Some sample solutions:
· The century-old tree, *a sturdy, large-leafed oak that long had shaded the market square,* was destroyed by lightning last Wednesday.
· Last Wednesday the century-old tree in the center of the market square was destroyed by lightning, *some of which also set fire to Farmer MacGregor's barn.*

1. My dentist filled two cavities, causing me much pain.
2. The carrier delivered only half the mail assigned to him that day.
3. Professor Snodgrass always gives good grades.
4. The laser is now being used in surgery.
5. Steve knew that when he opened the door he would see the one thing he was most afraid of.

Choosing Participial Phrases

Not only can participles and participial phrases, like other adjectival modifiers, help you make your writing tighter, livelier, and more specific, but since these phrases are related to verbs, they can also bring their own verbal quality to your sentences. They can provide a sense of action and a sense of time to the subjects and objects they modify. Notice, when you study the list of sample options, how phrases dominated by the present participle (the *-ing* form of the verb) lend a quality of immediate and continuing action to their descriptive function. And see how phrases dominated by the past participle (the *-ed* form of the verb) add a sense of completed action to their descriptive function. Notice also that the more distant past participles (the *having* and the *having been* forms of the verb), besides describing a noun, convey a sense of action having taken place before the time of the sentence:

SAMPLE OPTIONS

- *Straining and tugging,* their muscles rippling, the athletes pulled at the rope.
- *Whistling merrily,* the boy walked to the end of the pier.
- The witch, *riding high above on her broomstick,* looked out at the black night.
- *Accomplished and poised,* the ballerina stepped out on the stage.
- The young man clearly was a dandy, *top-hatted and affected in his speech.*
- *Having heard the tragic news,* the once-joyful comedian sat down and wept.
- The trainer, *having been badly mauled by the lion,* decided not to return to the cage for a few days.

TRY IT OUT

A. Combining Kernels. Combine each set of the following kernels into a single sentence, using at least one participial phrase.

Sample problem:
- The hordes of Attila the Hun rode out of the East.
- They pillaged.
- They raped.
- They terrified the inhabitants of the land.

Some sample solutions:
- *Pillaging, raping, and terrifying the inhabitants of the land,* the hordes of Attila the Hun rode out of the East.
- *Riding out of the East,* the hordes of Attila the Hun pillaged, raped, and terrified the inhabitants of the land.

1. Dan mowed the lawn.
Dan silently cursed his mother.
Dan's mother made him work hard.
2. The mourners went to the graveyard.
The mourners were shaken by the tragedy.
The mourners were stunned by the tragedy.
3. Willy Loman was confronted by the knowledge of a hopeless life.
Willy Loman killed himself.
4. The journalist eyed the politician coldly.
The journalist asked pressing questions.
5. Marie Antoinette did not realize the trouble she would be causing herself.
Marie Antoinette said, "Let them eat cake."

B. Compose Your Own. Compose your own sentences by adding at least one participial phrase to each of the following sentences. Don't be afraid to experiment creatively.

Sample problem:
· The clown silently wiped away a tear.

Some sample solutions:
· *Ridiculously costumed, jauntily capped, and smiling painfully,* the clown silently wiped away a tear.
· *Having remembered the days of his youth,* the clown silently wiped away a tear.

1. The instructor could not explain to the class what he wanted them to do.
2. My brother read the sports section of the paper from beginning to end.
3. Pericles addressed the Athenians.
4. Her dentist skillfully filled the cavity.
5. Every vacation Jean rereads her high school yearbook.

A Word of Warning

If there is anything more uncomfortable than to tell a joke and have it met by serious lips and unsmiling eyes, it is to be perfectly serious about a statement and have it greeted with chuckles. That is the almost universal reaction to dangling or misplaced modifiers. I would be less than honest if I did not warn you that along with all the exciting possibilities adjectival constructions offer, in their use lurks the potential pitfall of the dangling modifier, a pit into which all of us stumble from time to time. Misplaced modifiers are modifying words or phrases that are so positioned in a sentence that they seem to apply to a noun to which they are not intended to refer. The results range from the hilarious to the mildly amusing, depending upon the degree of inappropriateness of the match. These following examples include modifiers of all the kinds we have been discussing thus far (the modifiers are underlined; the words they modify are circled):

Faulty

- <u>Walking upside down on the ceiling</u>, (I) saw a huge black fly.

Faulty

- <u>Studious and bright</u>, (the examination) was a snap for Charley.

Faulty

- <u>A serious student</u>, (Charley's teacher) praised her highly.

Faulty

- The briefcase was the favorite possession of (Lawyer Brown), <u>being cracked with age and filled with a jumble of papers and official document</u>.

Faulty

- <u>Badly in need of repair and rattling at every window</u>, I still find that old ramshackle house appealing.

HOW NOT TO MISPLACE YOUR MODIFIER

Dangling and misplaced modifiers, though immensely distracting to the reader, are easily corrected. You can remove the error simply by placing the modifier near the word it describes, taking care to supply the referent if it has been omitted. If the resulting sentence sounds awkward, you may want to rephrase it further. You might, for instance, edit our sample sentences in this way:

- I saw a huge black fly walking upside down on the ceiling.
- The examination was a snap for Charley, who was studious and bright.
- A serious student, Charley was praised highly by her teacher.
- Cracked with age and filled with a jumble of papers and official documents, the briefcase was the favorite possession of Lawyer Brown.
- I still find that old ramshackle house appealing—though it is badly in need of repair and rattles at every window.

You can always correct such errors when you edit and revise your compositions, and so you need not worry about dangling modifiers while writing your first drafts. Still, to avoid such danglers in the first place, here are some rules to bear in mind:

1. Keep all modifiers as close as possible to the noun described.
2. When you begin a sentence with a modifying phrase, make sure it refers to the main subject of your sentence.

TRY IT OUT

A. Undangling Dangling Modifiers. Revise the following sentences to correct the misplaced modifiers.

1. Jumping into bed, the sheets were cold.
2. Having studied Roman history, not just one, but many coliseums remain standing throughout what was once the Roman world.
3. After being scolded at school, Denise's grandmother scolded her again when she came home.
4. The lunchroom was hateful to Professor Snerd, full of loud, unpleasant sounds and always smelling of stewed cabbage.

B. Combining into Essay. Combine one of the following sets of sentence kernels to create an effective essay. Try to include some adjective clauses, appositives, participial phrases, or other adjective phrases within it.

Aztec Cannibalism

1. The Aztec Indians were a tribe.
2. Their tribe had an empire.
3. The empire was important.
4. The empire was influential.
5. The empire once occupied a part of Central America.
6. The occupied part was substantial.
7. The Aztecs practiced cannibalism.
8. The practice went on during the fifteenth and sixteenth centuries.
9. Accounts provide evidence of this cannibalism.
10. The accounts were contemporary.
11. The accounts were by Spanish conquistadors.
12. Piles of skeletons provide evidence.
13. The skeletons are limbless.
14. The evidence is irrefutable.

15. The Aztecs were lightning fast.
16. The Aztecs were efficient warriors.
17. The Aztecs would attack their enemies.
18. The Aztecs would capture a number of their enemies.
19. The Aztecs would then swiftly retreat.
20. The Aztecs were excited.
21. Their excitement was from the battle.
22. Their excitement came from their own religious fervor.
23. The Aztecs marched their captives.
24. They marched them to the top.
25. The top was on one of their temple-pyramids.
26. The Aztecs performed a rite there.
27. The rite was one of the most important in their religion.
28. The rite was the sacrifice of the prisoners.
29. They would cut out the prisoners' hearts.
30. They would offer them to the gods.
31. There would be a feast.
32. They would give three limbs to each successful warrior.

33. The successful warriors had captured the prisoners.
34. They would give the remaining limbs to the priests.
35. They would give the remaining limbs to the elite class.
36. The elite class were the rulers of the Aztecs.
37. They fed the torsos to the animals.
38. The animals were hungry.
39. The animals were waiting.
40. The animals were carnivorous.
41. The animals were kept in the Royal Zoo.

42. Anthropologists believe this:
43. This system of cannibalism was ritualistic.
44. It was used by the Aztecs.
45. It was used for a purpose.
46. The purpose was nourishment (of themselves).
47. The nourishment was during periods of famine.
48. These periods were frequent.
49. The famine was in Central America.
50. The famine was throughout the fifteenth and sixteenth centuries.

CHOOSING ADVERB CLAUSES AND PHRASES

The adverbial function is more complex than the adjectival. True, the adverb modifies and describes the verb just as the adjective does the noun. But the adverbial function also includes placing the verb's action in time and space, marking it for degree and frequency, and providing it with causal, conditional, contrastive, and other such relationships. Using adverbial clauses and phrases in your writing enables you to make important connections for your readers.

Using Adverbials

Like adjectival constructions, adverbials can be single words:

quickly	seldom	affectionately
luckily	often	indoors

phrases,

in the garden	during the day
although tired	at the stroke of noon
whenever needed	after bathing
with candor	despite preparations for war
while singing	

or clauses:

- When she was happy . . .
- Before the game ended . . .
- Because I love you . . .

Adverbial constructions differ from the adjectival, however, in their movability. When you let an adjective construction stray too far from the noun it modifies, the sentence can suffer from a dangling modifier. In contrast, you have a great deal of freedom in placing adverbials. For many adverbials, almost any position will do:

Beginning	· *Frequently,* the invalid turned to her window to look at the birds.
Middle [after subj.]	· The invalid *frequently* turned to her window to look at the birds.
Middle [after verb]	· The invalid turned *frequently* to her window to look at the birds.
Middle [after comp.]	· The invalid turned to her window *frequently* to look at the birds.
End	· The invalid turned to her window to look at the birds *frequently.*

Even adverbial clauses, which are regularly placed at the beginnings and ends of sentences, can be used effectively in midsentence. Directly after the subject, for instance, is a position that offers an interesting—almost adjectival—effect. Compare:

- Greg, *though he was quaking with fear,* climbed to the very top.
- *Though Greg was quaking with fear,* he climbed to the very top.
- Greg climbed to the very top *though he was quaking with fear.*

Furthermore, although you may let a misplaced adjectival get by you once in a while, if you are a native speaker of English you should have no trouble with misplaced adverbials. You will catch them right away because they will sound "funny." A popular song of a few years ago (and a recent movie) played on the quaint humor inherent in the misplaced adverbial with such lines as "Throw mama from the train a kiss."

REVISION DECISIONS

If almost all positions in a sentence—except the downright ludicrous—are correct for adverbials, then you may wonder on what to base your placement decisions. The answer is to base them on the principles of sound, coherence, and emphasis. First, check on the general sound of the sentence. Does the order you selected sound awkward when you read it aloud? Does it sound awkward when you read it together with its neighboring sentences in the paragraph? If so, how might you reorder it to give it a comfortable sound?

Next, check for coherence. If the adverbial construction in question looks back to the preceding sentence, place it near the beginning of your sentence:

- She sought refuge in a cabin in the remote hills of Kentucky. But *through those hills* stalked a hungry cougar.

If the adverbial refers to the next sentence, place it at the end:

· She sought refuge in a cabin *in the remote hills of Kentucky.* But through those hills stalked a hungry cougar.

Finally, consider the matter of emphasis. As you will recall from Chapter 5, the end of a sentence is the part that ordinarily receives most attention from readers. The beginning of the sentence is second in importance. And the middle of the sentence draws the least of readers' notice—except, that is, when internal punctuation interrupts and gives the sentence other beginnings and endings within. (See page 206 for examples of how emphasis can be modified by commas or dashes.)

How do these principles apply specifically to placing mobile adverbials? First, they can remind you to make sure that an unimportant adverbial does not occupy the focal final spot in the sentence. Although the "invalid's window" sample sentences listed earlier are all grammatically correct, the one with *frequently* in the final position has an awkward ring not present in the other versions. The final *frequently* creates an anticlimactic sort of effect you might wish to avoid:

Awkward

· The invalid turned to her window to look at the birds *frequently.*

Again, if you want to create interesting dramatic effects, try clustering prepositional phrases at the beginning of a sentence. The old Thanksgiving song makes good use of just such a strategy:

· Over the river and through the woods, to Grandmother's house we go.

Adverbial prepositional phrases not only can set a sentence in place and time, but when clustered in this way can also provide the sentence with a rhythm that may be compelling. This sort of opening can supply an especially telling introductory effect:

· *On the eastern shores of the Mediterranean, amid the ruins of an ancient civilization,* the embattled nation of Israel continues her struggle to exist.

In summary, after all other considerations have been met and you still cannot decide where to place your adverbial constructions, ask yourself: how important is the idea in this adverbial to the purpose of the sentence? Just how much emphasis do I want to give it? And then, guided by the principle of emphasis, find it an appropriate home.

TRY IT OUT

A. Combining Kernels. Combine the following kernel sentences into effective sentences containing adverbs, adverb prepositional phrases, and other adverb phrases.

Sample problem:
- Wordsworth wrote something.
- The daffodils fluttered.
- They fluttered in the breeze.
- The daffodils danced.
- They danced in the breeze.
- The daffodils were beside the lake.
- The daffodils were beneath the trees.

Some sample solutions:
- Beside the lake, beneath the trees, daffodils were fluttering and dancing in the breeze, just as Wordsworth wrote.
- According to Wordsworth, some daffodils, while fluttering in the breeze, danced beside the lake and beneath the trees.

1. A small colony carried out its life processes.
The colony was made up of antibiotic cells.
The colony was in a petri dish.
The colony was on top.
The colony rested on some agar-agar.
2. The snow fell.
Its fall was soft.
Its fall was quiet.
Its fall was unending.
3. The flood obliterated everything.
It obliterated along its path.
This happened after it pushed past the dam.
Its pushing was ruthless.
This also happened after the flood rushed downstream.
4. Napoleon's army proceeded.
Its progress was made on the frozen steppes of Russia.
Its progress was dogged.
Then it was halted.
The halt was irretrievable.
The halt was in snow.
The halt was in blood.

B. Compose Your Own. Compose your own effective sentences by adding adverbs, adverb phrases, and adverb prepositional phrases to the following sentences.

Sample problem:
- Abraham Lincoln faced the crowds.

Some sample solutions:
- *While standing precariously on a makeshift platform, in the heat of the summer's sun, shyly and awkwardly the young* Abraham Lincoln *first* faced the crowds.

· *On a quiet day, not long after the roar and the blood of the great battle, a weary* Abraham Lincoln *stood on the very field of the battle and sadly but triumphantly* faced the crowds.

1. The General Assembly of the United Nations passed a resolution.
2. The 35-year-old pitcher haggled for a raise in pay.
3. The grandfather's clock struck the hour.
4. The brown bear roams Admiralty Island.

Choosing Adverb Clauses

A special word should be said about the adverb clause, because you may find it among the most useful of constructions. The clause simultaneously conveys its own information and expresses a specialized relationship to the information in the attached sentence because it is a sentence headed by an adverbial subordinating conjunction. This conjunction relays the particular adverbial relationship while it connects and subordinates the clause to the other sentence. The boxed section suggests some of the more useful of these adverbial conjunctions. They are grouped there in terms of the relationships they express.

Adverbial Conjunctions

Relating by Time	**Relating by Cause**	**Relating Conditionally**
When	Because	If
Whenever	Since	Only if
Before	In view of the fact that	Provided that
Even before		Unless
Until	**Relating by Contrast**	Not unless
Once	Although	Whether or not
As soon as	Even though	Assuming that
As long as	While	In case
While		Only
After	**Relating by Place**	
Since	Where	
	Wherever	

The following sets of sentences show something of the power of these adverbial subordinators and sample the tremendously varied relationships they make possible. Suppose, in composing a history paper, you are working with these two ideas:

· War broke out.
· The King refused to compromise.

Taken by themselves, and unsubordinated, they permit the reader only to speculate on the nature of the event they both describe. But if you combine them with an adverbial conjunction, you can make the meaning unmistakable.

TIME

For example, you can let the reader know in what order the actions took place. If the king refused first, you could write:

- *After* the King refused to compromise, war broke out.
- War broke out *after* the King refused to compromise.
- The King refused to compromise *before* war broke out.
- *Before* war broke out, the King had refused to compromise.

Which one you chose would depend upon the subject you wanted to focus on and upon what exactly you wanted to imply. You could be even more precise about the timing. For instance, you could advance the time of the breakout of war by writing:

- *Once* the King refused to compromise, war broke out.

And advance it yet further by:

- *As soon as* the King refused to compromise, war broke out.

Or stress the concept's recurring nature with:

- *Whenever* the King refuses to compromise, war breaks out.

You can even use the adverb clause to tell the sequence of events in such a way as to assign a cause:

- The King kept refusing to compromise *until* war broke out.

CAUSE

Some causal implication is inherent in almost all time relationships: By revealing the time sequence, you also hint at the reason for the action. But with specifically causal conjunctions you can be completely direct about the cause.

- War broke out *because* the King refused to compromise.
- *Since* the King refused to compromise, war broke out.

CONDITION

But what if the action has not taken place, yet you want to assert that if the conditions were right, the event certainly would happen? You could write for instance:

- *If* the King refuses to compromise, war will break out.
- War will break out *if* the King should refuse to compromise.

Or you might want instead to make a negative prediction:

> · *Unless* the King refuses to compromise, war will not break out.

Or, on the other hand,

> · War will break out *whether or not* the King refuses to compromise.

CONTRAST

And if this last prediction proved false, you might want to express the contradiction involved in such a turn of events:

> · *Although* the King refused to compromise, war did not break out.
> · War did not break out *even though* the King refused to compromise.

Despite the length of this list, we have by no means exhausted the possible relationships you might create by using adverbial conjunctions. By becoming sensitive to the subtle distinctions involved in these relationships, you can learn to choose the wording that most accurately reflects each relationship as you perceive it.

Adverb-Clause Strategies

In using adverb clauses you will find that you have two important options besides the choice of an appropriate adverbial conjunction. You have to decide which of the two ideas to put into the adverb clause and where to place the adverb clause in the sentence.

SUBORDINATION

Fortunately, in most cases, there is a sure way of determining which idea to put in the adverb clause. An adverb clause is a subordinate clause; and, in a sentence, the main clause is meant to carry the major thrust. By the very nature of English grammar, then, the main clause will be perceived as containing what the sentence "really" says. The rest, however interesting or important, will be seen to be of lesser significance. In choosing to put either the King or the war of our example into an adverb clause, then, you are making a subtle statement about the comparative importance of the material, both within the sentence and in the general context.

POSITION IN SENTENCE

Your decision about placing the adverb clause should, of course, be helped by the principles of adverbial placement we have already discussed (pages 231–232). But with the clause some special considerations come into play.

Emphasis. The English sentence has a natural order, as we have seen:

Natural sentence order = Subject (and its modifiers) + Verb (and its modifiers)

Since adverbial constructions are considered verb modifiers, we can suppose that when a sentence is written in its natural order, the adverb clause will be at the end. This supposition is supported by the punctuation rule that traditionally advises you to separate the two clauses with a comma when the natural order is inverted—that is, when the adverb clause opens the sentence:

- When the moon is full, some men go mad.
- Some men go mad when the moon is full.

The principles of emphasis would then seem to suggest that you use the "natural" order of main clause + adverb clause when you intend no special emphasis and when you want to be as simple and direct as possible. Even an emotional statement such as the following appears more matter-of-fact in the natural sequence:

- She might never see him again if the plane came late.

On the other hand, if you should want to emphasize this sentence, you can get your reader to pause at the comma—and perhaps ponder the implications of the statement—by reversing the order:

- If the plane came late, she might never see him again.

Such an order also has the effect of giving added significance to the *if,* the adverbial conjunction which would otherwise be buried in midsentence. To focus even greater importance upon the adverb clause, you might place it back in the emphatic end position but break the quick rhythm of the natural order with a pause-inducing comma—or better yet, an emphatic dash:

- She might never see him again—if the plane came late.

Context. There are other reasons besides emphasis for breaking the natural order. One reason occurs when the internal logic of the sentence seems to demand that you place the adverb clause first. Not reversing the "normal" order in the following sentence, for instance, would violate the actual chronological sequence:

- After a volcano explodes, a geyser of lava is released and, flowing irresistibly, destroys everything in its unpredictable path.

Another reason to switch the order of a sentence is to achieve a smooth transition to the sentence following. Such alterations occur frequently because the material in the main clause, usually composed of ideas directly related to the focus of the paragraph, is often echoed in the next sentence. In order to achieve an uninterrupted flow of ideas, the clause containing this material should be as close as possible to the new sentence. For example, you would probably avoid using the "normal" order if the following sentence were part of a paragraph discussing Arab influence:

- *Although the United Nations began so hopefully,* its very nature has been perverted by such occasions as PLO chieftain Yasser Arafat's machine-gun-adorned address. The very fact that this address was permitted to take place vividly illustrates the power that the oil-rich Arab countries can exert in the world.

Faulty
- The United Nations' very nature has been perverted by such occasions as PLO chieftain Yasser Arafat's machine-gun-adorned address *although the United Nations began so hopefully.* . . .

In this example the "normal" order violates the internal logic of the sentence itself. Placing the adverb clause first not only makes more sense but also permits an appropriate follow-up sentence.

TRY IT OUT

A. Combining Kernels. Combine each of the following sets of kernel sentences into effective sentences containing at least one adverb clause. In each case, don't hesitate to try a number of subordinating conjunctions and differing placements of the clauses to find the one you feel most precisely expresses the suggested ideas.

Sample problem:
- The pizza has shrimp and anchovies.
- I am determined to eat the pizza.

Some sample solutions:
- *Even if* the pizza has shrimp and anchovies, I am determined to eat it.
- I am determined to eat the pizza *whether or not* it has shrimp and anchovies.

1. Louis B. Leakey was looking for the remains of early man.
   Louis B. Leakey made an astounding discovery.
2. The violinist tunes his A string too sharp.
   The A string will surely break.
3. Drunken drivers frequently cause automobile accidents.
   Drunken drivers have impaired reactions.
4. It seemed a ridiculous thing to do.
   The daredevil was resolved to go over Niagara Falls in a barrel.
5. My father hears Reverend Green preach a sermon.
   My father falls asleep.

B. Compose Your Own. By using different adverbial conjunctions and thus adding differing adverbial clauses, create from each of the following sentences three interesting sentences that differ from one another in meaning and intent.

　　Sample problem:
· The train whistle blows at night.

　　Some sample solutions:
· *Whenever* the train whistle blows at night, my dog scampers under my bed.
· The train whistle blows at night *whether or not* there are cars waiting at the crossing.
· *Although* the train whistle blows at night, I sleep well.

1. Popeye continued to eat his spinach.
2. Many people believe in the presence of poltergeists.
3. There is scarcely a village in England that does not have a memorial recording the human devastation of World War I.
4. The dance had been the happiest evening of her young life.
5. Snoopy may well be the world's most beloved cartoon character.

C. Combining into Essays. Combine the following sentence kernels into effective essays. Make use of adverbial constructions where they seem appropriate. Feel free to experiment.

On ESP

1. Many people call extrasensory perception "hogwash."
2. They are skeptical.
3. A number of cases of ESP have been reported.
4. These cases seem to indicate experiences.
5. Some people have had experiences.
6. These experiences were psychic.
7. These experiences were real.
8. These experiences take a form.
9. The form occurs frequently.
10. The experience is a person knowing something.
11. The person is extra perceptive.
12. He or she knows it suddenly.
13. He or she knows it somehow.
14. A loved one is in danger.
15. A loved one is in pain.

16. There is an ordinary case.
17. The perceptive person will have a dream.
18. The perceptive person will have a hallucination.
19. The perceptive person will have a vision.

20. The perceptive person will have a sudden impulse.
21. The perceptive person will have an intuition.
22. The intuition may be a certain feeling.
23. Something is wrong.
24. Or the intuition may be a different feeling.
25. A friend needs help.

26. There was an instance.
27. The instance was during World War II.
28. A lady dreamed this.
29. The dream was of her brother.
30. Her brother asked a nurse something.
31. The nurse should not touch his leg.
32. A bullet had just been removed.
33. The bullet had been in his leg.
34. The lady found out something.
35. Her discovery came later.
36. Her brother had been shot.
37. The shooting had been on that very day.
38. The wound was in the leg.
39. Her brother had undergone surgery.
40. The surgery removed the bullet.

41. There is another example.
42. This example is also authenticated.
43. A nineteen-year-old planned to attend a funeral.
44. He went home instead.
45. He felt something.
46. He felt it for some reason.
47. He must see his mother.
48. He arrived home.
49. He called to his mother.
50. His mother left her chair.
51. His mother came to him.
52. A truck crashed.
53. The crash was at that very instant.
54. The truck came through the living room wall.
55. The truck smashed a chair.
56. His mother had been sitting in that chair.

57. There are volumes of evidence.
58. The evidence is similar.
59. Many people still are skeptical.
60. They do not believe in ESP.
61. They have had no personal experience with ESP.

> **62.** Only a few people have had experiences with ESP.
> **63.** This is a fact.
> **64.** This fact gives ESP its special value.

CHOOSING NOUN CLAUSES AND PHRASES

Noun constructions offer yet another set of options to help you build your writing style and revise your written work.

Choosing Noun Clauses

A noun clause is a clause that functions like a noun by serving in its entirety as the subject or object of a sentence, clause, or phrase. In some ways the advantages of using noun clauses are similar to those you gain in using adjective or adverb clauses. In enabling you to combine two sentences, all subordinate clauses permit you to relate two ideas more precisely and to subordinate one to the other. The noun clause, which joins the rest of the sentence by means of *that* or a question word (*why, how, what, who, whose, where, whatever, whoever, wherever,* and so on), accomplishes this end by standing in for the subject or object of a sentence that is indefinite or not clearly defined. For instance:

- Pedro wanted her to know something.
- Pedro loved her.

can become

- Pedro wanted her to know *that he loved her.*

or

- *That he loved her* was *what Pedro wanted her to know.*

or

- *What Pedro wanted her to know* was *that he loved her.*

In addition to the advantages shared with all subordinate clauses, noun clauses (and noun phrases) offer some special benefits for revision. Most important, perhaps, noun clauses provide a good way to avoid using "this" to mean "All that I have just said"—the sort of indefinite pronoun reference that readers often interpret as sloppy thinking. Consider these examples:

- Leslie had copied from René's paper.
  René was very angry about *this.*

can become

- René was very angry *that Leslie had copied from his paper.*

- How did Houdini do his famous disappearing-elephant trick? No one ever found *this* out for certain.

can become

- No ever found out for certain *how Houdini did his famous disappearing-elephant trick.*

Although you may be less familiar with the possibilities of noun clauses than with those of the other clauses, they can be truly useful additions to your stylistic repertoire.

TRY IT OUT

A. Combining Kernels. Combine the following sets of sentence kernels into effective sentences containing at least one noun clause.

Sample problem:
- I think this.
- I know something.
- Whose woods are these?

Some sample solutions:
- I think *that I know whose woods these are.*

or (more poetically, as Robert Frost originally wrote it)

Whose woods these are, I think *[that] I know.*

1. National Guardsman PFC Alfred Amos wondered this:
   Was his battalion going to train at Camp Grayling in Michigan?
2. The Burger Doodle waitress sweetly informed her customer something:
   Escargots are not on the menu.
3. The society matron lost all her money.
   This fact did not keep her from putting on aristocratic airs.
4. She would never go hungry again.
   Scarlett O'Hara swore this to herself.
5. Maria forgot to tell me something about the party.
   Where is the party going to be?
6. Two objects cannot occupy the same space.
   This is a law of physics that cannot be refuted.

B. Compose Your Own. Create effective sentences by adding at least one noun clause to each of these sentences.

Sample problems:
· I would not have directed you that way if I had known that _____.
· The pilot flew _____.

Some sample solutions:
· I would not have directed you that way if I had known *that the bridge was out.*
· If I had known *that your co-star was coming down with the mumps,* I would not have directed you that way.
· The pilot flew *wherever his imagination took him.*

1. Alice had a dream that _____.
2. Napoleon wondered whether _____.
3. Edison explained how _____.
4. _____ is a well-known fact.

Choosing Noun Phrases

In many situations where you can use a noun clause, you also have the option of employing a noun phrase—either a gerund phrase or an infinitive phrase. The gerund is the *-ing* form of the verb when it is used as a noun: the *singing,* the *climbing.* Gerund phrases are phrases that are dominated by a gerund:

· *The singing of the Vienna Boys Choir* filled our hearts with joy.
· *Climbing the peaks of the Colorado Rockies* is strenuous fun.

The infinitive is the "to" form of the verb: *to sing, to climb.* It too can be substituted for a noun:

· *To climb the peaks of the Colorado Rockies* is strenuous fun.
· It fills our hearts with joy *for the Vienna Boys Choir to sing.*

Noun phrases share with noun clauses the advantage of avoiding the indefinite pronoun. After all, the samples above might just as easily be written:

Faulty   · The Vienna Boys Choir sang. *This* filled our hearts with joy.
Faulty   · *You* climb the peaks of the Colorado Rockies. *It* is strenuous fun.
         · *One* climbs the peaks of the Colorado Rockies. . . .

So if you catch yourself using the usually too colloquial *you* or the usually too formal *one* or the indefinite referents *this* or *it,* you might think through what you want to say and see if the sentence wouldn't be more effectively phrased with a gerund or an infinitive phrase. These examples illustrate some alternatives:

Faulty
· Children watch violence on television. *This* is harmful.

can be phrased:

· *Watching violence on television* is harmful to children.

or

· *For children to watch violence on television* is harmful.

Faulty
· *You* buy beer and peanuts in college. *It* is an old custom.

can be phrased

· An old college custom is *buying beer and peanuts.*

or

· *To buy beer and peanuts* is an old college custom.

Another important advantage to using infinitives and gerunds arises from their verbal nature. They partake in the "acting" or "doing" that is the essence of the verb, and they thus impart a vitality to the sentence that nouns cannot match. Examine, for instance, the following comparable sentences:

· Against all odds, Carolyn continued *the maintenance of her position.* (nominalization)
· Against all odds, Carolyn continued *to maintain her position.* (infinitive)
· Against all odds, Carolyn continued *maintaining her position.* (gerund)

· If the sun disappeared, *our existence* would cease. (nominalization)
· If the sun disappeared, we would cease *to exist.* (infinitive)

I think you will agree that the sentences containing the nominalization seem static and weak compared to the sentences with the gerund and infinitive phrases.

You should find that gerund and infinitive phrases come in handy when you want to infuse the vitality of verbs into your writing. But try them out for yourself.

TRY IT OUT

A. Combining Sentences. Combine each of the following sets of kernels into effective sentences containing at least one gerund or infinitive phrase.
Sample problem:
· Octavian would seize control of the western part of the empire.
· This was his goal.

Some sample solutions:
- Octavian's goal was *to seize control* of the western part of the empire.
- *Seizing control* of the western part of the empire was Octavian's goal.

1. The magician diverts the attention of the audience.
   This is the most important ploy of the magician.
2. The children would swim and play in the sun all summer.
   This is the desire of every schoolboy and schoolgirl.
3. One drives on the expressways.
   It requires the utmost in concentration.
4. You should keep minor surgical wounds from becoming infected.
   It is one of the most important aspects of podiatry.
5. People slice carrots.
   It can be a dangerous activity if one doesn't know how.

B. Compose Your Own. Substitute a gerund phrase or an infinitive phrase for the blank in each of the following sentences.

Sample problem:
- _____ was a foolish thing for Van Gogh to do.

Some sample solutions:
- *Sending his ear* to the prostitute who had mocked him was a foolish thing for Van Gogh to do.
- It was foolish *for Van Gogh to send his ear* to the prostitute who had mocked him.

1. _____ can be very dangerous.
2. The Marine sergeant said he wanted all his recruits _____ .
3. _____ requires courage, bravery, skill, and a certain amount of stupidity.
4. _____ is Ralph's secret wish.
5. Next to completing these exercises, my favorite activity is _____ .

C. Combining into Essays. Compose effective essays from the following three sets of sentence kernels. Use noun clauses and phrases where they will enhance the writing. Don't hesitate to experiment with your constructions. Be creative.

Escaping the Tower

1. The Tower of London is huge.
2. The Tower of London is solid.
3. It seems an impenetrable prison.
4. These facts would seem to suggest something.
5. No one could escape from this prison.
6. Yet this idea is not precisely so.
7. The Tower has had a long history.
8. Some prisoners have managed.

9. They have escaped.
10. But such escapes have been few.
11. The escape requires strength.
12. It requires daring.
13. It requires courage.
14. It requires a great deal of luck.

15. Some escaped.
16. Almost all these managed it in the following way.
17. They used a rope.
18. They scaled down the wall.
19. They swung across the moat.
20. They accomplished this somehow.
21. Bishop Rannulf Flambard escaped by this method.
22. He was the first.
23. Henry I imprisoned Bishop Flambard.
24. Henry I was a son of William the Conqueror.
25. The escape was in 1100.
26. What did Bishop Flambard do to escape?
27. He got the guards drunk.
28. He supplied them with wine.
29. His act was gracious.
30. He slipped out.
31. He slipped between the bars.
32. The bars were on his window.
33. He slid down.
34. He slid on a rope.

35. Others tried to escape.
36. They were not so fortunate.
37. It was less than a century later.
38. Griffin was the son of Llewellyn.
39. Llewellyn was Prince of Wales.
40. Griffin also tried to escape.
41. He also used a rope.
42. His rope was made of knotted sheets.
43. Griffin was midway down.
44. The rope broke.
45. Griffin fell to the ground.
46. Griffin broke his neck.

47. There is a fear.
48. Prisoners might suffer a fate.
49. The fate would be the same as Griffin's.
50. There is also another fear.
51. The Tower has a size.

52. That size is imposing.
53. So most prisoners do not attempt this:
54. They do not escape.

SPICING YOUR STYLE WITH PARALLELISM

A writer's style is, to a large extent, defined by its rhythms. The more effectively you manage the rhythm of your sentences, the more effective will be your writing style. The patterned repetition that is rhythm can exert extraordinary power. Rhythm's emotional appeal would seem to be basic to human nature. Research indicates, for example, that newborn infants gain weight better and cry less when a recording of a beating heart plays in their nursery, perhaps reminding them of the security of the womb. Rhythm also satisfies intellectually. It imposes pattern and order upon otherwise disordered impressions.

Rhythmic sentences are created through parallelism. In addition you will find parallelism a useful way to link ideas to reveal their essential relatedness. How is parallelism achieved? Through repetition. The trick is to make sure the elements you wish to emphasize are repeated and are arranged in such a way that the repetition is instantly clear to the reader. Notice the repetition in the following well-known examples of parallelism:

SERIAL PARALLELISM

- I came,
  I saw,
  I conquered. (Julius Caesar)
- We cannot dedicate—
  we cannot consecrate—
  we cannot hallow—this ground. (Abraham Lincoln)

BALANCED PARALLELISM

- Spare the rod and spoil the child. (English and Biblical proverb)
- Hear the instruction of thy father and forsake not the teaching of thy mother. (Bible)

CONTRASTING BALANCE

- To err is human, to forgive divine. (Alexander Pope)
- Every sweet has its sour; every evil its good. (Ralph Waldo Emerson)

Although achieving such parallel effects involves repetition of both sound and meaning, you will find that the most significant repeated element is syntax. You can create parallelism by linking together identical grammatical structures and by combining them in one of the two ways that emphasize this identity: in a series (vertical parallelism) or in a balance (horizontal parallelism).

Serial Parallelism

When you have a number of ideas you want to tie closely together, you can do so most impressively by first forming them into parallel structures and then linking them together in a series by repetition. In doing this you can exercise a great deal of freedom. You have the choice of repeating any kind of sentence element you want. You can, for instance, choose single words or words and their modifiers from any of the parts of speech. For example, nouns:

· A *rag* and a *bone* and a *hank* of hair. . . . (Rudyard Kipling)

Or adjectives:

· A *real* and an *irresistible* and an *inexorable* and an *everlasting* enemy. (John Donne)

Or verbs:

· I shall never *ask,* never *refuse,* nor ever *resign* an office. (Benjamin Franklin)

Or adverbs:

· We are swallowed up, *irreparably, irrevocably, irrecoverably, irremediably.* (John Donne)

Or you can choose to form the ideas into parallel phrases. For example, participial phrases:

· . . . any nation so *conceived* and so *dedicated.* . . . (Abraham Lincoln)

Or infinitive phrases:

· The problem for modern parents is to find ways *to give their children a sense of usefulness, to make them feel that they are a vital part of a general family enterprise.* . . . (William Raspberry)

With prepositional phrases you have two choices. You can keep the objects identical and vary the prepositions:

· . . . that government *of the people, by the people, and for the people.* . . . (Abraham Lincoln)

Or you can vary the objects and keep the prepositions constant:

· *With* malice toward none, *with* charity for all, *with* firmness in the right as God gives us to see the right. . . . (Abraham Lincoln)

Clauses of all kinds also can be used in parallel constructions. For example, noun clauses:

· We hold these truths to be self evident: *that all men are* created equal; *that they are* endowed by their creator with certain inalienable rights; *that among these rights are* life, liberty, and the pursuit of happiness. . . . (Thomas Jefferson)

Or adverb clauses, such as these "unless" clauses:

> · For *unless all the citizens* of a state are forced by circumstance to compromise, *unless they* feel that they can affect policy but that no one can wholly dominate, *unless* by habit and necessity *they have* to give and take. . . . (Walter Lippmann)

Or these "if" clauses:

> · *If we wish* to be free; *if we mean* to preserve inviolate these inestimable privileges for which we have been so long contending; *if we mean* not basely to abandon the noble struggle in which we have been so long engaged. . . . (Patrick Henry)

Or adjective clauses, as, for example, those in the same Henry sentence from which we have just quoted:

> · . . . privileges *for which we have been* so long contending . . . struggle *in which we have been* so long engaged, and *which we have pledged* ourselves never to abandon. . . .

You can also put ideas into parallel main clauses or sentences:

> · We cannot dedicate—we cannot consecrate—we cannot hallow—this ground. (Abraham Lincoln)
> · We have petitioned; we have remonstrated; we have supplicated; we have prostrated ourselves at the foot of the throne. . . . (Patrick Henry)

CHOOSING CONNECTERS

In constructing parallel series, you also have a variety of connecting elements to choose from. You can join the parallel parts together with commas or semicolons or periods. Each of these kinds of punctuation is exemplified in the previous examples. Or if you choose to use conjunctions, you have your choice of the whole array of coordinating and subordinating conjunctions. What is more, you can decide exactly how often you want to use conjunctions. You might choose to use the conventional sequence of items that concludes with a conjunction:

> · Life, liberty, *and* the pursuit of happiness.
> · Never ask, never refuse, *nor* ever resign. . . .
> · A jug of wine, a loaf of bread, *and* thou. . . .

In another case you might want to depart from the norm and eliminate the conjunction in order to instill a note of urgency and achieve a brisk, no-nonsense approach:

> · I came, I saw, I conquered.
> · We have petitioned; we have remonstrated; we have supplicated; we have prostrated ourselves at the foot of the throne. . . .

To see just what is achieved by this omission, try adding a conjunction at the conventional place: for example, "I came. I saw. *And* I conquered."

Or on the other hand, you might prefer to achieve the emphasis that goes with departing from the norm by instead adding conjunctions after each of the parallel items. These additions have the effect of slowing the rhythm of the sentence and giving extra weight to each of the items:

· *Neither* snow, *nor* rain, *nor* heat, *nor* gloom of night. . . .
· A real *and* an irresistible *and* an inexorable *and* an everlasting enemy. . . .

If Donne had used the conventional system, he would have lost most of the force of his phrase: "A real, irresistible, inexorable, and everlasting enemy" is far weaker. In most cases you should be completely consistent with repeated conjunctions, adding the same one after all items in the series you choose to connect in this way. Nevertheless, you have the freedom occasionally to add them selectively and thus arrange your series in groups. Note, for example, how Lewis Carroll groups the items by his intermittent use of "and" and "of" in this line:

· Of shoes—*and* ships—*and* sealing wax—of cabbages—*and* kings.

For so formal a construction as parallelism, you thus have a surprising amount of freedom. There are, in fact, only two rules to follow when you work with this strategy:

1. Make the elements in the series as nearly equivalent as possible.
2. Put the most important, or the longest, element last.

MAKING THE TERMS EQUIVALENT

To achieve parallelism, the major term in all the items in a series must be of identical parts of speech, or as we said earlier, all the items must have "identical structures." But the technique loses much of its force if the parallelism is not extended further. The modifiers, for instance, should also be equivalent. Think how much less effective Kipling's line would have been if he had not described the vamping woman as

· *A* rag, *a* bone, and *a* hank of hair

but had instead called her

· Rags, a bone, and the hank of hair

or

· A rag, the bone, and hanks of hair.

Though it is often neither feasible nor wise for you to carry exact parallelism through every portion of every element in a series, still you should try for at least a measure of parallel construction throughout. Take, for example, Patrick Henry's "if" clauses cited earlier (page 249). They differ in many respects. The first is brief, the others are more lengthy; the last is negative, the others are positive; the first is passive, the others are active;

and so on. Yet these structures have much more than the initial "if" in common:

If	we	wish	to	be free . . .						
If	we	mean	to	preserve . . .	for	which	we	have	been	so	long contending
If	we	mean	not	basely to abandon . . .	in	which	we	have	been	so	long engaged
					and	which	we	have . . .			

It is also usually a good idea—for the sake of clarity as well as for rhetorical effectiveness—to repeat an introductory word throughout the series. Note, for example, that Lincoln did not write:

· With malice toward none, charity for all, and firmness in the right

But rather

· *With* malice toward none, *with* charity for all, *with* firmness in the right

BUILDING TO A CLIMAX

One of the major advantages in using serial parallelism is the possibility the technique offers of working toward a climactic point. Almost every one of our samples illustrates the fulfilment of this possibility. And you should find it worthwhile to organize climactically too. Furthermore, if you are not careful to arrange your items in order of importance, you run the risk of creating the sort of anticlimax that your readers may find ludicrous. If Patrick Henry, for instance, had been less careful in ordering his clauses, his great plea for independence might have petered out in this way:

· We have prostrated ourselves, we have remonstrated, we have even petitioned.

You can avoid running into similar problems by remembering to conclude your series with the item you want your readers to consider most important.

When you master the subtleties of creating parallel structures, you should find this technique a highly effective way to demonstrate the relatedness of a group of ideas, to organize these ideas in a creative sequence, and to develop a pleasing rhythmic quality in your prose.

TRY IT OUT

Model Your Own. Choose your own topic and closely imitate the structural pattern of the following famous parallelisms.

Sample problem:
· Neither snow, nor rain, nor gloom of night stays these couriers from the swift completion of their appointed rounds.

Sample solutions (subject: study)
· Neither sneeze, nor cough, nor sleepless night keeps this student from the grave consideration of her assigned homework.
· Neither friend, nor notes, nor book of text can help this student in the desperate study for his forthcoming exam.

1. "I came, I saw, I conquered."
2. "I shall never ask, never refuse, nor ever resign an office."
3. "A loaf of bread, a jug of wine, and thou, beside me singing in the wilderness."
4. "With malice toward none, with charity for all, with firmness in the right as God gives us to see the right, let us strive on to finish the work we are in."
5. Try your hand at the sample problem quotation.

Balanced and Contrasting Parallelism

The other form of parallel structure you might try is balanced parallelism. You can use balanced parallelism to reinforce a statement by repeating a particular sentence structure in a parallel way or by dividing the statement into balanced halves. For example:

· Eat not to dullness; drink not to elevation. (Benjamin Franklin)
· What we attain too cheap, we esteem too lightly. (Thomas Paine)
· A man's heart deviseth his way, but the Lord directeth his steps. (Bible)

Although the two kinds of parallelism distinguished in this chapter are alike in that both are composed of similar items linked together by similar placement, they differ in structure. If you picture serial parallelism vertically as a column of parallel items, then you might picture balanced parallelism horizontally as a balance scale or a teeter-totter with a single item (or group of items) on each side of the balance point. The balance point, which can be a mark of punctuation or a conjunction or simply a pause, separates the balanced items (see Figure 8.1). As with serial parallelism, the

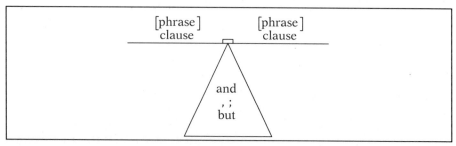

Figure 8.1. Balanced or Contrasting Parallelism

similarities in the balanced pairs usually go beyond repetition of function words and syntax to include an actual similarity of sound. The pairs of words balanced for their meanings in the preceding examples, for instance, are similar in number of syllables and in initial and final sounds: *attain/ esteem, deviseth/directeth, his steps/his way.*

Balanced parallelism is not only useful for pointing up the correspondence of like statements, but also is particularly effective in revealing the contrast that lies at the heart of some concepts. In such contrasting parallelism, the balanced halves are the contradiction or the antithesis of each other. For example:

- We must all hang together or, assuredly, we will all hang separately. (Benjamin Franklin)
- Hatred stirreth up strifes; but love covereth all transgressions. (Bible)
- It matters not how a man dies, but how he lives. (Samuel Johnson)

Because balanced (especially contrasted) parallels express ideas so succinctly and neatly, and often so wittily, many proverbs and maxims are written in this style. But you must not think that the writing of short, pithy statements is its only—or even primary—use. Parallelism can impose its proverblike quality upon even commonplace sentences. It often adds an air of wisdom and makes memorable much professional writing that does not strive for an especially proverbial sound, and in this way it can contribute to your own. The following passages from essays in Part Four exhibit the typical effect:

- The Harvard psychiatrists *worry about cheating children out of* their childhood. I *worry about cheating them out of* something more profoundly important; their self-respect as responsible, contributing human beings. (William Raspberry, page 424, paragraph 16)
- That response is a (by now) ritualized series of diversions and evasions that subtly but quickly *make us feel better* while also *making the hostages' situation worse.* (Greenfield, page 420, paragraph 1)

PAIRED CONJUNCTIONS

One important strategy for building balanced constructions is to employ paired conjunctions: both . . . and . . . ; not only . . . but also . . .; neither . . . nor . . .; more . . . than . . .; less . . . than . . ., among others. The pairs offer even inexperienced writers a useful form upon which to construct a balanced sentence. Professional writers frequently employ the conjunctions to good advantage:

- Terrorism [*not only*] attacks our compatriots on airplanes. . . . *But* it *also* attacks our most fundamental, settled assumptions. . . . (Greenfield, page 420, paragraph 4)
- We *not only* wear kids' clothes and eat kids' food; [*but*] we [*also*] dream kids' dreams, and make them come true. (Alexander, page 413, paragraph 15)

· *The point* of these observations *is not* that of determining who received the worst treatment. *Nor is it* to minimize the legacy of black slavery and disenfranchisement. *The point is* to question propositions concerning black socioeconomic progress. . . . (Williams, page 441, paragraph 4)
· Shallow understanding from people of good will is *more* frustrating *than* absolute misunderstanding from people of ill will. (Martin Luther King)

Because of its highly structured nature, balanced parallelism lends itself to some rather spectacular effects. For instance, with appropriate subject matter you can achieve a double pairing, such as these famous lines of John F. Kennedy:

· Ask not what your country can do for you; ask rather what you can do for your country.

Or you can work for the round-robin sort of balance that characterizes the nursery song which begins: "For want of a nail a shoe was lost / For want of a shoe a horse was lost / For want of a horse. . . ." Disraeli, for example, used this technique:

· Experience is the child of thought, and thought is the child of action. (Benjamin Disraeli)

VARIATIONS

On the other hand, you need not feel bound by the rigidity of the balanced parallel form, for variations not only are permitted, but in many cases also enhance the effectiveness of the construction. You should feel free, for instance, to interrupt the parallelism with an aside or a parenthetical phrase:

· We must all hang together or, *assuredly,* we will all hang separately. (Benjamin Franklin)

And although, as we have seen, balanced parallelism demands the pairing of elements on both sides of an imaginary balance point to achieve the balanced effect, it is not necessary—indeed, it is sometimes damaging—to spell out the parallelism linking every element. Authors often substitute a pronoun for an important noun in the second half of the pairing. In doing so they avoid the awkward and somewhat ponderous effect that repetition would involve. Journalist Lance Morrow, for example, writes:

· Faith defies proof; science demands *it.*

Note how the statement would have been weakened, had he kept the complete parallel:

· Faith defies proof; science demands *proof.*

Similarly, you have the option of skipping some parallel wording in the second half of the balance, as in these examples:

- Pride goeth before destruction, and a haughty spirit [goeth] before a fall. (Bible)
- Character is much easier kept than [it is] recovered. (Thomas Paine)
- Every sweet has its sour; every evil [has] its good. (Ralph Waldo Emerson)

Decisions on just how much of the pattern to repeat require the sort of subtle judgment that comes with practice and experience. But sophisticated judgment of this sort is well worth acquiring. For contrasting and balanced parallelism are techniques that can add to the wit or profundity of what you have to say and can also enhance the rhythmic effectiveness of your writing.

TRY IT OUT

A. Compose Your Own. Compose your own balanced sentences by filling in the blanks with a pair of parallel clauses, phrases, or words.

Sample problem:
- During the Civil War the North had not only _____ , but also _____ .

Some sample solutions:
- During the Civil War the North had not only a just purpose in their support of the Union, but also a moral cause in their opposition to slavery.
- During the Civil War the North had not only superiority of arms, but also dominance in manufacture and industry.

1. I consider myself knowledgeable not only about _____ , but also about _____ .

2. For there to be a prolonged period of true world peace, there would have to be either _____ or _____ .

3. In the past ten years people have been concerned more with _____ than with _____ .

4. Not only is Otis _____ ; he is also _____ .

5. Next summer I would much rather _____ than _____ .

B. Model Your Own. Look back over the examples in this section on balanced parallelism and select two to use as models. Using your own subject matter, closely imitate the structure of the two famous quotations you have chosen.

Sample problem:
- "Every sweet has its sour; every evil its good." (Ralph Waldo Emerson)

Sample solution:
- Every hot dog has its mustard; every reward its frustration.

Combining Serial and Balanced Parallelism

We have discussed the two kinds of parallelism separately so that you might understand the structures more clearly. But in actual practice, writers tend to build these constructions into each other in complementary ways—especially where they want to heighten the rhetorical excitement. By analyzing the following examples from the essays in Part Four, you can gain insight in managing the sophisticated stylistic tools parallelism offers.

TRY IT OUT

Count and identify the parallelisms in the following examples. Find the parallel elements, and link them together on your own copy by spacing them in a parallel way and/or by underlining or encircling. Use colored pens or pencils if available.

Sample problem:
· Children today not only exist; they have taken over. God's Country has, to an astonishing degree, become Kids' Country—in no place more than in America, and at no time more than in the period Halloween-to-New Year's Day. (Alexander, page 411, paragraph 2)

Sample solution:
· Children today not only exist ; Δ they have taken over. [contrasted bal.] God's Country has, to an aston Δ ishing degree, become Kids' Country. [balance]
⎧ — in no place more than in America,
⎨ and in no time more than in the period Halloween-to-New Year's Day.
⎩ [Serial par.]

1. On campuses covered with ivy and lined with palm trees, I met young women who've been encouraged to consider life plans that will include careers as well as families, aspiring as well as caretaking. (Goodman, page 418, paragraph 2)

2. [How many parallelisms can you find here?]
Liberals are temperamentally inclined to see the world as a harmonious carnival of sweetness and light, where good will prevails, good intentions are rewarded, the race is to the swift, and a benevolent Nature arranges a favorable balance of pleasure over pain. . . . Conservatives know the world is a dark and a forbidding place, where most new knowledge is false, most improvements are for the worse, the battle is not to the strong, nor

riches to men of understanding, and an unscrupulous Providence consigns innocents to suffering. (Will, page 438, paragraphs 2 and 3)

TRY IT OUT

Combining into Essays. Write effective essays from the following sets of sentence kernels. Use parallel constructions when they seem appropriate.

Desensitizing

1. Our society has become brutalized.
2. Murder fills it.
3. Rape fills it.
4. Theft fills it.
5. Other violent crimes fill it.
6. We have become insensitive.
7. Our insensitivity is to tragedies.
8. The tragedies are real-life ones.
9. There is a cause for our insensitivity.
10. Our ears are barraged.
11. The barrage consists of violence.
12. The barrage is constant.
13. The barrage is the news.
14. There is another cause.
15. Our eyes are assaulted.
16. The assault is by death.
17. The death is staged.
18. The assault is by mayhem.
19. The mayhem is staged.
20. The assault is on television.
21. We have reached a point.
22. At this point a crime does not lead to shunning.
23. The crime is well publicized.
24. The crime is violent.
25. The shunning would be general.
26. The shunning would be by the public.
27. The shunning would be of such crimes.
28. The crime leads rather to an occurrence.
29. The occurrence is increased.
30. The occurrence is of crimes.

31. A study is recent.
32. The study is from Northeastern University.

33. The study shows something.
34. The death penalty functions.
35. The function is less effective as a deterrent.
36. The deterrent is to violent crimes.
37. The function is more of an encouragement.
38. The encouragement is to violent crimes.
39. A study was made in New York.
40. The study covered the years 1907 to the present.
41. The study found this:
42. A month follows each execution.
43. Two more homicides take place in that month.
44. Two is the average.
45. These homicides are more than an uncommon occurrence.
46. The occurrence is usual.
47. The month is ordinary.
48. Researchers conducted the study.
49. Researchers attribute this situation.
50. The attribution is to the "brutalizing effect."
51. The effect is on society.
52. The violent event has a "brutalizing effect."
53. The event is publicized.
54. It is publicized highly.
55. The researchers observed another effect.
56. People commit suicide.
57. The people are visible.
58. The people are admired.
59. The people are famous.
60. Then other people commit suicide.
61. They follow the example.
62. Here is an instance.
63. Marilyn Monroe committed suicide.
64. This provoked more than 250 suicides.
65. The 250 is estimated.
66. The suicides were in her own country.
67. This provoked another 100 suicides.
68. The 100 is estimated.
69. The suicides were in Britain.

70. Thus our senses become desensitized.
71. Then each tragedy spurs suffering.
72. Each tragedy is new.
73. Then each violent event spurs suffering.
74. Each violent event is new.
75. The suffering is additional.
76. The suffering is innocent.

ASSIGNMENT

Making good use of the rhetorical and stylistic strategies you now command, write on one of the following topics.

1. Imagine you have been elected student representative to a blue-ribbon commission making recommendations to the president of your college or university for a new plan of education. What do you see as the most effective path for educating college students? Be specific in your recommendations and persuasive in their support.[2]

2. If you have recently changed your mind on an issue of some importance, write an essay explaining the change and persuasively setting forth your new point of view.

3. Respond to a recent article in the newspaper or in a newsmagazine such as *Time, Newsweek,* or *U.S. News and World Report.* Present the author's position fairly; then, by citing specifics, either agree or take issue with his or her point of view.

4. Some say the family is becoming an "endangered species." Identify a family problem you have some knowledge of and write an essay discussing it in terms of its causes and its consequences. Possible topics may include: stepfamilies, "live-in" relationships, divorce, midlife crises, elder family members, in-laws, postponed children, single parents, sibling rivalries.[3]

[2]Suggested by Professor Linda Young of California State University, Sacramento.
[3]Suggested by Professor Thomas Whissen of Wright State University.

Chapter 9

Convincing Your Readers Through Style

Making Decisions About Words

Writers, as we've said, create their writing styles through choices of sentence structure (syntax) and of words (diction). In Chapter 8 sentence-combining exercises offered you experience in making syntactic decisions. By providing ready-made diction, they freed you from any perplexing decisions about words. In Chapter 9, on the other hand, you will be confronting dictional decisions directly. Here you will have the opportunity to explore the practical considerations involved in choosing your words effectively.

FINDING THE PRECISE WORD

Although deciding upon words would seem to be a complex process, there is only one overriding consideration behind every choice: precision of meaning. Without a doubt, that word or phrase is best which most precisely conveys your intended meaning to your reader.

TRY IT OUT

To get some notion of the significance of precise diction, let's examine the words of a professional sentence or two.

1. Greenfield's thesis sentence from "Accepting the Unacceptable" appears below. Copy it, replacing the bracketed words with blank slots x and y.

... This latest episode of kidnapping and terror has ... illustrated once again our [permanent disadvantage] _____ (x) in dealing with people who do these things and our penchant for [deepening the disadvantage] _____ (y) by the way we respond. (page 420, paragraph 1)

a. To understand just how well these words carry the exact sense of what Greenfield wants to convey, try substituting for *disadvantage:* (i) "hindrance," (ii) "obstruction," (iii) a synonym of your choice. In each case comment on the effect of the change on the meaning of the sentence and on your (the reader's) acceptance of that meaning.

b. Now try the following phrase substitutions: (i) [x]"steadfast impediment," [y] "enhancing the handicap"; (ii) [x]"undeviating obstacle," [y] "exacerbating the encumbrance"; (iii) a set of phrases of your choice. Again comment upon the effect of the changes.

2. Try similar substitutions for the bracketed phrases in the following sentences. Use your dictionary or thesaurus. Comment on what you discover.

a. ... Many of these students maintain a kind of [conspiracy of silence] with men. They [secrete] away some levels of feelings and hopes until it is "too late." (Goodman, page 418, paragraph 4)

b. Each year the Cubs [charged] onto the field to challenge anew the theory that there are limits to the changes one can ring on pure incompetence. (Will, page 439, paragraph 6)

c. Children are a relatively modern [invention]. (Alexander, page 411, paragraph 1)

The Try It Out examples suggest how important it is in writing effectively to find the word or phrase that most exactly reflects your meaning and your purpose.

The Richness of the English Vocabulary

When it comes to finding the expression that exactly indicates the thought, we who write in English are particularly blessed. Many believe that the English vocabulary is more eloquent than that of any other language because of its abundance. English has come to encompass a great number of the words and phrases that enrich and enliven other languages. The English that we speak and write today is basically a mixture of the language of the Anglo-Saxon inhabitants of the British Isles (Old English) and that of their Norman conquerors (Old French). Latin, the language of the church and the universities, enriched this mixture, as did a generous smattering of Hebrew and Greek from the same sources, along with some remainders of Danish and Celtic that survived from earlier times. The early disposition of English to gather to itself the linguistic treasures of other cultures continues to this day and has produced the extraordinarily rich vocabulary from which we can choose our words and phrases.

SYNONYMS

There is scarcely a concept for which there are not at least two or three forms of English expression. That with which we think, for example, is variously called *mind* (Old English derivation), *reason* (Old French), *intellect* (Latin), or even *psyche* (Greek). But this multiplicity of synonyms does not fully account for the richness of English. Even more important is the variety of nuances and shades of meaning offered by these synonyms. Competing words of identical meaning do not exist long in a language together. Either one word becomes dominant and drives the other out of use or their meanings differentiate enough so that both are needed to give a full range of expression to a concept. Thus, though synonyms can substitute for one another in certain contexts, they cannot be interchanged in all situations. If, for example, you want to write about *publicizing* something, you have a wide range of synonyms from which to choose: *broadcast* (OE),[1] *publish* (OF), *propagate* (L), *spread* (OE), *promulgate* (L), *disseminate* (L). Which you choose depends a great deal on the nature of the material you wished to publicize. You might, for instance, *broadcast* a game, but you wouldn't *promulgate* it. You might *promulgate* a doctrine, but you would not *spread* it. And although you might *spread* fertilizer, you surely would not *propagate* it.

Synonyms not only vary in the identity of what they refer to (their denotation), but they also differ in the tone they convey and in the value judgments they imply (their connotation). The Latin-derived *promulgate* or *disseminate* suggests a more formal tone than the Old English *spread* or *broadcast*, which, like most Anglo-Saxon-derived words, carry with them the informality of ordinary speech. Yet these words do not suggest the casualness of other synonyms of *publicize* such as *ballyhoo* or *hawk about.* On the other hand, even the Latinate words are less formal or less ennobled than the Biblically allusive synonym *give tongue.* This list of words, more or less synonymous with *publicize,* can also illustrate the fact that synonyms do not have equivalent emotional weight or moral value. Ask yourself, for example, what is likely to be more important: that which is *promulgated* or that which is *gossiped about?* Which is more likely to be believed? Or even more likely to be true?

Because synonyms, as you have seen, are *not* completely interchangeable, their abundance in English offers you great room for choice. Within this abundance, you can find just the word or phrase that will most precisely (1) express your exact thoughts, (2) indicate the level of formality

---

[1]The abbreviations after these synonyms follow the conventional manner of signifying a word's linguistic derivation: Old English (OE), Old French (OF), Latin (L).

and tone of voice you mean to project, and (3) imply the moral and emotional value you intend. These elements of meaning overlap, of course, in every word; but because each is a truly significant consideration in your choice of diction, let us examine each element individually.

Choosing Words for Exact Expression (Denotation)

It would, I know, be helpful if I could supply some absolute rules to guide you in choosing the words that will most effectively express every idea that you may want to write about. The problem is that in stylistic matters there is almost no "always," almost no "never." A way of writing that one good author is careful to avoid, another uses to eloquent advantage. Consequently, though I can offer you two precepts to follow, these precepts are only *usually* useful; and I suggest that you follow them with thoughtful reservations.

RULE 1: CHOOSE THE MOST SPECIFIC TERM

When you are writing about concrete ideas, select the word or phrase that most accurately summons up the sense picture (not necessarily visual) that you have in your mind's eye and will best convey it to your reader. Ordinarily, use the most specific term available. For most purposes,

- "Joey took a picture of *an animal* at the zoo" is weak.
- "Joey took a picture of *a bear* at the zoo" is better.
- "Joey took a picture of the zoo's *polar bear cub, Whitey*" is good.

In most circumstances, you should probably avoid using a word (like *animal* in the sentence about Joey) that does not call up a specific mental image. And you should be particularly wary of words like *nice* that, despite their original specific meanings, have now fallen into vague general use.

An Important Reservation. By emphasizing the importance of finding the specific term, I do not mean to say that good writers should always shun words signifying general concepts. For instance, although Greenfield is especially precise in her diction, she does not hesitate to use an expression of extreme generality when generality itself is her immediate concern. In the sentence we analyzed in the preceding Try It Out, for instance, she writes: "people who do *these things.*" Although this is the sort of vague expression that good writers ordinarily avoid, Greenfield uses it here to demonstrate her point about our inability to face the specific hideousnesses of terrorism.

The rule is to be precise. If you need a general term, choose it deliberately. But if—as is usually the case—generality is *not* your purpose, then good writing requires that you select the particular word that most specifically holds your meaning.

Finding the Appropriate Specific Expression.   You can use questions to guide your search for the right specific word. If you are working with a concept like "building," you would probably want to first think of a word that expresses function. Do you want to refer to a *residence?* a *house of worship?* a *tavern?* a *factory?* a *hotel?* a *hospital?* or a *store?* Having selected a term, you would then try to make it more specific: Is the *residence,* for instance, an *apartment building?* a *two-family house (duplex)?* a *farmhouse?* a *county seat?* Is the *house of worship* a *church?* a *mosque?* a *meeting house?* a *temple?* a *synagogue?* Is the *tavern* an *inn?* a *restaurant?* a *bar?* a *pub?* On the other hand, you might prefer to distinguish the building by size: Is the *residence* a *high-rise?* a *mansion?* a *cottage?* a *bungalow?* or a *hut?* Is the *church* a *cathedral?* or a *chapel?* You might even want to distinguish the building by the nationality of its occupants. If so, you might choose to call it an *igloo,* a *hogan,* a *hacienda,* or a *chalet.* Perhaps the building you want to discuss is not intended for human occupation: you might then decide to refer to it as a *kennel,* an *aviary,* a *stable,* a *barn,* a *dovecote,* or even a *garage.* The more precisely the word you choose fits your idea, the better you will be able to communicate that idea, and the better your writing will be.

RULE 2: PREFER STRONG VERBS AND VIVID NOUNS; BE SPARING WITH MODIFIERS

If you admire a spare, clean style of writing, you will be wise to let strong verbs carry much of your meaning wherever feasible. Verbs such as *secrete, charge, challenge* (featured in the preceding Try It Out) directly express action and are described as "strong." In contrast are verbs grammarians describe as weak: the various forms of the verb "to be" (*is, are, was, were, has been,* and so on) and other such verbs that must be completed by an adjective or a noun (*seem, appear, become,* and so on). Most authorities consider the weak verb-complement construction to be less forceful. For example, note the vigor of Will's choice of the verbs *gird* and *wilt* in the following sentence:

> . . . When other kids' teams *were girding* for Homeric battles at the top of the league, my heroes *had wilted* like salted slugs. . . . (page 439, paragraph 6)[2]

Surely the sentence is more satisfying as Will phrases it than it would be if he had used "weak" verb constructions:

> · When other kids' teams *were getting* ready for Homeric battles . . . , my heroes *were* like salted slugs.

---

[2]Italics are used throughout this chapter to call attention to particular words. Unless otherwise indicated, you may assume that italics in quotations are mine, not the original authors'.

Effective writing is also built upon vivid and explicitly suggestive nouns. Examine, for instance, the following sentence from William Raspberry's essay:

> This *sense* of *uselessness,* I am convinced, lies behind the shocking *statistics* on teen-age *pregnancy,* youthful *homicide* and *suicide, crime, alcoholism,* and *drug abuse.* (page 423, paragraph 9)

Raspberry's sentence is a strong one mainly because of the force of its precisely chosen nouns. It gains much of its leanness from the absence of optional adjective and adverb modifiers. Where strong verbs and vivid nouns carry the meaning, few modifiers are required. Excessive use of these modifiers can add bulk or wordiness to your prose. Raspberry's one optional adjective *shocking* works well because it is a persuasive word in this context—and because it is alone. A writer must resist the temptation to embellish every noun with an adjective and every verb with an adverb. Think what such a method might have done to Raspberry's sentence:

Faulty

> · The *futile* sense of *utter* uselessness, I am *firmly* convinced, lies *dangerously* behind the *startling* and shocking statistics on *aimless* teen-age pregnancy, *malevolent* homicide and *pathetic* suicide, *miserable* crime, *wasteful* alcoholism, and *deplorable* drug abuse.

Though every modifier in this revision is completely appropriate to its context, the overkill lends a ludicrous—almost ironic—tone, even to a subject as serious as Raspberry's.

Similarly, you will find that qualifiers like *very* and *really* often weaken where they are meant to make expression more emphatic. The best way to avoid problems with excessive modifiers is to take care in your choice of nouns and verbs to make these essential words as vivid and explicit as possible.

An Important Reservation. Unquestionably, thoughtless or excessive use of modifiers can cause writing difficulties. Yet good writers often put modifiers to vigorous use. Examine, for instance, this sentence of Thomas's from "Late Night Thoughts . . .":

> I cannot listen to the last movement of the Mahler Ninth without the *doorsmashing* intrusion of a *huge* new thought: death everywhere, the dying of everything, the end of humanity. (page 428, paragraph 2)

Few readers would prefer the sentence with the optional modifiers omitted.

As a further caution in advising the use of strong verbs, it is only fair to point out that such constructions do not predominate in the main clauses of most professional expository writers—including those represented in this text. The verb "to be" and the other linking verbs *become, appear, seem, feel, believe, think,* and so on) are among the most useful building blocks of our language. Perhaps because of their very colorlessness, they provide an all-purpose serviceability, which even professional authors employ in a high proportion of sentences. I would not, therefore, suggest you avoid these verbs, but recommend rather when you use "weak" verbs that you be careful to make your nouns, adjectives, and adverbs as precisely meaningful as possible. Note the precision with which these parts of speech convey the subtleties of their author's meaning in the following examples:

> Perhaps the most *poignant victim* of the twentieth century is our sense of continuity. (Tucker, page 432, paragraph 8)

> . . . It was not so much the *promise of the kill* that took men away from their *warm homes* and sent them through the *cool shadowy woods;* it was something more *human,* more *mystical*—something even *simpler.* (E. B. White, page 436, paragraph 2)

TRY IT OUT

A. Classifying Words. Classify the following sets of words. Feel free to use your dictionary.

Sample problem: Classify the following beds by their occupants:

cradle, crib, sofa-bed, sleeping bag, bunk, berth

Sample solution:

cradle, for an infant	sleeping bag, for a camper
crib, for a toddler	bunk, for a sailor
sofa-bed, for a guest	berth, for a passenger

1. Classify the following ways of imbibing by their appropriate beverage (example, "sip tea"): sip, drink, chug-a-lug, quaff, take-a-nip, swallow.

2. Classify the following kinds of wood by their function (example: "posts, for building fences"): posts, lumber, boards, timber, beams, cords.

3. Classify the following adjectives in terms of the nouns they might appropriately describe (example: "extinct dinosaurs"): extinct, obsolete, archaic, old-fashioned, passé, antiquated.

4. Classify the following verbs in terms of their appropriate objects (example: "predict future"): predict, prophesy, give prognosis, foretell, dope out, forecast.

B. Distinguishing Synonyms. Though Roget's *Thesaurus* implies that the words in the following pairs are synonymous, there are subtle distinctions in their meanings. Choose six pairs and write a sentence for each member, making these distinctions apparent. Don't hesitate to use your dictionary.

1. ample / excessive
2. ecstatic / happy
3. answer / explain
4. old / venerable
5. weather / climate
6. vitality / animation
7. eager / anxious
8. prejudice / bias
9. repudiate / deny
10. suppress / repress

C. Distinguishing Confusing Word Pairs. These pairs of words are often confused. Choose the six pairs that have most puzzled you, and write a sentence for each member, distinguishing their meanings.

1. affect / effect
2. principle / principal
3. credible / credulous
4. flaunt / flout
5. persecute / prosecute
6. climactic / climatic
7. imply / infer
8. proceed / precede
9. assume / presume
10. elicit / illicit

Choosing Words for Appropriate Implication (Connotation)

If denotative meanings of the sort we have been discussing were the only meanings words had, your task of choosing words would be much less complicated. Unfortunately, then your language would also be far less expressive. But almost all words, in addition to signifying a particular object or concept, are also rich in implications and hidden nuances. In short, they *connote* as well as *denote* meaning.

To distinguish between the concepts of connotation and denotation, let's examine two lines from Alfred Noyes's poem about a dashing young highwayman and Bess, the girl he loves. Noyes describes the highwayman's sweetheart as

> · Bess, the landlord's daughter,
> The landlord's *red-lipped* daughter.

The denotative meaning of the italicized phrase is that the blood vessels near Bess's oral orifice are close to the surface—hardly an adequate summation of a key phrase in a romantic poem. Nevertheless, most readers would agree that the phrase is poetically apt, for readers instinctively know that "red-lipped" *means* a good deal more than it denotes. Clearly, in addition to their denotative meaning, the words *red* and *lipped*, when used together in this way, have sensual connotations so descriptive that Noyes, having only two syllables in which to sum up his heroine, justifiably chose these two. The connotative meaning of words and phrases is an important factor to keep in mind when you make your decisions about diction.

CONNOTATIONS OF FORMALITY AND INFORMALITY

One important kind of connotation that a word conveys is degree of formality, a connotation that often determines where you may use the word appropriately. Consider, for instance, the varying levels of formality in the following words that express *haste*. Do you think they are used appropriately?

· The diplomats *hastened* from the room.
· Mother *hurried* home from the grocery.
· When the sergeant said, "Snap to it!" the soldiers *snapped to it.*
· "Take the loot and *scram!*" hollered the masked man.

A set of synonyms for almost any noun, verb, adjective, or adverb can be arranged on such a scale of formality, from the ceremonial and learned terms of the formal level of style to the colloquialisms and slang of the extremely informal level. Connotations of formality correspond fairly well to the traditional concept of levels of usage: the High, Middle, and Low Styles. The writers and rhetoricians of times past believed that it was important to adapt the level of their language to the "kind" of speech they were giving or literature they were writing. They used the High Style for epics and tragedy and the Low Style for farcical comedy. (Think, for example, of the contrast between the language of Shakespeare's heroes and that of his clowns.) The Middle Style was the basic language of satire and of expository prose. Although the "Doctrine of Kinds," with its insistence on a strict match between level of usage and literary genre (or "kind"), has long since been discarded, the traditional concept continues to be a useful tool in the study of diction to this day. For example, it is still convenient to divide synonyms into categories representing the modern equivalents of the three major stylistic levels. Consider the style levels in Figure 9.1.

Formal / Learned Style	Middle Style	Colloquial Style
hasten	hurry	snap to it scram
intrepid valiant	courageous brave	plucky spunky gutsy
pedagogue educator	instructor teacher	grinder crammer
peruse contemplate	study learn	grind bone up
astutely	cunningly shrewdly	slickly
arduous	difficult	tough

Figure 9.1. Three Stylistic Levels

By developing an ear for connotative levels, you can control much of the tone of your writing. But what level of words should you choose?

THE MIDDLE STYLE

For most of your expository writing, the Middle Style is best—the clearest and the least pretentious. Since Middle-Style expressions are the common language of most of our thinking, these words usually come naturally to mind. Ordinarily, you will think and write *hurry,* for example, rather than *hasten, go* rather than *scram,* and there will be no problem in making your choice.

Nevertheless, there will be times when your first thoughts will not reflect the middle level. At these times a more formal or a more colloquial term will seem to conform most closely—most precisely—with what you want to say. It is then that the stylistic question arises: Should you go with the most precise term? In most cases, I would answer yes.

THE LEARNED STYLE

On the formal side, if you are addressing a scholarly subject and are writing for an audience who will understand your terminology, use the terms, however technical, which will most accurately convey your meaning. Similarly, if you find a word precisely reflecting your meaning that carries connotations appropriate to a more formal tone than the one you are trying to convey, then go with accuracy of meaning. Professional writers almost always do. E. B. White, for example, who is famous for his simple, lucid prose, consistently chooses the most precise expression—whatever level it may connote. In one sentence of his "Distant Music of the Hounds," White enriches his prose with several rather learned expressions without ever abandoning the basic Middle Style he maintains throughout the essay:

> Christmas in this year of crisis must compete as never before with the dazzling complexity of man, whose *tangential* desires and *ingenuities* have created a world that gives any simple thing the look of *obsolescence*—as though there were something *inherently* foolish in what is simple, or natural. (page 436, paragraph 3)

For another example, Alexander, whose style is more informal than White's, does not hesitate to vary it with a learned word where appropriate. She describes chess champion Bobby Fisher, for instance, as "the *quintessential* smart boy of every school." (page 413, paragraph 10)

You should feel free to follow the example of these professional writers and choose your words because of the precision with which they express your meaning—even if from time to time you must use expressions that are more formal or more learned than the Middle Style.

THE COLLOQUIAL STYLE

Similarly, you may occasionally take the option of choosing words that are more colloquial than the rest of your prose. Sometimes a colloquial word or even a slang expression can come closer to your meaning than any other term. Or sometimes when you feel the tone of your work getting too stuffy—perhaps too scholarly, perhaps too intense—you can regain a more conversational flavor by including an informal expression or two. Professional authors vary their writing in this way. Turner, for instance, writing for the readers of *Science* magazine, occasionally uses a colloquial word or phrase to lighten the intense tone of his scholarly article. For example, he writes:

> At about the time Chillingworth *set up shop* as the town's physician, Dimmesdale's health began to deteriorate. (page 434, paragraph 5)

Charles Slack uses such diction to add a conversational intimacy to his scientific essay for the readers of a popular journal:

> Can twenty *flunking* students of varying intelligence raise their math and English a full year's level in only thirty working days? (page 425, paragraph 1)

Note that both *set up shop* and *flunking* convey their intended meaning with singular precision and that both phrases tend to enhance, rather than detract from, the established tone.

YOUR DECISION

Make precision of meaning and tone your criterion for deciding whether to include an expression. But of course, consistency is also important, and the rhetorical stakes are high. If a word or phrase appears inappropriately learned or technical, it will be judged (and you, its author, will be judged) pompous or pretentious. If you go too far in the other direction and select terms that your readers judge off-color or too slangy, your seriousness and your taste will be open to question. These are the dangers. And yet, in the past, a judiciously mixed style was warmly approved by no less an authority than Aristotle; and in the present, it can be a real delight—as most of the essays in this book demonstrate.

TRY IT OUT

A. Classifying Synonyms. Place the synonyms in these lists on a continuum according to the formality of their connotations. For at least two of the words, write sentences that clearly express their meanings and are internally consistent in tone.

Sample problem:

Difficult, arduous, tough

Sample solution:

- After his *arduous* climb, the hiker removed his boots and relaxed his weary limbs.
- It has been a *tough* day for all the kids.

1. skeert, fearful, skittish, timorous, timid
2. ease, effortlessness, facility, piece of cake
3. dexterity, skill, adroitness, savvy, know-how, ability
4. quibble, pussyfoot, bicker, dodge, equivocate
5. drink, imbibe, wet-the-whistle, quaff, tipple
6. effervescence, fizz, froth, foam

B. Rewriting for Level of Style. The following sentences are written in exaggerated versions of either the Formal (Learned) Style or the Colloquial Style. Rewrite them in the Middle Style by selecting words and phrases appropriate to that stylistic level.
    Sample problems:
- Cool it, man. He's really with it.
- You tend to obfuscate the significance of your conceptualizations by utilizing unintelligible encoding.

    Sample solutions:
- Don't get angry. He understands the situation.
- You tend to blur the meaning of your thoughts by using language difficult to understand.

1. The butterfingered oaf seemed bound and determined to louse up the job.

2. Hang loose, Jack. I'll catch you on the backtrack.

3. Your inordinate capacity for public expectoration tends to nullify certain of your aspirations toward upward social mobility.

4. The incomparable absurdity attending your gyroscopic maneuvers makes you a farcical partner on the dance floor.

5. Your old lady's a real trip!

6. As I enumerate the unpalatable consequences of your proposed endeavor, I begin to abhor the entire prevailing circumstance.

CONNOTATIONS OF VALUE AND INTENSITY

Almost every English word not only expresses a particular connotation of formality or informality but also evokes a positive or negative response. This built-in value judgment varies widely. Synonyms of almost any noun, verb, adjective, or adverb can be arranged along a scale from highly positive to extremely negative and probably cover a number of gradations in between. Take, for example, this list of words roughly synonymous with "understanding" or "wise":

sagacious   astute   discerning   knowing   shrewd   canny   cunning   sly   slick

$\longleftarrow \hspace{10cm} \longrightarrow$

positive   *negative*

Should you want to use a word to represent an odor, you would have to decide just how good or bad a smell you intended before choosing one of these:

fragrance bouquet aroma scent redolence rankness putrescence stench stink

$\longleftarrow \hspace{10cm} \longrightarrow$

positive   *negative*

Sometimes a scale of values is not so much a measure of good or bad as of the intensity in the value connoted. All the following, for instance, have a connotation that is at least somewhat negative, yet there is a wide variance in the emotional intensity each conveys:

dishabille   disarray   disorder   messiness   dirtiness   sloppiness   squalor

$\longleftarrow \hspace{10cm} \longrightarrow$

less intense   *more intense*

SLANT

Our outlook on any subject is expressed by the evaluative connotations of the words in which we choose to discuss it. As columnist Sydney Harris suggests,

> I am opposed to your "newfangled ideas" because I believe in "the value of tradition," but you are opposed to my "sensible reforms" because you are "blindly clinging to the past."
> My outburst was "indignation"; yours was "anger"; his was "petulance."
> I am "cautious"; you are "timid"; he is "cowardly."
> My crude friend is "a diamond in the rough"; yours is "a touch on the common side"; his is "a loudmouthed boor."
> The ceremony I approve of had "dignity and grandeur"; the ceremony I disapprove of had "pomp and ostentation."
> Our country is engaged in "security measures"; your country is engaged in an "arms race"; his country is engaged in "stockpiling weapons."
> I am a "realist" when I am doing to you that which, if you were doing it to me, I would call "ruthless." ("Antics with Semantics: 5," *Leaving the Surface* [Boston: Houghton Mifflin, 1968], pp. 269–270.)

Harris's gentle irony points to the subjective quality of our language. This subjective quality is also known by the more negatively evaluative words "slant" or "bias." Because this quality is so universal—practically inevitable—I am not sure much is gained by criticizing it. After all, an outlook may be biased and still be correct. A reasonable approach is to acknowledge that every communication has a built-in point of view, a built-in bias, and take that bias into account as you form your own reactions.

You can even make your biases work for you. First, be aware of your own prejudices. Before attacking any writing job, examine your own thinking on the matter and determine exactly where you stand. If you are going to write about a legislative investigation, for instance, decide whether you regard it (to quote Harris again) as a "probe," a "fishing expedition," or a "witch hunt." If you are planning to analyze the beliefs of a social, political, or religious group, be straight with yourself as to whether you think of their ideas as "creed," "dogma," or "superstition" (269). However you answer, acknowledge to yourself that this answer is inevitably slanted—at least to some extent—by the sum total of your life experiences. Then, having decided how strongly you want to project this point of view, select the words and phrases that will convey the particular slant you want to project.

Words and phrases selected in this way should both express your specific meaning and suggest the value you wish to put upon it. If, in addition, they can withstand the tests listed in the accompanying box, your chosen terms should serve you well. When you can control the value connotations of the words you choose, you will command one of the most powerful features of rhetoric, for much of the persuasive ability of your prose lies here.

Choosing Words and Phrases: A Checklist

1. Is the term appropriate to the subject you are writing about and the tone you have established?
2. Do you have sufficient evidence to support the value connotations your term suggests, as well as its specific meaning?
3. Will this term be so offensive to your audience that they will not be able to give fair consideration to the thrust of your argument? (The question of what is offensive language is discussed on pages 168–171.)
4. Does this term both denotatively and connotatively reflect the truth as you view it? The answer to this question is important, even if you wish to sidestep questions of morality (though I am not convinced that a writer ever *can* sidestep such questions). Even the suspicion of insincerity in your reader's mind can rob you of your persuasive power—not only for the point at issue, but often for the entire composition.

With power, however, should go responsibility. You should use this skill thoughtfully, for words can matter quite a lot. It can matter very much, for instance, to a careful worker whether he or she is evaluated as "conscientious" or as "meticulous" or as a "finicky fussbudget." And, for another example, it can matter to the conscience of a people whether they see their armies on foreign soil as "conquerors" or "liberators." It is thus truly important that you understand the value judgments inherent in the words you use and that you choose your words with care.

TRY IT OUT

A. Arranging by Value. Arrange these sets of synonyms along scales from positive to negative *connotative value.* Then choose at least two words from each group and use them in sentences that clearly distinguish their meaning. Use your dictionary as needed.
  Sample problem:
  scheme, plan, connive, conspire, plot

  Sample solution:

plan	plot	scheme	conspire	connive

positive → *negative*

  In an old inn where highwaymen once *conspired* together, the local Boy Scouts gathered to *plan* their next cookout.

1. sentimental, tender, warm-hearted, maudlin

2. generous, extravagant, unselfish, prodigal, wasteful

3. caution, cowardice, carefulness, plucklessness, chickenheartedness

4. inquire, question, examine, grill, interrogate, put through third degree

5. old, experienced, seasoned, senior, venerable, aged, senile

6. impulsive, capricious, impetuous, heedless, thoughtless, uncalculating, inconsiderate

B. Ordering by Intensity. Arrange the words in each of these sets in order of *intensity of meaning,* from the least to the most intense. Then use at least two of them in sentences that distinguish their meaning.
  Sample problem:
  adversary, opponent, enemy, rival, antagonist

Sample solution:

rival   opponent   antagonist   adversary   enemy

← ——————————————————————————————————— →

least intense   *most intense*

The two boys had been *rivals* in their studies, *opponents* on the sporting grounds, and in their maturity became deadly *enemies* on the field of battle.

1. apathy, indifference, callousness, dispassion, insensitivity

2. drizzle, downpour, rain, shower, deluge

3. falsify, lie, dissemble, be untruthful, fib

4. abandon, leave, forsake, withdraw, desert

5. interest, passion, concern, enthusiasm, absorption

6. disease, malady, pestilence, ailment, plague

C. Evaluating Synonyms. Find four synonyms for each of these words. Arrange the five terms in the order of least to most formal, least to most positive, least to most intense in meaning, or any other appropriate order. Clearly label the scale. Then choose at least two words from each set and use them in sentences that distinguish their meanings.
    Sample problem:
    intemperate

Sample solution:

immoderate   intemperate   indulgent   dissipated   debauched

← ——————————————————————————————————— →

least intense   *most intense*

After many years of *intemperate* living, the Marquis de Sade surrendered himself completely to *dissipation*.

1. stale

2. competence

3. clumsy

4. curiosity

5. desire

6. flee

D. Rewriting for Connotation. Since words and phrases carry strong value connotations in addition to surface meanings, sentences with identical denotative meanings can evoke either positive or negative interpretations.

Rewrite the following positive statements to convey an overall negative impression by substituting expressions with negative connotations.

Sample problem:
Thomas, who was included in neither gathering, was nonetheless concerned with the success of both enterprises.

Sample solution:
Thomas, who was invited to neither party, nonetheless officiously intruded in the planning.

1. The intriguing character of Laura's verse captivates her readers and wins their enthusiastic notice.

2. Jimmy danced about with eager anticipation as he breathed in the tangy fragrance of the bubbling stew.

3. As she slipped lightly into the puddle, Jan exclaimed with surprise.

Rewrite the following negative statements to convey positive impressions by substituting appropriate positively charged words and phrases.

4. The stubborn cop grilled the hapless suspect unmercifully.

5. Andrew took a cavalier attitude toward his scientific studies and, though able enough, performed his experiments in a frivolous, disdainful manner.

6. Grunting with disgust, Nan hurled the book onto the sod.

E. Writing Job Evaluations. For each of the people described in the following summaries, write three one- to two-sentence job evaluations. In each set, one evaluation should be positive, one neutral, and one negative.

Sample problem:
Millicent Smythe does tidy, careful work. Her clothing is always bandbox fresh, and she never has a hair out of place. Except for current work and a small green plant, Ms. Smythe's desk is completely clear. She reworks each assignment until it meets her own high standard.

Sample solution:
Millicent Smythe is an unusually conscientious worker, whose extra care produces exceptionally reliable work.

Millicent Smythe is meticulous in her concern with the details of her work, which she executes in a neat, tidy fashion.

Millicent Smythe is a finicky fussbudget, who concerns herself almost excessively with minutiae.

1. Jerome M. Caldwell is quick to accept the decisions of his supervisors and is diligent in carrying them out. He is always ready with a compliment or a pleasantry when in contact with his superiors, and he is readily available for such encounters. Caldwell wears a carefully groomed moustache.

2. Jennifer L. Peterson is first to arrive in the morning and last to leave in the evening. She brown-bags it at lunch with the most recent edition of the journal in her field. She socializes very little at the coffee machine. Ms. Peterson usually wears well-tailored tweed suits.

3. B. Michael Pennington has a hearty manner, a sturdy handshake, and an impressive knowledge of the latest stories and jokes. He always wears a vest and is often difficult to find at his desk. Both his expense account and his volume of sales are high.

ACHIEVING PRECISION THROUGH IMAGERY

So far in this chapter I have advised you to choose the words and phrases that most precisely capture the meaning of what you want to say. And this is good advice. But sometimes you cannot find a word or even a phrase that exactly conveys the meaning you have in mind. There are times when the word or phrase that could communicate exactly what you mean seems simply not to exist—especially when you are dealing with concepts that are not concrete (like "buildings," "huts," "two-toed sloths") but rather abstract (ideas such as "freedom"—to be "free," "freely"; feelings such as "love"—"to love," "loving," "lovingly"). If you question whether with all the abundant resources of the English language such a lack of vocabulary could actually be, then think of how you might describe, for instance, the feeling of nausea. Whenever I have asked students to try this experiment, they have always responded with facial grimaces, gestures of hands clutching throat or abdomen, and a chorus of moans and gargles sounding like "Yecch" or "Gwrrk." If someone starts a semi-medical description ("There is a constricted feeling in my throat . . ."), he or she is inevitably booed down by those who feel that this sort of language is very far from what they are feeling. But when in frustration some people start sputtering "It's like . . . it's like . . . ," they are coming very close to the answer. Because our language does not have the words and phrases to express all our ideas and feelings directly, writers find that they sometimes need to be indirect, to tell instead what "it's like." They resort, in short, to comparison—to what we call "imagery" or "metaphor"—in order to communicate fully. Though imagery is the language of poetry, it can be very useful to the writing of prose as well.

The Objective Correlative

In order to use imagery effectively in your writing, you'll find useful a little technical understanding of what makes imagery work. The most helpful definition I know is T. S. Eliot's discussion of the objective correlative:

The only way of expressing emotion in the form of art is by finding an *objective correlative;* in other words, a set of objects, a situation, a chain of events which shall be the formula of that *particular* emotion; such that when the external facts, which must terminate in sensory experience, are given, the emotion is immediately evoked.[3]

Eliot means that when you can't find the words to express a feeling or an abstract idea directly, you should look for something objective, something that can be understood by the senses, to compare your abstraction or feeling with. He calls this compared thing an *objective correlative.* (We'll call it "o.c." for short.) If you have chosen well, your o.c. will call up in your readers something very close to the indescribable feeling or ideas you have been wanting to express.

How does it work? For example, let's take that feeling of nausea already mentioned. There is a stanza in "The Highwayman" where Noyes aims at conveying just such a feeling. In it he sets up an evil stablehand, a man full of sick fancies, as the betrayer of the dashing highwayman who is the hero of the poem. Noyes wants the image of Tim the ostler literally to turn the reader's stomach:

> And dark in the dark old inn-yard, a stable-wicket creaked
> Where Tim the ostler listened; his face was white and peaked;
> *His eyes were hollows of madness, his hair like mouldy hay,*
> But he loved the landlord's daughter, the landlord's *red-lipped* daughter,
> *Dumb as a dog he listened,* and he heard the robber say. . . .

If your response to these lines is similar to the way you felt when you attempted to express the feeling of nausea, then Noyes's objective correlatives of "mouldy hay" and "hollows of madness" worked for you.

Images of Form

Comparison is thus the basis of imagery. An image is a comparison. Writers have distinguished four forms of comparison: metaphor, simile, connotative language, and symbol. Any image you compose will take shape in one of these forms. The forms differ because of the differences in the relationship of the o.c. to the idea it expresses. In metaphor, the o.c. is *equated* to the idea or feeling. Directly or subtly there is always an equal sign. The o.c. is said *to be* the idea or feeling. In simile, the relationship is a little more distant. The o.c. is shown rather to be *similar* to the subject. The writer uses the word "like" or "as" to convey this similarity. With connotative language, the comparison is only implied by the connotations of the words used to

[3]"Hamlet," in *Selected Essays 1917–1932* (New York: Harcourt Brace Jovanovich, 1932), pp. 124–125.

Imagery

Definition: Imagery is comparison. The image centers on an objective correlative (o.c.) to which the writer compares an indescribable idea or feeling to evoke a similar idea or feeling in the reader.

Forms of images	Subject	Comparison	Objective correlative
METAPHOR:	*Subject*	=	*o.c.*
Example:	Tim's eyes	"were"	"hollows of madness"
SIMILE:	*Subject*	*like (as)*	*o.c.*
Examples:	Tim's hair	"like"	"mouldy hay"
	Tim's listening	"dumb as"	"a dog"
CONNOTATIVE			
LANGUAGE:	*Subject*	*implies*	*o.c.*
Example:	Landlord's daughter's sensual attractiveness	implied by	"red-lipped"
SYMBOL:	*Subject*	=	*itself*
		AND *stands for o.c.*	
Example:	Tim, the ostler	=	the stablehand, a character in the poem
		AND *stands for* stealthy, unseen evil	

express the ideas. And in symbolism, the o.c. has both a literal and a symbolic meaning—that is, at one time the o.c. both means itself and stands for something else, just as the American eagle is both a bird and a symbol of American strength and freedom. The accompanying boxed section illustrates how each of these forms works.

Using Imagery in Expository Prose

Our examples so far have been taken from a poem, and it is true that imagery is the language of poetry. Nevertheless, imagery is also useful for prose writers. Prose writers, like poets, sometimes want to convey an inexpressible feeling and, more often than poets, need to clarify an abstract idea. Furthermore, since prose writers are not confined to the condensed language of poetry, they are free to expand and elaborate upon an image. Each of these expansions has its own uses and its own name:

- Expanded metaphor = Extended metaphor
- Expanded simile   = Analogy
- Expanded symbol   = Allegory

The following quotations show how the authors of the essays in Part Four make use of the various forms of imagery. The examples should give you some ideas about how you too might employ these forms.

EXAMPLES OF METAPHOR

Some metaphors indicate the comparison directly:

Quotation	o.c.	=	Inexpressible Feeling or Idea
"When I reach my time I may find myself still hanging around in some sort of midair, *one of those small thoughts, drawn back into the memory of the earth.*"[4] (Thomas, 429: 3)	An immortal thought in the earth's memory		The author, after death

Other metaphors work through more subtly indicated comparison:

Quotation	o.c.	=	Inexpressible Feeling or Idea
"The desert's *cancerous* growth" (Golden, 415: 5)	An evergrowing cancer		The ever increasing desert
"If I were not such a First *Amendment* junkie" (Greenfield, 422: 10)	Addiction		The author's passion for the First Amendment

Extended metaphors work on the same principle. Here the comparison is extended or elaborated on. Not only is the subject equated to the o.c., but its qualities are spoken of in terms of the qualities of the o.c.

Quotation

The students, male and female, are the latest victims of *two-track talking, two-track teaching.* After my week at school, I wonder what will happen if young women don't learn that they have much more to fear from what they don't say. I wonder what will happen if more campuses don't involve their

---

[4]Italic type throughout the section highlights the o.c.'s.

male students in thinking about lives *gauged together,* rather than on these *separate tracks.* (Goodman, 419: 17)

o.c.	=	Inexpressible Feeling or Idea
Original o.c.: Trains on two separate tracks		Lives of noncommunicating women and men
Expanded o.c.: Tracks should be gauged together		To share a life, women and men must begin communicating their intimate thoughts—especially about a shared life

EXAMPLES OF SIMILE

The following examples illustrate simile:

Quotation	o.c.	"Is Like"	Inexpressible Feeling or Idea
"The cellos subside and disappear *like an exhalation*" (Thomas, 429: 7)	A sigh		Thomas's perception of cello music
"The mother lives *as junior partner* with the man who is, after all, the daughter's father" (Goodman, 418: 8)	A subordinate in business		The mother's position with her husband

The analogy, an expanded simile, permits the reader to view one set of ideas in terms of another:

> [My emotion on hearing of my friends' divorce] was an anger similar to that I feel when I see abandoned foundations of building projects—piled bricks and girders and a gash in the ground left to depress the passerby. (Tucker, 431: 3)

> One [formulation] holds that the hostages are "being treated well," so long as they get some food and soap and are not being physically beaten. It reminds me of that old standby about how the woman had been raped "but not harmed" by her assailant. The absence of a bash to the face in neither case constitutes absence of harm or good treatment. (Greenfield, 421: 6)

EXAMPLES OF CONNOTATIVE LANGUAGE

Almost all words that are not simply function words project various connotative meanings in addition to their literal or denotative meanings, as you learned earlier in this chapter. Connotative language becomes imagery when writers use the connotations of a particular word or phrase to stand as an objective correlative for the feeling or abstract idea they are trying to express.

Quotation

[To call terrorism war] is to elevate these *grubby* criminal acts to a status they don't deserve. (Greenfield, page 421, paragraph 7)
· [*grubby,* which denotes "dirty, full of grubs" here implies "low, beneath contempt"]

Quotation

At age seven . . . I fell *ankles over elbows* in love with the Cubs. (Will, page 438, paragraph 4)
· [*Ankles over elbows,* an allusion to "head over heels," implies the coltishly awkward enthusiasm of the seven-year-old.]

IMAGES OF FORM: EXAMPLES OF SYMBOLISM

Some symbolism also indicates comparison directly:

Quotation

There was a little device we noticed in one of the sporting-goods stores—*a trumpet* that hunters hold to their ears so that they can hear the *distant music of the hounds.* Something of the sort is needed now to hear the incredibly distant sound of Christmas in these times, through the dark, material woods that surround it. (White, page 436, paragraph 1)

o.c.	= *and* stands for	Inexpressible Feeling or Idea
Ear trumpet	=	"A device we noticed in [a] sporting-goods store"
	and stands for	A way to perceive real values obscured by materialism
Music of the hounds	=	The distant barking of the hunting dogs at night
	and stands for	The true and natural values

And other symbolism indicates comparison subtly:

Quotation

People used to grow up with *trees,* watch them evolve from saplings to fruit bearers to gnarled and unproductive grandfathers. Now, unless one is a farmer or a forester there is almost no point to planting trees because one is not likely to be there to enjoy their maturity. (Tucker, page 432, paragraph 8)

o.c.	= *and* stands for	Inexpressible Feeling or Idea
Tree	=	A large leaf-bearing, wooden-trunked plant
	and stands for	Stability and continuity in a disconcertingly fragmented world

---

TRY IT OUT

1. In the first paragraphs of his "Late Night Thoughts on Listening to Mahler's Ninth Symphony," Thomas explicitly sets up a metaphor that he extends throughout the essay:

   > I took *this music* [Mahler's Ninth] as a metaphor for reassurance, confirming my own strong hunch that the dying of every living creature, the most natural of all experiences, has to be a peaceful experience. . . . *The long passages on all the strings at the end.* . . . I used to hear as Mahler's idea of leave-taking at its best. . . . Now I hear it differently. I cannot listen to *the last movement of the Mahler Ninth* without the door-smashing intrusion of a huge new thought: death everywhere, the dying of everything, the end of humanity.
   >
   > o.c.: Mahler's Ninth = then: reassurance about death
   > now: threat of a nuclear holocaust

   Find the rest of this extended metaphor in other passages of the essay, and show how both the objective correlatives and the meanings of the continuations of the metaphor become more specific.

2. More often than not, symbols are also extended in this way. Find the continuations of the symbols in the two examples cited, and briefly explain them.

   a. There was a little device we noticed in one of the sporting-goods stores—*a trumpet* that hunters hold to their ears so that they can hear the *distant music of the hounds.* Something of the sort is needed now to hear the incredibly distant sound of Christmas in these times, through the dark, material woods that surround it. (White, page 436, paragraph 1)

      o.c.: Ear trumpet = "A device we noticed in [a] sporting goods store"
      and stands for A way to perceive real values obscured by materialism

   b. People used to grow up with *trees,* watch them evolve from saplings to fruit bearers to gnarled and unproductive grandfathers. Now, unless one is a farmer or a forester there is almost no point to planting trees because one is not likely to be there to enjoy their maturity. (Tucker, page 432, paragraph 8)

      o.c.: Tree   = A large leaf-bearing, wooden trunked plant;
      and stands for Stability and continuity in a disconcertingly fragmented world

Images of Content

Though all images take the shape of one of the basic forms—metaphor, simile, connotative language, or symbol—images can vary enormously in content, in the nature of their objective correlatives. Many o.c.'s refer to the sense impressions of ordinary experience: "like bees among flowers" (Tucker, page 432, paragraph 8), "as a rabbit track in snow leads eventually to the rabbit" (White, page 437, paragraph 4). But as a shaper of images, you also have a number of other kinds of o.c.'s available to you. Three of the most useful of these are called *hyperbole, personification,* and *allusion.*

HYPERBOLE

If the emotion or the idea you want to express seems inexpressible because it is so big, so vast, so overwhelming that it makes any regular image an understatement, and if only an exaggeration will do to convey that vastness, then you can turn to hyperbole. In hyperbole, the objective correlative is wildly exaggerated. Will uses hyperbole with reckless abandon in his essay on the Chicago Cubs:

> Spring . . . became for me an experience comparable to *being slapped around the mouth with a damp carp.* Summer was like *being bashed across the bridge of the nose with a crowbar—ninety times.* My youth was like *a long rainy Monday in Bayonne, New Jersey.* (page 438, paragraph 5)

The italicized o.c.'s all relate to what Will considers the unspeakable agony of a boyhood as a devoted Cubs' fan. Will phrases his hyperboles as similes. But they, like the other images of content, can be phrased in any of the forms. Thomas, for example, uses a hyperbolic metaphor when he writes that

> If I were sixteen or seventeen . . . I would know for sure that the *whole world was coming unhinged.* (page 429, paragraph 9)

Thomas also makes hyperbole out of connotative language:

> [When I was sixteen] the years stretched away *forever ahead, forever.* (paragraph 9)

PERSONIFICATION

In personification, another image of content, the objective correlative is human. Personification thus adds human appeal to nonhuman objects by endowing them with the characteristics of human beings. There are two kinds of personification. One kind turns an abstraction into a human being, like the characters in the old morality plays: Faith, Hope, Charity, and Bad Deeds. This form, though perhaps used more extensively in past centuries, is not uncommon even today and is employed especially effectively with ironic intent. Alexander, for instance, in characterizing the youthful affectations of the middle-aged, writes:

> New hair sprouts, transplanted, on *wisdom's* brow. (page 411, paragraph 3)

This sort of personification can also be used quite seriously, as Greenfield writes:

> We give *terrorism* a friendly face. (page 420, paragraph 4)

The other kind of personification attaches human characteristics to the nonhuman. Williams, for example, ascribes uniquely human activity to an impersonal system of economics when he speaks of *"unfettered* free enterprise" (page 442, paragraph 7). And Thomas personifies our earth as he writes:

> The life of the earth is the same as the life of an organism: the great round being *possesses a mind;* the mind contains an infinite number of thoughts and memories. (page 429, paragraph 3).

ALLUSION

Another way you can expand the metaphoric universe of your writing is to tint your o.c. with the unmistakable color of another piece of literature. Thus, through *allusion,* you include the world of the other work within your own. With an allusion you provide your readers with a shorthand "memo" that will take them to the work in question for the relevant idea and then back to your writing again. Tucker, for instance, uses a metaphoric allusion in this way when he refers to Dreiser's *American Tragedy:*

> In some respects, this freedom [to divorce easily] can be seen as social progress. Modern couples can flee the corrosive bitterness that made Strindberg's marriages nightmares. *Dreiser's Clyde Griffiths might have abandoned his Roberta instead of drowning her.* (page 432, paragraph 6)

Those readers who are familiar with Clyde Griffiths, the hero of *An American Tragedy,* can understand from a phrase what might otherwise have taken several paragraphs to explain.

Allusion is not confined to literary objective correlatives. With it you may draw in historical figures and events as Tucker did when he alluded to Strindberg. You may also allude to works of art or music, as Thomas does so masterfully throughout his "Late Night Thoughts on Listening to Mahler's Ninth Symphony."

Allusion can also be highly effective when used ironically. Shana Alexander provides the pastime of jogging with an exaggeratedly noble allusion to "America the Beautiful":

> Sages jog from *sea to shining sea.* (page 411, paragraph 3)

Allusion helps readers experience the pleasure of recognition and of sharing their author's knowledge. And, as long as reader and author actually do share in the knowledge alluded to, allusion can be a highly persuasive strategy. There is a problem, however, in the heavy reliance the author of allusions must place on the reader's having shared his or her experience. If readers have had no personal contact with *mouldy hay,* for instance, they can still imagine enough about it to find meaning in the metaphor; but if they know nothing about Strindberg or have never heard "From sea to shining sea," these images may well fall flat, endangering their authors' points as well.

Thus the question arises: Should you use an allusion that goes right to the heart of what you want to say even though you are not sure that it will be understood by all your readers? With my bias for placing precision of meaning above all other considerations, I would have to say, yes, use the allusion that will precisely carry your point. But hedge your bets. In the phrasing of your allusion (or in addition to your allusion) include enough hints of your intended meaning to be sure that your readers will take your point. Will, for example, ends his essay on the Cubs with a wonderfully witty *tour de force* of allusions. Those readers who recognize every quotation undoubtedly enjoy it most. Those readers (and they are probably in the majority) who find vaguely familiar echoes in his phrases should enjoy it thoroughly. But Will provides enough clues so that even those readers who are unaware of the source of any of his quotations can still understand his meaning and can find the passage a pleasure to read:

Allusion	Source
Do not go gently into this season, Cub fans: Rage, rage against the blasting of our hopes.	Do not go gentle into that good night. / Rage, rage, against the dying of the light. ("Do Not Go Gentle into that Good Night," Dylan Thomas)
Had I but world enough, and time, this slowness, Cubs, would be no crime.	Had we but world enough, and time, / This coyness, lady, were no crime. ("To His Coy Mistress," Andrew Marvell)
But I am almost halfway through my allotted three-score-and-ten, and you, sirs, are overdue. (page 440, paragraph 15)	The days of our years are three score years and ten. (Psalm 90, Bible) Overdue. (Radio announcer quoted earlier in essay)

Creating Images

This review of the metaphoric possibilities open to you demonstrates the kind of precision of meaning you might be able to achieve by using imagery in your writing. But you may still be in some doubt about how to go about actually composing such images. First, metaphors and similes, and certainly connotative language, may occur to you spontaneously as you write. When they do, be bold. Add them to your writing just as they occur to you, even if they seem a bit showy at first. Remember, you can always go back and revise or even delete.

But what about the times when the images do not come, yet you feel a certain precision is missing in your prose that a good metaphor might take care of? At these times, you have two good sources: your subconscious and your conscious mind.

SEARCHING YOUR SUBCONSCIOUS MIND

Try freewriting (see page 42) on a point that is troubling you. Then examine carefully what you have written for bits and pieces of metaphors and subconscious images that may have come to you unaware. If you do free writing regularly, you can accumulate a storehouse of imagery to turn to as you need it.

Similarly, if you keep a journal, you can read back over your recent entries for ideas and associations. Even if you do not keep a journal with any regularity, it is a good idea to keep a small notepad in your pocket or purse, so that if a striking comparison should occur to you while you are going about your activities, you will be able to preserve it for future use.

The poet Donald Hall, who is also a teacher, recommends daydreaming as a place to start building your images. Because dreams put you in direct contact with your own image-making faculty, he believes they can be an especially rich source of metaphoric material. Hall suggests that you analyze your dreams for images and the words that accompany them. The crazier they are, he feels, the more fruitful these images are likely to be. Hall writes: "We may start dreaming; we end up thinking."[5]

SEARCHING YOUR CONSCIOUS MIND

Your first step in a conscious search for imagery is to take your topic—or a person, place, or situation important to your topic—and deliberately associate physical objects and sense impressions with it. Make these associations as concrete and specific as possible. For example, if you were writing about rioting in the inner city, you might feel the need for an image to describe the tensions that occur just before a riot breaks out. By consciously employing your senses and your imagination, you might produce these associations:

- a street smelling of melting asphalt
- obscene graffiti on crumbling walls
- lounging figures
- the feeling of boredom
- the feeling of restlessness
- the rank odor of sweat and unwashed underwear
- unmirthful joking
- oppressive heat

[5] *Writing Well,* 3rd ed. (Boston: Little, Brown, 1979), pp. 110–11.

Your second step is to find an objective correlative that will make your associations real to your reader. Returning to our example, you might single out the oppressive heat and its triggering effect upon the riot and try it for various comparisons. What first comes to mind? Perhaps "hotter than blazes." But you will probably want to discard all such hackneyed phrases because their o.c.'s are so familiar that they no longer evoke sense images in readers' minds. You may also want to discard "as hot as a blast furnace" because it also may not seem like a fresh comparison to you or because it is not really an accurate description of city heat (that is, unless you decide to strive for hyperbole).

How do you find a fresh comparison? Search your recent memory. Where have you felt heat recently? Perhaps in a plant conservatory. You might try out:

> · The atmosphere was hot and heavy with unfallen rain, like the perpetual moist heat of a conservatory of plants.

The conservatory is indeed a fresh comparison, and one that accurately describes the feeling of heat. But is it as completely appropriate a reference to your basic subject as you could find? The best metaphors take the reader beyond a simple sense comparison into the heart of the concept being considered. So why not try again? Can you remember another recent experience with heat? How about the heat you may have felt when walking by piles of burning trash? How about:

> · The air was oppressive with the sort of acrid heat that surrounds a heap of burning rubbish.

Here your image is directly related to your basic subject matter and could also foreshadow your descriptions of the wanton fire-setting that will follow.

Though you may find a totally appropriate image difficult to discover, the result is certainly worth the effort. Total appropriateness of metaphor is one of the hallmarks of the professional writer. You will find it again and again in our collection of essays. Tucker, for example, achieves it in his selection of an image to express the rapidity of change in contemporary lives. He writes:

> We change addresses and occupations and hobbies and life styles rapidly and readily; much as we change . . .

He could have conveyed the notion of rapid change perfectly well if he had chosen the simile: "much as we change underwear" or "change dollar bills." But he underlines the comparison fundamental to his point by writing "much as we change *TV channels*" (page 432, paragraph 8). With similar appropriateness, White metaphorically equates modern Christmas with the gift within a gaudily bedecked package when he writes:

> To perceive Christmas through its wrapping becomes more difficult with every year. (page 436, paragraph 1)

Hidden Metaphors.   Yet another way to develop your imagery is to make use of the metaphors hidden in the very words that must be used to discuss the subject. Many words in common use are actually metaphors. Goodman, for instance, writes about the "gap" between men and women in the public-opinion-poll figures on the question of married women's activities' being "best confined to the home." *Gap* literally means "a small fissure or cleft as in a mountain." Goodman puns upon that meaning, creating this image to strengthen her point:

> But a *gap* between men and women exists even on this easy question. It grows into a *chasm* as the issues of sharing and partnership become more complicated. (page 419, paragraph 15)

Thus, if you are having difficulty uncovering appropriate imagery, you might check to see whether any of your key words actually have more than one meaning. Perhaps you will be able to derive some useful imagery from the literal sense of such words.

Negative Metaphors.   When you are bogged down in your efforts to discover an appropriate image for conveying an important idea, you might try thinking of a negative rather than a positive comparison. What is it that your subject is *not* like? Greenfield answers this question with this striking negative image:

> We call these shoot-and-pitch men "militants" . . . *as if they were merely agitating for pure air and happy whales.* (page 421, paragraph 5)

In similar negative fashion, Lewis Thomas ironically describes the television Civil Defense pitchman as "more dependable looking than most high school principals" (page 430, paragraph 10).

PRACTICE MAKES INSPIRATION?

Composing effective images is, of course, to some degree, a matter of inspiration. But inspiration comes more often to a mind that is ready to recognize it, knows what to do with it when it arrives, and even has ways of encouraging its coming. The following sets of exercises are offered as the sort of practice that can lead to such receptivity.

TRY IT OUT

A. Composing New Images. The following images long ago lost their impact. Find a new simile, metaphor, allusion, or other image to illustrate each of these abstractions. Suggest a context in which your image would be appropriate.

Sample problem:
Red as a rose

Some sample solutions:
· She blushed a painful tomato-juice red (for an essay on vegetarians)
· Red as the cover of a copy of "Quotations from Chairman Mao" (for an essay on radicalism)

1. Pure as the driven snow
2. Green as grass
3. Ugly as sin
4. Bitter as gall
5. Dead as a doornail
6. Jolly as old St. Nick
7. Life is the pits.
8. Hungry enough to eat a horse.

B. Describing with Metaphors. Describe five of your classmates in metaphoric terms. Make one description into an extended metaphor.

C. Creating Personification. Try turning the following abstractions into personifications.

Sample problem:
Laughter

Some sample solutions:
· "Laughter holding both its sides" (Milton)
· Her laughter hung in the air as if waiting for its presence to be recognized.

1. The sea
2. Autumn
3. Joy
4. Thirst
5. A computer
6. A mosquito
7. A guitar
8. A football

D. Creating Hyperbole. Create a suitable hyperbole for each of the following superlative situations.

Sample problem:
A truly excellent fiddle player.

Some sample solutions:
· "He fiddled all the bugs off a sweet potato vine."
· "He fiddled up a whale from the bottom of the sea."
· "He fiddled down a 'coon from a mile high tree." (Stephen Vincent Benét, "Mountain Whippoorwill")

1. A child's really grimy face
2. An enormous sandy beach

3. True love

4. A politician with disgusting ideas

5. A delectable meal

E. Creating Allusions. Create at least two metaphors or similes for each of the following. Include as many allusions as you can.

Sample problem:
Your favorite toddler

Some sample solutions:

· Holding the big bat determinedly in his tiny hands, Jamie stood at the plate, *a miniature Babe Ruth.*
· Two-year-old Susie, *like the dormouse at the Mad Hatter's Tea Party,* had the habit of falling asleep at the table.

1. One of your professors

2. A basketball triumph

3. An elderly relative

4. A scene from a movie or television drama

5. Your room

6. An idea of your choice

AVOIDING IMPRECISION

This chapter has detailed ways in which you can achieve precision of meaning by carefully choosing your words, phrases, and imagery. This goal of precision is well worth striving for, but sometimes deep-rooted habits or desires can prevent you from achieving it. The two most destructive of such tendencies are the desire to be impressive and the habit of lazy thinking.

Resisting the Desire to Be Impressive

Although the desire *to impress* is a natural human wish that can be useful in your writing, the desire *to be impressive*—though equally human—is misguided and can produce the opposite of the wished-for results. Trying to be impressive so often backfires because inexperienced writers tend to be mistaken in their notions about what sort of writing actually is impressive.

THE SIZE MISCONCEPTION

Probably the most important such misconception can be summed up in the catch phrase "big is better." Those who subscribe to this notion think that great numbers of long words give a composition an impressive tone. And so they search for opportunities to ornament their writing with the likes of *antidisestablishmentarianism.* If a word they want to use does not seem impressive enough, they pile prefixes and suffixes on it until it reaches a satisfying length. By this means they create such monstrosities as *directionality* or *scrutinization,* as in "Our goal is to establish directionality in the development of educational programs" or "He gave the summary careful scrutinization." To get a word like *directionality,* the writer had to begin with the perfectly good noun *direction* (which is already an extension of the verb *direct*), add a suffix to turn it into the adjective *directional,* and add yet another suffix to turn it back into a noun again. If the writers of the sample sentences had not used the elongated terms, they would have produced writing both more direct and more effective:

- Our goal is to establish direction.
- He gave the summary careful scrutiny.

Many of those who try to impress by size also try to impress by quantity. They like to pile up adjective upon adjective, adverb upon adverb. Not content with making their point soundly once, they restate it again and again. Those who hold with this way of thinking seem to believe that if one figure of speech in a sentence is good, three are better and six are really terrific. In their writing you would find long passages of what is usually called "purple prose." The following excerpt, for example, is typical:

Faulty
- No more time to think. No more time to ponder. The momentous decision must be made now or never. Was it her voice that, after a moment that seemed an eternity, harshly gasped out her final and eternal decision.

Such writers seem to share the mistaken idea that, since effective writing often involves touching the readers' emotions, they can achieve even greater effectiveness by wringing their readers' hearts. The believers in quantity do not seem to understand that they can lessen the impact of any idea or device, however effective, by overdoing it. They overlook altogether the remarkable persuasiveness of honest simplicity.

THE ODDITY MISCONCEPTION

Some inexperienced writers not only believe that "bigger is better," but also that "the more singular, the more significant." Unfortunately, the only words people generally consider unusual are words that are not comfortably lodged in their own vocabularies. We all tend to think of words that we know well and use without self-consciousness as ordinary. Thus, writers who wish to strive for unusual diction often find themselves forced to select for their writing words and phrases with which they are largely unfamiliar. Such writers comb their thesauruses for synonyms and often seem unaware that synonyms cannot be interchanged in all contexts. Actually, interchanging synonyms without regard to connotations or other nuances of meaning can be the source of downright embarrassing sentences. The following examples are typical:

Faulty   · The nurse was *interminably* helpful. [Did the writer mean "unceasingly"?]
Faulty   · She was well known for her *soporific* conversational style. [Did the writer mean "relaxed"?]
Faulty   · The graduate's father glowed with paternal *superciliousness*. [Could the writer have meant "pride"?]

Guide to Using a Thesaurus

1. Use your thesaurus to spur your memory when you have a word on the "tip of your tongue" but aren't able to bring it to your conscious mind.
2. Try your thesaurus when you have used a word several times and you feel you are beginning to establish a repetitive pattern.
3. Do *not* use your thesaurus to find a word that will seem more impressive than your original term.
4. And most important, *never* select from a thesaurus a word you do not already use comfortably, a word you do not already have in your working vocabulary.

SIMPLER REALLY IS BEST

Throughout this chapter I have insisted that your best choice is that word or phrase—whatever its length or degree of familiarity—which most precisely expresses your meaning. And such precision should remain your chief goal. Nevertheless, an important exception must be made: Since the whole purpose of precise wording is to communicate your thoughts to your reader, communication itself must always be your most important consideration. If, for instance, you knew that a word like *antidisestablishmentarianism* most precisely conveys your meaning, but you had reason to believe that much of your readership would not have that expression in their vocabularies, then you would be wise to trade precision for understanding and select a briefer, more widely known term.

In fact, because of most modern readers' desire for speedy comprehension of their reading material, you should probably conclude that, where there is a choice, smaller and simpler is usually better. The eye takes in the small word quicker than the longer, and the mind decodes and processes the more familiar term faster than the more unusual word. For these reasons, large, long, and complex wordings not only do *not* impress but, by impeding reading, can actually annoy readers. Readers who feel bored, confused, or intimidated are not likely to see the writer as an impressive intellectual, but rather as an inconsiderate show-off. The truth is that even the best-chosen diction that aims at being impressive tends to divert its readers' attention and thus to distract from the purpose. In general, therefore, good writing, like good acting, should move its audience without calling too much attention to itself.

GOOSEMYER by parker and wilder

GOOSEMYER by Brant Parker and Don Wilder. © 1980 Field Enterprises, Inc., by permission of North America Syndicate, Inc.

TRY IT OUT

Editing for Simplicity. Edit the following sentences by choosing words and phrases that are less pretentious or less emotionally charged.

Sample problem:

Insofar as excessive trepidation will incapacitate my vocational advancement, I will endeavor to vanquish this inadequacy.

Sample solution:

I will try to get over my shyness because it may harm my career.

1. The fragile Dolly-Lou was rendered prostrate by the callous insensitivity, hard-heartedness, and searing cruelty of Joe's cold-blooded indifference.

2. The guilt-ridden child went back to school intending to obliterate, exterminate, eradicate, and annihilate all signs of yesterday's mischief.

3. Consequently, the operator of the motor vehicle determined that it would be advantageous to maneuver his conveyance to a position perpendicular to where it was now located.

4. He gazed into her eyes with fervent ardor, his limbs trembling, his heart beating wildly, forlornly hoping against hope that Susan would choose to sit at the empty desk next to his.

5. Last evening's frankfurter occasioned the production of intermittent cadences in my abdomen, a condition whose immediate cessation I profoundly coveted.

Avoiding Lazy Thinking

Another important obstacle to using precise diction is the almost universal human tendency to be lazy in our thinking. Such laziness accounts for most of the repetitiveness and wordiness that mar so much written work. We don't want to make the effort to come out with the phrase that exactly expresses what we have on our minds, and so we include a number of similar wordings, each of which comes near to what we really want to say. Careful editing should clear up this problem; but again out of sheer laziness, most of us don't bother to keep on striving for a single precise expression but settle instead for a half dozen near hits.

CLICHÉS

Lazy thinking is behind the unfortunate tendency of many writers to compose in clichés. Clichés are automatic verbal responses that carry almost no meaning. They are the fixed phrases that come to mind before we give a subject serious thought. Some clichés are fillers, empty words that hold the space while we wait for our ideas to come together. For example:

In this day and age . . .   When all is said and done . . .
As luck would have it . . .   In the society of today . . .

Other clichés are sets of words that "sort of seem to *belong* together," one word triggering the whole phrase. *The Harvard Lampoon* (with tongue in cheek) suggests the following as "phrases [that] occur only as indivisible units, even though they appear to be constructed of discrete words":[6]

furtive glance   insurmountable odds
catlike quickness   abject poverty
limpid pools   lightning-quick reflexes
waning interest

Other such automatic phrases have the further disadvantage of being redundant (see page 174); that is, part of the phrase necessarily implies another part. Nonetheless we continue to use the parts together because one word seems naturally to summon up the rest. Here are a few typical examples:

evening sunset   morning sunrise   white snow
high mountains   fast speed   at this point in time

But clichés do not start out as clichés. On the contrary, when most of these phrases were introduced, they were so effective at conveying their points that they were used again and again. Over the years they simply lost their meaning. Many clichés are dead metaphors that had their origin in colloquial speech. You may recall a truly original way of describing an

---

[6]*The Harvard Lampoon Big Book of College Life,* Stephen G. Crist and George Meyer, eds. (Garden City, N.Y.: Doubleday, 1978), p. 108.

overcrowded room that has already died from overuse: *wall-to-wall people.*
Other examples include:

bite the bullet	the pits
heavy into	game plan
the name of the game	sight for sore eyes
gross	

Other clichés are made from words that have succumbed to the tendency of language to become more general in meaning. Though such terms have precisely defined meanings, these meanings are rarely intended by those who use them, as the accompanying table shows.

Word	Meaning	Usually used to mean
nice	precise	having a positive quality
classic	having stood the test of time	very nice
awesome	filling one with awe	extremely nice
divine	fit to be worshipped	extremely nice
fantastic	having to do with fantasy	wildly nice

If you are to aim for precision in your diction, clearly you will have to learn to avoid such clichés. But how can you tell when you have written a cliché? Whenever a word or a phrase seems to come automatically to your mind, you should check it objectively for both literal and figurative meaning. If it evokes no specific or appropriate sense image in the context in which you want to use it, you can be fairly sure you are burdened with a stock phrase or a cliché.

Gobbledygook.   Of all the clichés, the kind that most interfere with precision of expression today are those associated with jargon, trendy pseudo-technical terms that can turn your writing into gobbledygook. Turn back to page 180 and review the section on jargon and gobbledygook for a description of what to avoid.

TRY IT OUT

Editing for Freshness. Test the following sentences for the presence of stock phrases or clichés. If you discover any, edit them out and rewrite the sentence in a fresher, more effective way.
Sample problem:
Meryl regretted that his chances for advancement were *so few and far between.*

Some sample solutions:
Meryl regretted that he had such infrequent opportunities for advancement.
Meryl regretted that chances for his advancement came up so rarely.

1. Joe and Mabel were determined to devote their retirement to pursuing the finer things in life.

2. Although the mountain climber noticed the sky becoming dark and stormy, he resolved to stay on until the bitter end.

3. Felicia took advantage of this golden opportunity to get some rest, and so she went back to her room, where she turned on her radio and lounged around to her heart's content.

4. Last, but not least, we announce the retirement of our long-time board member, J. George Jones, who plans to return to his hometown in the west, where he will be gone but not forgotten.

5. Unlike her predecessors, Katherine Parr, Henry VIII's last wife, survived her experience in good spirits, went into her widowhood none the worse for wear, and lived to a ripe old age.

6. The diplomat showed his true colors when he began playing fast and loose with his country's economic commitments.

7. Nowadays, it goes without saying that getting involved in a deep and meaningful relationship is easier said than done.

8. As luck would have it, the newlyweds had many trials and tribulations trying to make ends meet in this day and age.

A Final Word on Style

In these chapters on style, I hope you have come to see that an appealing style is neither accidental nor beyond your reach. You mold your style by the decisions you make in specific choices of syntax and diction. Those decisions are most successful that make your meaning clearer and more accessible to the reader. In choosing your syntax, you should construct your sentences with rhythms that are both harmonious and varied and with a rhythmical emphasis that coincides with your purpose and your point. In choosing your diction, you should select the words and phrases that most precisely express what you want to say, what you want your reader to understand. In general, when other considerations are equal, you should aim for the simpler, shorter, clearer word or structure. All this advice is fundamentally sound; yet it may well be that H. L. Mencken's counsel is even more useful:

> The essence of a sound style is that it cannot be reduced to rules—that it is a living and breathing thing, with something of the devilish in it.[7]

[7]"Literature and the Schoolma'm," *Prejudices: Fifth Series* (New York: Knopf, 1926), p. 197.

ASSIGNMENT

1. Write an essay in which you put into words an insight you have gained or a set of ideas you have come to understand in one of your other courses. Define your point carefully and explain and support it by specific reference to the facts upon which it is based.

    Because you will be dealing with ideas and the relationship of facts to ideas, you may be confronted with the problem of vagueness. It will, therefore, be especially important for you to choose your diction so as to express your meaning with as much precision as possible.

2. Choose one word that has interesting meanings—denotative and connotative—associated with it. Learn all you can about the word through dictionaries (especially the *Oxford English Dictionary* [*O.E.D.*]), dictionaries of slang, histories of the English language, and other reference works available in your library. Draw associations with the word from your own experience (free writing or brainstorming may help). Then formulate a thesis based on all the ideas you've gathered and write an essay. Here are some words that are interesting to me:

romance	spectacle	circus	guest
fantastic	deem and doom	chamberlain	host

    And here's one student's introduction and thesis for such an essay:

    > I always thought what I'd been reading in the lawn swing over summer vacations were "romances." You know, those dollar novels with cover pictures of impassioned, embracing (or near-to-embracing) couples framed in vine-entangled scrollwork. But when my medieval lit teacher assigned a "romance," I found that this kind of reading was another story altogether. Knights and armor and wan fair maidens were a far cry from a modern breezy couple finding each other among the dunes by a secluded beach house. Despite the obvious differences, though, there's still a touch of the medieval in the modern word "romance."

3. Write an essay in which you compare two advertisements in the ways their writers attempt to appeal to particular audiences. Develop a thesis and support it with specific details gleaned from your analysis of the ads' pictorial and dictional features. The discussion of diction in this chapter should help your analysis.[8]

---

[8]Suggested by Professor Linda Young of California State University, Sacramento.

PART
THREE

Writing Special Kinds of Expository Essays

Two specialized kinds of expository writing are particularly important in the academic setting: research papers and critical analyses. You are almost certain to encounter them during your college career. At base, both of these special papers are expository, and so all the strategies for effective expository writing we have already discussed apply to them as well. But in addition, each has a number of distinctive characteristics; and since some of these are rather technical, both kinds of writing warrant individual study.

The purpose of Part Three, then, is to prepare you for the day when, without preliminaries, your professor will announce: "Write a research paper on an idea in this course that has interested you, and turn it in on November 25" or "Read a work from the handout list and write a critical analysis of it for Monday." In the following chapter you will find an abundance of practical guidance so that you may be knowledgeable about these two genres and feel confident of dealing with them successfully.

Chapter
10

The Research Paper:
An Interdisciplinary Approach

There comes a time—sometimes quite early in your college career—when you can no longer write from your personal experience alone, when you must turn to books or other sources to find your information. Perhaps the syllabus for your Comparative-Religions course includes a final essay on aspects of Buddhism, Hinduism, or Islam; or your Biology professor concludes a lecture on microbes by assigning a report on "The Virus of Your Choice"; or in thinking through an issue for your composition assignment you find your current information too limited to express your point of view. Then suddenly you are writing a research paper. You find that you are no longer in the freewheeling realm of individual writing but rather in the highly conventional territory of scholarly research. In this territory you are obliged to play by the scholars' rules. But if you are like most inexperienced writers, you probably don't know these rules. This chapter aims to help you learn them.

THE PRINCIPLE OF THE THING

You might not even be sure of what exactly a research paper is. Let's begin with a definition:

A research paper is a specialized form of expository writing in which a writer attempts to add to the world's accumulated scholarship by making some definite statement based on a careful study of

already existing data or ideas on a particular topic (or, optionally, on ideas developed experimentally by the researcher).[1]

The Expository Nature of a Research Paper

The scholarly research paper, then, whatever the discipline, is at base an *expository essay,* the same sort of essay we have been discussing throughout this book. Its nature, like that of all expository writing, is the development of a point, a thesis. In most cases, writing a research paper is much like writing other kinds of expository prose—you set out your thesis in an introduction, support it logically in the body of the paper, and restate it most convincingly in the conclusion.

SCHOLARLY PURPOSE OF A RESEARCH PAPER

How then is the scholarly research paper distinguished from other expository writing? The difference lies partly in its purpose, for the goal of research is an attempt "to add to the accumulation of the world's scholarship." This goal may at first strike you as far-fetched. You may wonder how any paper you might produce right now could serve so lofty an end. Yet, when you think about it, you may discover that by finding out what has been said on a topic and by taking it one step further, or at least by considering it in writing from a new and individual point of view, you really do contribute to scholarship in general. And although you may never have considered yourself a scholar, in doing research and writing it up, you in fact become one. For research is what scholars do, and writing research papers is one way scholars talk to each other. Although the chances may be slight that your first research paper will be among those few beginning papers each year that form the kernel of later dissertations or scholarly articles, still, by following the methods and conventions of research in writing these early papers, you are gaining the key that will open up the world of scholarship to you.

SPECIAL SOURCES OF A RESEARCH PAPER

The most important difference between the research paper and other forms of expository writing is the source of its subject matter. Instead of writing from personal knowledge, in the research paper—all across the curriculum—you will be basing your work and your conclusion upon *a careful study of already existing ideas or data.* The most difficult part of writing a research paper is distinguishing between these ideas and your own comments and conclusions. Scholars in the various fields of study

[1]Because the disciplines differ markedly in conventions for conducting and writing about experimental research, discussion here focuses on nonexperimental research.

have worked out varying, though essentially similar, research procedures and writing conventions to help you keep the distinguishing line clearly drawn. These procedures and conventions are what cause a research paper to appear to be so different from other sorts of expository prose. Yet they are the most helpful tools you have for writing a successful research paper.

A Basic Assumption—A Moral Obligation

With the research paper thus defined, there are practical principles to keep in mind as you set out to write. These principles concern the authorship of your paper. Who is the author of your research paper? You are. Whose point will you make in its thesis and support throughout the paper? Your own. Even though you will be working with other people's ideas, sometimes even with other people's words, you remain the single force, the unifying intelligence behind your paper. You are the only person sitting in the driver's seat.

YOU, THE AUTHOR

Even if you are working with a subject that is completely new to you, a subject so unknown that you necessarily find yourself heavily dependent upon the thoughts of others, in writing your research paper you must make yourself master enough of the new material that the way you present the work, the way you structure the ideas, will be exclusively your own. And even if you find yourself quoting or paraphrasing extensively, your thesis statement (and ordinarily most of the surrounding introduction and conclusion) should be completely in your own words. Similarly, all your topic and subtopic sentences, as well as all the sentences introducing your quoted or paraphrased source material, must be your own. For better or for worse, you are uniquely the author of your research paper.

PLAGIARISM

Because your research paper is so exclusively your own, its readers have every reason to assume that all phrasing and ideas not definitely assigned to someone else were created by you. You are thus obliged to acknowledge explicitly the source of all ideas and all wording that come from someone besides yourself. To give you some notion of the seriousness of this obligation, I prefer to speak plainly. Permitting the words or ideas of others to pass as one's own is a particularly ugly form of theft called "plagiarism." Some people, in fact, view plagiarism as even more immoral than ordinary theft. They argue that ordinary thieves steal only material objects, but plagiarists steal thoughts and ideas—surely substances of far greater worth.

As a writer of a research paper you are under strong moral obligation not to quote so much as a two-word phrase without acknowledging the mind who created that phrase. But questions of morality aside, crediting your sources is of value to you because it makes your paper more persuasive. Every time you cite or refer to the author of a quoted or paraphrased passage, you add to your own still unrecognized voice the weight and authority of the voices of the well-known people who have influenced your thinking.

ESTABLISHING YOUR TOPIC

Your first major step in working on your research paper is choosing your topic. It is possible that your instructor has relieved you of this responsibility by assigning a specific topic. Or it may be that when you learned of the general subject, a specific question related to it—perhaps one that you have long been interested in pursuing—came immediately to mind. On the other hand, since research papers are often assigned before you have had an opportunity to become acquainted with the subject, you may be approaching the problem with a blank mind. In any case, there are at least four standards by which you can judge how good a research project is likely to develop from a particular topic:

1. The topic should truly intrigue you. Do you have genuine curiosity about marketing goods in Japan? About recent challenges to Einstein's theory? If so, good. Go to it. If not, find a topic among those appropriate to the assigning course that will retain your interest through much reading and over the considerable length of time you must expect to spend in its company.

2. Ideally the topic should be narrow enough for you to be able to consider all the available resources on it. If this goal cannot be met, then you can so narrow your approach that you can make yourself expert, at least, on that portion of your subject which most concerns you. For example, marketing goods in Japan is too broad, but you might be able to cover marketing fast foods in Hokkaido (Japan's northernmost island).

3. The topic you select for investigation should show potential for yielding a possible thesis. In fact, even at this early stage you may want to project a trial thesis or hypothesis. But if you do start your research with a specific hypothesis, always remember that it is only a supposed thesis, and keep your mind open to other possibilities. For instance, you might project the hypothesis that although fast foods do well in Tokyo with its fascination for things western, they will not sell in the provincial Hokkaido. Yet you might decide quite the contrary when you learn that the population of this atypically chilly Japanese isle has been enjoying beef and potatoes since the late nineteenth century, when these foods were introduced there

by the University of Massachusetts Agricultural Experimental Branch (now the University of Hokkaido).

4. The topic you pick should be one for which the necessary resources are available to you. The books, magazines, or printed records you need should be obtainable from the library you have access to. If your topic needs nonprint resources, these also should be where you can obtain them.

· In particular, you should be able to see *primary source material* on your topic. Primary sources contain the material that is "straight from the horse's mouth." If you are writing on the Civil War, for instance, you might find primary source material in the official documents of the political leaders, the diplomats, and the generals who supervised the war effort; or in the diaries and letters of the soldiers who fought in it; or in the poems, stories, journals, or histories of contemporary observers, whether they were scholars, novelists, or the woman- or man-in-the-street. Primary source material is always the most direct, most relevant material. Usually, the more heavily a writer relies upon such sources, the more interesting will be the resulting paper.

· It is also often useful to have *secondary source material* available on your topic. Authors of secondary source material discuss or interpret primary sources. When you read a modern history of the Civil War or a critical study of *Hamlet,* you are reading secondary material. Your own research paper, if you base it mainly upon primary sources, will itself be a secondary source. Although you probably will not want to quote much from secondary material, you should find it useful in helping you interpret your topic. More important, secondary works sometimes offer the best opportunity you will have to examine the primary material that is not available to you locally. Although the secondary authors select the material they quote to fit their own theses, you may find some of that material valuable in supporting yours.

Beginning Your Search

Whatever the discipline, the purpose of your preliminary browsing is first to get some understanding of what your topic is all about and then to gather enough information about it to narrow it into manageable size and to define a question on which to focus your research.

HUMAN RESOURCES

Where do you start? Especially if you are unfamiliar with the assigned subject, you will need to get some preliminary information just as quickly as you can. You can talk to people—a college campus abounds in experts on all sorts of subjects—and you can turn to books and other printed sources. Perhaps your most helpful preliminary resources are librarians. Although I suppose there must be some exceptions, librarians as a species are knowledgeable professionals, eager to share their knowledge. They want to help you master the complexities of their library's particular system so that you will feel at home working there. The librarians I know truly enjoy helping students understand where to find and how to use their library's reference tools. You really need not hesitate to bring your "Where can I find . . . ?" questions to them.

PRINTED SOURCES ACROSS THE CURRICULUM

As for printed matter, when you find yourself with an unknown or almost unknown topic, the best place to find out what it is about is usually a good encyclopedia.

Encyclopedias.   Though there are few encyclopedia articles I would recommend as sources for your completed paper, I do suggest that you start your inquiry there. You may want first to get your bearings in a general encyclopedia, where you may well find a comprehensive survey of the subject, a list of related articles, and a bibliography for future research. Then you might want to do more specific or technically detailed background searching in such specialized encyclopedias as the *Encyclopedia of Education* or the *Encyclopedia Judaica* or the *Encyclopedia of Management,* for example.

Card Catalogue.   Sources for narrowing your topic and finding your research questions will also vary with your field of investigation and the nature of your study. Whenever contemporaneity is not the issue, your library's card catalogue offers a useful starting point, for there you can discover what books your library offers on your subject. Thumbing through tables of contents and skimming prefaces and introductory chapters of these books should not only give you an idea of what they cover, but also a fairly strong idea of the approaches the authors take and their points of view. Many works will also offer a bibliography that will come in handy later when you concentrate your study.

Periodical and Abstract Indexes.   As useful as bound books can be, however, even the most recent will offer little help in formulating really current research questions. For contemporary issues, your wisest starting place may be the most recent volume of a periodical index, where the entries are collected chronologically. Perhaps you are already familiar with the *Reader's Guide to Periodical Literature,* which lists articles in the popular magazines. Scholarly journals are indexed by discipline; examples include: the Social Sciences Index, the Education Index, and the Humanities Index.

Articles are listed under subject headings as well as by author and title. In addition, many of the indexes in the social, natural, and physical sciences provide extraordinarily useful abstracts (summaries) of listed works. Among these are: Biological Abstracts; Chemical Abstracts; Psychological, Sociological, and Geological Abstracts; as well as the more general ERIC (Educational Resources Information Center) abstracts; and Dissertation Abstracts International, which yearly summarize Ph.D. theses in all branches of the arts and sciences.

Defining Your Research Question

Having selected a few likely books, articles, or abstracts, you may again face the problem of how to proceed. Just what are you to look for in them? I recommend that you browse with the intent not so much of narrowing your subject as of discovering a question on which to focus your research. For the purpose of all your reading and inquiry will be to answer that question, and the answer you find will provide the thesis of the paper you will write.

Preliminary browsing can help you define your research question in one of two ways. You might either (1) pursue one of the questions about your subject that has intrigued previous scholars, or (2) follow up a question your preliminary reading raises in your mind.

DISCOVERING YOUR TOPIC'S CENTRAL QUESTION

Even skimming material on a subject often reveals the issues related to it that have been of greatest scholarly concern. Most of the writers on the subject of Shakespeare's *Hamlet,* for instance, have dealt with the critical question of what causes Hamlet's delay in avenging his father's murder. And, as another example, many students of concentration-camp psychology have pondered why the victims of camp atrocities so seldom rise up against their captors. If such central scholarly questions about your subject should interest you, you could devote your research to investigating the varying opinions put forth as answers to them, then evaluate these answers, and perhaps arrive at a comparable opinion of your own.

DEFINING YOUR OWN ISSUE

If, on the other hand, such longstanding questions do not appeal to you, your preliminary readings may lead to an aspect of your subject which, though it has attracted little earlier attention, is intriguing to you and about which you would like to learn more. You would then need to define your own investigative question. For example, one student of mine, while looking for a topic for a research paper in his history course, found an ambiguous passage in the text about the closing of the Korean War. The author did not make it clear whether John Foster Dulles's policy or the perceived self-interest of the Kremlin forced the final compromise in that war. The student really wanted to know and decided to research the question for his paper.

Whether you choose to follow up a standing question in your field or one from your own curiosity, your research project will be a search for a satisfying answer. And the thesis of your paper will embody this answer.

TRY IT OUT

1. Investigate the resources of some of the best-known reference tools by answering the following questions:
   a. What are the names and claims to fame of three women listed in *The Dictionary of National Biography* (DNB) or in *The Dictionary of American Biography* (DAB)? Or in the more recent *Dictionary of Literary Biography*?
   b. Look up a word of your choice in the *Oxford English Dictionary* (OED). When and in what work was it first used? What was its meaning at that time?
   c. Examine *Dissertation Abstracts* for the year of your choice. Give the title and author of a dissertation from each of three academic disciplines.

2. Primary source material is ordinarily the best source material. Where might you find primary source material to help you answer the following research questions?
   a. How did the critics first react to _____ [an old movie of your choice] when it was originally shown?
   b. What was the headline in the *New York Times* on June 22, 19 — [your choice of year]?
   c. What are the most recent findings of researchers on _____ [disease of your choice]?

3. Take either your assigned research subject or one of the following general subjects and narrow it to a topic of workable size.

Hamlet	Quakers
Nazi concentration camps	General Robert E. Lee
PCVs	The Keynesian Theory
The poems of Robert Frost	Dyslexia

   a. Read an article on your assigned topic or one of these subjects in a major encyclopedia, and suggest two specific issues or questions that you feel would offer good possibilities for research.
   b. Browse through three books (or articles) listed in the bibliography

accompanying the encyclopedia article or three listed in your library's card catalogue or in one of the periodical indexes. Again suggest two potential research questions.

c. Compare your sets of questions from exercises (a) and (b). Are the sets identical? If not, how do they differ?

4. Compose a tentative hypothesis for your research topic.

THE CRUCIAL NOTE-TAKING STEP

Once you have a fairly clear notion of the specific question you want to investigate, you are ready to start taking notes. Note-taking is the most critical procedure involved in a research-writing project. In fact, failure to master this skill will almost certainly result in disaster. Let me tell you a sad story about a typical student who was confused about note-taking.

Tale of a Confused Note-taker

Once upon a time a research paper was assigned. The very next day we find a jeans-clad figure sitting in the library hunched up over his notebook. Intensely concentrating, he pushes an unruly lock of hair out of his eyes and gets a firmer grip on his pencil. Several heavy books with dark covers and small print lie open before him, and he works with each in turn. "P. Q. Snerd, *The Vanishing Aardvark,*" he dutifully copies at the top of a page from a looseleaf notebook and dutifully adds the name of a publishing house, its city, and a date. "Pp. 86–93" finishes the heading. He then turns to page 86, glances at it, and begins to scribble rapidly. Skipping *the, and,*

and *however*, abbreviating lengthy constructions, and omitting difficult words and dull arguments, the student reproduces—more or less—what Snerd had written. As ideas come to him, the student, pleased with his understanding and insight, writes them on the same sheet. Once in a while he attempts to paraphrase a sentence, always carefully preserving its essential structure or its distinctive wording. When he has filled a looseleaf page from the chapter by Snerd, he turns to a book by Smith and fills two more pages in the same way. He repeats the process with the works of Jones and Brown. Then, feeling shyly satisfied with his good day's work, he packs up his notebook and wends his way home. The days pass, filled with the usual college joys and sorrows, and suddenly the due date for his paper is very close. The student turns eagerly to his notes. But he finds he is no longer able to remember which words and ideas are his and which are Snerd's (or Smith's or Brown's). Nevertheless, the student knows that from these notes a paper must be constructed, and he begins writing.

* * * * *

This story of the beginning of a research paper has only two possible endings; and both are sad. In one ending, the student reads over his notes and rather likes them. "Not bad at all," he thinks. And so, leaving the notes basically as is, he corrects them for spelling and punctuation, affixes the appropriate footnotes, and creates his first draft. All that is needed further is to write transitional sentences connecting the sequence of sources to one another, to copy these pages neatly, and to turn in the finished research paper.

In the other ending to the story, the student reads over his notes and falls in love: "Snerd really has it. She is totally right. She says just what I have always thought!" (or "She says just what I wanted to say"). But what to do? The prof insists that at least four sources be cited. The answer our student finds is to use Snerd as the base of the paper and to fit in a little of Smith and Jones and Brown where they seem most natural.

The first of these papers is organized according to the order in which our student chanced to read his sources. The second follows the structure of a botched version of a single author's arguments. Both papers, despite their references, can be technically considered plagiarized. Because the poor student could not know where his words ended and those of his sources began, he could not mark off quotations. Thus, much of the wording that would seem to be his own was actually written by someone else. The structure of the second paper is also plagiarized. And the first paper has no structure at all. Neither paper, in short, offers anything to reward all the time and effort that went into its creation.

The bad news is that such papers as these are the almost inevitable results of the student's rather typical note-taking methods. The good news is that the proper use of note cards can solve the problems of random organization and unconscious plagiarism, which so badly mar many student papers. Skillful note-taking can also make research and writing a good deal easier.

The Purpose of Note Cards

The immediate purpose of notes is to serve as a memory aid, a way to keep the information you need readily available to you long after the source books, journals, and magazines have been returned to their shelves and the people you have interviewed are no longer available. Scholars do their note-taking on index cards (usually the 4- by 6-inch size). You may well wonder how the form in which you store your information could make any difference. Yet surprisingly, when you try to use note cards, you will find that they do make a remarkable difference. Only note cards permit you to record facts and ideas individually, separate from the original author's arguments. Only when each item can be considered on its own does it become the sort of raw material you can integrate with your own creative thinking on the issue you are yourself pursuing.

The eventual purpose for notes is to serve as the "inventory of ideas" (see Part One), from which you will define your thesis and organize your paper. With note cards your inventory of ideas is in concrete form. The separate note cards permit you to relate ideas to one another in a physical way. To organize, you arrange your cards in appropriate stacks. To test the effectiveness of various organizational schemes, you simply rearrange the stacks of cards.

Note cards can, finally, be of great use to you when you credit your sources within your research paper, as well as when you document them in your footnotes and bibliography. Note cards are, in fact, the most effective way of solving the thorniest problem researchers face: keeping "what is mine" clearly separate from "what is thine."

Note-Taking Procedure

By carefully following the conventions outlined in the guidelines (pages 312–313), you will produce note cards from which you can write a well-organized, well-documented research paper. But these rules leave many questions of procedure unanswered. Let's approach the process step by step.

STEP 1: MAKING BIBLIOGRAPHY CARDS

You go to the library and assemble some books and articles on your subject. What then? The first thing you should do is glance through the material to eliminate anything that does not bear directly on the issue you have chosen to research. Then, before you write anything else, make a bibliography card for any book or article that seems to be even a remotely possible source. Even if you do not use the book during this day's note-taking, you'll have the bibliography card to help you find it again quickly. Just jot down all the pertinent bibliographic information (see Figures 10.1 and 10.2)—and don't forget the library code number. When you have finished, alphabetize your bibliography cards for storage. Three sample cards appear in Figure 10.4.

1. Make two kinds of cards: Bibliography Cards and Note Cards.
2. Bibliography cards contain only the information you will need to make your bibliography—plus the library code number to help you relocate the work. (See Figures 10.1 and 10.2.)

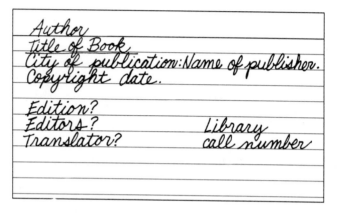

Figure 10.1. Bibliography Card for a Book

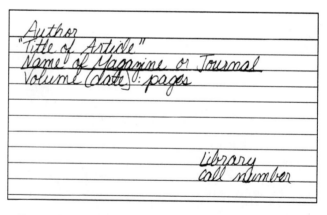

Figure 10.2. Bibliography Card for a Journal or Magazine

3. Note cards, however, demand care. Give each of your note cards a three-part structure, with an option for adding a fourth part. The parts are: (1) a brief heading summarizing the contents of the card; (2) the author's last name and the number of the page on which the recorded material was found; (3) the note itself; and (4) your own comment (optional) on the note. Figure 10.3 shows this structure.

Figure 10.3. Four-part Note-card Structure

4. Record only *one* idea on each note card.
5. Limit your note cards to one of these three forms: (1) exact quotations; (2) lists of facts or figures; and (3) (rarely) brief summaries of long passages.
6. Do *not* try to paraphrase quotations on your note cards.

STEP 2: DECIDING WHAT INFORMATION TO RECORD

You open a likely book, use the index or the table of contents to help you find the relevant material, and begin to read. When should you make a note? There are two ways of solving the problem, and neither is completely satisfactory. You can take down everything that touches your topic to any significant degree and risk ending up with a sizable batch of unused note cards. Or you can limit your note-taking to points that you can foresee using in your paper, and risk passing up ideas you will badly want later on.

I recommend taking few notes until you have settled on your research question. (If a passage looks useful, you can hold the place with a paper

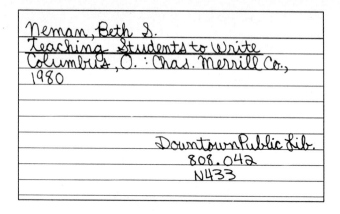

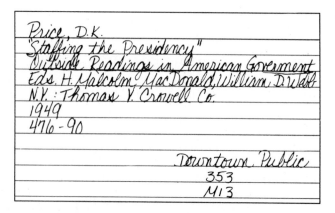

Figure 10.4. Sample Bibliography Cards

marker.) But after you have defined a hypothesis, it saves time and effort in the long run to err on the side of too many notes. After all, discarding material that later becomes unrelated is far easier than trying to retrieve a passage you neglected.

As a rule of thumb, if you are in doubt about copying a note from primary source material, go ahead and make the note—even when it is quoted in your secondary sources.

STEP 3: DECIDING WHEN TO COPY A DIRECT QUOTATION

You decide that a passage is important to your work and should be recorded. Should you quote it exactly? The answer almost always is yes, go ahead and get the author's exact words. At note-taking time you really can have no notion of how you will want to use particular material when you actually come to write your paper. You do not know whether you will want to quote it, paraphrase it, or discuss it in combination with material on other cards. You'll find you often want to have the author's exact words available when it comes time to make that decision. For a discussion of circumstances when a quotation card is not your wisest choice, see Alternative Step 5 (page 317).

STEP 4: DECIDING HOW MUCH TO QUOTE

Common sense decrees that you will want to copy onto note cards as little material as feasible. Consequently, what you need to do is to locate the significant part of a passage, the words or sentences in which the author sums up the essence of the idea you want to remember. Then you'll be ready to record, word for word, the significant words or sentences only. To streamline the note-taking, do not copy down extraneous material such as "as we said earlier" or "let us examine the facts" or even material important to the author's argument but not closely related to your concerns. Instead replace the omitted matter with marks of ellipsis: three periods (. . .)—or four (. . . .) if a sentence ending occurs in the omitted material. You may want to add or change a word or two to clarify the sense of a passage out of context, or even insert numbers to clarify ideas. If so, enclose any material you add in brackets [ ]. (See Figure 10.5.)

Finally, in recording quotations be sure to limit yourself to one idea per card—even if several ideas related to your work appear on the same page of a source.

STEP 5: MAKING YOUR QUOTATION CARDS

Leave the top line of your note card for the summarizing phrase that will label the recorded passage, and begin the next line by writing the last name of the source's author and the number of the page on which the quotation appears. Because you have already made a bibliography card for the book or article from which you are quoting, the last name of your author should be sufficient identification. If you use two authors with the same name, add identifying initials. If you use two works by the same author, also include a shortened title.

After the author and page number, copy the passage, omitting irrelevant material and clarifying meaning as Step 4 describes. If the passage you are quoting runs onto another page, insert the new page number at the appropriate place in your recorded material. When you have finished copying a quotation, carefully proofread your card for accuracy.

STEP 6: SUMMARIZING THE CONTENTS ON THE TOP LINE

Read over the material you have quoted on your note card. Analyze it in terms of your research purpose and summarize it as precisely as you can on the top line of the card. The summary line will permit you to work with the card later by simply glancing at the heading rather than by having to take the time to read the entire card. And even at this early stage it is useful to analyze the information you have discovered and to come to terms with it. Figure 10.5 provides an example of this process.

SOURCE PASSAGE

The Israelis not only have restored some of the water collection systems left by the ancient Nabateans in the Negev desert, but are letting the runoff nourish flourishing orchards of almond and pistachio trees. Another strategy for making the Negev bloom: drip irrigation systems that feed small amounts of water directly to the roots of plants with the help of computer monitors. (Golden, page 416)

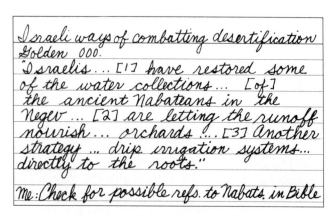

Figure 10.5. Making a Quotation Card

STEP 7: ADDING A PERSONAL NOTATION

If quoted material inspires you with thoughts of your own, skip a line and jot them down. But make sure to add your initial or some other sign to indicate just whose thoughts they are. See Figure 10.5 or, for another example, you might add this kind of cryptic personal note:

- Me: A's approach conflicts with other proofs here.

ALTERNATIVE STEP 5: MAKING LIST CARDS OR SUMMARY CARDS

What if you cannot foresee any possible future need to quote a particular passage exactly? And what if the information in question is strictly factual or numerical and would be more clearly recorded in a numbered list or a vertical column? In such cases, it is appropriate to make a list card rather than a quotation card. The headings remain the same. If you wish to quote an actual phrase of your author's when making your list, remember to enclose it in quotation marks. Figure 10.6 offers examples.

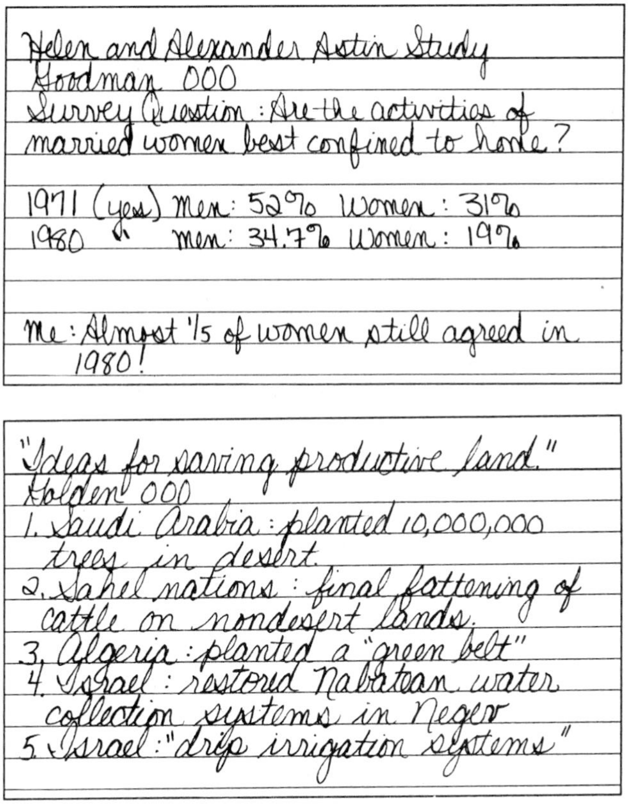

Helen and Alexander Astin Study
Goodman 000
Survey Question: Are the activities of married women best confined to home?

1971 (yes) Men: 52% Women: 31%
1980 " Men: 34.7% Women: 19%

Me: Almost 1/5 of women still agreed in 1980!

"Ideas for saving productive land."
Holden 000
1. Saudi Arabia: planted 10,000,000 trees in desert.
2. Sahel nations: final fattening of cattle on nondesert lands.
3. Algeria: planted a "green belt"
4. Israel: restored Nabatean water collection systems in Negev
5. Israel: "drip irrigation systems"

Figure 10.6. List Cards, Simple and Complex

Occasionally you will read some background material that you want to remember, but that you do not expect to use directly in your paper.

You then may want to write a summary card. On such a card you would briefly summarize a much greater amount of material completely in your own words. If you should want to quote a phrase or two, you would surround it with quotation marks and be sure to include the page number. Figure 10.7 shows a sample summary card.

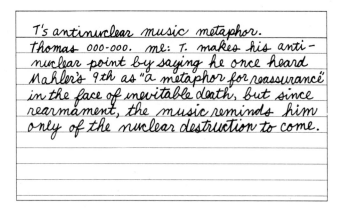

T's antinuclear music metaphor.
Thomas 000-000. me: T. makes his anti-
nuclear point by saying he once heard
Mahler's 9th as "a metaphor for reassurance"
in the face of inevitable death, but since
rearmament, the music reminds him
only of the nuclear destruction to come.

Figure 10.7. Summary Card

STEP 8: STORING YOUR CARDS

As you finish your research for the day and prepare to encircle your cards with a rubber band and depart, you have one more step to complete. In order to keep your thinking on your topic open and flexible, it is a good idea to arrange your cards *by idea* for storage. In disrupting the original ordering *by author,* you will help yourself think of the ideas as separate units to analyze and combine rather than only as member parts of their authors' arguments.

Usefulness of These Techniques

The note-taking conventions outlined here were developed by scholars to make their own research easier. And they can speed up your work too in the following ways:

1. *Using separate bibliography cards* keeps you from having to recopy the bibliographic information on every note card. These cards also make alphabetizing your final bibliography a breeze.
2. *One idea per card* makes your organizing task far easier, for you will be able to try out various combinations of structures simply by rearranging or reordering your cards.
3. Having a good *summary of included material at the top* of each note card saves you the time of repeatedly rereading each card during the process of "shuffling cards" to organize your paper.

4. *Quoting most information exactly* not only saves precious time during note-taking, but also gives you full information when you must decide how to use what your sources have to offer.

5. Writing the *source's name on each card* both refers you easily to the appropriate bibliography card and lets you know at a glance whose words you are working with. Having this information handy should be helpful when you are composing your paper and want to include an author's name.

TRY IT OUT

1. Write the information you would include on a bibliography card for each of the following:
   a. A book on your research topic—or one on your bookshelf
   b. A journal article on your topic—or one in a current magazine
   c. An editorial in today's newspaper
   d. An essay in Part Four of this book (choose one)

2. Compose the sort of brief summary of the following quotations that would be useful later in organizing a research paper. Your summary should fit on the top line of a note card.
   a. Subject of the paper: research into the causes of schizophrenia.

   Quotation: Kay, p. 401, "Wheat gluten, when [experimentally] introduced into the diet of schizophrenics, had the effect of exaggerating the schizophrenic symptoms and retarding the response to treatment."

   b. Subject of the paper: research into Bible-based pro- and antislavery arguments before the Civil War

   Quotation: Jay, p. 626. "It is wholly immaterial whether the ancient Hebrews held slaves or not, since it is admitted by all that if they did, they acted by virtue of a special and express permission from God, while it is equally admitted that no such permission has been given to us."

   c. Subject of the paper: research into critical opinion on why Hamlet delayed killing the king.

   Quotation: Harrison, p. 109. "*Hamlet* is usually considered a play of problems; and the problem which has chiefly exercised the critics is why did he delay? To which the answer is that in the play which Shakespeare wrote there was no delay."

   d. Subject of the paper: your research topic.

   Quotation: From one of your own note cards.

3. Let's say you are investigating the question of what makes Mahler's music distinctive. Read Thomas's essay in Part Four from this point of view and derive from it at least three note cards appropriate to your topic. Remember the following conventions in making your cards:

a. Identify each card by page number and author's last name.

b. Limit each card to a single idea central to your concerns in this project.

c. Quote the material accurately, replacing the phrases you omit with three periods (. . .) and enclosing words you need to add in [brackets].

d. For each card compose a useful summary of the passage quoted and write this summary on the card's top line.

4. Write bibliography and content note cards on your own research topic.

WRITING YOUR RESEARCH PAPER

Finding Your Thesis

Identifying a thesis for your research paper is not likely to cause you much difficulty. As you have been gathering your material, you have probably been testing out possible theses in your mind. If you began with a working hypothesis, you have probably been adding to it, changing it, or exchanging it for a thesis that will work better. If you began with a special question, you have probably found the answer to that question, and you should have little trouble formulating a thesis from that answer. In short, if you have been writing good theses for your other expository papers, you probably do not need additional advice on formulating an effective thesis for your research paper.

Nevertheless, two common thesis problems seem to plague research-paper writers. One is the overly combative "I think such-and-such is great" (or "terrible") thesis. And the other is its opposite, the bland, self-evident thesis of the "such-and-such is an interesting subject" variety. The latter type is usually meant to mask papers that simply "talk about" their topics rather than come to grips with the questions concerning them. Although there is no need for your research-paper thesis actually to be controversial, still a less-than-exciting paper will result from an attempt to assert that "George Washington was the first President of the United States," for instance, or that "The Grand Canyon is an impressive sight." Perhaps more to the point, the biographical summaries or geographical descriptions that result from such theses are not really research papers. They do not "add to the accumulation of the world's scholarship by making a definite statement based on careful study of . . . data." You can avoid bland, unfocused papers of this sort by making sure you have an arguable point to prove. Try using the "although" clause approach from Part One to help you arrive at that point.

On the other hand, by emphasizing the controversial aspects of the thesis statement, I don't want to imply that a combative thesis is required. In fact, such theses are best avoided. The propaganda tracts and personal pronouncements they tend to produce are rarely successful as research papers. When you think about it, you can find so many interesting nonpersonal statements to make about socialism, *Paradise Lost,* or Buddha that you should easily be able to avoid having the point of your paper amount to "I believe it is good" or "I believe it is bad."

TRY IT OUT

1. Compose several possible working theses on your research topic.

2. Discuss them with a group of your classmates or submit them to your instructor, or both, and select your tentative working thesis.

Constructing Your Working Outline

Once you have found your thesis, constructing your outline or plan is perhaps the most vital step in the writing of your research paper. For making your outline requires you to think through the totality of your reading—and the ideas inspired in you by that reading—and then organize them into a clear and coherent whole.

NOTE CARDS AS AN INVENTORY OF IDEAS

In some ways, organizing a research paper is easier than organizing other sorts of expository essays. Your stack of note cards gives you a ready-made inventory of ideas, with every idea concrete and movable. You can group and regroup your note cards until the topics on their summary lines fall into natural subdivisions, the five or six major points that will become your paper. Then you can arrange these groups or points into the best possible order for presenting your thesis. As you write your outline, coordinate your stack of note cards with it. Discard any cards that do not contribute to supporting your thesis. Be merciless in striving for a tight structure.

GENERAL ORGANIZING TECHNIQUES

How do you discover the structure that will present your thesis most effectively? Inasmuch as a research paper is a form of expository prose, you can use the same techniques to design its structure that you use to organize other expository essays. In fact, it would be a good idea to reread pages 48–63 and review the strategies suggested there.

A SPECIFIC RESEARCH-PAPER ORGANIZING TECHNIQUE: F.D.R.

To the extent that research papers form a distinct kind of writing, some special considerations also apply. And all research papers share one important point: they are all grounded in fact. A good research paper is not simply a discussion of its writer's views. Its thesis must arise from full consideration of the facts being examined. When you decide upon the structure of your research paper, then, you must be sure to keep the placement of your factual material foremost. One professor, who is also a history buff and an admirer of President Franklin Delano Roosevelt, suggests that the best way to organize a research paper is never to forget F.D.R. That is, always remember:

- F   acts
- D   iscussion
- R   ecommendations

What F.D.R. means is that your *Recommendations* or interpretations (that is, your final statement of thesis) must be based upon the *Facts* that you have presented clearly and have weighed and *Discussed* as objectively as possible.

In the sample outlines from student papers shown in the boxed section, you will notice a number of organizational strategies suggested in Chapter 1. Despite the variety, every sample outline demonstrates an understanding of the principle of F.D.R. Thus, when you are stacking your note cards into the piles that will form the structure of the outline for your research paper, be sure to keep F.D.R. in mind.

A final word of caution may be in order. Since organizing is a crucial step in fashioning your research paper, you may want to schedule a conference with your instructor before moving on to the writing itself.

Guidelines: Sample Outlines

Research Paper on a Literary Topic

Thesis: None of the major theories suggested by literary scholars completely answers the central critical question in Shakespeare's *Hamlet*, the question of why Hamlet delays in killing the king. Yet a combination of these theories can offer a plausible explanation.

I. Introduction—stressing the variety of critical answers to the question (Leading to) ⟶ Thesis

II. Detailed presentation of the most plausible theories.
    A. Theory of melancholia (A. C. Bradley)
        1. Explanation
        2. Facts in the play it accounts for
        3. Facts in the play it does not explain
    B. Oedipal theory (S. Freud. Olivier's movie interpretation)
        1. Explanation
        2. Facts in the play it accounts for
        3. Facts in the play it does not explain
    C. Theory of practical impossibility (G. B. Harrison)
        1. Explanation
        2. Facts in the play it accounts for
        3. Facts in the play it does not explain

III. My theory. A combination of II A, II B, and II C.
    A. Explanation
        1. Hamlet's delay in Acts I, II, and III. Caused by Hamlet's melancholic (II A) and, to some extent, Oedipal (II B) preoccupation with the possibilities of his mother's guilt.
        2. Hamlet's delay in Acts IV and V. Caused by lack of practical opportunity (II C) until Hamlet actually does the deed.
    B. How this theory accounts for the facts in this play
    C. How it avoids the problems of the other theories

IV. Conclusion

Research Paper on a Scientific Topic

Thesis: Schizophrenia is caused by a chemical imbalance in the brain and thus should be treated chemically, not by psychotherapy.

- Introduction. Although clause: Until recently schizophrenia was treated through psychotherapy
  Leading to ⟶ Thesis
- Presentation of research that shows schizophrenia to be the result of chemical imbalance in the brain.
  Farley's research
  Plotkin's research
  Fisher's research
  Terensius's and Kline's research
- Possible cause for this imbalance
  diet
  virus
  genetic causes
- Failure of the psychoanalytic approach
- Recommendation: Drug therapy should replace psychotherapy for schizophrenia

Research Paper on a Historical Subject

Thesis: During the Civil War the Bible became the South's main justification for slavery and the North's foremost weapon against it.

Intro: Setting up the paradox

Anti-Slavery Use of Bible

Influenced Leaders | Quoted at Abolitionist Meetings

Quoted in Abolitionist Literature

Pro-Slavery Use of the Bible   Abolitionist Rebuttal

(Biblical Passages for Justification) X Interpretation of passages

X Explanation of Allusion

(Biblical History for Justification) The Patriarchs   Mosaic Law

The Patriarchs The Mosaic Law

Conclusion: ① The Bible an effective weapon

② Anti-Slavery arguments prevailed

TRY IT OUT

1. Analyze your working thesis, stack and restack your note cards, and develop a well-structured outline to support it.

2. Discuss your outline with a group of your classmates or submit it to your instructor, or both, and revise.

Writing the Paper

In writing your research paper, again keep in mind that this paper is at base an expository essay—though with its own conventions. You should, therefore, continue to think in terms of the usual three-part structure: introduction, body, and conclusion. All these parts should function in much the same way as in other kinds of expository writing.

GENERAL INTRODUCTION AND CONCLUSION STRATEGIES

When you write your introduction, for instance, first approach and then set forth your thesis in your usual way. Take your usual care not to bring any of your arguments into this section. And when you write your conclusion, read back over the rest of the paper, as you do ordinarily, and draw your final reflections on it, being sure to give your thesis its most thorough definition in the process. In your introduction and conclusion, you will be expressing your own ideas, and thus you will probably not include any quoted or paraphrased material—except possibly as a stylistic device.

SPECIFIC RESEARCH-PAPER INTRODUCTORY CONVENTIONS

Within this typical expository structure, however, the research paper has its own more specific conventions, expected by its scholarly readers. A team at the University of Rhode Island recently studied these expectations and discovered that, "regardless of field," the faculty surveyed expected "the opening section of an academic paper" to:

> [(1)] introduce the broad subject area and specify what limited aspects of it are to be examined and used as evidence for the conclusions. . . . [(2) to] cite previous research, usually in an attempt to limit the subject or problem and to provide an intellectual context for the study . . . [(3) to] specify the method of inquiry and [(4) to] state in some form (as thesis or hypothesis) the conclusions whose validity is to be demonstrated or tested.[2]

Faculty expectations are so strong for "these features" that, according to the Rhode Island researchers, they become grounds for evaluation" (823). It is important, then, to make sure that you cover each point in some way in your introduction.

THE BODY

The body of a research paper is typically expository in that it consists of major points set forth in topic sentences, backed up by subpoints, defined in subtopic sentences, and supported by evidence. But because this evidence is specific to the research paper, composed as it is of material from outside sources, specifically research-paper conventions (especially those for quoting and paraphrasing, discussed in the next section) become important here.

Yet as you write your paper, you will probably be even more conscious of expository structure than usual because you will be working with a stack of cards that you have arranged to coordinate point by point with your outline. You will work down your outline, point by point, considering the cards that relate to a particular point and determining how you will approach each point from the sort of information the relevant cards contain.

It is possible that you will experience something almost akin to pleasure in this process. You may find a kind of delight in combining your well-organized outline and your well-coordinated note cards in a puzzle-building sort of way. And certainly there is a joy in watching the whole

[2]Robert A. Schwegler and Linda K. Shamoon, "The Aims and Process of the Research Paper," *College English* 44 (Dec. 1982): 822. Copyright © 1982 by the National Council of Teachers of English. Reprinted with permission.

project fall into shape. Nevertheless, you must be careful not to let such pleasure lull you into thinking that writing a research paper is really just putting together the parts of a puzzle. Such thinking can lead to a final paper that is merely a patchwork quilt of quotations, a paper where the material and not the author is in charge. To avoid producing such a paper, approach each section with these questions in mind: What point do I want to make here? How can I best use the information in this sub-stack of cards to make it convincingly?

Quoting and Paraphrasing (and When Not to)

There are two major ways you can make use of the material on your cards. The fact that you have the exact words of the author permits both options. On the one hand, you can read over the cards associated with a particular point, digest the information they contain until it becomes part of your own thinking, and—putting the cards completely aside—make your point about the subject in your own way. You will probably write the greater part of your paper in this fashion.

On the other hand, many times paraphrasing or quoting the material on your cards directly is the right choice. You should quote (or paraphrase) when the author's words (or your version of them) are in themselves proof of whatever your passage is asserting. All primary source material can be quoted (or paraphrased) for this purpose—whether it is a statistical chart for a scientific paper, a literary passage for a critical analysis, an expert opinion when you want to weigh scholarly views, or even the words of the person on the street when you need mass opinion. To get a sense of the appropriate use of source material, contrast the following quotations and paraphrases as they make the same point in a student's paper on the use of the Bible in the Civil War dispute over slavery.

The first example shows the Abolitionists' dependence upon the Bible to reinforce their antislavery arguments. Note that the student makes the point first in her own words.

Use of quotation

The Bible was the backbone of the Abolitionist cause. "Take away the Bible," William Lloyd Garrison said, "and our warfare with oppression and infidelity, intemperance and impurity, is removed—we have no authority to speak and no courage to act" (qtd. in Nelson 177).[3]

Use of paraphrase

The Bible was the backbone of the Abolitionist cause. William Lloyd Garrison felt that if the Bible could not be used, then they would lose their best authority and would no longer have either the justification or the spirit to continue. (Nelson 177)

[3]Both quotations and paraphrases must be documented. See page 337.

In the next example she uses quotation and paraphrase to express the religious rationale of the slaveholders:

Use of quotation

There was a widespread belief in the South that slavery was somehow good for the slaves. The Reverend Phillip Schaff considered slavery as "a wholesome training school for the Negro taking him from the lowest state of heathenism and barbarism to some degree of Christian civilization." (qtd. in Cole 156).

Use of paraphrase

There was a widespread belief in the South that slavery was somehow good for the slaves. Reverend Phillip Schaff, for instance, thought that slavery was a means of educating the slave in civilization and in Christianity. (Cole 256)

INTRODUCING YOUR QUOTATION OR PARAPHRASE

In order to remain in the driver's seat and not let the authors of your sources take over your paper, it is important that you introduce your source material—whether quoted or paraphrased—yourself. Ordinarily you should give it two types of introduction. First you need to make your point or subpoint in your own words. Then, as you support your point with material from your sources, you introduce the author of the supporting material. A paper should not simply burst into quotation as birds burst into song. Wherever your voice—or your ideas—gives way to another's, you need to signal the change to your readers by such phrases as "According to Snerd" or "As Smith writes." Furthermore, mentioning the name of the person from whom you took the material not only clarifies the distinction between your voice and that of your sources, it also lends the authority of your source to your argument. And in addition, by eliminating the need to identify the source, it makes your parenthetical documentation less intrusive. (See page 338.)

Some Hints. The first time you mention an author or informant, you should give the full name. At this first mention, you might also want to add an identifying tag such as "Jane S. Doe, Professor of Literature at Johns Hopkins University" or "John Q. Doe, Agronomist with the Department of the Interior." In this first reference it is also often useful to mention the name of the work from which you are quoting as well: "According to Leslie L. Pickle in *Poltergeists for Fun and Profit* . . ." or "In *Poltergeists for Fun and Profit,* Leslie L. Pickle points out. . . ." In later references, citing the last name alone is sufficient: "Doe argues that . . ." or "As Pickle explains, . . ."

The accompanying set of guidelines should help you use quotations and paraphrases correctly and gracefully.

Guidelines for Use of Quotation and Paraphrase

1. *Point.* Introduce your point in your own words. Use the quotation or paraphrase for support only. Never simply insert it to speak for itself. *Your paper should make coherent sense with all quotations and paraphrases omitted.*
2. *Pertinence.* Use a quotation or a paraphrase only when your point could not be supported as well without it. Remember that too many quotations can produce a patchwork-quilt effect.
3. *Brevity.* Trim your quotations as closely as possible, leaving only the phrasing that is completely relevant to your point. Carefully shape the quotation to fit *your* context, but be accurate and true to the author's original meaning.
4. *Identification.* Give the quotation a source. Either name its author specifically ("William Garrison," "Reverend Phillip Schaff," "John Brown") or in general ("a famous New England poet"). Even when the paper is read aloud (so that quotation marks have no significance), a listener should be able to understand that a new voice is speaking and, for the most part, should be told whose voice it is.

Putting the Rules into Practice

Guidelines can suggest what you should do, but the individual context of each of your points and subpoints, the paragraphs themselves, must determine how you will put these suggestions into practice. Consider the following situation, which roughly approximates that of Eileen Power's "The Peasant Bodo," in her *Medieval People* (London: Penguin, 1939):

Your thesis is:

Although wars and kings have long been the mainstay of history books, the everyday life of common people is at least as historically significant. Take, for example, the medieval peasant.

Your outline is:

   I. Introduction: Although . . . → Thesis
  II. Sources of current knowledge about med. peasants
     A. Estate Book of Abbey St. Germain, 811-26.
     B. Charlemagne, *Instructions to Stewards,* 8??
     C. Aelfric, *Colloquium*
     D. Others
 III. What we can know about:
     A. Feudal relationships
       1. Peasant tenant privileges
       2. Peasant feudal obligations
         a. Rents
         b. Taxes
         c. Labor

    B. Peasant–Church relationships
      1.
      2.
      3.
      4.
    C. Important events in peasant life
      1.
      2.
      3.
 IV. Conclusion

Your present task is: Write the section for point III. A. 2. c.

Your point here is: Contemporary sources show how hard the medieval peasants worked to fulfill their feudal obligations.

Your note cards on this point include those shown in Figure 10.8.

Estate obligations of plowmen
Abbey St. Germain Estate Book 78
Me: Each tenant owed the manor labor of:
(1) field work - about 3 days a week, a specified unit of seasonal plowing. Ex. - "Winter: Sow 4 perches. Spring: 2."
(2) labor services - so many weekly (Ex. - 2 plowings) at steward's demand.
(3) handiwork - specified weekly number, as needed, of repairs, gathering, carrying, wood-chopping, ale-making, etc.

Peasant women worked too
Charlemagne 43, 49
"Women ... are to give at the proper time the materials, i.e., linen, wool, vermilion, wool combs, soap, grease, vessels and other objects that are necessary.... And let our women's quarters be well looked after, furnished w/ rooms w/ stoves & cellars & let them be surrounded by a good hedge, & let the doors be strong, so the women can do our work properly."

Figure 10.8.

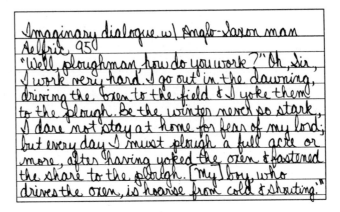

Obligations of other workers
Charlemagne 45
"[Each steward should have in his district]
good workmen, namely, blacksmiths, silver-
smiths, shoemakers, turners, carpenters,
swordmakers, fishermen, foilers, soap-
makers; men who know how to make beer,
cider & all other kinds of beverages, bakers
to make pastry for table, netmakers who
know how to make nets for hunting,
fowling, fishing...."

Imaginary dialogue w/ Anglo-Saxon man
Aelfric, 950
"Well, ploughman, how do you work?" "Oh, sir,
I work very hard. I go out in the dawning,
driving the oxen to the field & I yoke them
to the plough. Be the winter never so stark,
I dare not stay at home for fear of my lord;
but every day I must plough a full acre or
more, after having yoked the oxen & fastened
the share to the plough. [My boy, who
drives the oxen, is hoarse from cold & shouting."

Figure 10.8.   *(continued)*

How would you combine the information on these cards to make your point? It would surely depend upon how much emphasis you wanted to put on this idea. Perhaps you would want to use it in a rather minimal way, to make your point and get on to other ideas more important to your argument. You would probably then combine your sources as in A:

TOPIC SENTENCE

· According to contemporary sources, medieval peasants worked exceedingly hard, for they not only had to get their own living but also to fulfill their feudal obligations. . . .

SUPPORT A: SOURCES COMBINED AND SUMMARIZED

· . . . Plowmen had to plow and keep up the estate on which they were tenants. Skilled craftsmen had to furnish the estate with shoes, fish, swords, and everything the landholders needed for themselves or for gifts to the king. And the women were confined to their own quarters so as not to be distracted from weaving cloth and making pottery for the estate.[4]

The more specific you are in your supporting evidence, the more importance you give to your point:

SUPPORT B: SPECIFIED SOURCES PARAPHRASED

· . . . Estate books such as that of the Abbey de St. Germain specify the exact amount of field work, labor service, and hand work required for each farming peasant (78). Charlemagne's instructions to his stewards give us some notion of the product demands made upon blacksmiths, carpenters, swordmakers, and other skilled craftsmen (45) as well as those made upon peasant women (43, 49). Even fiction, such as the Anglo-Saxon Aelfric's "Dialogue with a Ploughman," confirm the peasants' heavy burden of toil.

If the point is one you truly want to emphasize, you might decide not only to paraphrase but also to quote directly:

SUPPORT C: SOURCES PARAPHRASED AND QUOTED

· . . . Estate books such as that of the Abbey de St. Germain specify the exact amount of field work, labor service, and hand work required of each farming peasant (78). Charlemagne's Instructions to his stewards give us some notion of the product demands made upon blacksmiths, carpenters, swordmakers, and other skilled craftsmen (45). The Instructions are also evidence of the particularly burdensome requirements placed upon women, who were to "be surrounded by a good hedge and . . . doors [that were] strong so that [they] can do our work properly" (49). Even fiction, such as the Anglo-Saxon Aelfric's "Dialogue with a Ploughman," confirms the peasants' heavy burden of toil:

> 'O sir, I work very hard. I go out in the dawning, driving the oxen to the field and I yoke them to the plough. Be the winter never so stark, I dare not stay at home for fear of my lord; but every day I must plough a full acre or more' (95).

As you become more experienced in research writing, you will begin to develop surer intuition about what sort of approach to take. To see how another student handled Power's material in a quite different way, turn to Bret Gilbert's paper, pages 445–447.

THE MECHANICS OF QUOTATION

A number of conventions have developed for transcribing quoted material. The purpose of these conventions is to make the quoted material instantly recognizable and to make the text as a whole easier to read. The most useful of these rules are listed in the boxed section.

---

[4]The material in this paragraph is derived from Abbey St. Germain 78, Charlemagne 43, 45, 49, and Aelfric 95. [A footnote is needed here because the multiple sources make parenthetical documentation cumbersome.]

Guidelines for Using Quotations

1. Brief quotations should be enclosed in quotation marks:

    > The power and force of the Old Testament were so much a part of Garrison that many associated the two together. Bates likens him to "a fiery Hebrew prophet" (454) and Wendell Phillips said that Garrison was "Taught of God . . . God endowed, and God-sent to arouse a nation" (Old South Leaflets 4:7).

2. A quotation that extends over three lines should be indented and blocked off. (You do not need to use quotation marks when you use this form. The indentation of itself says "quoted material.") For instance:

    > Wendell Phillips, like so many of his time, used Bible language and imagery in the remarkable oratory of his Abolitionist addresses. Take, for example, this excerpt from his "Dangers from Slavery" speech:
    >
    > > Then the wicked will walk on every side for the vilest of men will be exalted, and America, become the mock and scorn and hissing of the nations, will go down to worse shame than was ever heaped upon Sodom; for the lust of wealth, land and power, she will also have committed the crime against nature (Old South Leaflets 5:15).

3. Poetry should be quoted in lines, just as written:

    > The prose of *The Liberator* is interspersed with poetry, most of which has more passion than art:
    >
    > > God is a God of mercy, and would see
    > > The prison-doors unbarr'd—the bondmen free!
    > > He is a God of Truth, with purer eyes
    > > Than to behold the oppressor's sacrifice!

4. Brief portions of poetry (fewer than three lines) may be included within the text, but you should indicate the line divisions by slashes:

    > According to Stephen Vincent Benét's Bible-reading slave-trader, "It's down there, Mister, / Down there in black and white" (15).

Punctuation

Punctuate your quotations according to the following rules:

5. Carefully copy the author's punctuation (and spelling and wording) within the quotation.

6. When you trim the quotation to meet the requirements of your own introductory sentences and the point that you are making, substitute three periods [. . .] for any omitted words. Any additions or changes in wording that you have to make so that the quotation will fit the demands of your own text should be included in brackets [   ]. For example, the italicized portion of the following passage from page 31 of Prof. Scholar's book would read ambiguously if quoted out of context:

    > George Washington was the first president of the United States. *He was the father of his country.*

    To quote it so your readers would be sure about your subject and be aware you had changed the wording, you would enclose your own words in brackets:

    > According to Professor Scholar, "[George Washington] was the father of his country" (31).

7. A quotation within a quotation is indicated by single quotation marks (that is, an apostrophe on most typewriters):

   > Professor Researcher points out that "Edison tested the first record player with 'Mary Had a Little Lamb' " (21).

   Double quotation is awkward, however; avoid it if you can.

8. You have your choice of a variety of punctuation for introducing your quotation.

   a. You can make the quotation an integral part of the sentence by using no additional punctuation:

      > Thus both sides claimed to act "in strict accordance with the will of God" (Benét, 213).

   b. You can introduce the quotation informally with a comma:

      > According to F. C. Stifler, "The great Lincoln was nurtured on the Bible as few men ever have been" (42).

   c. Or you can introduce it more formally with a colon:

      > Lincoln's actions on slavery, as on all important issues, were governed by his creed: "What doth the Lord require of thee, but to do justly, to love mercy, and to walk humbly with thy God?" (Micah 6.8)

   d. You can use commas to interrupt the quotation by inserting its identifying tag:

      > "Take away the Bible," William Lloyd Garrison said, "and our war-fare with oppression . . . is removed" (Qtd. in Nelson 77).

   e. Or you can use a comma to put the identifying tag at the end:

      > The prophets were particularly outspoken on the subject. "Woe unto him . . . who useth his neighbor's services without wages," Jeremiah wrote (22.-13).

9. All punctuation that is part of a quotation itself goes *within* the quotation marks:

   > Khan wondered: "What killed Arthur Dimmesdale?"

   Periods and commas always go *within* the quotation marks—sometimes illogically:

   > Our national anthem is "The Star Spangled Banner."

10. *An Exception:* Parenthetical references follow the quotation marks and precede the punctuation, as in the earlier examples. Only when a quotation is separately blocked (as in example 2) do the parentheses stand outside the sentence.

TRY IT OUT

1. To practice the technique of quoting effectively, let's say that you are working for a research paper on a passage about the ancient Etruscan attitude toward death. Quote the note card in Figure 10.9—or portion of it—as you would for such a passage. Follow the quotation with the parenthetical reference: (466). Remember to identify your author and be sure to introduce your quotation with a statement of your own.

Etruscan Tombs: gay, filled with enjoyment of life
J.H. Plumb 466
"A rich caste of princes built tombs of singular
magnificence, filling them with amphorae, jewels,
and silver. And they adorned their walls with all
the gaeity they had enjoyed alive.... In their
tombs they hunted, played games, performed
acrobatics, danced, feasted; their amorous
dalliance was both wanton and guiltless.
Deliberately they banished death with the
recollected "gusto" of life."

Figure 10.9.

2. To try out the strategy of paraphrasing, rewrite the Etruscan passage for the same supposed paper by paraphrasing the material (or a portion of it). In order to paraphrase, restate the author's point in other words. If you need to use any of the original phrasing, be sure to enclose those portions in quotation marks. Ordinarily, you will be introducing your material with such phrases as "The author said *that*. . . ." (See examples on page 322.) Remember to include the parenthetical references: (466).

3. Which version of your Etruscan passage (the quoted or the paraphrased) do you think is most effective? Why? Would you prefer a mixed version combining both quotation and paraphrase?

4. This final exercise gives you the opportunity to practice putting together the kind of paragraph you will be writing in your research papers. Imagine that you have collected the note cards shown in Figure 10.10 from 1970s magazine articles for a section of your research paper on American fads of the 70s. Write a paragraph making use of the information they contain. You may quote and/or paraphrase or omit material as you choose. (See pages 328–329.) Be sure to make your own points and mention the authors by name. You might take the following as your topic sentence:

In the seventies fads were all-pervasive, self-preoccupied, and sometimes less than wholesome.

The Macho Fad
Wolfe 444   "[The men today]
are not only wacked-out, but tough
.... The evil that seems to fascinate
[them] most is violence. A lot of
men today have a kind of hairy
sentimentality about violence that
is somewhat like the girls and
Lady Brett."

The Hippy Fad
Wolfe 443   "In the women's
colleges...there is a whole generation of
young buds with pre-Raphaelite
hairdos and black-muslin stockings
who worship Guitar players and
Smoking Pot.... [These] girls all talk
about going down to the Village and
having affairs with coffeehouse
pot-head poets."

Examples of "me" Fad
Goodman 471
"The hyperindividualism of a movement like est....
"The 'isolation tank' seems to
suggest that the road to happiness
... is an internal route."

Figure 10.10.

Interest in the partic....fad is short-lived
Tucker 000
"Today, question often is not 'What do you do?'
but 'What are you into?' Macramé one week,
astrology the next, health food, philosophy,
history, jogging, movies, EST- we fly
from 'commitment' to 'commitment' like
bees among flowers because it is
easier to buy a new toy than to
repair an old one."

The "Me" Fad
Goodman 470   "The new
therapies- from the isolation tank on-
offer us ways to 'get into ourselves'.
Those who aren't 'doing their own
thing' or 'finding themselves' are 'getting
in touch' with their feelings.'... The
range of the new therapies is
characterized by a frenzied
search inward."

Figure 10.10. *(continued)*

CREDITING AND DOCUMENTING

Documenting sources is an important part of your research paper. You need to supply full bibliographical information both to give "credit where credit is due" and to allow readers the opportunity to obtain the sources themselves. Your readers might want fuller information than you offer, or they might decide to follow up your research with some of their own.

What Should You Document?

The question of what should be credited is not always easy to answer. Too many text interruptions can be distracting and can leave the impression of a stuffy, fuddy-duddy sort of mind. But too few can amount to plagiarism. As you become more experienced in research, you will develop a feel for what should and what should not be credited. But until you develop this natural sureness, it is best to avoid the greater of the two evils. In other words: When in doubt, document. Here are the rules:

1. All quotations *must* be credited.
2. All paraphrases *must* be credited.
3. Material that is not directly quoted or paraphrased from your source should be credited whenever it is, in any way, exclusive to its author. You do not need to credit it if it is common knowledge. The test should not be "Did I know this information before?" but rather "Can this information be found in an encyclopedia or in almost any book on the subject?" For example, you may not immediately know the birthday of Czar Nicholas of Russia, but there would nevertheless be no reason to document such a fact because it is available in any number of sources. Information that needs documentation includes:
   - Interpretations
   - Opinions
   - Challengeable data, including:
     - Statistics
     - Results of surveys
     - Results of studies

Remember the results of research are only as good as the people who did the work. Your reader has the right to know who they are.

Documenting with Ease

Despite its importance, the very idea of documentation can arouse feelings of panic in inexperienced writers. But, as it is with unfamiliar dogs, the bibliographic bark is much worse than its bite. The social and physical sciences long ago streamlined their systems. And now, with the conventions newly established by the authoritative Modern Language Association (MLA), the documentation hound has been defanged in the humanities as well. The essential information can now be communicated without seriously inconveniencing either writer or reader.

THE MLA SYSTEM OF DOCUMENTATION

Since the MLA practice is so widely followed, let's begin with it. In summary, to use these conventions, you as writer should:

1. present your bibliographic information in full in a List of Works Cited at the conclusion of your paper.
2. provide information specific to the individual reference (page numbers, for example) in parentheses within the text itself:
   . . . ," according to Professor Smith (367).
   When you do not identify your source directly in your text, you also include within the parentheses the author's last name or whatever information your reader will need to find the appropriate entry in the alphabetized Works Cited list:
   . . . ," as scholars have found (Smith 367).
3. resort to footnotes only when the material within the parentheses (several author's names, for example) becomes so lengthy and cumbersome that it disrupts the reading of your text.

And that's really all there is to it. But although this summary accurately reflects how to credit your sources in general, I'm sure you will still have questions about how to use the system in specific situations. Let me try to answer your questions.

What Goes Between Source Parentheses? In order to distract your reader as little as possible, parentheses interrupting the text should contain as little as possible. Since there is no need to duplicate information, I recommend that you identify your source in the text itself. As you introduce your quotation or paraphrase, it is a good idea to mention the author(s) name(s). In the absence of a known author, you can cite the title—or a clearly recognizable shortened version of the title. With the work clearly identified, your usual citation for both books and articles is a single, uncluttered page number within parentheses, directly following the cited material or at the first natural pause after it. To further decrease distraction, *The MLA Style Manual* suggests that the page number or numbers stand alone without an abbreviated *p.* or *pp.* or further punctuation: (170), for instance. All other parenthetical references are variations on this standard notation.

The boxed list of examples should provide you with models for handling a variety of documentation situations.

Parenthetical InText Documentation: MLA System Models

All citations refer to the List of Works Cited on page 342.

When you cite the author's name in your text:
E. B. White also makes this point (133).

When you do not identify your source in the text:
This point has been made before (White 131).

When you refer to a passage quoted in another work:
Jemshed Khan argues that "Chillingworth poisoned Dimmesdale with atropine from herbs gathered in the forest" (qtd. in Turner 434).

When you cite an author who has more than one work listed in your Works Cited, distinguish the work in the text or by including an (abbreviated) title as well as the author's name in the parenthetical note:
- In Successful Writing: A Rhetoric for Advanced Composition, Maxine Hairston reports on her research, which showed that successful business professionals "seem to believe . . . writers should observe the conventions of standard English" (245).
- A recent survey shows that the "men and women who occupy positions of responsibility in the business and professional world . . . seem to believe that writers should observe the conventions of standard English" (Hairston, Successful Writing 245).

When you refer to a work listed by title in your Works Cited, include an (abbreviated) title. But if you abbreviate, remember to begin with the word that begins the entry in your Works Cited so your reader can locate the full reference easily. Dictionary or encyclopedia references are alphabetically listed and need no page numbers.
According to the editors of the Funk and Wagnalls Encyclopedia, though barber and surgeon were once one, by the time of the Rennaissance "the surgical practice of the barber was restricted to bloodletting and toothpulling" ("Barber").

When you refer to a passage in a multivolume work, include the volume number and separate it from the page number with a colon:
God is a God of mercy, and would see
The prison-doors unbarr'd—the bondmen free.
(Old South Leaflets 4:6)

When you cite a classic work of literature, available in many editions, the page number of your particular copy is of less value to your reader than the canto, chapter, act, scene, or line of the work. The conventional citation is the division number first and then the line, separated by a period:

When your reference is to a Biblical passage, cite chapter and verse:
All through the Bible, the principles of freedom and equality are stressed: "Have we not all one father? Hath not one God created us?" (Malachi 18.8)

When your reference is to a verse play, cite Act, scene, and line. Use Roman numerals for the Act and scene:
When Hamlet learns who murdered his father he exclaims, "O my prophetic soul!" (I.v.40).

> *When your reference is to a long poem,* cite book or canto and line:
>
>   At the end of Milton's Paradise Lost, Adam and Eve, "with wand'ring steps and slow, / Through Eden took their solitary way" (12.648–49).
>
> *When your reference is to a work of prose,* begin the entry with the page number of your edition followed by a semicolon:
>
> - In Dickens's Great Expectations, Pip has to learn not to consider his relatives "coarse and common" (139; ch. 18).
> - Despite her insanity, Blanche Dubois makes her final exit with dignity, saying: "I have always depended on the kindness of strangers" (Williams, Streetcar , 142; sc. 11).
>
> And finally, when you refer to a work as a whole, mention the author's name and you need not interrupt your text with any citation at all:
>
>   Achtert and Gibaldi carefully edited the new MLA Style Manual.

When Should Footnotes (or Endnotes) Be Used?   Important as in-text notation is, it cannot replace footnotes altogether. If your parenthetical notation is too lengthy, it will distract your reader. And so, when you want to provide a quantity of information that might interrupt the argument you are pursuing in the text, use a footnote. Add a number (raised a half space above the line of print) referring to a note that will contain the additional information.

Your instructor will tell you whether to place these notes at the "foot" of the appropriate pages in the traditional manner or whether to follow the method, recommended by the MLA, of placing your notes in a list at the end of your paper, just preceding the List of Works Cited. The content of the notes will be the same in either case. And in both cases, you should number the notes consecutively throughout the paper.

The list on page 341 suggests situations where foot- or endnotes are appropriate.

How Do You Make a List of Works Cited?   If you have made your bibliography cards carefully, you should have no trouble at all in constructing your List of Works Cited. All you will need to do is alphabetize your cards by author (or title where there is no author) and copy the information in list form. The author's name is written last name first to make the alphabetizing clearer. The rest of the entry is indented under that name. The MLA suggests the system in the boxed format. Note especially the recommended punctuation and order of items.

In writing each entry in your bibliography, follow the model for sequence and punctuation. Do not be concerned if your entries do not have some of the items listed in the model. Since the model is meant to include all possibilities, you can expect to omit some items in any given entry. If there is no author, for example, you should begin with the title of the

---

Foot or End Notation: MLA Models

When you want to call your readers' attention to sources beyond those you refer to in the text:
> [3]See also Bloom 38–44 and O'Brien 109–117.
> [4]Snerd strenuously disagrees. See 98–99.

When you base a paragraph on multiple sources (as in Medieval Peasant, Support Example A, page 332):
> [5]The material in the preceding paragraph is derived from Abbey St. Germain 78; Charlemagne 43, 45, 49; and Aelfric 95.

When you have referred to a secondary source and want to provide the original source:
> [6]Jemshed Khan, "The Scarlet Letter—A Rash Conclusion?" *New England Journal of Medicine*, 311 (August 9, 1984): 416 (qtd. in Turner 434).

The rare occasions when you need to use footnotes to comment upon the text. Though it is ordinarily wisest to omit comments you cannot work into the text, sometimes you need to add a point to clarify an idea or to define a troublesome concept. And once in a great while you might make an "It is interesting in this connection that . . ." note. (See the Sample Research Paper, p. 350.)

List of Works Cited: MLA Model Entries

A Book

Author's Last Name, First Name. "Name of Article." <u>Title of Book</u>. Ed.[itor's] Name. (or) Trans.[lator's] Name. 3rd ed. Place: Publisher [Unless published before 1900], Date. 3: 3–33. [Volume and pages included only when your reference is limited to a specific article or section, e.g., "Introduction."]

Magazine or Journal Article

Name, Author's. "Name of Article." <u>Title of Journal</u>, [Volume] 3 (1933): [pages] 30–33.

---

article; if that also is missing, with the title of the book. Because articles in books are rare, except in anthologies, that item will frequently be omitted. You need not be uneasy if an exception to these models should arise. Your own good sense will show you how to manage it in a way consistent with the format.

The accompanying alphabetized list of works cited parenthetically in Chapter 10 demonstrates the MLA conventions for a wide variety of bibliographic entries you may have cause to use.

List of Works Cited: MLA Models

Article in Alphabetized Familiar Reference Work
(Note absence of publishing information)

"Barber." Funk & Wagnall's Standard Reference Encyclopedia. 1967 ed.

Book with a Single Author

Dickens, Charles. Great Expectations. New York: Washington Sq. Press, 1963.

Anonymous Book or Pamphlet

Education Directory; Higher Education 1967–68. Part 3. Washington, D.C.: U.S. Govern-
    ment Printing Office, 1968.

Anonymous Newspaper Article

"Fossils Strengthen Evolutionary Link between Dinosaurs, Birds." Richmond NewsLeader
    Aug. 14, 1986: A2.

Multiple Works of One Author

Hairston, Maxine. Contemporary Composition. 4th ed. Boston: Houghton Mifflin, 1986.
---. Successful Writing: A Rhetoric for Advanced Composition. New York: Norton, 1981.
    Milton, John. *Paradise Lost.* New York: Norton, 1975.

Work Preceding 1900 (Publisher unnamed)

Old South Leaflets. Eds. Directors of the Old South Works. 8 vols. Boston: 1896–1900.

Separately Published Work in Anthology

Shakespeare, William. Hamlet. The Complete Works of William Shakespeare. Eds. Hardin
    Craig and David Bevington. Glenview, Ill.: Scott, Foresman, 1973. 899–943.

Reprinted Article

Turner, Perry. "What Killed Arthur Dimmesdale?" Science 85. Oct. 1985: 81–82. Rpt. in
    Writing Effectively. Beth S. Neman. New York: Harper & Row, 1989.
Williams, Tennessee. A Streetcar Named Desire. New York: Signet, 1947.

Work with More Than Three Editors

---. The Glass Menagerie. An Introduction to Literature. Eds. Sylvan Barnet, et al., 6th ed.
    Boston: Little, Brown, 1977. 889–949.

Article in Anthology

White, E. B. "The Distant Music of the Hounds." The Second Tree From the Corner. New
    York: Harper & Row, 1949. 131–33.

TRY IT OUT

A. Practicing Parenthetical Documentation. Quote or paraphrase from the following writers or articles. Remember to introduce the topic in your own words and suggest the speaker, either specifically or in general. Follow the directions for each item and include parentheses documenting each appropriately:

1. Make a point about nuclear deterrence and support it by *quoting* Lewis Thomas. (page 428)

2. Make a point about nuclear deterrence and support it by *paraphrasing* Lewis Thomas. (page 428)

3. Make a point about desertification and support it by citing Fred Golden's statistics. (page 415)

4. Make a point about changing views on working women and support it by citing the Astin study (in Ellen Goodman's article, page 418).

5. Make a point on a topic you are studying and support it from your note cards in any one of these ways.

B. Practicing Bibliographic Citation. Make a brief List of Works Cited, including the following items:

1. Ellen Goodman's article as reprinted in this volume.

2. Lewis Thomas's article as originally published.

3. An article on Iroquois Indians from the 1978 edition of the *Encyclopaedia Britannica*.

4. An article on the front page of today's newspaper.

5. A book of your choice from your shelf.

THE APA DOCUMENTATION SYSTEM

In most of the social-sciences, authors document their scholarly writing by following the conventions recommended by the American Psychological Association. If you are writing your research paper for a social-science course—psychology, sociology, education, anthropology, or the like—you may well be asked to use this system. Because it is very similar to the new MLA system, you may confidently follow much of the process discussed above—if you are careful to make the changes described here.

HANDLING APA INTEXT CONVENTIONS THAT DIFFER FROM THE MLA

1. The focus of the social sciences is time-centered, and thus the APA asks you to put the date of the research under discussion into the text itself along with the author(s)'s last name.
2. It is not customary to use first names, initials, or titles in the text unless surnames are duplicated.
3. Page numbers are often omitted in the parenthetical references.

Parenthetical InText Documentation: APA System Models

- Bryant studied teacher preparation (1978) and concluded. . . .
- A recent study of teacher preparation (Bryant, 1978) demonstrates.
- Bryant found in 1978 that. . . .
- Similarly, a 1985 study (Frankel, Manogue, & Ronald) showed. . . .

HANDLING APA LIST OF WORKS-CITED CONVENTIONS THAT DIFFER FROM MLA

1. Indicate the author's name by surname and initials. Use an ampersand (&) before the last when citing multiple authors.
2. When an author has written more than one listed work, repeat the name in later references. With a single author, list his or her works chronologically with the most recent first. With multiple authors, alphabetize within the group by the second name listed.
3. The date of publication immediately follows the author's name in bold type.
4. Capitalize only the first word in titles. Omit article titles and continue to underline (italicize) titles of books and journals.
5. Underline (italicize) journal volume numbers and separate from page numbers by a comma.

List of Works-Cited: APA System Models[5]

Single Author, Monograph, Government Document

Bryant, J. (1978) The development and control of the teacher preparation program at Wilmington College [Monograph]. Columbus: Ohio State Department of Education.

Chapter in a Book, Multiple Authors, Editors

Frankel, J. & Borman, K. (1983). Gender inequities in childhood social life and adult work life. In K. Borman, D. Quarm, & S. Gideonse (Ed.), Women in the workplace (pp. 113–135). Hillsdale, N.J.: Ablex.

---

[5]Note alphabetized character of the list.

Journal Article, Repeated Reference: Multiple Authors

Frankel, J., Manogue, M. A., & Ronald, J. (1985). Women's life patterns: An exploratory study. Journal of Creative Sociology, *132* (2), 145–147.

Book, Two Authors

Hope, M. & J. Young (1986). The faces of homelessness. Lexington, Mass.: Lexington Books.

THE NUMERICAL DOCUMENTATION SYSTEM OF THE PHYSICAL SCIENCES

No one set of documentation conventions is accepted by all the scientific disciplines or even by all the scholarly journals of a particular science, as the style guides of the American Chemical Society (ACS) and the Council of Biological Editors (CBE) make clear. Yet with minor variations, most scientific journals prefer either a system very similar to that of the APA[6] (see above) or a numerical system keyed to the List of Works Cited.

1. To use the Numerical System, number your references parenthetically as you use them.
2. If you should repeat a reference, use the number where it first appeared.
3. Then, instead of alphabetizing your List of Works Cited, list the items numerically to correspond with the reference numbers within the text.

Parenthetical InText Documentation: Numerical System Models

- In completing his research, Bates (2) found. . . .
- His study was soon corroborated (4, 6–8, 10), and. . . .
- Willeke and Pavlik (3), however, disagreed.

The bibliographic format in the model is the format suggested by the Chemical Society. Note the difference in punctuation, the omission of titles in journal entries, and the use in these entries of italic type for *journal* and *volume number* and bold type to signify the date.

List of Works Cited: Numerical System Model

Book

(1) Dodd, J. ACS Style Guide: A Manual for Authors, 4th ed.; American Chemical Society Publications: Washington, D.C., **1978**; pp. 111–115.

---

[6]Journals in the biological sciences usually prefer the APA model.

Journal Article

(2) Bates, N. Tappi.[7] **1969,** *52,* 1157–61.

Portion of Book

(3) Willeke, K.; Pavlik, R. E. in <u>Generation of Aerosols and Facilities for Exposure Experiments</u>; Willeke, K., Ed.; Ann Arbor, Mich.: Ann Arbor Science, **1980;** Chapter 20.

Which System of Documentation to Use

It should be abundantly clear by now that no particular system of giving credit where it is due has been divinely inspired. I have shown you three well accepted systems, and there are others. Because none is more "correct" than another, I recommend that you follow whatever system of documentation your instructor suggests, and follow it as consistently as you can. If you do not know your instructor's preference, the MLA conventions (described on pages 338–342) should serve you well.

TRY IT OUT

1. Choose three of your own bibliographic cards—a book, a journal article, and an article in a book are preferable. Then, using these cards, make three mini-Lists of Works Cited, following in turn the conventions of the MLA, APA, and numerical ACS systems.

2. It is sometimes helpful to try out techniques by modeling your own work after that of those who have used the techniques successfully. Therefore, in this next exercise you are asked to write paragraphs on your own subject, using your own note cards, but copying the strategies of the Sample Student Research Paper.
   a. The student author of the research paper develops her point in this passage from the end of the second paragraph by a combination of quotation and paraphrase:

   > Wendell Phillips, too, was influenced by the Holy Book. He believed that the Bible was the "final authority on human bondage"; he even went so far on these grounds as to curse the Constitution because it condoned slavery. (in Madison, 64)

   Follow the pattern of this passage in making a point of your own and backing it by combining a quotation and paraphrase from your notes.

---

[7]Journal of the Technical Association of the Pulp and Paper Industry.

b. Note the pattern of the first paragraph, page 357, of the Sample Research Paper: the topic sentence, the explanation setting up support for the sentence, and the four supporting quotations with their parenthetical documentation. Imitate this pattern by making a point relevant to your subject in a topic sentence, explaining it in another sentence, and then backing up the idea with at least two quotations from your note cards.

A Sample Student Research Paper

THE OUTLINE

THE INFLUENCE OF THE BIBLE ON THE SLAVERY QUESTION

Thesis: Both of the opposing sides in the American
        Civil War realized the importance of the
        Bible in the slavery controversy and put
        it to constant persuasive use.

   I. Introduction

 II. The Influence of the Bible on the Anti-

     Slavery Movement

     A. The influence of the Bible on the North-

       ern leaders

       1. Abraham Lincoln

       2. John Brown

       3. Wendell Phillips

       4. William Lloyd Garrison

     B. The Bible used to foster the Abolition

       movement

Formal outline for inclusion with finished paper.

Compare with working outline, page 326.

       1. Technique of a religious revival

       2. Poetry and novels

       3. <u>The Liberator</u>

III. The Influence of the Bible on the Pro-Slavery Movement

    A. Pro-slavery feeling aroused in the South

       1. Former mild feeling

       2. Apologies change to assertions

    B. The Bible justification of slavery

       1. "Cursed be Canaan"

       2. Slavery sanctioned by God and prevalent among the Hebrew people

          a. Patriarchs

          b. Mosaic Law

IV. The Abolitionist Rebuttal

    A. Interpretation of "Cursed be Canaan"

    B. Interpretation of slavery among the Hebrews

    C. Slavery forbidden

    D. Equality stressed

V. Conclusion:

    A. The Bible an effective weapon

    B. The North "prevailed"

THE PAPER

THE INFLUENCE OF THE BIBLE ON THE SLAVERY QUESTION

Use of epigraph.

> The will of God prevails. No doubt, no doubt
> Yet, in great contest, each side claims to act
> In strict accordance with the will of God.
> Both may, one must be wrong. (Benet 213)

During the Civil War the Bible became the South's main justification for slavery and the North's foremost weapon against the institution.

Quotation from Benét epigraph.

Thus both sides claimed to act "in strict accordance with the will of God." This was entirely possible for them to do, in all sincerity. There are ample grounds in the Bible upon which to base either a violently antislavery or a strongly proslavery point of view, for the Bible is in some ways a very contradictory book. With differing interpretations, the Bible can be made to prove many viewpoints. Both of the opposing sides in the

THESIS

slavery controversy realized the effectiveness of the Bible and put it to constant use.

The Bible was the backbone of the Abolitionist cause. "Take away the Bible," William Lloyd

Primary source quotation as recorded in a secondary source.

Garrison said, "and our warfare with oppression and infidelity, intemperance and impurity, is removed--we have no authority to speak and no courage to act" (qtd. in Nelson 177). The powerful leaders of the North were so thoroughly steeped in the Bible from the days of their childhood that it naturally had a large influence upon their lives. According to F. C. Stifler, "The great Lincoln was nurtured on the Bible as few men ever have been" (42).[1] His actions on the slavery question, as on all important issues, were governed by his creed: "What doth the Lord require of thee, but to do justly, to love mercy, and to walk humbly with thy God." (Micah 6.8)

The spirit of John Brown, which legend tells us walked the night and could not rest until the last slave was free (Benet), was a direct product of the Bible, for this first and most ardent of the Abolitionists followed the Scriptures to the point of fanaticism. He studied the Bible with such zeal that his speech and writing acquired the flavor of the Old Testament. He was known throughout the land as a "Terrible Saint" or "God's angry man" (Madison 41, 43). Wendell Phillips, too, was influenced by the Holy Book. He believed that the Bible was the "final authority on human bondage";

[1]Stifler cites an interesting conversation that Lincoln once had with an agnostic friend: "You are wrong, Mr. Speed; take all of this book on reason that you can and the rest on faith, and you will, I am sure, live and die a happier and better man" (42).

Quotation from a secondary source.

Biblical quotation and documentation.

Combination of direct quotation and paraphrase.

Contentual footnote.

he even went so far on these grounds as to curse the Constitution because it condoned slavery (Madison, 64). Phillips, like so many others of his time, used Bible language and imagery in the remarkable oratory of his Abolitionist addresses. For example, this excerpt from his "Dangers from Slavery" speech:

Quotation from a primary source.

> Then the wicked will walk on every side for the vilest of men will be exalted, and America, become the mock and scorn and hissing of the nations, will go down to worse shame than was ever heaped upon Sodom; for the lust for wealth, land, and power, she will also have committed the crime against nature. (Old South Leaflets 5:15)

Perhaps William Lloyd Garrison did more with the Bible to further his cause than any other Abolitionist, both in his fiery speeches and in the Liberator, his daring newspaper. Even his first antislavery address was marked by constant Biblical allusion:

Long quotation indented and blocked off.

> Thus saith the Lord God of the Africans, Let this people go, that they may serve me; I ask them to proclaim liberty to the captives, and the opening of the prison to them that are bound; to light up a flame of philanthropy that shall burn till all of Africa be redeemed from the night of moral death and the song of deliverance be heard throughout her borders. (Old South Leaflets 8:10)

The power and force of the Old Testament were so much a part of Garrison that many associated the

Short quotations incorporated into the text.

two together. Bates likens him to "a fiery Hebrew prophet" (454), and Wendell Phillips in his beautiful eulogy said that Garrison was "Taught of God . . . God endowed, and God-sent to arouse a nation" (Old South Leaflets 4:7) Thus, the influence of the Bible was extended into the minds of the leaders of the Abolition movement, and their voices carried it to the people.

There were many ways in which the people received the spirit of Abolition, and in most of these the Bible played a major role. There were monthly prayer meetings. Songbooks and hymnals filled with Biblical phraseology appeared by the score. Time and time again the techniques of a religious revival and a Fourth of July rally were intermingled (Nelson 176). Abolitionist propaganda was also spread through poetry and novels, and again the Bible influence was very apparent. The most stirring novel of the era, Uncle Tom's Cabin, was written by Harriet Beecher Stowe, members of whose family had been ministers for generations, and who, consequently, was brought up on the Bible.[2] The famous New England poets, who lashed out so strongly against slavery, did so

Footnote identifying primary source, quoted in a secondary source.

[2]From an autobiographic passage by Harriet Beecher Stowe (qtd. in Nelson 178).

*Secondary
source
credited with
quotation.
Statistics
credited.*

with an enormous fund of Scriptural knowledge as background. Whittier, for example, according to Nelson, "wrote biblically as naturally as he breathed." In 285 of his poems are 816 passages drawn from the Bible (176). For instance, as the controversy was coming to a head, he wrote:

> He flung aside his silver flute,
> Snatched up Isaiah's stormy lyre,
> Loosened old anger spent and mute,
> Startled the iron string with fire. (qtd. in Nelson 176)

Lesser poets, too, drew from this unending source:

*Poetry quoted
in indented
lines.*

> Though hearts be torn asunder,
> For freedom we will fight:
> Our blood may seal the victory
> But God will shield the right![3]

The publication that most aroused the ire of the proslavery enthusiasts and the admiration of the Abolitionists was William Lloyd Garrison's <u>Liberator</u>. It was a newspaper composed of a series of antislavery essays and poems. Throughout there are many Bible references and some of the writing style is reminiscent of the Hebrew Bible. The prose is interspersed with poetry, most of which has more strength than style:

*Footnotes
citing specific
anthologized
material.*

[3]Lucy Larcom, "The Nineteenth of April" (<u>Bugle Echoes</u> 38).

```
God is a God of mercy, and would see
The prison-doors unbarr'd--the bondmen
  free!
He is a God of truth, with purer eyes
Than to behold the oppressor's sacrifice![4]
```

Thus by words and actions the Abolitionist movement advanced in the North with the Bible as the cornerstone of the whole effort.

Summarizing conclusion of the first discussion.

"Although" introduction of the second discussion.

Until so much antislavery sentiment had been aroused in the North, the Southerners had looked upon slavery as a necessary evil. They condoned it because they believed it an economic necessity, but were mildly apologetic about the institution on moral grounds. There was, however, a widespread belief that it was somehow good for the slaves. The Reverend Phillip Schaff considered slavery "a wholesome training school for the Negro--taking him from the lowest state of heathenism and barbarism to some degree of Christian civilization" (qtd. in Cole 256). There was also a feeling that God had willed the superiority of the white race. After much reflection, Alexander Stevens came to this conclusion. He said:

No need for quotation marks in blocked quotations.

> A proper subordination of the inferior to the superior race was the natural and normal condition of the former in relation to the

[4] "The Salvation," stanzas 10, 12. The Liberator Jan. 1, 1832 (Old South Leaflets 4:6).

latter. . . . The assignment of that position in the structure of society to the African race amongst us was the best for both races and in accordance with the ordinance of the Creator. (199)

More often, however, this belief was confined to the much vaguer feeling expressed by Benet in his description of Mary-Lou Wingate:

> In heaven, of course, we should all be equal,
> But until we came to that golden sequel,
> Gentility must keep to gentility
> Where God and breeding had made things sta-
>   ble,
> While the rest of the cosmos deserved
>   civility
> But dined in its boots at the second-table.
>   (162)

Perhaps the South would have continued to apologize for slavery, but for the denunciations of the Abolitionists; for few had ever before considered it in the light of a "scriptural blessing," as historian Lloyd terms it (164). But after the severe attacks of Garrison and the others, the South, on the defensive, thoroughly investigated the matter.

Phrase quoted for its stylistic appeal, appropriately credited.

Elaborate proofs were prepared justifying slavery on Biblical grounds. These were completed by intensive research and were intricately planned. The Old Testament justification of slavery fell into two principal arguments. The first:

Note effective lead-in to Biblical point.

that from the beginning the Negro race had been condemned to servitude; and the second: that God Himself had expressly sanctioned the institution of slavery. The proof of the first argument was found in Noah's angry prophecy to Canaan, Ham's son:

> Cursed be Canaan: a servant of servants shall he be unto his brethren. (Genesis 11.25-28)

Because legend tells that Ham was the founder of the dark races, this point became quite influential. Even Benet's Bible-reading slave-trader used this as his excuse for his infamous work. The poem reads:

Literary evidence.

> He touched the Bible. "And it's down there, Mister,
> Down there in black and white--the sons of Ham--
> Bondservants--sweat of their brows." His voice trailed off
> Into texts. "I tell you, Mister," he said fiercely,
> "The pay's good pay, but it's the Lord's work, too.
> We're spreading the Lord's seed--spreading his seed--". (15)

The second argument was put into a syllogism by Lloyd:

Southern Biblical Argument.

> *Whatever God has sanctioned among any people cannot be in itself a sin.
> *God did expressly sanction slavery among the Hebrews.

> *Therefore, slavery cannot be in itself a
> sin. (189)

*Topic
Sentence.*

All that was needed to complete the argument
was concrete Biblical evidence of the two premises. Passages were found and pointed out in detail by the Southern clergy. Several quotations

*Explanation
setting up
support.*

were always cited proving the existence of slavery in patriarchal times. Among the ones most
often quoted were the commandment to Abraham concerning circumcision, which particularly specifies, "he that is bought with thy money" (Genesis

*Biblical
support.*

6.9), and the advice of the angel to Hagar,
Sarah's runaway servant: "Return to thy mistress
and submit thyself under her hands" (Genesis 11.-
13). The complicated proofs continued by placing
emphasis on the Mosaic law. Frequently stated
were the long passages regulating the conduct toward "bondservants" (Leviticus 25.44-46; Exodus
21.2-6, 20-21). But perhaps repeated with most
regularity was this one quotation, which stressed
the property idea:

*Blocked long
Biblical
quotation.*

> And ye shall take them for a possession; they
> shall be your bondsmen forever: but over
> your brethren, the children of Israel, ye
> shall not rule one over another with rigour.
> (Leviticus 25.42-43)

Thus, with no mention of the later sections of the
Hebrew Bible, the arguments for the Old Testament

justification of slavery were complete. Now
firmly convinced that slavery was consistent with
the will of God, the South sent out its challenge:
"You cannot abolish slavery, for God is pledged to
sustain it!"

*Northern
defensive
Biblical
argument.*

The North accepted the challenge and answered the South's every argument with clear-cut
logic. Their first point was that the proslavery
evidence pertaining to the Mosaic law was really
inconclusive because it related exclusively to
the "regulation of the Hebrew social system"
(Drisler 3). William Jay said, "It is wholly immaterial whether the Jews held slaves or not,
since it is admitted by all that if they did, they
acted by virtue of a special and express permission from God, while it is equally admitted that
no such permission has been given to us" (626).
Several technical denials were made to the
"Cursed be Canaan" argument. It was pointed out
that there is no reason to believe that Noah's
curse extended to the other children of Ham
(Drisler 3). Furthermore, the Hebrew Bible speaks
of a vast Canaanite family in which there were
both Negroes and whites (Gasparin 104).

*Northern
Biblical
argument.*

The North's most conclusive arguments, however, were not defensive. In the later sections of

the Bible there are many passages which actually forbid slavery; but even within the five books of Moses several quotations may be found that prohibit slavery and slave trade as well. Among these are:

> And he that stealeth a man and selleth him or if he be found in his hand, he shall surely be put to death. (Exodus 21.16)

and

> Thou shalt not deliver unto his master a bondman that is escaped from his master unto thee. (Deuteronomy 23.16-17)

The prophets were particularly outspoken on the subject. "Woe unto him . . . that useth his neighbor's services without wages," Jeremiah wrote (22:13). And all through the Bible, time and time again, the principles of freedom and equality are stressed:

> Have we not all one father? Hath not one God created us?. (Malachi 18.8)

Thus the North argued that there is little to be gained in following literally all of the ancient laws set down in the Bible for a specific people in a particular set of circumstances, but that the <u>ideas</u> expounded in the Scriptures are just and right.

Concluding restatement of thesis

The Bible thus proved to be an excellent weapon, not only because of its variety in inter-

leading to

pretations, but because of its widespread appeal. As we have seen, the Bible arguments influenced all men from the very lowliest to the greatest leaders of the time in both sections of our country. As for the right of the matter, from our modern perspective, the Northern Biblical arguments would seem to have had the clear logical and moral superiority, and, as we know, they prevailed.

*author's
concluding
evaluation.*

THE BIBLIOGRAPHY

LIST OF WORKS CITED

Primary Sources

Benet, Stephen Vincent. John Brown's Body. Garden City, N.Y.: Doubleday, 1928.

Holy Bible. Authorized King James Version. Cleveland: World Publishing Company, 1955.

Bugle Echoes: A Collection of Poems of the Civil War, Both Northern and Southern. Ed. Francis F. Browne. New York, 1886.

Drisler, Henry. Criticism of John H. Hopkin's "Bible View of Slavery." New York, 1863.

Gasparin, Agenor Etienne. The Uprising of a Great People. New York, 1862.

Jay, William. Miscellaneous Writings on Slavery. Boston, 1853.

Old South Leaflets. Eds. Directors of the Old South Work. Boston: 1896-1908.

Stephens, Alexander H. Recollections of Alexander H. Stephens. Ed. Myrta Lockett Avary. New York: Doubleday, 1910.

Secondary Sources

Bates, Ernest Sutherland. American Faith. New York: Norton, 1940.

Cole, Arthur Charles. A History of American Life: The Irrepressible Conflict, 1850-1865. Vol. 7. New York: Macmillan, 1934.

Lloyd, Arthur Young. The Slavery Controversy. Chapel Hill: U of N. Carolina P, 1939.

Madison, Charles A. Critics and Crusaders. New York; Henry Holt, 1947.

Nelson, Lawrence Emerson. Our Roving Bible. New York: Abington-Cokesbury, 1945.

Stifler, Francis Carr. The Bible Speaks. New York: Duell, Sloan & Pierce, 1946.

ASSIGNMENT

Write a research paper of some five or six typed pages (1250 to 1500 words) answering a question raised by one of the following subjects from a variety of disciplines or on a topic one of your instructors will advise. I have included questions with some of the topics as suggestions of ways such general subjects can be made approachable.

- The Holocaust in World War II (Why were there so few instances of rebellion on the part of the victims of the Nazis?)
- Battered Wives (What causes this phenomenon, and how can it be remedied?)
- *Hamlet* (Why did Hamlet delay so long in "sweeping to his revenge"?)
- Japanese Markets (To what extent are western marketing techniques applicable? Why?)
- *Beowulf* (To what extent is it a Christian work?)
- The Aztec Indians
- Cancer
- Men in the Life of Queen Elizabeth I
- The Great Depression
- Versions of the Faust Legend
- REM (Rapid Eye Movements) and Deep-Dream Sleep
- Evolution
- Charlie Chaplin and the Notion of the Sad Clown
- Nuclear Energy
- Gregorian Chants
- Rights of Divorced Fathers
- Frank Lloyd Wright and His Contribution to Architecture
- Political Cartoonists
- The Great Schism in the Catholic Church
- Jazz
- Affirmative Action
- The Problem of Evil: Some Answers from Myth and Philosophy
- The Homosexual and the Law
- Cloning
- Paul Robeson: Figure of Controversy
- Hemingway: Macho or Mushy
- Astrology
- President Johnson's "Great Society"
- Lizzie Borden: Guilty or Innocent?
- Ollie North: Hero, Dupe, or Villain?
- Salem Witchcraft
- Ellis Island

- The Creation of Living Organisms for Commercial Use
- Alimony Laws
- The Insanity Plea in Our Court System
- Utopian Satire
- DNA

Chapter

11

The Critical Analysis

Like the research paper, the critical analysis is a specialized form of expository writing. It is specialized both in subject matter, which is limited to works of literature and other art forms, and in approach, which is almost exclusively analytical and interpretive. It is, nevertheless, important to remember that every critical analysis is an expository essay, and everything we have said about expository writing holds true for it as well.

THE NATURE OF A CRITICAL ANALYSIS

A critical analysis is a frequent assignment in college courses. You may be asked to write such a paper about an essay, story, novel, play, movie, or even a composition of music or dance or a work of visual art. Or you may be asked to write a comparative analysis of two or more such works. Sometimes a critical essay is required when the assignment or exam question doesn't mention "critical analysis" at all. You should write a critical analysis, for instance, if you were given an assignment similar to any of these:

- Comment on Lewis Thomas's use of imagery in "Late Thoughts on Listening to Mahler's Ninth Symphony."
- Tell how Kate Chopin's "The Story of an Hour" fits in with contemporary feminist concepts.
- In many novels and plays, minor characters contribute significantly

to the total work. They often have certain functions, in particular, as instruments in the plot, foils for the main characters, commentators on the action or theme, and the like. Write a well-organized essay showing how minor characters function in a work in which they appear importantly. (Adapted from a nationally standardized test question.)

When a critical analysis is called for, what specifically should you expect to write? Despite common misconceptions, you should *not* plan to write simply a summary of the work, nor an evaluation of its merits, nor an expression of the thoughts it raises in your mind—although any of these elements may form part of your paper. What you should expect to write, rather, is an interpretation of the work (or works). And you should expect to do so in terms of the way the author chooses to get his or her meaning across. Whatever kind of literature or art you will be dealing with and whatever the approach you select or are assigned, the heart of your critical analysis will be your answer to these two analytical questions:

1. What does the author actually say? (meaning)
2. How does he or she say it? (method)

The emphasis you place on your answer to each of these questions will vary, but the presence of both is unavoidable, for they are the essence of the critical analysis. How do you come to your answers to these questions? By a process known as *close reading.* The first step in planning your critical analysis, then, is to make a close reading of the work that is your subject.

Close Reading

Close reading begins with a concentrated phrase-by-phrase reading of a passage or a work. I recommend that you do this reading aloud. You may also want to take notes as you go along. Professor Elaine Maimon suggests that you even copy down selected passages in order to "get inside the author's rhythms and style."[1] In any case, take care to mark any word or reference you don't fully comprehend, and be sure that you understand it clearly before you are ready to pull your impressions together.

BE CONSCIOUS OF THE AUTHOR

The purpose of close reading is not only to understand the author's meaning fully. It is also to discover what the author does to affect your thinking and your emotions. Reading closely, then, differs from the usual varieties of reading not so much in the more intense attentiveness involved

---

[1] *Writing in the Arts and Sciences,* Cambridge, Mass.: Winthrop, 1981.

(although this attentiveness is certainly required) as in the attitudes it demands of you as reader. Ordinarily, as a reader, you think of the work you are reading as a way you may gain knowledge or pleasure. In order to do close reading, however, you must view the work rather as the creation of an author for a particular reason or set of reasons. Cleanth Brooks, Robert Penn Warren, and John Thibout Purser label a work of literature "the presentation of an author's way of looking at life."[2] Your job as a critical reader is to discover what way of "looking at life" is being presented. To do so, you read with the author's purpose foremost in your consciousness. Ask yourself continually: What is the author attempting here? Why would the author include this passage? This effect?

READ LITERALLY

Reading for the author's intent does not mean searching your imagination for hidden meanings and strange symbolisms, as students sometimes believe. Actually, quite the contrary is true—at least at the start. Close reading is first of all a reading for *literal* meaning. Ask yourself as you read: What do the words really say? What do they explicitly mean? What does the syntax literally convey? Only after you have established the literal meaning should you look for hidden interpretation or symbolic significance. Of course, you must delve beneath the surface in order to discover just what the author is trying to get at, but all the clues for a valid interpretation are present right there in the words themselves.

To show you what I mean, let's close-read the first paragraph of George Will's Chicago Cubs essay (page 438) together:

> A reader demands to know how I contracted the infectious conservatism for which he plans to horsewhip me. So if you have tears, gentle reader, prepare to shed them now as I reveal how my gloomy temperament received its conservative warp from early and prolonged exposure to the Chicago Cubs.

What does the passage mean, literally? Here's my reading: In answer to a reader's query, Will is going to explain how he became infected with the disease of conservative philosophy by growing up a fan of the Chicago Cubs, and it will be a sad story. What can we discover beneath the surface? The metaphors *contracting an infection* and *horsewhipping* indicate a lack of sympathy on the inquiring reader's part. Why does Will use them? Could he intend the essay to be a defense of conservatism as well as an explanation? Surely *horsewhip* is hyperbole and the quotation about shedding tears is inappropriately strong. Does he mean to be ironic? Let's reread.

No. Will doesn't seem to mean the opposite of what he says; it's more like tongue-in-cheek. Why does he adopt this tone? Perhaps he is trying to win over even the skeptical?

---

[2] *An Approach to Literature* (New York: Appleton-Century-Crofts, 1964), p. 4.

WONDER AT THE UNUSUAL

As you read, look for anything that seems, on the one hand, part of a pattern or odd or out of place, on the other. Notice, for instance, repetition, parallels, metaphors, intriguing openings, interesting conclusions. When anything seems to be calling attention to itself as out of the ordinary, try to reach some conclusion as to why the author put it there and how it fits into the pattern of the work as a whole. (Why does Will call conservatism an infectious disease? Why does he compare his tale with Antony's on Caesar's murder? How in the world does he mean to connect his political philosophy with the Chicago Cubs?)

BE AWARE OF YOUR OWN REACTIONS

You should also be sensitive to your own reactions and look for the author's purpose behind any unusual response you discover in yourself. Ask yourself: Why do I respond to that tone, situation, character, image, argument in that way? Does the author intend me to feel this way? What did she or he do to provoke this response? (Is Will writing a serious essay? Then why am I smiling?)

By exploring in this way the methods your author uses to influence your relationship with the material, you should be able to arrive at a tentative interpretation of the work. Close reading thus is double-edged. You study the author's methods to understand the meaning, and once you have established a tentative meaning you look for methods that will support or argue for your interpretation of it. The accompanying guidelines should be helpful in both searches.

Guidelines for Close Reading

1. *Clues from the overall structure.* Start with the overall structure. How is the work organized? What are the beginning, middle, and end? How does the gross structure contribute to the creation of the overall impression you have decided is the author's purpose?
2. *Clues from the individual parts.* Examine the work part by part. Which parts do you see as most important in contributing to the author's purpose? How do they do so? How do they fit into the whole? Are there portions that do not seem to contribute to, *or* perhaps seem even to contradict, your interpretation? Can the discrepancies be reconciled? If not, can your interpretation be adjusted to fit the new elements?
3. *Clues from substructures, motifs, patterns.* Within the overall structure, are there any secondary structures or motifs? Are there unusual elements within the work, ideas or stylistic constructions that catch your attention? Why do you think the author included them? Do they form a pattern? How do they contribute to the author's purpose? to your interpretation?

> **TRY IT OUT**
>
> Try out the Guidelines for Close Reading on Will's "The Chicago Cubs Overdue" or a work your instructor suggests. Answer the relevant questions in writing.

Planning the Structure of Your Analysis

Your close reading should provide you with preliminary answers to the two analytic questions: What does the author say? and How? These answers can become the foundation for organizing your critical essay. Because the critical analysis is such a specialized form of writing, it is possible to set up a model or format for a thesis that can help organize a wide variety of such essays. The format includes answers to both of the analytic questions:

· In *Such-and-Such Work,* Author So-and-So suggests . . . [(1) meaning] by . . . [(2) method].

Since structures are derived from theses, it is even possible to set up a model outline. A typical structural plan will, of course, also reflect the interplay of the two main elements, meaning and method. Here is such a plan:

  I. Introduction leading to thesis.
 II. Interpretation supported by [opening passages, for example].
III. Interpretation supported by [overall patterns of imagery, for instance
       Pattern A
       Pattern B
       Pattern C].
 IV. Interpretation supported by [for example, resolution of conflict].
  V. Conclusion: Full expression of interpretation [with reference to title, for instance].

In practice, of course, composing your thesis and planning the structure of your critical essay is not nearly so cut-and-dried. Although the basic pattern usually holds, the variations are infinite, determined as they are by the nature of the specific assignment and your specific approach to it. Let's look at variations of the basic thesis and structure that might be produced by writers working from the sample assignments offered at the beginning of this chapter:

· When the assignment places the emphasis upon a specific method:

Assignment: Comment upon Lewis Thomas's use of imagery in "Late Night Thoughts on Listening to Mahler's Ninth Symphony."

Thesis: In "Late Thoughts" Lewis Thomas uses the symbolism of his changing response to sounds to convey his anguish at the possibility of a nuclear holocaust.

1. Introduction—Including explication of Thomas's point of view
2. Symbolism of the sound of Mahler's Ninth
   - Then: symbolized "reassurance" in the continuity of life
   - Now: symbolizes demolition of all life
3. Terrifying new sound: the television speaker
   Symbolizing matter-of-fact acceptance of nuclear war
4. Concern for youthful interpreters of new sound
5. Conclusion

- When the assignment places the emphasis upon the meaning: (Here the author's point is to be applied to an externally existing idea.)

Assignment: Tell how Kate Chopin's "The Story of an Hour" fits in with contemporary feminist concepts.

Thesis: By portraying Mrs. Mallard's inner acknowledgment of the joy that freedom from her kind and loving husband would bring to her, Kate Chopin prefigures an important feminist theme: that even the kindliest "imposition of one person's private will upon another" causes unspeakable agony.

1. Introduction—including brief summary of plot
2. Chopin's point: implicit in Mrs. M's feelings
3. How Chopin develops the point: progression of Mrs. M's feelings
   - Initial response
   - Gradual awareness
   - Paradoxical ending
4. Conclusion: Application of Chopin's point to contemporary feminist theory

- When the assignment gives you elements to work with, but the subject and emphasis must be your own.

Assignment: In many novels and plays, minor characters contribute significantly to the total work. They often have certain functions, in particular, as instruments in the plot, foils for the main characters, commentators on the action or theme or the like. Write a well-organized essay showing how minor characters function in a work in which they appear significantly.

Thesis: In *Hamlet*, Shakespeare presents a number of men of action—Fortinbras, Laertes, even Horatio—as foils for his thoughtful hero. In doing so Shakespeare points up the seriousness of Hamlet's struggle with inaction and thus underlines Hamlet's eventual discovery that action itself is not what is important, but rather that "the readiness is all."

1. Introduction—including explication of Shakespeare's theme of "There is Providence in the fall of the sparrow" and "The readiness is all."

2. Theme developed through contrast: thoughtful Hamlet vs. active foils
   - Hamlet and Horatio
   - Hamlet and Fortinbras
   - Hamlet and Laertes
3. Shakespeare's direct statement of theme: Hamlet comes to understand (no longer rejects himself)
4. Conclusion

But what about the assignment when you are thrown altogether upon your own resources: "Write a critical analysis of . . .," for instance? This sort of assignment should not cause you special worry. After all, any one of the previous samples could have been composed for it. What you need to do when the assignment is general in this way is to discover an approach to a work that will permit you to discuss the aspects of it you find most interesting. When you do your close reading for such an assignment, use a list of the items that caught your attention as an inventory of ideas, and find connections and patterns among them. Then take those patterns that most impressively point to your interpretation of the author's thesis, theme, or meaning, and use them to support it.

Sometimes you will be asked to (or decide to) write a critical analysis in which you will be expected to compare two or more works in some respects. The following question from a standardized exam is typical of such comparative assignments:

· The struggle to achieve dominance over others frequently appears in fiction. Choose two stories in which such a struggle for dominance occurs, and write an essay comparing the purposes for which the author uses the struggle.

In order to plan the structure for a critical analysis coming out of such a question, you might try thinking back to the useful "although" clause format. This format will help you subordinate one work to the other, for it is difficult to produce a unified essay if two important subjects are given equal treatment. Though the word and concept "although" need not, of course, be used, a workable format for such an analysis might go something like this:

· Although many authors, such as Author 1 in "story 1," focus their stories on the struggle to achieve dominance over others for comedic or lightly satiric purposes, Author 2, especially in "Story 2," explores this topic in order to set forth his particularly brutal view of the nature of the universe.

Solving the Technical Problems

The writing and rewriting stages of the writing process are, as we have said, much the same for critical analyses as they are for the rest of expository writing. There are, however, a few technical problems that you may run into here which are specific to this kind of writing. These problems all evolve from the delicate relationship between the material in your critical analysis and the work you are dealing with.

HOW MUCH TO SUMMARIZE?

Perhaps the most difficult problem of this sort you will encounter is deciding how much of the subject work to recount. The least successful attempts at critical analysis are plot summaries, with their dull recounting of "and then, and then." You will certainly want to avoid boring your readers in this way. And yet, if you proceed with your interpretive analysis as if the work were as familiar to your readers as it is to you, you run the equally grave risk of utterly confusing them. Your readers then would be in the position of a person who joins a group already deep in conversation and tries unsuccessfully to catch enough clues to gather what they are saying—a very frustrating position indeed.

The solution lies in maintaining a delicate balance. A good rule is to assume that your readers have read the work, but that this reading was done several years ago. Following this rule, you should summarize whatever material is necessary to make your points clear, but only as much as the demands of your thesis and arguments require. More specifically:

1. Always identify the work (or works) you will be analyzing by title and by author in your introduction.
2. In order to orient your readers, be sure to include somewhere early in your paper a brief summary of the basic points or plot of your work—if only a sentence or two in length.
3. Never introduce a point without giving enough background from the work to make the point comprehensible to your readers. Never attempt to explicate a passage without quoting the passage.
4. On the other hand, do not get caught up in retelling the story, in rearguing the article. Keep your attention focused upon your purpose of developing your *own* critical thesis.

HOW TO DISTINGUISH YOUR AUTHOR'S PURPOSE FROM YOUR OWN?

Another problem in writing critical analyses is the blending of the two theses involved in this kind of writing: your author's thesis—theme, meaning—and your own. It is not difficult to confuse the two, but it is important that you do not. No matter how heartily you may agree with your author's view of life, your thesis can never be identical with your author's. The following thesis, for example, would be appropriate for a critical analysis:

- In "Accepting the Unacceptable," Meg Greenfield persuasively argues that the United States' response to terrorism is not only ineffectual, but actually damaging.

On the other hand, the following thesis would *not* do for a *critical analysis* of Meg Greenfield's article, even though it might lead to a good enough essay on a similar subject:

· The United States' response to terrorism is not only ineffectual but actually damaging.

When you undertake to write a critical analysis, you commit yourself to a purpose that is basically literary or scholarly and whose object is an external work of art.

Inexperienced writers sometimes forget this purpose in another way and use the work as a springboard for expressing their own ideas. The critical analysis one student wrote to answer a question on the significance of Cordelia's death at the conclusion of *King Lear,* for example, was less than successful because the student could not separate her own experience from that of Shakespeare's character:

Faulty

· The death of Cordelia proves my point that you have to do, think, and say exactly what your elders want you to or you shall perish. . . . It's as though elders need to control your every thought and movement.

Comparisons with your own experience and analogies to other literary works can be helpful to you in explaining your author's meanings, but make sure you do not let such material intrude upon your discussion of the author's intent. Let me suggest some practical ways to help you avoid such difficulties:

1. Get into the habit of speaking in terms of the author, "William Raspberry argues . . .," "Lewis Thomas uses his Mahler symphony metaphor to . . .," "Kate Chopin develops the character of Mrs. Mallard for. . . ."
2. Keep close to the work itself. When you leave it to make comparisons with external experience or other works, be sure that your purpose remains interpretive.
3. Quotations can keep you on the track.[3] Use them freely—but keep them brief. A well-chosen excerpt can supply irrefutable proof for the point you are making. Furthermore, if you include (in moderation) the words of an author who writes with wit and charm, you cannot help but enhance the effect of your own style.

WHICH METHODS OR STRATEGIES TO CITE?

Some writers inexperienced with critical analyses are so pleased with the strategies they have discovered in their close reading that they are

---

[3]For information on the technical aspects of including quotations in your written work, see pages 333–334.

tempted to fill their papers with them in a random "Lookee, here's a meta-phor" fashion. For instance:

Faulty

· Meg Greenfield uses contrasting parallelism in "Ac-cepting the Unacceptable." She writes: "That re-sponse . . . makes us feel better while also making the hostages' situation worse." (page 420, paragraph 1)

This practice has made far too many analyses focusless and inane. To avoid it, take care that every example you include not only demonstrates a point, but that you have clearly drawn the connection between the example and the point it supports. You might, for instance, edit our faulty example in this way:

· By phrasing our response to terrorism as a contrasting parallelism, Meg Greenfield sharpens our sense of the futility of a response "that makes us feel better while also making the hostages' situation worse." (page 420, paragraph 1)

WHEN TO USE OUTSIDE SOURCES?

Unless your instructor tells you otherwise, your critical analysis should be based upon your own reactions to the work in question. Ordinar-ily, critical analyses are not meant to be research papers and should not involve you in a search of the literature for the critical opinions of others.

This is not to say that all outside sources are forbidden. On the con-trary, let me encourage you to use reference books to gain background that will enrich your understanding of the work you will be analyzing. For example, you should certainly use a dictionary to understand an unfamil-iar word. And you will also want to look up in an appropriate source any references that are unfamiliar to you. You can find explanations for refer-ences to Greek or Roman gods and goddesses, for instance, in dictionaries of classical mythology; and you can look up biographical information in the *Dictionary of National Biography* (British) and the *Dictionary of Ameri-can Biography* (American). There are many such sources. Ask your refer-ence librarian to help you locate the appropriate volume to look up any-thing that puzzles you in your close reading.

HOW MUCH TO EVALUATE?

Evaluation is not required for a well-written critical analysis (except, of course, for reviews, which are written to advise readers on whether or not the work in question is worth their time). In fact, unnecessary evalua-tive passages can give a critical essay a less than professional sound. Such comments as the vague "I liked it because it was interesting" or the obvious

"I think Faulkner is a pretty good writer" are better left unsaid. And yet an aptly observed evaluative remark can enhance your critical analysis. If you want to include some evaluation in your analysis, here are some practical suggestions:

1. Base your evaluation firmly upon your analytical and interpretive findings.
2. Do not mingle your evaluative comments with analysis and interpretation. The concluding paragraphs are an especially appropriate place for evaluative material.
3. Evaluate the work according to how well the author succeeds in doing what he or she has set out to do. If you are writing a critical analysis of Wagner's *Lohengrin,* it would be appropriate to comment (if you believed it to be so) that by making the music rise too often to the heights of magnificence, Wagner hardens the listener to the effects of the crescendo and thus loses some of its impact. On the other hand, it would not be appropriate to comment (no matter how truly) that you do not care for the stories about Teutonic mythology that form the basis for Wagner's operas.

The Conventions of Critical Analysis

1. It is conventional to use the present tense for critical analysis. Write "Shakespeare *develops* his theme by . . .," not "Shakespeare *developed* his theme by. . . ."
2. It is conventional to credit the author with conscious manipulation of strategy as, for example: "Shakespeare develops his theme by. . . ."
3. And although you need not hesitate to use "I" where appropriate, your name standing as the author of the essay is usually sufficient identification for matters of opinion. Therefore, avoid writing "*I think* Shakespeare develops his theme by. . . ." And do not hesitate to write "Shakespeare develops his theme. . . ."

Writing a Review or Critique

In the same way that a critical analysis is a kind of expository writing, a review (or critique, as it is sometimes called) is a kind of critical analysis. It is a critical analysis whose purpose is to provide the reader with a guide to the book, essay, drama, musical performance, or other artistic work it discusses. Because it has this specific purpose, you might call a review an "evaluative critical analysis."

Except for your handling of the summary and the evaluation, you write a review just as you write a critical analysis. The summary of the work that you include in a review is, oddly enough, both more nearly complete and more limited than that which you use in writing other critical analyses. It needs to be more thorough because the purpose of the review is to acquaint your readers with the work. But on the other hand, if as a reviewer you are recommending the work, you must be careful not to give away so much that your readers will no longer need (or want) to experience it themselves.

The importance of evaluation is a more serious difference between other kinds of critical analyses, where an evaluative passage is optional, and reviews, which require evaluation. In reviews even the thesis itself may well be judgmental:

· This movie is well worth seeing because. . . .
· The world of literature is little enriched by this author's first novel because. . . .

Like all critical analyses, a review is concerned with what the author is trying to say and how he or she goes about saying it, but in the review, as these sample theses indicate, the analytic function backs up the evaluative.

Evaluative techniques tend to differ as well. In reviews, as in all critical analyses, you evaluate a work in terms of its author's goals. In a review, however, it is also appropriate to include your judgment as to the worth of these goals. I have suggested that your personal response to a work has little place in most critical analyses, but in a review you need not hesitate to include personal impressions if you can validate them with evidence from the work.

Analyses of Particular Kinds of Literature

In order to write a good critical analysis of a work, you need to have not only an understanding of the conventions of the critical analysis in general, but also knowledge of the techniques and strategies specific to the kind of art (the *genre*) that you are dealing with. The following sections outline the specific techniques that should be most helpful for your critical writing. Please note, however, that I do not attempt a comprehensive discussion there of all the valid approaches to literary or artistic analysis or appreciation. My intention is, rather, to augment your instructor's presentation of these matters, and to offer enough examples of techniques specific to each kind of literature to provide a guide for writing critical analyses about each of them.

ANALYZING EXPOSITORY WRITING

Let's begin with expository writing, the subject of this book. In working through *Writing Effectively* you have done a good deal of thinking about how to write expository prose. To compose a critical analysis of this sort of writing, you only have to reverse this thinking from the writer's point of view to that of the reader, from how you can get across what you have to say to how another author has done so. The territory then should already be familiar.

Finding the Author's Meaning

There is another reason why expository writing may be the easiest kind of writing for you to approach critically. Only in expository writing do authors express their meaning directly. Most of the time, as we have seen, authors state their theses in an explicit sentence or two, and where they do not, they imply the thesis so clearly that readers should have no difficulty in formulating it for themselves. But, for this reason, finding the author's meaning is not as central to analysis of expository prose as it is to analysis of other kinds of creative expression. Your task in writing an analysis of expository prose is more likely to focus on determining your author's way of viewing the thesis and discovering the means by which he or she attempts to persuade you to this point of view.

Determining the Author's Viewpoint

To discover your author's approach, you need to think a bit about the tone of the piece. How literally does your author intend her or his words? What connotations do the words convey? What value judgments are implied? Is your author always speaking to you in a straightforward way or is there some irony (see page 394) in the tone? Read between the lines. Is your author trying to communicate something that is not written on the paper? Look at these lines of Lewis Thomas's, for instance:

> The man on television, Sunday midday, middle-aged and solid, nice-looking chap, all the facts at his fingertips, more dependable looking than most high-school principals, is talking about civilian defense. . . . It can make an enormous difference, he is saying. Instead of the outright death of eighty million American citizens in twenty minutes, he says, we can, by careful planning . . . get that number down to only forty million, maybe even twenty. (page 430, paragraph 10)

Thomas describes the man on television as solid and dependable, but experienced readers catch the hints that let us know Thomas is talking about appearance only ("more dependable *looking*") and are not surprised to discover that Thomas believes him to be unsound. We recognize the ironic twist Thomas places on "enormous difference" to let us know that, unlike the televised speaker, Thomas believes that twenty million and eighty million dead are equally horrifying. Like other sophisticated writers, Thomas makes his point here by implication only. He never spells out his idea in words. When you prepare to write a critical analysis, you must be sure to catch all such implications.

Discovering the Author's Methods

Once you are clear in your understanding of your author's thesis and of his or her approach to that thesis, you will want to begin looking for the techniques your author uses to persuade you of the truth of that way of thinking. What are the rhetorical techniques specific to expository writing? They are the strategies for writing persuasively and effectively, the very strategies that this book has been concerned with throughout. In order to review them for your work with critical analysis, I can think of no more helpful arrangement than one that has been traditional with rhetoricians since the days of Aristotle. You'll find this arrangement in the accompanying boxed section (page 378).

These are among the most important rhetorical techniques available to the author of expository prose. Before you write your critical analysis, study the work to discover which of these techniques—or what varieties of them—your author employs.

An Example

How might you apply your knowledge of the techniques of expository writing to creating your own critical analysis? To get some ideas, let's follow student Anna Adams as she set about writing a critical analysis of Ellen Goodman's "The Cult of Impotence."

First, she read the essay with great care.

The Cult of Impotence[4]

Ellen Goodman

If they ever dig down through layers of future generations, looking for artifacts that tell something about mid seventies America, let's hope they find John Lilly's isolation tank. It will tell them a great deal.   1

The California physician and psychoanalyst has designed an enclosed   2
tank, with 10 inches of water heated to precisely 93 degrees and room for exactly one person. Why? As he told *People,* "Lying on your back, you can breathe quite comfortably and safely, freed from sight, sound, people and the universe outside. That way you can enter the universe within you."

Think what Greta Garbo could have done with that. Think what we do   3
with it—"free" ourselves from other people and the environment, enter the "universe within."

Rhetorical Strategies Available to Expository Writers

I. Appeal to Ethical Sense (see pages 91–96, 304–305).
   A. Presentation of the author as a good person, a likable person, a believable person.
   B. Presentation of the author as a knowledgeable person, personally experienced in this area and/or well studied in it.
   C. Presentation of the author as a fair-minded, reasonable, understanding person.
   D. Presentation of the author somewhere on the scale of objective observer to impassioned advocate (see pages 96–97).
II. Appeal to Reason (see pages 101–103).
   A. Clear, coherent presentation of thesis.
   B. Clear, though less forceful presentation of (or allusion to) the opposing point of view ("although" clause usually preceding thesis presentation).
   C. Logically consistent presentation of supporting material ("arguments").
   D. Supporting material ("arguments") that are internally logical and consistent.
   E. "Arguments" based upon fact, statistics, authority, logic.
III. Appeal to Emotion.
   A. Devices associated with poetry.
      1. Imagery (see pages 277–291)
         a. Metaphor, simile, symbol, connotative language
         b. Personification, hyperbole, and allusion
      2. Rhythmic, emotion-heightening language
      3. Repetition and variation (see pages 70–71)
   B. Devices associated with fiction (see pages 389–397).
      1. Narrative, anecdote
      2. Dramatization dialogue
      3. Characterization
      4. Specific detail (see pages 119–124)
      5. Irony
   C. Devices of sentence structure (see Chapter 8).
      1. Parallelism
      2. Balance and antithesis

4   The "isolation tank" is as good a symbol as any of a time when we are making a positive value out of our sense of impotence in the world, and a cult out of the fragmentation of society and missed connections of our personal lives. Over the last few years—driven by events more complex than the labels "Vietnam" and "Watergate"—we have turned inward, to the search for personal solutions. We are no longer convinced of the possibility of social change or even the capacity to "do good." Every change reverberates.

5   We have discovered that when you cure typhoid you get overpopulation, and when you raise the standard of living you destroy the environment. It is

no wonder that we "work on" an area that seems more within our control and power: ourselves.

   This self-centering is not only a retreat from the world, but a byproduct   6
of the current condition of our lives. The newest definition of American individualism is aloneness.

   In the years since 1960, the number of "primaries"—people living   7
alone—has risen by 87 percent while the number of families has risen only by 23 percent. Fifteen million of us live alone. Fifty million of us are single, widowed or divorced. At least partially in response to this, the new therapies—from the isolation tank on—offer us ways to "get into ourselves." Those who aren't "doing their own thing" or "finding themselves" are "getting in touch with their feelings." The West Coast greeting, "What are you into?" is most aptly answered with one word: myself.

   In the hyperindividualism of a movement like est, we are trained to be   8
self-reliant, totally responsible to and for our own lives. The range of the new therapies is characterized by a frenzied search inward. The "isolation tank" seems to suggest that the road to happiness, peace, fulfillment, understanding, is an internal route. As Dr. Lilly says, "If you are able to retire deep inside yourself, you can find the quiet place which nobody can penetrate. This way you can isolate yourself in your deep inner core."

   But then where are you? Then what? The impulses to more self-aware   9
ness, self-exploration are positive ones—but not if they lead to a dead end of navel-gazing, a permanent retreat from others and the problems of the world. At a time when we seem in almost perilous need of personal connection and social solutions, the tendency toward the isolation-tank psychology can be a sad perversion of the old American individualism.

   I am reminded of a brief exchange Peter Marin had with a man "into"   10
mysticism, and which he repeated in a piece written for *Harper's* last year. He wrote:

> He was telling me about his sense of another reality. "I know there is
> something outside of me," he said, "I can feel it. I know it is there. But
> what is it?"

> "It may not be a mystery," I said, "Perhaps it is the world."

In close-reading the article, Anna underlined significant passages, scribbled over the margins, gave the article a good deal of thought, and came out with an analysis something like the following:

```
         Inventory of Ideas: Notes
Title: Almost a miniature thesis of itself: [We have
    made a] "Cult of Impotence."

Introduction:
Striking symbol of the isolation tank
Use of precise facts (10 inches of water; 93 degrees).
Use of quotation of inventor (Inventor = a psychia-
    trist, a doctor, an authority in our society).
```

Quotation starts as simple explanation, ends in dramatic irony.
First mention of the key phrase: "the universe within."
Allusion to Greta Garbo: "I vant to be alone." (apt, but left unstated).
Brings in readers with "we" (reinforces earlier use of "let's").
Thesis Statement: The "isolation tank" is as good a symbol as any of a time when we are making:

—
 +   our sense of impotence
a positive value   in the world
_____

                              the fragmentation of society
                              and mixed connections of
     a cult   our personal lives.
_____

(Note mixed diction, emphasized by antithetically balanced sentence structure.)

Support:
Answers the questions:
A. Why do we "vant to be alone"?
   1. Despair over events beyond our control; feelings of helplessness (Vietnam, Watergate).
   2. Can't even do good without doing bad (Cure typhoid → overpopulation; raise standard of living → destroy environment).
B. How is the aloneness manifested in our society?
   1. Statistics on those living alone.
   2. Popularity of self-reliance movements → leads back to the psychiatrist's self-absorption tank (and another telling quotation).

Leading to Conclusion: Negative Evaluation
Open criticism built upon earlier preparation
   "Navel gazing"
   "permanent retreat from others and problems"

```
Leads to restatement of thesis (more strongly--and
   openly--worded):
      "At a time when we seem in almost perilous need of
      personal connections and social solutions, the
      tendency toward the isolation tank psychology can
      be a sad perversion of the old American individu-
      alism."
Conclusion:
Conclusion introduced by final statement of thesis.
Argument summed up by a quoted anecdote.
      Contrasts cult view of "the universe within" with
      "the world without."
```

Having determined what Goodman was saying and how she said it, Anna had to decide what she herself wanted to say about it. She developed a working thesis and drew an outline from it:

Anna Adams's Working Thesis and Preliminary Outline

```
Thesis: G. persuades that although the "universe
        within" may appear delightful, it
        actually is only a (rather selfish) way to
        hide from reality.

1. Introduction  →  Thesis

2. How G. wins readers by joining in their
   attraction to "individualism":
   ·tone
   ·logic
   ·content

3. How G. retains readers even when she turns and
   attacks extreme "individualism":
   ·tone
   ·logic
   ·content

4. Conclusion. [use final anecdote]
```

Anna Adams's Draft Critical Analysis
of Goodman's *Cult of Impotence*[5]

Ellen Goodman's Response
to the "Me Decade"

Self-awareness was the trend word for the 1970s.
More than a fashion fad, "finding yourself" (7) or
"getting into yourself" (7) had become a way of
life. Individualism was taken to the point of isolation. In adopting John Lilly's isolation tank
as the perfect symbol for the me decade, Ellen
Goodman points out that American individualism
meant aloneness--replacing reality with the
"universe within" (2). In the isolation tank
Goodman found a symbol which not only summed up
the beliefs of the me generation, but which also
expressed what was wrong with the entire value
system. In "Cult of Impotence," Goodman persuades
the reader that although the "universe within"
may appear to be delightful on the surface, retreating into oneself is nothing more than a way
to hide from reality.

The heart of Goodman's persuasiveness is the
tone of the article. With her open manner and

---

[5]Anna has documented her quotations by parenthetic reference to Goodman's paragraphs.

friendly voice, Goodman shows she understands the attractiveness of individualism as well as its dangers. Goodman includes the reader in her "we" from the very beginning:

> Think what we do with it--"free" ourselves from other people and the environment, and enter the "universe within." (3. Emphasis mine.)

Almost involuntarily, the reader pauses and imagines a life free of the demands of other people and other things. Consciousness only of oneself and one's own needs could almost be a paradise.

Goodman then offers explanations for why Americans felt the need to find the "inner self" in the 1970s. With Vietnam and Watergate, Americans were confused and afraid. It appeared as though the world itself was out of control. Everything that people tried to do to improve life--cure diseases, raise living conditions--ended in disaster--overpopulation, environmental destruction. Disgusted and bemused, the me generation turned to the only thing that could be controlled--the Self.

Readers are swept along with Goodman not only by the friendly conversational quality of her tone, but by her logical offering of explanations as to why the "universe within" is needed. Again, readers find themselves understanding and sympathizing with the me generation and its need to "find itself."

However, Goodman does not praise this value system, but rather criticizes it. And, although she, too, seems to place a high value on being one's own person, Goodman is able to convince her readers that retreating into oneself is not the answer.

Goodman's argument seems objective because of her use of specifics. She is not someone speaking from emotion. She uses exact facts in describing the isolation tank, for example: It holds "10 inches of water heated to precisely 93 degrees" (2). In addition, she uses statistics to emphasize the degree of isolation and aloneness of our population. "In the years since 1960, the number of primaries . . . has risen 87%. Fifteen million of us are single, widowed, or divorced" (7).

After reading these impressive statistics, readers are forced to modify their image of self freedom. It can no longer only mean being able to control oneself and one's world. It takes on the new meaning of a terrible loneliness. Readers see themselves isolated, lonely, and limited--

limited only to that which is inside them. And, as Goodman points out, "But then, where are you?" (9) Goodman can then openly express her contempt for the "universe within." After all the time one spends "finding" herself, she only finds herself "at a dead-end of navel gazing" (9). At this point, Goodman forcefully restates her thesis:

> At a time when we seem in most perilous need of personal connections and social solutions, the tendency toward the isolation-tank psychology can be a sad perversion of the old American individualism. (9)

Goodman then reinforces her point by putting her arm around the reader and relating an anecdote that sums up the entire argument: "I know there is something outside of me . . . I can feel it. I know it is there. But what is it?" To this Goodman has only to reply, "Perhaps it is the world" (10), and the reader must agree.

TRY IT OUT

1. Choose an essay from the collection in Part Four (or from another source) and answer each of the questions in *one* of the following sets,[6] supporting your answer with as much detail as you can.
   a. What is the author's thesis? Does he or she state it explicitly or merely

[6]These questions are adapted from a departmental Freshman Composition examination at Miami University (Ohio).

imply it? Describe in detail the rhetorical devices he or she employs to develop and sustain the thesis.

   b. What is the author's attitude toward the subject? Do his or her selection and treatment of details contribute to a particular tone that aids in unifying and developing the thesis? What is that tone? Cite specific words, phrases, allusions, and details, and specify their tone and effect.

   c. What is the relationship between the final paragraph (or paragraph cluster) and the rest of the essay? Show how the structure of the essay prepares us for the author's comments in the final paragraph. Does he or she organize the material in such a way as to create a pattern of development that leads logically to the final comments? Show how.

2. From your answers to the questions, compose a thesis for a critical analysis of the essay.

3. Use the thesis to construct a structural plan for such an analysis.

ANALYZING A NARRATIVE WORK: A STORY, DRAMA, OR NARRATIVE POEM

In expository writing authors convey their ideas about the world to the reader by stating them more or less directly. In narrative writing, authors convey their ideas more subtly—by telling a story.[7] As Brooks and Warren put it:

> **A narrative tells of a significant conflict, usually involving human beings, that is resolved in such a way as to imply a comment on human values, feelings, or attitudes. (Adapted from *An Approach to Literature*, page 9)**

Translating this definition into terms associated with fiction: the constituents of narrative writing are *characters* involved in a *plot* that will be resolved to bring out a *theme*. In writing a critical analysis of a narrative work, then, your task is to explain the theme and show how your author uses the characters and plot to arrive at it.

   In order to address the problems of writing a critical analysis of a narrative work in a practical way, we will need to work with a specific example. The following story is especially interesting for one so brief.

---

[7]Stories, novels, dramas, and narrative poems are all works of narrative literature and share in the techniques and conventions of storytelling. In addition, narrative poems and enacted drama participate in the techniques and conventions specific to poetry and to the theater. See the later discussions of these forms.

The Story of an Hour

Kate Chopin

Knowing that Mrs. Mallard was afflicted with a heart trouble, great care was 1
taken to break to her as gently as possible the news of her husband's death.

It was her sister Josephine who told her, in broken sentences, veiled 2
hints that revealed in half concealing. Her husband's friend Richards was
there, too, near her. It was he who had been in the newspaper office when
intelligence of the railroad disaster was received, with Brently Mallard's
name leading the list of "killed." He had only taken the time to assure himself
of its truth by a second telegram, and had hastened to forestall any less
careful, less tender friend in bearing the sad message.

She did not hear the story as many women have heard the same, with 3
a paralyzed inability to accept its significance. She wept at once, with sudden, wild abandonment, in her sister's arms. When the storm of grief had
spent itself, she went away to her room alone. She would have no one follow her.

There stood, facing the open window, a comfortable, roomy arm-chair. 4
Into this she sank, pressed down by a physical exhaustion that haunted her
body and seemed to reach into her soul.

She could see in the open square before her house the tops of trees that 5
were all aquiver with the new spring life. The delicious breath of rain was in
the air. In the street below a peddler was crying his wares. The notes of a
distant song which someone was singing reached her faintly, and countless
sparrows were twittering in the eaves.

There were patches of blue sky showing here and there through the 6
clouds that had met and piled above the others in the west facing her window.

She sat with her head thrown back upon the cushion of the chair quite 7
motionless, except when a sob came up into her throat and shook her, as a
child who has cried itself to sleep continues to sob in its dreams.

She was young, with a fair, calm face, whose lines bespoke repression 8
and even a certain strength. But now there was a dull stare in her eyes, whose
gaze was fixed away off yonder on one of those patches of blue sky. It was not
a glance of reflection, but rather indicated a suspension of intelligent thought.

There was something coming to her and she was waiting for it, fearfully. 9
What was it? She did not know; it was too subtle and elusive to name. But she
felt it, creeping out of the sky, reaching toward her through the sounds, the
scents, the color that filled the air.

Now her bosom rose and fell tumultuously. She was beginning to recog- 10
nize this thing that was approaching to possess her, and she was striving to
beat it back with her will—as powerless as her two white slender hands would
have been.

When she abandoned herself, a little whispered word escaped her 11
slightly parted lips. She said it over and over under her breath: "Free, free,
free!" The vacant stare and the look of terror that had followed it went from
her eyes. They stayed keen and bright. Her pulses beat fast, and the coursing
blood warmed and relaxed every inch of her body.

She did not stop to ask if it were not a monstrous joy that held her. A 12
clear and exalted perception enabled her to dismiss the suggestion as trivial.

She knew that she would weep again when she saw the kind, tender 13 hands folded in death; the face that had never looked save with love upon her, fixed and gray and dead. But she saw beyond that bitter moment a long procession of years to come that would belong to her absolutely. And she opened and spread her arms out to them in welcome.

There would be no one to live for during those coming years; she would 14 live for herself. There would be no powerful will bending her in that blind persistence with which men and women believe they have a right to impose a private will upon a fellow-creature. A kind intention or a cruel intention made the act seem no less a crime as she looked upon it in that brief moment of illumination.

And yet she had loved him—sometimes. Often she had not. What did it 15 matter! What could love, the unsolved mystery, count for in face of this possession of self-assertion which she suddenly recognized as the strongest impulse of her being.

"Free! Body and soul free!" she kept whispering. 16

Josephine was kneeling before the closed door with her lips to the 17 keyhole, imploring for admission. "Louise, open the door! I beg; open the door—you will make yourself ill. What are you doing, Louise? For heaven's sake open the door."

"Go away. I am not making myself ill." No; she was drinking in a very 18 elixir of life through that open window.

Her fancy was running riot along those days ahead of her. Spring days, 19 and summer days, and all sorts of days that would be her own. She breathed a quick prayer that life might be long. It was only yesterday she had thought with a shudder that life might be long.

She arose at length and opened the door to her sister's importunities. 20 There was a feverish triumph in her eyes, and she carried herself unwittingly like a goddess of Victory. She clasped her sister's waist, and together they descended the stairs. Richards stood waiting for them at the bottom.

Someone was opening the front door with a latchkey. It was Brently 21 Mallard who entered, a little travel-stained, composedly carrying his gripsack and umbrella. He had been far from the scene of the accident, and did not even know there had been one. He stood amazed at Josephine's piercing cry; at Richards' quick motion to screen him from the view of his wife.

But Richards was too late. 22

When the doctors came, they said she had died of heart disease—of joy 23 that kills.

Preparing to Write

The first step in writing any kind of critical analysis is close reading. In reading narratives closely you will want to go beyond your observation of those interesting parallels, unusual strategies, and symbolic touches that attract attention. You will want, in addition, to make special note of the major elements of narration: plot, characters, theme, and point of view. Let me sketch each of these briefly, using Kate Chopin's story for illustration.

Point of View

Perhaps the most crucial question you can ask when you are trying to gain insight into a story is "From whose point of view are we seeing the action?" What the story actually is varies with the eyes of the beholder. Authors present their stories from points of view that range all the way from the complete subjectivity of one character's perspective to an objectivity that goes beyond the author's view to a strict dramatization of action and dialogue (see Figure 11.1). The reader's job is to interpret the story in terms of this point of view.

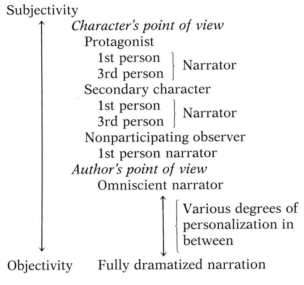

Figure 11.1 text:

Subjectivity

Character's point of view
  Protagonist
    1st person ⎫ Narrator
    3rd person ⎭
  Secondary character
    1st person ⎫ Narrator
    3rd person ⎭
  Nonparticipating observer
    1st person narrator
Author's point of view
  Omniscient narrator
    ⎧ Various degrees of
    ⎨ personalization in
    ⎩ between

Objectivity   Fully dramatized narration

Figure 11.1. Points of View

From what point of view is "The Story of an Hour" written? It begins in the author's own voice:

> Knowing that Mrs. Mallard was afflicted with a heart trouble, great care was taken to break to her as gently as possible the news of her husband's death. (1)

The narration continues in this fairly objective manner until Mrs. Mallard goes to her room alone. Here Mrs. Mallard's point of view takes over. Chopin continues using the third-person *she* because with it she can get outside her heroine and provide the reader with external description of her character. But from this time until close to the end, not only are we privy to Mrs. Mallard's thoughts, but the narrating voice even takes on the colorations of Mrs. Mallard's own:

There would be no one to live for during those coming years; she would live for herself. . . . And yet she had loved him—sometimes. Often she had not. What did it matter! (14–15)

How reliable a narrator is Mrs. Mallard? How close are her views to Chopin's own? This is perhaps the central critical question of the story, and the way you answer it will, to an important extent, determine your interpretation of the story.

Plot

CONFLICT

Plot begins with *conflict*, the struggle between two (or more) antagonists. In a complex story, determining the central conflict may be difficult, but you must come to a decision in order to understand the story well enough to write a critical analysis. In "The Story of an Hour," the conflict clearly takes place within Mrs. Mallard, the central character. To identify the conflicting parties within her requires an interpretation of the story. Is it her own spirit opposed to her internalization of the will of society as represented by her sister, Josephine, and her husband's friend, Richards? Or is her inner antagonist her husband, Brently? Much of the way you eventually interpret the story will be based upon this determination.

CHRONOLOGY

Plot can be considered as the way that a conflict is worked out in time. The plot of any particular story is a *chronology* of the incidents that set up, intensify, and then resolve the conflict.

You can often think through a plot more clearly if you diagram it as a time line (see Figure 11.2).

Climax

| Situation | X | X | X | X | X | Dénouement (end) |

Figure 11.2. Plot as a Time Line

In Figure 11.2, the word *situation* stands for the given, the way things are after the introductory passages of the work and before complications in the conflict set in. Each X marks an incident in the conflict, a dramatic episode in the development of the action. The curved line represents the pattern of emotional intensity. The notion of *climax* is a concept about which experts disagree: some see it as the moment of greatest emotional intensity, others as the point where the outcome becomes inevitable. When these points in the action do not coincide, you must decide where the climactic point really occurs. As for the *dénouement,* most stories still have some sort of brief conclusion to round them off and return readers to their own world again. You could work out the plot of "The Story of an Hour" along either of the plot lines sketched in Figure 11.3.

Situation	X	X	X
Mr. Mallard listed as a casualty in a railroad accident	Josephine and Richards gently break news. Mrs. M. overwhelmed by grief.	Mrs. M. alone in room, reluctantly accepts feelings of freedom and joy.	Mr. M. returns; Mrs. M. sees him and dies.

Figure 11.3. Plot Line for "The Story of an Hour"

CLIMAX

Where do *you* place the climax? In "The Story of an Hour" the movement of greatest emotional tension may or may not coincide with the final revelation. Your choice depends upon how much emphasis you feel Kate Chopin puts upon her heroine's death. Does she show that Mrs. Mallard cannot come to terms with the demands that society and her husband place upon her freedom and succumbs to them in death in a final climactic scene? Or does Chopin make a climax of Mrs. Mallard's triumphal moment of understanding of the central importance of personal freedom? If so, then does Chopin mean us to take her heroine's death, interrupting only what will once again be a freedomless life, as the dénouement rather than the climax of her story? Again, a crucial interpretive question.

REVERSAL

Another element of plot that Aristotle, for one, considered essential is *reversal,* a sudden turnabout in a major character's thinking or fortunes. Reversal gives tension to a story much as the "although" clause gives tension to an essay. And like the "although" clause, it may be implied rather than explicit. Explicit reversal is an important part of the sample story's plot. To the original situation, Brently Mallard's reported death, Mrs. Mallard reacts with a quick, intense grief for her loss. In the second episode, she experiences a reversal of emotion, and her grief turns to joy in her new freedom. In the final episode, the situation itself has reversed, and Mr. Mallard appears. Mrs. Mallard again experiences a sudden intense grief, this time at the loss of her new-found freedom. Her heart cannot stand the reversal, and she dies. Kate Chopin's story is classic in its plot.

FORESHADOWING

For a plot to succeed it must be plausible. Authors are never completely free in their creativity. In exchange for your "willing suspension of disbelief," as Samuel Taylor Coleridge called it, authors make a silent promise to keep their work within the laws of probability and cause and effect (even though life itself is not always so careful or so neat). Every event, therefore, must be *foreshadowed*, prepared for. Take an example from Chopin's story. People do not usually fall over dead when they hear bad news—dramatically moving or rhetorically convenient though such sudden demises may be for authors. But Kate Chopin carefully foreshadows her heroine's death, and so we accept it. She tells us in the very first line that "Mrs. Mallard was afflicted with a heart trouble" (1) to such an extent that "great care" (1) needed to be taken in telling her about her husband. She also lets us know that Mrs. Mallard was not one of those people who first greet news "with a paralyzed inability to accept its significance" (3), but rather one who gives herself immediately "with sudden wild abandonment" (3) to a storm of grief. With this foreshadowing, in addition to all the emotional strain the reader knows Mrs. Mallard has undergone within the hour, her death does not seem improbable.

Character

In reading closely, you will want to find out as much as you can about each of the characters in the story. You can judge the characters by what the author tells you about them and by what they do. You can also try to understand them by what they say and what other characters say about them—although you cannot always believe what a fictional character says.

What do we know of the characters in Kate Chopin's story? We know that Josephine and Richards are kind, considerate people who can be counted upon even in an emergency to do the right thing. They broke the sad news to Mrs. Mallard in a kind, capable way, and Josephine was lovingly there for her sister when she needed her. On the other hand, beyond the obvious concern for Mrs. Mallard's health, is there not just a touch of what might be a habitual condescension in Josephine's imploring into her sister's keyhole:

> "Louise, open the door! I beg; open the door—you will make yourself ill. What are you doing, Louise? For heaven's sake open the door." (17)

Is there not just a trace of a stronger personality dominating a weaker one—for her own good?

We know of Brently Mallard only from his wife, who comes to believe that she has been wronged by him. Yet even in her perhaps prejudiced eyes he is a "tender" (13) and "loving" (13) man with only "kind intentions" (14). It is clear that Kate Chopin wants to underscore Mallard's basic kindness to make the issue of his dominant will more clear-cut. Though we do not see any example of this dominance, we know from his wife's private thoughts that she, at least, believed that she suffered from it. What is the nature of what Mrs. Mallard refers to as "powerful will bending her in blind persistence" (14)? Perhaps Josephine's speech gives us echoes of it.

And how does Kate Chopin want us to regard her central character? She tells us that Mrs. Mallard is repressed and yet strong (8). She shows us that she is one who experiences powerful emotions with "wild abandonment" (3). Still we see the reluctance with which she accepts the unconventional insight that comes to her:

> She was beginning to recognize this thing that was approaching to possess her, and she was striving to beat it back with her will. (10)

In Mrs. Mallard, Chopin shows us a woman who has the courage to be completely honest with herself. And yet, what about her moral character? Does Chopin want us to regard her feelings about her loss of her husband as "a monstrous joy" (12)? Or are we to sympathize with them?

Theme

Such questions lead directly to a consideration of the theme, the "what the author is trying to say" that is the heart of the critical analysis. Although the theme does not exactly provide the summary of a work's entire meaning that a thesis does, the theme is the idea that informs every part of a story and gives it its reason for being. How do you find it? Brooks and Warren's definition points to one good method. If a narrative work consists of "A significant conflict that is resolved in such a way as to imply a comment on human values, feelings or attitudes," then you should be able to find that comment—the theme—by *identifying the conflict* and *noting how it is resolved.* The procedures suggested in the accompanying box should be helpful.

Determining the Theme of a Narrative Work

1. Precisely identify the conflict in your story. (Do not take a general conflict, such as "man against nature." Choose, rather, specifics, such as "Joe vs. the Antarctic.")
2. Ask yourself: What is the outcome of the conflict? Who wins?
3. Generalize on your answers to (1) and (2) and formulate a tentative theme.
4. Test your tentative theme to see if it is consistent with all the significant features of the story that you have noted in your close reading. Ask yourself, Is this what all the elements of the story seem to be aimed at? Is this what the author really says?

Let's work together through the steps listed in the boxed guidelines to try to discover the theme of the Chopin story.

POSSIBLE THEME A

1. Conflict: Mrs. Mallard vs. (an internalized) Josephine and Richards, or more specifically, Mrs. Mallard's view on marriage vs. conventional views.
2. Resolution: Conventional views win. No sooner does Mrs. Mallard come to terms with her joyous feelings of freedom from being a wife than she is faced with the continuation of that state. No longer able to face continuing in that role on society's terms, she dies.
3. Generalization (and tentative theme): It is impossible (alternative theme: it is unnatural) for women to try to strive for lives of "self-assertion."

POSSIBLE THEME B

1. Conflict: Mrs. Mallard versus Louise Mallard.
2. Resolution: Louise wins—at the loss of her life.
3. Generalization (and tentative theme): Freedom of will is the most important value; it alone makes life meaningful or even worthwhile.

Both of these tentative themes, different as they are, seem to be based on valid interpretations of the story, depending upon how the evidence is read. The question turns on Kate Chopin's use of irony.

Irony

Although irony is not an essential feature of narrative writing, many authors find it a highly effective tool for developing themes in their stories. In the sixteenth century, Wynken de Worde defined the term in a way that has never been bettered: "Ironye," he wrote, is "that which sayeth one thing but giveth to understand ye contrarye." The three basic kinds of irony differ mainly in who presents the irony.

- In *verbal irony,* the *speaker* means the contrary of what he or she says or writes.
- In *dramatic irony,* the *author* means something contrary to what the *speaker* says.
- In *circumstantial irony* (or the *irony of fate*), *fate* sees that events turn out contrary to human expectations—often almost as if in mockery of these expectations.

VERBAL IRONY

Kate Chopin uses no verbal irony in "The Story of an Hour." Neither she in her own voice nor any of her characters when they speak say anything that is the opposite of what they mean—as, for example, does Flannery O'Connor in this sentence from "Good Country People": "Mrs. Hopewell had no bad qualities of her own, but she was able to use other people's in such a constructive way that she never felt the lack." Chopin does, however, use both of the other kinds of irony to quite remarkable effect.

IRONY OF FATE

Irony of fate is deeply ingrained in Chopin's story. There is a grim ironic laughter behind every reversal of the plot. We find it, for example, in the fact that Mrs. Mallard should experience her husband's death—for which she has already mourned—with joy. And we discover even more when, after that forbidden joy, her husband turns out to be alive. The fateful chortle is there again when, after Mrs. Mallard has exchanged a fear of a long life for a wish for it, her original death wish is granted.

DRAMATIC IRONY

As for *dramatic irony,* it is this which gives the final sentence its bite and its pathos:

> When the doctors came, they said she had died of heart disease—of joy that kills. (23)

The doctors thought that Mrs. Mallard's feeling upon seeing her husband alive was a joy so sudden and profound that her heart could not stand the strain. Chopin has given us readers to understand quite the opposite. And yet on second thought, we can see in a final irony of fate that it may well have been joy that killed Louise Mallard—though not the joy the doctors had understood. For had she not experienced the joy of freedom, its loss would not have affected her.

Interpretation

Which of the two proposed themes you favor depends primarily on whether you interpret Chopin's use of Mrs. Mallard's point of view ironically or not. If you read her character ironically, then you will find dramatic irony in passages such as this:

> She did not stop to ask if it were not a monstrous joy that held her. A clear and exalted perception enabled her to dismiss the suggestion as trivial. (12)

You would thus see Mrs. Mallard's joy as monstrous, her feelings toward her kind husband as lacking in gratitude, and her ennobling of the idea of self-assertion as selfish and egotistical. To support this interpretation, you would concentrate upon the hysterical quality of such phrases as "feverish triumph in her eyes" (20) and "approaching to possess her" (10). With this interpretation, you might conclude that Chopin wants the reader almost to relish the irony implicit in Mrs. Mallard's final descending of the stairs "like a goddess of Victory" (20).

On the other hand, you may choose to identify Kate Chopin's views closely with those of her heroine. Then you would find no irony in her use of the phrase "clear and exalted perception" (12), but see it rather as Chopin's way of overriding any tendency of the reader to echo Mrs. Mallard's fear that hers might be "a monstrous joy" (12). With this interpretation, you would emphasize Chopin's use of spring imagery and note her attaching to it the symbolism of both life and freedom:

> She could see in the open square before her house the tops of trees that were all aquiver with the new spring life. . . . She felt [something coming to her] creeping out of the sky, reaching toward her through the sounds, the scents, the color that filled the air. . . . "Free, free, free." . . . She was drinking in the very elixir of life through that open window. (5, 9, 11, 18)

You might also attach symbolic importance to Chopin's pointedly calling her heroine (alone among the characters) by her married title: *Mrs.* Mallard, thereby equating her with her married state. Readers do not even learn Louise Mallard's given name until after her belief in her husband's death has set her free to be an individual person of her own.

In supporting this interpretation, you would also stress the power of Kate Chopin's insight into a woman's soul. You would back up this view by artfully quoting portions of the story to point out the psychological truth of Mrs. Mallard's experience. First the grief. Then the dazed state. And then the gradual release of the old feelings and the reluctant acceptance of the new freedom. Finally, the passionate embrace of a true sense of self.

With this interpretation, the ecstasy of that "brief moment of illumination" (14) becomes the climax of the story, overshadowing even the ironies of the final scene. For if you see the story in this way, you would understand that the knowledge that comes to Mrs. Mallard in that moment is in itself the theme of the work: that "to impose a private will upon a fellow-creature" is "a crime" (14); and that it is no less a crime whether it proceeds from "a kind intention or a cruel intention" (14). Viewed in this light, the final scene becomes yet another means for Chopin to reinforce the importance of Louise Mallard's insight. For this scene, so interpreted, dramatically demonstrates that after such a realization, life with her husband on the same basis is no longer possible for Louise Mallard. Reading the story in this way adds a final irony, for it makes the doctors righter than they knew when they spoke of the "joy that kills" (23).

A number of differing valid critical analyses could be written for 'The Story of an Hour'—as they could for all good short stories. The following is a workable outline for a critical analysis of Chopin's story based upon the second interpretation just sketched:

```
Thesis:  In "The Story of an Hour" Kate Chopin uses a com-
         plex system of plot reversals and multiple iro-
         nies to convey powerfully to her readers the
         idea that a life of submission to the will of an-
         other--even if the other is a kind and loving
         person--is not a life that is worth living.

  I. Introduction
 II. Brief summary of plot in terms of its reversals and
     ironies
```

III. Chopin's stress on the importance of Mrs. M's moment of insight
   A. Credibility of Mrs. M.'s point of view.
   B. Her relationship to Richards, Josephine, and Mr. M.
   C. Symbolic building to the moment: spring and life-renewing imagery.
   D. Psychological truth of Mrs. M.'s experience.
   E. Symbolic use of title: <u>Mrs.</u> first and individual name, <u>Louise</u>, afterward.
IV. The nature of Mrs. M.'s insight
V. Conclusion: The importance of the insight (and final ironies)

TRY IT OUT

1. Choose a piece of narrative writing and identify the parties to the conflict upon which its plot is founded. Who wins the conflict? Suggest a tentative theme by generalizing from the conflict and its resolution.

2. In narrative works that you are familiar with, find examples of (a) verbal irony, (b) dramatic irony, and (c) irony of fate. Explain how each example contributes to its author's purpose in the work as a whole.

3. Find one example of narrative writing in which a character narrates the story. Find another, like "The Story of an Hour," which, though told in the author's own voice, is written from a character's point of view.

ANALYZING A POEM

Some people are intimidated when they are asked to analyze a poem. These people tend to think of poetry as a different species of writing altogether—loaded with conventions that are more technical and more intellectually demanding than those associated with any other genre, but at the same time possessing meanings that are totally emotional, abstract, and other worldly. Neither of these contradictory impressions comes anywhere near the truth. To begin with, since some of the conventions and techniques of poetry are borrowed frequently by other genres, there is nothing particularly exclusive about them. Furthermore, when these conventions are approached in a unified and logical way, they are not especially difficult to understand.

The techniques of poetry are, for the most part, comprehended under *imagery*, the language of poetry, and *rhythm*, the sound of poetry. All imagery (sometimes called metaphor) can be understood in terms of comparison—comparing the indescribable thing, feeling, idea that the writer wants to express with a describable object that the reader can comprehend. (You will find a fuller discussion of imagery on pages 277–291.) In a similar way, all that is distinctive in the sound of poetry (except onomatopoeia) can be related to the notion of repetition. Although a complete explanation of the conventions of poetry is not appropriate here, the boxed sections, "A Guide to Imagery" and "A Guide to the Sound of Poetry" (pages 403 and 404) do offer a key to the vocabulary of both the language and the sound of poetry that may be helpful to you in writing critical analyses.

As for the mystique about the meaning of poems, I will grant that authors convey their ideas and feelings about life even more subtly in poetry than they do in stories. And because these ideas are more condensed in poems, the form more rhythmical, and the language more imaginative than is ordinarily found in prose, explicating the meaning may be more central to analyzing a poem than to writing about a work of another genre. But the meanings you will be searching for themselves will be far from distantly abstract. All good poetry is deeply rooted in the actual—in the things of the world that you can see, hear, smell, taste, and feel with your hands. Further, in order to get at the full meaning of a poem, you have to come to terms with both the connotative and the denotative meanings of the words actually written upon the page and with the basic subject-verb-object syntax of the clauses and sentences. It is not any airy notion, then, but the linguistic and physical realities behind each poem that make the close reading process for poetry probably the most demanding. The following hints for close reading offer a useful approach.

Reading a Poem Closely

READ THE POEM ALOUD

Poetry is as oral as music and is not meant to be read with the eyes alone. Really listen to the poem as you read it. How does the sound contribute to the poem's meaning? To the emotional atmosphere the poem creates? Be on the lookout for such sound delights as the breathlessness of Shakespeare's skylark:

> . . . and then my state,
> Like to the lark at break of day arising
> From sullen earth, sings hymns at heaven's gate.

The nasal quality of Pope's sneeze:

> Sudden with starting tears each eye o'er flows,
> And the high dome re-echoes to his nose.

STRAIGHTEN OUT THE POEM'S SYNTAX

You cannot begin to comprehend a poem unless you can understand what each of the sentences means. Take, for example, the first lines of Shakespeare's Sonnet 73:

> That time of year thou mayst in me behold
> When yellow leaves, or none, or few, do hang
> Upon those boughs. . . .

The first thing to do is to cut through poetic inversion (not to mention four hundred years of language change) and realize that Shakespeare means: You see in me that time of year when a few yellow leaves (or none at all) hang upon the bough. Although it may sound prosaic, the first questions you must ask yourself when you begin reading a poem are: What is the subject of the first clause? What is the verb?

BE SURE YOU KNOW THE MEANING OF EVERY WORD

Make sure that you know the meaning of each word in the poem, both literal and implied. If you are not really sure, look it up. Because poetry is such condensed expression, every word counts.

READ LITERALLY

This advice is particularly important when you approach metaphors and other imagery. Ask yourself: What exactly is the comparison? Then try to visualize it (or to imagine its smell, taste, or touch). Let's return to Sonnet 73:

> That time of year thou mayst in me behold
> When yellow leaves, or none, or few, do hang
> Upon those boughs which shake against the cold,
> Bare ruin'd choirs, where late the sweet birds sang.

What does Shakespeare intend us to think of when we read these lines? He compares his time of life with the autumn of the year. But in developing his images to make the time of the year more vivid and more specific, he extends the comparison to include himself as well. How can you get at Shakespeare's imagery? You can picture black, almost leafless branches silhouetted against a gray November sky. Try to feel them "shake against the cold"—as an old man might, perhaps. Then let the image in your mind of the bare boughs in silhouette transform itself into a silhouette of an equally bare "ruin'd choir," that is to say, the choir portion of one of the church or abbey ruins that dot the English countryside. Finally, imaginatively enter into Shakespeare's comparison of the special loneliness shared by the once-lively choir loft and the once-lively branches. Now that their respective choristers, the choirboys and the birds that once filled them with life and singing, are gone, the choir and the branches—and, by analogy, the poet himself—are left empty and useless and bereft.

NOTICE ANY UNUSUAL PLAY OF RHYTHM OR DICTION

Decide what the poet means by any unusual rhythmic patterns or plays on words that you find. What effect, for instance, does Shakespeare achieve by so frequently breaking up his second line with pauses? And why does he break the logical ordering of the words?

> When yellow leaves, or none, or few, do hang. . . .

Might he mean to slow the reader down and add a tone of sadness? And what about the word *cold* at the end of the third line? Is it meant to stand as the object of the phrase "against the cold" in the second line? Or is it the first adjective in the words describing "choirs" in the third line? Or is it meant to "look before and after" and function in both ways? And what does Shakespeare gain by adding the adjective *sweet* in "where late the sweet birds sang"?

DECIDE HOW THE FORM CONTRIBUTES TO THE MEANING OF THE POEM

For example, how does the three quatrain-couplet form of the Elizabethan sonnet help Shakespeare to organize his imagery in Sonnet 73? How does Coleridge use the conventions of the medieval ballad to enhance the Gothic effects of his "Rime of the Ancient Mariner"?

RELY ON YOUR CLOSE READING TO PLAN YOUR ANALYSIS

When you have satisfied yourself that you have a clear reading of your poem, plan your critical analysis. Back up your interpretation with the formal, metaphoric, and sound effects you have noted. Use these discoveries only in an interpretive way, however; by themselves they have no significance. Do *not* write:

Faulty

· Shakespeare's "That Time of Year" is a sonnet with 14 lines of iambic pentameter verse and an Elizabethan sonnet rhyme scheme that divides it into a 4 / 4 / 4 / 2 pattern.

Write instead:

· In "That Time of Year," Shakespeare works on a separate comparison to his aging self in each of the three quatrains of the sonnet and concludes with an ironic comment on the rest in the final couplet.

A Sample Critical Analysis

Let's look at a critical analysis published in *Explicator,* a scholarly journal in the field of English literature. First the poem:

We Real Cool[8]
    The Pool Players.
    Seven at the Golden Shovel.

We real cool. We
Left school. We

Lurk late. We
Strike straight. We

Sing sin. We
Thin gin. We

Jazz June. We
Die soon.
           Gwendolyn Brooks

The following critical analysis was written by Barbara B. Sims.

Brooks' "We Real Cool"[9]

The economy of Gwendolyn Brooks' eight-line poem "We Real Cool" parallels the brevity of the lives of her subjects, the pool players of the Golden Shovel.

Each line has two stresses, monosyllabic words in pairs which characterize the players. First, they tell the reader they are "real cool." This one descriptive phrase conjures up an image of the black young man of the streets, lounging before the pool hall, shucking and jiving, attired in a hip costume of colorful slacks, high-heeled boots, and Super Fly hat, playing a transistor radio loudly. At this point the tone is one of self-congratulation, as if being "real cool" is where it's at. Of course, the players "left school."

The second stanza begins syntactically in the second line of the couplet with the word "We," which is set curiously apart at the end of the line. The "We" is positioned as if to suggest that the identity of the players, individually and collectively, is less important than their clothes and activities.

Stanza 2 tells that the players "lurk late" and "strike straight." The connotations of these phrases tell us that all the activities of the cool people are not as innocent as playing pool and hanging around the set. Mugging, theft, and rape, among other crimes, are suggested by the word "lurk," while "strike" is reminiscent of the gangland "hit," which signifies murder.

The cool people are proud of their way of life, however, for they "sing" (praise) sin. When they drink, they "thin gin" (gin and 7-up?).

The final stanza refers to the players' interest in women—one of insincerity or playfulness. They "Jazz" June. Abruptly, Brooks concludes the poem: "We / Die soon."

Until the last line, the element of bravado in the diction and rhythm has made the activities of the street people seem somehow defendable, if not

---

[8]From *The World of Gwendolyn Brooks* (New York: Harper & Row, 1976). With permission of the author.

[9]*Explicator* 34 (April 1976), 39–40. Reprinted with permission of the Helen Dwight Reid Educational Foundation. Published by Heldref Publications, 4000 Albemarle St., N.W., Washington, DC 20016. Copyright © 1976.

downright desirable. A certain pride in being outside the conventions, institutions, and legal structures of the predominant society is conveyed. Escaping the drudgery and dullness of school and work has left the lives of these drop-outs open to many romantic possibilities.

However, the tone changes dramatically when the reader learns the street people "Die soon." At once their defiant and complacent attitudes seem quite pathetic, and the reader wonders whom the cool people are trying to kid about the desirability of their disorderly lives.

COMMENT

In her critical analysis, Barbara Sims sets up her thesis and then explicates Brooks's poem line by line to support it. Her thesis sentence very neatly takes the point the author is trying to make—which Sims sees as an ironic comment on the "brevity of the lives of [Brooks's] subjects"—and ties it together with the most significant and comprehensive of the ways Brooks has gone about saying it—that is, "the economy of the poem" with its eight brief lines, its 24 words.

While explicating the verse, Sims brings in and accounts for each of the curious features she must have noted in her close reading, among them the oddly placed "we" and the increasing repugnance of the sequence of expressions. In such a spare poem, most of the imagery lies in the connotative language, especially in the strong expressions. Sims not only accounts for the meaning of these images but helps us to visualize them.

Sims also attends carefully to the tone of the poem throughout her essay and, at its end, discusses the dramatic—almost paradoxical—change of tone in the poem's closing line. In her account of this change, Sims is able to bring us back to her main point and to conclude with a more precise and more strongly worded restatement of her thesis.

TRY IT OUT

Write an explication of the following poem:

Jenny Kissed Me

Jenny kissed me when we met
Jumping from the chair she sat in;
Time, you thief, who love to get
Sweets into your list, put that in:
Say I'm weary, say I'm sad,
Say that health and wealth have missed me,
Say I'm growing old, but add,
Jenny kissed me.

Leigh Hunt, 1784–1859

A Guide to Imagery

All imagery is basically comparison, the finding of the most precise literary notation to serve as the objective correlative for the emotion or idea to be evoked.

Form

1. *Metaphor.* When the objective correlative is equated with the compared item.
   - "To see the cherry hung with snow." (cherry blossom = snow)
2. *Simile.* When the comparison is pointed to explicitly by *like* or *as.*
   - "Apple blossoms look *like* snow."
3. *Connotative language.* When the comparison is implied by the connotation of the words employed.
   - "I met a traveler from an *antique* land."
4. *Symbol.* When the objective correlative has at least two layers of meaning.
   - "And miles to go before *I sleep.*" (Means both a distance to cover before bedtime and much to do before death.)

Content

1. *Hyperbole.* When the objective correlative is wildly exaggerated (implying a superlative emotional coloring).
   - "He fiddled all the bugs off the sweet-potato vine."
   - "Forever and a day."
2. *Allusion.* When the objective correlative refers to a literary source (taking on the emotional coloration of the source).
   - "No, I am not Prince Hamlet, nor was meant to be."
3. *Personification.* When the objective correlative is human or has human characteristics.
   - "And *Laughter* holding both his sides."
   - "He [the eagle] clasped the crag with crooked *hands.*"
4. *Synesthesia.* When the imagery involves a confusion of the senses.
   - "*Moulten golden notes*
     And all in tune.
     What a *liquid ditty* floats."
5. *Metonymy* (including *synecdoche*). When the objective correlative is the part that stands for the whole (or is closely related to it).
   - "Your smile had caught fire at Orly."
6. *Paradox* (and *oxymoron*). When the objective correlative expresses seeming contradiction.
   - "And if some lover, such as we,
     Have heard this *dialogue of one.*"

A Guide to the Sound of Poetry

Rhythm

Definition: movement with regular occurrence.

Meter

Definition: patterned rhythm (of English poetry).

1. foot (stressed syllable **/** and unstressed **∪**)
   a. *iambic:* soft   loud   ∪ /
      - "Shall I compare thee to a summer's day?"
   b. *trochaic:* loud   soft   / ∪
      - "Blessings on thee little man"
   c. *anapestic:* soft   soft   loud   ∪ ∪ /
      - "For the moon never beams without bringing me dreams"
   d. dactylic: loud   soft   soft   / ∪ ∪
      - "This is the forest primeval. The murmuring pines and the hemlock."
2. line
   a. dimeter, trimeter, tetrameter (1b and c), pentameter (1a), hexameter (1d), heptameter, octometer
   b. free verse—irregular rhythm
   c. blank verse—unrhymed iambic pentameter
   d. alexandrine—iambic hexameter
3. stanza
   a. couplet, triplet, quatrain
   b. sonnet: fourteen iambic-pentameter lines
   c. heroic couplet: iambic-pentameter couplet

Variation

1. caesura (a pause in mid-line)
   - When yellow leaves, or none, or few,
2. non-end-stopped line (making phrasal pattern at variance with metric pattern)
   - Like to the lark at break of day arising ○
     From sullen earth, sings hymns at heaven's gate.
3. varying degree of stress on syllables: *Spondee* (/ /) and *Pyrrhic* (∪ ∪)
4. substitution of feet: *Anacrusis* (+), syllables added, and *Catalexis* (−), syllables subtracted from feet.

Sound Devices

1. *Onomatopoeia:* the word imitates the sound.
   - "How they *clang* and *clash* and *roar.*"
2. *Rhyme*—repetition of final accented sound.
   Masculine: bat / cat
   Feminine: batty / catty
   Triple: battiness / cattiness

3. *Alliteration*—repetition of initial sounds.
   - "What a *t*ale of *t*error now their *t*urbulency *t*ells."
4. *Assonance*—repetition of vowel sounds.
   - "This b*o*dy dropped n*o*t d*o*wn"
5. *Consonance*—repetition of consonant sounds.
   - "And wa*s* a ble*ss*ed gho*s*t."
6. *Repetition* of words and phrases:
   - "I *galloped*, Dirck *galloped*, we *galloped* all three."
     Sometimes used to achieve the effect of a refrain (repetition of final line or lines, as in the old ballads).
   - "It's lilac-time in London; it's lilac-time in London."

ANALYZING A PERFORMANCE

Drama tells a story. Like all narrative literature, a play or a movie consists of characters involved in a plot in order to present a theme. The discussion of narrative literature earlier in this chapter, therefore, can help you write critical analyses of the plays you read. But drama is meant for the stage. And writing a critical analysis of performed literature differs from writing such essays about their literary versions in two important respects.

First, the question "What is the author saying" about a performed drama or a movie is not nearly as important as, "What is the acting company, or the director or producer, saying?" Although the author's story and theme are fundamental to any production, what you really want to get at in your analysis is the meaning of the entire theatrical experience, and that involves the way the author's material is interpreted in actual performance. Second, the methods by which the author and, in this case, the director and the company "go about saying it" must also be expanded to include not only the techniques of storytelling discussed earlier but also the techniques that go into producing the particular sounds, motion, spectacle of the production. A thorough discussion of these elements is beyond the scope of this work, but the boxed list (pages 406–407) offers examples of the sort of questions you will want to ask yourself when you prepare to write an analysis of a particular performance.

Movies

All the discussion that applies to stage drama applies to motion pictures as well. But film drama adds an extra dimension: the eye of the camera. Dramatic narration is the most objective of the narrative points of view. When readers read a play or a work that is heavily dependent upon dialogue (such as one of Hemingway's stories), they have a sense of being free to make their own interpretations. When the narrative is produced on the

Guidelines for Analysis of a Performance

Background

1. If the work is of an identifiable genre (Theatre of the Absurd, Restoration Comedy, Senecan Tragedy, or other type), what are the characteristics of this form? What are the authors of the works of this kind trying to accomplish in them? Is there anything you should know about the traditional staging or costuming or musical accompaniment of such drama? How closely does your particular production follow the traditions of the genre? In what ways does it depart from them, and why?

2. If the play is written in or set in another time or another place, are there historical, geographical, philosophical, or social facts that would shed light on the performance? Does this presentation try to suggest that other time or place? If so, how? To what extent? If not, why not?

3. If you are familiar with the work in written form, how closely does your production follow the script? How does this performance handle those ambiguous elements which must be interpreted anew with each production? (If you are watching *Macbeth,* for example, does the director have the Banquo actor appear as Banquo's ghost at Macbeth's feast, or is the ghost to be taken as only a figment of Macbeth's overwrought imagination?)

4. If your production is based upon a drama (or story) that is one of a series, or has a strong autobiographical flavor, are there any essential facts that you should know about your author's life or works? (I urge you to use such material cautiously, however, and to concentrate your analysis upon the performance itself.)

Action and Characters and Theme

All the suggestions about analyzing narrative literature are pertinent here. In addition, the following questions may be helpful:

1. How are the acts divided? How are the scenes arranged? Is there any particular pattern in the scenes or subscenes? How are subplots handled? What is the function of each scene in the overall pattern?

2. By what gestures, intonations, and attitudes does each actor delineate the character he or she portrays? Is there any interaction between particular characters that is especially telling? How personally or how distantly do the actors relate to the audience? If there are asides, soliloquies, or direct audience address, how are they handled? How does the audience respond to them? Do the comic characters encourage the audience to laugh *at* or *with* them? How much empathy do the noncomic characters elicit? How closely is the audience expected to identify with the protagonists (central characters)? What emotions—sympathy? antipathy? indifference?—do they arouse?

3. If the drama is a tragedy or if it has tragic overtones, what is the basis for the tragedy? Is it caused by a flawed hero? A flawed society? Fate? Some combination of these causes? How does the audience feel at the close of the tragedy? Does a *catharsis* take place, washing away the tragic emotions? Despite the downfall of the leading character(s), is there anything hopeful about the ending (the return of order, for instance)? How is this hope conveyed?

Setting and Stage Business

1. Can you find any motifs or symbolic representations in the dialogue, props, or, perhaps, in a repeated action of one of the characters? What does this motif or symbol seem to mean the first time it appears? Does it take on additional meaning as it is repeated? If so, what?

2. What is the nature of the sets and scenery? Are they realistic or do they merely suggest the place? Is there a symbolic quality about them? If so, what are they meant to express? How does the lighting contribute to the background of the drama? Do any special lighting effects stand out in your memory? What is their significance?

3. How do the costumes affect the mood of the production? Do they help characterize individual characters? If so, how?

4. If there is any particular stage business beyond that which would normally accompany the dialogue, what is its significance? If you have noticed any special patterning in the positioning of the actors upon the stage, what meaning can you give it?

Evaluative Questions

1. How did the audience respond to the play? Were they attentive? Were they fidgety—coughing, fanning, whispering together? Did they laugh in the appropriate places? Were they hushed in the appropriate places? Did they respond warmly and appreciatively at the close?

2. Did you find the action plausible? Did it seem to be true to the laws of logic and of cause and effect? Did the characters seem to act in ways that were psychologically consistent with what you were given of their characters? In short, were you able to suspend your disbelief?

3. Was the production a unified and satisfying experience for you? Why or why not?

stage, the author's words are given interpretation by the actors and the director. Although playgoers are guided in making their interpretation of the material in this way, the point of view is still usually general and remains relatively objective. Movies, on the other hand, return you to the controlled point of view. Here the camera directs your ideas and guides your thoughts while it focuses your attention.

Thus, in order to analyze movies critically, you must be conscious of where the camera is directing your attention and try to understand why. In addition to the points explored above, you will want to ask yourself questions such as: Why that distant shot? Why that close-up? Why this particular juxtaposition of images? of scenes? of characters? Why a darkening or a lightening? Why the concentration on this curious object? Why is the camera concentrating with such emphasis on the mouth (or the teeth) of the speaker? Why is it not focusing on the speaker at all? Where is it directing our attention instead? Are the listener's reactions more important? Is there something in the setting to which the speaker's words are supposed to relate? Why is this scene hazy? Why is this one extra sharp in its contrasts? Why is part of the scene out of focus?

The more motion pictures or television dramas you watch and the more literature you read from the viewpoint described here, the more observant you can train yourself to be. You will become more and more aware of the two kinds of strategies that call attention to themselves: (1) repetitions (or parallels), and (2) deviations from the norm. You will become more and more insightful in understanding why the author employs these techniques and why they appear where they do. In gaining these skills you should not only be able to write effective critical analyses, you should also find yourself getting even more pleasure from your viewing and your reading.

ASSIGNMENT

1. Try a self-focused critical analysis. Choose one of the essays in Part Four or another essay, story, drama, or poem, as your instructor directs you, and, using the tools suggested in this chapter, write a critical analysis of it.

2. Or write a critical analysis with an assigned focus. Select an essay, story, drama, or poem with an intriguing title and explain how the title is related to the meaning of the work as a whole—and to your understanding of that meaning.[10]

3. Write a critical analysis of Elizabeth Jane Stein's student paper, "The Blues Don't Knock on Nobody's Door" (page 458), showing how revising her first draft (page 462) helped her present her thesis more convincingly.

---

[10]Topic suggested by Professor Edward A. Kline of Notre Dame University.

PART
FOUR

A Sampler of Professional Essays and Student Papers

ESSAYS BY PROFESSIONAL WRITERS

The professional essays in Part Four are included for your reading enjoyment and to stimulate your thinking and writing. They are all written by authors of high reputation and were selected for the diversity of their views and for their interest to readers. Because these essays are effectively written, they may also contribute to your thinking about the writing process and serve as a testing ground for your beliefs about writing and for the claims made throughout the book.

409

Getting Old in Kids' Country

Shana Alexander

Children are a relatively modern invention. Until a few hundred years 1
ago, they did not exist. In medieval and Renaissance painting, you see
pint-size men and women wearing grown-up clothes and grown-up expressions, performing grown-up tasks. Children did not exist because the family as we know it had not evolved. In the old days, most people lived on the
land, and life was a communal affair.

Children today not only exist; they have taken over. God's Country has 2
to an astonishing degree become Kids' Country—in no place more than in
America, and at no time more than in the period Halloween–to–New Year's
Day. It is during the frantic family skedaddle from pumpkin to holly that
Kids' Country runs in its jumpingest high gear.

But it is always Kids' Country here. Our civilization is child-centered, 3
child-obsessed. A kid's body is our physical ideal. Weight-watchers grunt
and pant. Sages jog from sea to shining sea.[a] Plastic surgeons scissor and
tuck up. New hair sprouts, transplanted, on wisdom's brow. One way or
another we are determined to "keep in shape," and invariably this means
keeping a kid's shape—which we then outfit in baby-doll ruffles, sneakers,
blue jeans.

The food we live on is kids' food: pizza, hot dogs, fried chicken, ice 4
cream, hamburgers. This bizarre diet is the reason we have such trouble
maintaining our kids' bodies. The stuff we now drink has thrown the beverage industry into turmoil. Our consumption of soft drinks has risen 80
percent in a decade. Americans not only are switching *en masse*[b] from hot
coffee to iced tea, and from bitter drinks to sweet. The popularity of alcoholic soda pop—the so-called "fun" wines like Thunderbird and apple
wine—has jumped 168 percent in five years.

Children hate spinach, vitamins, and *haute cuisine.*[c] They like their 5
food kooked, not cooked; you pop, thaw, dissolve, or explode it into eatability. To buy it you push around a wire perambulator, and at the end of the
supermarket line you get prizes of colored stamps.

---

[a]A phrase from the patriotic song "America the Beautiful."
[b]In large numbers; "all together" (French).
[c]Elegant cookery (French).

In Kids' Country, every day must be prize day. Miss America, Miss   6
Teenage America, Miss Junior Miss America, and probably Miss Little Miss
America trample each other down star-spangled runways. Volume mail-
order giveaways will shortly silt up our postal system entirely. All day long
TV shows like *Concentration, Dating Game, Hollywood Squares,* and *Jack-
pot* hand out more toys: wristwatches, washing machines, trips to Hawaii.

The rest of the world may be in fee to the Old Boy Network,[d] carried   7
on to the point of senility, but here there are no elder statesmen left.
Seniority in an American politician no longer denotes wisdom, only power
or tenure. The old age of the present Congress is a major hindrance. No one
considers the Heberts and Eastlands to be Athenian men.[e]

Our contemporary heroes are a series of golden boys. A direct line   8
links Charles Lindbergh to Billy Graham to the astronauts to John F.
Kennedy—and to his kid brother.[f]

The philosopher-kings[g] of Kids' Country are professors like Erich   9
Segal and Charles Reich,[h] who saw in Woodstock and the flower children[i]
a new golden age of innocence he called Consciousness III. The totem
animal in Kids' Country just now is a talking, philosophizing sea gull who
soars on vast updrafts of hot air, and the Kids' Country bogeyman is a
wicked movie mafioso[j] with a heart of gold.

The ideal American parenthood is to be a kid with your kid. Take him   10
to Disneyland, take him fishing, take him out to the ball game.[k] Our national pastimes are kids' games, and we are all hooked. When the Redskins
are blacked out in Washington, the President holes up in New York so as

---

[d]Term referring to the special relationship, particularly useful in business or
professional life, that exists between men who share a similar (often elite) background.

[e]When Alexander wrote this essay, Representative F. Edward Hebert (Democrat, Louisiana) was 75 and Senator James O. Eastland (Democrat, Mississippi) was
73. Although both had served in Congress close to forty years, neither was especially
acclaimed for the sort of wisdom that brought renown to ancient Athens.

[f]All made significant achievements at an early age: Lindbergh, the first solo
transAtlantic flight at 25; Billy Graham, a successful evangelist at 28; John
Kennedy, the youngest man, 43, ever elected president; Robert Kennedy, attorney
general at 35.

[g]Plato's ideal rulers.

[h]Professor-authors who idealized youth in such books as Segal's *Love Story*,
a tribute to young lovers, and Reich's *The Greening of America*, a book in praise
of the ecological and humanitarian passions of youth in the 1960s.

[i]Woodstock, New York, was the site of a celebrated rock concert and "happening" in July 1969, attended by an estimated 400,000 flower children.

[j]The animal symbol of "Kids' Country" is the philosopher seagull hero of
Richard Bach's bestselling *Jonathan Livingston Seagull*. Its villain is the "Godfa-
ther," protagonist of the popular movie of that name.

[k]Allusion to the popular song "Take Me Out to the Ball Game."

not to miss the big game. Bobby Fischer,[l] the quintessential smart boy of every school, turns the whole country on to chess. *The Boys of Summer*[m] becomes a best-seller. In nostalgia's golden haze, we disremember the poet's full line, "I see the boys of summer in their ruin."

In Kids' Country, we do not permit middle age. Thirty is promoted 11 over fifty, but thirty knows that soon his time to be overtaken will come. Middle-aged man must appear to run, even if it is only running in place. Often the big kid outruns his heart. In our over-sixty population, there are ten widows for every man.

Like a child's room, Kids' Country is a mess. New York City seems 12 about to disappear under its load of litter, graffiti, and dog droppings. How is it that China can eliminate the house fly, and we can't even clean up Central Park?

In Kids' Country, not so ironically, Mommy and Daddy are household 13 gods, and so we have two immense national holidays, elsewhere virtually unknown, called "Mother's Day" and "Father's Day." Without them, the American small businessman would be in even worse shape than he already is.

Ours is the first society in history in which parents expect to learn 14 from their children, rather than the other way around. Such a topsy-turvy situation has come about at least in part because, unlike the rest of the world, we are an immigrant society, and for immigrants the only hope is in the kids. In the Old Country, hope was in the father, and in how much family wealth he could accumulate and pass along to his children. In the growth pattern of America and its ever-expanding frontier, the young man was ever advised to Go West.[n] The father was ever inheriting from his son; the topsy-turviness was built-in from the beginning. A melting pot needs a spoon. Kids' Country may be the inevitable result.

Kids' Country is not all bad. America is the greatest country in the 15 world to grow up in *because* it's Kids' Country. We not only wear kids' clothes and eat kids' food; we dream kids' dreams, and make them come true. It was, after all, a boys' game to go to the moon.

The stirring spoon has done its job. As a people we thrive. By the time 16 they reach sixteen, most American kids today are bigger, stronger—and smarter—than Mommy and Daddy ever were. And if they are not precisely "happier," they may well be more "grown up." But because this is a civilization with no clear rites of passage, life in Kids' Country seems to me to be

---

[l]United States chess champion at 14, world champion at 28.

[m]A series of vignettes about baseball and baseball players by Roger Kahn. The full quotation is from a poem by Dylan Thomas, among whose favorite themes is the sweet brevity of youth.

[n]Allusion to Horace Greeley's famous editorial advice: "Go west, young man" (1859).

in many ways the exact opposite of medieval and Renaissance life. If in the old days children did not exist, it seems equally true today that adults as a class have begun to disappear, condemning all of us to remain boys and girls forever, jogging and doing push-ups against eternity.

Shana Alexander   Born 1925. Journalist, lecturer, and television commentator. Alexander started out as a reporter and staff writer for such publications as *PM* and *Harper's Bazaar.* She later worked as a columnist and contributing editor for *McCalls* and *Newsweek* and as a commentator for CBS radio and television. She is the author of five books, including *The Feminine Eye* and *Appearance of Evil: The Trial of Patty Hearst.* This article was originally published in *Newsweek,* December 11, 1972.

Earth's Creeping Deserts

Fred Golden

Outside the great conference hall in Nairobi, 16 fountains sent up 1
sparkling plumes of water, and black Mercedes limousines glistened in the
bright East African sun. Inside, some 1,500 delegates from 110 nations sat
in air-conditioned comfort. The splendid setting of the meeting could
hardly have clashed more jarringly with its purpose. At the U.N.'s invitation, the representatives had gathered in the Kenyan capital last week to
discuss and devise ways of containing what an increasing number of experts regard as a major environmental danger: the creeping, seemingly
relentless spread of the earth's deserts.

More than a third of the earth's land mass is desert or desertlike, and 2
one out of seven people—some 630 million—dwell in these parched regions. In the past, they have been able to scratch out a livelihood—barely.
Now, largely through man's own folly, their fragile existence is threatened
by a deadly disease of the land called, awkwardly but accurately, "desertification."

In only half a century, an estimated 251,000 sq. mi. (650,000 sq. km.) 3
of farming and grazing land has been swallowed up by the Sahara along
that great desert's southern fringe. In one part of India's Rajasthan region,
often called the dustiest place in the world, sand cover has increased by
about 8% in only 18 years. In the U.S., so much once fertile farm land has
been abandoned for lack of water along Interstate 10 between Tucson and
Phoenix that dust storms now often sweep the highway.

For most Americans, desertification is not a problem. But for many 4
of the 78 million people who in recent years have had the ground under
them turn to dust or sand, there is no easy escape. Washington's Worldwatch Institute estimates that the lives of perhaps 50 million people are
jeopardized. As their fields and pastures become no-man's lands, the dis-
possessed add to the tide of ecological refugees who have already swollen
the Third World's ranks of unemployed and destitute. Unable to feed themselves, they place new strains on the food supply and create a tinderbox for
social unrest. Warns U.N. Secretary General Kurt Waldheim: "We risk
destroying whole peoples in the afflicted area."

The deserts' cancerous growth came to worldwide attention in the 5
early 1970s with the great drought and famine in Africa's Sahel, the band
of impoverished land across the Sahara's southern flank. More than

415

100,000 people perished before the rains finally came in 1974, and that was not the end of the tragedy. Hundreds of thousands of tribesmen remain in camps, and the desert's encroachment has not halted. Senegal told the U.N. meeting that it feared its coastal capital, Dakar, would soon be engulfed.

Droughts and crop failures have always been a harsh fact of life in arid regions. But the Sahel's calamity was worsened by distinctly modern factors. Improvements in public health had vastly expanded population. New wells lulled the Africans into thinking they were no longer so completely dependent on the slim rainfall. They enlarged their herds and planted more cash crops like cotton and peanuts. For a while, the land withstood the strains. But when the rains ceased, the crops failed and the cattle stripped the fields of virtually every blade of grass around the overworked wells. Soon the thin layer of topsoil vanished, and there was nothing but rock, sand, and dust. The Sahara had won. 6

Other countries have committed the same sad mistakes. In the Sudan, which could be turned into the pita[a] basket of the Arab world, traditional crop rotation has been all but abandoned—with disastrous reductions in yields. In Tunisia, mechanized plowing cut so deeply into the thin layer of topsoil that much of it loosened and blew away. 7

There are still many gaps in scientific understanding of the complex desert ecology. But there has been no shortage of ideas for saving productive land. Using its oil wealth to good advantage, Saudi Arabia has planted some 10 million tamarisk, acacia and eucalyptus trees to help keep the dunes from overwhelming its al-Hasa oasis near Hofuf. Taking a cue from the cattle drives of the old American West, seven Sahel nations are involved in a scheme, dubbed Solar, that would allow nomads to continue to raise cattle on marginal Sahelian rangeland. But when it comes time for fattening before marketing, the time when the cattle make their greatest inroads on pastureland vegetation, they will be marched to the wetter and hardier lands in the south. 8

Another idea, already acted on by Algeria, would create pockets of trees, shrubs and other barriers against the Sahara in a so-called green belt across the breadth of North Africa from Morocco to Egypt. The Sahel nations are talking of a similar desert project in the South. 9

The Israelis not only have restored some of the water collection systems left by the ancient Nabateans[b] in the Negev desert, but are letting the runoff nourish flourishing orchards of almond and pistachio trees. Another strategy for making the Negev bloom: drip irrigation systems that feed small amounts of water directly to the roots of plants with the help of computer monitors. 10

---

[a] Arab bread.

[b] A people with a genius for water engineering, who built a flourishing civilization in Israel's Negev region from 200 b.c.e. to 200 c.e., when Rome conquered and the land was wasted by wars.

Though the U.N. conference featured an Arab-led walkout during the 11 Israeli delegate's Negev report and other outbursts of rudeness and rancor, the Nairobi proceedings made some encouraging progress. Scientists presented many carefully prepared technical analyses of desertification and ways to combat it. The U.S. pitched in with an offer to train a cadre[c] of 1,000 Peace Corps volunteers for antidesertification work. Before the delegates disband this week, they are expected to adopt a 15-point plan that calls for a worldwide effort against the deserts' encroachment with everything from the planting of new vegetation to the settlement of nomads to control grazing.

Some scientists feared that the document placed too much faith in 12 technological—rather than "human"—solutions, but the plea nonetheless represents a milestone. For the first time, the international community is committing itself to the fight against the growth of deserts. While the document leaves action up to individual countries, the incentive to collaborate—perhaps even with old enemies—is great. To many countries, doing battle against the deserts is the only alternative to poverty, starvation and chaos.

Fred Golden   Journalist and author with a strong scientific bent. A lifelong resident of New York City, Golden worked briefly for the *Newark News* and the Associated Press before joining *Time* where, since 1969, he has headed the Science Section. Among his many books are *The Moving Continent* and *Quasars, Pulsars, and Black Holes: Colonies in Space.* This article was originally published in *Time,* September 12, 1977.

---

[c]A nucleus of trained leaders, around which a larger organization can be developed.

The Communication Gap

Ellen Goodman

I went back to college this week or, to be more accurate, back to 1
colleges. For five days I had an extensive course on the generation born
circa 1960. I gathered enough material for a thesis on The Communication
Gap Between the Sexes, Phase II.

On campuses covered with ivy and lined with palm trees, I met young 2
women who've been encouraged to consider life plans that will include
careers as well as families, aspiring as well as caretaking. I met young
women who talk regularly with each other in and out of class about marriages of mutuality, about futures of equality.

But when I asked how often, how easily, these same women talked 3
about their ideas and ideals with the men in their lives, I sensed an uneasy
quiet.

Gradually, I realized that many of these students maintain a kind of 4
conspiracy of silence with men. They secrete away some levels of feelings
and hopes until it is "too late," until false expectations are already set.

This silence grows in part from the old female fears—can I be ambi- 5
tious and feminine? can I be "liberated" and loved?—that live right below
the surface of this change.

Vulnerability and uncertainty, the anxiety about being accepted and 6
acceptable, are most acute in the first years away from home. To many of
these students, words like women's rights, equality and, surely, feminism,
are too risky to say in mixed company.

The fear is something they brought with them from home to campus, 7
from childhood to adulthood. After all, most of these twenty-year-old
daughters of forty-five-year-old mothers grew up in traditional, or transitional homes.

More than one talked freely about the double messages delivered by 8
parents. One mother still tells her daughter regularly to make a partnership
marriage. Yet the mother lives as junior partner with the man who is, after
all, the daughter's father.

Another father urges his daughter on to success, a flourishing career. 9
Yet the same man expects and wants service from the woman who is, after
all, her mother.

In their families, far more was said about changing roles to daughters 10
than to sons.

Now, in college, too, "women's issues" are still largely a single-sex 11 subject. The classes, the lectures, the guidance sessions are overwhelmingly taught by women to women. Few teachers—like few parents—talk with young men about the real lives they will jointly lead.

The job of communicating with men, changing their ideas, again falls 12 onto women. It falls heavily into the middle of all other issues raised in that emotional world we call a relationship.

The old reluctance of women to share their new aspirations is also 13 founded in the very real continuing gap between the expectations of men and women.

I know that men have changed in tandem with the times. When Helen 14 and Alexander Astin did their study of incoming freshmen in 1971, 52 percent of the men and 31 percent of the women agreed that "the activities of married women are best confined to home." When they asked again last year,[a] only 34.7 percent of the men and 19 percent of the women still agreed with that "confinement."

But a gap between men and women exists even on this easy question. 15 It grows into a chasm as the issues of sharing and partnership become more complicated.

So, the new silence has grown out of the old silence. The students, 16 male and female, are the latest victims of two-track talking, two-track teaching.

After my week at school, I wonder what will happen if young women 17 don't learn that they have much more to fear from what they don't say. I wonder what will happen if more campuses don't involve their male students in thinking about lives gauged together, rather than on these separate tracks.

We may graduate a whole new generation, sadly unprepared to live 18 together. We may graduate another crop of men who will be stunned and saddened at middle age, to discover that their wives do not, did not, want the life plan they thought was mutual.

Is this pain and disillusionment being nurtured now in the soil of our 19 silence?

Ellen Goodman   Born 1941. Pulitzer prize–winning feature writer and syndicated columnist. A Bostonian, Goodman has written for the *Detroit Free Press* and *Boston Globe* and now is published through the *Washington Post* Writer's Group. She writes primarily on feminist topics and other social and ethical issues. This article was originally published in the *Boston Globe,* March 1981.

---

[a]In 1980.

Accepting the Unacceptable

Meg Greenfield

1 Perhaps by the time these words appear the hostage crisis will have come to a bloodless—or bloody—end. Perhaps not. But whatever its ultimate outcome, this latest episode of kidnapping and terror has already illustrated once again our permanent disadvantage in dealing with people who do these things and our penchant[a] for deepening the disadvantage by the way we respond. That response is a (by now) ritualized series of diversions and evasions that subtly but quickly make us feel better while also making the hostages' situation worse.

2 The permanent disadvantage is not our fault. It is built in and has three main elements. First, people who urgently want something are always at a great advantage over those who merely want to be left alone—as those air travelers in particular did and as Americans in general do insofar as the conflict in the Middle East is concerned. Yes, those who wish to be left alone will struggle mightily to defend their country against military or even economic aggression. But these isolated, recurrent assaults aren't seen as that kind of threat.

3 Second, our permanent disadvantage rests on the unbearable choice we face between trying to save the lives of innocent victims and trying to face down their tormentors without yielding. No one has figured out a way to do this well because there is no way. We try to do both.

Assumptions: 4 Finally, it is in the nature of this kind of terror that its victims—meaning all who don't practice, understand or condone it—will at once turn and run from its reality, insisting on seeing it as something different from what it is. Terrorism attacks our compatriots on airplanes, and that makes us sad or angry on their behalf. But it also attacks our most fundamental, settled assumptions about how we can expect people to behave in relation to us, what we can count on them to feel and do—or not do. Those assumptions are central to our sense of personal security. And so this kind of attack frightens and disorients us and we try very hard to describe or rename or wish it away. We give terrorism a familiar face, an understandable motive, an explanation that makes it somehow less menac-

---

[a]A strong inclination.

ing. We try to doll it up to look just like the family next door. And meanwhile the terrorists continue to shoot the odd helpless passenger and pitch him out the airplane door.

We call these shoot-and-pitch men "militants,"[b] by the way, as if they were merely agitating for pure air and happy whales. And by implication, anyhow, we absolve the bulk of them from their crime by designating a certain few among them as "extremists," the others who did the tying up but not the shooting presumably being something else. This inapt language is part of our evasion, part of the effort to see the assault in less terrifying terms than it deserves. 5

I am always struck by a couple of particularly bad formulations that are used in these episodes. One holds that the hostages are "being treated well," so long as they get some food and soap and are not being physically beaten. It reminds me of that old standby about how the woman had been raped "but not harmed" by her assailant. The absence of a bash to the face in neither case constitutes absence of harm or good treatment. By the very act of their capture our hostages are being brutally mistreated. 6

The other especially unfortunate formulation is that which holds that we are in a "war" with terrorism. But war, with its rules and its purposes and its causes, for all its irrationality and evil, is exactly what we are not in. And to say we are is to do several things. It is to elevate these grubby criminal acts to a status they don't deserve; it is to cast, at least indirectly, all Americans as enemy civilians or belligerents[c] and thus fair game; and it is to misdescribe the nature of the assault itself. Soldiers may behave thuggishly, but there is a difference between soldiers and thugs. And there is a difference too between being a prisoner of war and being a hostage hauled off a plane. 7

All these slightly "off" terms start to get thrown around very early in each hostage episode. Within the first 48 hours we begin to transform the perception of what has happened. We call these ordeals "crises," but we drain the urgency from them. And as it is with our national "problems," we do not try to resolve them so much as we colonize them. Everybody moves in. Outrage over the fact of the kidnapping diminishes. The captivity of the victims becomes simply a given. The hostages almost are forgotten as politicians, press and public around the globe begin to communicate with each other courtesy of TV. The overwhelming purpose of all seems to be to tame the beast, to make it seem something else. 8

Resignation: It doesn't take long, you will observe, before we are all basing our conversation on unspoken premises that aren't much good from anyone's point of view—except that of the terrorists. In November of the first 9

---

[b]"Political activists."

[c]Those engaged in warlike behavior.

year of the Iranian hostage crisis you could hear people demanding that the captors entertain the prospect of delivering Christmas packages to their captured wards. Christmas arrangements! In November! What a way of saying that we were settling in for a nice long haul. Within a few hours of the TWA affair you could sense a similar resignation dropping down over the crime like a net. The lunatic professoriat took to the air and expressed its usual hostage-crisis baloney; we commentators did much the same; the so-called experts on terrorism scratched their heads; we heard all about the legitimate grievances of the captors; we heard how the hostages were being treated well; we got used to the idea.

Except that what we were getting ourselves used to was a very prett- 10 ied-up construction of the event. We had tamed it, rearranged it, made it safe for us, but not for the passengers of that ill-fated plane. If I were not such a First Amendment junkie, I sometimes think I would come out for mandatory silence in those first crucial hours of a hijack. We always say we won't pay ransom or give terms. But we give everything in the brief span of time. We give acceptance, credibility and respectability of a sort. We proceed to accommodate what has happened with too much understanding and too little complaint. It becomes, to the commentator and audience, more "interesting" than it is outrageous. We give it all away at the outset and wonder why it is so painful and costly to get our people back.

Meg Greenfield   Born in Seattle in 1930. A topnotch student at Smith College and a Fulbright scholar at England's Cambridge University, Greenfield was a reporter, editorial writer, and editor at the *Washington Post,* where she won the Pulitzer prize for Editorial Writing. She is currently a columnist with *Newsweek,* where this article was published, July 1, 1985.

Children of Two-Career Families

William Raspberry

1. Maybe you have to be crazy to argue with two Harvard psychiatrists—particularly two such insightful psychiatrists as Barrie Greiff and Preston Hunter.

2. So before I register my small objection to their article in the May–June issue of *Harvard Magazine,* let me say that nearly everything these two doctors have to say about the strains and stresses of dual-career families makes sense to me.

3. The only paragraph that arched my eyebrows included this sentence: "Dual-career parents . . . shouldn't overburden their children with responsibilities for themselves or their siblings, or for running the household; that only cheats them out of their childhood and confuses them about parental roles."

4. "Dual-career" families are defined as families in which both husband and wife have careers (as opposed to jobs) that require separate, major commitments outside the marriage.

5. The advice in the paragraph cited is calculated to help the children of these families deal with "the anger, hostility, rebellion and feelings of abandonment" caused by their parents' absence.

6. My fear is that the advice may feed another set of problems: the problems that stem from a general sense of uselessness.

7. It is my belief that many of the difficulties America's young people face today are the result of their sense of unnecessity. They are not needed to produce income, to maintain the family routine, to help in any serious way. As a result, they are likely to see themselves as part of no vital enterprise which they deem to be of overriding importance.

8. They may feel loved and well-provided for, but they are also likely to feel unnecessary.

9. This sense of uselessness, I am convinced, lies behind the shocking statistics on teen-age pregnancy, youthful homicide and suicide, crime, alcoholism, drug abuse—the whole range of things we refer to when we talk about the decline in character among young Americans.

10. And because it is harder for children of affluent families to feel necessary, it had seemed to me vital that they at least be given some responsibility for "themselves or their siblings, or for running the household."

11. Can it be only coincidental that teen-age suicide, drug abuse, etc.,

were practically nonexistent when most American families lived on farms, or in nonurban settings, where their children's contribution to the families' general welfare was taken for granted?

These children worked on the farm, or gathered firewood, or looked 12 after livestock and performed a whole variety of chores, not because their parents were concerned about developing in them a sense of responsibility but because their contributions were in fact necessary. Nor was there any concern that the performance of these necessary tasks would "cheat them out of their childhood."

But most of these tasks have no obvious counterpart in the typical 13 affluent, urban or suburban household. If they live in apartments or town-houses, today's youngsters don't even have lawns to mow.

Nor is it a problem only for the well-off. The children of urban tene- 14 ments may see themselves as equally unnecessary, playing no important role in their families' welfare.

Under the circumstances, it seems to me that the problem for modern 15 parents is to find ways to give their children a sense of usefulness, to make them feel that they are a vital part of a general family enterprise, and not just impediments to their parents' careers. It seems obvious to me that if children don't see themselves as valuable to others, they are unlikely to feel that they are valuable to themselves.

The Harvard psychiatrists worry about cheating children out of their 16 childhood. I worry about cheating them out of something more profoundly important: their self-respect as responsible, contributing human beings.

William Raspberry   Born 1935. Journalist, lecturer, and syndicated columnist. Formerly with the *Indianapolis Recorder*, Raspberry now is contributing editor of the *Washington Post*. He is also a television commentator and panelist and an instructor at Howard University. Raspberry writes mainly about racial issues, public education, and urban affairs. This article was originally published in the *Washington Post*, May 19, 1980.

If I'm So Smart, How Come I Flunk All the Time?

Charles W. Slack

Can twenty flunking students of varying intelligence raise their math 1
and English a full year's level in only thirty working days?

Dr. Lloyd Homme, chief of a special educational "fix-it" laboratory in 2
Albuquerque, New Mexico, said Yes and put teams of behavioral scientists
together with the flunking students to work on the problem. Any available
technology could be used—teaching machines, programmed instruction,
computer-assisted methods—to cram a year's knowledge into the boys.

Were the experiments a success? The scientists said Yes but the stu- 3
dents said No. When grades were measured using standardized tests under
strict laboratory conditions, marks went up more than one year on the
average. Meanwhile, back at the school, the students were still barely passing, at best. "The experiment was fine for the scientists. They proved their
theory on paper and made a name for themselves, but most of us were still
flunking in class," remarked one seventeen-year-old.

The only clue to the mystery was this common remark: "The teachers 4
ignore us—they've got it in for us."

At first the scientists on the team thought the complaint was just sour 5
grapes[a] and told the boys to work harder. When grades still failed to rise,
the scientists felt there might be some truth in what the young team members were saying. Not that teachers were to blame, necessarily, but there
still might be some negative bias. "You should see what goes on in class!"
said the boys.

"The only thing to do was to take them up on it, go into the classroom 6
with them and see what was holding back their grades," said Dr. Homme.

Hence, bearded behavioral scientists ended up in the back row of 7
math and English classes and made observations about the behavior of
students and teachers. Homme was surprised to discover that two simple
actions made the difference.

"With few exceptions, our students acted like dummies," said Dr. 8
Homme, "even though we knew they were ahead of the rest in knowledge.
They were so used to playing the class idiot that they didn't know how to

---

[a] An allusion to the Aesop fable about a fox who, after jumping unsuccessfully
ten times for a desirable bunch of grapes, concluded he didn't want them anyway
because "They're sour!"

show what they knew. Their eyes wandered, they appeared absent-minded or even belligerent. One or two read magazines hidden under their desks, thinking, most likely, that they already knew the classwork. They rarely volunteered and often had to have questions repeated because they weren't listening. Teachers, on the other hand, did not trust our laboratory results. Nobody was going to tell them that 'miracles' could work on Sammy and Jose."

In the eyes of teachers, students seemed to fall into three groups. We'll   9
call them *bright-eyes, scaredy-cats* and *dummies. Bright-eyes* had perfected the trick of

1. "eyeballing" the instructor at all times, even from the minute he entered the room.
2. never ducking their eyes away when the instructor glanced at *them.*
3. getting the instructor to call on them when they wanted *without* raising their hands.
4. even making the instructor go out of his way to call on someone else to "give others a chance" (especially useful when bright-eyes themselves are uncertain of the answer).
5. readily admitting ignorance so as not to bluff—but in such a way that it sounds as though ignorance is rare.
6. asking many questions.

Scaredy-cats (the middle group)

1. looked toward the instructor but were afraid to let him "catch their eyes."
2. asked few questions and gave the impression of being "under-achievers."
3. appeared uninvolved and had to be "drawn out," so they were likely to be criticized for "inadequate participation."

Dummies (no matter how much they really knew)

1. never looked at the instructor.
2. never asked questions.
3. were stubborn about volunteering information in class.

To make matters worse, the tests in school were not standardized and   10
not given nearly as frequently as those given in the laboratory. School test-scores were open to teacher bias. Classroom behavior of students counted a lot toward their class grades. There was no doubt that teachers were biased against the dummies. The scientists concluded that no matter how much knowledge a dummy gained on his own, his grades in school were unlikely to improve unless he could somehow change his image into a bright-eyes. This would mean . . .

1. Look the teacher in the eye.
2. Ask questions and volunteer answers (even if uncertain).

"Teachers get teacher-training in how to play their roles. Why   11 shouldn't students get student-training in how to play bright-eyes?" asked Homme.

Special training sessions were held at the laboratory. Dummies were 12 drilled in eyeballing and hand-raising, which, simple as they sound, weren't easy to do. "I felt so square I could hardly stand it," complained one of the dummies. "That was a first. Later, when I saw others eyeballing and hand-raising and really learning more, I even moved my seat to the front. It flipped the teacher out of her skull. She couldn't get over it."

Those who found eyeballing especially difficult were taught to look at 13 the instructor's mouth or the bridge of his nose. "Less threatening to the student," explained Homme. "It seems less agressive to them."

Unfortunately, not all of the dummies were able to pick up new habits 14 during the limited training period. Some learned in the laboratory but couldn't do it in the classroom. These became scaredy-cats—at least a step up. But for the majority, grades improved steadily once they got the hang of their new techniques. The students encouraged and helped each other to hand-raise and eyeball.

Teachers' comments reflected the improvement. "There is no doubt 15 that student involvement was increased by the program and as a result grades went up."

By way of advice to others wishing to improve their own eyeballing 16 and hand-raising, student Jose Martinez suggests: "Don't try to do it all at once. You'll shock the teacher and make it tough for yourself. Begin slowly. Work with a friend and help each other. Do it like a game. Like exercising with weights—it takes practice but it's worth it."

Homme agrees. "In fact, results are guaranteed for life," he says. 17

Charles Lee Slack   Born in 1929 into a scientific family, and educated at Princeton University, where he received a Ph.D. in Psychology, he was a research scientist and teacher at the National Naval Medical Center, Bethesda, Harvard University, University of Alabama, Brooklyn College, Columbia University, and New York University. Slack is now a freelance writer on educational, psychological, and other scientific issues. This article was first published in *Eye* magazine in January 1969.

Late Night Thoughts on Listening to Mahler's Ninth Symphony

Lewis Thomas

I cannot listen to Mahler's[a] Ninth Symphony with anything like the old melancholy mixed with the high pleasure I used to take from this music. There was a time, not long ago, when what I heard, especially in the final movement, was an open acknowledgment of death and at the same time a quiet celebration of the tranquillity connected to the process. I took this music as a metaphor for reassurance, confirming my own strong hunch that the dying of every living creature, the most natural of all experiences, has to be a peaceful experience. I rely on nature. The long passages on all the strings at the end, as close as music can come to expressing silence itself, I used to hear as Mahler's idea of leave-taking at its best. But always, I have heard this music as a solitary, private listener, thinking about death. 1

Now I hear it differently. I cannot listen to the last movement of the Mahler Ninth without the door-smashing intrusion of a huge new thought: death everywhere, the dying of everything, the end of humanity. The easy sadness expressed with such gentleness and delicacy by that repeated phrase on faded strings, over and over again, no longer comes to me as old, familiar news of the cycle of living and dying. All through the last notes my mind swarms with images of a world in which the thermonuclear bombs have begun to explode, in New York and San Francisco, in Moscow and Leningrad, in Paris, in Paris, in Paris. In Oxford and Cambridge, in Edinburgh. I cannot push away the thought of a cloud of radioactivity drifting along the Engadin,[b] from the Moloja Pass to Ftan, killing off the part of the earth I love more than any other part. 2

---

[a]Austrian composer, conductor (1860–1911, first name Gustav).

[b]A valley, renowned for its beauty, in the mountains of southeastern Switzerland, with the Moloja Pass on its eastern end. Ftan is a mountain village overlooking the valley toward its western end.

I am old enough by this time to be used to the notion of dying, 3
saddened by the glimpse when it has occurred but only transiently knocked
down, able to regain my feet quickly at the thought of continuity, any day.
I have acquired and held in affection until very recently another sideline
of an idea which serves me well at dark times: the life of the earth is the
same as the life of an organism: the great round being possesses a mind:
the mind contains an infinite number of thoughts and memories: when I
reach my time I may find myself still hanging around in some sort of
midair, one of those small thoughts, drawn back into the memory of the
earth: in that peculiar sense I will be alive.

Now all that has changed. I cannot think that way anymore. Not while 4
those things are still in place, aimed everywhere, ready for launching.

This is a bad enough thing for the people in my generation. We can 5
put up with it, I suppose, since we must. We are moving along anyway, like
it or not. I can even set aside my private fancy about hanging around, in
midair.

What I cannot imagine, what I cannot put up with, the thought that 6
keeps grinding its way into my mind, making the Mahler into a hideous
noise close to killing me, is what it would be like to be young. How do the
young stand it? How can they keep their sanity? If I were very young,
sixteen or seventeen years old, I think I would begin, perhaps very slowly
and imperceptibly, to go crazy.

There is a short passage near the very end of the Mahler in which the 7
almost vanishing violins, all engaged in a sustained backward glance, are
edged aside for a few bars by the cellos. Those lower notes pick up fragments from the first movement, as though prepared to begin everything all
over again, and then the cellos subside and disappear, like an exhalation.
I used to hear this as a wonderful few seconds of encouragement: we'll be
back, we're still here, keep going, keep going.

Now, with a pamphlet in front of me on a corner of my desk, pub- 8
lished by the Congressional Office of Technology Assessment, entitled *MX
Basing,* an analysis of all the alternative strategies for placement and protection of hundreds of these missiles, each capable of creating artificial
suns to vaporize a hundred Hiroshimas, collectively capable of destroying
the life of any continent, I cannot hear the same Mahler. Now, those cellos
sound in my mind like the opening of all the hatches and the instant before
ignition.

If I were sixteen or seventeen years old, I would not feel the cracking 9
of my own brain, but I would know for sure that the whole world was
coming unhinged. I can remember with some clarity what it was like to be
sixteen. I had discovered the Brahms symphonies. I knew that there was
something going on in the late Beethoven quartets that I would have to
figure out, and I knew that there was plenty of time ahead for all the
figuring I would ever have to do. I had never heard of Mahler. I was in no

hurry. I was a college sophomore and had decided that Wallace Stevens[c] and I possessed a comprehensive understanding of everything needed for a life. The years stretched away forever ahead, forever. My great-great grandfather had come from Wales, leaving his signature in the family Bible on the same page that carried, a century later, my father's signature. It never crossed my mind to wonder about the twenty-first century; it was just there, given, somewhere in the sure distance.

The man on television, Sunday midday, middle-aged and solid, nice- 10 looking chap, all the facts at his fingertips, more dependable looking than most high-school principals, is talking about civilian defense, his responsibility in Washington. It can make an enormous difference, he is saying. Instead of the outright death of eighty million American citizens in twenty minutes, he says, we can, by careful planning and practice, get that number down to only forty million, maybe even twenty. The thing to do, he says, is to evacuate the cities quickly and have everyone get under shelter in the countryside. That way we can recover, and meanwhile we will have retaliated, incinerating all of Soviet society, he says. What about radioactive fallout? he is asked. Well, he says. Anyway, he says, if the Russians know they can only destroy forty million of us instead of eighty million, this will deter them. Of course, he adds, they have the capacity to kill all two hundred and twenty million of us if they were to try real hard, and they know we can do the same to them. If the figure is only forty million this will deter them, not worth the trouble, not worth the risk. Eighty million would be another matter; we should guard ourselves against losing that many all at once, he says.

If I were sixteen or seventeen years old and had to listen to that, or 11 read things like that, I would want to give up listening and reading. I would begin thinking up new kinds of sounds, different from any music heard before, and I would be twisting and turning to rid myself of human language.

Lewis Thomas Born 1913. Physician, educator, medical administrator, and author. Having served as Professor or Dean of the College of Medicine at Minnesota, Yale, Cornell, and Rockefeller Universities, Thomas is now with the Sloan-Kettering Cancer Center. He also serves on numerous administrative boards and on the editorial boards of four medical journals. He is the author of many articles on biological subjects and two books, *Lives of a Cell* and *Medusa and the Snail.*

---

[c]American poet (1879–1955) whose style has been described as "intellectual dandyism."

On Splitting

Carll Tucker

One afternoon recently, two unrelated friends called to tell me that, [1]
well, their marriages hadn't made it. One was leaving his wife for another woman. The other was leaving her husband because "we thought it
best."

As always after such increasingly common calls, I felt helpless and [2]
angry. What had happened to those solemn vows that one of the couples
had stammered on a steamy August afternoon three years earlier? And
what had happened to the joy my wife and I had sensed when we visited
the other couple and their two children last year, the feeling they gave us
that here, in this increasingly fractionated world, was a constructive
union?

I did not feel anger at my friends personally: Given the era and their [3]
feelings, their decisions probably made sense. What angered me was the
loss of years and energy. It was an anger similar to that I feel when I see
abandoned foundations of building projects—piled bricks and girders and
a gash in the ground left to depress the passerby.

When our grandparents married, nobody except scandalous eccen- [4]
trics divorced. "As long as we both shall live" was no joke. Neither was the
trepidation brides felt on the eves of their wedding days. After their vows,
couples learned to live with each other—not necessarily because they loved
each other, but because they were stuck, and it was better to be stuck
comfortably than otherwise.

Most of the external pressures that helped to enforce our grandpar- [5]
ents' vows have dissolved. Women can earn money and may enjoy sex,
even bear children, without marrying. As divorce becomes more common,
the shame attendant on it dissipates. Some divorcees even argue that divorce is beneficial, educational; that the second or third or fifth marriage
is "the best." The only reasons left to marry are love, tax advantages, and
for those old-fashioned enough to care about such things, to silence parental kvetching.[a]

---

[a] Persistent complaining (Yiddish).

In some respects, this freedom can be seen as social progress. Modern 6
couples can flee the corrosive bitterness that made Strindberg's marriages[b]
nightmares. Dreiser's Clyde Griffiths might have abandoned his Roberta
instead of drowning her.[c]

In other respects, our rapidly-rising divorce rate and the declining 7
marriage rate (as more and more couples opt to forgo legalities and simply
live together) represent a loss. One advantage of spending a lifetime with
a person is seeing each other grow and change. For most of us, it is not
possible to see history in the bathroom mirror—gray hairs, crow's feet, yes,
but not a change of mind or temperament. Yet, living with another person,
it is impossible not to notice how patterns and attitudes change and not to
learn—about yourself and about time—from the perceptions.

Perhaps the most poignant victim of the twentieth century is our sense 8
of continuity. People used to grow up with trees, watch them evolve from
saplings to fruit bearers to gnarled and unproductive grandfathers. Now,
unless one is a farmer or a forester there is almost no point to planting trees
because one is not likely to be there to enjoy their maturity. We change
addresses and occupations and hobbies and life-styles and spouses rapidly
and readily, much as we change TV channels. In our grandparents' day one
committed oneself to certain skills and disciplines and developed them.
Carpenters spent lifetimes learning their craft; critics spent lifetimes learning literature. Today, the question often is not "What do you do?" but "What
are you into?" Macrame one week, astrology the next, health food, philosophy, history, jogging, movies, EST[d]—we fly from "commitment" to "commitment" like bees among flowers because it is easier to test something
than to master it, easier to buy a new toy than to repair an old one.

I feel sorry for what my divorced friends have lost. No matter how 9
earnestly the former spouses try to "keep in touch," no matter how generous the visiting privileges for the parent who does not win custody of the
children, the continuity of their lives has been broken. The years they spent
together have been cut off from the rest of their lives; they are an isolated
memory, no more integral to their past than a snapshot. Intelligent people,

---

[b]Despite the fact that August Strindberg (1849–1912) considered his first wife
to be ruthless, aggressive, and emasculating almost from the start, the Swedish
playwright remained married to her from 1877 to 1891. His second marriage,
though shorter, was equally unfortunate and was probably a partial cause of his
emotional breakdown, which coincided with it.

[c]In Theodore Dreiser's *An American Tragedy* (1925), the protagonist, Clyde
Griffiths, unwilling either to leave the girl he has seduced to her fate as an unwed
mother or to marry her himself, takes her out in a rowboat and permits her to
drown.

[d]Werner Erhard's *E*rhard *S*eminar *T*raining movement. Therapeutic program to enhance self-image. Its program consists of two weekends (sixty hours) of
"peak experiences" designed to help the participant "meet yourself face to face."

they will compare their next marriages—if they have them—to their first. They may even, despite not having a long shared past, notice growth. What I pray, though, is that they do not delude themselves into believing, like so many Americans today, that happiness is only measurable moment to moment and, in the pursuit of momentary contentment, forsake the perspectives and consolation of history.

There is great joy in watching a tree grow.   10

Carll Tucker   Born 1951. Author, columnist, editor, and publisher. Beginning as a reporter for the *Village Voice,* Tucker became a contributing editor of *The Saturday Review,* for which he wrote this article January 21, 1978. Since 1981 he has been associated with *The Patent Trader Newspaper,* Mount Kisco, New York, first as columnist and editor and now as president and publisher.

What Killed Arthur Dimmesdale?

Perry Turner

Remember high school English? Remember symbols? Remember the Scarlet A? When you studied Hawthorne's *The Scarlet Letter,* you probably spent a lot of class time discussing Sin and Guilt. But it could be your English teacher missed the point. Jemshed Khan, an ophthalmologist at the University of Missouri at Columbia, claims that too many of the book's readers are finding the same old profundities. What readers keep overlooking, maintains Khan, are all the signs of a great murder mystery. 1

The Scarlet Letter, for those whose memory is dimming, is the story of Hester Prynne, a young woman who, while her husband was away, took a lover and bore his child. As punishment, the colonial magistrates order her to embroider a scarlet A on her dress. Her former consort, the Reverend Arthur Dimmesdale, manages to conceal his role in Hester's predicament, but Hester's husband, the physician Roger Chillingworth, uncovers the culprit and insidiously torments him until, at the end of the novel, Dimmesdale bares his chest "with a convulsive motion" to reveal what most onlookers insisted was "a SCARLET LETTER—the very semblance of that worn by Hester Prynne—imprinted in the flesh." Shortly thereafter he dies. 2

But how did the minister come by his letter, anyway? " '[T]his burning torture' on Dimmesdale's chest," explained Khan in the August 9, 1984, issue of *The New England Journal of Medicine,* "was a diffuse nonpunctate erythematous rash. The rash, that is, of atropine poisoning." 3

It's certainly true that Chillingworth, the putative poisoner, was probably very well informed about atropine, an alkaloid produced by plants like henbane and deadly nightshade. He is observed to have "gathered herbs, and the blossoms of wild-flowers, and dug up roots, and plucked off twigs from the forest-trees, like one acquainted with hidden virtues in what was valueless to common eyes." And as a captive of the Indians, Chillingworth "had gained much knowledge of the properties of native herbs and roots." 4

It's also true that atropine produces symptoms much like those that start to plague Dimmesdale: flushing, for instance, and speech problems. At about the time Chillingworth set up shop as the town's physician, Dimmesdale's health began to deteriorate: "His form grew emaciated; his voice, though still rich and sweet, had a certain melancholy prophecy of decay 5 in it; he was often observed . . . to put his hand over his heart, with first a flush and then a paleness. . . ."

Atropine also makes the pupils dilate, and Hawthorne cagily observes 6 that "whether it were his failing health, or whatever the cause might be, [Dimmesdale's] large dark eyes had a world of pain in their troubled and melancholy depth." And then there's the matter of Dimmesdale's deteriorating coordination, another symptom of incremental atropine poisoning. By the last scene, in fact, his walk resembles "the wavering effort of an infant. . . ."

Nobody likes to miss the point, and soon after Khan published his 7 conclusions, scholars were hastening to concur. Barbara Storms, for instance, a University of Chicago student of literature, rejoiced over Khan's reading: "Gone is the heavy symbolic or allegorical structure put forward so often by literary scholars. The reader is left with the kernel of a possible truth rather than the chaff of rhetoric that only leads to more questions." Virginia McCormick, an English teacher at Allen High School in Allentown, Pennsylvania, took a less heady but no less approving tone: "[T]here is no reason," she declared, "that both theories—Dimmesdale's death as a result of a guilty conscience and his death as a result of herbal poisoning—cannot co-exist."

Others were less convinced by Khan's "possible truth." Eugene Arden, 8 an English professor at the University of Michigan in Dearborn, said that, toward the end of the novel, Dimmesdale "was in fact becoming the most powerful and persuasive deliverer of sermons in New England—not a feat likely in a person dying of atropine poisoning."

True enough, responded Khan, but toward the end of his life, Dim- 9 mesdale also rejected Chillingworth's "medicine" and thus regained enough vigor to continue preaching. "However," Khan said, "in his zeal he overexerts his weakened constitution. The combination of an exhausted physical state, and the residual effects of atropine (which may persist for four to nine days after ingestion) could have caused his death."

Some scholars are refusing to entangle themselves too deeply in a 10 point-counterpoint debate. Marcia Zorn, a former University of Dayton graduate student, complained that Khan's analysis "detracts from the higher truth and purpose of [Hawthorne's] parable—one that is not scientifically verifiable and was never meant to be."

So what *is* the higher truth here? It may be that the only indisputable 11 truth in *The Scarlet Letter* will come from neither physicians nor professors of literature but from the author himself. "A man burdened with a secret," Hawthorne advised, "should especially avoid the intimacy of his physician."

Perry Turner Born 1958. Professional writer. On the staff of *Science '83–Science '86* until its closing. Currently Associate Editor of *Air and Space,* the Journal of the Smithsonian's Air and Space Museum in Washington, D.C. This article was originally published in the October issue of *Science '85.*

The Distant Music of the Hounds

E. B. White

To perceive Christmas through its wrapping becomes more difficult [1] with every year. There was a little device we noticed in one of the sporting-goods stores—a trumpet that hunters hold to their ears so that they can hear the distant music of the hounds. Something of the sort is needed now to hear the incredibly distant sound of Christmas in these times, through the dark, material woods that surround it. "Silent Night," canned and distributed in thundering repetition in the department stores, has become one of the greatest of all noisemakers, almost like the rattles and whistle of Election Night. We rode down on an escalator the other morning through the silent-nighting of the loudspeakers, and the man just in front of us was singing, "I'm gonna wash this store right outa my hair, I'm gonna wash this store. . . ."[a]

The miracle of Christmas is that, like the distant and very musical [2] voice of the hound, it penetrates finally and becomes heard in the heart—over so many years, through so many cheap curtain-raisers. It is not destroyed even by all the arts and craftsness of the destroyers, having an essential simplicity that is everlasting and triumphant, at the end of confusion. We once were out at night with coon-hunters and we were aware that it was not so much the promise of the kill that took the men away from their warm homes and sent them through the cold shadowy woods, it was something more human, more mystical—something even simpler. It was the night, and the excitement of the note of the hound, first heard, then not heard. It was the natural world seen at its best and most haunting, unlit except by stars, impenetrable except to the knowing and the sympathetic.

Christmas in this year of crisis must compete as never before with the [3] dazzling complexity of man, whose tangential[b] desires and ingenuities have created a world that gives any simple thing the look of obsolescence—as though there were something inherently foolish in what is simple, or

---

[a]White here plays on "I'm Gonna Wash That Man Right Out of My Hair" from the musical comedy *South Pacific* (1949) by Richard Rodgers and Oscar Hammerstein.

[b]Only superficially relevant.

natural. The human brain is about to turn certain functions over to an efficient substitute, and we hear of a robot that is now capable of handling the tedious details of psychoanalysis, so that the patient no longer need confide in a living doctor but can take his problems to a machine, which sifts everything and whose "brain" has selective power and the power of imagination. One thing leads to another. The machine that is imaginative will, we don't doubt, be heir to the ills of the imagination; one can already predict that the machine itself may become sick emotionally, from strain and tension, and be compelled at last to consult a medical man, whether of flesh or of steel. We have tended to assume that the machine and the human brain are in conflict. Now the fear is that they are indistinguishable. Man not only is notably busy himself but insists that the other animals follow his example. A new bee has been bred artificially, busier than the old bee.

So this day and this century proceed toward the absolutes of conve-   4
nience, of complexity, and of speed, only occasionally holding up the little trumpet (as at Christmas time) to be reminded of the simplicities, and to hear the distant music of the hound. Man's inventions, directed always onward and upward, have an odd way of leading back to man himself, as a rabbit track in snow leads eventually to the rabbit. It is one of his more endearing qualities that man should think his tracks lead outward, toward something else instead of back around the hill to where he has already been; and it is one of his persistent ambitions to leave earth entirely and travel by rocket into space, beyond the pull of gravity, and perhaps try another planet, as a pleasant change. He knows that the atomic age is capable of delivering a new package of energy; what he doesn't know is whether it will prove to be a blessing. This week, many will be reminded that no explosion of atoms generates so hopeful a light as the reflection of a star, seen appreciatively in a pasture pond. It is there we perceive Christmas—and the sheep quiet, and the world waiting.

E. B. White 1899–1985. Pulitzer prize–winning man of letters and writer of essays and poems. White was a contributing editor of *The New Yorker* and columnist for *Harper's.* He has written 21 books, including essay collections such as *One Man's Meat;* books of humor, such as *Is Sex Necessary?* (with James Thurber); children's classics, like *Charlotte's Web;* and perhaps the most famous rhetoric ever, *The Elements of Style* (with William Strunk).

The Chicago Cubs, Overdue

George Will

A reader demands to know how I contracted the infectious conserva- 1
tism for which he plans to horsewhip me. So if you have tears, gentle
reader, prepare to shed them now[a] as I reveal how my gloomy temperament received its conservative warp from early and prolonged exposure to
the Chicago Cubs.

The differences between conservatives and liberals are as much a 2
matter of temperament as ideas. Liberals are temperamentally inclined to
see the world as a harmonious carnival of sweetness and light,[b] where
good will prevails, good intentions are rewarded, the race is to the swift,[c]
and a benevolent Nature arranges a favorable balance of pleasure over
pain. Conservatives (and Cub fans) know better.

Conservatives know the world is a dark and forbidding place where 3
most new knowledge is false, most improvements are for the worse, the
battle is not to the strong, nor riches to men of understanding,[d] and an
unscrupulous Providence consigns innocents to suffering. I learned this
early.

Out in central Illinois, where men are men and I am native, in 1948, 4
at age seven, I made a mad, fateful blunder. I fell ankle over elbows in love
with the Cubs. Barely advanced beyond the bib-and-cradle stage, I plighted
my troth[e] to a baseball team destined to dash the cup of life's joy from my
lips.

Spring, earth's renewal, a season of hope for the rest of mankind, 5
became for me an experience comparable to being slapped around the
mouth with a damp carp. Summer was like being bashed across the bridge
of the nose with a crowbar—ninety times. My youth was like a long rainy
Monday in Bayonne, New Jersey.

---

[a]"If you have tears, prepare to shed them now." Antony showing the dead
Caesar's armor to the crowd. *Julius Caesar* (III,ii,174).

[b]"Sweetness and light." Phrase originated by Jonathan Swift in *The Battle of
Books* (1704) and popularized by Matthew Arnold in *Culture and Anarchy* (1869).

[c]Allusion to *Ecclesiastes* 9.11: "The race is not to the swift, nor the battle to
the strong . . . nor yet riches to men of understanding."

[d]A contrasting continuation of the allusion to *Ecclesiastes* 9.11.

[e]"Plighted my troth." Literally, pledged my truth, my loyalty; similar to
phrase in traditional Protestant marriage ceremony.

Each year the Cubs charged onto the field to challenge anew the 6
theory that there are limits to the changes one can ring on pure incompetence. By mid-April, when other kids' teams were girding for Homeric battles[f] at the top of the league, my heroes had wilted like salted slugs[g] and begun their gadarene descent[h] to the bottom. By September they had set a mark for ineptness at which others—but not next year's Cubs—would shoot in vain.

Every litter must have its runt, but my Cubs were almost all runts. 7
Topps baseball bubblegum cards always struggled to say something nice about each player. All they could say about the Cubs' infielder Eddie Miksis was that in 1951 he was tenth in the league in stolen bases, with eleven.

Like the boy who stood on the burning deck whence all but he had 8
fled,[i] I was loyal. And the downward trajectory of my life was set. An eight-year-old could not face these fires without being singed, unless he had the crust of an armadillo, and how many eight-year-olds do?

Of the sixteen teams that existed in 1949, all have since won league 9
championships—all but the Cubs. And which of the old National League teams was first to finish in tenth place behind even the expansion teams? Don't ask. Since 1948 the Cubs have played more than 6,000 hours of losing baseball. My cruel addiction continued. In 1964 I chose to do three years of graduate study at Princeton because Princeton is midway between Philadelphia and New York—two National League cities. All I remember about my wedding day in 1967 is that the Cubs dropped a doubleheader.

Only a team named after baby bears would have a shortstop named 10
Smalley—a righthanded hitter, if that is the word for a man who in his best year (1953) hit .249. From Roy Smalley I learned the truth about the word "overdue." A portrait of this columnist as a tad would show him with an ear pressed against a radio, listening to an announcer say "The Cubs have the bases loaded. If Smalley gets on, the tying run will be on deck. And Smalley is overdue for a hit."

It was the most consoling word in the language, "overdue." It meant: 11
in the long run, everything is going to be all right. No one is really a .222 hitter. We are all good hitters, all winners. It is just that some of us are, well, "overdue" for a hit, or whatever.

Unfortunately, my father is a righthanded logician who knows more 12
than it is nice to know about the theory of probability. With a lot of help from Smalley, he convinced me that Smalley was not "overdue." Stan

---

[f]Battles between the great heroes that Homer describes in the *Iliad* and the *Odyssey*.

[g]Salting slugs (shell-less snails) draws the moisture from them.

[h]A headlong descent reminiscent of the leap the herd of swine took over the cliff at Gadara after Jesus had driven the demons out of a person and into the swine (*Matthew* 8.28–32).

[i]"The boy stood on the burning deck/Whence all but he had fled." Opening lines of the poem "Casabianca" by Felicia Dorothea Hermans (1793–1838).

Musial batting .249 was overdue for a hot streak. Smalley batting .249 was doing his best.

Smalley retired after eleven seasons with a lifetime average of .227. He was still overdue. 13

Now once again my trained senses tell me: spring is near. For most of the world hope, given up for dead, stirs in its winding linen.[j] But I, like Figaro,[k] laugh that I may not weep. Baseball season approaches. The weeds are about to reclaim the trellis of my life. For most fans, the saddest words of tongue or pen[l] are: "Wait 'til next year." For us Cub fans, the saddest words are: "This is next year." 14

The heart has its reasons[m] that the mind cannot refute, so I say: Do not go gently into this season, Cub fans; rage, rage against the blasting of our hopes.[n] Had I but world enough, and time, this slowness, Cubs, would be no crime.[o] But I am almost halfway through my allotted three-score-and-ten[p] and you, sirs, are overdue. 15

George Will Born 1941. Pulitzer prize–winning political columnist. Former college instructor and congressional aide, Will is now a Washington-based writer for *Newsweek* and the *National Review* and a syndicated columnist for the *Washington Post*. Will, who comes from a family including scholars and ministers, is known for his intellectual honesty, his wit, and his political conservatism. This article was originally published in *Newsweek,* July 11, 1977.

---

[j]The cloth in which, traditionally, a body was wrapped for burial.

[k]Hero of Rossini's opera *The Barber of Seville.*

[l]The complete quotation by James Barrie reads: "Of all sad words of tongue or pen, / The saddest are these—It might have been."

[m]*Le coeur a ses raisons,* from *Pensées (Thoughts)* by Blaise Pascal (1623–1662).

[n]Will plays on Dylan Thomas's poem to his dying father, "Do Not Go Gentle": "Do not go gentle into that good night. / Rage, rage against the dying of the light."

[o]A play on Andrew Marvell's poem "To His Coy Mistress": "Had we but world enough and time, / This coyness, Lady, were no crime."

[p]According to the Bible, "The days of our years are three score and ten, or by reason of strength, four score" [Psalm 110.10].

U.S. Blacks and a Free Market

Walter Williams

1   Does black socioeconomic progress necessarily depend upon whether blacks are liked by whites? Does it depend on the continuance of massive federal expenditures?

2   Well, if you asked the self-appointed black spokesmen, the answer to these questions would be "yes." But before we all agree, there are some important issues that must be raised. One issue is why is it that black entry, *en masse,*[a] into the mainstream of American society has these requirements, when it was not a condition for other racial groups? How do blacks differ from these other minorities?

3   One of the most distinguished features of American society is that we are a nation of racial minorities. What's more, casual reading of American history will show that none of these minorities was welcomed to our shores with open arms. They all faced varying degrees of open hostility and disadvantage. One need not go back too far in history to see in ads, "No Irish need apply," or, "Any color or country, except Irish." At one time Orientals were denied land ownership through the Alien Exclusion Act.[b] Japanese citizens were imprisoned.[c] Jews faced centuries of persecution and discrimination, which was not completely relieved when they came to our country.

4   The point of these observations is not that of determining who received the worst treatment. Nor is it to minimize the legacy of black slavery and disenfranchisement. The point *is* to question propositions concerning black socioeconomic progress which have now received an axiomatic status.

5   Some people attempt to explain away black difficulties by pointing out that blacks are a readily identifiable group and hence easily discriminated against. Well, what about Orientals? They are easily identified. But by virtually any standard of socioeconomic success, Orientals are at the top

---

[a]As a group (French).

[b]The Alien Land Acts of 1913 and 1920 in California (and similar acts in other states) provided that Orientals who were not citizens could not own property.

[c]In the fear-filled days following the Japanese bombing of Pearl Harbor in 1941, Japanese-Americans on the west coast were forced to go to internment camps.

of the ladder. Twenty-five percent of Orientals are professional workers compared to 15 percent for the general population. They have the second highest level of educational achievement. In addition, social disorganization among Orientals, as manifested by crime, juvenile delinquency and dependency, is lower than any other population group.

It is fairly certain that societal love cannot explain the assimilation of past disadvantaged groups. It is without any doubt at all that massive Department of Health, Education and Welfare (HEW) expenditures and affirmative action did not play a role. If we are not to subscribe to racist doctrines of group inferiority and dependence, the question still remains: How do blacks differ from past disadvantaged groups? 6

One of the major differences between blacks and other minorities is the kind of economic system they faced when they became franchised and urbanized. Minorities of the past faced a system of unfettered free enterprise. For example, a poor, uneducated Italian immigrant in the 1920s in New York could own and operate a taxi as a means to upward mobility. All he needed was industry, ambition, and a used car with the word "Taxi" written on it. Today, a black, Hispanic, or for that matter anyone else, seeking the same path to upward mobility would find that he needs more than a car, industry and ambition. He would have to buy a taxi license which costs $60,000. 7

Yesterday's disadvantaged could effectively acquire skills. Many jobs used a piece rate as a form of compensation and there was no federally mandated minimum-wage law. What this meant was that a person could be low-skilled and still employable. Being employable meant a chance of upgrading skills and income. For today's disadvantaged minorities such a chance is reduced. The minimum-wage law has the full force of a law which says, "If you cannot produce $3.10 worth of goods and services per hour, you shall never be employed." The effect of this law is revealed by the scandalous rate of unemployment among black youths. 8

A low-skilled person of the past could just walk up to a building site and offer his labor services. Today he must be a member of a union which has little incentive to grant him membership. Similarly, occupational licensing has an exclusionary effect. Historically, only the learned professions were licensed (doctors, lawyers and ministers); today there are over 500 licensed occupations—including poodle trimmer, peddlers and tree-trimmers. Numerous economic studies show that the effect of licensing is that of restricting entry and raising incomes of practitioners. 9

Therefore, what has happened is that when blacks received the franchise, they found that many markets were closed and hence the traditional sources of upward mobility. For too many blacks dependency has been substituted for self-initiative for lack of a better insight into the problems that they face. This misunderstanding has led their leadership to preside over the formulation of the first permanent welfare group in America's history. Ironically, this leadership, perhaps unwittingly, solidly supports 10 labor laws that seriously handicap the most disadvantaged while it vociferously supports other laws which increase dependence.

What disadvantaged people need are freer markets and a return to the 11 principles of the Bill of Rights—principles which the Supreme Court of the 1930s threw out when they gave the state and federal governments greater control over the individual's economic life. Black people need a fair chance to compete—nothing more and nothing less.

Walter Williams   Teacher and writer, Williams serves as Professor of Economics at Temple University, writes a syndicated newspaper column, and has been acclaimed as a leading voice for the new black conservatives. This article was originally published in the *Cincinnati Enquirer* (May 1980).

STUDENT PAPERS

Part Four also contains a group of papers from typical freshman students. They are all competent papers chosen for the variety of topics and techniques they exemplify. They have been included at the request of readers who are interested in how other students fulfill their writing assignments. (You will find other student essays serving as models for critical analyses (page 381) and research papers (page 347). Furthermore, many of the exercises throughout the text are at least partly student-composed, including the essays from which the sentence-combining Try It Outs were derived.)

PEASANT WORK AND PLAY IN MEDIEVAL FRANCE

Bret Gilbert

The life of the ninth-century peasant farmer was   1
truly a hard one. Most of the peasant's waking hours were
devoted to farming. He worked the fields year round from
sun up to sun down. His family worked equally hard year
round also. His very existence seemed to be for work.
Nevertheless, there was more to his life. Despite his tremendously hard and long hours, he still found some time
for leisure and enjoyment.

The peasant farmer's work was not only hard, but most   2
of it was done for someone else. Since most of his work was
part of his feudal obligation, he had little to show for
his trouble. We learn from the estate book of Irminon, the
Abbot of St. Germain, that each of the Abbey peasants was
required to do two types of labor:

> The first was field work: every year each man was
> bound to do a fixed amount of ploughing on the domain
> land . . . and also to give what was called a corvée,
> that is . . . an unfixed amount of ploughing, which
> the steward could demand every week when it was
> needed (812-13).

The second kind of labor required of the farmer was   3
called "handwork." The estate book specifies that "he had
to help repair buildings, or cut down trees, . . . or carry
loads"--anything, in fact, which wanted doing and which
the steward told him to do (815-17). The wives of these
farmers were also required to donate their work. According to the estate book, this work consisted of "spin[ning]

445

cloth or . . . mak[ing] a garment for the big house every year" (822).

The peasants' entire week, however, was not devoted to work. Upon the urging of the church, Charlemagne made a decree that was later renewed by his son that "no servile works should be done on Sundays, neither shall men perform their rustic labours" (in Faigniez, 51). The church meant these days when the people were freed from work to be reserved for going to church. But, as Eileen Power tells us, the peasant farmer was not happy with simply going to church on these days and then going home afterwards: "They used to spend their holidays in dancing and singing and buffoonery. . . . They were very merry and not at all refined, and the place they always chose for their dances was the churchyard" (30). Thus, on Sundays and holy days, for a short time, the peasants forgot about their work and just rejoiced in the pleasure of the moment, not worrying about the field they had to plow the next day. 4

Another release the farmer had from his arduous labor was the annual Great Fair of St. Denys, held outside the gates of Paris for an entire month. It was not unusual for the peasants to visit several times. Little booths with open fronts were set up by merchants from all over the world. In his <u>Life of Charlemagne</u>, the Monk of St. Gall describes the finery of the Frankish merchants who 5

> strutted in robes made of pheasant-skins and silk;
> or of the necks, backs, and tails of peacocks in
> their first plumage. Some were decorated with purple
> and lemon-coloured ribbons; some were wrapped round
> with blankets and some in ermine robes (149).

The Monk of St. Gall also described the excitement of the fair where one could hear "a hundred dialects and 6 tongues" and jokes and songs from all over the world (81-82). So the annual fair was also a place where the peasant farmer could forget his problems and simply enjoy life.

Though the medieval peasant was doomed to a life of hard work, he also had those beloved Sundays, holidays, and fair days. On these days the task at hand was not ploughing or cutting; it was singing, dancing, and laughing. And we can well believe he put enough energy into these few days to equal all the energy he put into ploughing the rest of the year.

7

List of Works Cited

Abbot Irminon. <u>Roll of Abbey St. Germain</u>, 811-826. Paris, 1886-95.

Faigniez, G., ed. <u>Documents relatifs de l'Histoire de l'Industrie et du Commerce en France</u>. Paris, [date unknown].

Monk of St. Gall. "Life of Charlemagne," <u>Early Lives of Charlemagne</u>. Ed. A. J. Grant. London: King's Classics, 1907.

Power, Eileen. "The Peasant Bodo" in <u>Medieval People</u>. London: Penguin Books, 1939.*

---

*All the material in this essay was derived from Power or from Power's documented quotations.

THERE'S NO PLACE LIKE HOME
Cheryl Jacobs

Ah! College life! No more peas or spinach, all the   1
ice cream I can eat. Staying out until 3:00 a.m. if I want
to. And no more fat jokes or washing dishes. This is the
life!

Or so I thought, until the fateful day about two   2
weeks after my arrival at this University when I discovered that my evergrowing bag of dirty clothes was not
going to get clean sitting in my closet. As I stuffed the
first load of clothes into that sinister looking machine
(that costs 50 cents of my own money), the realization
dawned on me that for the first time in my life I was really
on my own. Slowly I realized that I would never return to
that happy, secure, paid-for life with my parents. My future rested in my own hands now, and my life would never be
the same again. As I thought of this fact, standing in
front of that howling, dancing machine, the meaning of the
saying "You can never go home again," suddenly came clear
to me.

These words carry a special meaning for me because I   3
have never seen the house that I will be returning to at
Christmas. For only two weeks after my arrival at college,
my family moved from Beavercreek, Ohio to Washington,
D.C., and I was unable to accompany them. I returned to
Beavercreek over the recent midterm break, and I found
that I was now just a visitor, an outsider. My beloved home

now belonged to someone else. As I drove down that familiar street, I was mildly surprised and a little sad to see
my old house without the little orange Winnebago in the
driveway. The familiar garage was still messy, but with
someone else's junk. But when I saw an empty brick wall
where my father's pride and joy, a beautiful climbing
rose, had once stretched proudly, I was genuinely hurt. It
was hard for me to accept the fact that _my_ room was filled
with strange furniture and that _my_ closet held someone
else's clothes. It was sad to realize that my old home was
now just another house and Beavercreek was now just another town.

   I think often about my family at our new home in Wash-   4
ington D.C., and I realize that they will be different
also. Not because they have changed so much, but because I
have. These first few months at college have educated and
matured me in many ways. I am no longer that naive girl who
came to college last August, still looking at the world
through rose-colored glasses. That young girl made many
friends during her first carefree weeks of college--only
later to realize the superficiality of our relationships
and the simplistic social goals most of these people cher-
ished. I discovered that not every smile offered the
warmth and companionship of the friends I had left behind
and that glib words of promised friendship did not always
spring from the sort of solid values given me by my family.

   In addition, my good fortune and the optimism born of   5
it that had always sheltered me in the past had received a
great blow. One weekend, while visiting my sister at Ohio
State University, I witnessed two brutal accidents. In

the first, on our way to the stadium, we saw the bloodied and no longer human-looking remains of someone who minutes before may also have been traveling to the stadium. In the second, the disentangling of jersey-shirted bodies after an especially rough pile-up left one player motionless on the field. He never moved again, and he had been my friend. These accidents, which occurred within the time span of twenty minutes, forced me to see how cruel and how temporary life can be. It was time to grow up and face the reality of the world.

The words "you can never go home again" have a special meaning for me and I believe in them. Although it is hard to leave the security of my childhood behind, I know that it is for the best. I am looking forward to my future with new optimism and I know that even though I can never really go home again, I will always carry with me the comforting memory of my past; and I will make a new home for myself here, at this University and wherever my future may lead me.

THE ROOT OF ALL EVIL

Sheila Kenney

All Americans love to eat sugar. Even the most con-   1
scientious dieter may indulge every once in a while, even
though he knows that it is not good for him. But when the
stomach is growling, and a cherry pie has just been taken
out of the oven, still hot and spreading its sweet, fruity
aroma throughout the house, how could anyone in his right
mind refuse? Or for that matter, how could anyone refuse a
sundae dripping with strawberries and whipped cream? Or a
freshly baked donut smothered with chocolate and nuts? Or
a . . . ? Or a . . . ? The list goes on and on. So many of
America's favorite foods are composed of sugar. The typical American, however, does not realize just how much
sugar he consumes in the course of a normal day, and how
harmful this is to his health.

To prove just how much sugar Americans consume in   2
their lives, let's examine the types of food that the typical American eats in the span of 24 hours, starting with
the first meal of the day. Some Americans enjoy a good
wholesome, healthy breakfast of eggs, bacon, toast, and
juice. But what about those who don't have the time to sit
down for breakfast? They are content to eat a hastily
grabbed doughnut, Pop Tart, or a piece of last night's
leftover dessert. We all know that coffee is not coffee
without a teaspoon or two of sugar; toast is just not the
same without jelly; and cereal just doesn't taste good if

it's not smothered with sugar. Cereal is a type of breakfast food that most kids and mothers enjoy. Kids like it
because it's fun to eat and it tastes good. Moms like it
because it's easy and quick to prepare, and because their
kids like it. Have you ever picked up a box of cereal and
read its ingredients? Most cereals are practically dripping with sugar. Think about some of the popular brand
names of cereals. There are Sugar Pops, Sugar Frosted
Flakes, and Super Sugar Crisps, to name a few. All of them
contain the word "sugar" in their names. Of course, there
are some good nutritious cereals, such as Quaker Oatmeal,
Wheaties, and Life, which do not contain sugar. These cereals are dull and tasteless, so we solve this problem by
adding a little sugar or fruit to liven them up. Sugar!
Sugar! Sugar! This is only the beginning of the day, a day
in which three times this amount of sugar will be consumed.

After the typical American has eaten breakfast and   3
has gone to work or school, the hunger pains start again at
around the middle of the day. Lunch is usually a very quick
meal because of the short time allowed for those punching
a time clock and those who are between classes. Lunchpack-
ing is the easiest and most practical way of getting a good
meal. The typical lunchbox meal consists of a sandwich, a
piece of fruit, and a popular prepackaged snack, such as
Hostess Twinkies, Hostess Fruit Pies, and Little Debbie
Oatmeal Cakes. Again, sugar is prominent in the midday
meal.

On the way home from work or school, the typical   4
American may munch on a candy bar or drink a can of pop to

tide him over until suppertime. Supper is usually the typical American's most nutritious meal of the day. This meal
usually consists of a meat, vegetable, and a type of
bread. Sugar is usually not present. It is after the meal
is over and digested that sugar rears its ugly head. This
time it is in the form of Jell-O, pudding, cake, pie and
ice cream.

After examining how much Americans depend on sugar   5
in their daily diets, try to imagine how much damage the
long-term consumption of sugar must do to the physical
well-being of the typical American. It is easy to see what
sugar does to him when he struggles to zip up a pair of
pants that used to fit, and when he finds himself huffing
and puffing after walking up a relatively short flight of
stairs. Doctors despair at the consumption of sugar in the
diet because of the strain that extra weight puts on the
heart. Dentists despair at the consumption of sugar in the
diet because it promotes cavities and gum disease.

So the next time you feel those all too familiar hun-   6
ger pains coming on, instead of reaching for a quick,
ready-to-eat, sugary snack, why don't you try a nice juicy
apple, some crisp celery and carrot sticks, or some good
mild cheese and crackers. Your doctor and dentist will appreciate it, but most importantly, your body will too.

THE TECHNOLOGY-RESISTANT AMISH

Michael Reveal

The Amish are a slow-changing, distinctive cultural   1
group who place a premium on cultural stability rather
than change. Some people look at the Amish and consider
them backward, but actually they just want to be separated
from the world because they like a life of simplicity.
Their life is not affected by fads, material wealth, or
modern technology. They stay away from technology and
modern conveniences to reinforce their ideas that hard
work is necessary for the well-being of the mind and body.
But even though they believe strongly in hard work and its
benefits for the body, a still more important reason they
ignore technology is their strong religious faith and
ties to family and community. The Amish believe it better
to live a pure and spiritually clean life than to have the
benefits of modern society. Although the Amish have re-
sisted what Alvin Toffler calls the second technology
wave, and are not even considering the third wave, they
continue to prosper and in their farming are very competitive with their technologically advanced counterparts.

The roots of the Amish faith reach back to 16th-   2
century Switzerland where the Anabaptists, preachers of
adult baptism, were persecuted for nonconformism, and
forced to emigrate. They emigrated to all parts of the
U.S., the most distinct area being Lancaster County of
Pennsylvania. This area is blessed with some of the rich-

est soil in the nation and a climate ideal for farming. Let me take for my example the Amish who settled in this area.

Perhaps the most important general purpose of the Amish is to maintain a spiritual community separate from the world and close to the soil. Maintaining their spiritual community is accomplished rather easily because their lives are centered on their church community. This strict religious community causes obvious distinctions among the Amish which are best summarized by John Hostetler: "The Amish have a distinctive way of dress, their own language (Pennsylvania Dutch), a strong family unit, and a belief in appropriate technology" (61). The Amish are often called "plain people" because the clothes they wear are of plain fabric. For instance, the men are allowed only the different plain colors of black, grey, navy blue; while the women and children can wear a large variety of colors but only in dull shades. The fasteners on the outer clothing have to be hook and eye or buttons, but not zippers. To the Amish men zippers are too new and modern. All of these habits are basically intended to serve as symbols which are intended to form a separation. Hostetler explains:

> The shared conventions are given sacred sanction and biblical justification: unser satt leit (our sort of people) are distinguishable from Enlische leit (English people) or anner satt leit (other people) (138).

Ultimately, Amish clothing may be the most important way Amish can fight to stay different in the modern world and also to conform with old religious beliefs.

Their strict spiritual beliefs and emphasis on simplicity limit the Amish to using only horse- or mule-drawn machinery. For example, they use tractors only as sources of power for other machines, not for field work. And these tractors must be specially equipped, as Kline explains: "fitted with steel-treaded wheels so that they cannot be driven on roads in place of cars" (63). If Amish men are doing jobs such as baling hay that require mechanized power in the field, they use gasoline or diesel engines mounted on horse-drawn wagons. This method is directly related to some of the earliest mechanized agriculture methods, long outmoded by the development of rubber-treaded tractors and self propelled farm machinery. The same tasks are accomplished on modern farms by technically sophisticated machinery in about one-third the time.

Nonetheless, the Amish have proven their life of religious simplicity helps increase the quality of their products. Eventually, the higher quality of their goods makes them financially competitive with the larger quantities produced by modern farms. The most obvious example occurs when the Amish market their livestock. The highest quality of livestock is considered "premium" or "choice" on the quality grade-scale. The Amish livestock very rarely, if ever, receive a grade below "choice," and thus bring top prices.

The Amish find that these premium prices are necessary to continue their farming tradition. For example, an Amish farmer is expected to help his son and sons-in-law buy farms of their own when they become of age. This custom causes economic pressure, as an Amish farmer points out: "The biggest problem is high land prices. We might be at fault for that. We're increasing in population, but we don't like to spread out." (Quoted in Lee, 498) Douglas Lee further explains that when farmers bid for nearby land for their children, "prices have skyrocketed as high as $10,000 an acre." But the successful Amish farmers can afford the price.

The Amish people are a tightknit society, fighting hard to maintain their unique spiritual community closely related to the soil. Despite their rejection of any sort of technology, their strict adherence to a spiritually based work ethic has resulted in premium livestock and financial prosperity. Their success may be because the production of premium livestock is not their most important goal. As Lee states: "For the Plain People of Lancaster, Pennsylvania, success means children who join the church and carry on raising the most important crop on the farms: the next generation" (519).

7

Works Cited

Hostetler, John A. Amish Society. Baltimore, MD: The Johns Hopkins Press, 1968.

Lee, Douglas. "The Plain People of Pennsylvania," National Geographic, (April 1984), 492-519.

Kline, D. "Amish Farming: The Gentle Way of Life," Saturday Evening Post (March 1983), 62-63.

"THE BLUES DON'T KNOCK ON NOBODY'S DOOR"*
Elizabeth Jane Stein

The Defoe County Mental Health Center is an attrac-   1
tive, yellow frame building much like the homes surrounding it on the block. Inside, the feeling is informal and
relaxed, almost homelike. Other than the sign outside,
only the rack of drug information pamphlets and the reception desk give any clue to the Center's function. The nonclinical atmosphere is intentional and helpful, according to Becky P., PhD, Coordinator of Consultation and
Education for the Center. It is part of the goal of making
mental health services an integral part of the community
it serves.

Dr. P. attributes the beginning of the movement to-   2
ward community mental health centers to the Kennedy administration. However, she says, "Up to about five years
ago, most people depended primarily on a state hospital
for treatment." But with the recent release of thousands
of patients from state hospitals, the need for affordable
and accessible care in the community has increased considerably. Although community mental health centers are
not securing the level of government funding once available to state mental hospitals, in many ways community
health care comes closer to meeting the needs of the emotionally ill.

*Title of a song by Sid Wyche and John Denioa; Ragmop,
BMI.

Unfortunately, funding to the community mental   3
health centers has not kept pace with this need. Fees at
Defoe are on a sliding basis and run anywhere from $5.00 or
$10.00 to a maximum of $48.00 per hour. "But only one or
two people a year pay that much though that represents the
actual cost of an hour of treatment," Dr. P. said. Local,
state, and federal funds are supposed to fill the gap, but
they do not even come close. According to Dr. P., "There
has been no increase in funds to community health centers
proportional to the decline in state hospital population." She is hopeful that the situation will improve "as
the system evolves." But the bottom line remains that the
community health center is required to provide services
for people regardless of their ability to pay.

Despite the funding difficulties, delivering mental
health service on a community, outpatient basis has some
built-in advantages. The individual is treated within his
or her environment and is helped to adjust to living
within the community. This is an improvement over hospi-
talization, which tends to isolate the patient, making
eventual reentry into the community difficult. Also the
individual treated on an outpatient basis can better take
advantage of the potential support system of family and
friends.

Community mental health centers can also meet the   4
particular needs of the communities they serve. The Defoe
County Mental Health Center serves two distinct popula-
tions: people from the rural, farming community that sur-
rounds the Center and college students from nearby Defoe
College.

The Center's rural clients face some stresses unique 5
to rural life. "Agricultural life tends to tie family and
business together," Dr. P. says. "When you cannot have
clear separations between work, home, and family, you may
run into a problem." Rural life also means "more limita-
tion in expressing individual differences. There is a
need to conform to a rigid community standard and to hide
what's bothering you." Furthermore, living in a rural
village or town presents a problem of privacy. As Dr. P.
states:

> If you see a psychiatrist in, say, Cincinnati, no one
> will know about it. But in our small town, people
> know in spite of our efforts to protect privacy. They
> might see your car parked outside or see you walk in.
> Or the receptionist might be your uncle's wife.

The Center also gets a significant representation of 6
clients from Defoe College. What kind of problems bring
them to the Center? According to Dr. P., "Late adolescence
and early adulthood is a transitional time of tremendous
stress around questions of mating, finances, drugs, alcohol, eating, depression, even suicide. Mainly it's a time
of confusion, of seeking a self-identity. And certainly
drinking and romantic breakups greatly increase the risk
of depression." The stresses that bring individuals to
the Center may differ, but the Center's goal remains constant: "To teach people to cope with their stresses in
more constructive ways."

This "holistic" approach is another move community 7
health centers take toward a humane and healthgiving approach; and it is a move away from the typical hospital approach which treats psychological problems as a mental
illness--a disease to be treated with medication. Not

only is Defoe "more selective and sophisticated in the use of medication" than most hospitals, but according to P., "we don't even use the term <u>mental illness</u>":

> I think it's a poor term. People need to take more responsibility for their mental state and take an active role in helping themselves. The word "illness" implies something that happens to people beyond their control.

In fact, the Defoe County Mental Health Center sees its role as teaching as much as treating individuals and the community as a whole. The main focus of Dr. P's job is educating and training the public in order to eliminate the stigma of mental illness. Stigma can isolate people who are experiencing problems and prevent others from seeking the counseling they need. The Center sponsors Mental Health Awareness Week, a Mental Health Fair, and provides speakers to groups and schools. By increasing public awareness and emphasizing constructive ways for people to deal with their life stresses, the Center hopes to dispense preventive health care to the Defoe County community and to demystify the subject of mental illness.

Thanks to community health centers like Defoe, the 8 goal of affordable and accessible health care in the community is becoming a reality and is expanding to move the mental health field in a more humanistic direction.

"The Blues Don't Knock on Nobody's Door"
Elizabeth Jane Stein

The Defoe County Mental Health Center is [1]
an attractive, yellow frame building much like
the homes surrounding it on the block. Inside,
the feeling is informal and relaxed, almost
homelike. Other than the sign outside, only
the rack of drug information pamphlets and the
reception desk give any clue to the Center's
function.

This nonclinical atmosphere is inten- [2]
tional and helpful, according to B.P., Ph.D.,
Coordinator of Consultation and Education for
the Center. It is part of the goal of making mental health services an integral part of the community in which it serves.

Dr. P. attributes the beginning of the [3]
movement toward community mental health centers to the Kennedy administration. However,
she said, "Up to about five years ago, most people depended primarily on a state hospital for
treatment." But with the recent release of
thousands of patients from state hospitals, the

First Draft

need for affordable and accessible care in the
community has increased considerably.

Unfortunately, funding to the community 4
mental health centers has not kept pace with
this need. According to their brochure, "Defoe
County Mental Health Center is a contract
agency of the Defoe County Mental Health Board
. . . and is supported by local, state, and federal moneys as well as fees and contributions.
But there has been no increase in funds to community health centers proportional to the decline in state hospital population."

At the moment, the Defoe County Mental 5
Health Center has the capacity to treat about
300 people at any given time. There is a staff of
thirteen, including a consulting psychiatrist,
and headed by a licensed clinical psychologist.
Fees are on a sliding basis and run anywhere
from $5.00 or $10.00 to a maximum of $48.00 per
hour, "but only one or two people a year pay that
much though that represents the actual cost of
an hour of treatment," Dr. P. said. "The bottom
line is that we are required to provide services
for people regardless of their ability to pay."

Another option most people don't realize 6
is that most insurance plans will pick up at

FIRST DRAFT

least a portion of the fees. Insurance reimbursements can be markedly less if you choose a non-M.D. therapist. It is a conflict involving the prerogatives of money and power," said P. It brings to mind the recent stir between doctors and nurse-practitioners, whose right to do routine tests has been repeatedly challenged in court.

According to Dr. P., "Most medical doctors 7 (including psychiatrists) in this country are white males. Most of the subsidiary roles (nurses, therapists, social workers) are filled by women, sometimes minority women. These people earn substantially less. And we have the typical conflicts of money, power, and male supremacy."

It is an ironic struggle. A recent article 8 by Eugene Meyer, "The War Between Doctors and Nurses" (<u>Family Circle</u>, November 13, 1984) illustrates this irony through interviews with doctors and nurses now embroiled in legal battles. Molly Billingsley, a teacher of nurses at George Mason University, said, "Alot of people have suddenly realized that doctors are treating their ulcers, but never even asking them about their life styles. . . . We talk about

FIRST DRAFT

stress-reduction programs and the like--things
many M.D.s never mention."

This "holistic" approach to treatment   9
represents the thinking of the Defoe County
Center as well. Not only are they "more selective and sophisticated in the use of medication," but according to P., "we don't even use
the term mental illness." Dr. P. continued:

> I think it's a poor term. People need to take
> more responsibility for their mental state.
> The word "illness" implies something that
> happens to a person, beyond their control.

Call it whatever you like--statistics show 10
psychological problems are at an epidemic level
nationwide. One statistic that might be surprising is this: there is more psychological
stress in rural than in urban areas. "The agricultural life tends to tie family and business
together," B.P. said. "It also means more limi-
tation in expressing individual differences."
There is a need to conform to a rigid community
standard and to hide what's bothering you.

Another problem concerns privacy. As Dr.   11
P. states:

> If you see a psychiatrist in, say, Cincin-
> nati, no one will know about it. But in our
> small town, people know in spite of our ef-
> forts to protect privacy. They might see

FIRST DRAFT

your car parked outside or see you walk in.
Or the receptionist might be your uncle's
wife.

This creates a reluctance to go for help.   12
The stigma of mental illness is beginning to
fade, but it's fading slower in rural areas. The
Defoe Center puts education of the public
first. As its brochure states, "We educate,
train, and consult [providing] speakers to
groups and schools." They also sponsor Mental
Health Awareness Week, and a Mental Health
Fair. Education is the main focus of B.P.'s job.

What kind of problems bring people to the   13
Center? Often the problems of adolescence. According to Dr. P., it "is a transitional time of
tremendous stress around questions of mating,
finances, drugs, alcohol, eating, depression,
even suicide. Mainly it's a time of confusion,
of seeking a self-identity."

The major trend among college and high   14
school students is a lessening of drug use and
an increase in alcohol abuse. Alcoholism is
considered the nation's second most prevalent
disease, estimated to claim some 10 million
Americans. The Center estimates that there are
some 1,898 alcoholics out of a population of
32,801 (1975 census) in Defoe County. "Studies

FIRST DRAFT

have shown," Dr. P. said, "that the younger the
age at which people begin to drink, the more
prone they are to become severe alcoholics." So
far, studies have shown that the most successful treatment for alcoholism remains Alcoholics Anonymous and groups based on their principles.

Another problem the Center is seeing more   15
and more are cases of child abuse and domestic
violence. The statistics are frightening. One
out of every four little girls and one out of
every seven little boys will be assaulted. "The
overwhelming majority of abusers are men," said
P. "They have more difficulty dealing with
stress and fewer outlets for release than women
do." Growing public awareness may be the first
step toward helping the situation. Dr. P is herself a frequent speaker at local seminars.

What about depression--is T.S. Elliot's   16
famous line "April is the cruelest month . . ."
in fact accurate? According to statistics, the
two hot spots of depression and potential suicide are indeed the spring and also the Holiday
Season.

"Spring is a loaded time," Dr. P. said.   17
"The whole "Love is in the air' syndrome can be

FIRST DRAFT

depressing if you don't feel it." Christmas is

difficult too because the expectation of jolli-

ness can make despair deep."

   Dr. P. summed up in this way: 18

> All mental problems are complicated. Most
> thoughtful mental health practitioners are
> eclectic, realizing there is no one cure-
> all. People benefit from insight, from med-
> ication, and most of all from the empathy of
> a therapist.
>   What is needed is that the therapist be
> optimistic and hopeful about the person he/
> she is treating. People may feel hopeless at
> a particular time in their life, but nobody
> is hopeless. Everyone can be helped if they
> just reach out for it.

PART
FIVE

Revision Guide

Part Five offers you advice on the problems that writers have found most troubling in syntax, usage, capitalization, punctuation, style, and spelling. Items considered vary from the definitions of the parts of speech to the spelling of the parts of irregular verbs. But they are all catalogued here together alphabetically so that you can find any item easily when you need it. Each item is listed under the name it is usually called. However, if you usually think of an item under another name, you will probably find it cross-indexed under that title as well. So when you have questions while editing a preliminary draft or while making corrections to difficulties your instructor has pointed out on a finished paper, chances are you can find the answers here in the Revision Guide.

A/An

A and *an* are both indefinite articles. Use *a* before nouns that begin with consonant sounds and *an* before nouns that begin with vowel sounds.

- *a* sample; *an* example
- *an* apple, *a* banana, *an* orange, *a* pear, and two grapes
- *a* horse, *an* honest man

See **Article.**

Abbreviations

Although abbreviations are immensely useful in bibliographic and technical writing and in note taking and personal correspondence, they are rarely appropriate in expository prose. In this sort of writing you should avoid abbreviations except for those few forms that have become standard. These include:

Abbreviations Followed by Periods

1. Titles when followed by a name (Mr. Benson, Mrs. Steinem, Dr. Einstein)
2. Degrees after a name (Jane Pitt, Ph.D., or M.D., or M.S.W.)
3. Initials (R. W. Kane, M. Dorinda Young)
4. Others, such as A.M. and P.M. (which may be capitalized if you choose); Jr., Sr.; m.p.h. (miles per hour), r.p.m. (revolutions per minute)

Abbreviations without Periods

1. Government agencies (FBI, CIA, HUD)
2. Radio or television call letters (WKRP, WNRK, CBS)
3. Acronyms (initials that spell a pronounceable word: CORE, WAVES, VISTA)

Abbreviations That You Should Not Use in Formal Writing

Faulty

1. Days (Sun.) or months (Jan.)
2. Given names (Geo. or Chas.) unless that is how a well-known person identifies himself or herself
3. Cities and states (N.Y.C. or Cal.), except the commonly used D.C. for District of Columbia
4. Words in addresses (St., N. Blvd.)
5. Courses of instruction (Soc. 101)
6. Words preceding a number (vol., p.)
7. Military, religious, or political titles (Col., Rev., Hon.)
8. Latin abbreviations. *For example* is preferable to *e.g.*, *that is* to *i.e.* Even in bibliographic work, *Ibid.* and *op. cit.* have, for the most part, become obsolete.

Rules for Using Abbreviations

1. Abbreviations should not interfere with the regular punctuation of the sentence. If an abbreviation falls at the end of a sentence, regular punctuation prevails—except for the period, which is not added.

   · Shall we come at 6 P.M.?
   · It's already 6 P.M.

   Do not space between the period and the final punctuation mark.
2. Identify abbreviations that may be unfamiliar. Most readers would recognize WAVES as the women's branch of the United States Navy, but in using less-well-known initials or acronyms, write the title fully once with the initials, and then abbreviate all further references. Two alternatives are:

   · Mr. Jenkins took over the DPW (Department of Public Works) in December. The DPW now employs four hundred people.
   · Mr. Jenkins took over the Department of Public Works (DPW) in December.

Above/Below

Writers sometimes refer to their work as if it were written on a single long page. When they say, "We have already discussed this point, *above,*" they mean that they have discussed it earlier in the work; and when they say "We will have cause to refer to this point *below,*" they are suggesting a later discussion. Because the metaphor of a single long page can be confusing, this usage is becoming obsolete, and you should probably avoid it in your own work.

Accept/Except

Accept means to take or receive. *Except* refers to an exclusion.

   · We *accept* everything *except* personal checks.

Access/Excess

Access is a noun that means "the ability to get at or use" or "to get into something or some place." It can also refer to the door or entrance itself. *Excess* means "more than enough" (*excess* energy) or "more than a certain amount or degree" (in *excess* of a million dollars).

   · In an *excess* of misplaced creativity, she gained *access* to the only copy of the final exam.

Acronyms

See **Abbreviations without Periods.**

Active/Passive

A sentence is in the *active* voice when it contains a verb which tells that its subject is actively doing or being something.

> · The *dog chased* his tail.

A sentence is in the passive voice when it contains a verb that tells that something is being done to or being suffered by its subject.

> · The *tail was chased* by the dog.

The passive version of a sentence is often more awkward than the active version, and frequently confusing and less direct. Because the agent of the action can be omitted in the passive, writers sometimes use this construction deliberately to obscure.

> · (active) The political *candidate suggested* that his opponent, J. S. Bigsby, was not as circumspect about his finances as he should be.
> · (passive) *It was suggested* that J. S. Bigsby was not as circumspect about his finances as he should be.

Avoid the passive whenever you can. Use it only when you really mean to put the emphasis on the deed rather than upon the doer:

> · The man *had been killed* in the night by a person or persons unknown.
> · The courtyard *had been ransacked.*

Adjectives

See pages 190 and 216–217. See also **Articles, Pronouns: Demonstrative**, and **Pronouns: Possessive**, all words that also function as adjectives.

Adjective Clauses

See pages 219 and 216–236. See also **Commas: Parenthetical** for appropriate punctuation.

Adverbs

See pages 191 and 230.

Adverb Clauses

See pages 192 and 230–238.

Adverbial Conjunctions

See **Conjunctions**.

Advice/Advise

Advice is a noun.

· My *advice*, Raquel, is to avoid contact sports.

Advise is a verb.

· I would *advise* you to learn to play bridge.

Affect/Effect

When used as verbs, *affect* and *effect* have similar—though not identical—meanings. *Affect* means "to influence" and is used primarily in the emotional sense. *Effect* means to bring about.

· How did Marjorie's speech *affect* you?
· He lowered prices to *effect* economic change.

Affect is not used as a noun except in a narrow, technical sense (in the field of psychology). *Effect,* when used as a noun, means "result":

· The price change had little economic *effect.*

Aggravate/Irritate

Irritate means to annoy or to chafe:

· Try not to *irritate* your boss before you request a raise.
· The buckle on the shoe began to *irritate* the child's foot.

Aggravate means to make worse an already bad situation or irritation.

· His boss's irritation was *aggravated* by his request for a raise.
· The sore on the child's foot was *aggravated* by the rubbing of the buckle.

Remember, *aggravation* occurs only when a situation is already painful, angry, or unpleasant.

Agreement: Pronouns with Antecedents

A pronoun takes the place of a noun. (See **Pronoun; Pronouns: Demonstrative; Pronouns: Indefinite; Pronouns: Interrogative; Pronouns: Personal; Pronouns: Reflexive**; and **Pronouns: Relative**.) Somewhere in the words preceding a pronoun there must be a definite word (or phrase) for which the pronoun is a substitute. The pronoun must point definitely to that word or phrase and, in the case of personal pronouns, must resemble this antecedent in number (singular: *she, he;* or plural: *they*) and gender (masculine: *he, him, his;* or feminine: *she, her*). In the case of relative pronouns, the pronoun must also agree in humanity (human: *who, whom;*

or nonhuman: *which*). Demonstrative pronouns also must agree with their antecedent in number (singular: *this, that;* or plural: *these, those*).

- Jack, *who* was dressed in *his* red jacket, Jill, *who* wore *her* knitted cap, and *their* dog, *which* was clad in *its* warm blanket, shivered in *those* biting winds *that* greeted them on *their* winter walk.

Gender Related Antecedents

(See also **Gender.**) A gender problem arises in choosing a singular pronoun to replace or point to an antecedent of indefinite sex.

- A student needs to know how much *he? she?* should study.

Although for many years it has been inappropriate to assume such antecedents are masculine, no neutral pronoun has yet been fully accepted. You should, therefore, avoid the difficulty if you can by rewording or using the plural:

- Student*s* have to know how much *they* should study.

If you cannot avoid the problem and must use the singular, you can alternate usage or, as a last resort, adopt the awkward *his/her* or *his or her* format. When "the student" you are writing about is really yourself, you may use the pronoun signifying your own gender.

Gender Related Antecedents: Compounds

Agreement in gender is clear when both elements of a compound antecedent are of the same sex.

- Neither *Jack* nor *Tom* could find *his* shoes.

The gender of the pronoun becomes a problem, however, when the sex of the antecedents differs.

- Neither *Jack* nor *Jill* could find *his* or *her* shoes.

His or her can become awkward. *Their,* being plural, would be incorrect in a *neither/nor* context (see **Agreement: Subject and Verb**). In such cases, it is again better to rewrite, making the antecedent clearly plural:

- *Both Jack and Jill* searched for *their* shoes without success.

Ghostly Antecedents

A ghostly antecedent must be made to appear in sentences like these:

INCORRECT: Sally saw all her friends at Christmas. It had all the qualities of a class reunion.

It refers to a meeting or party that is never mentioned. The antecedent of *it* is a "ghost" that might appear correctly in this form:

CORRECT: Sally saw all her friends at Christmas at a *party that* had all the qualities of a class reunion.

Ghosts of this sort, like all ghosts, should be avoided whenever possible. Never use pronouns vaguely to mean "all the stuff I just said." (For ways of avoiding this error, see pages 171–172, and 243.)

Group Noun Antecedents

Use singular demonstrative pronouns with all singular antecedents, even when they designate a group.

INCORRECT: These kind of shoes . . . Those kind of stockings . . .
CORRECT: *This* kind of shoes . . . *That* kind of stockings . . .
These kinds of hats . . . *Those* kinds of caps . . .

Hazy Antecedents

When your reader cannot be quite sure which of two nouns is the antecedent for a pronoun, you have a hazy antecedent.

· Dad told John *he* had an appointment with the dentist.

He could mean either *Dad* or *John.* Rephrase:

· Dad mentioned *John's* dental appointment to *him.*

Agreement: Subject and Verb

Subject and verb must agree in number; that is to say, a singular subject takes a singular verb and a plural subject takes a plural verb.

· This *student likes* classes. These *students like* weekends.

When a sentence is inverted to begin with *here* or *there,* the verb still agrees with the subject—even though the subject now follows the verb:

· Here *is* your *coat.* Here *are* your *coats.*
· There *are* two *people* in the boat. There *is* one *person* in the boat.

Errors in agreement commonly occur in four situations: when a phrase comes between a subject and verb, when the subject is compound, when the subject is a pronoun, and when a singular subject appears to be plural.

Subject Accompanied by a Phrase
Rule: The subject of a sentence *cannot* be part of a prepositional phrase. And, of course, the verb must match the subject.

· All the *legs* of the lamb *were broken.* (*Of the lamb* is a prepositional phrase.)

Compound Subject
Rule A: When a sentence has two or more subjects (either singular or plural) that are connected by *and,* make sure the verb is plural:

- Both *Janet and Phil fail* to realize how much their whispering annoys their professor.

Exception: When two nouns are coupled together in such a way that they represent one thing, they take a singular verb:

- *Peanut butter and jelly is* my favorite sandwich.

Rule B: When two or more singular subjects are connected by *or, nor,* or *but,* use a singular verb:

- Neither *Washington nor Jefferson is* my favorite president.
- Not only *Mr. Perry, but* also *his partner, was* away.

Rule C: When one of the subjects connected by *or, nor,* or *but* is singular and the other plural, the verb agrees with the closer subject.

- Neither *George nor* the *dragons are* ready to fight.
- Neither the *dragons nor George is* ready to fight.
- *Is* either *George or* the *dragons* really going to fight?

Rule D: Singular subjects followed by *as well as, in addition to, no less than,* or *together with* require a singular verb.

- *John* as well as his friend *regrets* the incident.

Pronoun Subject
Rule A: Pronouns that refer to a single being take a singular verb: *each, every, everyone, everybody, somebody, anybody, nobody, no one, any, anyone, anybody, either, neither.*

- Everybody seems happy today.

Rule B: *None* and *all* may take either singular or plural verbs depending upon what they refer to.

- *None* of the soldiers *are* willing to volunteer.
- *None* of the pie *has* been eaten yet.

Rule C: Pronouns that take a plural verb include *several, both, many,* and *few.*

- *"Many are called,* but *few are chosen."*

Rule D: When *it* is the subject of a sentence, the verb is always singular, regardless of what follows the verb.

- *It is* the New York Yankees.

Rule E: Personal Pronouns. When personal pronouns are used with the verb *to be (am, is, are, was, were),* the verb must also agree with its subject in person:

· *She was* saying again and again: *"I am* to be Queen of the Prom. *You are* to be my partner."

In the case of a compound subject, the verb agrees in person with the closer pronoun.

· Neither she nor *I am* wrong.

Singular Subject That Appears Plural
Rule: All singular subjects, however they appear, take singular verbs.

1. *Singular words that end in "s".* Examples of such nouns that are singular in meaning include *dynamics, electronics, ethics, news, economics, mumps.*

   · Electronics has become a major field of study.

2. *Titles.* A title takes a singular verb even though it uses a plural noun or pronoun.

   · *"Sixty Minutes" is* aired on Sundays.

3. *Numbers.* Plural numbers take a singular verb when they are used to indicate a total or a unit.

   · *A million dollars is* the prize.

4. *Collective Nouns.* Collective nouns (singular forms that represent more than one person or thing considered as a unit) take a singular verb.

   · The *swarm* of bees *is* heading this way.

Exception: Collective nouns take a plural verb when they are not considered as a unit, but this syntax seldom occurs.

· The *jury were* not in agreement

If that sort of sentence sounds awkward to you, rewrite it as:

· The *members* of the jury *were* not in agreement.

All Ready/Already

Each of these expressions has its own meaning. They are not interchangeable. *All ready* means completely prepared.

· He is *all ready* for Saturday's game.

Already refers to time.

· She had *already* studied for the quiz.

If you are still in doubt, test to see if you can break the expression to add words. If you can, you know to write *all ready*.

> TEST: We are *all* of us *ready*.

All Right

There is no word spelled *alright*.

> · It was *all right* with Attila if his troops were too tired to loot, but he did insist on a little pillaging.

All Together/Altogether

These two expressions have different meanings and are not interchangeable. *All together* means collectively, everyone at one time or place.

> · *All together* now—pull!

Altogether means completely.

> · Your proposal is *altogether* unacceptable.

If you are still in doubt, test to see if you can break the expression to add words. If you can, then you know to use *all together*.

> TEST: *All* of us *together* now . . .

Allusion/Illusion

An *illusion* is something that appears to be, but does not really exist. *Allusion* comes from the verb *to allude* and means "the act of making a reference" or the reference itself. *Allusion* also refers to imagery that contains this sort of reference. See page 285.

> · In her lecture the professor made an *allusion* to Macbeth's *illusion* of Banquo's ghost.

A Lot

A lot consists of two words. Though it is proper to write such sentences as "He ate a lot of beans," the expression is too informal for most serious essays.

"Although" Clause

"Although" clause is a shorthand way of referring to that portion of the working thesis statement which sets up the point of view that the thesis itself refutes. By extension, the term *"although" clause* can also refer to that portion of the composition which presents an alternative way of thinking. The model "although" clause fits the format:

· (Although) others say *x*, *y* is closer to the truth.
· (Despite) *x* to the contrary, *y* is true.
· *X* may be so in some instances, but *y* is more usually accurate.

While identifying the "although" clause is highly useful in discovering a thesis and setting up the structure of a composition, you will not necessarily want to use it in its exact phrasing in your finished compositions.

Alumna/Alumnus

Both of these words refer to a graduate of a school, or even to a person who once attended a particular school. *Alumna* is feminine (plural, *alumnae*). *Alumnus* is masculine (plural, *alumni*).

· Karen is an *alumna* of Oberlin, Ann and Sue are *alumnae* of Chicago, Dan is an *alumnus* of Michigan, and George and David are *alumni* of Case Western Reserve. They are all *alumni* of midwestern universities.

When sexes are mixed, use the masculine form.

Ambiguity

An ambiguous sentence is one that can be understood in more than one way.

FAULTY: The doctor told him that weekly visits would no longer be a good idea.

Without further explanation of that ambiguous sentence, the patient might deduce either that he need not see the doctor again or that he needs to see the doctor more often or less often. In such situations, rewrite.

Ambiguity can also result from faulty punctuation.

· Marty said, "Sally is dead."
· "Marty," said Sally, "is dead."

In such instances, punctuation changes everything—especially for Marty and Sally.

Among/Between

Between is used when referring to two people or things. If more than two are involved, you should use *among*.

· Richie and Lynn made plans to divide the money *between* them, but Robbie, Russ, Susan, and Ruth decided that the money should be divided *among* all of them.

Although some people think that *between you and I* sounds more elegant, the correct form is *between you and me.* It is true that, although correct, *between him and her* sounds terrible. Reword such awkward phrases.

An

See **A/An.**

Angry/Mad

If you want to convey in writing the idea of rage, irritation, or fury, you should use *angry* and not *mad. Mad* means "mentally ill or deranged."

· I am *angry* about his treatment of the poor. I must have been *mad* to have voted for him.

Antecedents

See **Agreement: Pronouns and Antecedents.**

Antithetical Balance

See **Balanced and Contrasting Parallelism.**

Antonym

An antonym is a word that means the opposite or almost the opposite of another word. The antonym of *big* might be *little, small, tiny, diminutive,* or any other word with similar meaning.

Antonyms may reflect opposite action (lose-find), qualities (light-dark), or gender (boy-girl, rooster-hen).

Anxious/Eager

Both words refer to anticipation, but *anxious* implies a worried, fearful anticipation and *eager* refers to a joyful and enthusiastic anticipation.

· Cheryl was *anxious* about her test scores.
· Chris was *eager* to learn to drive.

Apostrophe

An apostrophe (') is a mark of punctuation that has two functions: to replace the missing letters in contractions and to indicate possession.

1. Use the apostrophe to punctuate contractions.

   · cannot = can't; has not = hasn't; do not = don't; would not = wouldn't; he is = he's; we have = we've; it is = it's; they are = they're

Exception: will not = won't

2. Use an apostrophe to signify ownership by adding it *after* the person(s) or thing(s) that the object(s) belong(s) to. Add an *s after* the apostrophe if the owner is single or has a non-*s* plural. You do not need to add *s* if the plural already has one.

   · John's dog; Harry's hats; a house's chimney; a dog's tail, a woman's magazine, the houses' chimneys; the dogs' tails; women's magazines

Exception: Omit the apostrophe from *its* when it is used as a possessive pronoun.

   · *Its* fur was mussed.

See also **Double Possessive.**

Articles

An article is a part of speech, one of three words *(a, an,* and *the)* that modify a noun. Articles are often classed with adjectives as modifiers of nouns. *The* is a definite article. *A* is indefinite. *An* is the indefinite article used with nouns that begin with a vowel.

   · Jan drove *the* car.

The makes the sample sentence refer to a particular car, one that has been identified earlier in the composition. Such is not the case in the following examples:

   · Jan drove *a* car.
   · Jan drove *an* automobile.

Here no particular car or automobile is intended. It is the general idea of this kind of motor transportation that is important.

As/Like

As and *like* both convey the idea of comparison. *Like,* however, is a preposition that is followed by an object. *As* is a conjunction that introduces a clause containing a subject and a verb—although sometimes the verb is "understood."

   · She doesn't type *as* neatly as George [does].
   · He has a voice *like* a German shepherd's.

- He looks *like* his father.
- He does not work day and night *as* his father [does].

Like cannot mean *as if* or *as though*.

INCORRECT: He raised his fist like he was going to hit him.

Use *as if he were* to correct the sentence.

As/Since

As is an adverbial conjunction that either indicates comparison (see As/ Like) or suggests the passing of time. It does not imply causality. *As,* therefore, can mean *while,* but it should never be used to mean *since* or *because*.

INCORRECT: *As I had to wait,* I brought along a book.
CORRECT: I read a book *as I was waiting* in order to pass the time.
CORRECT: *Since I had to wait,* I brought along a book.

Assure/Ensure/Insure

All these words have the sense of providing sureness, certainty. *Assure* carries the idea of promise; it is frequently used to suggest avoiding worry or concern.

- I *assure* you that the monster is really dead.

Ensure means to make certain.

- This pass will *ensure* your admittance to the trial.

Insure almost always refers to the business of paying to protect the value of life or property.

- We tried to *insure* our house against mud slides, but the cost in California is too high.

Auxiliary Verbs

Auxiliary verbs combine with action verbs so that these verbs can express a greater variety of time and purposes. There are two kinds of auxiliary verbs: helping verbs and modals. Helping verbs are the forms of *be* and *have* that combine with present and past participles.

- Joey *was fighting*. Jane *has been playing* in the mud. Gina's mittens *were left* behind. Aunt Selma *will be tempted* to spank.

Modals include such verbs as *should, would, may, can, must, do*. They are used before the present-tense form of verbs as well as before verbs that have helping-verb attachments.

· Aunt Selma *would have been tempted* to spank the children, and *might* even *have spanked* them, if she *did* not *remember* the old saying: "You *can catch* more flies with honey than with vinegar."

Await/Wait

Await takes an object. You can *await* my *arrival, await* the baby's birth, *await* the *holidays. Wait* does not take an object. You just *wait.* But if there is an object to deal with, you can *wait for* something. *Wait on* means to serve (as in a restaurant). *Wait on* never means the same as *wait for:*

INCORRECT: Let's not *wait on* him to get here.
CORRECT: Let's not *wait for* him to get here.

Bad/Badly

Bad is an adjective, *badly* an adverb.

· The painter had done a *bad* job, and so the house was *badly* painted.

Problems arise when the word is used with verbs like *feel.* When *feel* is used as a linking verb, it takes a predicate adjective. Thus, *I feel bad* means I feel ill. (*I feel badly* suggests that something is wrong with my sense of touch.)

Balanced and Contrasting Parallelism

See pages 252–255.

Be

The verb *to be* is an irregular verb that, alone among the verbs in our language, has retained most of the Old English inflections. Even today, both the present and the past tense forms change with first, second, and third person in the singular and the plural.

I *am*	I *was*
You *are*	You *were*
He, she, or it *is*	He, she or it *was*
We *are*	We *were*
They *are*	They *were*

The past participle is *(have, has) been.* The verb *to be* is particularly important because not only is it the verb most often used in English, but it also combines with the participles of the other verbs to form other tenses and the passive voice. (See **Auxiliary Verbs; Active/Passive.**)

Begin—Irregular Verb

They begin; they began; they have begun.

Below

See **Above/Below**.

Beside/Besides

Beside means "at the side of." *Besides* means "furthermore" or "in addition to."

· I like to walk *beside* you. *Besides,* I have no other friends.

Between/Among

See **Among/Between**.

Biannual/Bimonthly/Biweekly

Biannual means once every two years. *Biennial* means the same. A *biennium* is a two-year period. *Bimonthly* means every two months. *Biweekly* means once every two weeks.

· Tony owned so many pieces of property that he could inspect them only *biannually.*

See also **Semiannual**.

Bite—Irregular Verb

They bite; they bit; they have bitten.

Blame for/Blame on

Blame on is incorrect.

INCORRECT: He *blamed* his stiffness *on* the required daily exercise. (He does not really mean to blame his stiffness.)

CORRECT: He *blamed* the required daily exercise *for* his stiffness. (Here the exercise rightly takes the blame.)

Brackets

Use brackets ([ ]) when you are quoting another author and wish to include your own editorial comment or to add a word or words to make that author's syntax conform to your own in the surrounding material.

In the Quotation

- By mid-April, when other kids' teams were girding for Homeric battles at the top of their league, my heroes [the Cubs] had wilted like salted slugs and begun their gadarene descent [like the headlong descent of the herd of swine at Gadara after Jesus had transferred to them the demons who had been bedeviling the local populace] to the bottom. (Will)
- My heroes had wilted like salted slugs and begun their gadarene descent to the bottom. [Note Will's use of classical and biblical imagery.]

In Your Text

- In "Chicago Cubs, Overdue," George Will speaks of the Cubs baseball team of his childhood as "[his] heroes [wilting] like salted slugs."

See also **Ellipsis Points** and pages 315, 352.

Break—Irregular Verb

They break; they broke; they have broken.

Bring—Irregular Verb

They bring flowers; they brought flowers; they have brought flowers.

Bring/Take

You *bring* something *here.* You *take* something *there.*

> INCORRECT: Red Riding Hood, *bring* your Grandma some goodies.
> CORRECT: Red Riding Hood, *take* your Grandma some goodies, and don't *bring* the wolf home with you.

Can/May

Can indicates ability; *may* indicates permission.

- I *can* climb to the top of that tree if my mother says that I *may.*

Capital/Capitol

The only time you use *capitol* is when you refer to the center of government, the building itself. All other uses are spelled *capital.*

- We visited the *capitol* when we toured Columbus, Ohio's *capital.*
- That is a *capital* idea.
- I should reinvest my *capital.*
- He committed a *capital* crime.
- Do we need *capital* letters?

Capitalization

Use capital letters only when absolutely necessary. There are a number of occasions when they are necessary.

1. Capitalize the proper names of particular persons, places, or things.

   · We drove our Chevrolet Impala to see Uncle James and my three aunts in South Dakota.

2. Capitalize beginnings of sentences and lines of verse.

   · Little Bo Peep
   Has lost her sheep
   And can't tell where to find them.
   · Some girls are very careless.

3. Capitalize the pronoun "I" and the interjection "O."

   · And then I prayed, "Help us, O Lord."

4. Capitalize important words in titles. Do not capitalize articles or conjunctions and prepositions less than five letters long unless they are the first word of the title.

   · *A Man for All Seasons, Catcher in the Rye,* "Rock Around the Clock," *All About Eve*

5. Capitalize personal titles and titles of high office.

   · Mr. and Mrs. Abercrombie met the Secretary of State and his private secretary.

6. Capitalize the first word of outline headings.
7. Capitalize names of days, months, holidays, and holy days.

   · This year Yom Kippur fell on Thursday.
   · St. Patrick's Day is always on March 17.

8. Capitalize school courses but not general areas of study.

   · She always enjoyed geography, but Geography 101 was a difficult course.

9. Capitalize adjectives derived from proper nouns.

   · "Has anyone seen an American ship?" asked Cho Cho San.
   · I have studied my English lesson for hours.

10. Capitalize directional words only when they designate a specific area.

    · The South has always been noted for its hospitality, but birds fly north in the spring.

11. Capitalize nouns or pronouns referring to the Deity.

· Do not lightly invoke the name of God.
· The priest called to Him in prayer.

12. Capitalize seasons only when personified.

· Here comes Old Man Winter again.
· A winter in Buffalo is a numbing experience.

Some "don'ts" and "not necessaries":

1. Sometimes a.m., p.m., jr., and sr. are capitalized, but it is unnecessary.
2. Never capitalize the word *the* before a periodical title, such as the *Cincinnati Post,* the *Philadelphia Inquirer.*
3. Some writers capitalize the first word after a colon, especially if a full sentence follows.

· OPTIONAL: There are three things you must do: Pay attention to directions, trust the leader, and bring insect repellent.

Catch—Irregular Verb

They catch balls; they caught balls; they have caught balls.

Cite/Sight/Site

Cite, sight, and *site* are unrelated words that happen to be pronounced the same.

· I can *cite* the article in the zoning laws that prohibits a construction *site* from being filled with rubbish and becoming a distasteful *sight.*

Clauses

See pages 189–193, 216–222, 234–239, and 241–243.

Collective Nouns

A collective noun names a class of persons or things: *family, convention, herd, jury.* It is plural in meaning and singular in form. When it refers to a unit, it requires a singular verb. When its parts are not acting as a unit, it requires a plural verb.

· The committee is in agreement. The committee are not in agreement.

The singular verb is most often used.

Colloquial Language

Colloquial language is informal language used in everyday speech but seldom appropriate to formal writing. The more colloquialisms you use in writing, the more informal your writing becomes.

> · If Harvey *totals* his father's car again, he will really be *in a jam.* He's definitely *spacy.*

Colons

The colon (:) is a mark of punctuation that has limited use. It signifies "namely," "to wit," "that is," or "Let me explain" and thus is used to introduce examples or to set up explanations. The following instances are typical:

> · The food we live on is kids' food: pizza, hot dogs, fried chicken, ice cream, and hamburgers." (Alexander) [The colon here may be translated "namely."]
> · None of this is cheap: the capsule costs four thousand dollars, and then there are the freezing costs. (Plumb) [(Translate this colon "that is."]
> · The American way of death is not novel: seen in proper historical perspective, it reaches back not only down the centuries but down the millenniums, for it is a response to a deep human need. (Plumb) [Here the colon could be translated "Let me explain."]

You should also use colons in the following technical ways:

1. Follow the salutation of a formal letter with a colon (Dear Sir or Madam:).
2. Separate with a colon hour and minutes (9:45), volume and page of a periodical (*Saturday Review* 16: 197), and place of publication and publisher (New York: Harper & Row).
3. In dialogue follow the speaker's name with a colon:

> · Penny: The sky is falling!
> · Foxy: Come hide in my cave, my dear.

4. Use a capital letter after a colon when a question follows.

> · The question must be asked: What can be done?

Commas

The comma (,) is a mark of punctuation that is used to signify a pause, but not a full stop, within a sentence. Note the following rules for its use.

Main Clauses
Rule: Use a comma to separate the main clauses of a compound sentence when the second (or further) clause is introduced by a coordinating con-

junction *(but, and, or, nor, for,* and *yet).* Unless such a sentence is very short, insert a comma after the first clause, before the conjunction.

· The Scout leader tried to keep the boys together, for he did not want to search the zoo at closing time ever again.

Caution: Do not use a comma between main clauses that are not also separated by a coordinating conjunction. Such sentences require a full stop—that is, a semicolon or a period.

· The Scout leader tried to keep the boys together; he did not want to search the zoo again.

It is also wise to use a semicolon for this central separation if you have used commas within the clauses. See **Comma Splice.**

Introductory Phrases and Clauses
Rule: Use commas to set off introductory phrases and clauses.

· After the rain, [or "After the rain was over,"] the team returned to the practice field.

Parenthetical, Extraneous, or Interrupting Sentence Elements
Rule: Use commas to surround interrupting material to set it off from the rest of the sentence. (Always use two commas for such interruptions unless one side is already marked by some other mark of punctuation or the beginning of the sentence.) Some examples:

1. Interrupting phrases:

   · *Limping badly,* Jan ran, *or tried to run,* all the way around the stadium.

2. Adverbials:

   · Harry returned, *nevertheless,* and brought the money with him. He had already spent some of it, *however.*

3. Appositives:

   · Beatrice, *the waitress in the smart beige uniform,* spilled the punch on Dr. Miller.

4. Mild interjections:

   · *Well,* let's go. *Why,* here's Charley.

5. Direct address:

   · *Bill,* wait for us.

6. Nonessential *who, which, that* clauses. Set off adjective clauses *only* when the material they contain is parenthetical and not essential to the meaning of the sentence.

ESSENTIAL: no commas—Gert would never forget *the dog that wagged its tail* so pathetically.

NONESSENTIAL: commas—Gert would never forget *Rover, who wagged his tail* so pathetically.

If you still are unsure, ask yourself: What do I actually mean? Do I mean to limit the noun or don't I? Take, for example: *John saw the priest who was standing in the garden.* If your point is that John saw the priest, then the fact that he was standing in the garden is only parenthetical—a bit of interesting, though nonessential—information, and you would use commas:

NONESSENTIAL: John saw the priest, who was standing in the garden.

But if you want to distinguish the priest in the garden from another—say, chatting by the sweets table—then the clause becomes essential to your meaning and you should not use commas:

ESSENTIAL: John saw the priest who was standing in the garden [walk over and speak to the priest at the sweets table].

See also pages 203–205 and 218–219.

Quotations
Rule: Use commas to set off direct quotations.

· "Why," she asked, "are you always late?"

Elements in a Series
Rule: Use commas to separate parts of a series. The comma is optional before the final conjunction.

· We brought pots, pans, dishes, and glasses.

Miscellaneous
Rule: Use commas in certain more technical situations.

1. Between the day and year in dates (Sunday, December 7, 1941)
2. Between places in addresses (Philadelphia, Pennsylvania)
3. Between names and titles or degrees (Patrick Sanders, Jr., or Jane Killane, Ph.D.)
4. To divide numbers of more than four and sometimes more than three digits, separating groups of three (6345; 6,345; 1,233,987)
5. After the salutation or closing in letters (Dear Grandma, and Yours truly, Marie)

Clarity
Rule: Use a comma to promote clarity.

· Mr. Smith, our dean has been arrested.
· Mr. Smith, our dean, has been arrested.

In the case of the comma, fewer is better. Use commas only as needed. Many novice writers overdose on commas.

Comma Splice (Comma Fault)

A comma splice, sometimes called a "comma fault," produces a run-on sentence when a comma is incorrectly used in place of a period or in place of a semicolon between independent clauses. See also **Comma, Semicolon,** and **Run-on Sentence.**

When two independent clauses are not connected with a coordinating conjunction *(and, but, or, nor, yet, for,* and *so),* you have separate sentences and should divide with a period or a semicolon, not a comma.

> INCORRECT: Everyone applauded Paul, he was a star.
> CORRECT: Everyone applauded Paul. He was a star.
> CORRECT: Everyone applauded Paul, *for* he was a star.

When two independent clauses are joined by an adverbial connective *(indeed, therefore, however, nevertheless),* a semicolon is called for.

> INCORRECT: Her dress was perfect, nevertheless, the bride looked unhappy.
> CORRECT: Her dress was perfect; nevertheless, the bride looked unhappy.

Exception: If a sentence has three or more independent clauses that are parallel, the comma is an acceptable divider.

- "Children disobey their parents, students ignore teachers, teens sneer at police, and young men ignore the draft-registration laws," said Grandpa.

Comparison of Modifiers

Most adjectives and adverbs have two degrees of comparison: comparative and superlative.

- Adjective: pretty, prettier, prettiest
- Adverb: beautifully, more beautifully, most beautifully

Most adjectives of one or two syllables form comparatives and superlatives by adding -*er* and -*est.* Longer adjectives are preceded by *more* and *most.*

- tall, taller, tallest; beautiful, more beautiful, most beautiful

Some adjectives use both forms.

- This was the *happiest* day of my life. She was the *most happy* bride we had ever seen.

Some adjectives have irregular forms of comparison.

- good, better, best; little, less, least; bad, worse, worst

When comparing two persons or things, use a comparative adjective. When comparing three or more persons or things, use a superlative adjective.

> · Meg is the *smarter* of the two. Jane is the *smartest* girl in our class.

Remember always to complete comparisons.

> INCORRECT: Scrooge was certainly the stingiest.
> CORRECT: Scrooge was certainly the stingiest man in London.

Complement

The complement, as its name implies, is the part of the sentence that completes the verb. Most frequently it takes the action of the verb and serves as its object. *Ball* is the *direct object* of the verb *hit* in this example:

> · Ray hit the *ball.*

Sometimes, however, the complement refers to the subject. If it is an adjective describing the subject, it is called a *predicate adjective:*

> · Ray was *courageous.*

If the complement is a noun (or pronoun) equated with the subject by a form of the verb "to be," it is called a *predicate nominative:*

> · The ball was a hard-hitting *missile. (ball = missile)*

In sentences with a predicate nominative, the predicate nominative and the subject may be reversed without changing the meaning of the sentence.

> · Your trash may be my *treasure.* My treasure may be your *trash.*
> · The caller is *he.* He is the *caller.*

See also **Predicate.**

Complement/Compliment

A *complement* is that which completes. In grammar it refers to the part of the sentence that completes the verb (see the preceding entry). It can also mean the full quota—of a ship's crew or an army unit, for instance. Although pronounced the same, *compliment* is an unrelated word meaning words of courtesy or praise or, when used as a verb, the giving of such words.

> · He *complimented* the Captain on filling his ship's *complement* so quickly.

Complex Sentence

See pages 195–196.

Compound Sentence

See page 195.

Compound-Complex Sentence

See page 196.

Conjunctions

A conjunction is a part of speech used to join words, phrases, or clauses.

1. Coordinating conjunctions join words, phrases, and clauses of equal grammatical rank such as two independent clauses. They are *and, but, or, nor, for, yet,* and *so.*
2. Subordinating conjunctions introduce subordinate clauses. Some of these are *after, although, as, because, unless,* and *while.*
3. Correlative conjunctions are always used in pairs: *either/or, neither/nor, both/and, not only/but also,* and *whether/or.*
4. Adverbial conjunctions are used as conjunctions between independent clauses (*therefore, however, furthermore, nevertheless, thus,* and others).

Connotative Language

See pages 281–282 and 403.

Consist in/Consist of

Consist in refers to abstract elements that contribute to a complete effect.

· His charm *consists in* an open smile and a kind disposition.

Consists of is more often used to refer to parts of a whole list.

· The dessert *consists of* egg, chocolate, sugar, and whipped cream.

Contact

Contact is a noun that is frequently used as a verb. Its use as a verb will probably be generally accepted in the future, but now it is best to avoid it in most formal writing.

> AVOID: She expects you to *contact* her by Thursday.
> CORRECT: She expects you to *make contact* with her by Thursday.
> BETTER: She expects you to *call* (or *telephone* or *write*) her by Thursday.

Continual/Continuous

Continual means "repeated over and over, but with pauses or breaks." *Continuous* means "without interruption." Drumbeats are *continual.*

Droning is *continuous.* A good way to remember the *-ous* is: *o*ne *u*ninter-rupted *s*equence.

- Their *continual* bickering bored their friends.
- The *continuous* downpour stopped the game.

Contractions

A contraction is a shortened form of a word in which an apostrophe takes the place of the omitted letter or letters.

- *Isn't* that your dog, *Ma'am?*
- *He's goin'* on down the road.
- *It's* time to go.

See also **Apostrophe**.

Contrast to/Contrast with

When *contrast* is used as a verb meaning "to compare," it is followed by *with.*

- Coaches should not *contrast* a girl's ability *with* that of her teammates.

When *contrast* is used as a noun, it is followed by *to.*

- Barry's work was slovenly in *contrast to* his partner's.

Coordinating Conjunction

See **Conjunctions**.

Copulative Verbs

See **Linking Verbs**.

Correlative Conjunction

See **Conjunctions**.

Could Have/Could of

See **Would Have/Would of**.

Council/Counsel

Council is a noun that means a group of advisers or people who deliberate. *Counsel* as a noun means advice. *Counsel* as a verb means to give advice.

· The city *council* is in session every Thursday.
· Your *counsel* on marriage problems has always been helpful.
· When you *counsel* your clients, remember their economic problems.

Councilor and *counselor* are preferred spellings, although *councillor* and *counsellor* are also correct. *Counselor* is also used to mean attorney.

Criteria/Criterion

The singular form is *criterion;* the plural is *criteria.* Say the *criterion is,* the *criteria are.*

Dangling Modifiers

Dangling modifiers are parts of sentences which become so disconnected from the words they are meant to describe that the sense of the sentence is changed or lost.

Dangling Participles

INCORRECT: Jumping into bed, the sheets were cold.

The sheets, in this sentence, are jumping into bed. The actual word being modified is omitted.

CORRECT: Jumping into bed, John found that the sheets were cold.

Now John is jumping, not the sheets.

Dangling Adverbial Modifiers

INCORRECT: When he was six years old, Pat's teacher taught him to read.

(That's not bad for a six-year-old teacher.)

CORRECT: When Pat was six years old, his teacher taught him to read.
INCORRECT: After being out until 2 a.m., Paul's mother grounded him.

(Being out late made her cranky.)

CORRECT: Because Paul stayed out until 2 a.m., his mother grounded him.

The noun and pronoun being modified must be clearly identified and be placed as close as possible in the sentence to the modifier.

Dash

The dash (-- on the typewriter) is a mark of punctuation that should be used sparingly in formal writing. It is used instead of the colon in informal writing and instead of the comma for added emphasis. It may be used to include incidental information:

- Some scientists feared that the document placed too much faith in techno-logical—rather than "human"—solutions. (Golden)

It may also be used to set up an informal series:

- Any available technology could be used—teaching machines, programmed instruction, computer-assisted methods. (Slack)

Or it may be used to achieve emphasis, contrast, or change in the sentence's direction:

- Eugene Arden . . . said that toward the end of the novel, Dimmesdale "was in fact becoming one of the most powerful and persuasive deliverers of sermons in New England"—not a feat likely in a person dying of atropine poisoning. (Turner)

Demonstrative Pronouns

See **Pronouns: Demonstrative**.

Denotative Meaning

The *denotative meaning* of a word or phrase is its explicit meaning as compared to its connotative or implied meanings. For example, the denota-tive meaning of the phrase "a traveling salesman and a farmer's daughter" ignores the overtones suggested by the long lineage of off-color jokes on the subject. The words simply denote their stated meaning: an itinerant mer-chandiser and an agriculturalist's female offspring. See **Connotative Lan-guage**.

Dependent Clauses

See **Clauses; Adjective Clauses; Adverb Clauses; Noun Clauses**. See also pages 192–193, 216–222, 234–239, and 241–243.

Differ from/Differ with

Differ from means "not the same as." *Differ with* means "disagree."

- The Quakers and the Catholics in our organization *differ from* one another in their form of worship but do not *differ with* one another in their belief in religious freedom.

Different from/Different than

Different from is always correct although it may sound awkward at times. *Different than* is possible only when *different* precedes a clause in which some words are understood rather than stated.

· Angie found that she felt no *different* being in love for the eighth time *than* [she felt being in love] the first.

In all other instances, stay with *different from*.

· My dreams are *different from* yours. Our style is *different* in every way *from* yours.

Direct Object

See **Complement**.

Disinterested/Uninterested

A *disinterested* person has no personal connection, no opinion, is neutral. An *uninterested* person just doesn't care, although he may or may not have a stake in an issue.

· They looked for a *disinterested* person to act as referee. When they found someone, he was *uninterested* in the job.

Dive—Irregular Verb

They dive; they dived or they dove; they have dived.

Doesn't/Don't

Does and *Doesn't* are singular. *Do* and *Don't* are plural.

· Sally *doesn't* look her best in red. Her sisters *don't* either.

Be especially careful not to use *don't* with a single subject because it is one of the nonstandard constructions that people find most distracting.

Do—Irregular Verb

He doesn't; they do; they did; they have done. See **Doesn't/Don't**.

Dots

See **Ellipsis Points**.

Double Negative

Although speakers of standard English in Shakespeare's day believed that the more negative words one used in a sentence the more emphatically negative it became, today's standard English abides by the theory that negative words cancel each other out and thus turn a statement positive. You should, therefore, be careful to avoid a double negative (an error that readers find especially bothersome).

> INCORRECT: No one never came. [Means "Somebody always came."]
> CORRECT: No one ever came.

There is one construction, however, in which a double negative subtly reinforces a positive meaning:

- It is *not uncommon* to hear crying from the Kindergarten on the first day of school.
- She sold the set for a *not inconsiderable* sum.

Not uncommon is a cautious way to say *common*. *Not inconsiderable* means "considerable."

Double Possessive

Possessive case can be expressed with an apostrophe or by using *of* (John's brother, brother of John). In some sentences, you will need to use a double possessive, an apostrophe and *of,* in order to make your meaning clear.

- *We saw a painting of Whistler* means that Whistler was the subject of the painting.
- *We saw a painting of Whistler's* means that Whistler was the painter.

There is also room for choice. The following examples are both correct.

- He was a friend of Whistler.
- He was a friend of Whistler's.

See also **Apostrophe.**

Due to

Due to is acceptable when describing a noun. It follows a linking verb.

- Her success was *due to* working hard—and being the President's daughter.

Due to may *not* be used as an adverb explaining a verb.

> INCORRECT: He died *due to* an extreme cold.

Instead use *because of, on account of, owing to.*

> CORRECT: He died *because of* an extreme cold.

Due to the fact that is wordy and pretentious. Avoid using it.

Eager

See **Anxious/Eager**.

Effect

See **Affect/Effect**.

Elicit/Illicit

Elicit means "to draw out."

· Try to *elicit* more information from that witness.

Illicit means illegal or not allowed.

· She was engaged in the *illicit* manufacture of alligator belts.

Ellipsis Points

Use ellipsis points—that is, three periods (. . .)—when you interrupt a quotation in order to indicate the omission of a word, words, or sentences. Ellipses help you make the syntax of the quoted material conform to your own writing. (See **Brackets**, punctuation often useful in this connection.) Ellipses also permit you to leave out those portions of the quotation which are not relevant to the point you are making.

Whenever you omit part of a quotation, be sure that you do not alter the author's essential message. Sometimes advertisements use ellipses to deceive.

· [Original quotation] The *Times* critic called it "The biggest mess of a movie this season."
· [Advertisement using a misleading ellipsis] The *Times* critic called it "The biggest . . . movie this season."

Rules for Use

1. When you type ellipses, space between the dots.
2. When the omission is at the end of the sentence or includes the end of a sentence, you need a fourth dot (the period).

   · The President said, "Ask not what your country can do for you. . . ."

3. An unfinished or interrupted sentence in recorded conversation, however, ends with only three dots.

   · Marion began, "But if only I . . ."

4. The ellipsis should not be used to indicate a pause in speech.

> WEAK: Tom mumbled, "I . . . uh . . . I don't . . . uh . . . think so."
> BETTER: Tom mumbled, "I—uh—I don't—uh—think so."

Emigrate/Immigrate

Migration refers to moving from place to place. The move may or may not be permanent. You can *migrate to* a place or *migrate from* a place. "Migrate to" is *immigrate*. "Migrate from" is *emigrate*.

- Stanislaus *emigrated from* Poland in 1923. He *immigrated* to the United States.
- Stanislaus was an *emigrant from* Poland. He was an *immigrant to* the United States.

Ensure

See **Assure/Ensure/Insure**.

Euphemism

A euphemism is a more pleasant or less offensive way to state what the speaker or writer considers an unpleasant or unmentionable idea.

When the word *pregnant* was too blunt for sensitive company, euphemisms included "she has something in the oven," "they are expecting a bundle of joy," "the stork will arrive with a package from heaven," and other sayings today considered more offensive than *pregnant.*

Doctors call pain *discomfort.* Teachers call children *socially immature* when they bite one another. When a weight lifter gets fat, he claims he is *bulking up.*

The use of euphemisms presents a moral issue when it is intended to blur the reality of something a writer does not wish to admit. For example, many thoughtful people believe it is immoral to call the destruction of vast areas of vegetation *defoliation* or to refer to munitions used to kill people as *anti-personnel materials.*

It is usually wiser to avoid using euphemisms when the plainly stated original idea would do as well.

Everyday/Every Day

Everyday is a compound word when used as an adjective.

- Just wear your *everyday* clothing.

When referring to a frequency in time, write *every day* as two words.

· We shall help you *every day* until you finish.

Except

Some grammarians consider *except* a conjunction that should be followed by the subject of an understood clause:

· They all arrived early *except she* [did not].

Others consider *except* a preposition to be followed by an object:

· They all arrived early *except her.*

While they try to decide, stick with the objective. Use *except me, except us, except him.* See also **Accept/Except.**

Exclamation Point

The exclamation point (!) is a mark of punctuation that indicates excitement. It may also signal fear or surprise or other strong emotions. A sentence can take on new meaning when followed by an exclamation point.

· Who is singing *Thunder Road?* It's Bruce Springsteen.
· Who is that in the lobby? It's Bruce Springsteen!

Overused, however, the exclamation point loses its impact. Save it only for moments of strongest excitement. Such moments are very rare in expository writing.

Fall—Irregular Verb

They fall; they fell; they have fallen.

Farther/Further

Farther and *further* both mean "more" or "to a greater extent." *Farther* refers only to actual distance in space that can be measured. *Further* refers to time or other abstract measurement.

· Which family lives *farther* from the railroad tracks?
· I changed my opinion upon *further* consideration.
· *Further,* as a condensed version of *furthermore,* "further" has an additional or *further* use as an adverbial connective.

Faulty Parallelism

See **Parallelism, Faulty.**

Fewer/Less

Fewer is used with number; *less* is used with quantity.

- There were *fewer* than six people on the sign-up sheet.
- There was *less* noise tonight.
- We had hoped for *fewer* cases of chicken pox this year.
- We had hoped there would be *less* chicken pox this year.

With *fewer,* you can count the number of cases.

Exception: You can use *less* with a number when it refers to a collective sum (*less* than 30 years old or a salary *less* than $25,000).

Figurative Language

Figurative language is language used to express meaning that goes beyond its literal interpretation. Historically, figurative language is considered to be composed of individual "figures of speech" (or "flowers of rhetoric," as they were known for centuries) that served the masters of rhetoric as persuasive tools in their appeal to the emotions of their audience. Of the more than 200 such figures that were once codified, writers still find a good number that remain useful today. Among these are **Parallelism** and **Irony**, which are separately defined here.

In recent years, however, the term *figurative language* has ordinarily been equated with *imagery,* the discussion of one idea or thing in terms of another. **Imagery**, which includes images, i.e., figures, of form—Metaphor, Simile, Connotative Language, Symbol, Allegory, Analogy—and images of content, including Personification, Hyperbole, Allusion, Synesthesia, Metonymy, Synecdoche, Paradox, and Oxymoron, is discussed on pages 277–291 and 399–403.

Figures of Speech

See **Figurative Language**.

Firstly

This is not an acceptable form. Many people use *firstly, secondly, thirdly.* It is better to use *first, second,* and *third* as adverbs.

- *First,* I don't know how to drive. *Second,* I have no car. *Third,* I'm afraid of driving in city traffic.

Flied

See **Fly**.

Flowers of Rhetoric

See **Figurative Language.**

Fly—Irregular Verb

They fly; they flew; they have flown. *Flied* is correct only in sentences about the ball park, where Pete *flied out* to third.

Fragment

A fragment is a portion of a sentence that is punctuated as if it were a sentence.

- Though it is not a sentence.
- Which was a surprise.

Occasionally, an experienced writer employs a fragment effectively.

- What's wrong with nondiscrimination, with simple fairness? *Two things really.* (Raspberry)

But in general, fragments—like all structural errors of the sentence—are especially distracting to readers and thus are best avoided.

Funny

Funny is best used to mean "amusing," rather than "peculiar" or "suspicious" or "unusual." If you do not mean "amusing," find a more precise word than *funny*.

Further

See **Farther/Further.**

Gender

Gender is a grammatical term designating masculine and feminine (and neuter). With our new understanding of the way language reflects societal values and may even condition behavior, the old rules, with their implications of women's subordinate status, have been superseded. Grammatical gender has thus become politicized, and many people are now particularly sensitive to gender usage. You must, therefore, be especially careful in your use of gender-designating words.

Many male/female distinguishing nouns are completely appropriate: *rooster/hen, man/woman, cow/bull.* Other differentiating nouns are less strongly entrenched but are still used: *actor/actress* and *host/hostess.* Others have become obsolete: *aviator/aviatrix, author/authoress, poet/poetess.* Others, such as *Negress* and *Jewess,* are completely unacceptable.

Some well-meaning efforts to avoid discriminatory language have resulted in such infelicities as *councilpersons, congresspersons,* or *chairperson.* When you can, it is wiser to avoid such awkwardness and choose terms such as *councilors, legislators (senators, representatives),* or *chair.*

Pronouns also have gender. *He, his,* and *him* are masculine; *she, her,* and *hers* are feminine; and *it* and *its* are neuter. Plural pronouns are the same for all three genders: *they, their, theirs, them.* Problems arise when singular pronouns must agree in gender with their antecedents. When the subject is of mixed or unknown gender, things become tricky. Since the old rule of using the masculine term in such cases is now obsolete, it is better to avoid the problem altogether and stick with a plural subject: "The students, they. . . ." In the rare cases where the plural simply cannot be used, *he or she,* though awkward, is correct.

Gerund

See page 191 and pages 243–244.

Get—Irregular Verb

They get hives; they got hives; they have gotten hives.

Go—Irregular Verb

They go; they went; they have gone.

Good/Well

Good is an adjective, modifying nouns and pronouns. *Well* is an adverb, modifying verbs and adjectives.

After linking or sensory verbs, *good* is usually used because it describes the subject rather than the verb.

· Gardenias smell *good.* Pizza tastes *good.* Country music sounds *good* to many people.

In all those sentences, a more descriptive or precise word than *good* might have been found *(fragrant, delicious, pleasant),* but in no case should *well* have been used.

In referring to physical well-being, *well* usually follows *feel.*

· He feels *well* for the first time since football season.

Well follows most other verbs.

· He eats *well,* sleeps *well,* dances *well,* and lies *well.*

Got/Gotten

Got is incorrectly used to mean "to have." Because "have" itself always accompanies it, *got* in this sense is redundant.

> INCORRECT: Jerry *has got* thirty-five horses.
> CORRECT: Jerry *has* thirty-five horses.

Gotten, when used to mean "acquire" or "purchase," however, is not incorrect—although it is considered a bit awkward.

- Jerry *has gotten* thirty-five horses.
- BETTER: Jerry has acquired thirty-five horses.

Great

Great should be reserved for occasions for which the meanings "extensive," "remarkable," or "very large" are required. Do not use *great* to describe the way one feels or one's skill at something. These uses are too informal for writing.

> INCORRECT: He played a *great* game of tennis today. It's *great* to be here with you. This is a *great*-looking office.

Hang/Hanged, Hang/Hung

When discussing *hanging* as a means of executing a person, the past tense and the participle forms are *hanged.*

- He *was hanged* for the murder of his mother-in-law.
- The *hanged* man was revived and lived a long life.

When using *hang* in any other sense, use *hung* for the past and participle forms.

- She *hung* the picture upside down.
- The picture *was hung* upside down.

Healthful/Healthy

Healthful foods, activities, and environments contribute to your health. They keep you *healthy.*

Helping Verb

See **Auxiliary Verbs**.

Historic/Historical

Historic things are a part of history. Mt. Vernon is a *historic* home, Gettysburg is a *historic* battleground, segregation is part of a *historic* struggle.

Historical things are based on history. We have *historical* novels, *historical* research, *historical* studies.

Use *a,* not *an,* before *historic.*

Homonym

A homonym or homophone is a word that sounds the same as another word but is different in spelling and meaning.

- The *knight* rode out each *night* in search of dragons.
- Charlie *threw* the discus *through* a window.

Hopefully

Hopefully is rapidly becoming the most misused word in the language. *Hopefully* is not an adverbial conjunction like *however.* It is an adverb that modifies a verb. Although it is becoming acceptable to many in its conjunctive form, here is the strict interpretation: In the sentence, "Hopefully, I will run five miles tomorrow," *hopefully* must modify run. Unfortunately, the writer does not really mean that she will run full of hope. She means that she hopes she will be able to run that far, and that is what she must state:

> CORRECT: I hope that I shall be able to run five miles tomorrow.
> I hope I have made this point clear.

Hyphen

Hyphens (-) join two or more words or parts of words together to form a compound word (father-in-law, good-bye, ex-champion). But since not all compound words or prefixed words take hyphens, your dictionary will have to be your guide for words that include hyphens in their regular spelling.

Compound Adjectives

Always use a hyphen, however, when you use two or more words as a single adjective—even when these words are not ordinarily punctuated in this way:

- Marcia enjoyed sentence combining.
  Marcia enjoyed her sentence-combining course.
- Joseph was well dressed.
  Joseph was a well-dressed representative of his company.

· It was a good talk between mother and daughter.
It was a good mother-and-daughter talk.

Avoiding Confusion

Be sure to use a hyphen when it is needed to avoid confusing similar words.

· The International House co-op. The chicken coop.
· Re-cover the furniture. Recover from your illness.

Hyphenation in Word Division

If you must continue a word on the next line of type, you should follow some rules for dividing.

1. Divide between syllables.
2. Never divide a one-syllable word.
3. The part of the word on each line must have one vowel sound and must be pronounceable (not *ear-th*).
4. Do not leave one letter alone on a line *(a-gent)*.
5. Leave a single long vowel at the end of a syllable *(ho-tel, ta-ble, fa-mous)*.
6. Do not permit a short vowel sound to end a syllable *(bas-ket, wag-on, plan-et)*.
7. Words ending in *le* keep the consonant preceding *le* with the *le (sta-ble, ma-ple, mar-ble, am-ple)*.

   Whenever possible, go to the next line and write the whole word. You will avoid confusing errors and your work will be easier to read.

If . . . Were

When *if* or *as if* or *as though* is used to express a condition that does not exist or a situation that is only wished for or desired, you should follow the subject by *were* even if that subject is singular:

· *If* the world *were* flat . . .
· . . . led the prayers *as if* he *were* the Pope.
· . . . *wished* she *were* Queen Elizabeth.

Illicit

See **Elicit/Illicit.**

Illusion

See **Allusion/Illusion.**

Imagery

See **Figurative Language** and pages 277–291 and 399–403.

Imply/Infer

The speaker or writer *implies* (suggests, hints). The listener or reader *infers* (draws conclusions).

- He *implied* that he was wealthy by mentioning that his wife had left her sable coat outside Gucci's in the Rolls Royce.
- We *inferred* from his remarks that he was wealthy.

Indefinite Antecedent

See **Agreement: Pronouns and Antecedents.**

Indefinite Pronouns

See **Pronouns: Indefinite.**

Indefinite Reference

See **Agreement: Pronouns and Antecedents.**

Independent Clauses

See pages 189, 195.

Indirect Object

An indirect object is the noun or pronoun *to whom* or *for whom* a thing is done. Sometimes the words *to* and *for* are not written but are understood.

- Paula gave the present to *me.*
- Paula gave *me* the present.
- He gave [to] *Kim* all the help she needed.

The indirect object takes the objective form of the pronoun. You cannot say: He gave *she* and *I* his blessing. You must use *her* and *me.*

Individual

The word *individual,* both as an adjective and as a noun, carries the sense of singleness, of separate entity. It should not be used synonymously with a word as general as *person.* Avoid such expressions as "Joe is a terrific individual."

Infer

See **Imply/Infer.**

Infinitive

See page 192 and pages 243–244.

Ingenious/Ingenuous

Ingenious means "inventive."

> · Kathleen devised many *ingenious* ways for avoiding Latin class.

Ingenuous means "unworldly," "innocent," and "artless."

> · The sophisticated bachelor found the young singer's *ingenuous* frankness irresistible.

Input/Output

Input and *output* are part of the jargon of the computer world and are not usually appropriate in any other context. Under no circumstances should they be used as verbs.

Inside/Inside of

Use *inside* (meaning "within") without adding *of*.

> INCORRECT: He is *inside of* the house.
> CORRECT: He is *inside* the house.

Use *inside of* only when referring to limitations of time or distance.

> · We can be with you *inside of* an hour. We saw six leveled homes *inside of* a two-block area.

Insure

See **Assure/Ensure/Insure**.

Intensifiers

Intensifiers such as *very, most, quite, somewhat,* and *fairly,* which modify adjectives and adverbs, are traditionally, though somewhat illogically, classified as adverbs. *Be sparing* in your use of intensifiers—especially *very* and *quite,* which often create the opposite of the intended effect, making the phrase less strong. Think, for example, of your reaction if I had said instead: *Be quite sparing. . . .*

Interjections

Interjections are words that are grammatically unnecessary to the rest of the sentence but which are used to express emotions such as surprise, dismay, fear, or pain *(Oh! Wow! Hallelujah! Ow!).*

Intransitive and Transitive Verbs

A *transitive* verb takes a direct object.

- He *punched* his little brother.
- His mother *saw* him do it.
- He will not *do* it again.

(*Brother, him,* and *it* are objects.)
     An *intransitive* verb does not take a direct object.

- Birds *fly.*
- The man *died.*

Most verbs can be used as either transitive or intransitive.

- The gourmand *ate* his *dinner.* (transitive)
- The gourmand *ate* for hours and hours. (intransitive)

Most dictionaries list verbs as *vt* or *vi* immediately following the entry.

Irony

Irony is a rhetorical strategy in which the intended meaning is opposite from what is said or implied. Scholars distinguish three kinds of irony:

1. *Verbal Irony.* Here the speaker means the contrary of what he or she says or writes.

   - One of the *worst insults* kicking around today is any word that means in effect *"wholesome."* You are a wholesome person. How would you like to be called that? (Wolfe, emphasis mine)

2. *Dramatic Irony.* Here the author means something contrary to what the speaker says.

   - In the October 1973 war Israel . . . also suffered an acute understanding of the *"conscience of the West"* under oil pressure. (Will, emphasis mine)

3. *Circumstantial Irony* (the "Irony of Fate"). Fate sees to it that circumstances turn out contrary to human expectations—almost as if in mockery of these expectations.

· *"Silent Night,"* canned and distributed in thundering repetition in the department stores, has become one of the greatest of all *noisemakers,* almost like the rattles and whistles of Election Night. (E. B. White, emphasis mine)

See also pages 98–99 and 394–395.

Irregular Verbs

See **Regular Verbs** and the separate listings of the most common irregular verbs, individually alphabetized throughout the Revision Guide.

Italics (Underlining)

Underlining in a manuscript or typescript indicates italic script in typeset material. Such underlining has a number of uses.

1. *Titles.* Always underline the title of a separately published work.

    · Tom Sawyer = *Tom Sawyer;* Macbeth = *Macbeth.*

    See also **Titles**.

2. *Foreign Words.* If you use a word or a phrase from a foreign language, you must underline it. Many words from foreign sources, such as *kimono, chauffeur, spaghetti,* or *poltergeist,* have come into such customary use that they are now considered to be English words as well and need not be italicized. Occasionally, however, you will need to use a foreign word or phrase that has not yet become assimilated into English and for which there is no precise English equivalent. Examples of such terms include chutzpah (Yiddish), or sturm and drang (German), or in medias res (Latin). A word of caution: If you overuse foreign expressions, some readers may charge you with affectation.

3. *Words as Words.* Underline words or phrases when you are discussing them as words.

    · How do you define sincerity?

4. *Emphasis.* Underlining can also be an effective way of calling attention to a word or phrase you want to emphasize. Use this sort of italicization sparingly, however. Like the exclamation point, it can easily be overdone and become counterproductive. Sometimes a portion of a quotation you are using may be italicized and sometimes you may choose to emphasize part of a quotation in this way yourself. In either case, be sure to let your reader know whether you or the author is the source of the italics: (Emphasis mine) or (Emphasis Smith's).

Its/It's

It's is a contraction meaning *it is* or *it has* and should not be confused with the possessive *its*.

- The lion has a thorn in *its* paw, but *it's* not my job to remove it.

Judge

Correct spellings are *judge, judging, judged. Judgment* is preferred, but *judgement* is also correct.

Kind/Kinds

The singular form is usually used but causes some confusion in verb agreement. Most grammarians would accept "What *kind* of clothes *are* these?" Some writers try to avoid the problem by using "What *kinds* of clothes *are* these?" This is not a correct use of *kinds*. The plural form should be used only for classifying things specifically.

- How many *kinds* of birds are in Farleigh Woods?

A more precise word might be *species*, but *kinds*, if used, should be plural.
     This *kind* of problem *keeps* cropping up (not "These *kinds* of problems *keep* cropping up").

Kind of/Sort of

Although it is always appropriate to speak of "this kind of scholar" and "that sort of apple," the use of *kind of* and *sort of* as qualifiers should be restricted to informal occasions. Edit out such expressions if they occur in your formal written work.

> WEAK: This kind of writing is *sort of* sloppy and its content is *kind of* vague.
> BETTER: This kind of writing is sloppy and its content is rather vague.

Know—Irregular Verb

They know; they knew; they have known.

Lay—Irregular Verb

Hens lay eggs; hens laid eggs; hens have laid eggs.

Lay/Lie

Lie can mean "to tell an untruth." It can also mean "to recline." In either case, it does not take an object.

- The gangster *lied* to the judge.
- The judge will *lie* on the couch.

Lay means "to put" and always takes an object.

- *Lay* your coat down.
- *Lay* your bets.

People sometimes are confused by these two verbs because their parts are irregular and *lay* is the past of *lie* (Today I *lie* down; yesterday I *lay* down). See **Lay—Irregular Verb** and **Lie—Irregular Verb**.

Leave/Let

Leave means to withdraw or go away. *Let* means to allow or permit. If you say, *"Leave me alone,"* you mean "Remove yourself from my presence." If you say, *"Let me alone,"* you are saying, "Allow me to be by myself," either physically or symbolically.

- *Let* her go to the movies. *Let* them stay out until midnight.
- *Leave* the notes on the desk. Be sure you *leave* early.

Lend/Loan

You might *lend* me ten dollars or *loan* me ten dollars. Either is acceptable (twenty would be even more acceptable), but *lend* has a more formal sound and would be a better choice when you need a verb. *Loan* is always the correct noun.

- He tried to get a *loan* from the bank.

Do not say, "He tried to get the loan of Joe's car." Say, "He tried to borrow Joe's car."

Lets/Let's

Lets means *allows*

- Becky *lets* her sister borrow her clothes.

Let's means *let us.*

- Let's try to get there early.

Never use *let's us,* as in *let's us* be there early.

Lie—Irregular Verb

They lie down; they lay down; they have lain down. See also **Lay/Lie.**

Like

See **As/Like.**

Linking Verbs

Linking verbs (also known as copulative verbs) are verbs that take a predicate adjective or a predicate nominative instead of a direct object: they link rather than act. Linking verbs include all the forms of the verb *be* and other verbs such as *seem, appear, feel, look, remain, become.*

· Jane *seems* so confident and *appears* so self-possessed that I *become* all elbows and knees whenever she *is* around, *remain* miserable while she *is* near, and *feel* totally foolish as soon as she *is* away.

Literal Language

In literal language, the words mean exactly what they say. Such is not the case with figurative language.

LITERAL: His lying destroyed the relationship.
FIGURATIVE: His lies were the worm in the apple of love.

The word *literally* is misused when used like this: She was *literally* as big as a house. He *literally* turned green with envy. These things are done figuratively, not literally. See also **Figurative Language.**

Lowercase

Lowercase, often marked *lc,* refers to the small letters of the alphabet as opposed to capital letters.

· The author e. e. cummings always used lowercase for his name.

Mad/Angry

See **Angry/Mad.**

Main Clauses

See pages 189, 195.

May

See **Can/May**.

Media/Medium

Media is the plural form of *medium*. Television *is* a *medium* of communication. So is radio. So is the newspaper. They *are* all communications *media*.

It is incorrect to say "The *media is* treating the President harshly."

Memento/Momentum

Two totally unrelated words, *memento* and *momentum* are frequently jammed together to form a nonword, *momento*. A *memento* is a remembrance or souvenir. *Momentum* popularly means "forward push" but has precise technical definitions as well. There is no such word as *momento!*

Misplaced Modifier

See **Dangling Modifier.**

Mixed Metaphor

A mixed metaphor consists of two or more implied, unrelated comparisons of the same thing.

- The plane *shot* across the heavens, a great *bird tearing* through clouds, a silver *knife* in the sky.

In revision, the writer must first choose between bird and knife metaphors (and bullet, if you want to include *shot*), and then continue with that single comparison. Mixed metaphors are usually a sign of an inept writer.

Modals

See **Auxiliary Verbs.**

Myself

Myself is used primarily when the first person (I) is acting.

- I gave [to] *myself* the injection. (indirect object)
- I hurt *myself.* (object)
- I felt sorrow within *myself.* (object of preposition)

Myself should never be used in place of *I* or *me.*

> INCORRECT: Jerry and *myself* were the only ones who cared.
> INCORRECT: They invited Joanne and *myself* to come with them.

Negative

Negative words deny the verb. They include *not, never, no,* and *none.* If you use two in one clause, you cancel the denial.

> · I *don't* have *no* tuition. I *never* had *no* tuition.

These sentences as they stand literally mean "I do have tuition," "I had tuition." See **Double Negative.**

Neither/Nor

Neither . . . nor can be used only when referring to two elements.

> · *Neither* she *nor* her mother, . . .
> *Neither* soccer *nor* tennis, . . .

When both elements are singular, the verb is singular.

> · Neither *she* nor her *mother is* angry.

When both elements are plural, the verb is plural.

> · Neither the *cowboys* nor the *Indians were* depicted realistically.

When one is singular and the other is plural, the verb agrees with the closest one.

> · Neither the doctor nor his *instruments were* prepared.

None

None is considered singular because it means *no one.*

> · *None* of the boys *is* able to sing.

In some cases it is considered acceptable to use *none* as a plural when it means no persons.

> · *None* of the two hundred victims *were* from our town.

When the number meant by *none* is unclear, use the singular. Be consistent throughout the sentence.

> INCORRECT: None of the girls has their purses.
> CORRECT: None of the girls has her purse.

Nonrestrictive Clause

See **Comma; Adjective Clauses**.

Nothing

Nothing always takes the singular verb.

- *Nothing* but pain and injuries *has* plagued him all season.

Nouns

See page 190.

Noun Clauses

See pages 192–193 and 241–243. Never set off a noun clause with punctuation because noun clauses act as subjects or objects and no punctuation should ever come between a subject and its verb or a verb and its object.

Noun Phrase

See pages 191–192 and 241–243.

Number

When the word *number* is used as a noun, it usually takes a singular verb.

- The *number* of unemployed *is* appalling.

When the article *a* is used, as in *a number*, use a plural verb.

- *A number* of unemployed *are* planning disturbances.

See **Plurals**.

Numbers

Under most circumstances, spell out numbers from one to twelve and write larger figures (13, 874, 69,998,303) in numeral form. Dates and times (December 2, 1931 at 2:40 A.M.) should, as a rule, be given in numerals; and if you must begin a sentence with a number, it is usually wise to spell it out.

Objective Correlative (O.C.)

See pages 271–291 and 403.

Object of a Preposition

Pronouns that are objects of prepositions are always in the objective form. People who do not understand grammar and who want to sound genteel or elegant make some common errors.

> INCORRECT: There was bad feeling *between she and I.*

Although it may sound awkward to say *between her and me,* it is correct. The objects of the preposition *between* must be objective *(her* and *me).* If it sounds too bad, say *between Mary and me, between us,* or reword in some other way.

Object of a Verb

See **Complement.**

Only

When *only* is used to mean *no more than,* it should be placed as close as possible to the word it limits.

> INCORRECT: He *only* has *an hour.*
> CORRECT: He has *only an hour.*
> CORRECT: Phil jumped from the bridge *only an hour ago.*
> INCORRECT: Phil *only jumped* from the bridge an hour ago.

The incorrect version implies that the only thing Phil got around to doing an hour ago was jumping from the bridge, although there were other things he might have done besides.

Only should not be used as a conjunction.

> INCORRECT: He wanted to sing, *only* he had a sore throat.

Use instead *but, however,* or whatever conjunction seems appropriate.

Opportunity

Opportunity can be followed by *of, for,* or *to.*

- He had the *opportunity to* steal the emeralds.
- The police used that *opportunity for* questioning him.
- It was the *opportunity of* a lifetime.

You can see that *opportunity for* is followed by a noun or noun form (gerund). *Opportunity to* is followed by a verb.

Opposite

See **Antonym.**

Output

See **Input/Output**.

Pair

Pair takes a singular verb when both parts act as one *(pair* of socks *is). Pair* takes a plural verb when the two parts are not acting as one.

· That *pair are* always arguing.

When speaking of more than one pair, it is correct to use *pairs*.

· She owns six *pairs* of jeans.

Parallelism

See pages 247–256.

Parallelism, Faulty

Whenever you use parallel constructions, it is important to make sure that the parallel elements are syntactically alike. Awkward, even ludicrous, effects result from faulty parallelism. When parallel verbs are in different tenses, for instance:

INCORRECT: Lady Macbeth *urged* her husband to kill, *had seduced* him into the deed, and continually *washes* her guilty hands.

Or if parallel phrases are of different kinds:

INCORRECT: *With* heavy hearts, *with* stout resolve, and *having been* up all night, the Siamese twins decided to part their ways.

Parentheses

Parentheses ( ) are marks of punctuation used to enclose a word or phrase that qualifies or explains what has gone before or repeats what has gone before in a different way.

· My cousin will arrive (unless he loses his way again) in time for dinner.
· My little brother (a pest as usual) told my date I planned to marry for money.

Parenthetical remarks tend to interrupt the text, however; so be careful not to overuse them.

Participles

See pages 191, 216–217, and 221.

Parts of Speech

See pages 190–191.

Period

A period (.) is a mark of punctuation used at the end of a complete statement or command. It is also used to conclude most abbreviations. See **Abbreviations**. According to the *MLA Style Manual,* periods also separate Biblical chapter and verse (*Genesis* 4.12), dramatic act, scene, and line (*King Lear* V.ii.9–13), and book or canto and line (*Iliad* 7.22).

Personal Pronoun

See **Pronouns: Personal**.

Picnic

In adding endings, a *k* must be inserted so that the *c* followed by *i* will not have the sound of *s.* Correct spellings are *picnicked, picnicking, picnickers.*

Plurals

Most plural nouns are formed by adding *-s* to the singular. Exceptions: Nouns that end in a consonant and *y* form the plural by changing *y* to *i* and adding *-es (hobbies, parties).* Nouns that end in *s, sh, ch, x,* and *z* add *-es* to form the plural *(buses, matches, foxes, buzzes, pushes).* Some nouns ending in *f* add *-s (chiefs).* Others change the *f* to *v* and add *-es (thieves, leaves).*

A final group of nouns form plurals irregularly *(children, geese, deer, women).* When in doubt, look them up.

Compound Nouns

Although most compound nouns form their plurals regularly by adding *-s* to the end *(spoonfuls, cross-examinations),* a few where the significant word comes first add the *-s* to that portion of the word *(fathers-in-law, senators-elect).*

Possession or Possessives

See **Apostrophe; Double Possessive**.

Possessive Pronouns

See **Pronouns: Personal.**

Precede/Proceed

Precede means to go before. *Proceed* means to continue on or to go forward.

· The Queen *preceded* the Crown Prince as the royal party *proceeded* down the marble hall.

Predicate

The predicate is that part of a sentence which indicates what the subject is doing or being. It always includes a verb and may also include its modifiers and complements.

· Jack *selects.* Sally *shovels.* Artie *is never ready.* Perry *is running away.*

A simple predicate is the verb alone. A compound predicate is two or more verbs having the same subject and joined by a conjunction.

· Manuel *studied* and *wrote* for hours each day.

See also **Complement.**

Predicate Adjective

See **Complement.**

Predicate Complement

See **Complement.**

Predicate Nominative

See **Complement.**

Prejudice/Prejudiced

Because the *d* sound at the end of *prejudiced* is difficult to pronounce, people sometimes think that the passive verb *to be prejudiced* is spelled in the same way as the noun *prejudice.*

CORRECT: Her heart was filled with *prejudice.* For one reason or another she was *prejudiced* against almost everyone on her corridor.

Prepositions

A *preposition* is a part of speech that relates its object, a noun or pronoun, to another element in a sentence.

- He sings *in* the church choir. *In* relates *choir* to *sings.* (adverb phrase)
- He is part *of* the mob. *Of* relates *mob* to *part.* (adjective phrase)

about	below	in	since
above	beneath	inside	through
across	beside	into	to
after	between	like	toward
against	beyond	near	under
along	by	of	until
among	down	off	up
around	during	on	upon
at	except	outside	with
before	for	over	within
behind	from	past	without

Preposition at End of Sentence

It is sometimes correct form to end a sentence with a preposition. Some prepositions may fall at the ends of sentences: for example, *what it's all about, a chair to stand on, a pace to keep up with.*

To paraphrase Winston Churchill, the old rule of never putting a preposition at the end of a sentence often causes unwieldy constructions "up with which no one should have to put."

On the other hand, never make the mistake of using the preposition twice.

> INCORRECT: *With* whom did you come *with? To* what do you attribute your long life *to?*

Prepositional Phrase

See pages 191, 222, and 230.

Principal/Principle

Principal means "first" or "head" or "most important" and can be used in this meaning both as a noun and as an adjective. It can also refer to a sum of money that earns dividends.

- Mr. Steinmetz is *principal* of Jimmy's school. (noun)
- He had one of the *principal* roles in *Brigadoon.* (adjective)
- She lived on the interest and did not have to use the *principal* in her account.

A *principle* is a rule by which a person lives or by which an organization is conducted.

· Loyalty to her employers was a guiding *principle*.

Proceed

See **Precede/Proceed.**

Pronoun

A pronoun is a word used in place of a noun. Pronouns are classified as **personal, relative, interrogative, indefinite, demonstrative, reflexive.** See individual listings. See also **Agreement: Pronouns with Antecedents,** and **Gender.**

Pronouns: Demonstrative

Demonstrative pronouns imply that the speaker or writer is pointing at a specific object or person. They may be used as nouns, but are usually more effective when you use them as demonstrative adjectives. The demonstrative pronouns are *this* (plural: *these*) and *that* (plural: *those*).

· *This plate* is wet. *That towel* is dry. Why not dry *this* with *that?*

See **That/This.**

Pronouns: Indefinite

Indefinite pronouns include such terms as *such, any, some, each, all, either, none, one, somebody, something.* See **Agreement: Subject and Verb.**

Pronouns: Interrogative

Interrogative pronouns, which are almost identical with the relative pronouns, introduce questions.

· *Who* is in charge here? *Which* is the right direction?

Pronouns: Personal

In ancient days all English nouns and pronouns were inflected—that is, had different endings or forms to indicate the person they represented and to show their syntactic function in a sentence. But now only our personal pronouns change form to correspond with the person represented, and only these and the relative pronouns signify whether they are serving a subjective or objective or possessive function.

In speaking of yourself as the subject of a clause or sentence, use *I*. When joined together with others, use *we*. To make these pronouns the object of a verb or of a preposition, use *me* and *us*. When substituting a pronoun for other people and using it as a subject, choose (as appropriate) *he, she, they*. If you want one of these for an object, use *him, her, them*. (See also **Gender**.)

Choosing Subjective or Objective Forms

Most of the time choosing the correct form is fairly straightforward. Few speakers of English would ever say, *"Me* went to the store" or "Pat took *I* to the picnic." But some people have problems when another name or phrase intrudes:

· Jane and *I* went to the store. Pat took Joe and *me* to the picnic.

If you are ever troubled by a pronoun decision of this sort, simply remove the extra words and test the construction with the pronoun standing alone in its place.

With the Verb "To Be"

The verb "to be" acts as an equal sign, equating the subject on one side with the complement on the other. Therefore, when the complement is a pronoun it should, traditionally, be written as a subject:

· *It was he* who had saved the cat from the flames.

You should follow this rule in your writing, although in recent years speakers of Standard English have become more relaxed about following it in their speech. Most would not hesitate to answer a telephone query with "It's *me."*

With "Than" and "As"

Than and *as* are not prepositions that take objects, but conjunctions that begin clauses where the verb is often not stated, but understood. When the subject of such understood verbs is a pronoun, it should, naturally, be in its subject form:

· Joan is a better swimmer *than I* [am]. Roy is almost as tall *as he* [is].

Occasionally, the subject and the verb are both understood and the pronoun is meant to be the verb's object. Be careful with your choice of pronoun in such cases. The meaning can differ markedly:

· She likes Jody better than I [like Jody]. She likes Jody better than [she likes] me.

With "Between"

Since *between* is a preposition, it should be followed by an object. Thus the correct form should be *between you and me* or *between her and me*. If this construction persists in sounding awkward to you, you might choose rather to reword and write *between Mary and me.*

Possessive Pronouns

The correct forms are:

My hat. It's *mine.*   *Your* hat. It's *yours.*
Her hat. It's *hers.*   *His* hat. It's *his.*
Its hat. It's *its.*   *Our* hats. They're *ours.*
Their hats.   They're *theirs.*

The main point to notice is that even though *its, hers, yours,* and *theirs* add *-s* to signify possession, none of them takes an apostrophe.

Please note also that forms common to a number of dialects, such as *youse, you-all, mines,* and *his'n,* are not included among the standard personal pronouns.

Pronoun Reference

See **Agreement: Pronouns and Antecedents.**

Pronouns: Reflexive

Reflexive pronouns are formed by adding *self* (or *selves*) to personal pronouns. They include *myself, himself, themselves, itself,* and so on. A reflexive pronoun is used to emphasize a noun or pronoun by repeating it within the sentence in another form.

· *I* inspected the property *myself.*
· I couldn't believe that the *star himself* had arrived.

Reflexive pronouns should never be used as a substitute for an appropriately used personal pronoun.

INCORRECT: She taught Larry and *myself* to swim.
CORRECT: She taught Larry and *me* to swim.

Pronouns: Relative

Relative pronouns include *who, whoever, which, whichever, that, whom, whomever, what, whatever, whose.* Like all pronouns they take the place of nouns. Relative pronouns serve as the subject or complement of adjective clauses describing the noun for which they substitute.

· Mary, *who* understood the situation, . . .

Use *who* and *whom* for persons and animals with personality, *which* for inanimate things and other animals, and *that* for any of these.

· The cat, *which* was red, began to purr.
· The small, ancient lady, to *whom* it belonged, began to purr also.

See also **Who/Whom** and page 319.

Proved/Proven

Prove is no longer an irregular verb. The regular *-ed* form, *proved,* is now preferred to *proven* when combined with *has* or *had.*

· He *has proved* his point. It *has been proved* to my satisfaction.

Proven is still the appropriate adjective, however: *proven* facts, *proven* ability.

Punctuation

See **Apostrophe; Brackets; Colon; Comma; Dash; Hyphen; Parentheses; Period; Question Mark; Quotation Marks; Semicolon.**

Question Mark

A question mark (?) is used to indicate a question or an uncertainty.

1. Use a question mark at the end of a sentence that asks a question.

· Where will you be on Tuesday?

2. Do not use a question mark after an indirect question.

· He asked what I wanted for my birthday.

3. A question mark may be used to indicate that the writer is uncertain or questions the truth of a statement.

· The war that raged from 1812(?) to 1815.
· The movie queen was born in 1952(?).

A question mark shows the end of a question. It therefore goes inside quotation marks when a question is being quoted and outside the marks when the sentence containing the quotation is a question itself.

· The child asked, "Why is the sky blue?"
· Have you ever heard the saying, "All in good time"?

Quite/Really/Very

Quite, really, and *very* are intensifiers; that is, they are meant to emphasize the adjective they describe and make it stronger. They are so overused, however, that in most cases it is questionable whether they achieve that end. Like exclamation points, they can add a gushy rather than an emphatic quality.

> LESS EFFECTIVE: Professor Jones is *really (quite, very)* well known.
> STRONGER: Professor Jones is well known.

When you are tempted to prop up a colorless or weak adjective in this way, try substituting a more expressive or colorful adjective. You might, for instance, replace *very funny* with *hilarious, quite silly* with *ridiculous, really big* with *mammoth* or *colossal.*

Quotation Marks

Quotation marks (" ") are punctuation marks used to enclose short direct quotations.

- As Teresa Ferster Glazier reminds us, "Every quotation begins with a capital letter."

Do not use quotation marks for indirect quotations, which are usually introduced by *that* (unless you are including the exact words of your source).

- Professor Glazier reminds us that we should begin our quotations with capital letters.

Use quotation marks around the title of a poem or short story or song or any piece of writing that is not separately published.

- "The Barefoot Boy" is a poem by John G. Whittier.

Use single quotation marks (' ') as substitutions when you need to use quotation marks within a quotation.

- "Recite 'The Barefoot Boy' for me," Aunt Matilda demanded.

Use quotation marks to begin and end all parts of quotations that are interrupted by nonquoted material, but do not insert them at the end of each sentence when the quotation continues on.

- "Play hard," the coach advised, "and don't be afraid to block the other side. But always keep strictly to the rules of the game."

See also **Quotations** and **Italics.**

Quotations

Be sure that you indicate all quoted material, even if it is only a phrase. Enclose short quotations within quotation marks, and block off with wide margins any quotations that are longer than three lines of type or script. In double-spaced typescript you will ordinarily single space your quotations. Quotation marks are unnecessary when you use whole blocks of quoted material.

> George Will insists that "the differences between conservatives and liberals are as much a matter of temperament as ideas," and goes on to detail these differences:

>> Liberals are temperamentally inclined to see the world as a harmonious carnival of sweetness and light, where good will prevails, good intentions are rewarded, the race is to the swift, and a benevolent Nature arranges a favorable balance of pleasure over pain. Conservatives . . . know better. (p. 449)

If you omit any part of a quotation, use ellipses (three dots) to indicate the omitted material (see **Ellipsis Points**). If you need to add any words of your own to a quotation, enclose them in brackets [   ].

Whenever possible, identify the source of your quotation. If such attribution is not possible or desirable, you still must not burst into quotation as birds burst into song, but use such introductions as "Authorities agree that . . ." or even "It has often been said. . . ." See also pages 326–336.

Raise/Rise

Raise is a regular verb.

· They raise sheep; they raised sheep; they have raised sheep.

Rise is irregular. *Raise* takes an object; *rise* does not. Things *rise* unassisted, but if they need help, they must be *raised.* You can *raise* the window, *raise* the roof, *raise* Lazarus. Steam can *rise;* heat and bread can *rise.* See **Rise—Irregular Verb.**

Real/Really

Real and *really* are not interchangeable. *Real* is correctly used only as an adjective.

· My pearl came from a *real* oyster.

In writing, *real* should not be used as an intensifier.

INCORRECT: Joe was *real* impressed with my pearl.
CORRECT: Joe was *really* impressed with my pearl.

Usually it is more effective to eliminate the *really* altogether.

· BETTER: Joe was impressed with my pearl.

See also **Quite/Really/Very.**

Reason Is Because

Although this construction is used in a number of oral dialects, it is *not* Standard English and must be avoided in written work. Write "The reason is *that.*"

· The reason Lisa did not come to the square dance *is that* her new shoes pinched her feet.

Reason Why

Reason why is incorrect usage because *why* is unnecessary.

INCORRECT: I wish I knew the *reason why* he stopped calling Dorothy.
CORRECT: I wish I knew *why* he stopped calling Dorothy.
CORRECT: I wish I knew his *reason for* not calling Dorothy.
CORRECT: I wish I knew the *reason* he stopped calling Dorothy.

Redundancy

Redundancy refers to unnecessary repetition, a form of wordiness to watch for as you edit your work.

· 6 *a.m.* in the *morning* (A.M. *is* morning)
· *Dr.* Phillips, *M.D.*
· his *honest sincerity*
· the *sickly invalid*
· *each* and *every*
· *three different* attorneys

The accompanying list of common redundancies may help in revising your writing.

adequate *enough*
advance planning
am in possession of (use "have")
a percentage of (use "some")
appear *to be*
appointed *to the post of*
ascend, hoist, raise, lift *up*
as never before *in the past*
as to whether
at an early date (use "soon")

atop *of,* inside *of*
at some time *to come*
attach, assemble, collaborate, co-operate, fuse, join, merge, unite *together*
barracks (or dormitory) building
best of health (use "well" or "healthy")
big *in size*
biography *of his life*

blue *in color*
but nevertheless
christened *as*
classified *into groups*
close proximity
consensus *of opinion*
continue *to remain*
descend *down*
due to the fact that (use "because")
during the time that (use "while")
entirely complete
final completion, settlement, outcome
first priority
frown, smile *on his face*
give due consideration to (use "consider")
give rise to (use "cause")
good benefit
grateful thanks
habitual custom
had occasion to be (use "was")
important essentials
in this day and age (use "today")
invited guest
joint cooperation
last of *all*
little duckling, baby, sapling, smidgeon
lonely isolation
made an approach to (use approach)
made a statement saying (use "stated" or "said")
made *out* of

more superior, preferable
mutual advantage *of both*
never *at any time*
new beginning, creation, innovation, record, recruits
one *and the same*
over *with*
passing phase, fad, fancy
past history
penetrate *into*
protrude *out*
quite unique
recall, recoil, return, revert *back*
results so far *achieved*
separate and distinct (use "separate" or "distinct")
separate *apart*
serious danger
sink, swoop *down*
take action on the plan (use "act")
termed *as*
the house in question (use "this house")
body of *the late . . .,* widow *of the late*
throughout *the length and breadth*
today's modern woman (use "today's" or "modern")
total annihilation, extinction, reversal
true facts
usual customs
violent explosion
weather *conditions*
young infant, baby, teenager

Referent

See **Agreement: Pronouns with Antecedents.**

Reflexive Pronouns

See **Pronouns: Reflexive.**

Regard

With regard to and *in regard to* are both correct usage.

- Our conversation *with regard to* financing your project has been recorded.
- *In regard to* your ideas, we are in total opposition.

Do not use *in regards to* or *with regards to*.
When *regard* is used as a verb, it is followed by *as*.

- I *regard* this *as* a damaging statement.
- He will *regard* your interest *as* an invasion of his privacy.

You would not say *"regard it* an invasion" or *"regard it to* be an invasion." Just use *as*.

Regardless

The word *regardless* must be followed by *of*.

- My parents will send me to college *regardless of* my poor grades.

Irregardless is not a word.

Regular Verbs

Most verbs are regular verbs. They are called *regular* because they form the past tense and past participle by adding *-d* or *-ed* to the present form.

- They *seem;* they *seemed;* they *have seemed.*
- They *walk;* they *walked;* they *have walked.*

Irregular verbs form the past tense and past participle in a variety of ways. The forms of the more common irregular verbs are included alphabetically in this guide.

Relative Clauses (i.e., Adjective Clauses)

See pages 192–195 and 216–221.

Respectful/Respective

Respectful refers to the state of showing honor or deference to someone (*respectful* toward the flag). *Respective* means belonging to each individual.

- She was *respectful* to all her teachers.
- State your *respective* qualifications when your names are called.

Restrictive/Nonrestrictive Elements

See **Commas, Parenthetical.**

Ride—Irregular Verb

They ride; they rode; they have ridden.

Ring—Irregular Verb

Bells ring; bells rang; bells have rung.

Rise—Irregular Verb

The sun rises; the sun rose; the sun has risen.

Run-on Sentence

A run-on sentence is a group of words that contains more than one main (independent) clause but is punctuated as if it were a single sentence.

> INCORRECT: When the air had cleared, we saw our favorite car still coming on strong it still had a chance to win!
>
> CORRECT: When the air had cleared, we saw our favorite car still coming on strong. It still had a chance to win!
>
> CORRECT: When the air had cleared, we saw our favorite car still coming on strong; it still had a chance to win!

Substituting a comma for the period or the semicolon in the edited versions would be as incorrect as the first example. See also **Comma Splice.**

Semiannual/Semimonthly/Semiweekly

Semiannual means happening or appearing twice a year. *Semimonthly* means twice each month. *Semiweekly* means twice a week. Our newspaper will appear *semiweekly* on Tuesdays and Fridays. See also **Biannual.**

Semicolon

A semicolon (;) is a mark of punctuation that joins two or more closely related independent clauses when no coordinating conjunction (such as *and, but, or, nor, yet, for* is used. It is particularly valuable when an adverbial connective, ordinarily followed by a comma *(therefore, however, indeed, nevertheless),* is present.

· Marcia has always been athletic; she plays tennis and golf well.
· Marcia plays tennis and golf well; however, her basketball skills are only mediocre.

A semicolon can also separate the elements of a series if one or more of those elements contain commas.

· In reading, many children have trouble with comprehension; with phonics, especially vowel sounds; and with visual memory, including the learning of sight words.

Warning: A semicolon indicates a full stop—much as a period does. Be careful *not* to use it as a substitute for a comma, but confine your use of it to the two situations just outlined.

Sensual/Sensuous

The differences in usage between *sensual* and *sensuous* are subtle. *Sensual* is most often used when the senses under discussion involve sexual gratification. *Sensuous* is used to mean appealing to all or any of the five senses.

· The director suggested the *sensual* pose, the breathy voice, the provocative smile.
· We enjoyed the *sensuous* fragrance of magnolias.

Sentence

See pages 187–200.

Sentence Fragment

See **Fragment.**

Serial Parallelism

See pages 248–256.

Set—Irregular Verb

They *set* the table today; yesterday they *set* the table; they have *set* the table.

Set/Sit

Set takes an object. *Sit* does not take an object. You cannot *sit* something; you must *set* it.

- *Set* the books on that chair, and *sit* over here with us.
- *Set* the clock, *set* the table, *set* the child on his bench.
- *Sit* down.

See **Set—Irregular Verb** and **Sit—Irregular Verb**.

Shake—Irregular Verb

They shake; they shook; they have shaken.

Shall/Will, Should/Would

Originally, *shall* and *should* were used to express future intent when their subjects were *I* or *we* (first person). *Will* and *would* were used the rest of the time. If writers or speakers wanted emphasis, they could reverse these combinations *(I will. He should.)* Now the distinction is fading and *will* and *would* are used most of the time in speech and less formal writing. Although it is no longer essential, in formal writing you might still want to maintain the distinction. And in one case of *should,* you should do so. For when *should* is combined with a second-, or third-person subject, it still retains some of the emphatic sense of *ought;* and if you use *should* indiscriminately, it can give an officious, mandatory tone to your work.

- Commanding: You *should* eat your spinach.

Shine—Irregular Verb

Without an object:

- The sun shines; the sun shone; the sun has shone.

With an object:

- They shine their shoes; they shined their shoes; they have shined their shoes.

Should

See **Shall/Will; Should/Would.**

Should Have

See **Would Have/Would of.**

Sight

See **Cite/Sight/Site.**

Simple Sentence

See pages 187–195.

Sing—Irregular Verb

Birds sing; birds sang; birds have sung.

Singular

See **Plurals**.

Sink—Irregular Verb

Ships sink; ships sank; ships have sunk.

Sit—Irregular Verb

They sit down; they sat down; they have sat down. See also **Set/Sit**.

Site

See **Cite/Sight/Site**.

Slang

See **Colloquial Language**.

So

In more formal writing, *so* should be used not as an intensifier, but as a comparative.

> WEAK: Jane was *so* pretty.
> BETTER: Jane was *so* pretty that I could not take my eyes off her.

So/So That

So stands alone when it expresses a consequence of some action.

> · He smashed the car, *so* he has to walk.

So is always followed by *that* when it means *in order that*.

> CORRECT: He needed a ride *so that* he could get there by Friday.
> INCORRECT: He needs a ride *so* he could get there by Friday.

Sort of

See **Kind of/Sort of.**

Spelling

Because the spelling of English words does not always coincide in any universally regular manner with the way they are pronounced, memorization of the spelling of individual words and the determination to look up the rest is the only sure method. There are, nevertheless, a number of rules that you may find helpful:

Double Vowels

The following rules, which will probably have the vaguely familiar ring of your early school days, can still be of use when you can't remember which way to order your vowels.

1. For most double vowels
   Rule: When two vowels go walking, the first one does the talking.

   · pea ch, boa t, pou r

   Exceptions: Dipthongs such as *ou* and *oi* and the *i* and *e* combination.
2. For *i* and *e* combinations
   Rule: *I* before *e*
   Except after *c*.
   Or when sounding like "ay,"
   As in *neighbor* and *weigh*.

   · frie nd, belie f, recei ve, thei r

Adding Suffixes That Begin with Vowels
(-ed, -ing, -able, and so on)

3. For words that end in *e*
   Rule: Drop the *e* before adding the suffix.
   Explanation: The final vowel *e* serves to keep the central vowel sound long, and the vowel in the suffix will serve the same purpose.

   · *mope, moping, moped.* Chris sat around and *moped.*

4. For final accented words that do *not* end in *e*
   Rule: Double the final consonant before adding the suffix.
   Explanation: The double consonant prevents the vowel in the suffix from turning the central vowel sound long. The doubling thus keeps the vowel sound short.

   · *mop, mopping, mopped.* Chris *mopped* the floor.

5. For words that end in *y*
   Rule: Change *y* to *i* and add suffix. When the suffix is *-s,* change it to *-es.*

   · marry, married, marries

   Exceptions: (a) Keep the *y* when the suffix is *-ing*

   · marrying

   (b) Keep the *y* when the word is a proper noun

   · Jenny's

The K Sound and the S Sound

Problem: In English the letters *k* and *c* both carry the K sound, and *s* and *c* both carry the S sound. It is difficult to sound out the spelling of words with these sounds in them. Part of the problem can be handled by rules, however.

6. For syllables beginning with a K sound
   Rule: Spell with a *k* when followed by *i* or *e*. Spell with a *c* when followed by *a* or *o* (and usually *u*).

   · *ki*tchen *ke*ttle, *ca*tching *co*ld, *cu*bs

7. For words ending with a K sound
   Rule: Spell with *-ck* when the final syllable is stressed. Spell with *-c* when the final syllable is unstressed.

   · si*ck*, pic*c*nic

   For adding suffixes (beginning with *i* or *e*): You can keep the K sound if you begin the suffix with a *k*.

   · picni*cking*, picni*cker*

8. For words with S sounds
   Rule: Spell with *s* whenever the S sound is followed by an *a* or an *o* or a *u.*

   · sat [cat], sot [cot], sub [cub]

   Unfortunately, both *s* and *c* can be used before *i* and *e*, so when you are not sure here you will have to look up the spelling.

Combined Words

9. **Rule:** Words formed by combining two words retain all the letters of both words, even if a letter repeats.

   · roommate, withheld, overrule

10. Words formed by adding a prefix retain all the letters of both prefix and base, even if a letter repeats.

· misspell, unnatural, interracial, dissatisfied

The accompanying list of commonly misspelled words will also help you in revising. Memorize the spelling of any that are troublesome to you.

Spelling List

The following is a list of everyday words that have been found to be most frequently misspelled. These words are in such common use that people rarely take the time to look them up in a dictionary. Unfortunately, these words are also so common they are considered "simple," and thus when they are misspelled, they leave readers with an especially negative impression of the writer. If spelling is a problem for you, you can clear up a large proportion of it by a procedure that has worked for many others with a similar problem: First, identify your own particular troublemakers by having someone test you on this list. Then, make a deliberate effort to memorize the words you have missed. (You can use such memory tricks as closed-eyed visualization, idea-letter association, and repeated writing.) Finally, test out your troublemakers as many times as it takes for you to be sure you will not misspell them again.

absence	committee	friend	personal	succeed
accept	conscious	hoping	persuade	surprise
achieve	decision	immediately	planned	their
acknowledged	definition	intelligence	possession	there
advertisement	describe	its	presence	they're
alter	description	judgment	principle	thoroughly
argument	difference	knowledge	privilege	too
assistance	effect	library	psychology	traveling
athlete	embarrass	maintenance	receive	Tuesday
beautiful	especially	necessary	recognize	usually
beginning	exercise	neighbor	rhythm	Wednesday
believe	experience	ninety	science	
benefit	familiar	ninth	shining	
business	February	occasionally	similar	
characteristic	forty	opportunity	society	
circumstances	fourth	parallel	studying	

Stationary/Stationery

Stationary means not moving, remaining in one place. *Stationery* refers to paper, cards, and envelopes used to correspond by note or letter.

· The cabinets were *stationary*. She ordered monogrammed *stationery* to go on one of the shelves.

Steal—Irregular Verb

Thieves steal; thieves stole; thieves have stolen.

Sting—Irregular Verb

Bees sting; bees stung; bees have stung.

Stuff

Shakespeare said, "We are such *stuff* as dreams are made on." And if you also wanted to use the word in its original sense of "primary substance," you would be using it appropriately. But *stuff* used in its usual vague conversational sense is too informal for most writing situations. Search out and use a word that more exactly expresses your thought.

INCORRECT: We put all our *stuff* in one box.

If you can be precise, use *clothing, tools, supplies,* or whatever describes the contents of the box. If you cannot be precise, use *belongings* or *materials.*

Subject-Verb Agreement

See **Agreement: Subject and Verb.**

Subordinate Clause

See pages 192–193, 216–222, 234–239, and 241–243.

Subordinating Conjunctions

See **Conjunctions.**

Swim—Irregular Verb

Fishes swim; the fishes swam; the fishes have swum.

Swing—Irregular Verb

They swing, they swung; they have swung.

Syllabication

See **Hyphenation in Word Division.**

Synonym

A synonym is a word that means the same (or almost the same) as another word. *Rich* is a synonym for *wealthy, sick* for *ill, healthy* for *well, hurry* for *rush, swiftly* for *rapidly.*

Although words can be similar in meaning, the good writer is able to choose the word with the exact shade of meaning required. The best word is usually not the longest or most impressive word. It is the word that most precisely expresses the idea and the connotation you want to convey. See pages 260–277.

Syntax

Syntax refers to the way words, phrases, and clauses work together in a sentence. Syntax that is faulty or complicated leaves the reader confused.

Faulty syntax can be seen when subjects do not agree with predicates, when pronouns do not match antecedents, and when professors do not agree with students on sentence structure.

Take

See **Bring/Take.**

Than and Pronouns Following

See **Pronouns: with Than and As.**

That/This

This and *that* and their plurals, *these* and *those,* are demonstrative pronouns that point to or substitute for *specific* objects or persons.

· This tree. Those trees. That player. Those players.

Do not use demonstrative pronouns to signify "all this," "all that I have just said."

INCORRECT: We could all dress in costume, carve a pumpkin, and bob for apples as we used to do when we were children. *This* would be fun.

CORRECT: *This plan* would be fun.

See also **Agreement: Pronouns Antecedents, Group-Noun Antecedents.**

That/Which/Who

See **Pronouns: Relative** and **Who/Whom.**

Their/There/They're

Their and *theirs* are possessives. They express the idea of "belonging to."

· This is *their* furniture. The house is also *theirs.*

There can be used as an introductory word or as a word to tell place.

· *There* can be only twelve members. *There's* no reason to involve more people. Only the twelve members were *there.*

They're is a contraction that means "they are."

· *They're* leaving to pick up *their* notes, which they left *there* overnight. *There's* no doubt that *they're theirs.*

Thesis and Thesis Statement

See pages 3–9 and 82–87.

Thing or Things

Unless your purpose is to convey vagueness, try to avoid using the word *thing* (or *things*). Substitute a more precise word for it wherever you can in editing your work.

> WEAK: Robin finished the *thing* she was working on.
> BETTER: Robin finished the *project* she was working on.
> OKAY: It was just a *thing* of rags and tatters. (purposely vague)

Till/Until

Until is more often used than *till,* but either is acceptable and the meanings are the same. *'Til* is a seldom-used contraction for *until. 'Till* is not a word.

· Until tomorrow then.
· ". . . till the end of time."

Titles

Capitalize the first and every other significant word in a title.

· *The Decline and Fall of the Roman Empire* was written by Gibbon.

Underline (italicize) the title of every separately published work. These include full-length books *(Catch-22, The Third Reich);* magazines and journals *(The Ladies' Home Journal, College English);* operas or symphonies *(La Traviata);* plays, movies, and television shows *(Hamlet, The Attack of the Killer Tomatoes);* anthologies and encyclopedias *(Encyclopaedia Britannica).*

Put quotation marks around the titles of portions of books, such as chapters, works anthologized or otherwise included within books, short stories, essays, articles, songs, poems: "The Story of an Hour"; "Blacks and a Free Market"; "The Rime of the Ancient Mariner."

When you place a title at the beginning of a work of your own, you should neither underline it nor put quotation marks around it—except those portions, of course, which you would normally italicize or enclose with quotation marks.

To/Too/Two

Errors in using these words are probably the result of carelessness rather than lack of understanding. Watch for them when you proofread.

Two is always a number. *Too* means "also" and "overly" or "excessive." In other situations, *to* is the correct spelling.

· The *two* farmers walked *too* far *to* go *to* the store and *to* the market *too*.

Transitive Verbs

See **Intransitive and Transitive Verbs**.

Try and/Try to

Do not substitute *try and* for *try to*. Although this construction is often heard in conversation, it is not correct in writing.

INCORRECT: "We should *try and* remember the way back," she said conspiratorially.
CORRECT: "Yes, we should *try to* remember the way," he repeated ironically.

Underlining

See **Italics**.

Unique

Since *unique* means that the idea or thing it describes is the only one in the world, such expressions as *very unique* or *especially unique* are more than a little excessive and should be avoided.

Until

See **Till/Until**.

Used to

Never say *we use to* or *we didn't used to.* Say *we used to* and *we didn't use to.*

> CORRECT: We *used to* enjoy homemade ice cream, but we *didn't use to* get it in large quantitites because no one *used to* have a freezer.

Verbs

See pages 188–190 and **Regular, Intransitive, Active, Auxiliary,** and **Linking Verbs.**

Verbals, Verbal Phrases

See pages 226, 243 for **Gerund, Infinitive,** and **Participle.**

Very

See **Quite/Really/Very.**

Wait/Wait on

See **Await/Wait.**

Want/Wish

Want should be used when a direct object follows.

· Did she really *want* the mink *coat?*

Wish should be used with an indirect object.

· We *wish you* luck on your exams.

The English butler who asks, "Does madam *wish* her *tea* now?" is using incorrect grammar.

> You may use *wish for* or *wish to* in appropriate situations.

· We all *wish for* peace.
· Did Sandra always *wish to* be Miss Nebraska?

Well

See **Good/Well.**

When/Where

When and *where* should not be used after *is* to form a definition.

INCORRECT: A civil war *is when* two parts of the same government oppose each other with violence.

INCORRECT: A hole in one *is where* a golfer sinks the ball with one driving stroke.

CORRECT: A civil war is a war in which . . .

CORRECT: A hole in one occurs when a golfer . . .

Where at

At is not appropriate after *where*.

INCORRECT: Where's it at?

CORRECT: Where is it?

INCORRECT: He always knows where it's at.

CORRECT: He always knows where it is.

Which

See **Pronouns: Relative.**

Who's/Whose

Who's means *who is* or *who has.*

· Who's sending these threatening letters?
· *Who's* been eating my porridge?

Whose is a possessive form. It now may be acceptably used to refer both to people and to inanimate objects.

· *Whose* math paper is this?
· She avoided the tree *whose* bark John had carved.
· We know *whose* tapes are being pirated, but we don't know *who's* doing it.

Who/Whom

Who is used as the subject of a sentence or clause. *Whoever* follows the same rules. *Whom* and *whomever* are used as objects of verbs or prepositions or indirect objects. *Whomever* is awkward and seldom seen.

CORRECT: *Who* is your best friend? Your best friend is *whoever* has a car for Saturday night.

CORRECT: The person to *whom* you owe money is not always the person *whom* you want to see.

CORRECT: We asked *who* had been here longest. He is the one *whom* we wanted to interview.

CORRECT: We will present the keys to *whoever* wins the raffle.

In this sentence, a clause, *whoever wins the raffle,* is the indirect object, but *whoever* is the subject of the clause.

If the use of *whom* is correct but sounds stilted or awkward to you, try to rewrite the sentence, avoiding it altogether. See also **Pronouns: Relative**.

Will

See **Shall/Will; Should/Would**.

Wish/Want

See **Want/Wish**.

With

Do not use *with* to add a further thought to a sentence.

> WEAK: Janice and Albert always led the class *with* Patty trailing in third place.
> BETTER: Janice and Albert always led the class; Patty trailed in third place.

Would

See **Shall/Will; Should/Would**.

Would Have/Would of

Would have is correct. Never use *would of.*

> CORRECT: We *would have* come earlier. He *would have* helped you.
> CORRECT: We *would've* come earlier.
> INCORRECT: We *would of* come earlier.

The same rule applies to *could have* and *should have.*

Write—Irregular Verb

They write; they wrote; they have written.

Your/You're

Your is a possessive. *You're* is a contraction that means *you are.*

> · You're always leaving *your* coat on that chair.

Index